IBN AL-ʿARABĪ ON THE MYSTERIES OF THE PURIFYING ALMS

FROM THE *Futūḥāt al-Makkiyya*

(MECCAN REVELATIONS)

Muḥyī Dīn Ibn al-ᶜArabī

TRANSLATED BY

AISHA BEWLEY

EDITED BY

LALEH BAKHTIAR

SERIES EDITOR

SEYYED HOSSEIN NASR

GREAT BOOKS OF THE ISLAMIC WORLD

Library of Congress Cataloging-in-Publication Data

Muḥyī dīn ibn al-ᶜArabī, *On the Mysteries of the Purifying Alms* from the *Futūḥāt al-Makkiyya (Meccan Revelations)*
1. Islamic Law. 2. Sufism. I. Title.

ISBN: 1-56744-779-1 pbk
1-56744-780-5 hbk

Cover design: Liaquat Ali
Cornerstones are Allah and Muhammad connected by *Bismillāh al-Raḥmān al-Raḥīm* (In the Name of God, the Merciful, the Compassionate).

Logo design by Mani Ardalan Farhadi
The cypress tree bending with the wind, the source for the paisley design, is a symbol of the perfect Muslim, who, as the tree, bends with the wind of God's Will.

Published by
Great Books of the Islamic World, Inc.

Distributed by
KAZI Publications, Inc.
3023 W. Belmont Avenue
Chicago IL 60618
Tel: 773-267-7001; FAX: 773-267-7002
email: info@kazi.org /www.kazi.org

Contents

(Original Chapter 70 of the *Meccan Revelations*

FOREWORD

God's last plenar revelation to present humanity came in the form of a book, al-Qurʾan, which for Muslims is also *the* book and is in fact known also as *Umm al-kitāb* or Mother of All Books. While the peerless majesty of the revelation reduced the first generation of Muslims to silence, the echo of the Noble Book and its encouragement of acquiring knowledge could not but result in a culture which cherished books and honored scholars. This unmistakable emphasis of the Noble Quran on knowledge, combined with the synthetic power of Islam to absorb the learning of older civilizations to the extent that they conformed to the doctrine of unity (*al-tawḥīd*), gave rise to a vast and diversified intellectual life which for the past thirteen centuries has produced millions of works dealing with nearly every field of knowledge from the religious sciences, theology and philosophy to the natural sciences, from law to music, and from poetry to politics.

Islamic civilization was a lake into which flowed streams from many civilizations: Greek, Roman, Egyptian, Mesopotamian, Byzantine, Persian, Indian and even Chinese. In this lake the various elements became synthesized into a new body of water which itself became the source for numerous tributaries that have watered the various lands of *Dār al-islām*. Furthermore, Islamic civilization created works which had profound influence upon at least three major civilizations outside of the Islamic world: the Far Eastern, the Indian and the Western besides creating numerous masterly works whose influence has remained confined within the Islamic world. Such works in both categories contain a precious message for humanity as a whole and need to be made known by the world at large today.

Most treatises in Islamic civilization were written in the language of the Quranic revelation, Arabic, followed by the only other universal language of Islamic civilization, Persian. But important works have also been written in Turkish, Urdu, Bengali, Malay, Swahili, Berber, and numerous other languages including Chinese and, during this century, even English and French. Nor have all the works in Arabic been written by Arabs nor all the works in Persian by Persians. Numerous treatises in Arabic were written by Persians and later Turks, Indians, Berbers and Black Africans while many books in the Persian language were composed by Indians, Turks and Central Asians. The body of works written within the confines of Islamic civilization belongs to the whole of that civilization and in classical times, in fact, important books became known rapidly from Morocco to India and later Southeast Asia.

The Great Books of the Islamic World series seeks to make some of the most important works produced in Islamic civilization, primarily in Arabic and Persian, available in English so that these treasures of Islamic thought can be appreciated by those who do not possess the facility to benefit from them in the original languages. The audience to which the series addresses itself is predominantly the Western English reading public, but the series is also meant for Muslims themselves who have facility with the English language and also for non-Muslim and non-Westerners who are now becoming ever more knowledgeable in English and who might wish to gain deeper knowledge of the Islamic intellectual universe.

We hope that with the help of God, Exalted is His Majesty, this series will be successfully completed and that by providing a clear and readable translation of some of the great masterpieces of Islamic thought in English, this series will be able to create better understanding of Islam in the world at large and make accessible some of the treasures of traditional thought which, although Islamic in genesis, belong to all human beings who are interested in true knowledge in whatever form it appears. *wa mā tawfīqunā illā biʾLlāh*

Seyyed Hossein Nasr
Washington DC, June, 1997

EDITOR'S PREFACE

This work is a translation of a series of chapters of Muhyiddin ibn al-Arabi's great work, the ***Futūḥāt al-Makkiyya*** *(Meccan Revelations)*. This particular work, *On the Mysteries of the Purifying Alms*, is a translation of Chapter 70 of that work. Dr. James Morris, an expert on the life and works of the Shaykh al-Akbar, writes about these chapters of the ***Futūḥāt*** that they are "one of the most fascinating and potentially valuable sections of the entire *al-**Futūḥāt***—[they] offer what is almost certainly the most detailed and exacting phenomenology of spiritual experience in the Islamic tradition, presented in terms of an irenic reconciliation of contrasting legal interpretations of the basic ritual practices of Islam (purification, prayer, fasting, etc.)." (http://www.ibnarabisociety.org/articles/mr_introduction.html)

The works of these two giants of Islamic thought, Muhyiddin ibn al-Arabi (1165-1240 AD) and Abu Hamid al-Ghazzali (1058-1111 AD), on one of the five pillars of Islam, namely, purifying alms (*zakat*) are presented in this text. While Ibn al-Arabi answers whatever one would want to know about the purifying alms, al-Ghazzali summarizes the main points of the topic. Each one is valuable in its own right so while the text appearing here is that of Ibn al-Arabi, Appendix A presents the work of al-Ghazzali on the topic.

While both refer to the mysteries of the purifying alms, Ibn al-Arabi goes into much greater detail. The both agree about the subjects upon which the purifying alms is due and the types of persons to whom the Quran mentions should be the recipients. Ibn al-Arabi, however, adds that nothing belongs to the human being; ownership of everything belongs to God alone.

In addition to the usual eight types of property that require the purifying alms including certain types of livestock, land, gold and silver and trade, Ibn al-Arabi adds that the human being also owes the purifying alms for our limbs which he defines as: eye, ear, tongue, hand, belly, foot, genitals and heart. In addition is the voluntary charity due on our spirit and our soul. In regard to voluntary charity, he says this includes the saying of "God is Greater" and "there is no god but God."

Recognizing that the work of al-Ghazzali presented here is his summary in *The Alchemy of Happiness* of his *Revival of the Religious Sciences* and that his discussion on purifying alms is more intensive in the latter work, the difference between these two thinkers is not just in terms of quanitity. The difference is more significant in terms of quality or the mysteries involved in this pillar of Islam that Ibn al-Arabi expresses here.

Laleh Bakhtiar, Ph. D
Chicago, 2009

1 Introduction

The sister of the formal prayer is obligatory almsgiving;
so do not consider the text on this one and that
one to be the same.
Its formation is based on appraisal. This is why
the Throne of the Settling is traced back to division.
That is why it is divided into eight sorts of goods
in the divine law (*Sharia*).
It is the principle of the one who settles and is even-handed.
The Book mentioned them and their attributes.
It contains their sublime station.
Their property and themselves are purified and cleansed
by it and they are made absolutely pure
by the prayer of the one who takes up the Banner.
That is the Prophet Muhammad, the best of mankind
among his kind. He has highness which is above
levelness.
He obtained love because of his concern. Therefore, he did
not complain of separation, passionate love, or
ardent love.

1.1. The Difference Between Purifying Alms and a Loan

God Almighty said as a command to His servants: "*And perform the formal prayer and give the purifying alms and lend to God a good loan.*" (73:20) Here the loan is voluntary charity. The distinction between the two of them is that the purifying alms have a specific time, a minimum amount, and certain goods on which they are paid. A loan is not like that. Here voluntary charity are included under the category of a loan. It is as if He were saying: Give charity as a loan to God and He will multiply it for you. This is like what He said in the sound Tradition: "I was hungry and you did not feed Me." The servant said to Him: "How canst Thou be hungry when Thou art the Lord of the worlds?" God then tells him: "So-and-so asked you for food and you did not feed him. If you had fed him, you would have found that with Me." It is a very famous and sound Tradition. The loan which is not included under almsgiving does not have a specific time, amount or type of goods (upon which it is due). (235)

1.2. Purifying Alms and Charity

Prescribed alms and charity are two expressions which have the same meaning. God Almighty said: "*Take charity from their wealth that thou wouldst purify and and make them pure with it.*" (9:103) God Almighty said: "*Charities are only for the poor and the needy and for those who work to collect it and for those whose hearts were brought together and to free the bondsperson and the ones who are in debt and in the way of God and for the traveler of the way; this is a duty to God and God is Knowing, Wise.*" (9:60) He called it charity. The obligatory part of it is called both purifying alms and charity. The non-obligatory part is called voluntary charity. It is not called voluntary charity in the divine law. That is, the divine law (*Sharia*) does not apply this expression to it in spite of the fact that it has the meaning of growth, blessing and purification. (236)

In a sound Tradition, when the desert Arab mentioned to the Prophet that His messenger had claimed that they owed purifying alms on their property, the Prophet said: "He spoke the truth." The desert Arab asked: "Do I owe anything more than it?" He said: "No, unless you do so voluntarily." This is why it is called voluntary charity. He told him: "God did not make it obligatory for you. Whoever does something voluntarily, that is better for him. This is why He says after "*. . . and lend to God a fair loan, for whatever of good you put forward for your souls, you will find the same with God.*" (73:20) (237)

1.3. The Soul is Predisposed to Love of Wealth and Amassing It

Good is whatever action which brings you nearer to God, be it charity or anything else. In spite of this, the name "good" particularly applies to wealth. God Almighty said: "*And when the good afflicted him, begrudging,*" (70:21) that is, he is naturally disposed to do that. "*And whoever is protected from his own stinginess,*" (59:9) the ego (*nafs*) is naturally disposed to love of property and amassing it. (238)

God Almighty said: "*And he is more severe in the cherishing of good.*" (100:8) Here by "good" He means wealth. This is why generosity is an acquired and not an innate trait. This is why He named it "charity," that is, it is a harsh obligation for the soul since it abandons its own nature in doing that. That is why God made it dear when His Prophet said to the people: "Charity falls into the hand of the Merciful and He makes it grow as one of you would make his colt or young camel grow." (239)

1.4. Charity Falls Into the Hand of the Merciful

There are two matters here. One of them is that the asker is taking from the hand of the Merciful and not from the hand of the one who is giving the charity. The Prophet said: "It falls into the hand of the Merciful before it falls into the hand of the one who is asking." It is God who does the favor for the one who is asking, not the one who gives charity. God asked him for the loan. The one who is asking translates for God when he asks for the loan. Therefore, when the one who asks is a believer, he is not ashamed before the one who gives him the charity. He does not think that he has any excellence over him. The one who gives the charity gives God the loan which He asked for and will make it grow for him. This is part of divine jealousy and divine bounty. The other virtue is to teach him that it is entrusted in a place which will bring him profit and that all of this will be increased. Therefore he will be generous with it and be safe from the avarice of his ego. (240)

1.5. Part of the Nature of the Human Being is to Seek Profit in Trade

Part of human nature is to seek profit in trade and to make wealth grow. That is why the Tradition says that God makes charity grow. This is so that the servant will be naturally inclined to expend property for the sake of compensation, increase and blessings since it is purifying alms, even as he is inclined to amass wealth. It is natural for the soul to be avaricious. Therefore, God was kind to human nature since He did not bring it out of that to which it is naturally molded by calling it a loan. (241)

He sees that the merchant travels to distant places with great danger of loss of life and property. He spends money and gives it out because he hopes for profit, increase and capital growth. The soul finds joy in that. God asks him for the loan of all since he knows that He will advance it by two-thirds and by half. His joy at the one who advances Him all of it is greater and more complete. (242)

If one is miserly with charity after this bit of divine information and that their natural disposition is towards the doubling of wealth, that indicates that this miser has little belief in what we have just mentioned. If he had believed with certainty about his Lord and confirmed what He said about the soul regarding the loan and commerce of His servant, he would have hastened to that by his very nature just as he hastens to its like in this world sooner or later. (243)

When the servant makes a loan to a person on the basis of receiving a half or a third of the profits and then the one with the loan travels to a land and is absent for several years and he supposes that his money is lost or destroyed and he will have not profited at all, then the one with the loan does not deserve any censure at all when his wealth is destroyed. In spite of these possibilities, the human being is blind and gives his money and waits to see what he will obtain. He is quite content about it in spite of the fixed term, delay and uncertainty. (244)

When he is told: Give God a loan and take it many times over in the world to come without a third or a half, but with all the profit and the capital, you only need to be patient a little while and you will obtain all of that, the soul refuses and only gives a little. That only comes from lack of faith in the person himself since he is not generous with what his nature gives him of generosity while he loans to Zayd and Umar and is quite content as we said. Death is nearer to him than the strap of his sandal as Bilal said:

> Each person wakes up in the morning with his people
> while death is nearer to him than his sandal-strap. (245)

This is why God called it charity. It is a very difficult business for the soul. The Arabs say: A true (*sidq*) spear, that is, one that is hard, strong, and powerful, that is, the soul, experiences hardship and wounding by spending this wealth as Thalaba ibn Hatib stated. (246)

2 The Purifying Alms of the Hypocrites

God Almighty said about Thalaba ibn Hatib: *"And of them are some who made a contract with God* saying: *'If He gave us of His grace, we will be charitable and certainly we will be among the ones who are in accord with morality.'"* (9:75) God Almighty did not report that he said, "God willing." If he had said, "God willing," he would have done it. Then God said about him: *"Then when He gave them of His grace, they became misers with it and turned away and they were ones who turn aside."* (9:76) (247)

That was when God made purifying alms an obligation. The collector of the Messenger of God went to collect the purifying alms on Thalaba ibn Hatib's herds from him. He retorted: "This is the little sister of the *jizya*-tax!" and refused. God Almighty said what He said about him: *"He made the consequence to be hypocrisy in their hearts until a Day they will meet Him because they broke with God what they had promised Him."* (9:77) (248)

2.1. The Messenger of God Refused to Accept the Purifying Alms of Thalaba

When what God had sent down about him reached him, he brought his purifying alms to the Messenger of God but the Messenger of God refused to accept his charity because God had reported that He had named him a hypocrite. When the Prophet took charity, he purified the person by that, cleansed him and prayed for him as God had commanded him. God informed him that his prayer gave reassurance to the ones who gave charity. All these attributes are at variance with hypocrisy and what the hypocrite will find with God. Because of these conditions, he could not take the charity from him when he brought it to him after what God had said. (249)

After the Messenger of God died, Abu Bakr and Umar also refused to take it from him when he brought it to them when they were the caliphs. When Uthman ibn Affan became caliph, Thalaba brought it to him. Uthman took it with the interpretation that it was the due on goods which God had obliged in respect of this property. (250)

2.2. Criticism of What Uthman ibn Affan Did

This action of Uthman's is part of what he was criticized for. One must not criticize the judgment of one who strives with strenuous endeavor to arrive at a legal decision (*mujtahid*) in what his striving leads him to. The divine law has confirmed the judgement of the striver (*mujtahid*). The Messenger of God did not forbid any of his commanders from taking charity from this person. The divine command has come to give alms. (251)

2.3. The Judgment of the Messenger of God

The judgment of the Messenger of God may differ from someone else's judgment as we see. There were certain matters particular to the Messenger of God rather than anyone else because of the special quality entailed by prophethood in general or his prophethood in particular. God said to His Prophet regarding taking charity: "You will purify them and make them pure by it." He did not say: They will purified or cleansed by it. This is one of his special properties. He is compassionate and merciful to his community. He knew that if he took it, he would purify him and cleanse him by it. God had told him that Thalaba ibn Hatib was a hypocrite. The Prophet's good manners (*adab*) with God prevented him from taking it. Whoever so wishes stops where the Prophet stopped like Abu Bakr and Umar. (252)

2.4. Strenuous Endeavor to Arrive at a Legal Decision (*ijtihad*) is Allowed and Every Such Struggler (*mujtahid*) is Rewarded

Whoever wishes can stop at the general command of God as Uthman did. It is not necessary that anyone besides the Prophet purify and cleanse the one who pays the purifying alms. The caliph is the representative assigned to this purifying alms, that is, to the goods which demand it since the Messenger of God did not forbid anyone to do that nor did he command him to do what he stopped at and avoided. (253)

He allowed strenuous endeavor to arrive at a legal decision (*ijtihad*). Everyone who makes this strenuous endeavor takes note of the proof to which his strenuous endeavors led him. Whoever errs in his decision as a result of his strenuous endeavors has not carried out its due, yet both the one who errs and the one who is correct are the same, but not exactly so. (254)

3 Those Who Store Up Gold and Silver

Know that when God Almighty said: ". . . *and those who treasure up gold and silver and spend it not in the way of God, give to them tidings of a painful punishment,*" (9:34) that was before the obligation of giving the purifying alms which God prescribed for His servants in respect to their wealth. When God prescribed the purifying alms for His servants—the believers—God purified their wealth by it and removed the name "miserliness" from the one who gave wealth because of it by the very act of his giving it. God said about the one for whom almsgiving was sent down: ". . . *they became misers with it and turned away.*" (9:76) He described them as not accepting the judgment of God. He applied the attribute of being miserly to them towards the One who had blessed them and this miserliness is in respect of what God obliged them in their wealth. Then He explained about the painful punishment as being the state that he has. God Almighty said: " . . .*on a day it will be hot in the fire of hell. Then by it are branded their foreheads and their sides and their backs; it will be said: This is what you treasured up for yourselves.*" (9:35) (255)

3.1. The Repayment of Those Who Refuse to Pay the Purifying Alms

That is when the one with property sees the beggar turning to him. The lines of his forehead contract because he knows that he is going to ask him for some of his property. His forehead will be branded for that. The beggar will recognize that on his face. When the one who is asked pays no attention to the one who is asking and turns his side to him as if he had no awareness of him, his side will be branded for it. When he knows that the beggar is looking for him and that he must give to him, he turns his back to him and goes away and so God says that their backs will be burned because of it. This is the principle of those who withhold the purifying alms, that is, the purifying alms due on gold and silver. (256)

As for the alms on sheep, cattle and camels, that is another matter as is related in a text: "He will be thrown on his face on account of them on a very wide level plain . . . and they will gore him with their horns and trample him with their hooves and bite him with their mouths." This is particular to brows, sides and backs when burning is mentioned, and God knows best what He means. (257)

3.2 God Prescribed Purifying Alms as Purification for Property

God sent down the purifying alms, as we said, in order to purify property. It is difficult for the heedless and ignorant since they believe that they own what is specified for these goods and that it is part of their wealth. They do not know that what is stipulated is not their wealth. It is in their possession, but it is not actually part of their wealth. They are only told to bring it out. When they single it out, then they realize that it is not part of their wealthy. It is merely in their possession. This is the true situation. (258)

They believe that all that they have in their possession is their property and that they own it. Then God informed us that people have a due on their property which they should pay. It does not have any outward cause in which the ego can rely: No debt, nor selling other than what God Almighty mentioned about storing that up for him as a reward in the world to come. That is very difficult for the ego because of its partnership in the property. (259)

3.3. Property is God's Property and the Human Being is a Guardian of It

Since God knew that this is part of the natural mold of the soul, He removed that amount of property from their possession—rather He removed all property from their possession. He said: "*. . . and spend out of what He has made you ones who are successors in it.*" (57:7) That is to say, you only own what you spend of this wealth. This is disposing of it like guardians would do. The property belongs to God. When you are miserly with it, you are miserly with what you do not own since you are vicegerents in it and you are guardians for what you possess. (260)

He informed them that they are appointed vicegerents in it, and that is designed to make charity easy for them. It is a mercy to them. God said in effect: "As We commanded you to spend out of the property which you are appointed vicegerents over, so We commanded Our Messenger and representatives among you to take a certain amount from these properties which are in your possession. That is called the purifying alms. Its good reverts to you. Therefore, Our representatives do not dispose of what is your property. They dispose of that over which you have been made vicegerents as We allowed you to use it. If it is hard for you, the believer has no property and he has all property, sooner or later." (261)

3.4. Purifying Alms, as It is Charity, It is Hard on the Ego

I have informed you that since the giving of charity is difficult for the ego (soul), when a person spends charity, the reward is multiplied for him. He has the reward of hardship and the reward of spending. If he spends it without any hardship, then this is above the multiplying of the reward in a way that cannot be limited nor does it have any analogy. It is related about the one who is skilled in the Quran that he is joined to the angels, the noble scribes. The one who stammers when reciting the Quran has the reward multiplied for him because of the hardship he obtains in acquiring it and studying it. He has both the reward of hardship and the reward of recitation. (262)

3.5. Purifying Alms is Blessing in Property and Purification of the Ego

Purifying alms means that which purifies. When God removes the name of avarice and miserliness from the one who gives it, then avarice and miserliness have no control over him. Because the purifying alms contain growth and blessing, it is called "the purifying alms" because God makes it grow, as He said: *"He makes charity greater,"* (2:276) so purify yourselves by giving the purifying alms. It specifically has this meaning because its meaning exists in it. Purifying alms contains blessing for the property, purification of the soul and firmness in the way of life of God. Whoever is given these qualities is given much good. (263)

3.6. Purifying Alms is the Good Loan

As for His words on it: *"And lend to God a good loan,"* (73:20) goodness in action is that you see God in it. This is part of doing things beautifully or perfection of character (*ihsan*) and the Messenger of God used it to explain the concept of perfection of character (*ihsan*) when Gabriel asked about it. This is so that you know that property is God's property and that you own it when God lets you own it. After He lets you own it, He revealed to you in His kindness the aspect of the loan. He tells you in effect: "Do not let My asking you for a loan in this property distract you from recognizing that this property is actually Mine and not yours. (264)

"As it is not too grievous or difficult for you when you see someone using his property as he likes, so what I ask of you should not be too grievous or difficult for you in respect of that for which I have made you a viceregent. This is because you know that I am only demanding from you what I entrusted to you in order that you might give it to whomever I like among My servants. This amount of purifying alms I have not given to you at all. I have made you a guardian of it. It is not difficult for the guardian to carry out the trust and give it to its owner. When the alms-collector, who is the messenger and representative of the owner of the trust, comes to you, give him his trust cheerfully. This is the good loan. (265)

3.7. Perfecting Character (*ihsan*) Is That You Worship God As If You Were Seeing Him

Perfecting character (*ihsan*) is that you worship God as if you were seeing Him. When you see Him, you know that the property is His property and that the servant is His servant. He disposes of it and there is none to resist Him. You know that when you do these things, no benefit at all from them revert to God. When you do not do them, He is not harmed by that. All comes back to you. Therefore you must be in a state of perfecting your character (*ihsan*). You will be good to yourself. When you act with this trait of perfecting your character you will be protecting yourself from the avarice of your ego. Then this action will combine both the quality of perfecting character and God-consciousness (*taqwa*) for you, and so God will be with you. (266)

3.8. God Is With Those Who Have God-consciousness (*taqwa*) and Those Who Act in the State of Perfecting Character (*ihsan*)

Among those with God-consciousness (*taqwa*) is the one who is protected from the avarice of his ego by giving the purifying alms. "Among those who do good is the One who worships Me as if he sees Me and witnessed Me. Part of his seeing Me is his knowledge that I have only obligated him to dispose of what is Mine while its benefit reverts to him as a favor and a blessing, and he is praised for that." God has immense, overflowing bounty. (267)

3.9. Clarification: The Obligation of Purifying Alms on Property and the Soul

Know that God has obligated the purifying alms on wealth, that is, taken a little of it. He tells the owner of the property: "This amount which I have specified of property is not yours. You are entrusted with it." The owner of the property does not own the purifying alms. (268)

Then God Almighty placed our soul in the same jurisdiction as our property. He imposed almsgiving on them as He imposed it on property. Just as He commands almsgiving on property, He said to us about our soul (ego, self): *"He who makes it pure prospers."* (91:9) just as the one who has purified his property has won. Similarly He connected the soul to buying and selling in property and said: *"Truly God has bought from the ones who believe themselves and their property."* (9:111) He places buying and selling in both property and the soul. There is a question of jurisprudence in this sign. As He imposed the purifying alms on property and the soul, and the purifying alms on property is well-known, we will mention the purifying alms of the soul (ego) in detail in this book, God willing. (269)

3.10. The Purifying Alms of the Soul

I will also make the giving of the purifying alms on the soul, God willing, clear to you according to the basis which I have already mentioned. That is, namely, that the purifying alms are God's due on wealth. Wealth does not belong to the owner of the wealth. The same is true of the soul and therefore the purifying alms are due on the soul. It must be given to God from this soul so that he will be among the successful since He said: *"He who makes it pure prospers."* (91:9) and *"And whoever is protected from his own stinginess, then those are the ones who prosper."* (59:9) (270)

3.11. The Soul in Respect to Its Source Has a Possible Essence

Then we looked at the soul in respect to its source and said that the soul is made "possible" by its essence. If this is the case, no purifying alms are due on it. Nothing is due to God from a possibility of something existing. He is greatly Exalted. His existence is necessary and not just possible from any perspective. (271)

We found that this soul is described as existent, so we said that this existence by which the soul is described either belongs to it intrinsically or it does not. We saw that its existence is not the source of its essence and its essence is not described by it. We looked to see the one to whom it belongs. We found that it belongs to God even as we found that the specific amount in Zayd's property to which the purifying alms is due is because it is not Zayd's property. It is in his trust, his guardianship. (272)

3.12. The Essence of the Soul from God and for God

It is like that with the existence by which the soul is described. It does not belong to it. It belongs to God who brought it into existence.

Existence belongs to God, not to the soul. It is God's existence, not its existence. Therefore we said to this soul: "This existence by which you are described is not yours. It belongs to God. He bestowed it on you, so give it out to God and ascribe it to its owner. You still keep your possibility. You will not lack anything that is yours. If you do that, you will have the reward of those who know God with God. You will obtain a rank whose value is such that only God knows its true worth. That is the success which is going-on. God will make this existence go on for you and He will never take it from you. (273)

3.13. Existence and Bringing-into-Existence and Going-on and Making Go On

This is the meaning of His words: *"He who makes it pure prospers."* (91:9) That is, the one who has purified the soul or self has made it endure existent with the ability to escape from evil. That is to say, when you know that your existence belongs to God, God will make this gift endure for you and you will always be adorned by it. It is a going-on which is particular to the going-on of God. The loser who destroys it also goes on, but it is by God's preservation, not by the going-on of God. The polytheist who is one of the people of the fire does not think that his existence belongs purely to God because of what he associates with Him. The same is true for the atheist. (274)

We said that so that the one who has no knowledge would not imagine that God makes existence go on for the polytheist and the atheist. It is clear that the preservation of existence for those who are successful is not the same as its preservation for the people of the fire. This is why God says when He describes the people of the fire: *"Neither will it be decided a term for them so that they die nor will its punishment be lightened for them"* (35:36) as opposed to the attribute of the people of happiness who are in constant life. What a difference there is between the one who goes on by the going-on of God and exists by the existence of God, and the one who goes on by the preservation of God and exists by bringing-into-existence and not by existence. (275)

The gnostics have won this because they recognize that He is the One who deserves the attribute of existence. That is what they acquire from God, and this is the meaning of His words: *"He who makes it pure prospers."* (91:9) (276)

3.14. The Obligation of Purifying Alms on the Soul is Like Its Obligation on Property

Purifying alms is therefore obligatory on the soul as it is obligatory on wealth. Buying and selling occur in it as they occur in property. Something concerning this will come when we mention servants and their principle, and why the soul is not connected to the servant so that it would no longer have to give any purifying alms. Servants are connected to property by a certain aspect which we will discuss, God willing, as we will also mention what part of the human being must give the purifying alms according to the types of property on which it is obligatory. (277)

4 Do Not Claim Purity for Yourselves

As for His words: *". . . so ascribe not purity to yourselves."* (53:32) That is, God will not accept the purifying alms of the soul from one who ascribes himself as an associate to Him. Therefore He said: *". . . so ascribe not purity to yourselves."* He was saying to you, in effect: "When you consider that your "soul" is yours and not Mine, the purifying alms is My due and you are guardians over it. When you lay claim to it, you claim that you have given Me what belongs to you and that I am asking you for what is not Mine. The matter is different from that. Whoever is like this in giving does not purify himself. I only ask you for what is Mine, not what is yours until you meet Me. Then the cover will be lifted in the world to come and at that moment you will know whether your "soul" on whom the purifying alms is obligated, belongs to Me or you. Then your knowledge will not help you. This is why He said: *". . . so ascribe not purity to yourselves,"* that is, the "soul" that is not yours. It is His. (278)

4.1. The Soul of Jesus Was His in One Respect and in Another Belonged to God

Do you not see how Jesus ascribed his soul to himself from an aspect that is his and ascribed his soul to God by an aspect that belongs to God. He said: *"Thou knowest what is in my soul and I know not what is in Thy Soul."* (5:116) He related it to God, that is, "my 'soul'" is Thy Soul and Thy property. Thou hast bought it. Whatever Thou dost own, Thou dost know what Thou hast placed in it." He related himself to it. In respect to it as an individual, it belongs to him. In respect to its existence, it belongs to God and not to him. He said: "Thou knowest what is in my 'soul'" in respect to its source and I do not know what is in Thy Soul in respect to its existence. That is, in respect of what belongs to Thee. (279)

4.2. The Soul Has One Essence and Many Ascriptions and Relationships

Even if the soul is the same, the ascriptions vary because of the difference of the relationships. His words: *". . . so ascribe not purity to yourselves."* (53:32) do not conflict with what we mentioned of His words: *"He who makes it pure prospers."* (91:9) The Prophet said: "I do not declare anyone pure to God." God willing, in this chapter we will discuss the obligation of almsgiving, for whom it is obligatory, on what it is obligatory, how much is obligatory, from what amount it is obligatory, when it is obligatory and when it is not obligatory, with all the inward interpretations after we establish it outwardly by the judgment of the divine law as we did in the case of the formal prayer. This is in order to combine the outward and the inward dimensions to complete the form. (280)

4.3. The Reason for Joining the Outward and the Inward

There is no outward form that appears in the world in any creature for any reason that is manifest from forms or other things but that that very event has a spirit sending it to the senses. That spirit accompanies that form into existence by means of a certain phenomenal being: Angel, *jinn*, human being, animal, plant or mineral. To the senses, these are all the causes for the appearance of existence of that form. (281)

Since we know that God has connected a spirit of meaning to every sensory form by divine attention under the jurisdiction of a divine name or quality, we, therefore, interpret the Word of the Lawgiver inwardly. We do this step by step according to the principle that the spirit of whatever is in the outward dimension is reflected through the inward. The outward dimension is its sensory form and the divine spirit of meaning in that form is what we call the inner interpretation. When you traverse the valley, then you have learned about it, experienced it. These are the words of God Almighty: *"Then learn a lesson O those imbued with sight*! He said: *"Learn a lesson* (itabir*) O those imbued with sight."* (59:2) That is, learn from what you see with your eyes to what that form gives you of inner meaning and spirit. Then you will perceive it with your inner eyes. He commanded and urged this consideration. (282)

4.4. The Inflexible People Among the Scholars Stop at the Literal Meaning

This is a door which scholars neglect, especially the people who are inflexible and stagnated in the outwardly manifest. The only consideration which they possess is amazement. There is no difference between their intellects and the intellects of young children. These people do not learn at all to traverse from that outward form as God has commanded them. (283)

God has provided us with aptness in speech to be able to report about what we see. We know from God through the knowledge of unveiling, witnessing, and tasting. The interpretation of that is an opening from God which comes according to the principle of harmony. There are many individuals who cannot traverse, experience and learn from what is in themselves. There is many a person whose interpretation invalidates the soundness of what is in himself. God gives success. There is no Lord but Him. (284)

4.5. The Portion of Purifying Alms from the Divine Names

Know that since the meaning of almsgiving is purification as He said: *"Take charity from their wealth that thou wouldst purify them and make them pure with it."* (9:103) (His Word) refers to the divine name *al-Quddus* from among the divine names and qualities. That is, "the Pure." It also has whatever of the divine names possesses that meaning. Since the property which one gives in charity is not part of the property of the one who is told to give alms, but rather is a trust in his possession for its Owner, and only its Owner is entitled to it even if someone else has it, it is like a trust with him until he discharges it to its Owner. It is the same with the purifying alms of the soul. (285)

The soul has names and qualities or attributes which it merits. Those are the attributes which the "possible" are not entitled to because they are only "possible" and do not as yet have existence. God is entitled to these attributes when He is described by them so they can be distinguished from the attributes which are not fitting for Him. God, glory be to Him has described Himself with what is appropriate for the possible as an act of condescension on His part and as a mercy for His servants. (286)

4.6. The Purifying Alms of the Soul is to Give Out God's Due on It

The purifying alms of the "soul" is to give out God's due from it. Its purification is by that act of leaving the names and qualities or attributes which are not proper to it. Take your property from it and give Him what He owns from you. It is as He says: *"The command is altogether with God."* (13:31) That is sound. Our relationship to it is the relationship to the names and qualities or attributes in the view of the Asharites. All that is other than God belongs to God by God since only what is from Him can properly be said to be His. (287)

The Prophet said: The servant of a people is part of them. That is an incredible allusion. It is a statement which demands complete connection so that it can only be said that it is Him. It also demands absolute distance so that it cannot be said that it is Him since whatever is from you is not ascribed to you. A thing is not ascribed to itself because of it would have similarity. This is complete incomparability or transcendence. What is related to you is not what is from you. This is complete dissimilarity between you and it. There relationship in this question is like a person's hand to a person or a person's life to man. Life is part of a person's essence since he is alive and has animality. Life is ascribed to him even though it is part of his essence and his essence is only sound because of it. (288)

4.7. The Relation of the Possibles to the One Necessary by Essence

This aptness exemplifies an understanding of what we have indicated regarding the relationship of the possible to the One whose existence is necessary. The possibility of the possible is necessary in itself. This reality is still applied to it because it is its source and it is ascribed to it. What is its source may be ascribed to it. (289)

This is the meaning of His words: ""*The command is altogether with God.*" (13:31) That is, that by which you are described and that by which God is described belong to God entirely. So what is wrong with you? Do not understand your property when He says, in effect: "Give me your property." That is, that which is yours I have connected to you by the name of "possession." This is why He said: *"Take charity from their wealth that thou wouldst purify them and make them pure with it."* (9:103) That is, in effect, "Take from their wealth that which is not theirs. It is charity from Me to the ones I mention in My Book." God says: *"Learn a lesson O those imbued with sight?"* (59:2) He says that God made alms or charity obligatory for us on our wealth. He made our wealth a condition for charity. The condition is not the same as the thing alluded to, so the supplication is not the same as your wealth. Your wealth is the container for it. God has not asked you for what is yours. (290)

4.8. Purifying Alms on the Soul is More Definite than That On Wealth

The purifying alms on the "soul" is more definite than that on wealth. This is why God put it first when He spoke of selling. He said: *"Truly God has bought from the ones who believe,"* and then He adds: *"themselves and their properties."* (9:111) Therefore, the servant spends his "self" and his wealth in the way of God. What you will understand about that will come later, God willing. (291)

5 The Obligation of Purifying Alms

Purifying alms is obligatory according to the Quran, the *Sunna* and consensus. There is no dispute about it. (292)

5.1. The Purifying Alms of Existence: to Return What is God's to God

All that is other-than-God agree that the existence of what is other-than-God is from God. They return their existence to Him by this consensus. There is no disagreement about that among all that is other-than-God. This is the interpretation of consensus about the purifying alms of existence. (293)

We return what belongs to God to God. There is no existent and none who brings into existence except God. As for the Quran: *"Everything is perishing but His Countenance."* (28:88) Countenance refers to existence. It is the manifestation of the essence and sources. As for the *Sunna,* there is no power nor strength except by God. That is the interpretation of the purifying alms in the intellect and the divine law. (294)

6 The One Obliged to Pay Purifying Alms

Scholars agree that it is obligatory for every Muslim who is free, adult, sane, and who possesses the minimum amount. This is a place of agreement. They disagree about its obligatory nature for the orphan, madman, the servant, the People of the Pledge (*ahl al-dhimma*), and the one who lacks the minimum amount like the one who owes or is owed a debt or the one whose capital is tied up. (295)

7 The Interpretation of That About Which They Agree

7.1.1. The Muslim

The Muslim is one who submits to what is demanded of him. We mentioned that all that is other than God submits in referring its existence to God and that existence is only derived from God, and there is no going-on in existence except by God. (296)

7.1.2. Freedom

As for freedom, the like of that is that the one who is like this is free, that is, there is no ownership in his existence of any of God's creatures. (297)

7.1.3. Being Adult

5 Being adult is interpreted as having obtained discrimination between what his Lord deserves and what is not fitting for Him. When he recognizes the like of this, he has reached the limit where he must refer all affairs to God Almighty. That is the purifying alms which is obligatory on him. (298)

7.1.4. Sane

As for the intellect, it is that he understands from God what God desires of him when He addresses him in himself, when He inspires him or speaks to him on the tongue of the Messenger of God. Whoever limits his existence through the existence of his Creator has understood himself since the word for intellect (*aql*) is derived from the word for the hobbling-cord (*iqal*) of a beast. In reality, the hobbling cord is derived from the intellect. The intellect precedes the hobbling-cord. If he had not understood that when the beast is fastened by this rope, it is held back from going forward, he would not have called it a hobbling-cord. (299)

7.5. Owning the Minimum (*nisab*)

As for their statement about completely owning the minimum amount, his owning the minimum amount is the same as his existence, just as we have mentioned: Muslim, freedom, adulthood, and sanity. As for their words about full and complete ownership, the complete is that which is not lacking and has no imperfection in it. Imperfection is an quality of non-existence. He said: "It is non-existent." The perfect is existence. That is said in the words of Abu Hamid: "There is nothing more originally possible than this world. Its creation is the same as its existence. It is not other than that," that is, there is nothing in possibility more marvelous than its existence. It is possible in itself while its existence is derived. There is nothing more amazing in the "possible" than existence. It is obtained but the possible only obtains is existence from the Real. This is the meaning of the interpretation of their statement about complete possession. (300)

8 The Interpretation of That About Which They Disagree

As for the interpretation about what they disagree about, part of that is children. Some people say that the purifying alms is obligatory on their wealth. Some people say that there is no charity due on the wealth of the orphan. Some people make a distinction between what the earth produces and what it does not produce. They say that purifying alms are due on what the earth produces and that there are no purifying alms on anything else: Livestock, money and goods. Others make a distinction between money and other things, and say that there the purifying alms is only due on money. (301)

8.1. The Orphan is the One With No Living Father Who Has Not Yet Come of Age

The interpretation of what we have mentioned is that the orphan is the one with no living father who has not yet come of age, that is, he has not reached puberty in age, development, or by virtue of having had a wet dream. God Almighty said: *"He procreated not nor was He procreated."* (112:3) and He said: *"Glory be to Him that He should have a son!"* (4:171) God is not the father of any of God's creation and none of His creation is His son, glory be to Him and may He be exalted! (302)

Whoever considers that the obligation is on the property itself, says that it is obligatory. The one who takes the owner's obligation into consideration says that it is not obligatory for him because he is not under obligation. (303)

8.2. The Ascription of Existence to God and to the Source of the Possible

It is like that with the one who considers that his existence belongs to God. He says that almsgiving is not obligatory. There would be no one to accept it if it were obligatory. There is only God. The one who considers the relationship of existence to the possible itself—even while it is not described by existence—says that the purifying alms is obligatory and must be given since there must be a relationship due to an intelligible effect. (304)

8.3. Two Categories of Existents: Out-of-Time and In-Time

This is the reason why existent things are divided into two divisions: Out-of-time and in-time. The existence of the possible is an in-time existence. That is, this attribute occurred in it. In this division, he does not bother about whether this is in-time or out-of-time since, according to us, the in-timeness of a thing does not indicate that it did not have existence before its in-timeness. This is what God Almighty speaks about: "*Approaches them not a remembrance from their Lord, one that was renewed* (in-time). . . . " (21:2) Those are the out-of-time words of God which occur with them. It is as if you say: A guest happened to come to us one day. That does not indicate that he did not exist before that. (305)

3 Whoever thinks that in-time existence is not a right of the one described by it and that it is a right of another "possible," says that the purifying alms is obligatory for the orphan because it is a right of the Necessarily Existent (God) in what describes this "possible." This is like the opinion of the one who thinks that its obligation for the orphan in his property is a right of the poor in this property. Therefore the one who has disposal of the property gives out of that property. He is the guardian. (306)

8.4. Affirmation of Responsibility in the Source of the Oneness of God (*Tawhid*)

The one who thinks that alms is worship says that alms is not obligatory because the orphan has not reached the limit of obligation. We indicated that in sign:

The Lord is true and the servant is true.
Would that I knew who is the obligated one? (307)

This is for the one who is an adult while the child who is not responsible is the orphan. It is like that for all acts of worship in this fashion. The thing does not worship itself. When the one who recognizes this is very precise and makes it clear that there is only God, he is afraid of the pitfall into which the one without recognition falls. This is the one who is blamed by the Lawgiver who said that his actions will come to nothing. We seek refuge with God from disappointment! In that, the gnostic looks at the divine names, how principles are interdependent and their disparity in connections as we mentioned elsewhere. (308)

Acts of worship are obligatory for that reason and with this opinion in order to manifest that action in that place from that divine name upon which it is based. When a divine name addresses, it has jurisdiction in the state and the moment. It is then incumbent for this other divine name to move from this place to what is demanded of it. That is called worship. It is the furthest of what can be reached in affirming obligations in unity (*tawhid*) itself so that He is the One Who Commands-the One Who is Commanded, Speaker-Listener. (309)

8.5. The Interpretation of the One Who Makes a Distinction Between What the Earth Produces and What It Does Not Produce

As for the interpretation of the one who makes a distinction between what the earth produces and what the earth does not produce, its interpretation is what appears from the one described with existence. This is the "possible," in the things over which he has authority from whatever is the cause of its manifestation. If he ascribes the existence of that to what His existence is ascribed, he says that there are no purifying alms due. If he does not ascribe it and takes note of its manifestation, he says that it is obligatory. (310)

8.6. The One Who Makes a Distinction Between Money and Other Things

As for the one who makes a distinction between money, money belongs to what has the attribute of perfection or is like perfection. What is other than money is less than the degree of perfection or likeness to perfection. This is described as imperfection. He obliges alms for the imperfect in order to purify it of imperfection and does not oblige it for perfection. Perfection can only be in what is perfect since there is only perfection in Oneness. (311)

8.7. People of the Pledge and the Christians of the Taghlib Tribe

Part of that are the People of the Pledge (*ahl al-dhimma*). Most agree that the People of the Pledge pay no purifying alms. There is one group which states that the purifying alms is doubled for the Christians of the Taghlib tribe. That is, whatever is taken from the Muslims is taken from them. A certain group made that statement and related it from the action of Umar with them. It is as if they thought that the like of this is like seizing something, even if the roots are different. (312)

8.8. It Is Not Permitted to Take Purifying Alms from the Ungrateful

That which I believe is that it is not permissible for anyone to take the purifying alms from an unbeliever, even if it is obligatory for him along with all of the obligations. He does not accept some of what is obligatory for him except after he has acquired belief in that. If he is one of the People of the Book, we have a certain view. If the capitulation tax (*jizya*) is taken from them, the Lawgiver confirmed their religion which they have. It is prescribed for them so they must establish their religion. If the purifying alms is part of it and they bring it, it is accepted from them. God knows best. (313)

We should not seek to take the purifying alms from the polytheist. If he brings it, we accept it. God Almighty said: "*. . .and woe to the ones who are polytheists—those who give not the purifying alms. . . .* (41:6) God Almighty says: "*Say to those who were ungrateful: If they refrain themselves, what is past will be forgiven.*" (8:38) Here the ungrateful is rejected, not the monotheist. (314)

9 Interpretation of the Purifying Alms of the People of the Pledge (*Ahl al-Dhimma*)

God Almighty said: *"They regard not towards one who believes either ties of relationship or a pact."* (9:10) "Ties of relationship" or "wombs" refers to God. It is one of His names (*rahma*) and the pact is the contract and covenant. If the pact is made, then it is fulfilled by the purifying alms. The purifying alms for the People of the Pledge is performing what they agreed in the pact to do. The one who removes the purifying alms from them thinks that when those who make a pledge make a pact, then the two are equal in the contract. When the two are equal, they are made to be two likes. God Almighty said: *"There is not like Him anything,"* (42:11) so He does not accept the monotheism (*tawhid*) of the polytheist even though the polytheist affirms the oneness of God in His immensity when He says: *"We worship them not but that they may bring us near to God."* (39:3) This is undoubtedly monotheism. In spite of this, the divine law forbade its acceptance. (315)

9.1. The Proof of Monotheism is Monotheism Itself

Know that the proof is other than the proven. Monotheism is the proven while the proof is different. Therefore there is no monotheism here. Whoever makes the proof of the oneness of God to be the same as the oneness of God says that there the purifying alms is not obligatory. Therefore, there is no purifying alms due by the People of the Pledge. The purifying alms purifies. There must be belief in order to purify the soul. Belief itself is a sign of inner purification. A belief which we take notice of is only when the thing be named by the statement of the one who is aware of what he is speaking about. This or he does what he does based on the words of one who is aware. Belief in this sense is not through the intellectual proof itself. (316)

9.2. Unity (*Tawhid*) Pervades in Things

The knowledge of polytheism is one of the most difficult things to look into since oneness, unity pervades all things. The action in which something is associated with God is not sound at all. Whenever someone has a special rank, it is impossible for there to be a partner in it. However, polytheism, which is dealt with in the divine law, exists, and one is punished for it. (317)

10 The Ungrateful Are Addressed by the Principles and Secondary Rulings of the Divine Law

Know that the ungrateful are also addressed by the divine law. It is belief in all that the Messenger brought from God in the way of reports and the fundamental principles and secondary rulings. It is his words, may God bless him and grant him peace, in effect: "And that you believe in me and what I have brought." That is acting according to what the address demands of actions and non-action. (318)

Belief that voluntary charity is voluntary, is mandatory. It is one of the basic principles of the divine law. Giving voluntary charity is a secondary ruling. There is no difference between it and obligatory charity in respect of belief in them, even if the reward for them is not the same. That does not, however, detract from the basic principle. Even if the two are different from one aspect, they are joined together in the strongest aspect. (319)

10.1. Belief is the Root and Action is the Branch

Undoubtedly belief is the root and action is the branch of that root. This is why the believer never purely rebels without the rebellion being mixed with obedience. The one who mixes obedience and rebellion is the rebellious believer. If he rebels in a certain matter, he still believes that it is rebellion. Belief is obligatory, so he has done what is obligatory. The believer is rewarded in the very act of rebellion and his belief made is stronger. (320)

10.2. Purifying Alms is Not Acceptable in the Case of the People of the Pledge

No purifying alms are due from the People of the Pledge, meaning that it not acceptable from them when they pay it, even though it is obligatory for them, like all the other obligations of the divine law. This is because they lack the precondition which makes it valid. That is belief in all that the divine law brought, and not simply in it and some of what the divine law brought. If one believes only in the purifying alms or one of the obligations as obligations or some of the supererogatory practices as supererogatory practices while not believing in the other obligations or supererogatory practices, then his belief would not be accepted from him since he did not believe in all of it. (321)

In spite of this, we cannot ask the People of the Pledge for the purifying alms. If he brings it out of his own initiative, then we cannot reject it because he brought it to us without being asked for it. The ruler takes it from him for the Muslim treasury. He does not take it as purifying alms or reject it. If he refuses it, he has rebelled against the command of the Messenger of God. (322)

11 Purifying Alms on the Servant's Property

As far as the servant is concerned, people have three different opinions about it. Some say that he does not give any purifying alms at all for his property because he does not own it completely since the master can remove it. The master also does not own it completely because the servant has disposal of it. Therefore there is no alms on a servant's property. Another group believe that the master must pay the purifying alms of the servant because he can remove it from him. Another group say that the servant must pay the purifying alms for it since the place of its disposal is like the disposal of the free person. (323)

Our Shaykh and a group of people said that there is no purifying alms due on the property of the *mukatab* servant until he is free. Abu Thawr said that there is purifying alms on the property of the *mukatab* servant. (324)

That which I say is that either you think that the purifying alms is due on the property and do not take the owner into consideration, and in that case the ruler must take it from all property provided that there is the minimum amount and the one who possesses it has had it for a full year. Whoever thinks that the obligation of the purifying alms is due from the owners of the property has the various positions which we have mentioned in respect of that. It is most fitting that every one who looks at property is called upon to pay its purifying alms. (325)

11.1. Purifying Alms is Due on Property Itself

The interpretation of that is that the servant and what he owns belongs to his master. Whatever his master commands him to do he is obliged to obey him. The purifying alms is a right which God has obligated on property itself for certain categories. It is in the hands of the believers. Property is not impaired for the owner. That is, from the owner having the power to dispose of it. Purifying alms is a trust in the hand of the one who has this property in these categories. It is neither the property of the free person nor the servant. The ones who have it must pay it from what they have and can dispose of it, whether they are free or servants among the believers. All are servants of God. (326)

There is no purifying alms owed by the servant because he is merely handing over the trust. For him, the purifying alms means to connect this right to its owner. *"Truly God commands you to give back trusts to the people."* (4:58) He purifies property on which purifying alms are due by the purifying alms themselves. That is, by paying the purifying alms due on it. Purifying alms are obligatory for the master because he owns the servant. God has made it obligatory to be merciful in the same way that He is merciful as He says: *"He has prescribed for Himself mercy."* (6:12) He said: *"And My mercy encompasses everything. Then I will prescribe it for those who are Godfearing and give the purifying alms and those who believe in Our signs. . . ."* (7:156) *"It has been an obligation on Us to help ones who believe."* (30:47) and *". . . and live up to the compact with Me."* (2:40) Whoever sees the fundamental basis as we have mentioned has his own opinion regarding the property of the servant. (327)

12 Owners Who Have Debts

Part of that concerns owners who have debts which would absorb their property and absorb what property of theirs is subject to the purifying alms although they possess property on which the purifying alms is obligatory. (328)

12.1. Statements of the Scholars on the Property of Those in Debt

Some say that there is no alms on the property, whether it is grain or something else, until the debt is paid on it. After that, if there remains that on which the purifying alms is obligatory, then he should give the purifying alms. Otherwise he does not give it. One group stated that the debt does not prevent the purifying alms on grains being due, and it only prevents it on other things. One group said that the debt only prevents the purifying alms on coinage, unless he has goods from which his debt could be paid. It is not prevented by it. Another group say that the purifying alms is not prevented at all. (329)

12.2. Purifying Alms Is the Right of God and the Right of God Has First Right

The interpretation in that is that almsgiving is a form of worship. It is the right of God. The right is the first to be paid. A text has come about that from the Messenger of God. God made alms a right for the ones He mentioned in the Mighty Quran "*. . . and falsehood cannot reach it from before it or behind it —a revelation from One who is All-Wise, Praiseworthy.*" (41:42) The debt is an organized, advanced due. The debt should be paid before alms. (330)

13 Property Owed to Someone Else

Part of property which is owed to someone else while it is not in the possession of the owner is a debt. Some say that there is no purifying alms on it, even if he holds it until a year has passed while it is still in the possession of the lendee. That is my opinion. Some say that if he takes the loan, he pays the purifying alms after one year, even if it stays with the debtors for years since its root is compensation. If it is without compensation, like inheritance, then it is met after a year. (331)

13.1. There Is No Owner Except God

The inner interpretation of that: There is no owner except God, and whoever God gives property to He gives him ownership over it is in his hand inasmuch as he can dispose of it, then he must pay the purifying alms according to its conditions without regard for the passage of time. The Sufi is the child of the moment. He does not belong to what has passed or to what lies in his future, even if he can make an intention for the future and desire the past. However, he is in the state of the present. This is all of him and he is part of the moment, not part of the past or the future. (332)

13.2. The Time Elapsed Regarding the Property Is Not Taken Into Consideration

Therefore, he does not take into consideration the time that has passed while that property has been in the hands of the debtors. He constantly has an opening with God Almighty that the one in whose hand the property lies is God. The purifying alms is obligatory on it for the years in which he has had it. The Messenger of God said: "Perform the formal pilgrimage on behalf your father." He also commanded the guardian of the dead person to perform what the dead person owed of fasting Ramadan. That only brings the fruit of the action to the one for whom he performs the formal pilgrimage or fasts for what is obligatory on him. That has a different principle. (333)

13.3. The One Who Has the Greater Pilgrimage or Another Action Done on His Behalf

In spite of this, whoever performs the formal pilgrimage for him or performs whatever action he does, that is charity for the one who does this action for the person for whom he is acting, be he dead or alive. However, the living person does not have what is obligatory for him cancelled for him unless he is incapable of doing it. If his guardian does it, then he has the reward of the one who performs what is obligatory for him. That is only the formal pilgrimage according to what we have just mentioned. The reward does not go to the taker unless the person who is represented is dead. It is a reward in the other world. If he is alive, the borrower is his guardian. That is God. If he takes it, it gives it to him in the world to come and for the one who did it for him, here in this world. (334)

14 Intention and Action

Part of its interpretation refers to the person who desires to have property so that he might act correctly with it. Then God would write for him the reward of the one who acts. His intention is better than the one who does it, and He will write the fullest portion for him. He is in the protection of someone wise and does not have any of it in his possession. (335)

If he obtains what he desires, or some of what he desires which he can bring to performing that correct action, then it is obligatory for him to do that correct action which he intended. If he does not do it, the reward of what he intended is not written for him. Had he died before he obtained what he desired, the reward of what he intended would have been written for him. God Almighty said: *Your property and your children are a trial,* (8:28), that is, they are a test to establish the proof of the sincerity of the claim or whether it is a lie. (336)

15 Purifying Alms on Fruits Whose Source is an Endowment (*waqf*)

Part of this section is their disagreement regarding the purifying alms on fruits whose source is an endowment. Some say that the purifying alms is due on them. Some people say that there none is due on them. Some people make a distinction between what is an endowment for the poor—on which there is no purifying alms—and what is set up for specific individuals—on which the purifying alms is due. (337)

I say that the purifying alms is obligatory, whether it is for a specific or unspecified person. If it is for specific people, then they must pay the purifying alms. If it is not specific, then the ruler must take the purifying alms from it based on the principle of guardianship. (338)

15.1. Pure Action for God and That Which Contains Someone Else's Due

The inward interpretation of that fruit is the action of the human being who is obligated. The action can be purely for God like the formal prayer, fasting, and their likes, or there can be a due owed to someone else in it, like the purifying alms, although it is still prescribed that the person act. So he said: "This is for God and you. It is for you, and what do I have except God and you?" The Prophet said: "Whoever says: 'This is for God and you,' it is for you and God has nothing of it." Then he prescribed for the one who said this to say: "This is for God and then for so-and-so." He should not use the *waw* ("and") of partnership. This action which he does for him is for God, and it is like the purifying alms on property whose source is an endowment and which belongs to certain people. It is his words: "Then for so-and-so," with a preposition and not with the conjunction "and." It is those fruits which remain in the possession of the beneficiary of the endowment after giving the purifying alms. This is the interpretation of the one who thinks that the purifying alms are due on it. (339)

15.2. Purifying Alms are the Due of God and the Due of the Poor

The one who thinks that there is no purifying alms due for it, that is that nothing is due for God, follows the interpretation of the words of the Prophet: "It is for you. God has nothing of it." That is, God has nothing due from it. Whoever thinks that the purifying alms is the due of the poor, thinks in his interpretation that the purifying alms of the source of fruit is an endowment—and it is the action of this servant which is bound to his master—he is never freed. He says that the action belongs to God by the principle of the endowment system. The *houris* and their likes have a portion of that action which is designated alms as one of them said in respect to the strivers:

> The doors of Eden are open and the houris are looking down
> from them.
> Go ahead in whatever way possible and set out, O warriors!
> The gardens are before you,
> and in them are tender beauties.
> They are rare. The tents are already up.
> Our bride-price is steadfastness and constancy. (340)

15.3. Steadfastness and Constancy Are the Purifying Alms of *jihad*

They are in the position of the purifying alms on fruit whose source is an endowment. It is the words of God Almighty: *"And I created not jinn and human kind but that they worship Me."* (51:56) He only created them to worship Him, so they are bound to Him. Then He stipulated a portion for God in their actions, which are in the position of the fruit on the trees. That is, sincerity in action. It is part of action and the right of the one who does the action. That is what he obtains of reward for the action. That is in the position of purifying alms which the reward demands. This is the interpretation of the purifying alms of fruit whose source is an endowment according to the differences of opinion. God is the guide. (341)

16 Paying the Purifying Alms Due on the Produce of Rented Land

Part of this subject concerns the question of whether or not one should pay the purifying alms due on the produce of rented land. Some scholars say that the purifying alms is owed by the crop's owner. Some people say that purified alms is owed by the land owner and that the renter does not have to give anything. My position is the first one. The crop owner has to give it. (342)

16.1. Rented Land Is the Soul of the Obligated Person

The leader of the formal prayer, the caller to formal prayer (*muadhd-hin*), the one performing the struggle (*jihad*), the one who gives charity, and whoever takes a reward from his actions are among those who rent. The earth which is rented is the soul of the responsible person. Its produce is the actions which appear from this soul. The creator is God Almighty. God Almighty said: *"Is it you who create it or are We the ones who are the creators*? (56:59) The Owner of the land is the Lawgiver and that is God since He gave the divine law just as He gives success in agriculture. God said in report from one of His Prophets: *"My success is not but from God."* (11:88) (343)

16.2. God Broadcasts the Seeds of Guidance in the Land of the Soul

He—glory be to Him!—broadcasts the seeds of guidance and success in the land of the soul. Then the land of the soul produces according to what is planted in it. God has something due on it. Part of it is what the human being has a right in. What belongs to God is designated as the purifying alms. What remains is for the human being. The wage is prescribed. God buys ourselves from us and then rewards us for them by "the tenth" tax (*ushr*). He said: *"Whoever drew near with benevolence, then for him, ten times the like of it."* (6:160) Our good action is the tenth tax which We give Him from what He has planted in the earth of ourselves in the way of good which generates this righteous action. (344)

16.3. God is the Lord of the Earth, the Cultivator, the Hirer and the Renter

He—glory be to Him!—is the owner of the land, the cultivator, the hirer and the tenant. He is the one obligated to pay the purifying alms and He is the one who takes the alms as He said: *"Know they not that God is He Who accepts remorse from His servants and takes charities and that God is The Accepter of Repentance, The Compassionate."* (9:104). However, there are different aspects and relationships. He is the Giver and the Taker. There is no god but Him. There is no Doer except Him. He obliges since He is like that and He is obliged since He is like that. (345)

God Almighty said: *"He has prescribed for Himself mercy."* (6:12) That is, obligated it and made it obligatory. No one obligated that on Him. He obligated it on Himself as a favor from Him and bounty to us. He makes Himself known to us by the realities of His names and qualities, and all the divine roads are established on these names. *"Say: All is from God. So what is with these folk that they understand almost no discourse."* (4:78). (346)

16.4. The Good is from God and the Bad from Yourself

Then He took an oath and said within these words: *"Whatever of benevolence lit on thee is from God and whatever evil deeds lit on thee then is from thyself."* (4:79) It is what does you ill. You are the place of the effect of evil. Inasmuch as it is an action which is not described as evil, it belongs to the divine name which brought it into existence. The bringing into existence of the like of this action is good. It is only evil for the one who finds it evil or the one who makes it evil. That is the human soul since the one who experiences pain is the one who experiences it in himself. Its principle is manifest in him. It is not from the One Who Brings it into existence. There is no jurisdiction in it at all for the Doer. (347)

This is the meaning of His words: *". . . whatever evil deeds lit on thee then is from thyself."* (4:79). Good is like that. That is good with the human being, so it is also good in respect of the Real who brings it into existence. Good is ascribed to God. He brings it into existence in the beginning, even if it is good with you after it is brought into existence. However, it is only called good inasmuch as it is prescribed and it is only prescribed on the part of God. (348)

16.5. Evil, in Respect of God, is Good

This is why we said that the evil is good as far as God is concerned because there it is avoided. It is evil to the one who has it either in this world or in the next. Leaving action may be evil although that is not action, or action may be evil. It is like that with the good action. It can either be action or non-action. Divine success is what effects the action or non-action inasmuch as it is leaving it and inasmuch as it appears from him since it is an action. (349)

16.6. God Obliges the Servant to Act and Not Act

There is no right which is obligatory for the servant to not do or to do but that God has a due on it by which a judge is established as a representative from God. If what remains of that action or non-action is a right for God, it is a right for God from all its aspects and the servant has no right in it: Like the formal prayer and carrying out the punishment (*hudud*). If what remains of that action or non-action is a right of a creature, like beating, cursing, or usurpation of property, God has a right in it, and it is what we already mentioned. The creature also has a right in it. The right which God has is the same as the purifying alms which exists in all the actions of God in His creation. The judge is a representative in what he is appointed to do. If he likes, he can keep it, and if he likes, he can leave it according to the situation and what is beneficial. There is nothing held against him in that. It is called discretionary punishment (*tazir*) regarding that which has no punishment (*hadd*). He must cut off the hand of the thief. If he takes the property from his hand and returns it to his owner, then the judge can choose. If he wishes, he punishes him for that amount in which God has a prescribed right, and if he wishes, he does not punish him, but leaves that to God when He takes charge of him in the world to come without intermediary. (350)

17 When "*Land Revenue*" *Tax* is Transferred to the Muslims

Part of this section is the land of the "land revenue" tax (*kharaj*) when it is transferred to Muslims. That is the land which is in the possession of the People of the Pledge. Is there the tenth tax on it along with the "land revenue" tax or not? Some say that there is "the tenth" tax, that is, purifying alms on it. (351)

Know that purifying alms is either a due on land or a due of grain. If it is a due on land, then the purifying alms is not obligatory because two rights are not joined together in it: That would be the land revenue tax and the tenth tax. If it is the due on the grain, then land revenue tax is due from the land and the tenth tax from the grain. The dispute about the sale of land on which is the land revenue tax is well-known among scholars. (352)

17.1. Actions of the Body, and the Body and Passion

Bodily actions are in the position of agriculture and the body is in the position of the earth. Passion rules the land. When this land moves to the jurisdiction of the divine law, which is acting by what Islam demands, then the land revenue tax on the land is the rights which God has over it inasmuch as He gave it existence. That is knowledge which the intellect alone possesses by its perception. God has the land revenue tax on this land since it is praiseworthy to thank the Blesser. He is the One who bestowed it, glory be to Him! (353)

17.2. Two Categories of Muslims: Gnostic and Non-gnostic

When this land comes into the possession of Muslims, that is, into the divine law, and is transferred to them, then Muslims are divided in two divisions: The gnostics and the non-gnostics. When the gnostic plants righteous actions on this land, he sees that the purifying alms is the due of the action. That is, he refers the actions to their Actor. That is God—glory be to Him! (354)

The non-gnostic thinks that the action belongs to the physical faculties and that the land revenue tax is obligated on them. Therefore he thinks that the purifying alms is not obligatory since two dues are not joined together in it. He thinks that the action only belongs to himself. He is not a gnostic: *"And God places not a burden on any person beyond what He has given him."* (65:7) He said: *"That is their attainment of knowledge."* (53:30) (355)

17.3. It is Not Impossible that Two Dues Be Combined in the Land

As for our position in this question, it is that two dues are joined in the land. That is not impossible since the land is in the possession of the one who has it and that forbids someone else from using it without his permission. He owes something for it which is called the land revenue tax. When he plants it, then the state of the land changes since it is cultivated rather than uncultivated. Then there is another due obliged on it since it has cultivation. The tenth tax is obligatory for it since it is cultivated and the land revenue tax is obligatory for it since it is in his possession. That is the method by which we consider the interpretation. (356)

18 When the Tenth Taxed Land is Transferred to the People of the Pledge

As for tenth taxed land, when it is transferred to the People of the Pledge and he cultivates it, some say that there is no land revenue tax due on it and no tenth tax. Al-Numan said that when a member of the People of the Pledge bought land on which there is the tenth tax, it became land on which the land revenue tax is due. It is as if he thought that the tenth tax is the due on the land of Muslims and the land revenue tax is the due of the land of the People of the Pledge. Whoever thinks this, demands that when the land of the People of the Pledge moves to the Muslim, it reverts to being the tenth taxed land. (357)

18.1. Jurisdiction of the Intellect and Jurisdiction of the Divine Law Over the Soul

The intellect has jurisdiction over the soul in respect to its essence and investigation. The divine law has jurisdiction over the soul. When the intellect removes the soul from the power of the divine law by a doubt by which it buys, does God accept from it every action whose form is praiseworthy in the divine law? His action is from his intellect and not from the divine law. Some of us say that it is indeed accepted and he is repaid for it in this world, if he is not a monotheist and is a polytheist. If he is a monotheist, then it is accepted from him and he is repaid for it with a reward other than that of the believer. (358)

18.2. The Believer Has Two Rewards for His Action on the Day of Rising

The believer has two rewards for his action on the Day of Rising: A reward inasmuch as he is a believer acting by the divine law and a reward inasmuch as that action is part of good character and is good in itself. The Messenger of God spoke to Hakim ibn Hizam when he became Muslim. He had done much good during the Age of Ignorance: "You have become a Muslim along with the previous good which you did." Therefore God rewarded him for the good which he had done at the time of the Age of Ignorance. (359)

18.3. Good Demands Repayment in Itself

Good demands repayment in itself. When it is accompanied by belief, then the repayment is multiplied because of this extra attribute. It has another due. The principle of the divine law is the tenth tax and the principle of the intellect is the land revenue tax. (360)

19 When Purifying Alms Are Paid and Then Lost

When alms are paid and then lost, some people say that he is rewarded for it. Some people say that he is answerable for it until it is put in its proper place. Some people make a distinction between paying it after he has the ability to pay it, and paying it at the beginning of the time when it is obligatory and can be paid. Some people say that if he pays it some days after he is able to do so, and it is obligatory, then he is responsible. If he pays it at the beginning and is not remiss, he is not answerable. (361)

Some people say that if he is remiss, then he is liable, and that is my position. If he is not remiss, then he gives the remaining purifying alms. Some people say that he returns what has gone from all of it. There remain the very poor and the owner of the property when there are two partners in the remainder according to their portions of the portion of the owner of the property. It is like two partners, when some shared wealth vanishes and the two partners remain in that relationship in the remainder. (362)

The end result is that there are five positions about this question. The first is that he is absolutely not responsible. The second is that he is absolutely responsible. The third is that if he is remiss, he is responsible, and if he is not remiss, then he is not responsible. The fourth is that if he is remiss, he is responsible, and if he is not remiss, then he pays the remaining alms. The fifth statement is that they are two partners in what remains. (363)

19.1. If Some of the Property is Lost After the Obligation

If some of the property is lost after the obligation and it is said that it was possible to give the purifying alms, then it is said that he gives the remaining purifying alms. Some people say that the state of the poor and the state of the property owner is that of two partners who lose some of what they have. (364)

If the purifying alms is obligatory and it is possible to pay it, but he does not pay it until some of the property has been lost, then it is agreed that he is answerable. God knows best. This is with the exception of cattle according to the one who thinks that their obligation is completed, provided the messenger sets out with capability. That is the view of the school of Malik. (365)

20 The People of Wisdom and the Purifying Alms of Wisdom

The Messenger of God said: "Only give wisdom to its people lest you wrong it, and do not forbid it to its people and thereby wrong them." Spending wisdom is the same as the purifying alms. It has people as the purifying alms has people. When you give wisdom to other than its people while you suppose that they are its people, then it is lost as this property is lost after it is spent. It has not reached its owner. He is then answerable to the one who loses because he has been remiss since he was not firm in his recognition of the one who would lose this wisdom. Therefore he must bring it out a second time to the one who deserves it so that it is put in its proper place. (366)

20.1. When the One with Wisdom Puts It in the Wrong Place

As for the principle of two partners in that as was stipulated, when the bearer of wisdom puts it with other than its people according to his supposition, then he loses it. The one to whom you have given it is not its people so it is lost with him. He loses some of its due and the one who has given wisdom to other than its people must make good what has been missed when he looks at the state of the one who loses the wisdom. He is asked for the amount appropriate to him in order to make it good so that its people will obtain it. The due of the other is forfeited according to what he lacks of the understanding of the first wisdom which was wasted on him. (367)

20.2. The One Who is Asked for Knowledge and Conceals It

As far as the remaining case is concerned, there are many different aspects of interpretation based on this method. Some take the general statement of the Messenger: "Whoever is asked for knowledge and conceals it, God will bridle him with a rein of fire." Therefore when someone who is not one of the people of wisdom asks him for it and the wisdom is wasted, he says that he is not absolutely responsible. Others take the statement of the Messenger: "Only give wisdom to its people lest you wrong it." He says that he is absolutely liable. Its security is that he gives him the aspects of the answer to what he asks which befit him, even if that is not valid in the heart of the matter, like the "whereness" for the One who is not described as being enclosed. (368)

Whoever abandons the first answer for another answer in the question which is necessitated by the state of the one who is asking and the moment, says that he pays the remaining purifying alms and that the principle of what has passed and been lost is like the principle of property which is lost before it can be paid. Some say that he must look at the state of the one who is asking and when he does not do so, then he is remiss. If he does so and errs by a doubt which leads him to imagine that he is one of the people of wisdom, then he has not been remiss. This is the position of the one who says that if he is remiss, then he is answerable, and if he is not remiss, then he is not answerable. The fifth statement has already been discussed previously regarding the partner. (369)

20.3. Knowledge is a Trust with the Knower

The knower either believes regarding knowledge he has that they have it like the trust and so his principle in that is that of the guardian, or he believes that it is a debt which they have against him, and so his principle is that of the debtor. The principle regarding the trust, the debt and loss is well-known. The interpretation of those aspects has preceded about it, and God knows best. (370)

21 When Someone Dies After Purifying Alms is Obligated for Him

Some people say that it is paid from his capital. Some people say that if he bequeaths it, it is paid from the third. If not, there is nothing against him. Some say that one begins with it, even if it uses up the entire third. Some of them say that one does not begin with it. (371)

21.1. The Purifying Alms of Knowledge is Teaching It

The person among the people of the Path of God is given knowledge of God. We have stated that the purifying alms of knowledge is to teach it. A truthful, thirsting disciple comes and asks him about a question of knowledge which he does not know. This is the time when it is obligatory for him to teach it to him: It is like the obligation of the purifying alms when there is full power and the minimum amount. Then he did not teach him when he asked about knowledge. If God withholds that question from the knower, he will remain ignorant of it and seek it in himself and not find it. That is his death after the obligation of the prescribed alms. Ignorance is death. He said: *"Is he who has been lifeless and We gave him life. . . "*. (6:122) Or else the knower may be obliged to teach one who deserves it but then he teaches the one who does not deserve it. That is his death since he is ignorant of the worthiness of the one who deserves the wisdom and so he gives it to other than its proper people. (372)

In the first case, the sincere disciple is given that question, but it comes from seeing this knower when he hears him teach it to someone else or he learns it from the one that that person of knowledge has taught previously. That falls in the balance of the first person of knowledge, even if he is ignorant of it. So this means that he is rewarded for it and it is taken out of his capital. If that person of knowledge apologizes to the disciple and admits his penalty and wrong action, then God will give opening to the disciple by it. His admission is in the position of the one who bequeaths it. (373)

21.2. The Sick Person Only Owns a Third of His Property

As for bringing the purifying alms out from the third (which can be left as bequests), the sick person only owns a third of his property and no more. It is as if it were obligated on him in what he owns. It is like that with this knower. He only owns the excuse from himself in this state, and he does not know the other two-thirds. It is a favor, and there is no favor in teaching after this event and it is not obligated of him. He has forgotten it. In general, the one who has this state must renew his repentance for what he has fallen into and ask forgiveness of God in what is between him and God. *"Truly God loves the penitent."* (2:222). (374)

22 Their Disagreement About Property Which Is Sold After Purifying Alms Is Obliged

Some people say that the one who takes the purifying alms takes it from the property itself and gives the buyer back its price from the seller. Some people say that the sale is void. Some people say that the buyer can choose between letting the sale go through or returning it. The tenth tax is taken from the fruit or grain on which purifying alms is due. Malik says that the seller must pay the purifying alms and that is my opinion. (375)

22.1. The Servant Is Commanded to Pay the Purifying Alms of His Soul (*nafs*)

The interpretation of that: God Almighty said: *"He who makes it pure prospers."* (91:9) That is, the soul because he has made it become that on which alms is not obligatory. The servant is commanded to give the alms due on his soul. Then God has bought their souls from the believers. Then one of the believers sold himself from God after he was obliged to pay alms. When the servant believes, it is obligatory for him to pay the alms on his soul. He sells it from God after the purifying alms is obligatory. (376)

22.2. Purifying Alms Is the Property Itself and Purifying Alms is the Liability of the Responsible Person

So the purifying alms is either within the property itself or the liability of the responsible person. If it is the liability of the responsible person, then it is obligatory for the seller. If it is on the property itself, then its purifying alms is obligatory for the one who actually possesses that very property. Therefore the buyer brings it out of the property and the seller must return its price. When the obligation falls on the seller, then the seller must give the purifying alms of that amount of the property which he has. (377)

22.3. The Shaykh of Guidance Owns the Soul of His Disciples

Similarly the shaykh of guidance owns the soul of his disciples, and he pays their purifying alms according to the purifying alms which are obligatory for himself before he buys them from God. Since the purifying alms are obligatory for him on himself, he gives the purifying alms on the soul of the disciples whom he has. If he is someone who says that the sale is invalid, he revokes the purchase until the purifying alms is paid and then he buys it from God. If he is one who says that the buyer has the option of seeing the sale through or revoking it, that is up to God. If He likes, He accepts it and purifies it by the purifying alms, and if He so wishes, He returns it to the seller until he gives the purifying alms. (378)

23 Purifying Alms on Property Given Away

Part of this subject is their disagreement about purifying alms on property which is given away. Its interpretation is that the recipient can choose. If he likes, he accepts the gift and recognizes the due in it and gives its due to the one who deserves it and keeps the rest. If he likes, he returns what purifying alms is obligatory in it to the seller until he pays it. The recipient is God here. Those who have the purifying alms on the soul is what the Garden demands of them and whoever is in them: Is it their due from the soul of the believer? (379)

24 The Ruling About Someone Who Refuses to Pay Purifying Alms but Does Not Deny That It is Obligatory

Abu Bakr al-Siddiq, may God be pleased with him, believed that his judgement was that of the apostate and so he fought them and took their children as captives. Umar ibn al-Khattab, may God be pleased with him, differed from him in that and he set free those of them he had imprisoned. Most people follow Umar's position. One group believes that the one who refuses to do any of the obligatory things is ungrateful, even if he does not deny that it is obligatory. (380)

24.1. The Soul of the Believer is a Portion of the Garden

The interpretation of that: Know that the soul of the believer contains a portion of the Garden. Whoever is in it has purifying alms from it and God has that which remains. That is what it is valid to sell. The group of the realized among the people of the Path of God believe this because of the multiplicity of the classes for whom the purifying alms on their souls is obligatory. (381)

The Garden contains levels which demand what they deserve from the soul of the believer. That is the purifying alms. Castles seek for the soul to live in them and wives demand what they need from him. As the eight obligated limbs of human beings have the purifying alms on them for person, so they have a relationship in taking the purifying alms from another aspect. What is in the Garden is in the position of those who are allotted what befits them. (382)

24.2. The One Who Refuses to Pay the Purifying Alms Due On His Soul Wrongs It

Whoever refuses to give purifying alms for himself for any of these classes while he affirms that it is obligatory for him, is a wrongdoer and not a rejecter. This is with the exception of the formal prayer. If he abandons that, the divine law has called him ungrateful by the simple fact that he has abandoned it, and I do not know what is meant here. The one who refuses to give the purifying alms is a wrong-doer since he keeps someone else's due which they should have. After this, God willing, I will mention some of that for which purifying alms is obligatory. God speaks the truth and He guides to the path. (383)

25 Concerning That on Which Purifying Alms Is Obligatory

Scholars agree that the purifying alms is obligatory for eight categories among the products of minerals, animals and plants. The minerals are gold and silver. The plants are wheat, barley and dates. The animals are camels, cattle and sheep/goats. This is agreed upon and it is the sound position in our view. As for raisins, there is some dispute about them. (384)

25.1. Obligatory Charity and Voluntary Charity

Purifying alms is obligatory from the human being for eight limbs: Eye, ear, tongue, hand, belly, foot, genitals, and heart. There is obligatory charity on each limb and for each limb God demands it from the servant in the world to come. As for voluntary charity, every joint of the human being must pay charity as the Prophet said: "There is charity owing on every joint of the person in the morning." "*Sulama*" are the digital bones of the hand. They are also called *uruq*. Every glorification is charity. Every "there is no god but God" is charity. It is the same for praise and saying: "God is Greater" (*takbir*). (385)

25.2. The Purifying Alms of the Eight Limbs of the Human Being and Eight Categories of Wealth

The purifying alms which these limbs owe is the right of God Almighty which He made obligatory for the human being in respect of these eight limbs as He made it obligatory in these eight of gold, silver, and the rest of what I mentioned which is agreed to be subject to obligatory purifying alms. It is incumbent for the believer to pay God his due for every limb. (386)

The purifying alms on the eyes is what God has made obligatory for it in the way of its due, like lowering the eyes from forbidden things and looking at what leads to nearness with God: Like looking at the Quran, the face of the human being of knowledge, the faces of those who rejoice when you look at them, like family, children, and the like. It is like looking at the Kaba when you are near it. It is related that the one who looks at the Kaba receives twenty mercies every day. The one who circumambulates it receives sixty mercies. This is how to look at all the obligated limbs of the human being: They are used in what is appropriate and held back from what is not appropriate. (387)

25.3. Clarification of the Classes of Wealth

Know that these classes contain the products of the elements as we said. They are mineral, plant and animal. There is no fourth class. God made alms obligatory on specific classes of each genus among the products in order to purify the genus. There is no doubt that the whole class is purified of the claim in which it is obtained from person by possession. Its root is purity since it is absolutely the property of God. (388)

25.4. The Root from Which Things Appear

That is because the root from which things are manifest from His names is *al-Quddus*. That is the Pure in essence, pure from in-time things. When things appear in their sources and claims of property are acquired in them by ownership, then by the relationship of property they are moved from their basis to that which removes them from the basic purity which they had in relationship by someone else's ownership of them. The in-time is enough for the in-time. (389)

These classes have no action in themselves. God has obliged the purifying alms for them on their owner and made that their purification. God specified a minimum amount in them which returns to God from the command of God in order to relate them to their basic Owner. Purity is obtained. God made alms the purification of property. It is like that in the interpretation. (390)

25.5. The Eight Obligated Limbs Are Basically Pure

These obligated limbs are basically pure. They are in their first natural state and they continue to have that purity and integrity. Do you not see that they will be called upon to testify on the Day of Rising and that their testimony will be accepted by their basic purity and integrity. The root in things is integrity coming from a pure root. The wound is passing. God Almighty said: *"Truly having the ability to hear and sight and mind, each of those shall be that which is asked."* (17:36). He said: *On a Day when witness will be borne against them by their tongues and their hands and their feet as to what they had been doing."* (24:24) He said: *"And they will say to their skins: Why do you bear witness against us; they will say: We were given speech by God*

Who gave speech to all things." (41:21). He said: *"And you had not been covering yourselves to that witness be borne against you by your having the ability to hear or by your sight or by your skins except that you thought that God knows not much of what you do."* (41:22). (391)

All this is information from God to us that every part of us is a witness which is pure, just, and pleasing. That is good news which is better for us, *"except most of humanity knows not"* (12:21) the form of good in them. Since this is the truth of the matter, he hopes that the outcome will be good, even if he enters the fire. God is too majestic, immense and just to punish something disliked which is forced. He said: *"Whoever disbelieved in God after his belief—except for whoever was compelled to do it against his will while his heart is one that is at peace in belief, but whoever expands his breast to disbelief, on them is the anger of God and for them is a serious punishment."* (16:106). (392)

25.6. Connection of the Self is the Senses and Limbs

The principle of the person who is forced is confirmed in the divine law. We know the definition of the forced person about whom there is agreement, as well as the forced person about whom there is disagreement. It is agreed that the limbs of these people who are forced are also forced. There is no doubt that these limbs will testify against the managing soul which has power over them. The soul is the one from which God demands restitution for the limits He set the punishments. It will be asked about them. The soul is compounded of the senses and the faculties without it being disengaged from these natural, just, pure, pleasing bodily limbs whose words are heard. The ego is only punished by means of punishment inflicted on these bodies. They are what sense the sensory pains since the animal spirit pervades them. (393)

25.7. The Punishment of the Soul

The soul is punished by cares, sorrows, being overcome by illusions, and ruinous thoughts and what it sees of pains that its subjects experience as well as the changes which befall every category according to the punishment which befits it. The Lawgiver gave information that its end, since it believes, will be ultimate happiness because the one who is compelled is not punished for what he is forced to do. The limbs are only punished by pain through their sensation of it and also by pleasure in what they obtain in respect of their animality, so understand! (394)

Its form is that of the one who is compelled to commit fornication. There is some dispute about that. The soul is not punished for what it aspires to do as long as it does not act by what it intends with the limbs. The animal soul (*nafs al-ammara*) encourages its essence even though it is compelled by one aspect. The soul only act by these tools. These tools have no movement to action except by the desires of the soul. Even as action is by the whole, so punishment occurs by the whole. Then the integrity of the tools leads to the happiness of the believers at the end of the business. The sensory punishment is removed. (395)

25.8. The Removal of Punishment at the End of the Matter from the People of Belief

Then the judgement of the divine law removed that which it intended from the soul, and so the punishment of meaning is also removed from the believer. There no longer remains any spiritual or sensory of punishment for any of the people of belief. As the time for that action was short in the abode of this world by the existence of pleasure in it and "the days of bliss are short," such is the length of the punishment for the rational soul and the animal soul and its perception. The shortness of time corresponds to the time of the action. The breaths of worries are long. How long is the night for the people of pains! How short are the very same nights for the people of pleasures and bliss! The time of hardship is long for the person in hardship, and the time of ease is short. (396)

25.9. Statement: The Purifying Alms of the Human Being's Limbs Has a Minimum (*Nisab*) and a Time

Know that the purifying alms has a minimum amount and a year's length of time. That is, a specific amount of money and time. It is the same with the interpretation of the purifying alms on the limbs. They have a specific amount and time. The minimum amount is when the eye reaches the second glance since that is intentional and when he listens for the second time. It is like that for second things in all the limbs because of the intention and the specific amount of time which accompanies it. We will mention what is connected to this question by question according to what God casts into the thought about that. God gives success and guides to the Straight Path. (397)

26 The Purifying Alms of Jewelry

Scholars disagree about the purifying alms on jewelry. Some say that there is no purifying alms on it, and some say that there is. (398)

26.1. Interpretation of the Purifying Alms on Jewelry

Interpretation of that: Jewelry is what is used for adornment. Adornment has been commanded. God Almighty said: *"O Children of Adam! Take your adornment at every place of prostration,"* (7:31) and *"Say: Who has forbidden the adornment of God which He brought out for His servants and what is the good of His providing?"* (7:32) He ascribed adornment to Him as He related it to this world and not to Satan. The purifying alms is His due. What is related to Him does not have any due for Him since it all belongs to Him. There is no purifying alms for the adornment of God. (399)

26.2. God Has Prescribed that the Human Being Use It for Help in His Actions

Whoever takes it for the adornment of the life of this world and removes the adornment of God from it must give purifying alms for it. That is that he gives God a minimum amount in it by which he gives life to that which he related to himself. Then it is purified and cleansed as God set down that the human being should seek help by God and ask for aid from Him in the actions which He has obliged him to perform. He—glory be to Him!—is the Doer, not them. (400)

Similarly, there must be the purifying alms for the adornment of God which He has brought forth to His servants. They make the purifying alms obligatory then for that adornment as they make it obligatory for jewelry. (401)

27 The Purifying Alms on Horses

They disagree about horses. Most say that there is no purifying alms on horses. Some people say that if they are free-grazing and meant for breeding, then there the purifying alms are due from him; that is, when there is both male and female horses. (402)

27.1. Horses Are the Most Useful on Animals on Which One Can Struggle (*Jihad*) in the Way of God

The interpretation in that: This sort of animal and its like is part of the adornment of God. God said: *"And He creates horses, mules and donkeys for you to ride and as an adornment."* (16:8) It is part of the adornment of God which He brought out to His servants. Then it is a sort of animal which has attack and retreat. It is the most useful animal for being mounted on when striving in the way of God. Generally it belongs to God, and so God has no due in whatever belongs to God because it all belongs to God! (403)

27.2. The Body Is the Mount of the Soul

The mount of the soul is the body. Then the body, in its natural temperament and the composition of its natures, helps the pure believing soul to do what is desired of it in the way of turning to obedience of God. God has no due in whatever belongs to God because it all belongs to God. (404)

When the body helps at one moment and does not help at another moment because of flaws in it, then the soul is returned forcefully to what does not help and there the purifying alms are due on it. That is like the one who wants to perform the formal prayer and finds that there is laziness and brokenness in his limbs. He is kept back from it in spite of the fact that he desires it. Paying the alms at that moment is that he performs it and does not abandon it in spite of his laziness. At that moment it is weary (*saima*, weary, free-grazing). The interpretation of being used for breeding is used because there is both male and female in it, that is, the thoughts of the intellect and the that of the soul. (405)

28 On Free-grazing Camels, Cattle and Sheep, and Non-free-Grazing

Some people say that alms is obligatory for all of them, free-grazing and otherwise. Most believe that there is no alms on animals of these three sorts which are not free-grazing. (406)

28.1. Permitted and Non-permitted Actions

Interpretation of this: Free-grazing animals are all permitted actions, and the non-free grazing animals are what is other that is allowed (that is, neither disliked nor recommended, but allowable). The one who says that the purifying alms is due on free-grazing animals says that the allowed is when heedlessness accompanies it. They say that it is obligatory for a person to keep it in mind when he does an allowed action that it is allowable because the divine law allows it. Had it not been that the divine law allowed it, he would not have done it. This amount of reflection is its purifying alms. (407)

As for other than free-grazing animals, there are no purifying alms on them because they are all actions which are delimited by obligation, prohibition, recommendation or disapproval. In all of them, the servant has no choice whatsoever. All of them belong to God, and there is no alms on what belongs to God. (408)

Some of our companions connected the recommended and the disapproved to the allowable and said that purifying alms are due for them the same as with the allowable. Another group said that it is like the allowable. It contains what is like the forbidden and the obligatory, and what is like the allowable. If the moment is dominated by either of these two aspects, its principle is according to the judgement of the moment in it. That is that he has it in mind when he connects them to the allowable and in the moment when he connects them to the obligatory and forbidden. (409)

The form of resemblance is that the free-grazing is owned and the non free-grazing is also owned. The owner combines them both. However, it is firmer in respect to the non free-grazing because the owner is occupied with it and takes care of it. The free-grazing is not like that, even if it is owned. It is like that with the recommended and disapproved.

He can choose in action or non-action, so it is like the allowable. He is rewarded for doing them or for non-action, so it is like the obligatory and the forbidden. This is the most exact of the schools of the people in our opinion. (410)

28.2. The Actions of the Servant Are Related to Him and Related to God

Some say that purifying alms are due on all of it. He says that it is obligatory for all—free-grazing and non-free-grazing— because the actions which occur from the servant are related to the servant by the ascription of form, even if the proof demands the opposite of that. Therefore purifying alms are obligatory for all actions because they contain an ascription to the creation. (411)

28.3. The Form of Purifying Alms in Human Actions

The form of the purifying alms is that you keep present in your mind that all that occurs from you is by decree and the determination, with witnessing and complete presence in every action when you begin the action. That amount of time is the time of the purifying alms. It is in the position of the end of the year. The amount of that action in which one can return to God is the minimum amount of that action. This is from the school of those who know God. All actions belong to God in one respect and are related to the servant in another respect. One aspect does not veil them from the other just as one concern does not distract them from the other. (412)

29 The Purifying Alms on Grains

After they agree about these three categories, they disagree about plants. Some of them do not think that the purifying alms are due on anything except for those three species. Some of them say that there are purifying alms on all edible plants which are stored up. Some of them say that there are purifying alms due on all that the earth produces, except for grass, wood and reeds. (413)

29.1. The Heart is the Place of the Plants of Thoughts

Interpretation about them being plants: This species is particular to the heart. It is the place of the plants of thoughts, and their jurisdiction appears in it over the limbs. Every thought which grows in the heart and appears on the outward earth of his body has purifying alms due on it by the testimony of everyone who thinks that the one on whom it is manifested does it. Then he must purify it by returning it to God. That is its purifying alms. (414)

As long as it does not appear, whatever grows in his heart has not grown. Is he one who sees God in it or before it? If it is like that, then he does not have to pay any purifying alms on it. It belongs to God. Whoever sees God after it for its sake, that is the purifying alms itself, and so he has paid it. If he does not see God in any aspect, then those who know God deem that he must give purifying alms. The religious scholars of the People of the Path do not think that he has to give purifying alms because the Lawgiver did not take aspiration into consideration until the action takes place. Therefore it is a plant which does not owe any purifying alms as there is no punishment for it. (415)

29.2. The Food by which Everything Subsists

If the plants are among the thoughts which contain the food for the soul, then alms is obligatory for them for the soul's portion. If the soul's portion if subservient, no purifying alms is due. The food of this which is described is God by whom everything is established. Sahl ibn Abdullah was asked: "What is food?" He replied: "God." They said: "We have asked you about the food of forms." He said: "God." When they pressed him, he said: "What concern is it of yours? Leave the houses to their Owner and Builder. If He likes, He will fill them. If He likes, He will leave them in ruins." (416)

30 The Interpretation of the Minimum Amount

As for the minimum amount in the limbs, it is that you pass in every limb from the first to the second. However, this is from the first thing which is overlooked, not from the first recommended thing. No purifying alms are due for the first thing which is overlooked. It belongs to God. The second belongs to you, and so there must be the purifying lams due on it, whether it is in the first glance, the first listening, the first running, or the first thought. (417)

30.1. Every Movement Without Intention Has No Purifying Alms Due from It

In general, every movement by a limb which has no intention in it has no purifying alms due from it. When it is the second which follows it, then it is only from the soul by intention. Therefore purifying alms are obligatory, that is, its purification. Purifying alms on it is repentance from it and nothing else. It is joined to the first movement in purification for the sake of repentance. Repentance is its purifying alms. (418)

30.2. The Minimum in which Purifying Alms Is Obligatory for the Limbs

This is the definition of the minimum amount in which purifying alms is obligatory for all that purifying alms are obligatory on. There is no need to enumerate them in the outward prescribed principle of those classes because what we intend to do is to interpret. It is clear, so that it is sufficient for us and we do not need to go into details. We have already interpreted the time of alms. We still need to interpret the one who pays alms before its time. Some people forbid that, and that is my position. Some people permit it. (419)

30.3. The Purification of the Place for the Thought Before It Occurs

It is the purification of the servant for the thought before it occurs by predisposition to it while he knows what occurs to him in respect of the unveiling which he has. If it occurs, then there must be purification since there is no doubt that it has occurred. He does not overstep moments by affairs. The principle belongs to the moment. Whoever brings it out before the moment has invalidated the principle of the moment. (420)

31 Concerning Those to Whom Purifying Alms is to Be Paid

They are the eight categories which God mentions in the Quran: The poor, the destitute, those who collect it, those whose hearts are to be reconciled, servants, debtors, in the Way of God and the traveler. (421)

31.1. Paying Purifying Alms from the Actions of the Limbs

Their interpretation is the aforementioned limbs which bring out the purifying alms from their actions and it is returned to them. This is designated as their reward. There are the purifying alms in the actions of these limbs, and that is divided between them. Whoever purifies his glance by himself, has given the purifying alms of his hearing and begins to hear by his Lord. That is His words in effect: "I am his Hearing, his Sight," and so forth. Similarly he speaks, touches, and runs, and all of that is by his Lord and he is transformed in all of his actions by his Lord. (422)

32 Specification of the Eight Categories Among Which Purifying Alms is Divided in Interpretation

32.1. The Eight Categories Who Can Receive Purifying Alms

God Almighty said: *"Charities are only for the poor and the needy and the ones who work to collect it and for those whose hearts were brought together and to free the bondsperson and the ones who are in debt and in the way of God and for the traveler of the way."* (9:60) It says that God made it obligatory for these classes, and it is not permitted to give it to anyone else. There is some disagreement about giving it to just one category. (423)

32.2. Paying Purifying Alms to the Categories Which Deserve It and Not Individuals

I believe that whoever finds these categories, divides up the charity among them according to what he finds of them. However, it is divided up among the categories, not among individuals. If he only finds one person among a category, he pays him the share of that group. If he finds more than one person in that group, then he divides up the amount for that group among those who are present, no matter whether they are a few people or a lot. It is like that for those who collect it. His portion in that land is according to what groups exist. If he finds all of them, then each group gets an eighth, and so on to a seventh, sixth, fifth, fourth, third, half, and all. (424)

32.3. The Precedence of Categories Who Are Given Purifying Alms

Then we put ahead the one whom God put first when He mentioned them in giving. That is how I act here in specifying them in this chapter. When the Messenger of God came to the running between Safa and Marwa in the Farewell Pilgrimage, he recited God's words: *"Safa and Marwa are among the Waymarks of God,"* (2:158) and he began with what God began with. (425)

32.4. The Story of One of Ibn Arabi's Shaykhs

One of our shaykhs related a story to me about this. He said: "There was a person among the people of Qayrawan who wanted to go on the formal pilgrimage. He kept vacillating as to whether to go by sea or by land, and he did not prefer either of them. He said, 'I will ask the first person I meet and I will travel by whatever route he says.' (426)

"The first person he met was a Jew, so he was confused about the matter and whether or not he should ask him. Then he resolved to ask him and consult him. He said: "Muslim! Did not God say: '*He is the One who makes you travel in the land and the sea?*'" (10:22) Therefore he put first what God put first." This is the path. We begin with what God began with, and we put first what God put first. Whoever clings to that sees good in his actions. (427)

32.5. Purifying Alms Is the Right of God in Property

Interpretation of the poor to whom charity must be given: None but us among the People of the Path obliges that he take it. We think that it is obligatory for him to take it when he is given it and did not ask for it at all. If he truly achieves servanthood so that his rank in it is tested and it comes to him, then he takes it. Purifying alms, even if it is for these categories, is the right of God in this property. The servant must eat from the property of his master. It is his due. However, it is forbidden for the People of the House in particular because of this relationship, no matter whether or not they realize servanthood. If it had been by the realization of servanthood, then it would only have been forbidden for the Messenger of God and whoever follows in his footsteps. The matter is not like that. The People of the House are not entitled to dispose of God's rights. (428)

32.6.The Poor Is the One Who is In Need of Everything

In our opinion, the poor is the one who has no rank of poverty beyond him. He is the one who is in need of everything and nothing is in need of him. Up until this very moment, I have not seen anyone who has realized this attribute. God Almighty says by way of divine jealousy: "*O humanity! It is you who are poor in relation to God . . . .*" (35:15) and He refers to Himself in this sign as that which is all that he needs. "*And God, He is Sufficient, Worthy of Praise.*" (35:15) The poor person needs only God, whether or not this individual recognizes that. (429)

The divine seeker sees God as the source of everything. He is immersed and engulfed in his servanthood since he sees that God is called by the name of everything that he needs. There is nothing in existence but he needs it, whatever it is among all things. Nothing needs him since this *faqir* stops at this sign: *"O humanity! It is you who are poor in relation to God . . . ."* (35:15) *"And God, He is Sufficient, Worthy of Praise."* (35:15) He realizes this attribute, so God has obliged purification and alms for him since he had good manners with God and knew what God meant by this sign. It is one of the greatest signs. It is related in the Quran to those who know God and who understand what comes from God. There is no attribute of richness by God or by other than God that appears on him. He needs Him from that aspect, so absolute poverty is valid for him. It is as if God enriched him by what makes him among the rich by God. The one who is rich by God is the one whom creation needs and to whom he is radiant by his richness by his Lord. That one must not take this alms. (430)

God mentioned the poor first. The highest of them is the one who has the most intense need. It is not the destitute (*miskin*) or anyone else. The poor is the one who is broken. His back is bent and he cannot straighten his back. He never has any potion in uprightness. His head is always bent over because he is broken, so understand this allusion! (431)

32.7. The Needy is the One Who is Managed by Someone Else

And the destitute (miskin). *Miskin* is from *sukun* (stillness). It is the opposite of movement. Death is stillness. When the corpse moves, it is by someone else moving it, not by the corpse itself. The needy is the one who is managed by someone else. This is why it is obligatory to give him the purifying alms and one does not say that he takes it. He is not described by need or by lack of need. This is why we said that the poor has no one who has a more intense need than him. (432)

The needy is the same as the Muslim who has entrusted his affairs to God without any choice on his own part. Unveiling has given him that. This is why we connected him to the corpse. The needy is like the earth which God has made humble to us with a humility of essence under the might of every mighty one, whoever he may be. That needy one realizes that might belongs to God and that it is His might which is manifest in the very mighty one. That is a prophetic recognition. (433)

32.8. The Understanding of the Arabs and the Ranks of the Gnostics

God Almighty said: *"As for one who is soul-complacent, then thou atten-*

dest to Him and not upon thee is any blame if he purifies not himself." (80:5-6) Among those of realization, the pronoun "to Him" belongs to God, even if the sign came as a rebuke. However, this was in respect to the understanding of the Arabs. We remain with the witnessing of the Messenger of God his tasting, and his rank. The gnostics among us who have this station have one of the merits of the Messenger of God. Do not concern the mighty with that. We say that he is one of those whom God has made miserable through his might. (434)

This needy one is only humble to the attribute, and as far as he is concerned, this attribute belongs only to God in reality. The metaphor did not contaminate it at all. This needy one sees only God by his eye since he does not see any other might except His might with his eye or his heart. He looks at the abasement of all that is other-than-God with the eye with which they should be regarded. The creature who describes himself with might imagines that this wretched one is abased to his might. Rather, the abasement is to might in particular, and might belongs only to God. He has given this station its due. This is what the needy one is like to whom charity should be given. (435)

32.9. The Collector is the Guide to the Recognition of the Meanings

"The one who works to collect it."(9:60) The collector is the one who guides to recognition of these meanings and clarifies these realities. He is the teacher and the master, and he indicates them. He gathers them together by his knowledge of whoever is obligated to give it. He has some of it according to his work. The business in respect of him in it is only as we have already mentioned. It is more fitting for the guide to say what the Messengers said: *"My compensation is with God."* (10:72) This amount which they have may be from the divine alms so that they can take the alms of interpretation and not the alms of property. Outward alms is forbidden for the Prophets because they are servants. The servant does not take purifying alms inasmuch as it is related to creation, so know that! (436)

32.10. Those Whose Hearts Are Reconciled to Love of the Good-doer

". . .and for those whose hearts were brought together."(9:60) They are those who are reconciled to love of the Good-doer by goodness because their hearts are overturned and it reconciles them. It is that they are overturned in all matters to what their realities grant. However, it belongs to one source, and that is the source of God. This is what they are reconciled

to. Disparate sources do not own them since the matters in which they are reconciled are disparate. (437)

32.11. The Brooks Come from a Single Source

Since all brooks come from a single source, that source must be observed and there must be reconciliation to it. If heedlessness takes one away from it and that source/spring withholds its water, the brooks will not help him. They will dry up and the source/spring will vanish. If the spring is guarded and he is reconciled to it, then its brooks will penetrate deeply and its ways will be wide. (438)

32.12. Those Who Seek Freedom

"To free the bondsperson." (9:60) They are those who seek freedom from the bondage of all that is other-than-God. Causes have enslaved the servants of the world to such an extent that they only recognize these causes. The highest of them in bondage are those who are enslaved by the divine names. There is nothing higher than this enslavement except for the enslavement of the unity of the First Cause inasmuch as it is a cause, not in respect to its essence. In spite of this, they must not be enslaved by the divine names since they mainly look at the essence inasmuch as it is essence, not inasmuch as it is divine. Purifying alms are paid for the like of these servants. (439)

32.13. Those Who Lend God a Good Loan

". . . and the ones who are in debt." (9:60) They are the ones who have loaned God a good loan by His command. He said as a command: *"And lend to God a fair loan"* (73:20) attached to two obligatory commands. They are His words: *"And perform the formal prayer and give the purifying alms"* (73:20) The third is His words, *"And lend God a good loan."* (73:20) The loan is the third of three. However, He did not specify what you should loan Him as He did not specify what alms should be paid or the specifics of the formal prayer. It includes every prayer which He commanded us to perform and every alms and every loan. (440)

However, He described the loan as being "good" while He stressed it with a verbal noun. The reason for that is that in both the formal prayer and purifying alms, the servant is a servant by compulsion. In the loan, he is a servant by choice. Some people loan God a loan by choice. That is the one whom the command did not reach. What reached him was "loan God" or His words: *"Who is he who will lend God a fair loan."* (2:245) (441)

The first debtor takes the purifying alms which is given as charity by the principle of obligation, that is, it is obligatory for him. The second one takes it when the alms agent chooses him since he has singled him out rather than anyone else. This is especially true in the school of the one who thinks that the number of these classes is that it is spent among are the ones who have been mentioned. That is to say, it is not permitted to give it to anyone else. If he gives it to one class rather than another, then the obligation has been met. This is a question of some dispute. (442)

By this sign, "*. . . whoever lends to God*" and "*. . . lend God a fair loan,*" the lender does not take it by the principle of obligation. In another sign, the lender is commanded to take it by the principle of obligation because the one who is commanded performs an obligation and his repayment is obligatory. "*And it has been an obligation on Us to help ones who believe.*" (30:47) Belief is obligatory. "*Then I will prescribe it* (God's Mercy) *for those who are Godfearing and give the purifying alms and those who believe in Our signs.*" (7:156) All of these are obligations. Therefore, there is no doubt that He has made the reward of mercy obligatory for them. (443)

32.14. The Way of God: All the Paths of Good Which Bring One Near to God

"*. . . and in the way of God.*" It could be that He means those who strive and spend in *jihad*. The customary usage of the term, "*in the way of God*" in the divine law means *jihad*. It is the most apparent meaning in this sign. However, it is possible that by "*in the way of God*" He means all the ways of good which bring one near to God. (444)

As far as this category which is defined by the principle of what the Path demands by "*in the way of God,*" it is what this name, which is God, gives him rather than any other of the most beautiful divine names. He gives it in whatever noble qualities demand without interpreting any of the categories of creatures as God provides for His servants. It is whatever general benefit demands for every person, rather than for every animal and every plant, even to the tree which he sees is dying of thirst. He has with him that which he can use to buy something with which to water it from the alms property. He waters it with that and it is part of "*. . . in the way of God.*" He does not say this. (445)

32.15. Lesser Struggle and Greater Struggle

If God means those doing *jihad* in *the way of God*, it is well-known who those who strive in *jihad* are. Those who strive with themselves are also striving "*in the way of God.*" They help one another by that to do *jihad* against themselves. The Messenger of God said: "You have returned from the lesser *jihad* to the greater *jihad.*" He meant *jihad* against the soul and opposing it in its desires which turn one away from the path of God. (446)

32.16. The Traveler Is the "Child of the Path of God"

For travelers. Travelers are well-known. They, in the interpretation, are those who follow the Path of God because the *alif-lam* (definite article) belongs to the definition. They are an appositive for the genitive construction. The portion of these people among alms is that which is the divine purification which we mentioned earlier. (447)

32.17. Concluding Section

May God give you success! Then know that the matters which human beings takes charge of are all rights of God. Even if these rights are numerous, from a certain aspect they are contained in one of two divisions. One of them is the right creation owes God. It is the words of the Prophet: "Your soul has a right against you. Your eye has a right against you. Your wife has a right against you." The other division is the right of God for God. That is the words of the Prophet: "I have a moment in which only my Lord is enough for me." (448)

33 Purifying Alms Involves the Rights Due to God

33.1. The Eight Categories of Rights

This right which belongs to God is the alms of the rights which creation owes to God. All of these rights in general fall into eight categories of knowledge and action. They are in the position of gold and silver. Among the animals, the spirit, the soul and the body are opposite sheep, cattle and camels. In plants, they are opposite wheat, barley, and dates. (449)

33.2. What the Spirits, Self and Limbs Produce

In the interpretation, it is what the spirits, soul, and limbs produce of thoughts and actions. Sheep belong to the spirit, cattle to the soul, and camels to the body. We allotted sheep to the spirits because God made the ram the price of the spirit of a noble Prophet. He said: "*And then We took ransom for him with a sublime slaughter.*" (37:107) He made it "great" and made it a ransom for the son of Abraham, a Prophet, the son of a Prophet. There is no higher rank than sheep among the animals because of this sign. These are the sacrifices of this community. Do you not see it? It is also made the due of God in camels. It is one sheep for every twenty-five camels. He made a hundred camels the ransom for a soul who is not a Messenger or a Prophet. Then look at the rank of sheep compared to that of camels! (450)

33.3. Sheep-pens and Camel-pens

Then the Messenger of God commanded us to offer formal prayer in sheep-pens. The formal prayer is an act of drawing near to God. Its places are the mosques of God and therefore sheep-pens are among the mosques of God. They possess a degree of nearness. Camels do not possess this rank, even if they are greater in size. This is why we gave them to the bodies. Do you not see that one of their names is "*badana*" and the body itself is called "*badan*." The body is part of the world of nature, and there are two degrees of the world between nature and God. These are the soul and the intellect. Therefore nature is in the third degree of nearness, and it is quite far from divine nearness. (451)

Do you not see that the Prophet forbade the prayer in the resting-places of camels? He found fault with that because they are Satans. "Satan" is distance. One says "a deep (satan)" well when its bottom is very deep. The formal prayer is an act of nearness to God. Distance is the opposite of nearness. That is why he forbade the formal prayer in the resting-places of camels because of the distance which they contain. (452)

33.4. The Natural Body and the Spirit

It is the same with the natural body. Where is it in relation to the degree of nearness which the spirit has? It is the intellect. It is the first existent thing. It is breathed from Him when He said: *"That is when I have shaped him and have breathed into him of My Spirit."* (15:29) This is why we put the spirit in the position of the ram and the body in the position of the camel. (453)

33.5. Cattle Are the Opposite of the Soul

As for cattle being opposite the soul, they are below sheep in rank and higher than camels, even as the soul is above the body and below the intellect, which is the divine spirit. That is because when the tribe of Israel killed a soul and disagreed about it, God commanded them to sacrifice a cow and then to strike the corpse with part of it. Then the corpse came to life by the permission of God. Since the soul of the dead was brought to life by it, we recognize that there is a relationship between it and the soul and so we gave it to the soul. (454)

33.6. The Crop of the Intellect, the Soul and the Limbs

Then the spirit, which is the intellect, manifests what God has provided it with: That knowledge, wisdom and secrets which only God teaches him. All this knowledge, some of which is connected to phenomenal being and some of which is connected to God, are in the position of purifying alms on wheat because it is the finest kind of grain. The soul manifests the thoughts and appetites with which God has provided it and which only God knows. This is its plant and it is in the position of dates. The purifying alms of God in it is the first thought and the first appetite which is for the sake of God. We linked it to dates because the date-palm is our aunt. In relation to the intellect, it has the same position as the date-palm has in relation to Adam. It was created from the left-over clay of Adam. As for the limbs, God's provision in them is all actions. The actions grow and the portion of alms in them are the prescribed actions in which God is seen. (455)

33.7. The Obligation of Purifying Alms in the Actions of the Intellect, Soul and Limbs

These are the eight categories on which alms is obligatory. As for knowledge which is in the position of gold, what is obligatory for gold is obligatory for it. As for action which is in the position of silver, what is obligatory for silver is obligatory for it. As for the spirit, what is obligatory for sheep is obligatory for it. As for the soul, what is obligatory for cattle is obligatory for it. As for the limbs, what is obligatory for camels is obligatory for them. (456)

As for the gnoses which result from the intellect and the secrets which it produces, what is obligatory on wheat is obligatory for them. As for the appetites and thoughts which the soul produces, and the *waridat* which it generates, what is obligatory on dates is obligatory for it. As for the actions which the limbs produce and the forms of acts of obedience and other things which they generate, what obligatory on barley is obligatory for it. (457)

34 The Interpretation of Foods at Certain Moments

Know that the moments in the path of God which belong to those of knowledge and action are in the same position as food to put natural bodies right. As certain foods are the purifying alms of that group, so the divine moment is the alms of the moments of phenomenal being. There is food for the spirits in the moment as there is food for the animal and plant forms in foods. Actions are the food of limbs. (458)

34.1. Knowledge and Action Are Two Minerals/Mines

Knowledge and action are two minerals/mines. Divine desires are obtained when they exist, both in this world and the Next. Similarly, all goals of goods and desires are obtained by gold and silver. We will clarify what is connected to this category and these categories in the way of the right of God which is the purifying alms. (459)

35 Comparison of the Categories on Which Purifying Alms Must Be Paid by the Responsible Limbs of Human Beings

The poor are comparable to the genitals among the limbs. The needy are comparable to the belly. Those who collect alms are comparable to the heart. Those who are hearts are reconciled are comparable to the hearing. Servants are comparable to the sight. Debtors are comparable to the hand. Those who strive are comparable to the tongue. The traveller is comparable to the foot. (460)

If you consider this balance between these categories and these limbs according to what we have mentioned, you will find the wisdom of what we have indicated. Poverty in the genitals is clear. Wretchedness in the belly is apparent. The collector by the heart is plain. Those who are hearts are reconciled with the hearing is clear. The servants by the eyes is apparent. The debtor by the hand is eloquent. The striver by the tongue is plain. The traveller by the foot is the clearest of all. (461)

36 Concerning the Amount in Weight, Measure and Number

Muslim related from Abu Said al-Khudri that the Messenger of God said: "There are no purifying alms due on grain or dates until it reaches five wasqs (more than five sheep and less than ten), and there are no purifying alms due on what is less than five wasqs, and no purifying alms due on what is less than five awqiyas (that is, silver)." (462)

36.1. What Is Generated by Taking on the Character of the Divine Names in the Human Being

He used the "wasq" for grains, and they are plants. It is a well-known measure, and it consists of 60 saa's. Five wasqs is therefore 300 saa's. That is what is generated by taking on the character of the divine names, that is, the divine qualities from the qualities which are in the human being because we have related that God has 300 qualities. Whoever takes on the character of one of them, enters the Garden. All of them are qualities which the human being uses with creatures and with the one with whom they must be used according to the definition of the command of God. (463)

The purifying alms of the qualities is the quality which he uses with God. It is He who takes charge of the one who takes on character with Him. By his character, it is impossible for the human being to reach the pleasure of this world and it is better to prefer the Presence of God. That involves that with every category, he takes on the character of the divine quality which God uses with him. He is in harmony with God. (464)

36.2. The Specific Number and Number of Meaning

He said: "Nor in what is less than five." This is from the number of sources. It is only action that makes the source multiple, and not knowledge. The measure of knowledge is in the meaning, and the measure of action is in the sensory. (465)

36.3. The Symbolic Meaning of the Number Forty

"Nor in what is less than five awqiyas." The awqiya is forty dirhams. Forty in the awqiya is like the forty mornings. "Whoever is sincere in them, the fountains of wisdom appear from his heart on his tongue." Then they appear from the servant in five states, as there are five awqiyas in the purifying alms: A state in his outward aspect has an awqiya, and it is outward sincerity (*ikhlas*), a similar state in the inward aspect, a similar state in his limit, a similar state in his ascension, and a similar state in his whole. These are five states multiplied by forty which gives the result of 200. That is the limit of the *nisab*. There are five dirhams in it. There is a dirham from every forty dirhams. That is what is connected to every forty of the unity (*tawhid*) which is ascribed to this sort. The measures of the meanings and the spirits is the measure of His words: "*And they measured not God with His true measure.*" (6:91) The measures of sensory things are weights in actions. Measures are recognized by weights. (466)

37 The Time in Respect of What Is Watered by Irrigation and What Is Not

Al-Bukhari mentioned from the Messenger of God that there is half of the tenth tax (*ushr*) from what is watered by irrigation of the tenth tax of what is not watered by irrigation. (467)

38 The Master and Actions of the Disciple

It is the actions of the master (desired) and the actions of the disciple (desirer). The disciple is with himself for his Lord so he must pay half of the tenth tax. It is that he purify his action of what his soul manifests in it. The master is with his Lord, not with himself. Therefore he must pay the tenth tax, and it is his entire soul. He has no soul since all fatigue is lifted from it. It is the same with the interpretation in given knowledge and acquired knowledge. Only half of acquired knowledge is sincerely for God. All of given knowledge is for God. "All" designates the amount only of the amount of alms. It is what is related to God of that knowledge or that action, and what is related to the servant in respect of the presence of the servant with himself in that knowledge or action. (468)

39 Paying Purifying Alms from Other Than the Thing on Which the Purifying Alms is Imposed

There is a sheep for every 25-35 camels. Interpretation: "*Certainly the way of life is exclusively for God*?" (39:3) This refers to the purifying alms of actions since action requires sincerity. It is intention. (469)

40 About Two Partners in Purifying Alms

Al-Daraqutni mentioned that Sad ibn Abi Waqqas said that the Messenger of God said that there is not joint ownership of a water basin, shepherd and stallion. (470)

40.1. The Meaning of Two Partners

Section on the interpretation in that: God Almighty says: "*And cooperate with one another in virtuous conduct and God-consciousness.*" (5:2) Mutual help in a thing is sharing in it. This is the meaning of the two partners. (471)

40.2. The Meaning of the Basin

The basin is every action or knowledge which leads to the life of the hearts. It helps us with life according to what each of them needs from his partner in it. This is the heart in human being and the limb. They are partners. The limb helps the heart to act. The heart helps the limb to sincerity. They are partners in whatever they begin, whether it be action or seeking knowledge. (472)

40.3. The Meaning of the Shepherd

As for the shepherd, it is the meaning which guards the actions. It is presence and calling to mind. For instance, in the formal prayer, you cannot turn your face in any direction except the direction of formal prayer (*qibla*) and you cannot intend another act of worship. The heart and the senses share in it. (473)

40.4. The Meaning of the Stallion

As for the stallion, it is the cause which demands what that action or knowledge produces of acceptance and reward with God. They share in the wage. The soul takes what is appropriate to it of what knowledge gives it and the senses take what the body has if what it connected to it in the way of good form in the world to come and the meaning which is generated for them. This is the stallion, and they are partners in it. (474)

41 Actions in Which There Is No Purifying Alms

The Messenger of God said that there no purifying alms are due on working camels or battle horses. Al-Daraqutni transmitted it from Ali, may God be pleased with him. These are camels for work and horses and we have already discussed alms on horses. (475)

41.1. Forms Are the Agents of the Spirits

The forms carry the spirits because they do what they are obligated to do on them, and actions occur from them by means of the forms. There are no purifying alms due against the agent in his body. The purifying alms are due from the spirit which makes it act. The purifying alms is its intention and its fearful awareness. That us sincerity to God in that action. God Almighty said: "*Neither their flesh nor their blood attains to God, but your God-consciousness attains HIm.*" (22:37) (476)

42 Paying Purifying Alms from the Same Sort

Abu Dawud related from Muadh ibn Jabal that the Messenger of God sent him to the Yemen. He said: "Take the grain from the grain and take the sheep from the sheep and take the camel from the camels and the cow from the cattle." (477)

42.1. The Incentive to Pay Purifying Alms Outwardly and Inwardly

Outward alms is what the divine law limits by in the way of obligatory actions which have a correspondence in the recommended. The formal prayer is the purifying alms of the supererogatory prayers. It is obligatory or a prayer which the human being vows for himself or whatever form of worship it might be. It its the same with the inner dimension. Its purifying alms is of the same kind. It is that which incites him to the act of worship, that is, fear or desire. The inner alms in that is that it be what lordship desires of being obeyed. It is not awe or desire except at a greater distance. (478)

43 Concerning What Is Not Taken in the Purifying Alms

Abu Dawud mentioned in the Book of the Messenger of God: The very old and animals with defects should not be taken in the alms, nor the ram unless the alms collector so desires. (479)

43.1. Avoiding What Will Sully Acts of Worship

The very old is like the Word of God Almighty: "*When they stand up for formal prayer, they stand up lazily to make display to humanity. . .* " (4:142) He said: "Let each of you pray with energy." "Those with defects" are actions without intention, or intention without action when there is power to do the action and any impediment is removed. (480)

As for the choice of the alms-collector regarding the ram, its interpretation is that he does not injure the property owner. He may say that only such-and-such is acceptable. The intention at the beginning is enough in action. The obligated person is not obligated to more than that. When the obligated person calls the intention to be present in the entire action, he has that and he is thanked for it since he does the action better and brings something more precious in that. (481)

In general this chapter is to be fearfully on your guard against what will sully these acts of worship, like turning aside in the formal prayer and fiddling in it and speaking within the soul about forbidden and disliked things during the formal prayer and imagining them and the likes of these. This is like Jarur dates and the Hubayq dates (both forbidden by the Prophet to be used in payment of the purifying alms on dates. (482)

44 The Purifying Alms on Silver

44.1. Silver Is Action and Gold Is Knowledge

It was previously stated that silver is action and gold is knowledge. The purifying alms on action is the obligatory part of it. The purifying alms on knowledge is also the obligatory part of it. There are many supererogatory actions and knowledge whose purifying alms are obligatory ones since purifying alms are obligatory. Whatever there is of voluntary charity in the supererogatory is the presence of the servant in that action from its beginning to its end. The other alms, and I mean voluntary alms or charity, is that he intend by doing that to complete the obligatory actions. (483)

44.2. Completing Obligations from the Supererogatory

It is related from the Messenger of God that he said: "The first of the actions of the servant which He will look at will be the formal prayer. If it is complete, then it will be written for him as complete. If something is lacking in it, He will say, in effect: 'Look and see whether My servant has any supererogatory actions.' If he has supererogatory actions, God will say, in effect: 'Complete My servant's obligatory actions from his supererogatory actions,' that is, his actions will taken in his obligatory alms, fasting, and pilgrimage and whatever obligatory actions remain. If he intended by that supererogatory action to complete the obligatory or to exalt the presence of God entering into the servanthood of choice, neither desire for the Garden nor fear of the fire moves him to that." (484)

45 The Purifying Alms of Treasure-troves

Muslim related in his *Sahih* that the Messenger of God said that there is one-fifth for treasure-troves. That is, whatever wealth is found in the earth which was buried in the Age of Ignorance or by the rejecters. (485)

45.1. The Purifying Alms on What Is Embedded in Human Nature

Whatever is embedded in the human nature is a treasure-trove. It is love of leadership, advancement over fellow men, attracting benefits and repelling injuries. The one-fifth tax is due on it. (486)

45.2. The Purifying Alms of Leadership and Advancement Over One's Species

When he experiences leadership in his heart, by it he intends to exalt the word of Quran over the word of those who reject as it is in the heart of the matter. In the heart of the matter, the word of God is the higher and the word of those who reject is the lower. Here disbelief only means polytheism, nothing else. (487)

This is as the Messenger of God said about haughtiness in war concerning Abu Dujana when he took the sword from the Messenger of God by its right. He walked with it haughtily unsheathed between the rows. When the Messenger of God saw him like that, he said: "This is a gait which God and His Messenger hate except in this place." Its purifying alms is what we mentioned of the intention to humiliate the rejecters, reduce their power, and exalt the word of God, which is Islam, and lack of concern for the idolaters. (488)

45.3. Purifying Alms on Accruing Benefits and Repelling Injuries

It is like that for accruing benefits and repelling injuries. The purifying alms of accruing benefits is to intend by the benefit to help one to rise to God's obedience from sleep, eating, drink, rest, storing wealth, and the like of that. As for repelling injuries, he only repels them lest they come between Him and what he desires to do of establishing the obedience of

God and His religion and the happiness in the world to come to which it leads him. That is the fifth of its treasure-trove. If you were to ask: "How is it an injury to his religion?" I mean by it that if he does not repel that harm from himself, it will come between him and performing one of the obligations of God or between him and the means of good. Repelling it is the fifth of its treasure-trove which is in himself about repelling harm which will not lead to invalidating a specific obligation which he should perform or which is desirable. The Prophet was asked about the treasure-trove. He said: "It is gold which God created in the earth on the day when He created the heavens and the earth," that is, metals. (489)

46 The One Whom God Has Provided with Wealth Without Any Effort on His Part or Acquisition

It is related in a Tradition from the Messenger of God that he said about the acquisition of this type of property: "There are no purifying alms due on it until a year has passed while it remains in his possession." (490)

46.1. Noble Qualities Which Are Praised of Themselves

The interpretation of that is the noble qualities which appear on the servant which he does not bring in respect to drawing near to God. He will benefit by that in the world to come and he does not have to intend to draw near to God. There is certain dispute if he intends to draw near to God by that. It is better and more fitting in respect to him. (491)

The Tradition which has come about that is what Abu Dawud mentioned from Dabbaa bint al-Zubayr. She said: "Al-Miqdad went for a need. Then a large rat brought out a dinar from a hole. He kept bringing out dinar after dinar until he had brought out seventeen. Then he brought out a dinar and then he brought out a red scrap of cloth in which there was a dinar. Then al-Miqdad took them to the Messenger of God and told him about it and told him to take its alms. The Prophet said: 'Did you go near its hole?' He said: 'No.' The Messenger of God told him, 'God has blessed you with them.'" (492)

47 The Purifying Alms of the *Mudabbar* Servant

The transmitter, may God be pleased with him, said that the Messenger of God commanded us to give the purifying alms for the one whom we had promised to sell. (493)

47.1. The Intention to Do Good and Drawing Near to God

When a person speaks to himself within himself about doing some good or noble quality, he should intend nearness to God from what his soul tells him about that. (494)

48 On Purifying Alms Before Its Time

Some Imams say that it can be done based on a Tradition in Abu Dawud from Ali ibn Abi Talib relating that al-Abbas asked the Messenger of God about giving purifying alms early. He gave him permission to do so and said: "Once." Therefore he gave him verbal permission in this Tradition. If it is sound, it is an allowance in a special instance, and it is not used for analogy. (495)

48.1. The Intention for the Formal Prayer is Only Obligatory at its Beginning

The intention for the formal prayer is only obligatory at the beginning of the formal prayer. If a person intends it before he begins to perform ablution and keeps the intention until he actually starts the formal prayer, he is allowed to do that and he acquires much good. However, the formal prayer which is limited by the moment is not allowed before its time has come except in the school of the one who thinks that two formal prayers can be joined together at the beginning of the time. Therefore, it is not impossible to allow purifying alms to be paid early. Relaxation in this comes from His words: "*. . . are those who compete with one another in good works.*" (23:61) (496)

48.2. Looking at Fiancées

The like of this is also in the interpretation of the one who is allowed to look at his fiancées but is prevented from doing so because of modesty before God and fear that he might look longer than necessary. Therefore he does not do that until he has married her. I think that there are divisions in looking at fiancées. If the fiancée is one of the descendants of the Helpers and he does not look at her before the marriage-contract, then he rebels. If he looks at her face before the marriage, then his look is an act of nearness to God and obedience to His Messenger. As for those outside of the Helpers, this is not the case. However, it is more appropriate for him to look when he becomes engaged. (497)

48.3. The "In the Name of God" in Every chapter is Its Key

As for what we said about joining together two formal prayers when the second is added to the first, inwardly that is that he find the spirit of the Opening Chapter of the chapter which he means to recite in the *bismala,* "In the Name of God." The *bismala* in every chapter is its key. (498)

49 The Festival Marking the End of Ramadan

Scholars disagree about the principle of tax of the festival marking the end of Ramadan (*zakat al-fitr*). Some say that it is obligatory. Some say that it is *Sunna*. Some say that it is abrogated by the purifying alms itself. (499)

49.1. *Fatir, Fataqa and Fitr*

Interpretation of *fatir*: *"Praise belongs to God, One Who is the Originator* (fatir) *of the heavens and the earth."* (35:1) and *"Have not those who are ungrateful considered that the heavens and the earth had been interwoven and We unstitched* (fataqa) *them?"* (21:30) *Fitr* is to originate. From that, *"It is the nature originated* (fitra) *by God in which He originated humanity."* (30:30). (500)

48.2. The First of That Which God Opened Was the Hearing and Tongues

The first of that which God opened was the hearing of phenomenal beings while they were being brought into existence: which is the state of the connection of power between existence and non-existence by His word *"Be!"* by whose articulation they came to being to obey the command of God. That is, "the word of presence" The first thing to which their hearing was opened in the first existence was His words: *"Am I not your Lord? They said: Yea! We bore witness."* (7:172) This is particular to human beings while taking form is general. The first thing to open their tongues was their word: *"Yea! We bore witness."* The first thing that opens the intestines of the person who fasts is what they eat on the day of the festival (*fitr*) before going out to the place of prayer. The first of what will open the intestines of the people of the Garden will be their eating "the extra part of liver of the fish." (501)

49.3. What the Servant Must Know About the Tax (*Zakat al-Fitr*) on the Day of the Festival

The servant must know that the purifying alms on the festival day are for the attribute of everlasting support that is proper only to God Almighty. The fast belongs to God, not to the servant. This alms is obligatory for every person, free or servant, young or old, male or female. He must recognize what lordship demands of the attributes of everlasting support. In our opinion, only dates and barley are permitted, and nothing else is allowed in it. According to most scholars, any eatable foods are allowed. This is a matter of some dispute. (502)

49.4. The Food of Forms and the Food of Spirits

Food is that by which this natural growth is sustained. The food of the spirits is what nourishes them in the way of unveiling or belief. The growth of the articulate spirits is established by this amount of knowledge. Its alms is the knowledge of unveiling in particular. (503)

50 Its Obligatory Nature for Rich and Poor, Free and Servant, Male and Female, Young and Old

The Messenger of God said that it is obligatory for each young and old person. It is interpreted as the teacher and the knower. (504)

50.1. Freedom and Servanthood

The interpretation of the free and the servant is the one who has freed himself from the bondage of phenomenal beings. His moment is his witnessing as he is free of it. The servant is the one whose moment is contemplation of servanthood without looking at phenomenal beings. (505)

50.2. Male and Female

The interpretation of male and female is that the intellect is the male and the soul is the female. One can also consider that the one who looks at divine knowledge is the male and the one who looks at the knowledge of nature is the female. Each one is related to that which he looks at. (506)

50.3. Rich and Poor

The interpretation of the rich and the poor is the rich by God or the poor in need of God. (507)

50.4. The Four mudd, Four Humors, Four Levels and Four Ascriptions

He said that it is a saa of dates. The saa is four mudds. The growth of the saa is from four humors. Each has an element or the humor of a mudd in order to perfect the growth in spirit, intellect, body and rank. In it, he sees the four relationships by which his Lord is described when He brings his source into existence. The roots come from life, knowledge, will and power. Each attribute has a mudd so that the sum is a saa since by these relationships, it is valid that He be the Lord and you be the ruled, His servant. (508)

51 Paying the Purifying Alms on the Day of the Festival for Everyone He Must Provide For

Al-Daraqutni mentioned from the Tradition of Ibn Umar, may God be pleased with him, that the Messenger of God commanded *zakat al-fitr* from young and old, free and servant among those whose provision you are responsible for. (509)

51.1. The Intention of the Student with the Teacher in Teaching

When the master teaches the student, he intends to bring him knowledge which he has not obtained until he obtains the benefit which the shaykh intends. That is the purifying alms of his teaching. The virtue of that intention reverts to the student. The master gives the student the virtue which comes to him. There is opening for the master by the trueness of the student about what he does not have. The guardian is driven in this question to pay the purifying alms of the orphan's property which is in his care under his supervision. (510)

52 On Paying It for the Christian and the Jew

Abu 'l-Hasan al-Daraqutni, may God have mercy on him, mentioned it in his book from the Messenger of God that is, paying *zakat al-fitr* for the Jew and the Christian. (511)

52.1. General and Comprehensive Islamic Creed

It is the intention of good in the action of the one who is not one of your kind while its virtue reverts to you. I believe in what the Christians and the Jews believe which is true in their religion and their Book in respect to my belief in my Book. God Almighty says: "*All have believed in God and His angels and His Books and His Messengers.*" (2:285) This is the position from which it is paid. "I am one of those who gives him provision and my Book contains his Book, and my religion contains his religion. His religion and Book are included in my Book and religion." (512)

52.2. When the Soul Shares in the Action, It Seeks Its Portion

When the soul shares in the action, seeks its portion. This is the same position as that of the Jew and the Christian who say that Uzayr is the son of God and that the Messiah is the son of God. The believer must give purifying alms for it and it is by means of this quality. The Prophet stood up for the funeral of a Jew. He said: "Isn't it a soul?" (513)

52.3. "Christian" is derived from "*nasra*" (help) and Jew from "*huda*" (guidance)

This is the interpretation of giving the purifying alms for the Jew and the Christian. This is when the meaning is taken into account. When the expression is taken into account *nasra* and *huda*, then the purifying alms for them is only to intend the countenance of God by it. (514)

53 The Time of Paying *Zakat al-Fitr*

The Messenger of God commanded that the *zakat al-fitr* be paid before people go out to the place of formal prayer. (515)

53.1. Hastening to Bring Comforts to Those in Need of Them

Interpretation in that: It is hastening to bring comforts to those in need of them, and then he goes out to the place of prayer. It is His words: *"Put charity forward in advance of your conversing privately."* (58:12) The one who prays, speaks with his Lord and goes out to the place of formal prayer. That is better and purer for him. (516)

54 The One Who Is Excessive in Purifying Alms

The transmitter from the Messenger of God said that he said, "The one who is excessive in giving the purifying alms is like the one who withholds it." Abu Dawud related it. (517)

54.1. To Exceed the Limit Is to Decrease What Is Contained Within the Limits

Your soul has a right over you and your eye has a right over you. If you obligate it above its capacity, you will make it ill. That leads to the loss of much good. You are then like the one who withholds good in what he desires of good. You know that the soul acts by these limbs. When the tools are hampered and too weak to act since they were first carried to hardships, then you are like the one who refuses to act. We wrote on this meaning: (518)

Whatever work the carpenter does in occupation with his
tools,
They are permitted to be ruined in it.
To exceed the limit is to decrease
what is contained within the limits.

55 The Purifying Alms on Honey

Al-Tirmidhi mentioned from Ibn Umar from the Messenger of God that there is on a skin of honey for every ten skins. (519)

55.1. The Purifying Alms of Knowledge is Teaching It

It is the knowledge which the saint takes by means of revelation from that which is connected to other. He must disseminate it to its people since it is for their sake that he gives it. We particularly mentioned revelation rather than any other attribute since there are many attributes of the acquisition of knowledge when we liken it to honey. That is the result of revelation. God Almighty said: *"Thy Lord revealed to the bee."* Its alms is therefore is therefore teaching it. (520)

56 Purifying Alms Being Due from the Free, Not Servants

The Messenger of God said that there is no alms on the property of the *mukatab* servant until he is free. Al-Daraqutni mentioned it from a Tradition reported by Jabir. (521)

56.1. The Reason for the Free Person Owing Purifying Alms is the Claim of Ownership

As it is not permitted for the servant to take the purifying alms, the Messenger of God was forbidden alms because he has realized his servanthood. He did not leave it in any movement or stillness by which he would be free, through heedlessness or without heedlessness. His God chose concern for him in this ruling. Thus alms is not obliged in his property until he is free. The servant has no ownership with his master. (522)

The reason for the purifying alms for the free person is the claim of ownership. The servant has no claim in anything. The servant is the same as his value. That is the price for which he was purchased. As there is no claim conceivable in his price and no rejection in what his master commands him to do, so the servant and each servant has no regard for his price in the behavior of the master. He does not realize his servanthood and he does not recognize it by himself. This is the school of the group [the Sufis] without any dispute. (523)

56.2. The Basis of Manifestation is Claim

When the servant is like this with his master, then the servant vanishes and the master appears. The root of manifestation/appearance is a claim. In this state, the master stands with others in the attribute of the servant as a mark of honor to the servant. It is His words: "I was hungry and you did not feed Me. I was ill and you did not visit Me." Hunger and illness are among the attributes of the servant. Similarly, God said in response: "So-and-so was ill and you did not visit him. If you had visited him, you would have found Me with him." God is with the servant who is like this. When the servant is like this, he is with his Lord, so understand! (524)

57 Where Purifying Alms Is Taken

Abu Dawud related from the Prophet that alms is only taken in their lands. (525)

57.1. Bodies Are the Abodes of Spirits

The human being's abode is his body. Purifying alms are taken from the human spirits in the world to come. The bodies must be gathered. Purifying alms are only taken from the one for whom it is obligatory in his land (abode). Human spirits have no abodes except their bodies. (526)

58 The Ruler Taking Half of the Property of the One Who Does Not Pay His Purifying Alms after Purifying Alms Is Taken From Him

Abu Dawud related that the Messenger of God said in a Tradition that he took the purifying alms: "If anyone withholds it, we will take it and half of his property." It is one of the firm orders of our Lord." (527)

58.1. Purifying Alms Is Obligatory for the Human Being in His Actions

Whatever person possesses of his actions is divided into two divisions. There is a division particular to his limbs. The purifying alms which is obligatory for him in his actions is what God has made obligatory of his actions, supererogatory and permitted. When he does not pay the purifying alms on his property, then God looks at the actions which he did in the moment in which it was obligatory for him to perform the obligation of God. If it is noble qualities, he is not repaid for them with the reward which they deserve. The reward is withheld from him for the purifying alms of the action of the moment. If it is trivial, then the burden is multiplied against him. The one who has a blameworthy action in the state of leaving the performance of what is obligatory joins together two blameworthy actions of action and non-action. If he is doing an indifferent action, then he is only punished for leaving the obligation. (528)

58.2. Taking Half of the Property of the One Who Refuses to Pay Purifying Alms

As for taking half of his action, that is the half in which claim is conceivable. It is action. Responsibility is divided into action and non-action. Non-action has no claim in it. Action remains. God takes it from him by the proof that God is the Doer of that action. When that is unveiled to him, he does not have anything left with which to seek repayment since repayment is inasmuch as he acts. It has become clear to him that the Actor is God. He remains in bewilderment until God is gracious to him, either after punishment or before punishment and forgives him. This is the half of his wealth which is taken from him in the world to come when the Reckoning is conceivable. (529)

59 The Agent Being Satisfied with the Purifying Alms

Al-Harith ibn Abi Usama mentioned in his *Musnad* from Anas that he said: "A man came from the Banu Sulaym. He said, 'Messenger of God! When I give the purifying alms to your messenger, am I free of it before God and His Messenger?' The Messenger of God said, 'Yes, when you give it to my messenger, you are free of it and you have its reward. The wrong action would then fall upon the one who alters it.'" (530)

Abu Dawud mentioned from the Tradition of Jabir that the Messenger of God said: "A hated party will come to you. When they come, greet them and leave them what they desire. If they are just, it is for themselves. If they are unjust, it is against them. Please them. The end of your alms is their satisfaction. They should make supplication for you." This Tradition also contains what Bushayr ibn al-Khasasiyya said. He said: "We said, 'Messenger of God, the people of alms wrong us. Should we hide that amount of our property which they wrong by being excessive?' He said, 'No.'" (531)

59.1. The Purifying Alms-collector Is the Moment

The alms-collector is the moment. His satisfaction is that he be given in full what his state demands of that which he brings. If he brings harshness and force as a person finds in a thought in one of his actions, whatever action it may be of good, it is arduous and may lead to destruction. Abu Madyan, may God be pleased with him, said: "There is blood-wit in it for the killer." (532)

God Almighty says about the emigrant: . . . *death overtakes him, then surely his compensation will fall on God."* (4:100) The form of excess in it is that God has given your soul a right over you and your eye a right over you. You are excessive to yourself in that respect and that is His words about the chosen: *"to those whom We favored of Our servants. . ."* (35:32) It is the thought which occurs with whatever occurs. It is excessive and it is just. (533)

60 Hastening to Give Charity

Muslim ibn al-Hajjaj mentioned in his *Sahih* from the Messenger of God that he said: "Give charity. It has almost reached the point when a person will go out with his charity and the one to whom he gives it says: 'If you had come with it yesterday, I would have accepted it. Now I have no need of it.'" And he will not find anyone to accept it. (534)

60.1. The Obligation of Hastening Repentance

It is hastening with repentance. That is one of the obligations. If he puts it off until he dies, it will not be accepted. This is a very fine question. Few of our companions chance upon it. (535)

60.2. The Harshest of States for the Heart of the Desired *Madhjub*

It is that one who is desired might not turn in repentance and have an unveiling from God as an act of concern for him. The first of what is unveiled to him may be that God is the Creator of everything. He does not think that he himself has any outer or inner movement or any action, intention, or anything except God. There is nothing in his power. Then is repentance conceivable for someone who has this state or not? He sees that he is completed divested of actions. If he turns in repentance, is his repentance accepted in spite of this unveiling? (536)

Or is he in the position of the one who repents after sunrise for sunset? The sun of the reality has risen here for him from the sunset of his heart by the soundness of his knowledge. This is one of the difficult states for the heart of the desired attracted one (*majdhub-murad*). The acceptance of repentance and the acceptance of action is with the veil: the veil of the ascription of action to you. Here nothing emerges from him but that it is accepted. It is in his power. Acceptance is only from other. (537)

60.3. The Relationship of the Perceiver and the Relationship of the Doer

Know then that the relationship of the perceiver is not the relationship of the doer. The one who perceives accepts from the doer, and the doer disposes of this essence which is the place of the manifestation of the action, whatever action it may be. Repentance is conceivable from the one with this unveiling. Here God is the *al-Tawwab,* The Accepter of Repentance. This is the furthest witnessing. Therefore, let him hasten to acts of obedience in any state and not hesitate. The breaths are not his and responsibility is only here. On the Day of Rising when they are called upon to prostrate, it will a prostration of differentiation, not a prostration of test. In the call to prostrate, he differentiates those who prostrated out of fear and for the sake of appearances. In this world they are not differentiated since the form appears the same. (538)

61 The Effect Which Purifying Alms Has on Divine and Other Relationships

Part of that are His words: *"And whatever you spend of anything, He will replace it."* (34:39) Muslim transmitted in his *Sahih* that Abu Hurayra reported that the Messenger of God said: "There is not a morning that comes to the servants but that two angels descend. One of them says, 'O God! Give the spender a replacement!' The other says, 'O God! Give the withholder destruction!'" (539)

61.1. He-ness is the Source of the Essence

My brother, see how he made its He-ness (*huwiyya*) replace your decrease. You give life to the one to whom you give charity, as God gives you life by it in post eternal time because if God is not your life, then there is no life. If you said: "If that were the case, then the *ya* would have a *fatha* and the *lam* a *damma*," we said that He-ness is the same as His essence. He-ness follows the thing that is given as charity by a divine name by which that spender has life. His names are not other than Him. However, this is how the expression occurs for what is commonly understood in that since there are a variety of relationships. Our discussion about these meanings is with our companions who know what we say and indicate to them, based on the technical terms which are established with us for that. The outsider's objection is not accepted. (540)

61.2. he Tongue of the Angels Is the Tongue of Good

Do you not see that the angel said: "Give a spender a replacement" even though he is already promised that and His promise is true? Here spending is part of destruction and injury. That is, what he has must be damaged. He said: "Replace it with that whose effect is appropriate for the one for whose sake it was destroyed." He has the reward of the one who gives life. Do you not see that the other says: "O God! Give the withholder destruction!" because the angels are the tongue of good. (541)

The angel said: "O God! Give the withholder what you give the spender until his property is destroyed like that of his companion." It is as if he were saying: "O God! Provide the withholder with spending so that he spends. If Thou canst not, since Thou already knowest that he will not spend it freely, then destroy his property so that he has the reward of the one who is afflicted. We afflict good. Thou hast said: *"To God prostrates whatever is in the heavens and the earth, willingly or unwillingly."* (13:15) The property of this one is destroyed unwillingly, so prepare a reward for him from the one who experiences rest by it even if the one who is deprived of his property by loss did not intend that. This is a supplication for good for him. It is not what is supposed by the one who has no recognition of the ranks of the angels. The angel does not make a supplication for evil, especially in respect of the believer in His existence, how much more so it is with the one who accepts His unity and the one who accepts what comes from Him! (542)

61.3. The Supplication of the Angel Is Answered

There is no doubt that the supplication of the angel is answered for two reasons. One reason is because of its purity. The other is because it is a supplication for someone else. It is a supplication for the one who possesses wealth by the tongue of someone who has not rebelled against Him. It is the tongue of the angel since this exists among the tongues of the children of Adam although their tongues rebel. However, God Almighty said to Moses, in effect: "Call on Me with a tongue that has not rebelled against Me." He asked: "What is that?" He said: "The supplication of your brother for you and your supplication for him. Each of you has not rebelled against Me with the tongue of the other who makes the supplication for him. He only calls on Me with a pure tongue." He related the supplication to him because the supplicater represents the one for whom he makes the supplication. The tongue of the supplicater has not rebelled against God for the one for whom he makes the supplication. (543)

61.4. Your Spending Makes God Spend on You

Part of that is also what Muslim transmitted from Abu Hurayra. He reported that the Messenger of God said: "God, the Mighty and Majestic, told me: 'Spend and I will spend on you.'" God informs us that your spending makes God spend on you. This is part of the effect of charity in the divine relationship. (544)

61.5. Charity Extinguishes the Anger of the Lord

Part of that is what al-Tirmidhi mentioned from Anas ibn Malik. He said that the Messenger of God said: Charity extinguishes the anger of the Lord and repels evil from the dead. It is a Tradition which is rare and good. This is part of the effect of charity: It repels and puts out the fire of anger. On the Day of Rising, God will be angry with an anger that He has never been angry with before and will never be angry with the like of it afterwards in an aspect which befits His majesty. There is no doubt that the anger which He tells us about is known. What is not known is its relationship to God. It is not that anger is unknown or that it refers to what it produces in the person who is angry or that it refers to another meaning which we do not know. Had it been that, we would have been told what we do not understand. Then it would have no effect on us, and it would not be a warning. The goal is understanding of what we know. We are ignorant of the particular relationship since we are ignorant about the One it is related to, not what is related, so know that! (545)

61.6. What Happened to One of Ibn Arabi's Shaykhs in Morocco

This happened to one of our shaykhs from the people of Mawazana in Morocco. Certain matters about him were presented to the Sultan and the punishment for the would have entailed his execution. He was commanded to be brought present in shackles. A summons was given among the people that they all should be present so that he could question them about him. The people all said the same thing about him: that he should be killed. They said that he had done what necessitated it and that he was a *zindiq* (heretic). On his way, the shaykh passed by a man who was selling bread. He said to him: "Lend me half a loaf." He lent it to him and he gave it as charity to a passing individual. (546)

Then he was carried off and brought to sit in that great gathering. The judge had resolved that the people would testify against him regarding what he had said about him, and that he should be put to death in the worst possible manner. The judge was one of the people who hated him the most. He said: "People of Morocco! This is so-and-so. What do you say about him?" They all said in the same voice that he was a just, well-pleasing man. The judge was amazed. (547)

The shaykh told him: "Do not be astonished. This question is not very impossible. Which anger is greater? Your anger or the anger of God and the anger of the fire?" He said: "The anger of God and the anger of the fire." He said: "Which safeguard is greater—in weight and value—half a loaf or half a date?" He said: "Half a loaf." He said: "I repelled your anger and the anger of the assembly by half a loaf of bread since I heard the Prophet say: 'Safeguard yourselves from the fire, even with half a date,' and he said: 'Charity puts out the wrath of the Lord and repels evil from the dead.' God made that repel your evil from me and evil from the dead by half a loaf—in spite of your lowness and the greatness of my charity. My charity is greater than half a date, and your anger is less than the anger of the fire and the anger of the Lord." Those who were present marvelled at the strength of his belief. (548)

61.7. The Worst Death

The worst death is that a person die in a state which leads him to misery. God is only angry towards the wretched. So reflect on the effect of charity and how it affects the divine wrath, the worst death and the power of the fire. The one who gives charity for himself in anger is only by controlling himself in that. If it is owned by another in anger, then there is charity for it from where he is not aware. The Messenger of God said: "The strong one is not the one who makes others fall down. The strong one is the one who controls his soul in anger." Anger is a burning fire. This is part of a person's charity to himself. (549)

61.8. Putting Out the Fire with Charity and the Good Word

Then God mentions that He will not forgive a polytheist. In spite of this, God lightens the punishment for him according to the amount he expends. Abu Dawud mentioned from Aisha: "Muhammad! Where is Abdullah ibn Jidan?" He replied: "He is in the fire." That was hard for her. He said: "Aisha! Why is it that it is hard for you (to accept)?" She said: "He used to give food and keep up ties of kinship." He said: "It has been lightened for him by what you said regarding him." It was lightened for him by simply mentioning it among noble qualities. (550)

Al-Bukhari said in his *Sahih* that the Prophet said: "Guard yourselves against the fire, even with half a date. Whoever does not find half a date, then with a good word." The Prophet said that the good word is charity. Every glorification is charity. Every *"la ilaha illa Llah"* ("there is no god but God") is charity as well as other remembrances of God (*dhikr*) and actions which noble character demands. Muslim mentioned in his *Sahih* that Abu Hurayra said that the Messenger of God said: "A dinar which you spend in the way of God, a dinar which you spend to free a servant, a dinar which you give as charity to the very poor, a dinar which you spend on your family, the one which has the greatest reward is the one which you spend on your family." (551)

62 The One Who Gives of What He Loves

God said: "*You will never attain virtuous conduct until you spend of what you love.*" (3:92) Abdullah ibn Umar used to buy sugar and give it as charity. He says: "I love it," acting by this sign. The thing that the human being loves most is himself. If he spends it in the way of God, by that he has what will counterweight it. Whoever uses up something, must pay its price. God has used up the soul of this servant. He has commanded you to spend what you love. Its price is only the Garden with Him. This is when you do not find anything, you find God. He only exists in the absence of the things on which he relies. The soul of a person is the source of all things. It is destroyed, so its price is what we mentioned. Look then at how sublime the excellence of charity is! (552)

63 The States of Charity from Inward Knowledge

Announcing alms is from the name, the Manifest, and beginning with it, and the name, the First, and being based on it, it comes from His words: *"Say: If you have been loving God, then follow me and God will love you and forgive you your impieties."* (3:31) The ruler asks the people to give to those who are poor and in need when they come to him and he does not have anything in the treasury to give them. This is the heart which is empty of knowledge whose benefit passes to another of the limbs. Whoever has a good opinion of Him should ask the divine names to give him some of the states and knowledge which will help his outer and inner faculties to the actions which God has obliged that he do. (553)

63.1. The Heart Is Questioned about Its Flock

God informed the Messenger: "On the morning of every day, every joint owes charity." He made every glorification charity. He made every *"La ilaha illa Llah"* ("there is no god but God") charity as well as other things. These states require intention and sincerity. The intention comes only after recognition of the one to whom one is sincere. That is God Almighty. The Imam must ask for something with which to give as charity for every joint and on every joint. The heart is answerable for its flock which consists of all its outer and inner faculties. (554)

The prophetic Tradition which contains what we confirmed and considered is what Muslim transmitted from Jarir ibn Abdullah. He said: "We were with the Messenger of God at the beginning of the day. A group of people came who were barefoot, naked, ragged, and girded with swords. Most of them were from Mudar, indeed, all of them were from Mudar. The face of the Messenger of God fell when he saw the need that they had. He went inside and then emerged again and ordered Bilal to give the call to formal prayer and the declaration to perform the formal prayer. (555)

Then he led them in the prayer and gave a discourse and said: *"O humanity! Be Godfearing of your Lord Who created you from a single soul and from it created its spouse and from them both disseminated many men and women. And be Godfearing of God through Whom you demand mutual rights of one another and the wombs, the rights of blood relations. Truly God has been watching over you.*" (4:1) "*O those who have believed! Be Godfearing of God and let every soul look on what it has put forward for tomorrow. . . .*" (59:18) People gave charity from their dinars, from their dirhams, from their clothes, from a saa of wheat, from a saa of dates, until he said: "Even half a date." (556)

Then he said: "A person of the Helpers came with a purse and it was almost too big for his hand. Indeed, his hand was too small." He said: "Then people came one after the other until I saw that there were two piles of food and clothes and until I saw that the face of the Messenger of God was radiant as if it were of gold. The Messenger of God, said: 'Whoever makes a good custom (*Sunna*) in Islam has its reward and the reward of whoever acts by it after him without their reward being diminished at all. Whoever makes a bad custom in Islam has its burden and the burden of whoever acts by it after him without their burden being diminished at all.'" (557)

64 The Complaint of the Limbs to God about the Soul and Satan and What Evil They Cast at Them

The people of unveiling see and hear the complaint of the limbs to God Almighty about the foul soul which manages the body and disposes of the limbs in the evil which Satan casts to it along with the soul in respect of its luminous form. The animal receptive soul complains of the evil which Satan casts at it which it uses in the inner and outer faculties. When they are truthful in their complaint, God grants them security from what they fear and He provides them with acceptance of what the angels casts to them. He gives them success in using that casting for obedience to God Almighty and obedience to His Messenger so that those actions make him inherit witnessing of God and intimate conversation with Him in unveiling and witnessing without any intermediary. He speaks to them with an address that confirms blessings and favors. (558)

64.1. The Common People of Letters Do Not Hear the Complaint of the Limbs

The common blind people among the people of letters and forms are not aware: "*Unhearing, unspeaking, unseeing,*" (17:97) they do not use their intellect. They are unwilling to hear this complaint due to the intensity of their unwillingness to hear and the complete unwillingness to see. If they had done what God obliged then to do, God would have taught them the like of this knowledge and they would have seen Him with the witnessing of the eye as the People of God see Him and obtain Him. God said in respect to one of them: "*We taught him knowledge which proceeds from Our Presence.*" (18:65) "*So be Godfearing of God and God teaches you.*" (2:282) And "*If you are Godfearing of God, He will assign you a Criterion between right and wrong* (furqan)" (8:29) "*And He assigns you a light to walk by.*" (57:28). (559)

64.2. The Opening of the Treasures of Chosroes

The Messenger indicated what we mentioned in a Tradition which is general to what occurs in this world as well as indicating what we mentioned. It is what al-Bukhari transmitted from the brother of our ancestor,

Adi ibn Hatim. He said: "While we were with the Messenger of God a person came to him and complained of poverty. Then another came to him and complained about highway robbery. He said: 'Adi, have you seen Hira?!' I said: 'I have not seen it. I have been told about it.' He said: 'If you live for a long time, you will see a woman in a camel-sedan travel from Hira until she goes around the Kaba, not having any fear of anyone except God.' I said to myself, 'What will happen to the robbers of Tayy who have caused troubles in the land?' (560)

"'If you live a long time, the treasures of Chosroes will be opened up.' I said: 'Chosroes, son of Hurmuz?' He said: 'Chosroes son of Hurmuz. If you live long enough, you will see a person going out with his palm full of gold or silver, seeking someone to accept it from him, but not finding anyone to accept it from him. Each of you will meet God on the day he meets Him with no interpreter between Him and him to interpret for him. He will say: 'Did I not send you a Messenger who conveyed to you?' He will say: 'Yes indeed.' He will say: 'Did I not give you wealth and children and bestow bounty on you?' He will say: 'Yes indeed.' He will look to his right and only see hell, and he will look to his left and only see hell.'" (561)

Adi said: "I heard the Prophet say: 'Safeguard yourselves from the fire, even with half a date. Whoever does not find half a date, then with a good word.'" (562)

64.3. Security from the Greatest Fear

As for his words: "Do not fear anyone but God," it is the greatest fear. He has mastery and the kingdom of everything is in His hand. Where then is security? This clarifies our retreat. The person who is in the like of this state is in security in his property and in this world, and he is secure from himself and from the one who would harm him. This is what the Messenger of God meant. God is the One who provided him with security in that state, so he should fear God because of what there is in His unseen which he does not know, and the times of which he does not know. (563)

If this fearful one had feared God completely, he would have connected his fear to his religion. The path of Satan to his heart is not secure as the outward path is secure on which the travellers cross. When he fears God, his fear distracts from him property and himself. Had it not been that the way is not safe, this fearful one would have been in security. The only thought that occurs to him is about his religion since he fears that it will be stripped from him. This is to such an extent that if he had been touched by the destruction of the property or life in his path when thieves fall upon him, he might well be joyful at that and happy since it has a great reward in it which is stored up as well as expiation. His principle is that of the merchant who sells for a referred term with great profit. (564)

How excellent is the connection of prophethood to his words: "Do not fear anyone except God." Where is security? The Prophet only mentioned that to Adi since the normal security was obtained at that moment when the person complained that there were highway robbers. In that security, the Messenger of God included fear of God for those possessing intelligence. This is so that the discourse is general with security and specific with fear. It clarifies the states of the elite of God. That is, be the like of this state in your security: "Be fearful of God Almighty." This is one of the comprehensive statements for the one who looks and can see. (565)

65 Charity to the Nearest Kin and then the Next Nearest and the Consideration of Proximity in That

The nearest of a person's family to him is himself. God Almighty says about His nearness to His servant: "*We are nearer to him than his jugular vein.*" (50:16) It is as if He were saying that He is nearer to him than himself. His soul is more entitled to charity from him than anyone else, as God is more entitled to the loan since He is nearer to him than himself. Everyone who gives charity must give it to the creatures connected to him, then his limbs, and the nearest one to him after that. That is the family, then the child, then the servant, then the maternal relations, and the neighbor as he gives charity to his student and the one who seeks to benefit from him. (566)

When the gnostic of his Lord realizes that he is entirely light and that God is his hearing and sight and all of his faculties, then he is all Real. Whoever is part of the People of God, is the family of this person who is like this. There is no doubt about it. As the people of the Quran are the people of God and His elite are the family of this person whom we have mentioned, He is all Real as the Prophet said in his supplication: "Make me light," since he saw that God called Himself Light. He represents God among His servants. The one who gives charity to the People of God is the one who gives charity to his family when the one giving the charity is like this. (567)

65.1. Those Who Are Nearest to God Are the Most Entitled to Acts of Goodness

One day I was sitting with our Shaykh, Abu'l-Abbas al-Arabi in Seville. We—or someone—wanted to give some charity. One of the people in the assembly said to the one who wanted to give charity: "Near kin are more entitled to acts of goodness." The Shaykh immediately said, without any pause between the words of the speaker: "To God." O what comfort! By God, I only heard it in that state from God to such an extent that I imagined that it was such-and-such that had been sent down of the

Quran because of what I realized by it and what my heart drank." It was like that with all who present. (568)

Only the people of God should consume the blessings of God. They were created for these people while others consume them by the principle of subordination. They are the object of blessings. Other people, as we said, consume them subordinate to the whole. In respect to distinctions, there is not a single essence from him or accidental thing in him but that it glorifies God. Therefore he is one of the People of God. There is none in the world who is outside of this general kinship. The elite only acquire perception of this by unveiling. (569)

65.2. The Obedience of the Unity of Gatheredness and Obedience of the Units of the Whole

This question is one of the most abtruse questions in the Path of God since the sum only consists of these parts and the parts are the same as the whole. Therefore each part and section obeys the while the whole although the wholes foes not possess this attribute. It obeys by the obedience of the oneness of the whole. It is an obedience which is distinct from the obedience of individuals of this whole. (570)

65.3. The Greatest Reward Is for Spending on the Family

It is related in tradition about spending on the well-known outward family and its excellence. Its interpretation is only this. It is what Muslim transmitted in his *Sahih* from Abu Hurayra. He said that the Messenger of God said: "A dinar which you spend in the way of God, a dinar which you spend to free a servant, a dinar which you give as charity to the very poor, a dinar which you spend on your family, the greatest reward is the one which you spend on your family." (571)

66 Maintaining Relations with Kin and the Kin are a Twig from The Merciful

May God provide you with understanding from God! Understand that since kin (*rahim*) are a twig from the Merciful, whoever maintains kinship with them is joined to God. That is, to the one who is a branch from Him. Whoever cuts them off is cut off from God. Charity to kin is charity of joining to the Merciful. Charity to other than kin falls into the hand of the Merciful. There is no connection to the Merciful in it. (572)

66.1. The Adamic Form Is a Caliph

This Adamic form is a caliph. His station grants that he be the caliph outwardly by the form of the one who was made caliph. Whoever gives charity to himself by what he obtains of its life, has charity and joining to God, one of whose attributes is the Merciful. God created Adam in His form, in spite about their disagreement regarding the pronoun, "His." God Almighty said: *In the Name of God, the Merciful, the Compassionate,"* and He described God as the Merciful. (573)

66.2. When the Relationship is Distant, the Station is Great

Al-Tirmidhi transmitted from Salama ibn Amir that the Prophet said: "Charity to the destitute is charity to those of kin; it is two things: Charity and ties of friendship." According to our companions, whenever the relationship is strong, the station is great. The matter is not like that with us. Whenever the relationship is distant, the station is great. We wrote about that:

I saw my Lord with the eye of my Lord.
    I said, "My Lord." He said, "Thee." (574)

Some of the gnostics imagine that this sign is based on the first form. That is not the case. The pronoun of the speaker in this sign is the eye of the servant by his Lord, not by his own soul. Consider this. It is one of the most wondrous gnoses. It contains immense secrets and great knowledge. (574)

67 The Taker Giving Charity to the Giver from Whom He Took It

The soul gives charity to the intellect by accepting from it what it casts to it since there some souls which do not accept. The soul gives form to the soul of its disciples which are motherless orphans because their soul is dead to them. They have none to manage them except for this soul which belongs to their Shaykh. It gives charity to them by what God casts to it from the divine spirit since they are in the station of the state which is affected by the action. The soul of the disciple discovers matters which neither its station nor its state accords it. They are outside of its own acquisition. He imagines that God has given him an opening without any intermediary while that opening is from the state of the soul of this person who is the Shaykh. The disciple is enthralled by love in the room of the Shaykh and he has an immense reward with God because of that. There is no Prophet who did not say when he gave profit and conveyed the message and it was said to him: "*I have not asked you for any compensation; my compensation is with God.*" (10:72) That is, teaching which demands a reward. (575)

67.1. The Reward Which Does Not Remove You from Your Servanthood

This is the reward which does not remove you from your servanthood. You are a servant in the form of a wage-earner. It is not the reward of a wage-earner. The wage-earner is the one who is hired. He is an alien. The master does not hire his servant even though the work demands a wage, and he does not take it. The worker takes it. The worker-servant takes the wage from God so he resembles the wage-earner in taking the wage. He differs from him in the hire. What we have mentioned is confirmed by what Muslim transmitted from Bilal from the Prophet in his *Sahih*. He asked him about a woman's charity to her husband and to the orphans in her care. He said: "She has two rewards: the reward of near kinship and the reward of charity." (576)

68 Concerning Who Are the Parents of a Person's Self

The manager of his body and his faculties is the partial soul which is the soul of the human being. It is the child of his natural body which is its mother while the divine spirit is its father. This is why you say in intimate conversation: "Our Lord and the Lord of our celestial fathers and terrestrial mothers." *"That is when I have shaped him and have breathed into him of My Spirit."* (15:9) "Mary was pure and chaste, so We breathed into her of Our spirit," and that was Jesus her child. She is his mother. (577)

68.1. The Orphan is the One with No Father

The body was that in which a soul was formed by the spirit being blown into it The body is therefore the mother, and that from which it is blown is the father, although this child is like the orphan without a father since his intellect is not strengthened by looking at it. It is as if he had no intellect. He is in the position of the child who has no father to teach him knowledge and good manners. His vegetable soul fashioned him which is his body by the sound nature on which God created it. Therefore, its inner and outer faculties are in the very limit of purity and balance. (578)

The soul benefits from the knowledge which are in the position of a woman's charity to her orphan child. This person obtains from the side of his body divine knowledge as a repayment for what he gave as charity to himself whose value only God can reckon. Umm Salama, the wife of the Prophet said: "Do I have a reward for the children of Abu Salama when I spend on them and I have not left them such-and-such when they are my sons?" He said: "Yes. You have a reward for what you spend on them." Muslim transmitted it in his *Sahih*. (579)

69 THE ONE WHO GIVES CHARITY BY WISDOM TO THE ONE WHO DESERVES IT

It is charity. *"Found He thee not an orphan and He gave thee refuge?"* (93:10) He means the one who asks for knowledge. A person gives charity by knowledge to the people of God who are worthy of it. Wisdom should only be passed on to its people. That is considered to be charity with God. When he does not think that has any virtue for the one he teaches and he does not critically examine what he is asked to do as service in that in good manners, respect and exploitation in return for what he was given— if he fails to do that—that is not reckoned with God. (580)

We met our Shaykhs on that basis, and it is our Path. The divine law takes note of it in the knowledge of forms and its world. He said that when the Muslim spends on his family with expectation of the reward, then it is charity for him. That is, it falls into the hand of the Merciful. Muslim transmitted this Tradition from Abu Masud al-Badri from the Messenger of God. (581)

70 Divinely Given Knowledge and Acquired Knowledge

There are two types of knowledge: Given and acquired. Given knowledge has no measure. Acquired knowledge is what is obtained from piety and sound action. Specification and measure enter into it. Every piety and specific action has a specific knowledge which only it possesses. There is the one who is fears God for God, the one who fears God because of the fire, the one who fears God because of Satan, the one who does not fear God. Every act of God-consciousness has a specific action and a specific knowledge which is obtained by the one who has piety. (582)

70.1. A Person's Spending on Himself Which Is Considered Charity

A person's spending on himself which is considered charity is that by which he is nourished by acquired knowledge by which he has life after-time in this world and the world to come. That is because every correct deed is charity. The people of correctness in this world are the people of correctness in the world to come. There is none recognized/correct except God. There are no people except the People of God! (583)

70.2. The One Who Is Faithful to Himself is the One Who Guards His Honor

The one who is faithful to himself is the one who guards his honor. That is part of his charity to himself. To guard one's honor is not to let any blame fall on him from God, and nothing more. Then he is praised by the divine law and every divine tongue from angel, animal, plant, mineral and sphere and all except for *jinn* and men as well as by some of *jinn* and men. (584)

Is it conceivable that he guard his honor from all *jinn* and men? This is inconceivable because the root which is God does not have His honor protected from the tongues of His creation, although it is possible that He is elevated above honor/reputation. Since it is possible, then He has protected Himself—which is His honor—from there being any effect in Himself. It is not that He has protected His honor in what is said about

Him. That is the meaning of His words: *"And whatever you spend of anything, He will replace it."* (34:39) (585)

70.3. The Hand of God Spends and His Hand Takes

If a person spends, he hopes for glory on the tongues of creation. That is why he spends. If he desires to return the praise to God inasmuch as it is the blessing of God, then he spends in this business and does not see the spender. He spends in rebellion against Iblis and does not see the protection. Spending is only from the hand of God. The like of this is excluded in every spending since this is his state and his tasting. He does not find the reward to the one who returns except to its Giver. The hand of God gives and the hand of the Merciful takes from it.

The hand of God spends
  and the hand of the Merciful takes.
That which belongs to generosity is empty
  and that which the servant has is useless.
His signs distinguished a wonder.
  It is connected to the eyes.
Had you seen them in their transformation
  while they cross through phenomenal beings,
You would have said that my desires move them
  while they remain still by the proof. (586)

70.4. Every Correct Action Is Charity

What we have mentioned is confirmed by the indication of the Prophet that every correct action is charity and that what a person spends on himself and his family is written as charity for him. That by which a person guards his honor is charity for him. Whatever maintenance a person spends, it is up to God to replace it except for what is spent in buildings or rebellion. This Tradition was mentioned by Abu Ahmad from the Tradition of Jabir. Abdu 'l-Hamid—who is the source of Abu Ahmad—related that he said to Ibn al-Munkadir: "With what does a person guard his honor?" That is, what does it mean? He said: "He pays the poet and the one with a tongue." (587)

71 The Distinction Between Servanthood and Freedom

The relation of a person by servanthood to his Lord or to servanthood is better than his relationship by freedom to another so that he is called "free from the bondage of others." Freedom from God is not valid. When a person is in the station of freedom, he only sees the source of others because his freedom from them is established by his seeing them. In this station, he is absent from both his servanthood and servitude. The station of servanthood is more noble than the station of freedom in respect of a person. Worship is more noble than servanthood. (588)

The Prophet indicated the like of this in the Tradition of Maymuna bint al-Harith when she set free a servant girl that she owned in the time of the Messenger of God. He said: "Had you given her your to your maternal kin, you would have had a greater reward. The station of servanthood is weightier than the reward for freedom. (589)

71.1. The Disparity Between the Thankful Rich and the Patient Poor

Similarly poverty and need of God are weightier than richness by God. One of our Shaykhs, Abdullah al-Qalafat in Algiers, related something to me in about 590 AH. We had had some discussion about the comparison between the rich and the poor. I mean the thankful rich and the steadfast poor one. It is a question which they tackled for me and we were pulling the state of poverty and wealth in that. He told me: "I was present with one of the Shaykhs. He related to me from Abu 'l Rafi al-Kafif al-Malaqi, the student of Abu 'l Abbas ibn al-Arif al-Sanhaji that he said: (590)

"There two men together. Each of them had ten dinars. One of them gave one of the ten dinars as charity, and the other gave nine of the ten dinars as charity. Which of them was better? Those present said: 'The one who gave the nine.' He asked: 'Why do you prefer him?' They replied: 'Because he gave more in charity than his companion gave.' He said: 'Good, but you have missed the heart of the question and it is hidden from you.' He was asked: 'What is that?' He said: 'We assumed that they were equal in property. Therefore, the one who gave more charity entered into poverty more than his companion. He is better since he went first in the direction of poverty.'" (591)

71.2. The Sufis Do Not Stop with Rewards, but with Realities

This is not unknown to the one who recognizes the stations and states. The People do not stop with the rewards. They stop with the realities and states and what unveiling grants. This is why they are preferred to the scholars of forms. Had he given all of it as charity and remained in his root, with nothing, that would have been higher still. He lacks the degree and taste according to what he withholds of it. (592)

Do you not see what our Shaykh, Abu 'l-Abbas al-Sibti, may God have mercy on him, said about the one who is dying and wills away a third of his property in bequests? The dying person only owns a third of his property, so he spends out of what he has and he has nothing left for him. The Lawgiver allowed him to give the entire third away as charity, which is what he owns. He is praised for doing that in the divine law. He then meets God poor. As he left Him, so he returns to Him: empty-handed. Someone wrote some poetry with this idea:

When the child is born, he clenches his hand:
    evidence of the avarice built into the living.
When he dies, he opens it as a warning.
    "Look at me" I have left with nothing!"

He is better than the one who did not give that third as charity which is what he owns, or give less than a third as charity. He intends that what remains be charity for his heirs. There is a wondrous indication in it. (593)

72 The Excellence of Someone Who Leaves Charity for People After His Death in Either Property or Knowledge

The gnostic of God is dying, and there is benefit for people in knowledge of their Lord if he is able to speak and his tongue can be understood. Then a student transmits from him a question regarding useful knowledge about tawhid or something else, and those who are present and listening profit from it. Then that dying gnostic plucks its fruit and the student also plucks the fruit of his transmission with God. God will repay the dead person with a necessary repayment which comes from his striving. God said: "*The human being has nothing but what he endeavors for and that endeavor will be seen.*" (53:39) The best of what a person eats comes from his own earning. His child is part of his earning, and the student is certainly the child of the religion. Whatever a person strives for, he has that with God by means of the divine obligation with which He has obliged Himself. (594)

72.1. The Work of Others in the Principle of Representation

As for what another does for him by the principle of representation in which the dead person neither gave permission nor instructed to be done nor has he any action in it, God will grant him that station since someone else gave it to him. The dead person takes it, but not by means of the divine obligation. However, he absolutely must take it for it has come to him without him asking for it. It says in sound Tradition: "Take whatever comes to you without asking. As for something else, do not. Do not let your soul follow it." A whiff has come about that in the knowledge of forms in what Muslim transmitted from Aisha. A person came to the Messenger of God and said: "Messenger of God! My mother died suddenly and did not leave any will. I think that if she had spoken, she would have given charity. Will she have a reward if I give charity for her? He said: 'Yes.'" (595)

73 What the Next Formation Grants

God Almighty said: *"As He began you, you will revert to Him."* (7:29) and *"And surely you have known the first growth. Will you not then recollect?"* (56:62) He originated us without any prior example and we know that. Similarly He will restore us without any example. (596)

73.1. The Person Being In Different Places at the Same Time

Know that whoever knows the reward of the world to come and a person's relationship to it knows the next formation. It is not impossible for a person be in different places at the same time although logic considers this matter to be impossible. Unveiling testifies to its validity although it is logically impossible. What is not impossible is the divine relationship to every one who prays and converses with his Lord. The human being is created in respect to his reality on which he will be formed in the world to come "on the form." (597)

73.2. The Gnostic Being with Many of the Divine Names in Different States While the Source is One

The gnostic can be with many of the divine names in different states while the source remains one in the gnostic and the One Named. Every person sees Him according to his source which this person is obliged to manifest. Zayd may be in the state of prayer while Amr sees him as asleep, Khalid sees him writing, Muhammad sees him sewing, and Qasim sees him eating. The source is the same and all of that is actually seen by each onlooker. Each onlooker is in a different land than that of his companion, even as he will enter into whatever form he likes in the forms of the Market of the Garden. I have not heard anyone report about this station except for Abu Bakr al-Siddiq, may God be pleased with him, about entering all the eight gates of the Garden at the same time, and Dhu 'l-Nun al-Misri in his famous questions like the dead person whose friend sees him dead without movement while another person sees him alive and asking with his own eyes at the very same moment. (598)

73.3. Entering All the Gates of the Garden at the Same Time

As for the Tradition of Abu Bakr, al-Bukhari mentioned in his *Sahih* that Abu Hurayra said that he heard the Messenger of God say: "The one who spends out two kinds of actions in the way of God will be summoned from the gates of the Garden, 'Servant of God! This is better!' Whoever is among the people of formal prayer will be called from the gate of formal prayer. Whoever is among the people of charity will be called from the gate of charity. Whoever is among the people of obligatory fasting will be called from the gate of obligatory fasting, the gate of Rayyan (quenching)." Abu Bakr said: "No one called from these gates will feel distress." He said: "Can anyone be called from all of them, Messenger of God?" He said: "Yes, and I hope that you are among them, Abu Bakr." (599)

On the Day of Rising, God will call people to enter with a single call for the entry to the Gardens. One will enter by one gate, one by two gates, and one by three. The most universal of them will be the one who enters by the eight gates because the limbs which are under obligation are eight. Each limb has a gate. Do not be ignorant about it in the reward at the same time that a deed contains action and non-action, like lowering the eye while listening to admonition, while reciting, while fasting, while giving charity, while being scrupulous, while guarding chastity. All of that is with the intention which draws near to God Almighty. (600)

Every gate contains stages, like belief in God which has some seventy odd branches. The highest of them is: "there is no god but God," (*La ilaha illa Llah*) and the lowest is removing something harmful from the road. There is no greater harm than idolatry, and no greater road than the road of belief. So he seals it in the same way he began it, with: "there is no god but God," (*La ilaha illa Llah*). It is the negation of what is other than God which lays claim or has any claim to divinity made for it. Removing harm is the negation of harm in the road. The end of the circle is joined to the beginning and we incline to it. What lies between these two are the rest of the branches of belief. (601)

Whoever knows what we have said will enter all of the gates of the Garden at the same time. The formation which will exist in the world to come will allow these matters as our formation in this world grants that all the branches of belief can be in a person at the same time. This is not impossible. (602)

74 Giving What Is Good in Charity While Being Cheerful About It

Know that what is good in charity is that you give charity from what you own, while you only own what is lawful for you to own, while you are cheerful about it. The highest form of that is that in it you fulfill the trust which the divine law called charity in the language of forms. Then your hand is the hand of God when you give. This is why we said that it is a trust. Only their Creator profits by the like of this gift. The one for whom they were created deserves it. That is the creature. It is a trust with God from God for this servant to whom it was given. It is either given from Him to him or at the hand of another servant. This is the best charity because it is given out according to the limits of sound knowledge. (603)

74.1. The Hand of God Gives and the Hand of God Takes

When it arrives in the hand of the one to whom it is given, the Merciful takes it with His right hand. In the soul of this giver when he gives, the Giver is God. Then his hand is higher than the hand of the one who takes the charity and is the asker. That must be. The higher hand is the hand of God. It gives out. If this giver sees the hand of the Merciful taking from him when he gives it to the asker, then his hand remains higher than the hand of the Merciful inasmuch as the giver is God. The Merciful is one of the attributes and qualities of God. He does not take it from him exactly. What He takes from him is the piety of the giver when he gives. The most perfect of its aspects is that which we have just mentioned. (604)

The giver sees that God is the Giver and that the Merciful is the Taker and that mercy is the giver. It is charity. When the Merciful takes it with His right hand, He makes this servant its locus and the Merciful gives it to him. Only that is possible. Charity is mercy, and only the Merciful gives it by His reality. God accepts it inasmuch as He is described as the Merciful, the Compassionate, not in respect to the Pure Name. Charity falls into the hand of the Merciful before it falls into the hand of the asker. The tradition has come to this effect. (605)

74.2. Your Charity to Zayd Is the Same as Your Charity to Yourself

When the asker consumes the like of this charity, it bears him fruit in the form of obedience, guidance, light and knowledge. All of this is the result of care which the Merciful has in the charity. He will see all that power of this charity gives in the soul of the asker in the way of obedience, guidance, light and knowledge in the world to come in his balance and in the balance of the one who gave it. He is the charity-giver, the representative of God. He is told: "This is the fruit of your charity. Its blessings (*baraka*) has reverted to you and to the one to whom you gave it." (606)

74.3. The Best Charity

The best charity is that which a person gives to himself. This is present also with the one who gives charity in the most perfect aspects of himself. On the Day of Rising, it will not be said to the one who gave this sort of charity: "From where did you give charity, or to whom did you give it?" He is like this. If the taker is like him in this rank, then they are equal in happiness, although the giver of the charity is preferred by one degree, and no more. If he is not like this, it will be according to the attribute by which God established him. If it is voluntary charity, then it is an existential divine favor. If it is obligatory alms, then it is a divine favor. If it is a vow, then it is existential, divine, and compulsory. A vow causes it to be extracted from the miser. If this gift is a simple gift, then it is not part of this topic. This topic only concerns giving what is "charity." (607)

74.4. Charity Becomes Great in the Hand of The Merciful Physically and Spiritually

This charity becomes great in the hand of the Merciful both physically and spiritually. The physical part of it, inasmuch as it is sensory, is that it will be found physically in the Garden, visible to the eye. The spiritual aspect of it is in respect to what established it from lawful earning and taqwa in it, striving and cheerfulness when he gives it, and seeing what we mentioned of the divine matters in it. He will find it in the Slipping Heap in the general witnessing of God [in the world to come[. He will experience it at every moment when the balances pass him at the time when they are brought out while he is in the Garden. He is given witnessing as a favor from God in His Garden itself. None except the one who is like this sees it. (608)

Muslim transmitted it from Abu Hurayra. He said that Prophet said: "No one gives any charity except from what is good, and God only accepts the good. The Merciful takes it in His right hand. If it is a date, it grows in the palm of the Merciful until it is greater than the mountain, just as one of you raises his colt or young camel." All of that descends in his charity from the degree which we described. Its position with God is according to the extent of his knowledge and his intention. (609)

74.5. Charity Comes from the Name, The Rich, The Strong

Charity only comes from the name, the Rich, the Strong, Possessing firm power by means of graciousness without seeking any gratitude for it. If it is combined with seeking gratitude, then it does not comes from the name, the Rich. It comes from the name, the Transformer, the Wise, the Knowing. (610)

74.6. Charity and the Intention of the Good Loan

If it occurs to the charity-giver to give God a good loan by his charity, that is responding to the command of God. This subject is also connected to charity since he is commanded to give the loan while the loan may be the same as obligatory alms. If he seeks recompense so that he gets back more than what he loans, then he gives a loan outside of its proper limits. Charity is not described with the quality of the loan. He has not given the prescribed loan. "God would not forbid usury and then take it from us," as the Messenger of God said. (611)

So every loan which seeks benefit is usury. If is when this idea occurs to him when he gives it and so he is only giving it for that purpose. The giver, who is the lender, must be excellent in loyalty and he will be increased above that without it being a condition in the loan itself. God has promised to multiply the reward for the loan. However, the servant does not lend it for the sake of the reward, he lends it because of the command. Doing good will be repaid by God on the Day of Rising. (612)

74.7. God Will Deal with Us According to What He Prescribed for Us

This is the meaning of His word "good" when He described the loan. God will deal with us according to what He prescribed for us and not by anything else. Don't you see that His Prophet was commanded to ask Him on the Day of Rising to judge between His servants and Him by the Truth which He revealed. He said to him: *"My Lord! Give judgment between us with the Truth."* (21:112) The definite article in "the Truth" belongs to the well-known Truth with which he was sent. This is the basis for the states in which creatures will find themselves on the Day of Rising. Whoever wants to see the judgment of God on the Day of Rising should look at the judgment of the divine law in this world. It is completely identical, no more and no less. Have insight into your divine law. It specifies the Truth to which you will return. Do not be deceived. Be on your guard and have a good opinion of your Lord. Recognize the places where He addresses His servants in His Mighty Book and the *Sunna* of His Prophet. (613)

75 Concealing Charity

Know that concealing charity is a precondition for obtaining the sublime station which God has bestowed on the seven Abdal. The form of concealing that has various aspects. One is that the recipient does not know you and that you are very discreet in conveying that to him in any manner. There are many aspects to this. (614)

75.1. Charity Is Taken from God, Not from You!

One of them is that you teach him how to take it so that he is taking from God and not from you so that he does not think that you have any excellence over him because of what you have given him. Therefore, he does not show any abasement and poverty in your presence, and he obtains an immense knowledge of the One who gives to him. You are hidden from his eyes when you give to him since he is certain that he is only taking what is his. This is part of concealing charity. (615)

75.2. The Most Concealed Charity Is that Your Left Hand Does Not Know What Your Right Hand Gives

Part of it is that he conceals the fact that it is charity so that the recipient does not know that he is in the presence of the charity-giver. When the agent who is appointed by the ruler takes it, he takes it by force and might from you. When it is in the hands of the ruler, who is the guardian for it before God, then the ruler gives it to its eight owners and its owners take it with might and pride, not with abasement. It is their right in the hands of this guardian. When the taker is given it, he does not know who is the specific owner of that property. Therefore, the rich property owner has neither might nor favor in respect of this poor person. He does not know whether it was specifically his wealth that reached him. This is also part of concealing charity because the giver does not know specially who receives the charity, and the recipient does not specially know who gave it. There is nothing more concealed than this concealment. His left hand does not know what his right hand spends. This is the same as that. (616)

75.3. Those Whom God Singled Out for the Shade of the Throne

The Messenger of God mentioned what we said about concealing charity when he clarified the seven stages which belong to the elite of God who will be given shade on the Day of Rising with the shade of the Throne of the Merciful because they are among the people of the Merciful. Al-Bukhari transmitted it from Abu Hurayra from the Prophet. He said: "There are seven whom God will shade in His shade on the day when there is no shade but His: a just imam, a youth raised in worship of God, a person whose heart is attached to the mosques, two men who love each other in God and met and part in that, a person who is called by a woman of rank and says: 'I fear God,' a person who gives charity and conceals it so that his left hand does not know what his right hand spends, and a person who remembers God while he is alone and his eyes overflow with tears." (617)

76 The One Who Is Singled Out by the Owner of this Property Which He Possess Before He Gives It to Him as Charity

There are servants of God to whom it is unveiled that the provision which they possess belongs to so-and-so. They see the names of the owners on it although it is in their hands. When the one who is like this gives charity, is it then written for him as charity? We say: "Yes, it is written for him as charity inasmuch as God has ascribed ownership to him." If he received unveiling, that unveiling does not detract from it. Have you not seen that the dying person has the name of property removed from him and he is barred from him and he is barred from disposing of it and he is only allowed one third of it. Nothing that he says is heard about what is more than that because he is speaking about what he does not own. (618)

76.1. The Self is Naturally Disposed to Avarice

Know that the soul is naturally disposed to avarice. God Almighty said: "*And when the good afflicted him, begrudging.*" (70:21) and "*And whoever is protected from his own stinginess, then those are the ones who prosper.*" (59:9) The reason for that is that it is a possible. Every possible is in need of being connected to something whose existence dominates its non-existence. Its need is essential. As long as person's life is connected to his body, his need is before him and he sees his poverty and the eye brings it to him in his promise. He said: "*Satan threatens you with poverty.*" (2:268) He can only overcome his soul and Satan when he is strong by divine success. Then he fights his soul and Satan who aids it against him. This is why the Lawgiver called it charity—because it is brought out from strength and force. You say: "A true (*sidq*) spear," that is, strong and firm. (619)

If it had not been that he hoped for going-on and was certain of separation, it would have been easy for him to give property because it will be taken from him forcibly whether he likes it or not. Whoever wants the soul to be generous in that state may acquire that in another place according to what he is parted from. All of that comes from his desire, so he does not find generosity in the soul like this and God has not protected it from its avarice. (620)

In that vein, Muslim mentioned that Abu Hurayra said that a person came to the Messenger of God and said: "Messenger of God! What charity has the greatest reward?" He replied: "By your father, that you give charity while you are healthy and avaricious, fearing poverty and hoping to go on, and that you do not delay until it reaches the throat and then say: 'So-and-so has such-and-such.'" (621)

The one who is not protected from the avarice of his soul by God and reaches this limit and it is unveiled to him that a part of his property is for a certain person, then he should make that charity. When he makes it specific, he should tell himself that he is fulfilling a trust and that its moment has come. Then he will be gathered with those who fulfill trusts, not with those who give charity. No doubt of charity occurs to him if he wants to counsel himself. (622)

77 Types of Ownership and Transfer of Ownership Among the People of God

77.1. Ownership by Right, Ownership as a Trust and Existential Ownership

The gnostic says: "God knows this property of yours." He accepts it from Him with good manners and knowledge that it is a property which is deserved by the one who is entitled it and has a right to it. Property is a trust for the one who has possession of it as a trust. Property is existence for the one who exists from it. All things are the property of God in existence. They belong to the servant according to the state. What he must have in the heart of the matter of what will benefit him is property which he deserves. That is food and drink by which he is nourished when he takes nourishment, and it is not what is extra and outside of his way. The clothes he has are what protect him from the heart and cold. As for whatever is beyond this amount, it is a property which he has as a trust for the one to whom he gives it as well as what he spends on himself that we mentioned. (623)

77.2. The States of the Gnostics in Respect of Types of Ownership

The gnostic is one of two types. He may be one of those to whom the names of the owners of things are unveiled as written on them, so he keeps them for them until he gives them to them in the moment which the All-Wise decreed and specified that. He separates what is his and calls it merited property because his name is on it and he deserves it, from what belongs to someone else. He calls that property a trust because the name of the owner is on it. In the language of the divine law, all is his property in the outward judgment. This gnostic may be one of those to whom that is not unveiled. He does not recognize exactly whose provision he has. When it is unveiled to him, he acts according to his unveiling. The judgment belongs to knowledge in that. (624)

If it is not unveiled to him, then it is better for him to bring all of it out of his property as charity for God and his provision. He must bring it while he trusts what God has if what he deserves remains with God. If nothing remains for him with God, he will not helped by holding on to what is not his property in the divine law. In the heart of the matter, he does not deserve it by unveiling. He leaves it for him and is not praised. These are the states of the gnostics. (625)

77.3. The Person with Unveiling Spending from His Property

The person who is unveiled may spend all of his property by his unveiling because he sees that the name of someone else is on it, and so he does not deserve any of it. In form, he resembles the one who gives all his property without unveiling. If he does not have trust in God, then the divine law censures him if he gives out all of his property and after that has to ask people for charity. The charity of the one who is like this is not accepted, as has been related about that in the Tradition in al-Nasai about the person who was given two garments as charity. Then another person came to him to ask him for charity, and this first person who had received charity gave him one of the two garments. The Messenger of God rebuked him and said: "Take your garment." He did not accept his charity. (626)

If he knows that he will not have to beg or run the risk of it, then he can give out all of this property. It is by the measure of preference if he knows that, since he does not have unveiling. If he has unveiling, he acts according to his unveiling. Abu Dawud transmitted what is in harmony with what we mentioned from the Tradition of Umar ibn al-Khattab. He said: "One day the Messenger of God commanded us to give charity. That was consistent with the property which I had. I said: 'Today I will get ahead of Abu Bakr if I can get ahead of him one day.' I brought half of my property and the Messenger of God said: 'What have you left for your family?' I said: 'The like of it.' Abu Bakr brought all that he had and he said: 'What have you left for your family?' He said: 'I have left them God and His Messenger.' I said: 'I will never get ahead of you in anything.'" (627)

77.4. Treating the Self According to the Divine Law Which Rules It

The one who knows himself must deal with himself in the manner in which the divine law ruling him deals with it. The murid should not look at the thought which occurs to him in the moment and then be under the jurisdiction of his thought. He might err more than he is correct. Here, there is a distinction between the person of knowledge and intellect and the ignorant person. However, all of this is for the one among the people of God who has no unveiling. The Messenger of God was silent about Abu Bakr when he brought him all the property which he had because he recognized his state and station. He did not say to him: "Have you not kept anything for your family from your property?" He praised Umar for that in the presence in the Messenger of God and he did not rebuke him for it. Kab ibn Malik related in this Tradition, "Keep some of your property." Kab ibn Malik had stripped away all of this property as charity because of a thought which had occurred to him. The Messenger of God did not deal with him according to his thought. He dealt with him according to what his state demanded. He said: "Keep some of your property. It will be better for you." (628)

78 What the Gnostic Sees in the Bounty and Justice of God and the Deception of God Almighty

Part of the deception of God and His justice and overflowing favor is that He makes it clear to people where what is good for them lies. This is part of His favor. As for His justice and deception, it is that He deals with them according to their attributes. The gnostics in the like of this station look at the states of their souls and what God beings them inwardly and outwardly. They weigh that with the measure which the Merciful has set up in order to establish the measure with justice and not to lessen the measure. If the scales are equal, that is sound knowledge. If the scale of giving is heavier than the scale of the state, then he looks at the state. If it is part of what the divine law praises, then that is either a repayment given in advance or increase of favor. If the state is part of what the divine law censures, then that is deception from God. If the state is something which is neither praised nor censured, then that is justice from God leading either to favor if he thanks God and obeys Him in renewing those gifts, or it leads to hidden deception if he rebels against God in it. (629)

If he is concerned with asking forgiveness and repentance, that hidden deception is either met directly or he remains in the same state. If he remains in that state, it is deception within deception. If he takes steps in the matter, then that is part of the overflowing favor of God and the principle of deception is removed from him in this state. (630)

78.1. "The upper hand is better than the lower hand" is Part of Deception and Favor

Part of the deception of God and His overflowing favor is that "the higher hand is better than the lower hand." "Charity falls into the hand of the Merciful." There is deception and favor in that. It has been related that it falls into the hand of the Merciful before it falls into the hand of the asker. Al-Bukhari mentioned from Hakim ibn Hizam in what we have noted that the Prophet said: "The upper hand is better than the lower hand. Begin with your dependents. The best charity is that given by the wealthy. Anyone who refrains [from asking], God will spare him the need to and anyone who seeks to be independent, God will give him independence." This Tradition contains the details of what we mentioned regarding states. (631)

78.2. The Highest Wealth is Wealth by God

The highest wealth is wealth by God. Seeking to refrain here means being content with little. Effacement is used linguistically and "little" is meant by it. It is one of the opposites (*afw* = both surplus and effacement). Charity from a "wealthy person" is charity, and supplication from poverty is a supplication which is answered without a doubt. Where is the asker who is poor and the giver who is wealthy? (632)

79 The Soul's Need for Knowledge

79.1. Legal Knowledge, Divine Knowledge, and Knowledge Related to the Next World

Know that the soul's need for knowledge is greater than the need of the natural disposition for food to put it right. There are two knowledge: a knowledge which it needs as it needs nourishment and there must be economy in it and restriction according to the need. There is knowledge of the rules of the divine law. He only looks at it according to what need touches him in the moment. Its jurisdiction is connected to actions which occur in this world. You only take from it according to your actions. (633)

The other knowledge is that which has no limit. It is knowledge connected to God and the places of the Rising. Knowledge of the places of the Rising leads the one who knows them to prepare for every place with what befits it because the truth itself is what is sought on that day when the veils are raised. It is the Day of Distinguishing. The person of intellect must have insight into the business in order to prepare the answer for himself and others in the places where he knows that the answer will be demanded of him. This is why we connected it to knowledge of God. (634)

79.2. The One Who Seeks Knowledge Must Only Ask God About the Question

The one who seeks knowledge must only ask God about the question, not the question itself. Similarly, the asker must have presence with God so that the asker will get much from the question. God is the One who is asked. If that does not occur to him and he only sees the master and only seeks knowledge from him and that person of knowledge does not return him to God when he says: "God knows best," or tell him knowledge which will return him to God, that is what the Messenger of God indicated according to what Muslim mentioned of the Tradition from Abu Hurayra: "Whoever asks people for their property a lot, asks for burning embers. Let him do with a little or a lot." (635)

God wants His servants to return to Him with their requests, not to their likes except inasmuch as they learn from them how to ask God. That is the limit of their prescribed God-consciousness. He says: "*Be Godfearing of God*" by what He taught you of what you have learned by means of piety ". . . *and God teaches you*." (2:282) He—glory be to Him!—is the Teacher, whether the question is about knowledge or something other than knowledge, like the desires of the soul as His Lord said to Moses in what He revealed to him or spoke to him. "Ask Me—even for the salt which you put in your dough." (636)

He said in the area of allusion, not the area of explanation: "The Merciful, He taught the Quran" in whatever heart it is and is firm, and to whatever heart it descends. "*He created the human being. He taught him the clear explanation*," (55:1-4) in order to make clear to people what had been sent down to them. He ascribed teaching to Himself, not to anyone else. All of this comes from divine jealousy lest a creature other than the Creator be asked. He wants to spare His servants asking those who do not possess anything of this business. The Messenger of God pointed this out and he did not specify any particular question. He said: "Had you truly known what was in the question, no one would go to anyone else to ask for anything." (637)

The Messenger of God disliked questions and criticized them. He wanted people to act by what God taught them on the tongue of His Messenger. They should ask God in their actions to increase them with knowledge on top of their knowledge from Him. He Himself takes charge of teaching His servants. He is jealous and does not like for anyone else to be asked. If he asks someone else by the outward tongue, the heart is still present with God in the asking, and God is the One who is asked, the One who possesses the kingdom of everything in His hand by meaning. The outward name from God is this person. It is part of the sum total of the letters which are written on the outspread parchment of existence. This asker takes his answer from God either by the fulfillment of a need or by supplication. (638)

79.3. Asking the Ruler Is Better than Asking Someone Else

This is why it is better to ask the ruler than to ask anyone else because the existence of the Real is more manifest in him than in any of the rabble or common people. This is why begging is removed from those who asks kings. They are the representatives of God, and they are the place of the need of creation. They are commanded not to scold the beggar. God Almighty says to His Prophet, who is the greatest representative: "*And as for one who begs, scold him not*." (93:10) This is why God will question the representatives on the Day of Rising. He will ask the shepherds what they did for them. (639)

Now to return to the questions of charity here, the Messenger of God said: "Begging consists of lacerations with which a person injures his face. Whoever wants to, preserves his face. Whoever wants to, does not: unless he asks the one with power for something, he cannot avoid asking for something." This is the text which we mentioned. It is a Tradition which Abu Dawud transmitted from Samura ibn Jundub from the Messenger of God. (640)

79.4. Asking the Righteous Gnostics is Better than Asking Rulers

It is like that with asking the gnostics of right action, the people of fearful watching. It is better than asking the rulers unless the ruler has these attributes. The people with these attributes are nearer to God. By God's praise, we have seen some rulers who were like this in the religion, scrupulousness and establishing the truth by the Truth, may God have mercy on them. (641)

It is related in tradition that a person said to the Messenger of God: "Shall I beg, may God bless him and grant him peace?" He said: "No. If you must beg, then ask those of right action." When the gnostics are asked for something specific to them of the matters of this world, they ask God by God for the knower. (642)

79.5. The Best Charity Which God Bestows on Those of His Servants Who Have Drawn Near

Those who know God are those who are emptied by the contemplation of God. The remembrance of God distracts them from asking God. They are the masters of states. He gives them knowledge of Him, and it is the best that the askers are given. When they know Him with the knowledge of tasting, they only remember Him for Him by them and by Him. By this remembrance, He gives them something which makes them leave remembrance for Him by Him. He gives them the vision since the visions is higher than contemplation. It is the best charity which God bestows on those of His servants who have drawn near. (643)

80 Those Know God by God Given Knowledge That is *Laduni* Knowledge

Know that those who know God only take given knowledge from among the knowledge. It is directly given knowledge, the knowledge of Khidr and his likes. It is the knowledge in which they have no action at all by any thought, so that none of the impurities of acquisition soils it. (644)

The divine Self-disclosure which is free of possible matter from spirit, body, and intellect is more complete than the divine Self-disclosure in possible matters. Some Self-disclosures in possible matters are more complete than others. When the knower of God has a divine Self-disclosure dependent on another Self-disclosure which he has not obtained and then obtains after that so that he is given knowledge of Him which he did not have, he does not accept it in given knowledge. He connects it to acquired knowledge. (645)

80.1. Acquired Knowledge

Every knowledge which he acquires by supplication in it or by pure supplication is acquired. That is only good for the Messengers, may the blessings of God be upon them. They are part of prescribed acquisition. When they stop with their prophethood, not with their message, then their state with God is the state which we mentioned of leaving off seeking what is other than Him and supervision. They stand with God. They look at Him. They speak by Him in everything that is said and everything that is seen and stood with. (646)

80.2. Responsibility is Only Command or Prohibition

It is as if they spoke by Him and heard by Him. They remember worship as an act of devotion and they submit to worship as an act of worship. They strive without slackening in worship, and not through turning attention to it or seeking anything other than to fulfill what is demanded by the station of the One who obligated them inasmuch a He obligates, not from any other aspect, and in respect to the station of the one who is obligated. God gives them knowledge directly from them which they did not seek, so that it would be acquired by earning. (647)

One of His names is the Believer (*al-Mumin*). It is one of the attributes of the servant and not one of the names of the servant. If it had been a name, it would not be weakened. Since it is an attribute, it can be weakened, It is a Name of God and an attribute of the servant. This is good manners with God. In the meaning of what we indicated is related a Tradition which Abu Amr ibn Abd 'l-Barr al-Namiri mentioned from Khalid ibn Adi al-Juhani. He said: "I heard the Messenger of God say: 'Whoever has something good come to him from his brother without looking for it or asking for it should accept it and not reject it. It is provision which God has driven to him.'" This Tradition combines the command to accept and the prohibition against rejecting. All obligation is obtained in it. Obligation is what is other than command and prohibition. (648)

80.3. The Great Do Not Act On Anything Nor Reject Anything

Part of what supports the authenticity of this Tradition is what Muslim transmitted in his *Sahih* from Ibn Umar. He said that the Messenger of God used to give to Umar ibn al-Khattab. He said: "Messenger of God, give it to someone who needs it more than me." The Messenger of God said to him: "Take it. Enrich yourself with it or give it as charity. Take whatever property comes to you when you have not looked for it or asked for it. If not, then do not. Do not let your soul pursue it." The great do not ask anyone for anything. It is God that they see in things. They do not reject anything that they give to them. good manners with God is not to return to God what He gives you. (649)

80.4. The Trial of Knowledge Is Greater than the Trial of Property

The trial of knowledge is greater than the trial of property. The honor of property is an incidental honor which does not exceed people's mouths. The soul has no attribute in it. The honor of knowledge is an adornment with which the soul adorns itself. Its temptation is far greater. It is not removed from its owner whether he is either poor or rich, or in his ups and downs. Wealth can be taken from its owner by a thief who steals it, a fire, drowning, demolition, earthquake, natural disaster, sedition, or the ruler. Knowledge is in a protected fortress within you. It can never be reached. It clings to a person in both life and death, in this world and the Next. It is yours in every state. If it is yours at any moment, then it is yours in another matter. Even if afflictions strike you because of it, they will not be numerous. It is only by its honor since you did not act by it. You are only afflicted by failure to act by it, not by it itself. When you are saved, it takes you by the hand to its station. Its station is what it knows. What it knows is God and so it sets you down with God according to that knowledge. Therefore do not be among the ignorant. (650)

81 God's Obliging Purifying Alms on Products

81.1. Products Are Generated by the Movement of the Sphere and the Elements

Know that God has obliged alms on products. They are three: mineral, plant and animal. The minerals are gold and silver. The plants are wheat, barley and dates. The animals are camels, cattle and sheep. It is general to all products, and the name "products" is applied to them because they are produced from a mother and a father, from a sphere and its movement which is in the position of intercourse while it is the father and the elements are the mother. (651)

81.2. As Purifying Alms Is Purification, It is Deprivation in Property

Therefore, a person loves property as he loves the child. Don't you see that God connected it to the child in temptation? He says, Your property and your children are a trial." He put property before the child. *"God will enrich you out of His grace."* (8:28), when He deprives you of some of them. Purifying alms, even if it is purification of property and its owners are purified of the attribute of miserliness, is loss of property without a doubt. Therefore, its owner has the reward of the afflicted, and it is one of the greatest rewards. (652)

81.3. A Child is a Branch of the Parent as Maternal Relations is a Branch of The Merciful

A child is a branch of the parent "as kin (*rahim*) is a branch of The Merciful (*Rahman*). Whoever maintains ties with them, God will maintain ties with him. Whoever severs connections with them, God will sever connections with him." One of the poets said about children (and it is part of the poetry found in the Hamasa:

Our children among us are our livers walking on the earth.

He considered the child 'a piece of the liver'. (653)

81.4. The Heart of Every Person is Where His Property is

Jesus said to his companions: "Every person's heart is with his property. Therefore put your property in heaven and your hearts will be in heaven." He urged charity since he knew that charity falls into the hand of the Merciful. He said: *"Are you so safe from He Who is in the heaven . . . .?"* (67:16) The Prophet said: "Charity puts out the wrath of God." See how wondrous, fine, and sweet are the words of prophethood! (654)

Whoever joins the child to the parent and connects him to him has the reward of the one who joins maternal kin. Man must connect his property, inasmuch as it is a generated product, to its father from whom it was produced because it is a piece of him. The person who gives his alms has the reward of the one afflicted and the reward of joining maternal kin when he purifies his property by alms. (655)

81.5. Only the Believer or Gnostic is Capable of Patience in Loss of the Beloved

Patience in loss of the beloved is one of the greatest forms of patience. Only the believer or the gnostic is patient in that. The ascetic has no alms due from him because he does not have anything left on which alms is obliged since asceticism demands that. The gnostic is not like that since the gnostic knows that inasmuch as he joins the world together, he seeks property. Therefore he gives it its due. From that aspect, alms is obligatory for him. He is also ascetic from one aspect. This is why we preferred the statement of the one who said that alms is obligatory on property, not on the responsible party. He is responsible for spending it from the property since the property cannot bring it out itself. (656)

81.6. The Ascetic and the Gnostic

The gnostic has both rewards rewards as opposed to the ascetic. The gnostics are the Perfect Men. They have both asceticism and storing up, trust and acquisition. They have love in the entire world, even if the aspects of love vary. They love all that occurs in the world by love of God in bringing that event into existence, not in respect to the event itself, so know that! There is fine divine deception in that which only those of knowledge and manners are aware of. (657)

The gnostic knows that within him there is a portion within him which seeks what is suitable for it in the world. He gives everything with a due its due as God gives everything its creation. The Messenger of God said: "Your soul has a right over you. Your eye has a right over you." It is like that with every part of you. This is why it will testify against you on the Day of Rising when God calls on it to testify against you. (658)

Look at the wisdom of the Samiri since he knew what Jesus (?) had said about love of property being joined to the hearts. He fashioned the calf for them by what he saw of their ornaments because he knew that their hearts would follow their property. They hastened to worship it when he summoned them to that. (659)

81.7. The Common Person and the Gnostic

In respect to the sovereign secret, the gnostic is appointed as a viceregent in the property in his possession. He is like a caretaker over property which is placed in his charge. He brings out the alms from it and he has nothing in it. This is why we said that it is due on the property. The child does not have any obligation. The Prophet commanded trading with the property of the orphan so that charity would not consume it. (660)

The common person, even if he is like the gnostic in that it is general, does not know that. He ascribed the property to himself and so he is told, "your property," and brings out the alms from it. The gnostic brings it out as a caretaker and the common person brings it out by the principle of ownership. None believes in God more than them even though they associate. Each group is truthful in its state as is the one with a divine proof in what he is related to. (661)

81.8. The Love of the Gnostic

Had it not been for love, alms would not have been made obligatory so that they would be rewarded with the reward of the one who is deprived of what he loves. Had it not been for the relationship between the lover and the beloved, there would be no love nor would its existence be conceivable. Thus you know the love of the gnostic for his property from any relationship and his love for God from any relationship. His love for property and this world does not detract from his love for God and the world to come. What he loves in it is by a certain matter which is only in conformity in divine matters and in the world. Love God since He nourishes you from His blessings, and so the relationship is sound. (662)

81.9. Gnosis Is the Property of the Gnostic and Its Purifying Alms Is Teaching

One of His blessings is gnosis of Him. The gnostic seeks it from Him.

It is the relationship of a poor creature to one who is rich who seeks what he has in order to obtain it. The gnostic only seeks a matter in-time from Him since the gnosis which someone in-time has of the Out-of-time is gnosis which is located in-time. The relationship between him and gnosis is in-time. It is in the hand of the Recognized and love is connected to the Recognized by this relationship. Recognition of Him does not come to an end and does not stop. Love does not stop. This gnosis is obtained from soul-disclosure, and soul-disclosure does not end. Therefore gnosis is the property of the gnostic, and the alms of this property is teaching. It is a divine degree. God says: "*So be Godfearing of God and God teaches you.*" (2:282) He is the Teacher. This is why we said that teaching is a divine degree. (663)

81.10. The Eight Types of Purifying Alms and Eight Bearers of the Throne

He stipulated eight types of alms because of what it contains of the soundness of the knower. It lies in that by which the bodies are established by nourishment and fulfillment of needs. There is soundness for the body in these two matters. They are the eight bearers of the Throne. The Throne, which is the kingdom, is carried by them. Part of this reality is that the eight types join it. There is dispute on what is outside of them, and refers to them. The Throne is the Kingdom. and the bearers of this Throne which designates us are these eight types which carry it. This amount of property is called alms is like the wage for their carrying it. (664)

82 Why Property Is Called Property

Property is so called because it makes the souls incline to it. Souls incline to it because God has placed fulfillment of needs in it, and a person is naturally disposed to need because he is poor by his essence. He inclines to it by a nature which does not leave him. Had making do without property been a reality, it would not be property, and making do without in the world to come would have been a more complete station than it is in this world. The matter is not like that. God has promised to multiply the good reward with ten like it, or more, up to 700 times. Had little been a veil, more of it would have been a greater veil. (665)

82.1. The "Door" at which We Find God

Have you not looked at the place of soul-disclosure and unveiling? It is the world to come. It is the place of seeing and contemplation while you obtain all the appetites of the soul absolutely without any barrier, The word: "*Be*!" from every person rules in it. Had the like of this been a veil, the veil of the world to come would have been immeasurably denser and greater. Glory be to the One who put a door in everything! When that door is opened, he finds God there. He specified a divine aspect in everything. When it appears in soul-disclosure, he recognizes that aspect from that thing. (666)

Abu Bakr al-Siddiq said: "I have not seen anything but that I saw God before it." He only saw with his eye since God was his sight in that place. He saw Himself before seeing that thing. People are the place for that sight. That is why he said: "I have not seen anything but that I saw God before it." God called it alms because of what it contains of growth and increase. This is why you give little and find a lot. Had you given it for the removal of the veil, since it is a veil, the reward would have been many veils greater than this veil. By God's praise, what you gave is not a veil and what you reached from that is not a veil, so know that! (667)

82.2. The Behavior of the Gnostic and the Asceticism of the Ascetic

Look at how the gnostic behaves in this world. Do not apply his behavior to your behavior and your ignorance and evil. Woe to you! You think that doing-without in that is better than him. How far off the mark! *"Say: Are those who know on the same level as those who know not. . . ."* (39:9) For the gnostic, it is an attribute of Solomonic perfection. *"He said: My Lord! Forgive me and bestow on me a dominion such will not be fit and proper to another after me; truly Thou art the Giver."* (38:35) How this name fits the question! Do you think that he asked for what would veil him from God or that he asked him for what would distance him from God? (668)

82.3. The Perfect Solomonic Attribute and Muhammadan State

Then look at the fine good manners of the Messenger of God when God gave him power for the *ifrit* who attacked him. He wanted to take him and tie him to one of the pillars of the mosque so that people could look at him. Then he remembered the supplication of his brother Solomon. God repelled the *ifrit* and he slung awat. This is a Solomonic state which Muhammad obtained. He did not turn from it because of making do without it. It was his good manners towards Solomon which turned him away from that since Solomon had asked his Lord for a kingdom which none after him would have. (669)

We know from this story that his words about no one else having it meant that no one would manifest it visibly to people, even if some people acquire the power, like the Messenger of God with the *ifrit*. We know that he wanted to show that to the eyes of the people but then God answered Solomon's request when the Messenger of God remembered the supplication of his brother Solomon so that he did not proceed in this idea about displaying that. God completed this blessing for Solomon in the domain of obligation. He said to him: *"This is Our gift. Then showest thou grace or holdest back without reckoning."* (38:39) Any harm was removed from him in acting by the name of the Withholder and the Bestower. He was given an early garden in this world but that kingdom did not veil him from his Lord, the Mighty and Exalted! (670)

82.4. The Gnostic Combines Two Sources and Grasps Two Realities

Look then at the degree of the gnostic and how he combines both sources and grasps the two realities! He pays alms from the property in his possession as the caretaker pays it from the property in his charge, as He said: *"And spend out of what He has made you ones who are successors in it."* (57:7) He made him an owner in order to spend from a divine reality contained it from property which is kingdom-property by another reality in it. He is its guardian in respect of the divine Reality. May God place us among the gnostics of knowledge who know what He has lodged in it of delight! Amen. (671)

83 Property Accepting Different Types of Giving

83.1. The Types of Giving by which God and the Servant Are Described

Know that property accepts different types of giving. There are eight types and they have eight names. One type is called giving blessing. Another type is called the simple gift. Another type is called charity. Another type is called generosity. Another type is called a present. One type of called magnanimity. Another type is called liberality. Another type is called altruism. (672)

83.2. From What Divine Reality Does Altruism Appear in Phenomenal Being

A person gives by all of these eight types, and God gives by seven of them: All of them except altruism. If the non-Arab says: "From what divine reality does altruism appear in phenomenal being? He does not give by preference because He is Rich above need. Altruism is giving what you actually need, either by state or hope. It is that you give while you imagine that you need it and you give it in spite of this illusion. Then your giving is altruism. This is impossible in respect of God. Then has something appeared in existence which is not connected to a divine reality? (673)

83.3. The Essence, the Rank and the Form Which is Viceregency

We have said previously that absolute richness belongs to God in respect of His essence, free of any relationship of the world to it. When you relate this world to Him, you do not take the essence into consideration and you do not consider absolute independence. You consider the essence as "God," and so you consider the rank. That which the rank must have are those names by which you name Him. That is the divine form, not the essence in respect to its source. It is inasmuch as He is God. Then He gave you the form which is the caliphate and named you by all the names in a praiseworthy manner. He has given you that on which the relationship is based. This is the Most Beautiful Names. (674)

83.4. Altruism Is Giving Away What You Yourself Need

If you were to say that the giver no longer has what he has given, we would reply that this refers to what the reality of the giver is. If he gives something physical, then the giver loses it by giving. This is why we defined altruism as giving what you need. You do not turn your attention to whether what is given will remain or be lost. That refers to the reality of the matter which you have given, so know that! It is from this reality that altruism issues in the world and that there is no clarification after its clarification. (675)

83.5. Explanation of the Eight Types of Giving

Giving blessing is giving what is a blessing for the one to whom you are giving. It is in harmony with his nature and agrees with his desire. The gift is giving just to bestow. The present is giving in order to win love. It comes from love. The Lawgiver said: "Give presents to one another and love one another." Charity is giving from hardship and reluctance. That is because a person is naturally disposed to avarice. *"And whoever is protected from his own stinginess."* (59:9, 64:16). *"When good afflicted him, begrudging."* (70:21) When he gives in this fashion, his giving is only from force because of the natural disposition of the soul. (676)

83.6. Recognition of the Lord by Means of the Divine Law

In respect to God, this relationship is a reality of what comes from divine hesitation in taking the soul of the believer. There must be the encounter. He wants to take his spirit while He hesitates because of what He already knows. In respect to God, it is as if it were. In respect to the servant, it is not as if it were out of divine manners. The proof of the intellect casts the like of this away because of its incapacity and lack of recognition of what the worshiped divinity deserves. God is recognized by this reality which the servants have. Sound intellects accept it from the jurisdiction of their thoughts on it by the attribute of the words which it has when the intellects which are under the rule of their thoughts reject it. This is the recognition which the divine law demands of us: that we recognize our Lord by it and describe Him by it. It is not the recognition by which we affirm Him. That is part of what intellects cannot grasp. It descends in relationship to this recognition. It is affirmed through the judgment of the intellect. This is confirmed by divine report. By every aspect, He knows Himself better than we do. (677)

83.7. Generosity and Magnanimity

Generosity is giving after the request: in respect to both God and creatures. Magnanimity is giving before the request: for God, not creatures. When it is related to creatures, it is inasmuch as God has not sought this matter from him which creation has specified God has asked him to give voluntary charity and He was not specific. When the servant specifies a garment, dirham, dinar, or something else without being asked for that, that is the magnanimity of creatures. (678)

We said "not creatures" in that because he only gives for nearness to God on the basis of divine information. This is why we said: " . . . for God, not creatures." Since the divine law does not consider that, giving before the request does not exist in the world for the sake of nearness without any doubt. The desire of the Sufi is to act only in matters which acts which bring one near to God. That is necessary. He must observe the judgment of the divine law in that. (679)

83.8. Liberality and Altruism

Liberality is giving according to need and no more for some cause matter which the giver sees. If he gives more than that, it might contain destruction for the recipient. God said: "*And if God extended the provision for His servants, they would be insolent in the earth, but He sends down by measure whatever He wills.*" (42:27) Altruism is giving what you need at the moment or imagine that you need. God said: ". . . . *and hold them in greater favor over themselves even though they themselves had been in destitution.*" (59:9). (680)

83.9. Giving Is a Divine Matrix and Charity is a Phenomenal Matrix

All the giving which we mentioned is charity in respect to the servant since he is naturally disposed to avarice and miserliness. Similarly, the matrix in divine gifts of these eight types is giving, *wahb*. That is giving for the sake of blessing and nothing else. He is the Giver (*al-Wahhab*) in reality in all His giving as the servant is giving charity in all his giving because he is not free of desire and seeking compensation for his essential poverty. (681)

What is related to God by the principle of the non-essential is related to creation by the Essence. What is related to God through the Essence—like the Absolutely Rich—is related to creation by a non-essential relative connection. God said to His Prophet: "*Take charity from their wealth,*" (9:103) that is, what it is hard for them to give in themselves. This is why

Thalaba ibn Hatib said: "This is the little sister of the capitulation tax (*jizya*). since it was hard for him after he had made a contract with God as God informed us when He said: "*And of them are some who made a contract with God.*" (9:75) When God provided him with property and God made charity obligatory for him, he said that God had not informed him about it. (682)

He said: "*They became misers with it.*" (9:76) That is the attribute of the soul to which it is naturally disposed. When it rules the servant, God seeks to change it for another. We ask God for well-being! Similarly it is related, "If they turn away" from the spending which you ask of them and are miserly: "*And if you turn away, He will have a folk other than you in exchange,* (47:38) that is, with your attribute. They will give what they are asked. This is as He said: "*So if these were ungrateful for them, then surely We have charged a folk with them who will never be of the ones who are ungrateful for them.*" (6:89) The kingdom is too vast to be constricted to the existence of one thing. Charity is a matrix in phenomenal being, and pure giving (*wahb*) is a divine matrix. (683)

83.10. Nature Dominating Greed in the Highest Rank

Part of what will support what we mentioned is that the angels spoke from their natural disposition when they referred good only to themselves. Nature dominated them in that so that they did not agree with God when He wanted to manifest it in phenomenal being and make Adam a viceregent in the earth. He acquainted them with that and they did not agree with it because nature dominated their greed for the highest rank. They were veiled by the rule of nature so that they did not ascribe their lack of agreement with God to any imperfection. They had the form of jealousy for the divine Presence and preference for His immensity. They neglected to exalt Him. Had they agreed with the immensity demanded by Him, they would have agreed with Him, but they did not do so, even if they meant good. They said, "Why put on it one who will cause corruption on it and shed blood when we glorify Your praise and proclaim Your purity?" That is, we are more entitled than this. They preferred their view to God's knowledge of His creation. That is why He said to them: "*Truly I know what you know not.*" (2:30) He described them as lacking the knowledge which God had about this viceregent. They did not know it and so they praised themselves. Their question contains all that when they praised themselves, proclaimed themselves just, and took exception to others. They did not refer knowledge in that to God. This comes from the miserliness of nature towards rank. (684)

83.11. The Angels Are Subject to the Authority of Nature

This confirms what we believe: that the angels are subject to the authority of nature and that it has an effect on them. God said: *"I have had no knowledge of the lofty Council."* (38:69) Quarreling is part of the rule of nature. It is related that the angels of mercy and the angels of punishment quarrel about the person who dies between the two groups. He described them as quarreling. If it had not been that their rank was other than the soul and above air, its principle would have pervaded them. Whoever wants to understand the root of this business should look at the opposites in the divine names. This reality appears from there in all. (685)

The angels share with us in being ruled by nature, and part of its rule is miserliness and avarice in whoever is compounded of it. That comes from the name, The Withholder, among the names. Its cause in us is that poverty and need are essential for us and every possible entity. This is why possible things need that whose possibility is dominant. The one formed from nature is intrinsically avaricious and miserly, and generous only incidentally. God only made alms obligatory and purified the soul of avarice and miserliness by it because of this exact same matter. The obligatory part of it is harder for the soul than voluntary charity because of the compulsion which the obligatory has and the element of choice contained in the voluntary. In the obligatory, he is a servant under the rule of a master. In the voluntary, it is up to him to do this or not do it, however he wishes. (686)

84 Storing Up Comes from the Avarice and Miserliness of the Self

84.1. The Giving of Servanthood and the Giving of Lordship

Know that part of the avarice of the soul is storing up and uncertainty about until the moment of need. When the need is specific, then there is giving. Most of the souls of the righteous are like this. As for the common people, we are not speaking to them. We are speaking to the people of God according to the levels. Very few among the people of God seek for the people of need so as to bring them what they have, be it obligatory or voluntary. In the obligatory part of that, God has set down its classes and ranks in the minimum amount and specific time. The voluntary part of that does not stop at anything. Voluntary is giving of lordship. It is not limited. The obligatory is the giving of servanthood. It is according to what his master ordains for him. The giving of servanthood is better. The obligatory is better than the supererogatory. Where is compulsory servanthood in relation to voluntary servanthood. This group is very small among the righteous and I am uncertain about them. We are not obliged to seek for them. The one with need is the seeker. If it is specifically incumbent on me by a state or a request, then I give it. (687)

84.2. Those Who Give Out of Divine Generosity and Good Character

Those who are above this level which gives the definition of merit are also higher than these ones. They are the ones who give what is in their hands out of divine generosity and character. They give to the deserving and the one who is deserving in respect of the reality because he only takes by the attribute of poverty and need, and nothing else, whether these gifts are presents or pure giving or one of the other types of giving. It is like the rich merchant who has thousands. He crosses deserts and rides the seas and endures dangers. He exiles himself from his family and children and exposes himself and his property to destruction in his journeys. That is in order to seek a dirham more than what he already has. Therefore, the attribute of poverty rules him and blinds him to these terrors and makes hardships easy for him because of the strength of this attribute in the servant. (688)

Whoever looks in this manner, which is the truth, sees that whoever is given something and takes it deserves it since he recognizes the attribute by which he takes it from him. He takes it from him to fulfill a need of his since he is compelled to return to him and to veil his station by taking. That hand of his is a true hand as it is related that charity falls into the hand of the Merciful before it falls into the hand of the asker. He makes it grow as one of you would raise his foal or young camel. This is taking without thought of need at the present. He does not see the root which moved him to take it. It is that the reality of the possible demands that. (689)

His reality is veiled from this person when he takes this thing which he desires. We recognize it while he is ignorant of himself. He only gives from what he does not need, whether it is for a desire, compensation, or whatever. He is rich and without need of what he gives. And no one takes except what one who deserves or needs what he takes, whether it is by desire, compensation of whatever, because the need to care for what he takes is a need since it is only made to grow after he takes it, so understand! It is fine and deep because the divine ascription in taking care of something belongs to charity while the Absolute Rich is the One who deserves it. (690)

84.3. The Divine Ascriptions Are Not Denied by Someone Who Is Not a Sincere Believer

The divine ascriptions are not denied except by the one who is not a sincere believer. God said: *"Lend God a good loan,"* and He said: "I was hungry and you did not feed Me. I was thirsty and you did not let me drink. He made all of that clear. He did not forbid the ascription of these things to Him so as to make it clear that He is the Manifest in manifestations according to their predisposition. The upper hand spends, and it is better by every aspect than the lower hand which is the taker. The giver has a due and the taker has a due. They are not equal in rank, name or state." (691)

There is nothing but that it has an aspect and relationship to God, and an aspect and relationship to creation. This is why he called it spending. He said: *"Spend out of what We have provided you,"* (2:254) and *"they spend out of what We have provided for them."* (2:3) By this directive, He referred to the great men of knowledge because they are those who have giving inasmuch as it is spending since they have knowledge of the two relationships because it is derived from the tunnel which is the home of the *jerboa*. It is also called *nafiqa*. It has two doors. When something hunts it by one door, it goes out by the other door. This is like probable language when the one who utters it limits it to one aspect. He can say: "I meant the other possible aspect." (692)

84.4. Giving Has a Relationship to God and a Relationship to Creation

Since giving has a relationship to God and wealth, and a relationship to creation and need, God called it 'spending'. Those with knowledge spend by two aspects. They see God as the Giver and the Taker in what they give and they also see that their hands are the place in which the taking and the giving appears. One does not veil them from the other. These ones only see the deserving. Every taker takes according to the principle of merit. If it had not been that he deserved it, it would have been impossible for him to accept it from him. If he gave it as absolute wealth, that is impossible for him. Absolute poverty is not impossible for him. (693)

84.5. Those Who Look at Times of Need and Store Up

Some of those anticipate times of need and store up as we mentioned because of uncertainty which they have. Some store up by insight and some store up without insight. We do not consider it sound for the latter to store up because it does not come from insight and they are not among the people of God. The people of God are those who possess insight. As for the one who does so from insight, that may come from a divine command which comes to him and governs him, or not from a divine command. If it is from a divine command, then he is a pure servant and we have nothing to say about him. He is commanded as we think is the case of Abd 'l-Qadir al-Jili. This is his station, and God knows best what he is obliged to do in the world. (694)

If the storing up is not from a divine command, then it may be that he knows that this amount which is stored up is meant for such-and-such a person and that it will only reach him by his hand. Therefore, he keeps it by this unveiling. This is also among the aspects of Abd 'l-Qadir and those like him. On the other hand, he may recognize that it is for a certain person while he does not know whether it will reach him at his hand or the hand of someone else. Keeping the like of this is avarice in nature and joy at existence. He is veiled from that by his unveiling regarding the owner. That was the basis of our objections to from Abd 'l-Aziz ibn Abi Bakr al-Mahdi when he stored up. He stopped and could not find an answer. He was not storing up from insight that it would be at his hand or insight that that specific thing had an owner. It immediately came to light in our presence. In a case like that, he should not store up. (695)

The master of the Party, the intellect of his age, the just in state, Abu 'l-Suud ibn al-Shibl was correct when he said: "We leave God to dispose of us." He did not assail the divine presence. Had he been commanded to stop at a matter or had it been specified for him, he would have stopped with the specification. There is dispute among the people of God regarding that. If he is among the persons for whom it is specific that that stored item will only reach its owner by his hand at a certain time, some of them keep it until that time, and some of them say: "I am not a sentry. I will spend it since God did not command me to keep it. When the moment comes, if God returns it to my hand, I will give it to its owner. I will not be described as storing up between the two times because I am a treasury of God. I am not a sentry. I have dealt with it and devoted myself to it. He said: 'The heart of My servant contains Me.' I do not like to beset him in a matter which is not His.'" Know that! I have informed you about an immense business in this question. (696)

Purifying alms is only valid for a gnostic when he stores up because of a divine command or precise exact unveiling such that he already knows that this thing is under his care for someone else. Then that is valid for him. Outside of this, he is purified as the common are purified. (697)

85 The Divisions of People in Charity: The Givers and the Takers

85.1. There Are Four Types of People in Taking and Giving

Know that people fall into four divisions in what they give and what they take. One division regards what they give as important and what they take as unimportant. One group regards as unimportant what they give and think that what they take is important. One group thinks that both what they take and what they give are unimportant. The last group thinks that both what they give and what they take are important. This is why some of them select and do not see the face of God in things. Some of them do not select and see the face of God in things since they are aware of their absolute poverty. Their drinks vary as their contemplation and tasting varies according to their states. The state of the articulate soul is like the natural disposition of the animal soul. The natural disposition rules the body and the state rules of the soul. (698)

85.2. It Is Prescribed to Consider Charity Important

Know that it is prescribed to consider charity important. God Almighty said: *"Then eat of it and feed the ones who are in misery and the poor."* (22:28) He also said: *"And feed the ones who are paupers and the ones who were poor persons who do not beg,"* (22:36) that is, from the sacrificial camels which God made one of the Waymarks of God. He said: *"Whoever holds the Waymarks of God in honor, then it is, truly from hearts filled with God-consciousness. For you in that is what profits for a term that was determined. After that their place of sacrifice is at the Ancient House."* (22:32-33) That is, the body. He said in this story: *"They spend out of what We have provided them."* (2:3) We mentioned in the commentary on the spender from which spending, *infaq*, comes, that it has two directions/aspects. Similarly, here we obtain their meat from them and God obtains God-consciousness from us in them. Part of our God-consciousness is to exalt them, so considering charity important is part of this topic among some of the gnostics. This is why he considers important what he gives if he is a giver or what he takes if he is a taker. His witnessing is another tasting. (699)

85.3. The First Witnessing which Ibn Arabi Experienced on the Sufi Path

This is the first witnessing which we experienced in this area in this Path. One day, I was carrying something in my hand which the common people generally consider to be dirty and base. Those like us did not carry something like this because of what the souls contain of levity of nature and love of distinction over the one who is regarded with the eye of respect. I saw a shaykh who had some of his companions with him. His companions said to him: "Master, this is so-and-so advancing. He does not fall short in the Path. He strives against his ego. You see him carrying this in the middle of the market where people see him like that," and they told him what was in my hand. The shaykh said: "It may be that he is not carrying it in order to strive against his ego." They said to him: "What else can it be except this?" He said: "Ask him when he joins us." (700)

When I reached them, I greeted the shaykh. After he had returned the greeting, he said, to me: "Why are you carrying that which is in your hand when it is something dirty and despised? People of your rank among the masters of this world do not carry something like this in their hands because of its lowness and filth." I said to him: "Master! Far be it from you to have this view! This is not view of those like you! God Almighty did not consider it dirty or deposed when He created it by the power to bring it into existence as He connected power to bringing the Throne into existence as well as creatures which you consider to be important. So then how is it with me? I am a low and weak servant. Should I then consider as despicable or dirty what is like this?" He kissed me and made supplication for me and said to his companions: "Where is this thought in relation to the one who carries it in order to struggle against his ego?"

85.4. Various Aspects of Things Being Considered Important by the People of God

Considering charity important may be part of this subject for the giver and the taker. Considering things important has many aspects which the People of God take into account. God revealed to Moses, peace be upon him: "When someone brings you a rotten bean, accept it. I have brought it to you." The giver things that it is important since he represents God in conveying it. The taker thinks that it is important since God has bought it. Here the hand of the giver is the hand of God by witnessing and strong belief. God said that God says on the tongue of His servant: "God hears whoever praises Him." He relates the word to Him while it is the servant who says that. God said in a tradition: "I am his hearing, his sight, and hand and support." (702)

The people of unveiling may consider it important when they see, witness and hear the glorification of that charity, gift or present, or whatever. It glorifies God and exalts its Creator in the language appropriate to it. God said: *"There is not a thing but it glorifies His praise."* (17:44) They consider it great because it exalts God and is never heedless or slacks off, as the virtuous angels exalt Him. This is whether they are poor, lowly servants and people of affliction or well-off. They see blessings in them because they are involved in obedience of God according to what is said. How then is it with the one who sees this directly with his own eyes? Whatever giver or taker sees this, considers God's creation great since all of it is like this. (703)

He might also exalt it since he is poor and in need of that thing since God has made it a reason which he needs to obtain his need, whether he is a giver or a taker because this is what he sees. (704)

85.5. God is the One Named by Everything in Need, the Goal of All Worship

He might think that it is important since God Almighty said: *"O humanity! It is you who are poor in relation to God."* (35:15) In this sign, God says that everything is in need of Him. This is part of it. The names and qualities of God are exalted, and this is one of His names. This is something very fine. The only one who comprehends it is the one who has this witnessing. It comes from divine jealousy and divine sending-down. It is like His words: *"And thy Lord has decreed that you worship none but Him"* (17:23) in spite of what they worship in the earth things like stones, plants, and animals, and in the sky stars and angels. That is their creed about every worshiped thing: that it is a god, not that it is a stone, or a tree or anything else. This is in spite of the fact that they err in the relationship in their error about the worshiped. This is why God said: *"And thy Lord has decreed that you worship none but Him."* Part of His decree is that they believe in God whenever they worship what they worship. This is part of divine jealousy so that only the One with this attribute is worshiped. In the heart of the matter, that is God—glory be to Him! Charity is considered great by this unveiling. (705)

85.6. Different Aspects Why the People of God Consider Things Unimportant

As for the fact that some of them consider it unimportant, this is due to another witnessing. The witnessing of the people as well as their states, tasting and drinks rules them by their power and strength. Does not all that we mentioned about thinking that it is important actually originate from the rule which states, tasting, and witnessing have over people? (706)

85.7. The Possibility is an Attribute of Need which the Possible Has

Part of it is that he sees a possibility of the charity given if he is a giver or taken if he is a taker. The possibility is an attribute of need which the possible has as well as being a favor, a need, and a right. Therefore, the one who sees this considers everything to be unimportant, whether it is one of the most precious of things or something not precious at all. (707)

85.8. Ibn Arabi is a Witness Against His Time

Lack of importance might also be muddied for the one who gives for the sake of God and takes by the hand of God. I saw one of those I reckon to be one the people of God, although I do not testify to anyone's integrity before God as the Messenger of God commanded us and did. God forbade us to do that. A poor man asked him to give him something as charity for God. The man who was asked brought out a purse in which there were some pieces of silver, large and small. He began to search in it with his hand while that good man was looking at him. Then he looked at me and said: "Do you know what this giver of charity is looking for?" I said: "No." He said: "For the value of his station with God. He gives for the sake of God. When he sees a big piece, he turns away from it and says: 'We are not equal to this with God.' He relies on a smaller piece which he finds and gives to the beggar. That virtuous man said: "This is your value with God." (708)

85.9. Everything is Insignificant in the Presence of God

Is not everything insignificant in the presence of God? However, here divine generosity relies on divine jealousy. That is because on the Day of Rising, a caller will call people from before God: "Where is what you gave for the sake of other-than-God?" Then a massive amount property, estates and kingdoms will be brought. Then it will be said: "Where is what you gave for My sake?" Then dry crusts, small pieces of silver and some rags will be brought. God will be jealous about that that the like of this was given for His sake from His blessings. Therefore, he takes charity in His hand and makes it grow until it becomes like the mountain of Uhud or greater than it. He will show it to him before witnesses and will make what was given for other-than-God small and He will make it scattered dust. (709)

Therefore, the one who sees this and the likes of this—which would be too long to mention—must consider it insignificant. What we have told you about this is enough concerning what these four categories contain into which we divided the world at the beginning of this section. (710)

86 The States of People in Open and Hidden Charity

86.1. Interpretation of the Secrets in Charity

There are some people who keep charity secret since God has praised that in the excellent Tradition which says: "His left hand does not know what his right hand spends," as well as what has come about secret charity and God's concern for it, Therefore, he keeps it hidden because God knows what he spends, and not for any other reason. This is from sincerity and its like because God has preserved the People from hidden and open association, so he is among those who are sincere:

> There is only God. There is no Lord but Him.

This is because they see that God is the Doer in actions. They know that God only mentioned secrecy in the like of this and preferred it to openness in the opinion of the one who thinks this because he has knowledge of it even if he does not disclose it. It is not for the sake of sincerity and openness because secrecy and openness are equal in respect to these in the giver and the taker. Part of this is His words: "Whoever remembers Me in himself, I remember him in Myself. Whoever remembers Me in an assembly, I remember him in a better assembly than it." (711)

86.2. Interpretation of Making Charity Public

As for the one who gives charity publicly, this is not what he and his likes see. What dominates his heart and sight is that he sees God in everything. Every state of his consists of actions without doubt. This is all he sees in it for the one who has charity as we mentioned about the assembly. Whoever remembers Him in an assembly, he remembers Him in himself, so the remembrance of the soul comes first without a doubt. Not everyone who remembers Him in himself remembers Him in an assembly. This is a state which is added to the remembrance of the soul, not a rank above the one who remembers in himself. The remembrance of the soul is not perceived in both cases. It is hidden by every aspect. Public charity proclaims divine power to the one who hides or conceals it. It is outwardly manifest in possible manifestations. This is the path of our

Shaykh Abu Madyan. He would say: "*Say: God revealed it; after that forsake them.*" (6:91) "*Would you call to any other than God?*" (6:40) He made it public as he based himself on the prophetic inheritance. (712)

86.3. Showing-off and Sincerity with the Common and Elite People of God

As for what the common people of this path, like Abu Hamid al-Ghazzali, al-Muhasibi and their likes, mention about showing off and seeking sincerity, that is God's directive in the language of the common people to make that general to all. That is not the tongue of the one who sees only God. We are speaking with the people of God about that. Our Shaykh used to say to his companions: "Publicize obedience to God so that the Word of God is higher, as those others make public acts of rebellion and opposition and exhibit objectionable things. They are not ashamed before God." One of the masters asked the companions of an esteemed Shaykh: "What did your Shaykh command you?" They said: "He told us to strive in actions and to see our incapacity in them." He said: "By God, he has commanded you to pure magic! Why has he not commanded you to actions and seeing the One who makes them take place and grow?" This is part of this subject. (713)

86.4. The Perfect One Is the One Who Gives in Both States to Combine Both Realities

I have informed you about the fine points of secret and public charity in the souls of the People as well as the dispute among formal scholars regarding prescribed and voluntary charity. It is so famous that there is no need to mention it since we want to be concise and to the point. As regards open charity, there is the Tradition: "Whoever makes a good *Sunna*." (714)

As for the perfect one among the people of God, he is the one who gives by both states so that he combines the two stations and obtains both results. He sees by both eyes and travels both roads and gives with both hands. He makes it public in the moment in the place where he sees that God has made the public dominate, and he conceals it in the moment in the place where he sees that God has made secrecy dominant. This is better for the perfect among the people of God in the path of God. (715)

87 Voluntary Charity

87.1. Voluntary Charity and Self-imposition

Voluntary charity is servanthood by choice which is soiled by mastery. If it is not like this, it is not voluntary charity. He imposed it on himself as God has made mercy obligatory for Himself for the one who repents and acts correctly after doing evil by his ignorance. This is like it. It is soiled lord-ness which rules him. No one makes anything obligatory for God Almighty. He obliges on Himself that which He makes obligatory since He is The Obligator. Whoever gives from this obligation, is part of this stage. (716)

We make it obligatory that this divine rank is like that when it is done, and we oblige that it has a reward in harmony with this action. We give it itself to the one who gives this obligation from this stage. These are individuals among those who recognize voluntary charity. From that station, God rewards him when this is his drink. (717)

This is a very fine witnessed question of tasting, but I have not seen anyone who spoke about it before me unless that has not reached me. The people of God who have realized this station must perceive this, but perhaps God has not let it flow on their tongues or it has been impossible for some of them to express it. We have mentioned it in this book in another place more extensively and in a clearer manner. (718)

87.2. Voluntary Charity Is Higher than Obligatory Charity

According to this interpretation, voluntary charity is higher than obligatory charity. This voluntary type might also be obligatory by the obligation of God since the servant has made it obligatory for himself, as in the case of the vow. God makes it obligatory for him when the servant himself makes it obligatory. Other things than vows might be connected to this topic. The desert Arab said in the sound Tradition: "Messenger of God! Do I have to pay anything except alms?" He said: "No, not unless you do so voluntarily." It is possible that God makes that obligatory for him when he does it of his own free will. Then it is connected to the rank of the obligatory. Therefore, the reward may be the same although there is an added reward for the voluntary aspect in that. Therefore, it is higher than the basic obligation by this amount. God said: *"And render not your actions untrue"* (47:33) and He made it a prohibition. The prohibition is general to any action as opposed to the command. The beginning is necessary in the divine law. It is the most evident and therefore the prohibition between the obligatory and the non-obligatory are equal. The Messenger of God said that the supererogatory can be used to make up prayers and fasting. We do not think that that is allowed for obligatory matters. There is a question of dispute about making up the obligatory of that which has a set time. (719)

87.3. The Servant Is Compelled in His Choice

The meaning of the voluntary in all of that is only that the servant is a servant of his accord and the place for what his master obliges from him. By his essence, he accepts the obligation and what is made obligatory for him. The voluntary returns to its root and comes out of its root. It has an accidental quality. Whoever clings to the root constantly, always sees only the obligatory because he is directed, compelled in his choice to be like the root which brought him into existence. He said: *"The saying near to Me is not to be substituted and I am not unjust to My servants."* (50:29) What comes from Him is only by what He previously knew. The possibility is negated in respect to God. That is only what is. There is nothing but this in the divine Presence. He said in the Tradition of hesitation, "He must meet Me," that is, there must be death. He says: "The word of punishment has been realized on him," and He said: "The word is true from Me. I will fill. . ." (720)

87.4. Judgement Belongs to the Obligatory and the Possible Has No Source

There is only one matter in the root with God. There is only one matter which occurs in phenomenal being. Whoever knows it, knows it. Whoever is ignorant of it, is ignorant of it. This is accorded by the realities. Judgment belongs to the obligatory. The possibility has no source by any aspect. Since the One only has one reality from all aspects, then multiplicity does not have any aspect which it would emerge. Only the one emerges from it. If there are aspects of meanings or different relationships in the one, then outward multiplicity is not impossible for it because of these numerous aspects. (721)

87.5. Glory be to the One, Unified by the One and the Unity of Multiplicity!

Therefore, occupy yourself with this question. From here you will recognize where you have come from, who you are, whether you are one or many, from aspect the one accepts multiplicity and the multiple accepts oneness, and why the wisdom in multiplicity is vaster than wisdom in the one given that one is the root. How do the branches emerge from the principle of the root when there is none to assist them? Do the relationships which multiplicity grants in the root derive from the root or are they granted by the principles of the branch? There are not existent sources in the root. All of this is connected to this question. (722)

Glory be to the One, Unified by One, and the oneness of multiplicity! Multiplicity has a oneness particular to it. That is necessary. This is what designates the particular multiplicity. It is distinct from other than it. Distinction only occurs between things, ones or many, by oneness. Had two shared in it, distinction would not occur, and distinction is obtained. There must be oneness in the one and the sum. There is only one both in root and branch. Look, then by brother, at what I have told you! It is part of the subject of divine gnosis. Look at what the voluntary charity gives and how noble this relationship is! (723)

88 Reparation of the Purification of Alms

88.1. The Thing Is Only Purified by Itself

The Messenger of God obliged one sheep for every five camels although the category of sheep is not the category of camels. The root in this question is whether the thing can be purified by itself or purified by other than it. The sound root is that the thing is only purified by itself. This is the truth to which it is referred, even if the opposite occurs about the form. The root is preserved. (724)

88.2. Water and Death Differ in Form, Not in Root

Then God made purification by water and earth obligatory for worship. They are different in form, but not different in the root. The root is water: *"We have made every living thing of water."* (21:30) He said about Adam: *"He created him from earth dust."* (3:59) Therefore outwardly purification only occurs in the thing by that from which it was created, as animality embraces both sheep and camels, and property embraces sheep and camels, etc. If it had not been for this matter in which they share, purification would not be valid. This is why it is valid for some properties to be given in alms which are not the same category as those subject to the alms. (725)

88.3. The Making Pure of the Servant is His Recognition of Himself

The Messenger of God said about the purification of a person from ignorance: "Whoever recognizes himself has recognized his Lord." By his recognition, purification is valid for his recognition of his Lord. God is the Absolutely Pure. The servant is made absolutely pure by his recognition of himself. He is only purified by himself, so realize this! (726)

89 The Minimum Amount (*nisab*)

The minimum amount about which it is valid to say: "How much?" It is weight and measure. The lawgiver clarified the minimum amount of the measure and the minimum amount of the weight. (727)

89.1. "The Measure" is What Is Understood in the Presence of Mithal

Interpretation of this: The intelligible measure belongs to what has come in Prophetic tradition about the division of the intelligible in people "by one qafiz, two qafiz, or more or less." The Prophet connected it to measure, even if it is conceptual. He is the one who possesses the most complete, universal, glorious unveiling. We have already informed you that there are three presences: intelligible, sensory, and imaginary. The imaginary is that in which meanings descend into sensory forms, that is, appear by Self-disclosure in them since their refuge is only like that. From this presence, the Prophet divided the intellect by measure since God manifested the intellect to him in the form of measure, that is, the intellects, when God desired that. (728)

89.2. The Weighed Are Actions in the Presence of the Mithal

As for what is weighed, that is actions. They are also incidental meanings which present themselves to the doer, therefore God connected them to weight. He said: *"We will lay down the balances of equity on the Day of Resurrection."* (21:47) and *"Whoever does the weight of an atom of good will see it."* (99:7) Therefore action is included in weight and is weighed. However, that occurs in the presence of the mithal in which meanings are only perceived in sensory forms, like the divine Self-disclosure in sleep in which God is only seen as form. There are many traditions related about that which do not need to be investigated in order to realize that. It is something that every person knows since every person has imagination, both awake and asleep. This is why he interprets what he perceives by the imagination as the Prophet interpreted the form of milk as wisdom and the form of the shackle as constancy in the religion. (729)

89.3. Quantities of the Weighted a nd Quantities of Number

This is recognition of the *nisab* by what the *nisab* is, not by what the *nisab* is in such-and-such. That refers to the *nisab* from which alms is taken. Included in this subject is recognition of what one quantity is and what are many quantities. We have this single piece of gold or silver which may not be minted, and then it would be a single body. When it is weighed, its weight gives the minimum amount or more. Since it is one body, does that body have one quality of many qualities, that is, more than one? (730)

Know that number accords many and few qualities in the thing. Number is a quantity. This is from one to ten, to multiples of ten like 20, 30 to 100, 200 to 1000, 2000, and its amounts of numbers. When the weighed or measured thing which is one body has one of these numerical titles applied to it, it has one principle. If other titles of the numbers are applied to it, like 11, or 120, or 300, or 3000 or any complex number, then its qualities come from the number according to what is compounded. If the weighed thing is not one body, like dirhams and dinars, then it also has many quantities. If the number is complex and the weighed thing is a sum from ones, the number and weighed thing has quantities. If one of them is complex, and a sum and the other is not a sum or is not compound, what is not complex or a sum has one quantity and the complex and sum has quantities, so know that! (731)

Quantities occur in bodies when division occurs since bodies accept division without any doubt. Does separation by division return to unification or not? If it returns to unification as some of think, the one body has many quantities. If it does not return to unification as some of them think, then it only has one quantity. It is for this separation which we mentioned from quantities of weighed things and quantities of number, we have not seen anyone to whom it presented itself. It is something which is necessary. Whoever recognizes this question, recognizes whether the affirmation of the single jewel-essence, which is the part which does not accept division, is valid or not. (732)

89.4. Classes of Number in the *nisab* of Purifying Alms

Then you should know that part of the wisdom of the divine law is that it embraces all the classes of number in that on which alms is obliged. There is uniqueness and it is put in animals, and falls into three classes. Three is the first of the singles. It is the camels, cattle, and sheep. He put evenness in two classes, in the minerals, which is gold and silver, and in grains, which is wheat and barley. He put oneness into one class, and it is dried dates. This is by agreement. There is no dispute about it. Things taxed by alms outside of this have dispute. There is no agreement on them. There is both rare dispute and dispute which is not rare. (733)

90 The Purifying Alms of Silver

They agree that it is on five awqiyas of silver by the sound tradition. The awqiya is forty dirhams. This is the minimum amount in the silver whose alms is 2.5%. (734)

90.1. Each Group Has a Perfection Which It Reaches

Section on its interpretation: Each group has a perfection which it reaches. Perfection in the mineral class is obtained by gold. We will mention that under the alms of gold. Silver has half of the degree of perfection. The time required to obtain mineral perfection is 36,000 years. Silver is 18,000 years. It is half of the time of perfection. All minerals seek the degree of perfection. It may happen in the path that something comes between them and reaching the goal. The one who reaches the goal is called gold. Whatever is below this degree by some illness which happened to it is called by another name—silver, copper, lead, tin, iron, and mercury. (735)

90.2. The Formation of Gold

Gold comes from the unification of two parents by intercourse and formation in proportion and the overcoming of heat in the metals in all equally. Neither of the two parents of cold and dryness has what would effect this seeker of the degree of perfection before the power of the heat of the metal. When the traveller is like this, he reaches the goal and finds the source of gold. If any coldness comes upon him in his journey more than is needed, it makes him ill and comes between him and his goal. Then it has the name of silver. It is only one degree below gold. Perfection lies in four. It lacks perfection by one degree of the four. Four is the first perfect number. This is why it contains ten. Therefore silver is 2.5% (a fourth of ten) since it lacks one degree from gold by the dominance of cold. Cold is an active root and heat is an active root. Wetness and dryness are passive roots. Wetness follows cold since it is passive and under its influence. This is why silver is formed in half of the time in which gold is formed. (736)

90.3. Scientific Inimitability in the Quran

Since the passive indicates the active and seeks it by its essence, it is enough to mention the passive and we do not need to mention that which produces it since it contains it. God Almighty said: *"And on dry land and in the sea,"* (6:59) and He did not mention hot or cold. This is part of the eloquence of the Quran and its inimitability since He knew that the one who brought it: Muhammad, may God bless him and grant him peace, was not one of those who was occupied with natural sciences so that he would recognize this value. He knows absolutely that that is not from him and that it is *"a sending down successively from The Wise, The Worthy of Praise,"* (41:42) and that the One who said this has knowledge. He is God Almighty. The Prophet knew everything by the instruction and teaching which God gave him, not by his reflection, thought, and investigation. The only one who recognizes the value of prophethood is the one whom God acquaints with these matters. Look then at how wise the knowledge of the divine law is in making alms obligatory in these classes according to the well-known limit in every class for the one who looks and sees! (737)

91 The Minimum Amount of Gold

We will mention what is agreed upon regarding the *nisab* of gold, God willing. One group says that alms is obligatory on 20 dinars, as it is obligatory on 200 dirhams. Some say that there is no alms on gold until it reaches 40 dinars, and then it is one dinar. That is 2.5% because a tenth of 40 is 4 and a fourth of 4 is 1. Some say that there is no alms on gold until its value or exchange-rate reaches 200 dirhams. When it reaches that, then there is 2.5% on it whether it reaches 40 dinars or is more or less. This is in whatever is less than 40 since the interpretation of gold is what we have already mentioned. When it reaches 40, then it is interpreted by itself, not by the dirham, value, or exchange-rate. (738)

91.1. Interpretation of "The *Nisab* of Gold is 40 Dinars"

Interpretation of that: There is a dinar due on 40 dinars. That is 2.5% of that. We mentioned that silver is ruled by one nature while it is seeking the perfection which gold has obtained. That is coldness among the four natures. You take one nature from gold, and you remove it from the place of the balance. This is why one dinar is taken from the 40 which is the *nisab* of gold. It is 2.5% (a fourth of ten) because four times ten equals forty. Four is a tenth of forty, and one is a fourth of four. It is 2.5% (a fourth of ten). It is the one which silver took, and by which silver reaches the goal of the degree of perfection. It is less than gold by this amount. Therefore its alms is a dinar. (739)

91.2. Interpretation of "The *Nisab* of Gold is 20 Dinars"

This dinar joins with the 5 dirhams in being the 2.5% which is what is taken. 20 is a tenth of 200, and a fourth of 20 is 5, so there is 5 dirhams in 200. It is 2.5%. Whoever traces gold back to silver and says that there is a dinar in 20 a there is in 200 dirhams, or whoever says that it is by value and the exchange-rate for 200 dirhams, makes alms obligatory for whatever has this value and its exchange-rate in gold. This is in what is less than forty. No prohibition has been related about what is less than forty in gold as there has been a prohibition in silver. He said: "There are no purifying alms due on what is less than four awqiyas." He did not say:

"There is none on what is less than forty." This is why dispute is allowed about gold, but not allowed about silver. (740)

They are joined together by the 2.5% by every aspect. Then ten and the four are considered since it the four contains ten. It is multiplied by it and it is not multiplied by other than it because four contains its source as well as the numbers below it. Part of the sum is ten. This is why it is said that four is the first perfect number. Four is the source, and three is in it, so there is seven. Two is in it, so there is nine, and one is in it, so there are ten. Whoever multiplies four times ten is like the one who multiplies four by itself by what it contains. Therefore alms is obligatory since it looks at itself in that and does not look at its Creator and the One who brought it into existence. Therefore, God takes from it its contemplation of itself from it and calls that the alms for it. That is, its purification from claim. It remains for its Lord by its Lord. He did not specify any particular due for Him in it since all of it is His, not its. (741)

92 Awqas—It is What is Above the Minimum Amount in that Which is Subject to Purifying Alms

Scholars agree that the purifying alms is due on the awqas of animals, but there is none on awqas in grains. They disagree about the awqas of gold and silver. I say that there is no awqas in the alms of gold and silver since it is better to connect them to grains than to connect them to animals. Animals are next to plants, and plants are next to minerals. In principle it is better to connect it to what is nearest to it. The neighbor is more entitled to affinity. (742)

92.1. Perfection Does Not Accept Imperfection

Perfection does not accept imperfection. Purifying Alms is diminution (imperfection) of property. For this reason, when the animal is perfected by humanness, there is no alms on it. Things were only created to seek perfection. None is perfect except the human being. Gold is the most perfect mineral. This is why it does not accept imperfection by fire as do the rest of the metals. (743)

If you said that silver falls below the degree of perfection and is therefore imperfect and yet it has alms obliged on the awqas, we would reply that it shares with it in alms when it reaches the minimum amount in gold. That is not done for the rest of the metals. Had it not been that there was a strong relationship between the two of them, partnership would not have occurred in principle. That is why it is like that in the awqas. (744)

92.2. Alteration and Change in Forms

If you said, alms is decrease/imperfection of property, and whoever achieves perfection is not imperfect. Gold has achieved perfection and there is alms on it when it reaches the *nisab,* and it is gold in the *nisab* and gold in the awqas, so the principle of perfection is not removed from it, we said. I say the like of that and it is necessary if we proceed on this basis. However, we are dealing with another principle. It is change and transformation in forms in the divine soul-disclosure and the variety of relationships and interpretations in the divine presence. The source is one while the relationships are many. They are knowing, powerful, or creating. (745)

God did not make alms obligatory on the sources of the taxed inasmuch as they are sources, but since they are property in these particular sources, and it is not obliged in everything which has the name "property" applied to it. We take note that the ruling regarding alms on them is applied when they reach the minimum amount of property. We do not consider their sources. In awqas, we consider their sources, not the property so we remove alms from them. (746)

That is how we interpret the transformation of the soul-disclosure of creeds and rank without considering the Essence. We consider the essence in incomparability (*tanzih*) without considering rank or creeds. Since the root of existence—who is God—accepts interpretations, that reality pervades some existent things, or rather is general to existent things. We consider their existence in them differently: sometimes in terms of intelligible matters and sometimes in terms of legal matters. (747)

92.3. The Servant Is a Human Being and Has Perfection

Do you not see the servant? He is a person and he has perfection whether we consider the aspect of property in him or we consider the seller who has trade. We fix him with a value and we put him in a rank of property which is subject to alms. We pay out the alms from its value. (748)

92.4. The Manifestation of the Truly Real in the Presence of the Mithal

Do you not see that the perfectness of God does not accept any attribute from things in time? When it appears in soul-disclosure in the Presence of the mithal to the eyes which are limited by the shared senses, rulings then follow from this particular soul-disclosure. God says, "I was hungry and you did not feed Me. I was thirsty and you did not let Me drink. I was ill and you did not visit Me." When one looks at Him when the relationships are removed, He said: "*There is not like Him anything,*" (42:11) and He said: "*And truly God is independent of the worlds.*" (3:97) Whoever is rich above being proven is the proof of Himself because of the strength of His clarity. There is nothing more forceful in proving the thing than itself. (749)

92.5. Judgments Follow Interpretations

I have called your attention to the fact that rulings follow the interpretations and relationships. After a ruling from the Lawgiver has occurred in a certain matter so that it rules it, then we must look at what is considered in it so that it is governed by that ruling. This is what sets the knower above the ignorant. Since this is confirmed, then know that reaching maturity is by age, growth or maturity in the intellect. It is like the *nisab* in property. As when the *nisab* exists in property then alms is obligatory for it, so responsibility is demanded of the person of intellect when he becomes an adult. After becoming adult, the intellect takes deeper root as time passes just as property is increased by trade, and therefore awqas appears. Whoever does not find in the judgment of his intellect that God is absolutely the Doer and that the servant has no effect in the action must pay alms on awqas. Purifying Alms is the right of God in property. From his actions, he ascribes to God what must be ascribed. (750)

92.6. Ascription of Action to God or to the Human Being

Take two men. One of them relates to God what is related to Him by reality and relates to himself that part of his actions which should be related because of adab. This is like his words: "*I wanted to mar it,*" and "*So thy Lord wanted that they be fully grown, having come of age.*" (18:79, 82) It is like the words of Abraham: "*When I was ill, it is He Who heals me.*" (26:80) It is like His words: "*Whatever of benevolence lit on thee is from God and whatever evil deeds lit on thee then is from thyself.*" (4:79) The other person is someone who ascribes all of that action to a person logically and in the divine law like the Mutazilites, and those who only ascribes to God the creation of the power in the doer to do that action. (751)

As for the one who thinks that actions are only from God when his intellect is strong and that the servant has no effect in them, he does not think that there is alms on awqas because there is only what returns to God. He knows that all belongs to God as Shayban al-Rai said when he was questioned about alms. Ibn Hanbal and al-Shafii questioned him. He said: "In our school or your school? If it is in our school, then all belongs to God. We do not own anything. If it is in your school, then there is one sheep for every forty sheep." Shayban considered one matter and made alms obligatory. He considered another matter and did not make alms obligatory. The property was still the same property. (752)

93 Adding Silver to Gold

Some say that dirhams are added to dinars. When their sum reaches the minimum amount, then alms is obligatory. Some say that silver is not added to gold and that gold is not added to silver. That is my position. (753)

93.1. Interpretation of the One Who Does Not Think that They Are Added Together

The Prophet said: "Your eye has a right over you. Your soul has a right over you, so eat and sleep." The human being joins together his eye and his animal soul. However, God gave each of them a due particular to it. The right of the eye here is sleep, and the right of the growing nourished soul is food. (754)

93.2. Interpretation of the One Who Thinks that They Are Added Together

So one thing is not added to another. Sleep is not in the position of food, and food is not in the position of sleep. Nothing is added to anything else. The one thinks that sleep can be added to food. Food is a reason for obtaining sleep because of the wet vapors which are generated from it which cause sleep. Therefore, the eye obtains its right and the soul obtains its right. Therefore, there is no harm in adding gold to silver in order to obtain the right from that sum. (755)

94 Two Partners

Some say that there is no alms on two partners in their property until each of them has the *nisab*. That is my position. Some say that the rule about shared property is the same as the rule of property which belongs to one person. (756)

94.1. God Is the Partner Most Able to Dispense with Partners

When partnership occurs in person's action, God has no due in it and so there is no alms on it because God Almighty said, in effect: I am the partner most able to dispense with partners. Whoever does an action in which another one shares, I am free of it and he is the one who shares. God said: Whoever says: It is for God and for your sakes, it is for you and God has none of it. (757)

94.2. *Nisab* by Partnership Is Not Considered

One does not consider a *nisab* achieved through partnership. The two partners are subject to the principle of separation, even if they are joined together. If they are joined together, their conjunction is a proof of the existence of separation since there would be no joining had it not been for separation. Since the rule belongs to separation and neither of them reached the *nisab* in his property, there is no alms obliged on it. Purifying almsgiving, even if it is demanded from property, is only demanded from the one who is responsible for paying it. (758)

94.3. Property in the Public Treasury Does Not Have Any Purifying Alms Due on It

Do you not see that the property which is in the Treasury does not have any alms due on it because of creation's partnership in it, even though the minimum amount exists, and a year has passed if the ruler keeps it and does not part with it because of some benefit which he sees in that? Since creation are considered to be partners in that, none of their shares reaches the minimum amount and the owner of the property is not singled out. When the ruler names someone and pays to him that which reaches the minimum amount, then it has left the treasury and its owner is specified. That principle has been removed. When a year has passed, then he pays its alms. (759)

95 On the Purifying Alms of Camels

It is agreed that there is alms on them. We have mentioned their amount and *nisab* in the rules of the divine law. (1)

95.1. Purifying Alms Purifies Property from Avarice

The judgment of the Lawgiver about camels is that they are satanic. Therefore alms is obliged on them so that they will be purified of this relationship since alms purifies the owner of property from the attribute of avarice. Being satanic indicates distance. You say: "A deep (satanic, *shaytun*) well" when its bottom is very distant. He is called Satan because of his distance from the mercy of God when he refused and was proud and was one of the rejecters. (2)

95.2. When Actions Are Not Ascribed to God, They Are Far from God

When actions and deeds are not ascribed to God, they are far from God, so alms is obliged from them. That is the due which God has in them which returns to Him. When they return to Him, the robe of excellence is obtained. It is said that all of God's actions are good. Purifying almsgiving is obliged of the Mutazilite since he believes that the creation of the actions of the servants belongs to them. Purifying Almsgiving is obliged of the Asharite since he relates a question of the action to himself. (3)

95.3. There Is a Sheep in Every Five Camels

There is a sheep in every five camels. This is the same as the alms of silver. It is 2.5%. Therefore the principle of number which is alms which is paid applies. It is like the one who thinks that there is alms on awqas. He pays on dirham for every four dinars, and a dirham for every forty dirhams. This is as he pays a dirham for gold in awqas while silver is not the same class as gold. Similarly the sheep is given in the alms of five camels and it is not in the same class either. (4)

95.4. The Due of God Is Also Taken from the Limb

The due of God is also taken from the limb by burning by fire and by cutting off for theft. The responsible soul is the thief while it is not the same sort as the limb. It is purified of the principle of theft by cutting off the hand, as five camels are purified by paying a sheep while the sheep is not the same class as that which is subject to the alms. The principle of the awqas has already been discussed so there is no need to mention it here. (5)

96 Young Camels

Some people say that there is alms on them and some people say that there is no alms. (6)

96.1. The Judgment on the Responsibility of the Child Before He Is an Adult

The child is not obliged to be legally responsible until he comes of age, so there is no alms on young camels. The child learns the prayer and is beaten for not doing it when he is ten years old. He is not beaten on account except for omitting an obligation, even though he has not come of age, so alms is obliged on young camels. There is intelligence in the child, even if he has not come of age. Whoever takes reaching adulthood into consideration, says there is no responsibility. Whoever considers the strengthening of the intellect, obliges responsibility in what the divine law has laid down because its ruling applies in that. (7)

God said: "*We will cause them to join their offspring,*" (52:21) and He said: "*We gave him critical judgment while a lad.*" (19:12) Jesus said in the cradle: "*He gave me the Book and made me a Prophet and He has made me one who is blessed wherever I may be*" in the cradle and elsewhere. "*And bequeathed to me the formal prayer and the purifying alms so long as I am living and He has made me to be pious toward one who is my mother.*" (19:30-31) Part of his devotion to his mother was freeing her from what was imputed to her by testifying on her behalf. He stated all that he claimed in the past tense so that the listener would recognize that he had acquired all of that while he was still a child in the cradle. He mentioned that God had told him to perform the prayer and pay the alms as long as he was alive and that He had given him the Book and wisdom. Perception of the Book which he was given was hidden from the eyes of the people until it appeared at a later time. As for wisdom, he manifested it when he spoke the like of these words while he was still in the cradle. (8)

96.2. However Old a Human Being's Body is, His Life-span is Short

The human being is small in respect to his body since he has not spent much time in this form. The smallest period is the time of his formation, and then his period continues to extend until he dies. Whenever his body grows, his life grows smaller. Therefore, he never parts from the relationship of largeness and the relationship of smallness. His increase is his decrease, and his decrease is his increase. See how wondrous is this divine management! (9)

97 The Purifying Alms of Sheep

They agree that there is alms due on them. Success is by God. (10)

97.1. The Head of the Sheep is in the Position of the Perfect Human Being

God Almighty says about person's soul: *"He who makes it pure prospers."* (91:9) We have already discussed that. God put the head of a sheep in the station of the perfect human being. It is his price. See then how perfect is the rank of sheep! One of them ransomed a noble Prophet. He said: *"And then We took ransom for him with a sublime slaughter."* (37:107) God made it great to represent this noble Prophet and to take his place. Therefore, alms is obliged on sheep as the one who has purified himself has won. The poem says (11):

97.2. The Sacrifice and Ransom of the Sons of the Human Being

The ransom of a prophet is a two-horned sacrifice.
    Where is the bleating of ram compared to the humanity
    of the human being?
God the Great made it great as divine concern to us
    and him while he did not know from what measure it was.
There is no doubt that the camel has the greatest value,
    while it is less than the sacrifice of a horned ram.
Would that I knew whether by his essence, a small ram
    represented the vicegerency of the Merciful. (12)

98 The Purifying Alms of Cattle

Divine law scholars agree that purifying alms is due on all of them. (13)

98.1. The Relationship Between Cattle and the Human Self

The interpretation in that: God says about the human soul: *"He who makes it pure prospers."* The relationship between cattle and a person is very strong and forceful. This is why the corpse was brought to life by it when he was struck with part of the heifer. The blow is an indication of the attribute of force when a person disdained to allow the cause of his life to be a cow, especially when it had been sacrificed and its life had left it. This person who was struck by part of it was brought to life by its life. He refused when it was presented to him, so he was struck by part of it and brought to life by the attribute of force because of the disdain with which the human being was molded. (14)

98.2. Partnership Between the Human Being and Animal

God did that so that he would recognize the partnership between him and the animal in animality which is realized by definition and reality. This is why every animal is separated from others by its established division by which this is called human being, that is called cow, this is called sheep, etc. The human being only refuses in respect to his established division. Therefore, God taught him by what took place that animality is the same reality in all animals. He let him benefit from what he did not have. (15)

Similarly, that dead person was only brought to life by animal life, not by human life inasmuch as he is speaking. The speech of that dead person is not like the words of that cow in the tribe of Israel when it said, "I was not created for the like of this. I was created for cultivation." When the Prophet informed about this tradition which occurred among the Bani Israel, the Companions were amazed and said: "A cow who speaks?" The Messenger of God said: "I believe it." They did not see that God has made speak that which is more amazing than this since the skins will speak: *"We were given speech by God Who gave speech to all things."* (41:21) Here is a profound knowledge for the one whose inner eye has been unveiled by God. (16)

98.3. The Quality of the Interspace in the Human Being and in Cattle

He made alms obligatory for cattle as the relationship of the interspace between cattle and the human being is manifested in the soul. Cattle are between camels and sheep in the animals subject to alms. The human being is between the angel and the animal. The cow which manifested revival by its death and the blow with it also belonged to the interspace in its age and color. It was neither young nor old, but between that. This is a station of interspace. It was neither black nor white, but yellow. Yellow is the colour of the interspace between black and white. Realize what I have pointed out in this interpretation! It contains majestic meanings and secrets which only the people of sight and vision recognizes. (17)

99 Grains and Dates

You already know that alms is obligatory in that by general agreement. (18)

99.1. Purifying Alms of the Growing Self and the Fasting of the Elite and Common

Interpretation of that: It is the growing soul. It is that which grows by nourishment. Its alms in the human being is by fasting. However, it has a condition in the Path of God. It is that the person fasting abstain from eating in the day and then take what he would have eaten in the day and give it away as charity. That removes miserliness from him. In our opinion, if he does not do that and fills himself up in his evening meal with what he missed in the day, he has not abstained. This is what separates the fast of the elite people of God from the fast of the common people. (19)

The Messenger of God only had his morning meal as a mercy to the common people so that they would find something to emulate. The Messenger of God said: "Whoever fasts continuously, should do so until the morning meal." He also encouraged people to break the fast and to delay the morning meal." God Almighty said: "*And We have not sent thee but as a mercy for the worlds.*" (21:107) This is the interpretation of what is subject to alms in grains, Success is by God. (20)

As for dates, it is also agreed that there is alms due on them. That has already been discussed. (21)

99.2. The Palm Is the Aunt of the Human Being

The interpretation of dates in alms: Know that the Prophet made the date-palm our aunt, and likened it the believer when people asked him about it. That happened to the people of the deserts and also to Abdullah ibn Umar that it was the date-palm. He was right about what the Messenger of God meant. This Tradition is evidence for allowing people to make estimations. (22)

99.3. The Purifying Alms of the Believer from the Ascription of Believer

As alms is obligatory in the divine law on dates, so when the believer shares with God in this name, God then has a due in it as He has in all of the divine names. This due is called alms. The believer purifies himself of this relationship to him by being truthful in all his words, deeds and states, and by granting security to every fearful person. When he is truthful in all that, God confirms him because God only confirms the truthful and God only confirms him from His name, *al-Mumin*. Therefore the truthfulness of the servant reverts to the name of God, *al-Mumin*, as the form of the one who looks in the mirror returns to the looker so that God confirms him in that in which this servant is truthful. This is his alms from the ascription of belief to himself. He gives out the due of God from his belief by the words, deeds, and states in which he is truthful. (23)

99.4. The Property on Which Purifying Alms is Agreed and Not Agreed

Now the classes of property which they agree are subject to alms are complete. That which is subject to dispute is connected to it. The subject of dispute is either plant, animal or mineral. That has been made clear in the part on which there is agreement, so the dispute can be judged in it. In it, he should consider what is appropriate to that class, so that discussion will not be lengthy. We intend to be short and concise in this book as much as possible. The area is large and contains whatever matrices and fundamental principles are necessary in the Path of God. The offshoots and branches are also almost too many to be contained. Indeed, they are too many to contain. "*God says The Truth and He guides to the Way.*" (33:4) (24)

100 Estimation

It is agreed that one is allowed to estimate what there is on the palm trees and other things. That is to determine the *nisab* in it so it takes the place of measurement. (25)

100.1. Measure Is in the Rank of Knowledge and Guessing in the Rank of Opinion

The interpretation of that: It is a dangerous subject. He needs to recognize and to be precise in amounts and to have a sharp eye. God Almighty said: *"Perdition to those who were to guess"* (=*kharras; kharasa*= to guess, to estimate)!" (51:10) This is an indication which is connected to commentary, even if we did not intend commentary by it. However, it is close to the meaning, measure and weight being in the position of knowledge while estimation is in the position of probable opinion. The root is knowledge. (26)

100.2. When Knowledge is Impossible, We Judge by Opinion

When knowledge is impossible, then we judge by opinion. That is only in the judgements of the divine law, that is, the branches of the judgments. The judge only judges by the testimony of the witness while he is not absolutely sure about what he witnessed in that. The root in the prescribed judgment is probable opinion, even in happiness with God. God said, in effect: "I am in My servant's opinion of Me, so let My servant think well of Me." When good opinion of God dominates the servant, then the result is happiness. Similarly bad opinion of God ruins him. *"And that your thought which you thought about your Lord has dealt destruction to you and you have become among the ones who are losers."* (41:23). (27)

100.3. Judgment by Knowledge and Judgment by Probability

Scholars did not disagree about the one who judges between two adversaries by opinion. They disagreed about his rendering judgement by his knowledge. Opinion in this type of thing is basically agreed upon and is resorted to. Knowledge in that is a source of dispute. Even if God Almighty has knowledge, He still judges by witnesses. This is why it has come: *"He said: My Lord! Give judgment between us with The Truth."* (21:112) That is, by what Thou hast prescribed for me and with which Thou hast sent me. (28)

100.4. Gnosis of God by the Intellect is by Means of Estimation

In this way, gnosis of God by the intellect is by means of estimation. This is why it accepts the doubt which lessens proofs. Gnosis of God by means of the transmitted divine law is absolute and doubt does not lessen it with the believer at all. If the relationship is not known, then knowledge of God is by the divine law. It is that God informs His servants about what He has. He has more knowledge of Himself than His servants. (29)

100.5. Knowledge by God from God

Knowledge of Him from His is that he knows that He joins together connection and disconnection. This is not allowed in speculative proofs, that is, to join together two opposites in the subject. That only occurs here, so He does not let it rule His creation. Intellect, its speculation and reflection are part of His creation. When he says that the One who brought him into existence is not like this or is like this, there is no doubt that he is estimating. The estimator might be right and he might be wrong. Absolute knowledge of God is better than knowledge of Him by guessing, even if estimation is necessary in knowledge of God. (30)

101 What the Owner of Dates and Agriculture Consumes of His Dates and Agriculture Before the Harvest and Cutting Off the Fruit

Some say that he reckons that in the *nisab*. Some say that he does not reckon it. The estimation is left up to the owner of the property to estimate what he and his family consumed. (31)

101.1. Concern for Purifying Alms Affects the Forbidden

Dates and agriculture are result of the human being's actions. His actions are obligatory, recommended and indifferent/ allowed. As for forbidden and disliked actions, they are not included here, especially the forbidden in alms. It might be included in alms by a particular aspect in doing something forbidden. That would be that the believer basically does not have a pure act of rebellion without it being tarnished by obedience. They are those who mix a sound action with an evil one. The obedience which sullies every act of rebellion is the belief that it is rebellion. As it is obedience in the rebellion itself, so it is nearness in distance itself. That belief is its alms. (32)

So the forbidden action is purified by belief. It is the words of God Almighty: "*God will substitute for their evil deeds benevolence.*" (25:70) If he gives this amount while doing the act of rebellion, hope arises in the person that God will accept that. It is the words of God: "*And others have acknowledged their impieties. They have mixed acts that are in accord with morality with others that are bad deeds,*" (9:102) that is, return to them with mercy, acceptance, forgiving and the transformation of wrong actions. This is the divine concern of alms which affects the forbidden action. (33)

101.2. Purifying Alms Is the Right of God and the Right of the Human Being

As for acts of obedience, their *nisab* on which alms is obliged is their alms of the allowed from the one who does it in particular. It is that which the soul is given. Purifying almsgiving, even if it is a right of God, is only a right of God inasmuch as He has prescribed it. It returns to us. God has specified its camels by mentioning the classes from which it is taken. God gives charity to the human being by the allowed in the eight limbs from all his actions. That is the alms which God gives it from all its actions. That is by its poverty and need and action and its affection for obeying its Lord and being joined to Him by his belief and freeing its neck from the bondage of obligations at the moments of allowed things, even if they are included in them, that is, in the obligations since it is obligatory for him to believe that the permitted is permitted, etc. (34)

101.3. The Divine Law of the Permissible

If someone reckons it (the produce eaten by the owner) is counted against him in the *nisab,* that is because it is part of what is prescribed for him because the allowed is prescribed like the obligatory. This is why he acts in it as one who is allowed it, not by the direction of nature. If someone says that it is not counted against him, that is because it is allowed. He thinks that the obligation falls away in the allowed because the one who is obligated cannot choose. Obligation is hardship. Choice has no hardship, even if it entails bewilderment and hesitation. (35)

102 The Time of Purifying Alms

Most scholars from the early period agree that almsgiving is obligatory on gold and silver and animals provided a year has passed. None of the first rank disagreed about that in what has been transmitted to us except for Ibn Abbas and Muawiya because they did not have firm sound Tradition which they considered to be established from the Messenger of God about that. (36)

102.1. The Completion of the Time in the Year and the Completion of the Human Being in Intellect

Know that the year contains the perfection of time, so it is like the perfection-completion of the minimum. As alms is obliged by the completion of the *nisab*, so it is obliged by the completion of the time. The meaning of the perfection-completion of time is that it contains all of the four seasons. This is why one waits a complete year in the case of the impotent person (to dissolve a marriage) so that he can experience the four seasons. It does not change anything in his state, that is, it has no authority in his impotence since he lacks the predisposition for it to affect him. Man's perfection lies in his intellect. When he is complete in his intellect, his year is complete so he must pay the alms. It is that he knows what rights God has against him and strives to fulfill that. (37)

102.2. The Moment of Grains and Dates

The moment for grains and dates is the day when they are harvested. He finds it without the precondition of the year since the year has passed over the root. That is the effect that autumn, winter, spring, and fall has on it. It is as if it were not outside of the rule of the year by this interpretation. Some acts of worship are tied to the year like the hajj and fasting and what we mentioned of the classes of property subject to alms. Some obligatory acts of worship are not connected to the year like the formal prayer, the visitation, and supererogatory good actions outside of the formal pilgrimage. Its obligatory and supererogatory parts are equal in the year. (38)

103 The Purifying Alms of Mines

Some scholars think that it has both the year and *nisab* just like gold and silver. Some think that there is the *nisab* in it without the passage of a year like what the earth produces which is subject to alms. (39)

103.1. The Divine Names Are Matrices and Natural Pillars Are Matrices

The mine is nature from which bodies are formed. The souls of partial and natural bodies have four realities. When they are combined, then the world of bodies appears. In divine knowledge, it is that the world was manifested from God Almighty since He is The Living, The Knowing, The Transforming, The Powerful, and no more. Each name has a certain authority in the world, so it enters under the circle of these four matrix-names. (40)

103.2. Concerning the One Who Takes the *Nisab* Rather than Year into Account

Whoever takes into account the *nisab* without the year considers this. It is above time. When that which is formed from nature is formed from the human being, then the *nisab* is reached, and almsgiving is obliged. It is the connection of that to the four established attributes in the divine knowledge through which formation is valid. Nature is a tool, not a god. (41)

103.3. Concerning the One Who Takes the Year and *Nisab* Into Account

Whoever takes into account the passage of a year with the *nisab*, that is when what is formed from the human being is formed from the elements, not from nature. Nothing is formed from the elements except after the passage of time. That is the movement of the spheres above them. Therefore, its alms is limited by time. It is giving God's due from that formation by its relationship to a particular divine aspect which He has in every possible thing without consideration for its cause. This is the world of creation. The First Command is the world of the command in particular, so know that. (42)

104 The Passage of a Year on the Profits of Property

One group think that the year is considered in it from the day he can make use of it, whether or not the assets amount to the *nisab* or not. This is my position. Another group say that the year of the profits (revenues) is the year of the assets, that is, when a year has passed on the assets, then the alms of the profits is paid with it, whether the assets reach the *nisab* or is less than the *nisab* if both assets and profits add up to the *nisab*. This is unique to Malik and his companions. Another group makes a distinction between whether the capital which has been present for a year reaches the minimum or not. They say that if it is the *nisab* then there is alms for the profits and the capital together. If it does not reach the *nisab*, then he does not pay the alms. (43)

104.1. Actions are the Human Being's Property and their Profit Lies in Forms

Section on its interpretation: Actions are property and their profit lies in the forms that come from them. This is like the one who performs the formal prayer or the remembrance of God. From his formal prayer or remembrance of God, there is created for him an angel which asks forgiveness for him until the Day of Rising. The forms which cover actions are their profits. It is like the one who withholds alms. His property which is the amount of alms will come to him as a large bald snake with black spots over its eyes which will be placed around his neck. It will be said to him: "This is your treasure." (44)

104.2 Action of the Heart and Action of Bodies

There are two classifications of actions: Spiritual actions which are the actions of the hearts, and natural actions which are physical actions, sensory actions. One considers a year in sensory actions, but one does not consider the year in actions of meaning because they are outside of the jurisdiction of time. The *nisab* must be considered in both the meaning and the senses. The *nisab* has already been discussed. It is the amount before this in this book. (45)

The form of almsgiving in that profit is the good which reverts to the doer from it since he is described by the attributes of the religion by giving the alms in the poor, wretched and others. It is the words of the Prophet about the forms of angels created from actions. "It asks forgiveness for him until the Day of Rising." (46)

104.3. The Dream of Ibn Arabi of the Prophet in Mecca

I saw the Messenger of God in a dream while I was in Mecca. He was pointing at the Kaba and saying: "Dwellers of this House! Do not stop anyone from going around this House at any time of the night or day and from praying at whatever time he wishes of the day or night. God will create an angel for him from his prayer who will ask forgiveness for him until the Day of Rising." The confirmation of some of this tradition is what is related from the Prophet when he said: "Descendants of Abd al-Manaf! Do not stop anyone from going around this House at any time of the night or day and from praying at whatever time he wishes of the day or night." Al-Nasai transmitted it in his *Sunan*. God knows best. (47)

105 The Passage of the Year on Gains

It is what he uses in property outside of its profits. Some scholars said that scholars agree that when the property is less than the I and he makes use of other property with it without profit, and the sum of the two is equal to the *nisab*, then the year is met from the day when it is complete. They disagree about when he uses property while he has the *nisab* of other property over which a year has passed. Some of them say that he pays alms for the used property if it is the *nisab* and the year has passed and he does not add it to the property on which alms is obliged. That is my position. Others say that all gains have alms after a year has passed on the assets if the assets reach the *nisab*. They have the same opinion about profits. (47b)

105.1. The One Who Makes Use of Someone Else's Action Does Not Profit

"Whoever follows a good *Sunna* has its reward and the reward of whoever acts by it." He has made use of the action of someone else which did not come from his action, so it is his profit. It is action. The principle in that in the interpretation is based on what is in the outward principle as we have detailed in the schools according to their disputes and their disagreement as preceded above in the sections of interpretation before this. (48)

106 The Interpretation of the Passage of a Year for the Offspring of Sheep

Some scholars say that the year which applies the offspring is the year which applies to their mothers, whether the mothers reach the *nisab* or not. Some say that the year of the offspring is the year of the mothers only if the mothers reach the *nisab*. (49)

106.1. Interpretation of the One Who Isolates the Offspring of Sheep

Its interpretation: "*We will cause them to join their offspring,*" (52:21) and We have not joined them from any of their action. This is about those who believe and whose offspring follow them in belief. These offspring are in the position of the supererogatory good actions while the mothers are like the obligatory good actions. As one draws near by obligatory thing, one also draws near by supererogatory ones. It is related in traditions that supererogatory good actions result in divine nearness, so He gave it an authority in itself. This is the interpretation of the one who isolated the offspring of the sheep in principle. (50)

106.2. Interpretation of the One Who Joins the Sheep to the Mothers

The interpretation of the one who joins them to the mothers as we mentioned about both schools interpretation is that supererogatory good actions are obligatory ones and that their principle is that of the obligatory. This is why they are added to them. When a human being begins the voluntary prayer—which is the supererogatory one which is not obligatory for a person and which he can abandon without rebellion—or when he begins the fast or formal pilgrimage, he is obliged to perform the obligatory parts in them. Bowing, prostration, and standing are obligatory and necessary in the supererogatory prayer. The prayer is only valid by these pillars. (51)

This is why God says (in a Sacred Tradition, *hadith qudsi*): "Complete the obligations of My servant from his voluntary ones." The obligation of the obligatory is completed by the obligation of the voluntary, whatever action it may be. The due of God in supererogatory good actions is what they contain of the obligatory parts. This is their alms. Whatever excess there is in that reverts to the one who does it. This is why God is his hearing and his sight when he draws near by supererogatory actions. (52)

107 Gains from Animals

It has been interpreted like the interpretation of gains of coin. There is no need to mention it in this section. We brought it in order to point it out. (53)

108 Interpretation of the Passage of a Year on Debts for the One Who Thinks that There Is Purifying Alms Due on Them

Some people say that the year starts from the day when he takes the debt from his creditor. There is dispute among those who say that there is alms on the debt. Some say that one considers it from the beginning of the debt. If a year passes, then he pays the alms of the year. If many years pass, he pays alms for each year. The one with this school puts it in the position of present property. Some say that he only pays alms for one year, even if it remains for years with the one who has the debt. This is the only amount of alms due on it. I do not see that he has any proof in that. (54)

Interpretation in that: There is the obligatory pilgrimage for a dead person and the one who cannot perform the obligatory pilgrimage as is related in text. There is the fasting of the guardian of the dead person if he dies while he still owes some of the fast of Ramadan. It becomes a due of God for the guardian who goes on the formal pilgrimage or fasts. That due is the amount of alms which is in the debt. The claims which the debts owe are freed. This is as the one who owe debt has no alms in what he has because he does not own it. (55)

108.1. Whoever Thinks that He Has No Purifying Alms on the Debt

Whoever thinks that he has no alms on it long as it is with the debtor thinks that a person has only what he strives for. He does not have in his possession property by which he strove for good. The good in it is since he was generous to the debtor by giving him some property. He specifies that this action has the same station as alms so he does not need to give alms for it. (56)

108.2. What good is greater than the one who is generous to the servants of God?

Scholars confirm that the goal of purifying alms is to take satisfy a need. Had it not been for his need, the one who took the debt would not have taken it. The one who gives it has taken care of this need of his, so it is like alms in this way. This is the interpretation of the one who does not think that there is any alms on it until he takes it and a year has passed since he took it. (57)

108.3. The Verse Concerning Debts in the Quran

The sign concerning debts according to what we said is His words: *"Lend a fair loan to God,"* (57:18) and *"Who is he who will lend God a fair loan?"* (2:245) Since the loan takes care of need, that is why the Jews said: *"God is poor and we are rich,"* (3:181) that is, because of His poverty, He seeks the loan from us. They do not see what God means by that about the extent of His connection to His creation as has come in the *Sahih*, "I was hungry and you did not feed Me." It is like that, and the subject is the same. We have already discussed the loan at the beginning of the chapter. (58)

109 The Passage of a Year for Goods with the One Who Obliges Purifying Alms on Them

The interpretation of the year is above. I believe that there is no alms on goods since there is no text to that effect. It is as if were an extra law. It is free analogy without being divine law derived from established divine law. God knows best. (59)

Some scholars stipulate that there be money with the goods. Some of them consider the *nisab* in it. Some of them do not consider that. Most of the scholars, leaders and others say that its principle is the same. It is that whoever buys some goods and has them for a year, pays alms on them. Some people say that he pays alms for their prize and not their value, and that is what I say. (60)

109.1. Action Is Based on Firm Divine Law or Noble Character

The interpretation of this: Goods are dutiful actions presented to the human being in which he has no intention or they are actions in which intention is not a precondition. He has a reward for them as the Prophet said: "You have become Muslim with the previous good you have done," that is, you have its reward, even if you did not do that from a firm divine law. However, it is noble character, so it finds God and it is rewarded. If it had not been that deed which was presented has God's due in it by a certain relationship which it grants, it would not be praised. That is its alms from where he is not aware. (61)

110 Paying Purifying Alms Before the Year Has Passed

Some scholars forbid that. I say that it is forbidden outwardly, not inwardly. Some of them permit that. (62)

110.1. Interpretation of the Permission to Pay Purifying Alms Early

The interpretation of the permission: *"Put forward for your own souls."* (2:223) *"And whatever good you put forward for yourselves, you will find it with God."* (2:110) *"And compete with one another for forgiveness from your Lord."* (3:133) *"and those who give what they gave with their hearts quaking . . .are those who compete with one another in good works."* (23:61) The Prophet said about the one who brought testimony before it was asked of him, "The reward in it is greater than the reward of the one who brings the testimony after being asked to do so." (63)

110.2. Interpretation of the Prohibition Against Paying Purifying Alms Early

As for the interpretation of the prohibition, authority belong to the moment, so one must not do something in it which it does not demand. Here are fine points from knowledge of the sciences of the divine names. Can a name rule in the moment of the power of another name while the authority of the master of the moment continues? Can they share in the moment? Is it the rule of moment which rules the name by putting it under the authority of the ruled predisposition in it which the moment gives? Authority only occurs in its moment then? There are more questions of this sort, so know that. This is enough of the interpretation of the chapter of alms. Praise belongs to God. (64)

Appendix A
Al-Ghazzali's "Mysteries of the Poor Rate" from his *The Alchemy of Happiness* translated by Jay R. Crook (Muhammad Nur)

CONCERNING THE POOR RATE

Know that the obligatory poor rate[438] is one of the Pillars of Islam, for the Messenger (S) said: "The edifice of Islam is built upon five things: the Testimony that *There is no god but God, Muhammad is the Messenger of God;* formal prayer, the obligatory poor rate, fasting, and the (Greater) Pilgrimage." In the Traditions, it is related: "A fiery brand will be placed on the breasts of those who possess gold and silver and do not pay the poor rate so that it comes out of their backs. Whoever possesses animals[439] and does not pay the poor rate will be overcome by them on the Day of Resurrection so that they will gore him with their horns and trample him under their hoofs. When they have done all this, they will start over again. They will continue to do so until that time all people are called to account." This Tradition is found in two of the authentic books of traditions.[440] Therefore, (the poor rate) is incumbent upon someone possessing property and a religious obligation to know the rules for paying it.

EXCURSUS: CONCERNING THE DIFFERENT KINDS OF POOR RATE AND THEIR CONDITIONS

Know that the obligatory poor rate is of six[441] kinds:

THE FIRST KIND: THE POOR RATE ON LIVESTOCK. These are camels, cattle, and sheep. However, the poor rate is not paid on animals such as horses and donkeys. Four conditions regarding this poor rate must be observed: The first condition: They must not be animals that are fed fodder; rather, they must be grazers not requiring much expense. If, during the year, (the grazing animals) are fed enough fodder to be considered fodder-eating animals, then they are no longer subject to the poor rate. The second condition: They must be the property of the owner for the entire year. If they leave one's ownership, they are not subject to the poor rate. On the other hand, their offspring are counted, even if they are born at the end of the year and the poor rate must be paid for them following the principle of assets. The third condition: One gains wealth from that property and it is in one's control. However, if (the animals) are lost or taken from one by force, the poor rate does not apply to them, unless they are returned to him with all profit that would have been earned from them. Then, (the payment of) the poor rate for the past becomes obligatory. If someone is in debt, in an amount equaling the livestock he possesses, it is correct that he not pay the poor rate, for in truth he is poor. The fourth condition: One must possess the requisite wealth in an amount to be counted among the wealthy (and thus subject to the poor rate), for wealth is not obtained from a small amount. As for camels: Unless there be five (or more), (payment of the poor rate) for them is not required. For five camels, (the payment is) one sheep; for ten, two; for fifteen, three; for twenty, four. These sheep must be at least one year old. (If the payment is made) in goats, not less than two years old. If there be twenty-five camels, then it is one one-year old female camel. If there be none, then a two-year old male may given in its place. Thereafter, nothing additional is required until there are thirty-six. For thirty-six, a two-year old female is necessary; for forty-six, a threeyear old female; for sixty-one, a four-year old female; for seventy-six, two two-year old females; for ninety-one, two three-year old females; for one hundred and twenty-one, three two-year old females. After that, the calculation is that for every fifty, one three-year old female and for every forty, a two-year old female. As for cattle: No poor rate is required until their number is thirty. Then a one-year old is necessary; for forty, a two-year old; for sixty, two one-year olds. After that, the calculation is one two-year old for every forty, and a one-year old is given for every thirty. As for sheep: For each forty, one; for one hundred and twentyone, two; for two hundred and one, three; for four hundred, four. After that, the calculation is one for every one hundred not less than a year old. If it is male, then not less than two years old would be suitable.[442] If there are two persons whose sheep are held jointly and both are of sufficient means to qualify for the poor rate—and neither one of them is either an unbeliever or a self-ransomed slave[443]—then the two are as though they were one proprietor. If they both have no more than forty, then half a sheep is required (from each owner); if they possess one hundred and twenty, both together, one sheep is sufficient.[444]

THE SECOND KIND: THE POOR RATE OF TITHES.[445] Whoever possesses 800 manns[446] of wheat, barley, currants or raisins, dates, or some other edible thing suitable for eating and is the food of a class (of people) upon which they can subsist, such as chickpeas, rice, beans, etc., giving tithes on it is obligatory. Things that are not (basic) comestibles, such as cotton, walnuts, linen, and fruit, are not subject to the poor rate.

If one has 400 manns of wheat and 400 manns of barley, they are not subject to the tithe, for eligibility to pay the poor rate must be from one kind of goods. If there is no water (for cultivation) from a canal or an underground channel, and water is instead drawn from a well by buckets, then one half of one tenth is necessary.[447] It is not proper to give it for grapes and fresh dates; however, it is for raisins and (mature) dates, unless raisins are not made from such grapes. In that case, the tithe is lawful. It is necessary when the grapes have taken on their color and the wheat and barley kernels have hardened that they not be disposed of until they have first been appraised in order to find out how much the share of the poor will be. Then, after the amount has been made known and agreed upon, it is lawful to dispose of them all.

THE THIRD KIND: THE POOR RATE FOR GOLD AND SILVER. For every 200 drams of silver, five dirams[448] are required at the end of the year. For every twenty dinars, half a dinar: that is one tenth of one fourth.[449] Whatever is over this is calculated the same way. For silver, for golden and silver swords,[450] and for ornaments made of gold and silver on swords, animal harnesses, etc., and everything that is not permissible, the poor rate must be paid. However, ornaments which are—for a man or a woman—permissible to use are not subject to the poor rate. If one has gold and silver lent out to people that could be called in if one wished, it is subject to the poor rate.

THE FOURTH KIND: THE POOR RATE ON TRADE. If something is bought in the amount of twenty dinars, with the intention of trade, and the year ends, the cash poor rate becomes obligatory, and whatever profit has been made during the year is counted. At the end of every year, one must assess the value of the goods. Then, if the capital was originally gold or silver, (the poor rate) must be given in that form. If the goods were bought with cash, it should be paid in the coin most commonly used in the city.[451] If one has goods and intends to trade them, but does not buy anything with them, they are not counted at the beginning of the year. Whenever during the year the intention to trade is rescinded, the poor rate need not be paid. However, if it is cash and the person qualifies for paying the poor rate, the beginning of the (fiscal) year is calculated from the time when he becomes eligible to pay the poor rate.

THE FIFTH KIND: THE POOR RATE OF THE 'ID FESTIVAL. Every Muslim who, on the eve of the ('Id) Festival has more food than he himself or his family will consume during that day, [452] and has something in excess—not counting the house, clothing and necessities—must give a ṣāc[453] of foodstuffs of the kind that are his usual food. That is, three manns less one-third of a mann. If (one's staple food) is wheat, barley is not suitable. If it is of a kind of grain, it should be of the best kind. Flour, etc., should not be given in place of wheat grain, according to Shafi'i (R). This poor rate must be given for every person for whom thou providest (their) expenditure, such as women, children, parents, and bondmen. The 'Id poor rate for bondmen is joint; two are counted as one. One does not need to pay a poor rate for an unbelieving bondman. If a woman wishes to pay her own poor rate from her own property, it is lawful. If the husband pays it without her directive, it is lawful. This much of the rules of the poor rate must be learned. If some other circumstance occurs, one ought to know that he must ask about it and do so.

THE MANNER OF GIVING THE POOR RATE

Know that one must observe five things in giving the poor rate:

FIRST: The declaration of the Intention of the poor rate is a religious obligation. If one is appointing some one else to do this, at the time of the appointment, the Intention must be stated, or the representative must be instructed to declare the Intention at the time of its distribution. When the guardian of the property of an infant pays the poor rate on it, he should declare the Intention.

SECOND: When the year is ended, one should hasten; inexcusable delay is not seemly. The poor rate for the 'Id Festival should not be delayed and hurrying to do so during the month of Ramadan is lawful, but not before (the commencement of Ramadan). Pre-paying the poor rate on property is meritorious during the entire year, with the condition that the recipient of the payment remains poor until the end of the year. If the recipient dies before the completion of the year, or becomes solvent, or apostatizes, that payment must be made up.

THIRD: The poor rate must be paid of the same kind as the thing assessed. According to the Shafi 'ite school, it is not correct to give gold in place of silver, wheat in place of barley, or anything else of an equivalent value.[454]

FOURTH: Charity should be given where the property is, where the poor can see the property. If (charity) is given to a different city, the correct view is that the obligation of the poor rate upon that donor is not reduced (by the gift). FIFTH: The poor rate should be divided among eight categories of people, however many there are, so that each group is not less than three and the total is twenty-four. If the poor rate is one diram, according to the Shafi'ite school, it should be divided into eight equal parts. Then each part is divided among the persons of the category as they wish, even it is not equal. In these days, three of those (eight) categories (of poor rate recipients) are uncommon: the warriors for the faith, those who are to be reconciled, and the collectors. But the poor, the destitute, the captives to be ransomed, the wayfarers, and the debtors can be found.[455] According to Shafi'i, each person should give the poor rate to at least fifteen individuals. In the Shafi'ite school, there are two difficult problems: one is that substitution (of one kind of goods for another) is not permitted, and the other is that it must be distributed among all (qualified recipients). Most of the people follow the Hanafite school with respect to these two matters. We hope that that they will not be seized (for punishment on the Day of Resurrection) for this, if God Most High wills it.

DISCLOSING THESE PEOPLE: THEY ARE OF EIGHT CATEGORIES

THE FIRST CATEGORY is the Poor. This is a person who possesses nothing and cannot do any business. If he has food for the day and clothing on his body, he is not poor. If he has no more than one half of his daily sustenance, or has a shirt but no turban, or has a turban but no shirt, then he is poor. If he can earn money with some tool, but does not have the tool, then he is poor. If he is a student who, if he were to engage in some trade, would be held back in his studies, he is poor. Such persons are not often found, except children. The solution is to seek out a poor family man and give him the portion of the poor on behalf of his children.

THE SECOND CATEGORY is the Destitute. Anyone whose basic expenditures are greater than his income is destitute. Even if he has a house and clothing, but does not have the expenses for a year and he cannot depend upon his earnings, it is lawful to give him enough to complete the year. If he has carpets, utensils, and household furnishings, because he has need of them, he is (still counted among the) destitute. If he has something in excess of his need, he is not destitute.

THE THIRD CATEGORY is the Collectors of the Poor Rate. They collected the poor rate and distribute it among the poor. Their salary is paid from the poor rate.

THE FOURTH CATEGORY is Those Who Are To Be Reconciled. This is a great person who embraces Islam if he is given property. Others will be encouraged to accept Islam by his example.

THE FIFTH CATEGORY is the Bondmen to be ransomed. These are bondmen who purchase their freedom by giving their price to their master.

THE SIXTH CATEGORY is the Debtors: persons who have fallen into debt not by reason of vice and who are poor; or a person of means who has incurred debts for some good purpose to prevent social turmoil.

THE SEVENTH CATEGORY is the Warriors for the Defence of the Faith. These are warriors who do not receive payment from the public exchequer, even if they have wealth. They are given equipment from the poor rate funds.

THE EIGHTH CATEGORY is the Wayfarers. Travelers who do not have traveling provision, either passing through, or traveling from their own city, are given supplies and rent. It is lawful to accept the word of any person who declares "I am a pauper" or "I am needy," for one cannot be certain that he is lying. However, if the traveler or the warrior does not travel or go to battle, then the poor rate should be taken back from him. The other categories must be validated by the word of trustworthy persons.

THE INMOST SECRETS OF GIVING THE POOR RATE

Know that just as formal prayer has an external form and an inner reality that is the spirit of that form, so does the poor rate. If a person does not comprehend the inner mystery and the true nature of the poor rate, it is a spiritless form for him. Its secret lies in three things:

THE FIRST (SECRET) is that the people are commanded to the love and friendship of God Most High and there is no believer who does not claim this. Indeed, they are commanded not to love anyone more that God Most High, as is said in the Honorable Quran: *Say: If your fathers and your sons and your brethren and your wives and your kinsfolk and the wealth ye have acquired, and trade whose dullness ye fear, and dwellings ye love, are dearer to you than God and His Messenger and striving in His way, then wait till God brings His command to pass. And God guides not the transgressing people.* (Q. 9:24) There is no believer who does not claim that he loves God Most

High above all other things, and he supposes (to himself) that that is so. Therefore, there is a sign and a proof needed lest everyone take pride in an empty boast. So, since property is one of the things loved by man, he is tested with it and it is said: "If thou speak the truth in thy claim of love, sacrifice this one of thy beloved things so that thou may understand the level of thy love for God Most High." The persons, then, who have learned this secret, are of three classes:

The First Class was the truly righteous, who sacrificed all that they possessed and said: "We give for the love of God Most High." Others gave half of their possessions. When Abu Bakr[456] (R) brought all of his wealth, the Messenger (S) said: "What hast thou left for thy family?" He answered: "God and the Messenger of God." 'Umar (R) brought half of his wealth. The Messenger (S) asked: "What hast thou left for thy family?" He said: "As much as I have brought." The Messenger (S) said: "*The difference between you two is like the difference between your words.*"

The Second Class was the benevolent who did not spend all of their wealth at one time, as they did not have the power to do so. They kept their (property) and waited for the need of the poor and the payments of charity. They kept themselves the same as the poor. They did not stint in the amount of the poor rate, but when they came upon the poor, they treated them as though they were their own family.

The Third Class was that of the good, sound men who did not have the ability to pay more than five dirhams out of 200 dirhams. They contented themselves with their religious obligation and observed the command of God joyfully and promptly. They did not humble the poor when distributing the poor rate alms. This is the lowest degree, for anyone whose soul (dil) does not permit him to give five dirhams out of the two hundred which God gave to him, has no part in the love for God. Since he cannot give more than this, his love is very weak and he is counted among the miserly devotees.

THE SECOND SECRET is the purification of the soul from its miserliness and pollution. Miserliness in the soul is like a religious impurity that causes it to be unsuitable for approaching God Most High, just as an external impurity causes the body to be unsuitable for the presence of prayer. This impurity of miserliness will not be cleansed except by spending wealth. Because of this, the poor rate removes the impurity of miserliness as water washes the (external) impurities. And, it is for this reason that the poor rate and voluntary alms are forbidden to the Messenger (S) and his household, in order to protect his position from the dirt of the peoples' property.

THE THIRD SECRET is that the gratitude for the blessing that property is a blessing for the believers, the cause of their ease in this world and the next. Just as formal prayer, the Pilgrimage, and fasting are the gratitude for the blessings of the body, the poor rate is the gratitude for the blessing of property, so that when one finds himself self-sufficient with these blessings, and sees another Muslim, like himself, in need, he says to himself: "He is a servant of God Most High like me. I am thankful that He has made me unneedful of him and made him needful of me. Let me befriend him. It may be that this is a test; if I stint, I may be changed into his condition, and he into mine." Therefore, everyone must know these secrets of the poor rate so that his poor rate not be an empty form.

THE RULES AND DETAILS OF GIVING THE POOR RATE

If a person desires that his worship be living and not spiritless, and that his spiritual reward be multiplied, then he must observe seven duties:

THE FIRST DUTY: This is to hasten in giving the poor rate, before it falls due, by giving it throughout the year. In this, there are three benefits: One is that the eagerness to worship may appear (in the donor), for giving after it is obligatory is a necessity, because if one does not give, he will be chastised (in the Hereafter). Therefore, that payment will be made out of fear, not out of love. There will be with him that which comes from fear, not from love and compassion.

The second is that happiness may touch the souls of the poor early so that they supplicate for one with more sincerity because they see the happiness unexpectedly. And the supplications of the poor are a walled fortress against all calamities (for the donor).

The third is that one may be secure from the impediments of fortune, for there are many calamities in delaying. It may be that some impediment befall him, depriving him of this benefit.[457] When the soul conceives an eagerness for something, one should seize the opportunity, for that is the view of mercy. Be quick, lest Satan attack! *For the heart of the believer is between two fingers of the fingers of the Compassionate One.* The thought occurred to one of the saints, while in the privy, to give his shirt to some poor person. He called his disciple, took off his shirt, and gave it to him. The disciple said: "O shaykh! Why didst thou not wait until thou camest out (of the privy)?" He replied: "I was afraid that some other impulse would occur to me and prevent me from doing this."

THE SECOND DUTY: If one wishes to pay the poor rate in one lump sum, one should give it either in the month of Muharram[458] which is the first of the year and a sacred month, or in the month of Ramadan.[459] However much the occasion is nobler, so the spiritual reward is increased. The Messenger (S) was the most generous of mankind; he gave away whatever he had. At the month Ramadan, he did not keep back anything and gave all of it away.

THE THIRD DUTY: The poor rate should be given privately and not in public in order to avoid hypocrisy. In the Traditions, it is related: "Secret almsgiving quells the wrath of God Most High." In another Tradition: "Seven persons will be in the shade of the Throne of God tomorrow: one is the just ruler, another is the person gives alms with the right hand, giving in such a way that the left hand does not know of it.[460] See what his status is; that he is at the level of the just ruler!" And in the Traditions, it is related: "Whoever gives alms in secret, (the alms) are written among the secret deeds; if they are given in public, then they are written among the public deeds. If the donor says to another: 'I gave such-and-such alms,' then the deed is taken out of the records of secret and public deeds and written in the record of hypocrisy." For this reason the forefathers surpassed themselves in giving alms in secret to the point that there was one who would seek out a blind person and place the alms in his hand without speaking, lest the blind person recognize his voice. Another would look for a sleeping pauper and tie the alms to the man's clothing so that he would find them when he awoke and not know who had given them to him. There was another who threw them in the path the poor were taking. Another would give the alms to a representative who would then distribute them. All this they did so that the poor would not know (their benefactor)! Yet, they considered keeping their deeds secret from others even more important, for giving in public may lead to hypocrisy; even as miserliness is defeated[461] in the soul, hypocrisy is nourished. These traits are all destroyers. Miserliness is as a scorpion in the grave and hypocrisy is as a snake, which is stronger because they make the scorpion the food of the snake in order to strengthen the snake. One is saved from one destructive force to fall into another that is more difficult. The bite of this on the soul, when in the grave, will be as the bites of snakes and scorpions, as we found in the Prolegomena.[462] Therefore, the harm of giving (alms) in public is greater than its benefit.

THE FOURTH DUTY: (For one who) is secure from hypocrisy, and has cleansed it from his soul—such a person knows that if he gives in public, others will imitate him and their desire (to give) will increase—

for such a person, giving in public is better and more virtuous. This person must be one to whom praise and censure are equal, one who is proficient in the knowledge of God Most High.

THE FIFTH DUTY: That is that one not invalidate the charity with obligation or troubling. God Most High said: *Do not make your charity worthless by reproach and injury.* (Q. 2:264) This refers to injuring the poor with sour looks, knitting the brows, or speaking harshly to them, questioning them rudely, and looking upon them with contempt because of their poverty. This (attitude) arises from two kinds of ignorance and foolishness: One is that it is hard for some to give up property. For this reason, they are stingy and speak roughly. Whoever finds it difficult to give one dirham to receive a thousand is ignorant. By (giving) this poor rate, he will obtain the highest heaven and the pleasure of God Most High and redeem himself from hell. Why is this difficult for him if he believes in these things? The other is the foolishness that a person suppose he is nobler than the pauper is because of his wealth. He does not know that a person (the pauper) who will go to heaven five hundred years before he does is nobler than he and his status much greater! To God Most High, the poor have dignity and nobility, not the rich! The sign of their nobility in this world is that while the rich man busies himself with work, worldly concerns, and their burdens and calamities, his portion of such things is not greater than the amount of his need, and it is incumbent upon him to supply the needs of the poor! So, in truth, the rich man has been made the forced laborer of the poor man in this world, and in the next, the poor have been allotted five hundred years to await (the rich man's) arrival!

THE SIXTH DUTY: This is not to impose an obligation. The root of obligation is ignorance, and that is an attribute of the soul. It is to do some good deed for the poor and given them something from his own blessings, and (thus) to put the poor under his control. Then, if he thinks this way, its sign is that he expects the poor person to serve him and wait upon him, and to greet him first. In sum, he expects much respect and deference. If the poor person is deficient in this, he is more amazed at this than he was before. It may be that he says: "What (wrong) have I done to him?" All of this is from ignorance. Indeed, the truth is that the pauper did him a service by accepting his alms so that he may escape the fire of hell and his soul be cleansed of the impurity of miserliness. If a cupper[463] cups him without payment, he would be put under an obligation to (the cupper), for he let out that blood which could have been the cause of his death. Since he has received both purification and salvation because of the poor person, he should put himself under obligation to him! Also, the Messenger (S) says: "Alms first fall into the hand of God Most High; then, into the hand of the poor person." Since one gives to God Most High and the pauper is the representative of God Most High on His behalf, (the giver) must feel grateful to the poor person, and not expect gratitude from him. When one becomes informed of these three inner secrets of the secrets of the poor rate and reflects upon them, one knows that the imposition of an obligation is ignorance. The forefathers went to great lengths to avoid doing this. They stood before the poor person and placed it before him humbly. Then they begged him, saying: "Accept this from me." There are some who held it in front of them in their hands so that the pauper would take the coin from their hands. Thus, the pauper's hand was above theirs, for the upper hand is better than the lower hand. It is not fitting for a person to impose an obligation. 'Ayishah (R and Umm Salamah[464] (R) would send something to a poor person, and would say: "Memorize what supplication he utters"; so that they could give a reward[465] of a supplication for every supplication, this so that the alms would remain unrewarded.[466] Nor did they not hold the eagerness for supplication by the poor man proper so that he suppose that they had done the good deed (for that). The doer of the good deed is in fact the pauper who has taken this burden from thee.

THE SEVENTH DUTY: One should give from the best, most lawful, and most appealing part of one's property; for, that which is doubtful is not fit for nearness (to God). God Most High is pure and does not accept anything other than the pure. God Most High said: *And seek not of the bad to spend thereof (in charity) when ye would not take it for yourselves, save with disdain.* (Q. 2:267) That is: Why do ye spend as the portion of God Most High that thing which ye would accept with repugnance? If a person places the worst he has in his home before the poor man, he slights him. How can it be that one gives the worst to his Lord and the best to His servants?[467] The worst kind of giving is to give with aversion. Alms given without joy, it is feared, will not be accepted. The Messenger (S) says: "In almsgiving, it is possible for one dirham to take precedence over a thousand dirhams." It is that which is given of the best and given with joy.

THE RULES FOR SEEKING OUT A POOR PERSON

Know that when one gives the alms of the poor rate to any poor Muslim, he is fulfilling a religious obligation; but a person who is doing the business of the Hereafter should not stint in making the effort (to find a suitable recipient). The spiritual reward for the properly distributed charity is multiplied, so one should watch for (at least) one of these five characteristics:

THE FIRST CHARACTERISTIC: The one who is abstinent and pious. The Prophet (S) said: "*Feed the pious*." The reason for this is that they are aided by what they receive in their devotion to God, and the donor is a partner in the spiritual reward of that (devotion) which he has aided. A great and wealthy person would not give alms except to the Sufis. He used to say: "These are a people who have no ambition other than God Most High. When they are in need of something, they are distracted (from Him). And I, when I take my soul to the Divine Presence, I would prefer (them) to the attention of a hundred souls whose ambition is the world." These words were related to Junayd[468] who said: his doing this was a kind of tacit obligation upon them which they remedied by supplicating on his behalf. "This it the speech of one of God's saints." The man was a grocer and he had become penniless, because he had given away everything that he possessed. He would give the Sufis whatever they asked and not seek payment. Junayd sent the man some goods so that he might return to his trade, saying: "For a man such as thee, trade has no loss."

THE SECOND CHARACTERISTIC: The one who is one of the learned. He obtains the leisure to study by means of the alms. The giver shares the spiritual reward of knowledge.

THE THIRD CHARACTERISTIC: The one who conceals his need. He hides his own poverty and lives with the appearance of affluence: *The ignorant think (they are) rich because of their restraint.* (Q. 2:273) These are a people who keep the veil of the appearance of prosperity over their faces. It is not as though thou give to a pauper who is not afraid to beg.

THE FOURTH CHARACTERISTIC: The one who has a family or is ill. However much the need be greater, the greater is the spiritual reward (of giving to him).

THE FIFTH CHARACTERISTIC: The one who is a relative; (giving to him) is both a present and alms, and the person who is held as a brother in the love of God Most High—he, too, is of the degree of the relatives. If one finds a person possessing all of these qualities—or more— he takes precedence. When one bestows upon such persons, their high desires and thoughts and their supplications become one's fortress. This is a benefit beyond that which is the expulsion of miserliness from oneself and the giving of thanks for one's blessings. And one must not give the poor rate to 'Alawis,[469] nor to unbelievers, for this is soiling the people's wealth. The 'Alawi is vexed by this and (giving) this [charity][470] to an unbeliever is repugnant.

THE RULES FOR THE RECIPIENT OF THE POOR RATE

The recipient of the alms must observe five duties:

THE FIRST DUTY: He must know that since God Most High created His servants in need of goods, for that reason He did not place a great deal of property in their hands. However, He favored a group and protected from the activities and concerns of the world. He placed the burden of the pain and trouble of the business of the world and its preservation upon the powerful. He commanded them to care for those of His more beloved servants according to their needs, so that those precious ones could escape the burden of the world and might be of one mind and thought in their devotion to God Most High. Since by reason of (physical) needs they would become distracted, in accordance with their needs, they are supplied by the powerful so that the blessedness of their supplications and resolution may be an atonement for the powerful. Consequently, the poor person must receive that which he receives with the intention of using it for his self-sufficiency so that he may be free for devotion (to God). He must recognize the value of the blessing which the powerful have given him as a kind of impressment fee, so that he attend to worship. This is just as the kings of the world, not wanting their own personal (male) servants[471] to absent themselves from their service, do not permit them to engage in any worldly trade. They turn the villagers and the traders of the marketplace who are not fit to be their servants into their corvée[472] so that they (the kings) may receive from them the tolls and taxes imposed upon their activities and pay their personal servants. As the aim of the property (taken) from all is its use by a special class, the aim of God Most High from all mankind is the worship of the Divine Presence. For this reason, He said: *I did not create jinn and mankind except that they worship (Me).* (Q. 51:56) So, the poor person must accept everything he receives with this intention. For this the Messenger (S) said: "The wage of the giver is not greater than the wage of the taker, for (the recipient) takes out of need." This is the person whose purpose is the freedom from care for religion.

THE SECOND DUTY: The recipient receives it as from God most High and views it as from Him. He recognizes the wealthy donor as one utilized (by God) on his behalf, one who has been compelled to deliver it to him by means of (His) agent. His agent is the belief that has been given to him so that he might know that his salvation and happiness are bound up in (giving) charity. If he did not have this agent, he would not give a single grain to anyone. Therefore, (the recipient) should be grateful to Him who has obliged the agent. As (the recipient) knows that the hand of the rich giver is a means, he must view him as the medium and give thanks: *Whoever does not thank people has not thanked God*. For God Most High, as He is the Creator of the deeds of His servants, always lauds them and thanks them, just as He said: *How excellent a servant he was; lo! he was ever turning (to Us)* (Q. 38:44)[473] And He said: *Surely he was a truthful man, a prophet;* (Q. 19:41),[474] and the like, because whoever has been turned into the means of goodness, has been made dear. As He said: *There is blessedness for him whom I have created for goodness and I have caused goodness to flow on his hands*. So, one must know the value of His dear ones, and this is the meaning of gratitude. One must make a supplication for him and say: *May God purify thy heart in the hearts of the godly and increase thy work in the works of good deeds; may He bless thy soul amongst the souls of the martyrs*. In the Traditions, it is related: "Recompense everyone who does a good deed for thee. If thou art unable, then offer supplication to God on his behalf to fulfill the (obligation of) recompense. The perfection of gratitude is to conceal a defect in the alms and not to consider its meagerness as meagerness, nor to think it mean; just as the prerequisite of the giver is that he give, and even if it should be much, he must consider it unworthy and not magnify it.

THE THIRD DUTY: One should not accept anything that is not lawful. One should not accept anything from the property of oppressors. One should be wary of the property of usurers.

THE FOURTH DUTY: One should not accept more than one needs. If one accepts it for a journey, one should not take more than is necessary for one's provisions and lodging. If one is a debtor, he should not accept more than the debt. If it is for his family's sustenance, it should not be more than ten dirhams; one should not accept eleven dirhams, as that one (extra) dirham is unlawful. If there is something in the house of furnishings and clothing in excess (of need), it is not proper to accept the poor rate alms.

THE FIFTH DUTY: If the giver of the poor rate is not knowledgeable about the source of the portion he is giving, (the recipient) should ask: "Is this which thou art giving from the portion of poor or from the portion of the debtors?"[475] For example, if the recipient is not of that characteristic, and (the donor) gives the amount of the eighth of his poor rate to him, he should not accept it. According to the school of Shafi'i (R), the whole amount cannot be given to one person.

THE MERIT OF GIVING ALMS

The Messenger (S) said: "Give alms, even if all of it is but a date, for that will keep a poor man alive and slay sins as water extinguishes fire." And he said: "Take heed of hell; if it is all (but) half a date, so be it. If thou canst not (give that), then (give) a kind word." And he said: "No Muslim gives alms of what is lawful but that God Most High takes it in His Own gracious Hand. He nurtures it as thou nurturest thine own animals until the time that that date becomes as large as Mount Uhud."[476] And he said: "At the Resurrection everyone will be beneath the shade of his own alms until the time when judgment is made among created beings." And he said: "Almsgiving shuts seventy of the doors of evil." He was asked: "Which alms are more meritorious?" He answered: "Those which thou givest in health, for thou hast the expectation to live on and do not fear poverty; not those thou delayest until thy soul reaches thy throat[477] and then say: 'This to this person, that to that person,' for that will belong to that other person,'—whether thou sayest it (in words) or sayest it not (in words)."[478]

Jesus (A) said: "Angels will not come to the house of whoever disappoints a beggar and drives him away from its door for seven days." The Messenger (S) did not delegate tasks to others; rather, he would do them with his own hands. He would give alms to the needy with his own hand, and he would place the water of purification himself at night and keep it covered. And he (S) said: "Whoever clothes a Muslim, (the clothing) is kept by God Most High so that it will become like a cloak on him."

'Ayishah (R) gave fifty thousand dirhams in charity and wore a patched, mended tunic. She did not make a tunic for herself. Ibn Mas'ud (R) says: "A man worshipped God for seventy years, then he committed a great sin which voided all of that worship. Then, he passed by a poor man and gave him a round loaf of bread. He was forgiven for his sin and the deeds of seventy years of his obedience were restored to him." Luqman[479] said to a boy: "Whenever thou committest a sin, give alms."

'Abdullah bin 'Umar[480] used to give large amounts of sugar in alms and would say: "God Most High says: Ye will not attain piety until ye spend of that which ye love. (Q. 3:92) And I love sugar." Sufyan Thawri says: "The alms of whoever does not consider himself more in need of the spiritual reward of the alms than the poor person needs the alms are not acceptable." Hasan Basri saw a beautiful girl with a slave dealer and said: "Wilt thou sell her for two dirhams?" The other replied: "No." Hasan said: "Go, for God Most High sells the women of Paradise for two kernels of grain, and they are more beautiful than she." He meant alms.

Endnotes

438 The poor rate (*zakāt*) is an obligatory annual tax on certain kinds of property. Voluntary charity or alms is called *ṣadaqah*.

439 Animals of commercial value such as beasts of burden, cattle, sheep, and other livestock.

440 A reference to the six books of traditions compiled by pious scholars in the 3rd Islamic (late 9th and early 10th CE) century. They are all considered authentic by Sunni Muslims. Those by Bukhari and Abu Muslim are the most highly regarded of the six.

441 Both Persian texts have only five, the 'Id tax being the fifth. A comparison with the Arabic Revival shows that the fifth kind was the poor rate on mines, absent from the Persian texts. In the *Revival*, the 'Id tax is the sixth kind.

442 This calculation differs slightly from the one Ghazzali gives in the *Revival*. The relevant passage in that book says that poor rate becomes obligatory only when the number of sheep reaches 40; then a ewe in her second year or a goat in its third year must be given. Nothing more accrues until the number of animals is 121, then two must be given. For two hundred, three; for 400, four. Thereafter, one for every one hundred.

443 "a self-ransomed slave: (*mukātab*): a slave or bondman who has made an agreement with his master to work at some enterprise and gradually purchase his freedom.

444 Ghazzali, in the equivalent passage in *The Revival*, states that the poor rate for two owners who own a flock jointly is the same as for one owner with respect to the rules of the poor rate. If they jointly own forty sheep, they must give own; if three persons own a flock of 120 sheep, each must give a sheep.

445 Tithes (*mu*^{c}*ashsharāt*): literally one tenth; that is, a 10% tax.

446 Various weights are given for the weight of a mann. There are forty sers in a mann..

447 That is, the tax is 5%.

448 diram (dram): A weight that in Persia was, for example, one four-hundredth of a mann. In modern times equivalent of a gram.

449 That is, the tax is one fortieth, or 2.5%.

450 "swords" (***khanūr***, also ***khunūr*** or ***khunnūr***): AA in a footnote says this means 'swords.' Steingass gives additional meanings, including 'utensils, knives, pots, etc.,' plus other meanings referring to non-metallic things.

451 In this period, coinage was not a monopoly of the central government as it is today. Although there were letters of credit and other banking instruments, daily trade was conducted with coins, usually of copper, silver, and gold. These were issued by kings, governors, warlords and lacked standard weight and purity. Some coinages had a better reputation for purity than others. There was also considerable counterfeiting and adulteration. Coin clipping was also common. Certain coins were favored in one district but not in another. Recognizing this situation, Ghazzali does not declare a single standard, but leaves it to the custom of the place. Incidentally, for nearly two centuries prior to the oil era, the standard coin, because of its reputation and recognizability, in much of the Middle East was Austrian Maria Theresa dollar rather than any local issue.

452 That is, for the day commencing with the final breaking of the fast of Ramadan (*ifṭār*) and the festival following it. The first day of Shawwal.

453 ṣāᶜ: a dry measure given various values. Steingass makes it the equivalent of five and one-third raṭls, with each raṭl the equivalent of a pint.

454 That is, if the wealth which serves as the basis of the poor rate assessment is gold, it must be paid in gold; if it is wheat, it must be paid in wheat. The equivalent value in some other form or of some other kind is not acceptable.

455 The categories of the recipients of the poor rate are enumerated in the Q. 9:60. Extensive commentaries have been written about the exact meaning of these words and there are differences of interpretation and usage among the chief religious schools of Islam.

456 Abū Bakr: The first of the Rightly Guided caliphs, rgd. from AH11/632CE to AH13/634CE. He was the father of 'Ayishah. He was the only one of the four Rightly Guided caliphs to die a natural death.

457 By making him unable to pay the poor rate and obtain its spiritual reward.

458 Muharram is the first month of the Islamic lunar calendar. The lunar year gains about ten or eleven days on the solar year every year, so the dates vary. In the year 2001CE, for example, Muharram AH1422 began on the 26th of March. Twelve years earlier, in 1989CE, it began on

the 2nd of August. 459 Ramadan is the ninth month of the Islamic lunar calendar and the month of fasting. See previous Note.

460 Compare these words attributed to Jesus: "But when thou givest alms, let not thy left hand know what the right hand doeth, that thine alms may be in secret; and thy Father who seeth in secret shall reward thee openly." Matthew 6:3.

461 The remedy for miserliness is to give things away. See above.

462 See the Fourth Topic of the Prolegomena.

463 "cupper": a practioner of cupping, a method of drawing blood to the surface of the body by means of a glass vessel or cup evacuated by heat..

464 Umm Salamah: A wife of the Prophet. She and her first husband, Abu Salamah, were early converts to Islam and emigrated to Ethiopia due to the persecution by the Quraysh. There they had a son, whom they named Salamah. Then, they left Ethiopia and emigrated to Madinah where they had three more children. Her journey alone from Mecca to Madinah with her small child is well known. A non-believer, 'Uthman bin Talhah, happened to meet her on the road and, thinking that a woman should not travel alone such a long distance, escorted her courteously to Madinah. Abu Salamah was wounded at the battle of Uhud and later died in AH4/624CE. The Prophet was 57 years old when he contracted this marriage with the widow.

465 "reward": the text has *mukāfāt*, which in modern Persian usually implies retaliation and retribution; *quid pro quo*. In Arabic, however, and Ghazzali seems to be using it in the Arabic sense, it means 'reward, gratification.'

466 That is, the supplication (*du*ᶜ*ā*) of the poor person on their behalf would have nullified the spiritual reward of the charity, so they would ask the person charged to distribute the charity to memorize the words of supplication that the receiver would utter. Then they would supplicate on his behalf to balance that so that the charity would remain untainted by an expression of gratitude from the receiver. The poor man's supplication on their behalf was occasioned by receiving the alms; in the view of 'Ayishah and Umm Salamah.

467 "His servants": i.e., mankind, the people he would seek to impress.

468 Junayd: Abu al-Qasim bin Muhammad bin al-Junayd. He came from Nahavand in western Iran and began his career as a silk spinner. He went to Baghdad and became a famous Sufi theologian and jurist. He performed the Pilgrimage thirty times and died in AH297/910CE.

469 Alawis (ᶜAlawīyān): that is, descendants of the Prophet. The poor

rate is not given to descendants of the Prophet.

470 From the AA text.

471 "servants" (*ghulāmān*): or "bondmen, slaves." This term only refers to males, usually young. In Arabic, it means "boy, youth, slave, servant." The root gh, l, m can also have sexual overtones.

472 "corvee" (*sukhrah*): "forced labor, unpaid labor." The kings do not pay their subjects; rather, they levy taxes and fees upon them in order to support their rule over them.

473 In this particular citation from the Quran, the servant referred to is Job.

474 This refers to Abraham.

475 The question here is about which category the alms are being given from and whether the recipient is qualified to accept them.

476 Mount Uhud: A small mountain about three miles north of Madinah. It is famous as the site of a battle (AH3/625CE) in which the Muslims, who had disobeyed the orders of the Prophet, were defeated by the Quraysh.

477 That is, you are about to die.

478 That is, after death it will be someone else's property anyway.

479 Luqman: **Luqmān al-Ḥakīm**, in the Quran (Q. 31:1-19) one upon whom God had bestowed knowledge. Muslim commentators are not unanimous as to whether he was a prophet or not. Western scholars have often identified him with Aesop, the putative author of a Greek collection of fables and moral tales. Aesop is not a proper name, but means "the Ethiope," indicating an African origin. Other identifications have been proposed, but God knows best. The problem of Luqman is discussed in the translator's *The Old Testament: An Islamic Perspective*. The text of the discussion is also found in *From Monarchy to Hellenism in The Bible: An Islamic Perspective* series, extracted from the former volume.

480 'Abdullah bin 'Umar: See Ibn 'Umar.

General Index

Index to Quranic Verses

Books in English by or about Ibn al-Arabi

ALONE WITH THE ALONE: CREATIVE IMAGINATION IN THE SUFISM OF IBN ARABI Henry Corbin (A), Ralph Manheim (T) pp 454 "Henry Corbin's works are the best guide to the visionary tradition.... Corbin, like Scholem and Jonas, is remembered as a scholar of genius. He was uniquely equipped not only to recover Iranian Sufism for the West, but also to defend the principal Western traditions of esoteric spirituality."-- Introduction by Harold Bloom

In this book, which features a powerful new preface by Harold Bloom, Henry Corbin brings us to the very core of this movement with a penetrating analysis of Ibn 'Arabi's life and doctrines. Corbin begins with a kind of spiritual topography of the twelfth century, emphasizing the differences between exoteric and esoteric forms of Islam. He also relates Islamic mysticism to mystical thought in the West. The remainder of the book is devoted to two complementary essays: on "Sympathy and Theosophy" and "Creative Imagination and Creative Prayer." A section of notes and appendices includes original translations of numerous Sufi treatises.

Harold Bloom's preface links Sufi mysticism with Shakespeare's visionary dramas and high tragedies, such as The Tempest and Hamlet. These works, he writes, intermix the empirical world with a transcendent element. Bloom shows us that this Shakespearean cosmos is analogous to Corbin's "Imaginal Realm" of the Sufis, the place of soul or souls.

IBN ARABI: A MOVEMENT OF SUFI SPIRITUALITY IN THE MODERN WORLD Suha Taji-Farouki (A) pp 490 "A marvellous book ... historically and ethnographically well informed, with equally well-informed use of theory - handled with very considerable sensitivity - and lucidly written." Paul Heelas, author of The New Age Movement and The Spiritual Revolution "Empathetic in approach and immensely well-documented, this is an exemplary work. Its great importance for akbarian studies is its discussion of the way in which Ibn 'Arabi's teachings have been received and transformed in the modern world." Michel Chodkiewicz, author of *Seal of the Saints* and *An Ocean Without Shore* "A masterful and multifaceted study. This important book opens out to provide a much-needed critique of the sociology of Islam in the age of globalization." Victoria Rowe Holbrook, author of *The Unreadable Shores of Love and Beauty and Love* "The primary reference work on Beshara will be this thoughtful, intelligent and immensely well-researched book. We can learn a great deal from it." Peter Young, Principal of the Beshara School of Intensive Esoteric Education

CONTEMPLATION OF THE HOLY MYSTERIES: THE MASHAHID AL-ASRAR OF IBN ARABI IBN ARABI (A), Cecilia Twinch (T), Pablo Beneito (T) pp 136 A major work of mystical literature, this account focuses on 14 visions in the form of dramatic conversations with the divine, interspersed with dazzling visionary episodes regarding the nature of existence, humans' relationship with reality, and the way to achieve true happiness. The introduction presents a resume of Ibn Arabi's life and examines in detail the style and symbolism of the contemplations. Presented for the first time in English, this work is a superb example of Ibn Arabi's inimitable style and deep perception.

DIVINE GOVERNANCE OF THE HUMAN KINGDOM:INCLUDING WHAT THE SEEKER NEEDS AND THE ONE ALONE Ibn Arabi (A), al-Jerrahi al-Halveti (T) pp 300 A powerful but little known work, this volume contains three mystical texts. *Al-tadbirat*, the largest, is a fascinating treatise on the divine design and management of the world, and the central role the human model plays in the creative and governing process. The other two are *Kitab kunh ma la budda minhu lil-murid* (or, *What the Seeker Needs*), a brief guide for those want to follow the Sufi path, and *Kitab al-ahadiyyah* (or, *The One Alone*), an esoteric essay on transcendental unity.

DIVINE SAYINGS: 101 HADITH QUDSI: THE MISHKAT AL-ANWAR OF IBN ARABI by Muhyiddin Ibn 'Arabi (A) Stephen Hirtenstein and Martin Notcutt (T) pp 120

Much of the early scholarship on Ibn Arabi focused on his contributions to the intellectual sciences, especially metaphysics and spiritual psychology. Only gradually have scholars come to acknowledge the extent of his immersion in the transmitted sciences such as Quran and jurisprudence. As for the Traditions, it is difficult to overestimate the importance that he gives to the field. One must always keep in mind that his goal was to make the fullness of Muhammadan sanctity more accessible, that is, the whole range of spiritual perfections realized by Muhammad in act, word, and inner reality. As he says in a typical passage, 'Our vision of God in the Muhammadan form through the Muhammadan vision is the most complete vision that there may be. So we never cease encouraging people to achieve it, both orally and in this book' (*Futuhat* IV 184). In many ways it is the Traditions, Muhammad's own words, that provide seekers with the most immediate access to the Muhammadan form. Stephen Hirtenstein and Martin Notcutt have produced in *Divine Sayings* a beautifully translated version of Ibn Arabi's best known collection of Traditions, based not only on the published Arabic text but also several important manuscripts, with full scholarly apparatus. They have done a great service to all those who would like to gaze upon the Muhammadan form though the eyes of al-Shaykh al-Akbar. - William C. Chittick, Stony

Brook University.

This classic collection (and first critical edition) of 101 memorable *Divine Sayings* related by the Prophet, translated in full for the first time in English, is not just an indispensable key to the teachings of Ibn Arabi and the wider traditions of Islamic spirituality. These short sayings are also a simple, direct, immediately accessible summary of the most universal spiritual lessons: The all-encompassing primacy of God's Love and Compassion; the corresponding human tasks of attentiveness, perseverance, and true service; the practical centrality of purified intention and constant remembrance—and the interaction of all those elements at each stage along our spiritual path. - James W. Morris, University of Exeter. Anqa Publishing.

THE FOUR PILLARS OF SPIRITUAL TRANSFORMATION: THE ADORNMENT OF THE SPIRITUALLY TRANSFORMED (*Hilyat al-abdal*) Muhyiddin Ibn Arabi (A), Stephen Hirtenstein (T) pp 80 "One of Ibn Arabi's most accessible and widely studied works, the *Hilyat al-abdal*, highlights the practical foundation of spiritual discipline underlying all of his metaphysical and theological writings." —Professor James Winston Morris, Boston College

IBN ARABI William C. Chittick (A) pp 160
Muhyi ad-Din Ibn Arabi (1165 - 1240) was an outstanding Spanish-born mystic and one of the most prolific writers in Islamic history. He made major contributions to the fields of Quran commentary, jurisprudence, theology, philosophy, cosmology, and spiritual psychology, and he was also a great poet of love. Although he is known as the first spokesman for 'the oneness of being', his real focus was the diverse modalities of human perfection. He marks a transition in Sufism in practical instructions on healing the heart and aphorisms on the divine mysteries to an equal stress on the theoretical issues that had long been the topic of philosophy and theology.

IBN AL-ARABI'S BARZAKH: THE CONCEPT OF THE LIMIT AND THE RELATIONSHIP BETWEEN GOD AND THE WORLD Salman H. Bashier (A) pp 206

IBN ARABI - TIME AND COSMOLOGY Mohamed Haj Yousef (A) pp 254 This book is the first comprehensive attempt to explain Ibn 'Arabī's distinctive view of time and its role in the process of creating the cosmos and its relation with the Creator. By comparing this original view with modern theories of physics and cosmology, Mohamed Haj Yousef constructs a new cosmological model that may deepen and extend our understanding of the world, while potentially solving some of the drawbacks in the current models such as the historical Zeno's paradoxes of motion and the recent Einstein-Podolsky-Rosen paradox (EPR) that underlines the discrepancies between Quantum Mechanics and Relativity.

IBN ARABI AND MODERN THOUGHT: THE HISTORY OF TAKING METAPHYSICS SERIOUSLY Peter Coates (A) pp 214 These penetrating metaphysical and spiritual teachings cross the divides of culture and time, providing unexpectedly modern insight.

IBN ARABI IN THE LATER ISLAMIC TRADITION: THE MAKING OF A POLEMICAL IMAGE IN MEDIEVAL ISLAM Alexander D. Knysh (A) pp 449 This book examines the fierce theological controversy over the great Muslim mystical thinker Ibn Arabi (1165-1242). Even during his lifetime, Ibn Arabi's conformity with the letter of the Muslim dogma was called into doubt by many scholars who were suspicious of the monistic (unitive) tendencies of his metaphysical teaching, of his claims to be the Prophet's successor and restorer of the true meaning of the Islamic revelation, and of his allegorical interpretation of the Quran. Following Ibn Arabi's death, these misgivings grew into an outright condemnation of his teachings by a number of influential thirteenth through fifteenth century theologians who portrayed him as a dangerous heretic bent on undermining the foundations of Islamic faith and communal life. In response to these grave accusations, Ibn Arabi's advocates praised him as the greatest saint of Islam who was unjustly slandered by the bigoted and narrow-minded critics.

As time went on, these conflicting images of the mystical thinker became rallying points for various political and scholarly factions vying for lucrative religious and administrative posts and ideological denomination. In thoroughly analyzing the heated debates around Ibn Arabi's ideas throughout the three centuries following his death, this study brings out discursive strategies and arguments employed by the polemicists, the hidden agendas they pursued, and the reasons for the striking longevity of the issue in Islamic literature up to the present day. On the theoretical level, this book reassesses the validity of such common dichotomies as orthodoxy versus heresy, mainstream versus mystical interpretations of

Islam, and communalism versus individualism as well as other issues related to the history of Islamic thought.

IBN AL-ARABI ON THE MYSTERIES OF BEARING WITNESS TO THE ONENESS OF GOD AND PROPHETHOOD OF MUHAMMAD Ibn al-Arabi (A) pp 396 from Chapter 67 of the *Futuhat al-Makkiyya* translated by Aisha Bewley. The master of Islamic spirituality describes the first of the five pillars of Islam by not only disclosing its mysteries but detailing the rulings of the divine law as well.

IBN AL-ARABI ON THE MYSTERIES OF PURIFICATION AND THE FORMAL PRAYER pp 730 from Chapters 68 and 69 of the *Futuhat al-Makkiyya* translated by Aisha Bewley. Ibn al-Arabi delves into the mysteries of the Islamic practices of purification and the formal prayer. In exhaustive detail he explains possible issues that may arise from the point of view of the divine law as well.

IBN AL-ARABI ON THE MYSTERIES OF THE PURIFYING ALMS pp 280 from Chapter 70 of the *Futuhat al-Makkiyya* translated by Aisha Bewley. Ibn al-Arabi explains the mysteries of the Islamic practice of the purifying alms in a way no other scholar ever has. He opens up doors of intuition to the astute reader.

IBN AL-ARABI ON THE MYSTERIES OF FASTING pp 292 from Chapter 71 of the *Futuhat al-Makkiyya* translated by Aisha Bewley. Ibn al-Arabi relates mysteries of fasting from the gnostic (irfani) perspective while at the same time following the divine law in every detail.

IBN AL-ARABI ON THE MYSTERIES OF PILGRIMAGE pp 326 from Chapter 72 of the *Futuhat al-Makkiyya* translated by Aisha Bewley. Every detail that a pilgrim would want to know about the mysteries of the pilgrimage in addition to the divine law rulings is contained in this volume.

IBN ARABI: THE TREE OF BEING Shaykh Tosun Bayrak (A) pp 255

IBN ARABI: THE VOYAGE OF NO RETURN Claude Addas (A) pp 134 This is a concise introduction to the life and thought of Ibn 'Arabi, who is considered as the 'Greatest of Sufi Masters'. Written by the author of a best-selling biography of Ibn Arabi, *Ibn Arabi: The Voyage of No Return* traces the major events of Ibn Arabi's life: his conversion to Sufism; his travels around Andalusia and the Maghreb; his meetings with the saints of his time; his journey to Mecca; his travels in Egypt, Palestine, Mesopotamia, Anatolia and Syria; his most important books. The events of Ibn Arabi's 'inner voyage', however, are far more spectacular than those of his outer life and are here presented directly from the many autobiographical sections found in his writings. Through her detailed analysis of Ibn Arabi's works and her profound understanding of his ideas, Claude Addas gives us a comprehensive insight into the major doctrines of this most influential of Sufi, masters: the doctrine of prophethood and sainthood, of inheritance from the prophets, of the 'imaginal world', of the 'unicity of Being', of the 'Seal of the Saints', and many others. Addas also introduces the main disciples of Ibn Arabi down to the nineteenth century and traces both his unequalled influence on the course of Sufism and the controversies that still surround him till today. *Ibn Arabi: The Voyage of No Return* is essential reading for anyone interested in Islamic mysticism and is a genuine contribution to scholarship in this field.

IMAGINAL WORLDS: IBN AL-ARABI AND THE PROBLEM OF RELIGIOUS DIVERSITY William C. Chittick (A) pp 220

ISLAM AND THE LIVING LAW: THE IBN AL-ARABI APPROACH Eric Winkel (A) pp 128 Ibn Al Arabi, the mystic scholar of the 13th century, highlights the ambiguities of language and the polysemantic, multifaceted text of the Quran. With Al Arabi's help, Winkel expounds how narrowly religion is interpreted by most scholars. Al Arabi disturbs the comfort of man-made religion by his reflections on language, and Winkel's book takes up the same challenge.

JOURNEY TO THE LORD OF POWER: A SUFI MANUAL ON RETREAT Ibn Arabi (A), Abd al-Kerim al-Jili (Commentary), Rabia Terry Harris (T) pp 128 This is the first English translation of a 12th-century Sufi text dealing with spiritual ascent. Ibn Arabi's writings have influenced both Muslim and Christian traditions.

KERNEL OF THE KERNEL Muhyi al-Din Muhammad ibn Ali Ibn al-Arabi (A) pp 50

MECCAN REVELATIONS OF IBN ARABI, VOLUMES I AND II Edited and translations by Michel Chodkiewicz and William Chittick pp384 **MECCAN REVELATIONS OF IBN ARABI, VOLUME II** Edited by Michel Chodkiewicz (E) pp 270 Perhaps no mystic in the history of the world has delved as deeply into the inner knowledge that informs our being as did Ibn 'Arabi. He was born into the cultural and religious crucible of Andalusian Spain in 1165, a place and time in which Muslim, Jewish and Christian scholars learned from each other and from the Greek classics that were then being translated and circulated. Drawing from the most advanced philosophical and metaphysical thinking of his time and from his extensive knowledge of the religion of Islam, Ibn 'Arabi created an extraordinary mystical theology that essentially sprang from his own spiritual realization. Because of the advanced nature of his teachings he has been known for 800 years as the Sheikh al-Akbar, or the Greatest Master.

Because of the subtlety of his language and complexity of his thought, access to Ibn 'Arabi has always been difficult and translation daunting. Previously only short extracts were available in English. This volume, is the second of our acclaimed translation of Les Illuminations de la Mecque, and contains more of the "Greatest Shaykh's" wisdom for the first time in English, on such issues as the gnostic and the sacred law, the mystic properties of Quranic letters, the secrets of Forgiveness and the attainment of Divine Nearness.
This great book soars beyond time, culture and any particular form of religion. Describing what is fundamental to our humanity, it is astonishingly universal. Finally readers in the West have an entree into one of the most important, profound works of world literature.

MUHYIDDIN IBN 'ARABI - A COMMEMORATIVE VOLUME Edited by Michael Tiernan pp 380 This unique volume celebrates the 750th anniversary of the death of one of the world's mystical giants, Muhyiddin Ibn Arabi, known throughout the Muslim world simply as the Shaykh al-akbar (the greatest teacher). This text brings together, for the first time, works by eminent scholars and students of the Shaykh from many different countries.

MYSTICAL ASTROLOGY ACCORDING TO IBN 'ARABI Titus Burckhardt (A), Keith Critchlow (F), Bulent Rauf (T) pp 64 A unique work, providing the underlying spiritual principles (from the point of view of one of the greatest Sufi masters who ever lived) lacking in most modern books of astrology. It will complement and deepen anyone's personal library or collection of works on astrology.

PERFECT HARMONY (CALLIGRAPHER'S NOTEBOOKS) Ibn 'Arabi (A), Hassan Massoudy (I) pp 64 Among the other three volumes in Shambhala's series is Perfect Harmony: Sufi Poetry of Ibn Arabi, which pairs the poetry of the 13th-century Sufi mystic with contemporary calligraphy by Hassan Massoudy. In a moving afterword, Massoudy explains how he became involved in calligraphy as a child, and how his work is inspired by poetry.

PRAYER FOR SPIRITUAL ELEVATION AND PROTECTION Muhyiddin Ibn Arabi (A), Suha Taji-Farouki (T) pp 150 "The importance of having a stable text with full vocalization based upon the best manuscripts is evident. But the author's careful study of the chains of transmission and the detailed information about the recitation of the prayer in the contemporary world are also of the highest interest." Prof Michel Chodkiewicz

QUEST FOR THE RED SULPHUR: THE LIFE OF IBN 'ARABI QUEST FOR THE RED SULPHUR: THE LIFE OF IBN 'ARABI Claude Addas (A), Peter Kingsley (T) pp 347 The first serious biography of the most influential figure in the history of Islamic mysticism. It is based on an enormous amount of documentary evidence...In his voluminous writings Ibn Arabi recounted his visionary experiences, his journeys, real and imaginary, and his meetings with other mystics, both alive and dead.

Quest for the Red Sulphur: The Life of Ibn Arabi is undoubtedly a landmark in Ibn Arabi studies. Until the publication of this book, anyone who wanted to learn about the life of Ibn Arabi has had little choice of material to work from. This major study by Claude Addas is based on a detailed analysis of a whole range of Ibn Arabi's own writings as well as a vast amount of secondary literature in both Arabic and Persian. The result is the first-ever attempt to reconstruct what proves to have been a double itinerary: on the hand the journey that took Ibn Arabi from his native Andalusia to Damascus—and on the other hand, the 'Night Journey' which carried him along the paths of asceticism and prayer to the ultimate stage of revelation

RINGSTONES OF WISDOM (FUSUS AL-HIKAM) Ibn al-Arabi (A) Caner K. Dagli (T) pp 352 *The Ringstones of Wisdom* is one of the most influential and controversial books of Islamic civilization. This relatively brief but far-reaching text covers topics such as creation. prayer, the relationship with God with the world, and the interpretation of dreams.

SEAL OF THE SAINTS. PROPHETHOOD AND SAINTHOOD IN THE DOCTRINE OF IBN ARABI Michel Chodkiewicz (A), Liadain

Sherrard (T) pp 192 This is by far the best available explanation of the central importance of sanctity for understanding both the practical and the theoretical teachings of Sufism. - William Chittick; An extraordinarily good book about an extremely difficult thinker...Chodkiewicz not only knows the texts remarkably well, but also avoids and rejects certain errors of perspective common among other scholars. TLS

SELF-DISCLOSURE OF GOD: PRINCIPLES OF IBN AL-'ARABI'S COSMOLOGY William C. Chittick (A) pp 483 *The Self-Disclosure of God* continues the author's investigations of the world view of Ibn al-Arabi, the greatest theoretician of Sufism and the "seal of the Muhammadan saints." The book is divided into three parts, dealing with the relation between God and the cosmos, the structure of the cosmos, and the nature of the human soul. A long introduction orients the reader and discusses a few of the difficulties faced by Ibn al-Arabi's interpreters. Like Chittick's earlier work, *The Sufi Path of Knowledge*, this book is based primarily on Ibn al-Arabi's monumental work, *al-Futuhat al-makkiyya "The Meccan Openings*." More than one hundred chapters and subsections are translated, not to mention shorter passages that help put the longer discussions in context. There are detailed indexes of sources, Koranic verses, and hadiths. The book's index of technical terminology will be an indispensable reference for all those wishing to delve more deeply into the use of language in Islamic thought in general and Sufism in particular.

SEVEN DAYS OF THE HEART Pablo Beneito (A), Ibn Arabi (Author), Stephen Hirtenstein (T) pp 182 *The Seven Days of the Heart* is a collection of prayers for the nights and days of the week by one of the world's greatest mystics, Muhyiddin Ibn Arabi (1165-1240). This is the first time these extraordinary and beautiful prayers have been translated into English. There are fourteen prayers, full of the most astounding expressions of contemplation and devotion to God. This is a unique spiritual masterpiece, made available for the first time to English-speaking readers.

STATIONS OF DESIRE: LOVE ELEGIES FROM IBN 'ARABI AND NEW POEMS Michael Sells (A) pp 136 Islamic poetry is enjoying an influx of readers in English, but poems by such Sufi saints as Rumi and Ibn Arabi have suffered from terrible translations. Sells, who has proven his talents in the highly regarded anthology Early Islamic Mysticism (1996), is confident enough to include some of his own poems, inspired by Ibn Arabi's love elegies, alongside his versions of the master's work, and his deftly wrought, spare verses are quite good in their own right.

But Ibn Arabi is the star here, and these translations show the twelfth-century Muslim mystic at his very best. This is truly beautiful love poetry, and the oft-posed question of whether the beloved in it is God or a human quickly becomes irrelevant. Furthermore, by invoking the Beloved in both genders, Ibn Arabi invokes love that transcends gender and identity, and flies in the face of the stereotype of Islam as inherently sexist. Love for God and romantic love each is, as Ibn Arabi writes, "a garden among the flames." Truly a collection to be treasured. John Green

SUFI METAPHYSICS AND QURANIC PROPHETS: IBN 'ARABI'S THOUGHT AND METHOD IN THE FUSUS AL-HIKAM Ronald L. Nettler (A) pp 160 The *Fusus al-Hikam* is acknowledged to be a summary statement of the sufi metaphysics of the "Greatest Master", Ibn Arabi (d.1240). It is also recognized that the *Fusus* is a work of great complexity both in its ideas and its style; and, over the centuries, numerous commentaries have been written on it. Each of the chapters of the *Fusus* is dedicated to a Quran prophet with whom a particular "wisdom" is associated. In *Sufi Metaphysics and Quranic Prophets*: Ibn Arabi's Thought and Method in the *Fusus al-Hikam*, Ronald Nettler examines ten chapters from the *Fusus* which exemplify the ideas, method and perspective of the entire work. Concentrating on a detailed analysis of the text, the author brings out the profound connection and integration of scripture and metaphysics in the world-view of Ibn Arabi. Sufi Metaphysics and Quranic Prophets serves not only as an explication of Ibn Arabi's thought in the *Fusus*, but is also a great aid in the overall understanding of Ibn Arabi's theology.

SUFI PATH OF KNOWLEDGE William C. Chittick (A) pp 478 Translations of Ibn Arabi from the *Meccan Revelations.*

SUFIS OF ANDALUSIA: THE RUH AL-QUDS AND AL-DURAT FAKHIRAH M IBN 'ARABI (A) pp 173 This work was originally published in 1971. Muhyiddin Ibn Arabi was one of the greatest mystics whose influence was pervasive and profound. *Sufis of Andalusia* consists of biographical sketches of some of the contemplatives and spiritual masters among whom Ibn Arabi spent his early years.

SUFISM AND TAOISM: A COMPARATIVE STUDY OF KEY PHILOSOPHICAL CONCEPTS Toshihiko Izutsu (A) pp 493 In this deeply learned work, Toshihiko Izutsu compares the metaphysical and mystical thought-systems of Sufism and Taoism and discovers that, although historically unrelated, the two share features and patterns which prove fruitful for a transhistorical dialogue. His original and suggestive approach opens new doors in the study of comparative philosophy and mysticism.

Izutsu begins with Ibn Arabi, analyzing and isolating the major ontological concepts of this most challenging of Islamic thinkers. Then, in the second part of the book, Izutsu turns his attention to an analysis of parallel concepts of two great Taoist thinkers, Lao-tzu and Chuang-tzu. Only after laying bare the fundamental structure of each world view does Izutsu embark, in the final section of the book, upon a comparative analysis. Only thus, he argues, can he be sure to avoid easy and superficial comparisons. Izutsu maintains that both the Sufi and Taoist world views are based on two pivots--the Absolute Man and the Perfect Man--with a whole system of oncological thought being developed between these two pivots. Izutsu discusses similarities in these ontological systems and advances the hypothesis that certain patterns of mystical and metaphysical thought may be shared even by systems with no apparent historical connection.

This second edition of Sufism and Taoism is the first published in the United States. The original edition, published in English and in Japan, was prized by the few English-speaking scholars who knew of it as a model in the field of comparative philosophy. Making available in English much new material on both sides of its comparison, Sufism and Taoism richly fulfills Izutsu's motivating desire "to open a new vista in the domain of comparative philosophy."

TARJUMAN AL-ASHWAQ Muhyiddin Ibn Al-Arabi (A) pp 155
The *Tarjuman al-Ashwaq* or *Interpreter of Desires* by Ibn Arabi is acknowledged as one of the major works in Sufi literature.

THE REFLECTIVE HEART: DISCOVERING SPIRITUAL INTELLIGENCE IN IBN ARABI'S MECCAN ILLUMINATIONS James Winston Morris (A) pp 424 For centuries Ibn Arabi has been considered the "Greatest Master" of Islamic spiritual teaching, but Western readers have only recently had access to his greatest writings. This introduction to Ibn Arabi's *Meccan Illuminations* highlights the mysticism and realization of Sufi spiritual life, providing an intellectually penetrating look without requiring specialized knowledge. The development of several key themes and modes of reflection in Ibn Arabi's spiritual teachings are explored as are the gradually unfolding meanings that distinguish this important classical text of Sufi practice.

TWENTY-NINE PAGES: INTRODUCTION TO IBN 'ARABI'S "METAPHYSICS OF UNITY" A.E. Affifi (A) pp 80

UNIVERSAL TREE AND THE FOUR BIRDS (MYSTICAL TREATISES OF MUHYIDDIN IBN ARABI) Muhyiddin Ibn Arabi (A), Angela Jaffray (T) pp 135 "In the history of monotheistic spirituality, in particular its Western, Abrahamic branch incorporating Judaism, Christianity, and Islam, there is really no one, from taproot to topmost leaf tip, like Muhyiddin Ibn Arabi. This short, lyrical and evocative book, with a conceptual spine strong as tensile steel, makes a rich perspective palpably real to the reader through the eloquence of its imagery and the uniqueness of its author's unforgettable voice."

UNIVERSAL TREE AND THE FOUR BIRDS THE SPIRITUAL LIFE AND THOUGHTS OF IBN AL-ARABI
Stephen Hirtenstein (A) pp 256 "By far the simplest and most heartwarming rendition of Ibn Arabi and his teachings that I have come across. A wonderful contribution to the integration of spirituality in our modern scientific thinking by making Ibn Arabi accessible to the popular mind." -- Amit Goswami, professor of Physics, University of Oregon, author of The Self-Aware Universe

CPSIA information can be obtained
at www.ICGtesting.com
Printed in the USA
FSOW03n0601041016
25557FS

PAKISTAN'S FOREIGN POLICY 1947–2019

A CONCISE HISTORY

FIFTH EDITION

PAKISTAN'S FOREIGN POLICY 1947–2019

A CONCISE HISTORY

FIFTH EDITION

ABDUL SATTAR

Foreword by Agha Shahi

OXFORD
UNIVERSITY PRESS

OXFORD
UNIVERSITY PRESS

Oxford University Press is a department of the University of Oxford. It furthers the University's objective of excellence in research, scholarship, and education by publishing worldwide. Oxford is a registered trade mark of Oxford University Press in the UK and in certain other countries

Published in Pakistan by
Oxford University Press
No. 38, Sector 15, Korangi Industrial Area,
PO Box 8214, Karachi-74900, Pakistan

First Edition published in 2006

Second Edition published in 2010

Third Edition published in 2013

Fourth edition in Oxford Pakistan Paperbacks 2017

Fifth Edition published in 2020

ISBN 978-0-19-070257-1

Fourth Impression 2022

Typeset in Minion Pro
Printed on 63gsm Offset Paper

Printed by Mas Printers, Karachi

Acknowledgements
Photo Courtesy: National Archives of Pakistan, Islamabad
Author's personal collection

Contents

Foreword

Gaining independence by the exercise of the principle of self-determination, the nascent state of Pakistan wished, as its founding father repeatedly said, to build friendly and cooperative relations with its neighbours. Idealistic in inspiration, the state's foreign policy had soon to come to grips, however, with the reality of the challenge to its right to peaceful coexistence. The failure of its own efforts and those of the United Nations for the settlement of disputes in the wake of Partition—in conformity with the principles of international law and justice—illustrated the tyranny of power disparity in the region.

In order to ameliorate the situation, Pakistan did what many other states in a similar predicament had done: it began to look outwards for friends and allies to support its own efforts to safeguard the independence, strengthen the security, and build the economic sinews of the infant state. Resistance to hegemony in the regional context complemented Pakistan's policy of opposition to the Soviet policy of expansionism and subversion. However, Pakistan was not motivated by the Cold War or ideological considerations, as illustrated by its policy to develop friendly relations with the People's Republic of China, disregarding the objections and sanctions by its partners in military alliances led by the United States of America.

The failure of the allies to come to Pakistan's assistance and the powerlessness of the United Nations to restrain India from intervention and aggression in East Pakistan in 1971 convinced Pakistan's leaders of the need to develop nuclear capability for the purpose of deterrence. This was an aim the Pakistani leadership pursued with single-minded determination in the face of discriminatory sanctions and pressures, willingly bearing the burdens and sacrifices resulting from the discontinuation of foreign assistance.

Through diligent research, Ambassador Abdul Sattar has recapitulated the rationale of these and other major policy decisions (including that of opposition to Soviet intervention in Afghanistan in 1979), in order to write what he calls 'a plain history'. He has delineated the objective strategic considerations on the basis of which the government and its leaders made fateful decisions. He also draws on personal knowledge as an official in the Ministry of Foreign Affairs in the 1980s, when the Geneva Accords were negotiated for the withdrawal of the Soviet forces from Afghanistan, and as foreign minister when Pakistan decided on a policy reappraisal in the wake of 9/11.

The scholarly work he has produced accomplishes his laudable purpose of writing an objective history of Pakistan's foreign policy. The book provides an authoritative account for students of foreign policy, observers, and analysts to understand the past and benefit from its lessons in formulating effective strategies for the realization of the aims and objectives of the state: to strengthen security and accelerate economic and social progress to achieve a position of dignity and self-respect in the comity of nations.

I commend *Pakistan's Foreign Policy* to students and scholars at home and abroad, as well as to members of the security and foreign policy establishment in Pakistan, as it will facilitate a deeper understanding of the strategic compulsions that have driven decision-making in Pakistan's national security and foreign policy. It will also serve to inculcate a sense of history in the younger generation of Pakistanis and heighten the consciousness of their national identity.

Agha Shahi
(former Foreign Minister of Pakistan)

Agha Shahi (1920–2006), Nishan-i-Imtiaz, *was a statesman and a career Foreign Service officer. A diplomat and technocrat by profession, he joined Foreign Service in 1951 and held important diplomatic assignments in the United States of America, China, and the United Nations. He remained Foreign Minister from 1977 to 1982 during the military government of President General Zia ul-Haq and served as Foreign Secretary from 1973 to 1977, when he was appointed Foreign Minister.*

He also served as Pakistan's Permanent Representative to the UN and represented Pakistan in the UN Security Council from 1968 to 1969. For more than a decade, he led Pakistan delegations to UN General Assembly sessions, conferences of the Non-Aligned Movement, and the Organization of Islamic Conference.

Preface to the Fifth Edition

The world has been transformed. A new President in the United States has fundamentally changed relations with friends and allies, and renounced multilateral conventions evolved through years of negotiations such as the Global Convention on Climate Change. He has discarded the fifteen years old Pakistan-US Alliance. The Nuclear Agreement worked out by Five Plus Two (Germany and European Union) with Iran which lifted a dark cloud from South-Western Asia has been disowned by the Trump administration. A new alliances has been formed between the US and Saudi Arabia against Iran. The Narendra Modi government in India suspended dialogue with Pakistan and adopted a 'fierce' stance; incidents of exchange of fire across the border and the Line of Control increased in frequency and took mounting toll of innocent lives.

A revised edition therefore became unavoidable. I am glad that despite my advancing age I have been able to update the text and include extensive sections bearing on Pakistan's relations with its neighbours with memorable impact on Pakistan's foreign policy. A major addition are the chapters on 'Afghanistan: Ethnicity and Politics', 'Pakistan-China, Enduring Entente', and a section on 'Trump's Pakistan-Afghanistan Policy'.

I hope the revised edition will benefit students of Pakistan's foreign policy.

Abdul Sattar
Islamabad, May 2019

Note to the Reader

Abdul Sattar (1931–2019): distinguished diplomat and author, passed away on 23 June 2019 in Islamabad.

On 5 August 2019, the Indian Government revoked Article 370 of the Indian Constitution that guaranteed special rights to the Muslim-majority state of Jammu and Kashmir.

In view of the fast changing events, the Publisher has added a section, '5 August 2019: Annexation of the Valley' in Chapter 15: 'Kashmir: The struggle for *Azadi*'.

Chapter 1

The Emergence of Pakistan

Historical Background

The late nineteenth century marked the beginning of a seminal transformation in the political evolution of South Asia with the penetration of modern ideas of nationalism and self-rule. Until then, different parts of the vast geographical region inhabited by indigenous people and settlers of diverse races and religions were ruled by whoever conquered their lands. More often, the region was an aggregation of kingdoms and princely states, with kaleidoscopic boundaries expanding and contracting with the rise and fall of dynasties.[1] Over the millennia, the rulers were as often local as foreign. Some came with waves of migrations, others as invaders, and most who came from Central Asia settled in the land.

Following Alexander's invasion across the Sulaiman Range in 325 BCE, Chandragupta Maurya[2] conquered the Indus and Gangetic plains. His descendant, Aśoka (273–232 BCE), built a great empire that extended from Afghanistan to Kalinga (Orissa), and after his conversion to Buddhism spread the new religion throughout the land. In 200 BCE, Bactrians, from their kingdom between the Hindu Kush range and Amu Darya, advanced to occupy the Upper Indus Valley. Two centuries later, they were supplanted by Central Asian Kushans who ruled the region from Peshawar, as their capital, till the fifth century. Kanishka (CE 120–162), the greatest of the Kushans, extended the realm from Kabul to Kashgar and Kashmir in the north, to Sindh in the south, and to the Gangetic plain in the east. The Gandhara region became a meeting place of Buddhist and Hellenist arts and cultures, leaving a legacy of glorious sculptures. After the raiding forays of White Huns in the fifth century, the region was conquered by the Gupta rulers of central India, who unleashed a Brahminical reaction that wiped out Buddhism from the land of its birth.

The Arabs penetrated South Asia via the Indus delta in the eighth century. After pirates along the Sindh coast pillaged ships carrying Muslim pilgrims, the Governor of Basra sent a force under Mohammad bin Qasim in 711 to Debul. Two years later, Multan became the first Muslim province in South Asia. In the late twelfth century, Muhammad Ghori, a Turkic ruler of Ghazni, extended his realm eastwards to Delhi. His successors, Iltutmish and Balban, ruled the northern plains during the thirteenth century. The Delhi Sultanate was taken over by Khilji and Tughlak dynasties until the end of the fourteenth century. Amir Timur marched his army through Afghanistan into Punjab, and plundered and sacked Delhi before returning to Samarkand in 1399. The Sayyids and the Lodhi Afghans subsequently re-established the Delhi Sultanate. In 1526, Babar led his army from Kabul to supplant the last Lodhi Sultan.

Zaheeruddin Babar, a descendant of Amir Temur, and heir to the small fief of Ferghana, aspired to revive the empire of his fourteenth century ancestor. He captured Samarkand twice but was defeated and driven across the Hindukush to Kabul. Receiving an invitation from the Governor of Punjab, he marched down the passes to capture the Delhi Sultanate in 1526, and from his new capital at Agra he extended his realm, laying the foundation of the great Mughal Empire that rose to its zenith under Shah Jehan in the seventeenth century. After Aurangzeb, the dynasty went into decline in the eighteenth century. Its fall was hastened by European empire-builders who scrambled to pick up the pieces. Defeating France and Portugal, Britain put the pieces together to rule the expanding realm through the East India Company, before assuming direct imperial rule after a coalition of the aggrieved local elite tried to wrest power back from the Company in the name of the Mughal titular emperor in 1857. Calling it mutiny, the British suppressed the challenge in a savage manner. The last Mughal emperor was exiled to Burma, and Britain then assumed the reins of government directly until 1947.

The Central Asian people, who came with the waves of migrations over the centuries, mixed with local people and developed a syncretist culture with Persian as the court language. Immigrant scholars preached the message of Islam and Sufi saints won a cross-religious following by their exemplary piety, noble conduct, and service to humanity. The Muslim rulers did not impose their religion on local inhabitants nor exclude local allies from positions in the army and administration, though, like others before them, they gave preference to kin and clansmen. After the British took control, Muslims became suspect and were not only supplanted by loyal non-Muslims but subjected to suppression, exclusion, and expropriation. They were further marginalized because of their refusal to reconcile and adjust to the loss of power.

Sir Syed Ahmad Khan (1817–98), social reformer and political visionary, discerned the dangers confronting his community, and embarked on a campaign to awaken and inspire the Muslim people to abandon the boycott of the foreign rulers and to acquire contemporary education. He also founded a school that grew into the Aligarh Muslim University, where learned academics, some of them from Europe, were employed to teach modern subjects and prepare the Muslim youth for gainful opportunities in the professions and for participation in the expanding political and economic life of the land.

As contemporary ideas of self-government and nationalism began to stimulate political thought in the latter part of the nineteenth century, different ethnic and religious communities projected their futures in terms of their interests. The Muslim community, comprising a quarter of the population in British India, awoke to its predicament, characterized by economic disparities and social exclusion. The future looked bleak as they faced the prospect of a powerless 'permanent minority'. British India, Sir Syed Ahmad Khan argued in 1883, was 'a continent in itself inhabited by vast populations of different races and different creeds' which lacked 'the community of race and creed [that] make the English people one and the same nation.'[3] The idea of nationhood captured the imagination of the Muslim community as its leaders discerned the looming danger of political domination across the religious and social fault line. At first, they sought legal and constitutional safeguards to secure and ensure an equitable share in social and political institutions.

The rift began to widen after the founding of the Indian National Congress in 1886 with Allan Octavian Hume, a British ex-official, as its first Secretary General for two decades. Dominated by the Hindu elite, the Congress attracted few Muslims as their leaders advised them to keep aloof from this nominally secular party that sought to supplant the British in positions of power and influence. To protect and promote the rights of the Muslim community, its leaders with modern education and political vision established the Muslim League in 1906. The issues were joined in 1909 when the Congress opposed the Muslim demand for separate electorates that would ensure representation for Muslims in the government. The two communities also clashed over the British government's decision in 1905 to create the new province of East Bengal and Assam, which brought some relief to the Muslim majority from the domination and exploitation by West Bengal. To the consternation of the Muslim League, the Congress successfully pressured the British government to annul the division in 1911. More enduring, and in the end insoluble, were constitutional issues, as the League proposed and Congress opposed safeguards for Muslims.

Mohammad Ali Jinnah, a brilliant barrister with impeccable anti-colonial credentials, successfully promoted a compromise package for the future constitution. The package known as the Lucknow Pact, after its approval by both the Congress and the League in 1916, included separate electorates, provincial autonomy, a one-third share for Muslims in the central assembly, and safeguards in respect of legislation affecting any of the religious communities. The Indian National Congress, however, went back on its commitment in 1928, when it adopted the Motilal Nehru Report, recommending replacement of separate electorates with a joint electorate and the curtailment of provincial autonomy, thus striking a fatal blow to any prospect of harmonious politics.

The Muslim League's struggle evolved through four stages. At first, it sought an equitable share in political and social life. During the second stage, the League's emphasis was on constitutional safeguards for Muslims in provinces where they were a minority. As political thought progressed, they sought autonomy for Muslim-majority provinces and then finally raised their sights to an independent state. A profound grasp of the history and aspirations of the Muslim people led the influential poet-philosopher Muhammad Iqbal to conclude, as early as 1930, that the formation of a Muslim state amalgamating the Punjab, North-West Frontier Province, Sindh, and Balochistan, 'appears to me to be the final destiny of the Muslims.'[4] He also urged

Mohammad Ali Jinnah, then living in London, to return, as he was 'the only Muslim in India today to whom the community has a right to ask for safe guidance.'[5]

Quaid-i-Azam Mohammad Ali Jinnah. Courtesy of the National Archives of Pakistan.

The cleavage between the League and the Congress widened following the elections in early 1937. The Congress exploited its triumph by excluding League members from participation in governments in the provinces, adopting symbols of the Hindu raj, and promoting the replacement of Urdu with Hindi. Muslim leaders, realizing the consequences of disunity and factional politics before the election, now closed ranks under Jinnah's leadership. He galvanized Muslims by laying before them a lucid vision of political salvation. Eminent Muslims and the Muslim media began to call him Quaid-i-Azam, Great Leader.[6] In 1938, he was authorized by the League to explore the possibility of a suitable alternative political structure which would completely safeguard the interests of Muslims and other minorities in India.[7] The Sindh Muslim League recommended the devising of a scheme for Muslims to attain full independence.

The Second World War accelerated the political evolution. 'The British wanted to win the war first and transfer power afterwards; the Congress demanded power at once, and a Hindu-Muslim settlement afterwards; the Muslims insisted on a Hindu-Muslim settlement first.'[8] On 23 March 1940, a historic resolution was proposed at the Lahore session of the Muslim League demanding 'that the areas in which Muslims are numerically in a majority, as in the North-Western and Eastern zones of India, should be grouped to constitute Independent States in which the constituent units shall be autonomous and sovereign.'[9] It was to go down in history as the 'Pakistan Resolution'.[10] Muslim students in England had first suggested the name in 1932.[11]

Enfeebled by the war, the British announced their intention to depart. The Congress demanded transfer of power, claiming the right of succession as the largest political party. The Muslim League reiterated its 'divide-and-quit' demand, asking the British to first agree to the creation of Pakistan in regions where Muslims constituted a majority. In a last attempt to realize their dream of preserving the unity of their Indian empire, the British Cabinet Mission in 1946 proposed a constitutional plan based on the division of British India into three autonomous zones with the powers of the centre to be limited to foreign affairs, defence, and communications. The League first accepted the plan but later rejected it, because the Congress leader, Jawaharlal Nehru, asserted his party 'regarded itself free to change or modify the Cabinet Mission plan as it thought best.'[12] With the plan thus undermined by the Congress refusal to guarantee the autonomy of the zones, the League reverted to the demand for the partition of British India into sovereign states.

The British government then proposed the Partition Plan. After hectic consultations and negotiations, it was accepted by the leaders of the Muslim League as well as the Indian National Congress, and announced on 3 June 1947. Pursuant to the agreement, Pakistan was established through the exercise of self-determination by the people of the Muslim-majority provinces and parts of provinces of the British Indian Empire, either in popular referenda or by the votes of the elected representatives of the people.

The Congress grudgingly agreed to the partition, and some of its leaders projected the economic collapse of Pakistan. No one epitomized the contradictions in the Congress more strikingly than its spiritual leader, Mahatma Gandhi. He agreed that partition was 'inevitable' but also declared, 'So long as I am alive, I will never agree to the partition of India'.[13] The Congress leadership accepted the 3rd June Plan, but the highest organ of the party, the All-India Congress Committee, quibbled in endorsing the decision. Its resolution professed that the Congress 'cannot think in terms of compelling the people in any territorial unit to remain in the Indian Union,' but in another sentence harked back to its view that 'the unity of India must be maintained.'[14] In another contradiction, the Congress emphasized the 'unity of India' but tried to undermine the unity of Pakistan by suggesting that 'the referendum in the North-West Frontier Province should provide for the people voting for independence.'[15]

Apart from the difficult and divisive legacy of pre-Independence political rivalry, adversarial perceptions of history, differences of religions and cultures, and the clash of political ideologies, deep bitterness was engendered by communal rioting. This led to the massacre of hundreds of thousands of innocent people and the exodus of some fifteen million people who moved from the country of their residence to seek refuge in the other. Further worsening of relations and the perpetuation of tension was owed, in particular, to the failure to resolve the disputes that arose after Independence.

The 3rd June Plan gave only seventy-two days for transition to independence. Within this period, three provinces had to be divided, referenda organized in North-West Frontier Province and the Sylhet division of Assam, civil and armed services personnel given the opportunity to decide which country they would serve, and assets apportioned. The telescoped timetable prepared at the behest of Governor General Mountbatten seemed tailor-made to create formidable problems for Pakistan, which, unlike India, inherited neither a capital with a functioning secretariat nor the resources to establish and equip the administrative, economic, and military institutions of the new state. More daunting problems soon arose in the wake of Partition.

NOTES

1. 'Sometimes all India was a patchwork quilt of states; sometimes empires as that of the Guptas prevailed over great areas.' H. G. Wells, *The Outline of History*, The Macmillan Company, New York, 1921.
2. He was 'helped in his intrigue by an astute Brahmin of the name of Chanakya or Kautilya.' H. G. Rawlinson, *India*, Frederick and Praeger, New York, 1952, 65.
3. Speech in the Legislative Assembly, extract cited by Chaudhri Muhammad Ali, *The Emergence of Pakistan*, Columbia University Press, 11.
4. In his address to the annual session of the Muslim League at Allahabad, 1930, Iqbal said, 'I would like to see the Punjab, North-West Frontier Province, Sind, and Baluchistan amalgamated into a single State. Self-government within the British empire or without the British empire, the formation of a consolidated North-West Muslim State appears to me to be the final destiny of the Muslims, at least of North-West India.' Shamloo, *Speeches and Statements of Iqbal*, Al-Manar Academy, Lahore, 1948, 11–12.
5. Letter of Iqbal to Jinnah.
6. Although admiring Muslims and media called him by this honorific earlier, the Muslim League first used the title in 1937. Sharif Al Mujahid, *Quaid-i-Azam Jinnah*, Quaid-i-Azam Academy, Karachi, 1981, 41.
7. Resolution of the Muslim League, December 1938.
8. Chaudhri Muhammad Ali, *The Emergence of Pakistan*, Columbia University Press, New York, 1967.
9. The resolution states: 'No constitutional plan would be workable or acceptable to Muslims unless it is designed on the following basic principle, namely that geographically contiguous units are demarcated into regions which should be so constituted, with such territorial adjustments as may be necessary, that the areas in which the Muslims are numerically in a majority as in the north-western and eastern zones of India should be grouped to constitute independent States in which the constituent units shall be autonomous and sovereign.' Text quoted in Chaudhri Muhammad Ali, op. cit., 38.

10. The ambiguity was clarified by the Quaid-i-Azam. When asked whether the resolution asked for one or two states, he said 'one'. The next day newspapers referred to it as the 'Pakistan Resolution'. Stanley Wolpert, *Jinnah of Pakistan*, Oxford University Press, New York, 1984, 185.
11. The signatories of the pamphlet *Now or Never* were Mohammad Aslam Khattak, President Khyber Union, Choudhary Rahmat Ali, Inayatullah Khan (of Charsadda), and Sheikh Mohammad Sadiq of Mongrol, Kathiawar. They conceived the name Pakistan by combining P for the Punjab, A for Afghania (a synonym then for land of Pathans), K for Kashmir, S for Sindh and TAN for Baluchistan. Mohammad Aslam Khan Khattak, *A Pathan Odyssey*, Oxford University Press, Karachi, 2004, 15, 264.
12. Ibid., 67.
13. Abul Kalam Azad, *India Wins Freedom,* Orient Longman, Delhi, 185, 187.
14. Moin Zaidi and Shaheda Zaidi, eds., *The Encyclopaedia of the Indian National Congress*, S. Chand & Co., New Delhi, Vol. 13, 111.
15. Government of India records quoted in Chaudhri Muhammad Ali, 152.

CHAPTER 2

Foreign Policy Beginnings

Pakistan emerged onto the world stage on 14 August 1947, after a two-pronged struggle: first, for independence from colonial rule, and second, for freedom for the people of Muslim-majority areas from the looming threat of economic, social, and political domination by another people manifestly dismissive of their urge to preserve their separate identity. Neither British nostalgia for maintaining the unity of the 'Jewel in the Crown' nor the ambition of the Indian National Congress to step into the shoes of the departing colonial power conformed to the imperatives of the dawning era of self-determination and self-rule. The Muslim League had to wage a long, and at times bitter, political battle, but the issue was ultimately resolved through agreement. The British and the Congress leaders conceded the League's demand for the creation of two independent states to succeed the Indian Empire. Pakistan came into existence through the explicit exercise of the right of self-determination. The people of Muslim-majority parts of British India voted directly in referenda or through their elected representatives to join the new state.[1]

The foreign policy of Pakistan was to be moulded in the crucible of interaction with its neighbour India, but it was imbued from the start with the idealistic vision of the state's founding fathers. Quaid-i-Azam[2] Mohammad Ali Jinnah, the first head of the new state, was a man of ideals and integrity, committed to the principles of peace with faith and confidence in human capacity to resolve differences through the application of logic and law. Another exemplar was Liaquat Ali Khan, a barrister who became secretary general of the Muslim League in the 1930s and the first prime minister of Pakistan. He believed, like Jinnah, that Pakistan should be a progressive, democratic polity founded on Islamic principles of social welfare, religious tolerance, and the equal rights of all citizens. The first foreign minister, Zafrullah Khan, was a jurist of repute and

Chaudhry Sir Zafrullah Khan (first Foreign Minister of Pakistan). Courtesy of the National Archives of Pakistan.

throughout his tenure sought to promote the resolution of international disputes in conformity with the principles of the United Nations Charter.

The nation's mentors were dedicated, practical men, with implicit faith in the Muslim community's capacity to end stagnation and build a better future. An early titan was Sir Syed Ahmad Khan, who believed in the acquisition of 'education in its modern sense' to promote 'equal and proportionate progress' for all people. Mohammad Iqbal, a humanist scholar with profound insights into Islamic as well as western history and philosophy, rejected the concept of predestination and advocated constant human striving to shape a better destiny for mankind. His inspiring poetry, widely read in the early twentieth century, sought to inculcate the spirit of dynamism in society. Holding out the vision of Islam as a progressive faith, Iqbal argued in favour of revival and the active use of the Islamic doctrine of *Ijtihad* as a means of adaptation of temporal laws to resolve the social dilemmas arising from progress in science and industry.[3]

The Founding Father's Vision

In the one year he lived after the establishment of Pakistan, Jinnah laid the foundations of so many institutions and proclaimed principles of enduring value in so many diverse affairs of state—ranging from administrative, fiscal, and economic to constitution-making and formulation of foreign policy—that people marvel at his genius as well as feel more acutely the sense of loss at the all-too-brief time providence allowed him to guide the new state.

Manifest in the views Jinnah articulated is a modern intellect with a firm commitment to fundamental principles indispensable for the maintenance and promotion of international peace, progress, and prosperity of humankind, illustrated in the following excerpts from his speeches:

> There lies in front of us a new chapter and it will be our endeavour to create and maintain goodwill and friendship with Britain and our neighbourly dominion, Hindustan, along with other sisterly nations so that we all together may make our greatest contribution for the peace and prosperity of the world.[4]

> Our foreign policy is one of friendliness and goodwill towards all the nations of the world. We do not cherish aggressive designs against any country or nation. We believe in the principle of honesty and fair play in national and international dealings and are prepared to make the utmost contribution to the promotion of peace and prosperity among the nations of the world. Pakistan will never be found lacking in extending its material and moral support to the oppressed and suppressed people of the world and in upholding the principles of the United Nations Charter.[5]
>
> There is nothing that we desire more ardently than to live in peace and let others live in peace, and develop our country according to our own lights without outside interference, and improve the lot of the common man.[6]

Jinnah's concept of Pakistan as a Muslim, liberal, democratic, and modern nation-state naturally predisposed him in favour of close relations with democratic countries. During the Second World War, the Muslim League decided, under his leadership, to support the Allies against the Fascist powers. Jinnah paid special tribute to the United States of America as having 'acted as a beacon of light and had in no small measure served to give inspiration to nations who like us were striving for independence and freedom from the shackles of foreign rule.'[7] Equally warm were his words for the French ideals of liberty, fraternity, and equality.

The Soviet Union's record of rapid economic progress and its foreign policy of opposition to colonialism and imperialism impressed all educated people. The Soviet system, however, was unattractive to League leaders because of its restrictions on freedom, atheist ideology, and sponsorship of subversion in other countries.

Pakistan was, at first, averse to becoming involved in the ideological contest between the emergent blocs led by the US and the Soviet Union. As Liaquat Ali Khan said, the state started 'without any narrow and special commitments and without any prejudices in the international sphere.'[8] It was 'neither tied to the apron strings of the Anglo-American bloc nor was it a camp-follower of the communist bloc.'[9] Foreign Minister Zafrullah Khan echoed the same thought saying Pakistan followed the principle of 'Friendship towards all states, but with regard to each individual question, standing on the side of fairness and subject to that, to help and succour the weak.'[10]

Sharing an overarching sense of community with other Muslim peoples of the world, Pakistan remained true to the tradition of solidarity of the Muslim people of British India with the just causes of fraternal nations. Records of the Muslim League since the early twentieth century are replete with resolutions voicing deep concern over the injustices done by European powers to the Ottomans and the Arab countries, and extending support to the causes of the people of Turkey and Palestine. An admirer of Mustafa Kemal Ataturk, after Independence Jinnah recalled the 'deep sympathy and interest' with which the fortunes of Turkey were followed 'right from the birth of political consciousness among the Muslims of [British] India.'[11]

Preoccupied with developments in South Asia, the Quaid did not allow the political conflict of the pre-Independence period to cloud his vision. He transcended the bitter legacy and looked with hope and anticipation to future relations with Britain and India.

Proud of having achieved Pakistan 'peacefully by moral and intellectual force',[12] Pakistani leaders hoped that law and reason would govern relations between Pakistan and India. Jinnah expressed the hope that both countries would adhere to the principles of equity and justice and build peaceful and cooperative relations to the mutual benefit of their people. He said:

> Our object should be peace within and peace without. We want to live peacefully and maintain cordial and friendly relations with our immediate neighbours and with the world at large. . . . We stand by the United Nations Charter and will gladly make our full contribution to the peace and prosperity of the world.[13]

In another statement, Jinnah said:

> It is of vital importance to Pakistan and India as independent, sovereign states to collaborate in a friendly way to jointly defend their frontiers, both on land and sea, against any aggression. But this depends entirely on whether India and Pakistan can resolve their own differences. If we can put own house in order internally, then we may be able to play a very great part externally in all international affairs. The Indian Government should shed their superiority complex and deal with Pakistan on an equal footing and fully appreciate the realities.[14]

The bonds of geography were of obvious importance in relations also with other neighbours. Iran was a friend and brother; so was Afghanistan. Despite Kabul's challenge to the boundary agreement it had signed with the British Indian government as far back as 1893, Jinnah hoped that Pakistan and Afghanistan would soon 'secure and strengthen' the goodwill and friendship between the two fraternal nations. Similarly, he expressed 'warmest goodwill' towards Sri Lanka.

The Enduring Relevance of Principles

The thread that runs through the statements of Pakistani leaders—and which has a timeless value—is that the interests of Pakistan are best served by upholding the universally recognized principles of international law codified in the Charter of the United Nations. Their observance by all states, large or small, more or less powerful, is indispensable for the preservation of international peace and the promotion of cooperation among nations, to their mutual benefit.

Just as an individual cannot achieve fulfilment in isolation from the nation to which he or she belongs, a state too has to seek its destiny in cooperation with the world community. The successes as well as the failures of our foreign policy can be traced by whether or not it earned the nation a place of respect in the international mainstream. A policy that leads to isolation is inimical to the interests particularly of middle and small powers.

Friendship between states, as between individuals, is dependent on reciprocity, mutual goodwill, and respect for equity and justice. It cannot be promoted by attempts on the part of one to dominate or impose unilateral preference on the other. The UN Charter calls for peaceful settlement of disputes consistent with the principles of justice and international law. The Quaid reiterated that principle in offering friendship and collaboration with India.

In the catalogue of enduring principles enunciated by the Quaid-i-Azam, it is necessary also to mention his views on human rights, the state's responsibility towards citizens, and the obligation of citizens to be loyal to their state. In a speech to the Constituent Assembly on 11 August 1947, he said, 'You may belong to any religion, caste or creed—that has nothing to do with the business of the state. We are starting with the fundamental principle that we are all citizens, and equal citizens of one state.'[15] Remarkable for its perspicacious recognition of the implications of the transition from his role as leader of a political party to that of head of state, the speech symbolized an intellectual leap—so far his primary concern had been the future of the Muslim people; now it would be all citizens of the state. The nation henceforth was all the people of Pakistan, irrespective of their religion.

Characteristically, Jinnah was consistent in giving the same message to Muslims who remained in India. Four months later, at the last session of the Muslim League as its leader, he endorsed the bifurcation of the party. The meeting decided: 'It is obvious that the Musalmans of Pakistan and India can no longer have one and the same political organization.' The Muslims of India would no longer be guided from any source outside and they would aspire to equal rights and obligations as loyal citizens of India.

Giving Muslims of minority provinces the credit for the establishment of Pakistan, Jinnah told the session, 'Pakistan is going to be a Muslim State based on Islamic ideals. It is not going to be an ecclesiastical State. In Islam there is no discrimination as far as citizenship is concerned.'[16] In affirming the principle of equality of citizens, Jinnah emulated the precedent set by the first Islamic state in the *Misaq-i-Madinah* that provided for equal rights for all people, Muslims as well as Jews, Madinites as well as those who migrated from Makkah.[17]

Jinnah's vision of human rights anticipated the Universal Declaration of Human Rights. Adopted a year later, it proclaimed the principle:

> Everyone is entitled to all the rights and freedoms set forth in this Declaration, without distinction of any kind, such as race, colour, sex, language, religion, political or other opinion, national or social origin, property, birth or other status.

From the very beginning, Pakistan's foreign policy upheld the fundamental principles of international law, especially respect for independence, non-aggression, and non-interference in internal affairs as an indispensable condition for peace and progress. It extended goodwill towards all states and support for the legitimate causes of peoples, the cherishing of fraternal bonds with other Muslim nations and the desire for cooperation with all other states, especially its neighbours.

The Shadow of Partition

With the emergence of Pakistan and India as independent states, by mutual consent of the leaders of major political parties, old political controversies were relegated and the emphasis shifted instead to building peaceful coexistence and good-neighbourly cooperation, to the mutual benefit of the two. Jinnah urged such a course, but the transition from chequered past to beckoning future could not be achieved by Pakistan alone.

The Indian National Congress accepted the partition officially, but the resolution adopted by the Central Working Committee declared, 'The picture of India we have learned to cherish will remain in our hearts and minds.' Sardar Patel was 'convinced that the new state of Pakistan was not viable and could not last.'[18] Three days before the 3rd June Plan, Gandhi had declared, 'Even if the whole of India burns, we shall not concede Pakistan' and then, changing his mind a few days later, said, 'The two parts of India would ultimately reunite!'[19]

As the leaders of Pakistan grappled with the monumental task of establishing the government of the new state in a new capital, in the midst of myriad challenges, they were sustained by the strength of their faith and the support of the nation. Meanwhile, the civil administration and armed forces of British India were still in the process of division, and resources were meagre as India delayed or withheld Pakistan's share of financial and other assets. Complex partition problems were compounded by the unfair boundary award and the unanticipated tide of millions of refugees fleeing communal riots of unprecedented magnitude. Relations between the two countries got off to an inauspicious start and tensions mounted as unforeseen disputes darkened the South Asian horizon.[20]

Agreement on the division of the assets and liabilities of British India provided for a 17.5 per cent share for Pakistan, but India stalled implementation. The transfer of cash balances amounting to Rs 750 million was delayed for months, causing severe difficulties for Pakistan. Of the other assets, India 'dishonestly retained much of Pakistan's share.'[21] Of Pakistan's share of 165,000 tons of defence stores, India had transferred only 4,730 tons by 31 March 1948, and another 18,000 tons by 10 September 1949, expropriating the balance of 142,000 tons.[22] In contrast, Pakistan promptly transferred ninety fighter aircraft that were India's share. Indian leaders 'persistently tried to obstruct the work of partition of the armed forces'.[23] 'What mattered to them, above all else, was to cripple and thwart the establishment of Pakistan as a viable independent state.'[24]

Demarcation of boundaries in Punjab and Bengal was entrusted to the Boundary Commission headed by Cyril Radcliffe, a British jurist. Its mandate required it to do so 'on the basis of ascertaining the contiguous majority areas of Muslims and non-Muslims.' While it could also take into account 'other factors', it was expected to be just and impartial. But Radcliffe yielded to Governor General Mountbatten's pressure and awarded several Muslim-majority areas to India, including two *tehsils* (subdivisions) of Gurdaspur district providing it access to the state of Jammu and Kashmir.[25] Jinnah called the award 'unjust, incomprehensible, and even perverse' but urged, 'As an honourable people we must abide by it.'[26] Already in Nehru's thrall, Mountbatten had earlier helped promote Nehru's designs on Kashmir in his talks with the Maharaja in Srinagar. He was now indebted to Nehru for retaining him as governor general of independent India.

Apart from providing India with a road link to Kashmir via Jammu, the unjust boundary award, announced on 17 August 1947, three days after Pakistan's independence, added fuel to the raging fire of communal violence. Despite calls for the maintenance of peace by Jinnah and Gandhi, communal riots escalated as the partition was being effected. Although acts of savagery took place on both sides, the policy of the rulers of the princely states of Patiala and Kapurthala was particularly virulent. They unleashed local forces to kill and expel Muslim inhabitants. In a matter of weeks they liquidated the Muslim population of some 700,000. They also sent armed men to Jammu and Kashmir to assist the Dogra forces of this state in unleashing terror. Within weeks, a quarter of a million Muslims were 'systematically exterminated'.[27]

Suddenly, in April 1948, India cut off the water in the irrigation canals that flowed from headworks on the rivers Ravi and Sutlej, menacing agriculture in Pakistan. Ignoring principles of international law governing international rivers, it claimed 'seigniorage' charges for the water flowing to Pakistan. Facing the ruin of agriculture in the affected areas, Pakistan submitted under duress.

Tension between Pakistan and India built up as disputes between the two countries multiplied. Pakistan sought their resolution on the basis of law and equity, willing to accept impartial settlement. India, however, was intent from the start to impose its unilateral preferences. The divergence was aggravated by India's primordial inclination as a more powerful state to exploit power disparity to its advantage.

The Muslim World

For seven hundred years after the establishment of the first Muslim state in the seventh century, the dynamic Islamic civilization contributed to unprecedented advances in all fields of human endeavour, achieving glorious heights in arts and architecture, and extending the frontiers of knowledge in philosophy and historiography, geography and astronomy, mathematics and medicine, trade and commerce. Expanding across the continents of Asia and Africa, it established its sway also in parts of Europe, and contributed to its renaissance. Following the devastating invasions of the Mongols, the Muslim power declined, and by the eighteenth century, European empires colonized large parts of its former territories.

During its own freedom struggle, the Muslim League followed a policy of solidarity with other Muslim nations. Jinnah voiced the anguish of the Muslim people at the 'enormities' of European powers, which, following a policy of aggression, broke up the 'sacred land of the Crescent and Star and the blue and golden Bosphorus.' He advocated the cause of the Khilafat as the custodian of the holy places of Islam. Kemal Ataturk's heroic role in defending the Turkish homeland inspired the Muslim people in South Asia. Jinnah called him 'the greatest Musalman in the modern Islamic world.' Another issue that distressed the Muslim community was the injustice perpetrated on the people of Palestine. Addressing a meeting in Mumbai in 1945, Jinnah said, 'I have no enmity against the Jews. . . . But why should the Arabs be dumped with such a large number of Jews?'

As Governor General of Pakistan, he sent a cable to President Truman in December 1947 conveying Pakistan's 'shock at the UN General Assembly's decision to partition Palestine.'[28]

Support for the just causes of Muslim nations remained a priority objective of Pakistan's foreign policy. At the United Nations and other forums, Pakistan raised its voice in support of independence of Indonesia, Libya, Morocco, Sudan, Tunisia, and other former colonies. Spokesmen of some of these nations were given Pakistani passports to travel internationally to solicit the world community's support for their freedom struggle.

Pakistan's policy towards the Muslim world was motivated by an earnest desire for close cooperation in all fields in the belief it would accelerate the process of economic development and social reconstruction. Its leaders advocated collaboration in fields of science and technology, which was the key to progress in all fields. Pakistan even contemplated pooling of resources in order to strengthen mutual security.

Upon independence, Pakistan developed close relations with most Muslim countries, especially Iran and Turkey. The Shahanshah was the first head of state to visit Pakistan and was given a memorable welcome by enthusiastic crowds. Turkey, aware of the history of support by South Asia's Muslims and their admiration of Kemal Ataturk, responded with cordiality. Indonesia was impressed by Pakistan's support for its struggle. Saudi Arabia, the cradle of Islam, wished 'the new Muslim State great prosperity and progress'[29] and ever since has remained a fraternal friend and constant supporter. Pakistan's championship of the Palestinian cause evoked appreciation in the Arab world.

The start was promising. Pakistan hosted a number of conferences of representatives of Muslim peoples to deliberate on issues of common concern. While many appreciated the initiatives, others were less enthusiastic. Differences in policies emerged with the rise of Arab nationalism that emphasized the Arab bond virtually to the exclusion of non-Arab Muslim states. While Egypt leaned towards the Soviet Union for support against the UK and USA, Pakistan's security imperatives drove it into alliance with those powers. The Baghdad Pact provoked strong Arab denunciation on the additional ground that Iraq's membership was divisive of Arab unity. Pakistan's role at the first London conference on the Suez crisis further antagonized Arab sentiment against Pakistan.

Afghanistan

Pakistan looked forward to close, fraternal and good-neighbourly relations with Afghanistan, with which it shares multiple ties of geography and history, ethnicity, and culture. The economic interests of the two countries are intertwined. Pakistan provides access to sea for landlocked Afghanistan, which in turn is a bridge from Pakistan to Central Asia. Unfortunately, relations were clouded at the start as the Afghan government challenged the validity of the 1893 Anglo-Afghan treaty establishing the Durand Line as the boundary between Afghanistan and British India. Signed by Amir (King) Abdur Rahman Khan and reconfirmed in Anglo-Afghan treaties of 1905, 1919, and 1921, the treaty explicitly prohibited cross-border interference. But Kabul tried to fish in the troubled water as the British withdrawal became evident. In May 1947 the Afghan Foreign Minister argued 'As long as the British Government remained responsible for the control of the Frontier; the Afghans had nothing to say.' But now Kabul expressed 'concern at the possible fate' of the people of NWFP and demanded that they should be given an opportunity to decide whether they wished to 'rejoin' Afghanistan or form a separate independent state.[30]

In June 1947, the *Khudai Khidmatgar* leader, Khan Abdul Ghaffar Khan joined the fray, with backing from Mahatma Gandhi to demand an opportunity for the people of North West Frontier Province (NWFP) to choose 'a free Pathan state.' After that idea too, was rejected by the British government, he announced boycott of the referendum in which the people of the province voted overwhelmingly to join Pakistan.

On 30 September 1947, Afghanistan voted against Pakistan's admission to the United Nations. Graciously, it withdrew the negative vote twenty days later. Speaking on the occasion, Pakistan's Ambassador M.A.H. Ispahani, expressed the hope that the Afghan statement 'reflects more accurately the feeling of fraternity, friendship, and good-neighbourliness which exist between Pakistan and

Afghanistan.' That pronouncement proved prophetic as relations between the fraternal neighbours continued to develop in peace and cooperation.

In 1948, the elderly Ghaffar Khan explained that he had only wanted the province to be renamed 'Pakhtunistan'— the land of the Pashtun people—as the other provinces of Pakistan are named after the language of the people—Punjabi, Sindhi and Balochi. In 2010, his wish was fulfilled. At the initiative of the ruling Awami National Party in the province headed by Ghaffar Khan's grandson, Asfandyar Wali Khan, the NWFP was renamed Khyber Pakhtunkhwa—Khyber, land of Pakhtuns. The Durand Line boundary with Afghanistan was not affected.

NOTES

1. The Sindh assembly and representatives of Muslim-majority districts in Bengal and Punjab assemblies voted to join Pakistan. In Balochistan, a *Shahi Jirga* and members of the Quetta municipality decided unanimously to join Pakistan. In NWFP, Congress and Red Shirts boycotted the referendum, but 289,244 votes, representing 51 per cent of the total electorate, were cast in favour of Pakistan. Tribal *jirgas* declared in meetings held by Governor Cunningham, and confirmed in writing, that they were part of Pakistan. *See* 'The Tribal Areas' in Chaudhri Muhammad Ali, *The Emergence of Pakistan*, Columbia University Press, New York, 1967, 163–6.
2. The title given by the admiring nation during the freedom struggle means 'Great Leader'.
3. Allama Mohammed Iqbal's *Reconstruction of Religious Thought in Islam*, the key to his ideas on reformation, advocated that *Ijtihad* in modern times could be entrusted to elected members of parliament. Limited to temporal issues concerning *mu'amilaat* (worldly affairs) innovations would not relate to *ibadaat* (theological affairs). *See* Javid Iqbal's lecture on Iqbal's anniversary, *Dawn*, Islamabad, 10 November 2004.
4. Mohammad Ali Jinnah, *Speeches as Governor General, 1947–48*, Ferozsons, Karachi, 11.
5. Ibid., 65.
6. Ibid., 62.
7. Ibid., 67.
8. Prime Minister Liaquat Ali Khan, quoted in S. M. Burke and Lawrence Ziring, *Pakistan's Foreign Policy,* Oxford University Press, Karachi, Second Edition, 1990, from Sarwar Hasan, *Pakistan Horizon*, 4 December 1951.
9. S. M. Burke and Lawrence Ziring, *Pakistan's Foreign Policy,* Oxford University Press, Karachi, 1990, quoting from *Dawn*, Karachi, 9 March 1955.

10. Zafrullah Khan, Constituent Assembly Debates, 1948 (821).
11. Jinnah, *Speeches*, 32.
12. Radio broadcast, 31 August 1947. *Jinnah Papers*, ed. Z. H. Zaidi, Quaid-i-Azam Papers Project, Islamabad, Vol. VI, 1.
13. Statement on 11 March 1948.
14. Jinnah *Speeches*, 45.
15. *Jinnah Papers*, Vol. VI, 446–50.
16. Sharif Al Mujahid, *Dawn*, Islamabad, 26 December 2004.
17. Ibid.
18. Abul Kalam Azad, op. cit., 207.
19. *The Times*, London, of 5 June 1947, quoted in G. W. Choudhury, *Pakistan's Relations with India*, 84.
20. For information on the partition period, the author greatly benefited from Chaudhri Mohammad Ali, *The Emergence of Pakistan*, Columbia University Press, New York, 1967; S. M. Burke and Lawrence Ziring, *Pakistan's Foreign Policy*, Oxford University Press, Karachi, 1990; and G. W. Choudhury, *Pakistan's Relations with India, 1947–1966*, Pall Mall Press, London, 1967.
21. Ian Stephens, *Horned Moon*, Chatto and Windus, London, 1954, 215.
22. G. W. Choudhury, op. cit., 62.
23. John Connell, *Auchinleck*, 915–18.
24. Ibid., 220–2.
25. Others included Ferozepur, Zira, and Fazilka, which had a Muslim majority and most importantly included the Fazilka Headworks that controlled canals on the Sutlej, which irrigated lands on the Pakistan side.
26. Jinnah, *Speeches*, op. cit., 32.
27. *The Times*, London, 17 October 1947.
28. Noorani, A. G., 'The Durand Line Revisited,' *Criterion Quarterly*, January-March 2015. *Pak-Afghan Discord: A Historical Perspective, 1855-1979*, Pakistan Studies Centre, University of Karachi, 1990.
29. Ibid.
30. Ibid.

Chapter 3

The Kashmir Question, 1947–1957

The Dispute

The state of Jammu and Kashmir was one of some 500 quasi-autonomous princely states which exercised varying degrees of internal autonomy on the basis of treaties and agreements made during the period of colonial penetration, and recognized Britain as their suzerain. The British Indian Independence Act of 1947 affirmed the lapse of British suzerainty over the states. Theoretically, the states regained their sovereignty. However, the British Secretary of State for India clarified 'We do not, of course, propose to recognize any states as separate international entities.' Governor General Mountbatten advised the rulers of states to accede to India or Pakistan bearing in mind 'You cannot run away from the dominion government which is your neighbour any more than you can run away from the subjects for whose welfare you are responsible.' The British stance conformed to the partition principle and all but three of the five hundred states—Junagadh, Jammu & Kashmir, and Hyderabad—followed the British advice. In deference to the wishes of the Nizam of Hyderabad, Pakistan supported his preference for independence. Pakistan and India, however, adopted contradictory stances. When on 15 August 1947, the Muslim Nawab of Hindu-majority Junagadh announced accession to Pakistan; the Indian government protested arguing that the ruler's decision was 'in utter violation of the principle on which partition was agreed upon and effected.' Pakistan agreed to a referendum but India invaded and occupied the state. Meanwhile, India had no compunction in violating the partition principle in regard to Jammu and Kashmir. A majority of the state's population—77 per cent—was Muslim but its Hindu maharaja was instigated by New Delhi to first delay a decision and then on 26 October 1947 to announce accession to India. New Delhi instantly flew a military contingent to occupy Srinagar and large parts of the State's territory while pretending it had accepted the accession provisionally subject to the approval of the population. The Nizam of Hyderabad preferred independence, but India invaded and occupied the Hindu-majority state in 1948.[4]

Earlier, on 25 July 1947, Governor General Mountbatten had advised the princes to accede to Pakistan or India. This advice was consistent with the principle underlying the Partition Plan of 3rd June. On the basis of this principle the Indian National Congress had insisted on the partition of the provinces of Assam, Bengal, and Punjab.

All the princely states except Hyderabad, Jammu and Kashmir, and Junagadh followed the principle of partition and acceded to India or Pakistan.

The Maharaja's decision to accede to India followed events that testify to a pre-conceived design. In June 1947, two months before independence, Nehru betrayed his mind in a note to Mountbatten arguing: 'The normal and obvious course appears to be for Kashmir to join the Constituent Assembly of India,' falsely stating, 'This will satisfy both the popular demand and the Maharaja's wishes.'[5] Gandhi visited Srinagar in July and held talks with the Maharaja. After the meeting, the Maharaja appointed a chief minister who openly advocated accession to India.[6] Mountbatten connived in the Indian design on Kashmir by influencing Sir Cyril Radcliffe, the supposedly impartial chairman of the Punjab Boundary Commission, to award two Muslim-majority *tehsils* (subdivisions) of Gurdaspur district to India.

The ruler of Jammu and Kashmir, Maharaja Hari Singh, was notorious for his oppressive rule. Whilst decisions were being made on the partition plan, he incarcerated prominent leaders of the two major political parties, the All Jammu and Kashmir Muslim Conference, the most important Muslim party in the state and an ally of the Muslim League, and the National Conference, a secularist ally of the Indian National Congress.

Popular opinion in Jammu and Kashmir made its preference clear. The Muslim Conference adopted a resolution in July 1947 in favour of accession to Pakistan. Majority opinion, even in the National Conference, was also said to be of the same view, but it was decided to postpone a decision until its leader, Sheikh Abdullah, could be consulted. No political party favoured accession to India. Pakistan's independence day was enthusiastically celebrated in Srinagar with flags. The Maharaja ordered the flags torn down and closed down all pro-Pakistan newspapers.[7]

The Maharaja had other plans. First, he delayed the decision on accession and offered to sign a 'standstill' agreement with Pakistan and India.[8] Prior to this, in late July, he had ordered Muslims to deposit any arms they possessed with the state authorities. He strengthened garrisons in areas where rebellion was suspected. Assisted by elements of state forces sent by the Sikh rulers of Patiala and Kapurthala, who had already acceded to India, plus armed volunteers of the militant Hindu RSS, the Dogra force of the Maharaja 'wantonly plundered whole areas inhabited by Muslims and set fire to their homes.'[9]

Popular suspicion of the Maharaja's intentions was corroborated by his actions. Demonstrations were held in Poonch and Mirpur, and on 17 August, Sardar Abdul Qayyum Khan and his companions declared a revolt. Soon, 60,000 ex-soldiers who had served in the British army during the Second World War joined the revolt. In September, a freedom movement was launched by Sardar Mohammad Ibrahim Khan. It later established the Azad government of Jammu and Kashmir in the liberated territory.

In pursuit of his design, the Maharaja singled out Sheikh Mohammad Abdullah for release from jail on 29 September in response to Nehru's repeated demand. Abdullah immediately started a pro-India campaign. Addressing a public meeting he was permitted to hold in Hazaribagh on 5 October, he said, 'We will naturally go to that dominion where our own demand for freedom receives recognition and support.' That dominion, he left no doubt, was not Pakistan.[10]

Meanwhile, the Maharaja's forces embarked on a campaign of massacres and mass evictions, evidently designed to reduce the Muslim majority in the state. More than half a million people were driven out across the border towards Pakistan. In Jammu province, where Muslims were 61 per cent of the population, 200,000 Muslims were exterminated, and in some of the districts, the majority was reduced to a minority.

The plight of the Muslims evoked strong sympathy in Pakistan. The Government of Pakistan sent strong protests to the Maharaja but with little effect. To save their Kashmiri brethren from extermination, Afridi and Mahsud tribesmen from Tirah and Waziristan formed a *lashkar* and entered Kashmir on 22 October. Although they made short shrift of the state forces, they unfortunately displayed poor discipline, and killed a number of Christian missionaries in Baramula. By 26 October, they were on the outskirts of Srinagar but were diverted by looting.

New Delhi reacted instantly. The Indian Defence Committee had already met on 25 October and decided to rush arms aid to Kashmir. On Governor General Mountbatten's advice, it decided to first secure the state's accession. Secretary V. P. Menon flew to Kashmir and claimed to have obtained the signatures of the Maharaja on the document on 26 October. At the same time, the Maharaja set up an interim government and asked Sheikh Abdullah to join the state prime minister to carry out the responsibilities. On 27 October, Mountbatten accepted the accession. On the same day, the Indian air force flew paratroops to Srinagar. Pakistan lacked military strength to counter the Indian use of force, as India had withheld the transfer of Pakistan's entire share of the ordnance.

In an attempt to camouflage the 'utter violation' of the principles of the partition, the Indian government erected a smokescreen of promises to the people of Kashmir and the Government of Pakistan, Mountbatten stated in the letter of acceptance of the Maharaja's offer of accession:

> Consistently with their policy that, in the case of any state where the issue of accession has been the subject of dispute, the question of accession should be decided in accordance with the wishes of the people of that state, it is my Government's wish that as soon as law and order have been restored in Kashmir and her soil cleared of the invader, the question of the state's accession should be settled by a reference to the people.

Also, on the same day, Nehru sent a telegram to Liaquat Ali Khan:

> I should like to make it clear that the question of aiding Kashmir in this emergency is not designed in any way to influence the state to accede to India. Our view which we have repeatedly made public is that the question in any disputed territory or state must be decided in accordance with the wishes of people and we adhere to this view.[11]

The circumstances clearly pointed to a preconceived design, and the Pakistan government did not give credit to the hypocritical proviso or Nehru's assurance. On 27 October, the Quaid-i-Azam ordered General Gracey, the acting commander-in-chief of the Pakistan army, to send troops to counter the Indian attack, but he demurred and instead sought instructions from the Supreme Commander, Field Marshal Auchinleck, in New Delhi.

Another part of the Indian design to annex Kashmir under a cloak of legitimacy was the appointment of National Conference leader Sheikh Abdullah as administrator of the state. Meanwhile, the Muslim Conference was silenced and its leaders Ghulam Abbas and Mirwaiz Mohammad Yusuf remained in detention. (Months later, in early 1948, they were released but, barred from political activity, they decided to cross over to Azad Kashmir.)

Upon receiving news of accession, the people of Gilgit were outraged, and on 30 October, the Gilgit Scouts, the agency's force, ousted the Maharaja's governor, who had been appointed after the British government's lease of the territory expired on 15 August. At the request of the Scouts, Pakistan took over the administration of the agency.

On 30 October, the Pakistan government issued a public statement declaring that the Maharaja's accession to India was based on 'fraud and violence'. Pakistan would never recognize the accession which was 'fraudulent inasmuch as it was achieved by deliberately creating conditions with the object of finding an excuse to stage the "accession" . . . (which) was against the well-known will of an overwhelming majority of the population and could not be justified on any grounds whether moral or constitutional, geographical or economic, cultural or religious.'[12]

On 16 November, Liaquat Ali Khan proposed that the United Nations send its representatives to stop the fighting and the repression in Kashmir. On 21 November, Nehru replied it was not clear to him what the UN could do. Meanwhile, the Indian forces met with stiff resistance by the people as they proceeded to occupy the state and drive out Kashmiris.

At the United Nations

On 1 January 1948, India filed a complaint with the Security Council against Pakistan, under Article 35 of Chapter VI of the Charter, and asked the Council to call upon Pakistan to stop giving assistance to the invaders. In an attempt to reassure the Council of its own bona fides, the Indian complaint stated:

> In order to avoid any possible suggestion that India had taken advantage of the State's immediate peril for her own political advantage, the Dominion Government made it clear that once the soil of the State had been cleared of the invader and normal conditions were restored, the people would be free to decide their future by the recognized democratic method of plebiscite or referendum which, in order to ensure complete impartiality, may be held under international auspices.

The Security Council started consideration of the question on 15 January. By then, Pakistan had also filed a counter-complaint, charging India with genocide and refuting the validity of the Maharaja's accession. Pakistan requested the Security Council to (a) call upon India to desist from acts of aggression, and (b) appoint a commission to investigate its charges against India.

During the debate in the Security Council, Foreign Minister Zafrullah Khan spoke for five hours. After refuting the allegations made by the Indian representative, he concluded with the question 'What is to be done?' and suggested, 'Everyone who has gone into Kashmir should get out,' including Sikh bands, RSS volunteers, tribesmen, and Indian troops.

Acting under Chapter VI—Pacific Settlement of Disputes—and with the consent of both parties, the Security Council decided on 20 January 1948 to establish the UN Commission for India and Pakistan (UNCIP) in order to investigate the facts and exercise mediatory influence. Comprising selected members of the Council, the Commission visited Pakistan and India. On its recommendation, the Council adopted the first substantive resolution on 21 April 1948. Referring to the Indian complaint 'concerning the *dispute* over the state of Jammu and Kashmir' (emphasis added), and Pakistan's 'counter-complaints', and 'noting with satisfaction that both India and Pakistan desire that the question of the accession of Jammu and Kashmir to India or Pakistan should be decided through the democratic way of a free and impartial plebiscite,' the Security Council accepted UNCIP's recommendation for measures 'appropriate to bring about cessation of the fighting and to create proper conditions for a free and impartial plebiscite to decide whether the State of Jammu and Kashmir is to accede to India or Pakistan.'

Ignoring the Security Council's call to both sides to refrain from any action that might aggravate the situation, India embarked on a large-scale offensive in the spring. General Gracey then submitted to the Government of Pakistan his appreciation that the operation would lead to another serious influx of refugees from Kashmir into Pakistan and recommended that the Indian advance be stopped. Pursuant to his advice, the Government of Pakistan decided to send limited forces to hold defensive positions in the state. When UNCIP came to Pakistan in July, Zafrullah Khan informed the representatives that three brigades had been sent to reinforce the defence lines held in Azad Kashmir in May, as Pakistan could not sit back passively unmindful of the danger of the Indian army's invasion of Pakistani territory.

India seized upon the Pakistani decision to allege aggression. Both sides hotly debated the issue in the commission. Finally, on 13 August 1948, UNCIP adopted an elaborate three-part resolution providing for a ceasefire order by India and Pakistan, a truce agreement, and plebiscite. Pakistan was to withdraw its troops, as their presence in Jammu and Kashmir 'constitutes a material change in the situation' and territory vacated by them would be administered by the local authority under the surveillance of the commission. Also, the Indian government 'would begin to withdraw the bulk of its forces from Kashmir after the Commission had notified them that the tribesmen and Pakistani nationals had withdrawn and that the Pakistani troops were being withdrawn.' The resolution also contained the following key paragraph:

> The Government of India and the Government of Pakistan reaffirm their wish that the future status of the State of Jammu and Kashmir shall be determined in accordance with the will of the people and to that end, upon acceptance of the Truce Agreement, both Governments agree to enter into consultations with the Commission to determine fair and equitable conditions whereby such free expression will be assured.

On 5 January 1949, following the entry into force of the ceasefire, UNCIP adopted another resolution incorporating supplementary principles accepted by India and Pakistan about a truce, the appointment of a plebiscite administrator, and arrangements for the plebiscite. The resolution reiterated: 'The question of the accession of the State of Jammu and Kashmir to India or Pakistan will be decided through the democratic method of a free and impartial plebiscite.'

Although the British role in the Security Council was pro-India, most members brought an impartial and salutary approach to deliberations on the Kashmir question rooted, in the norms of international law in order to promote a solution consistent with the ethics of justice and the right of self-determination. Unfortunately, this spirit soon suffered attrition and some of the key members of the Security Council later adopted stilted positions on the basis of self-interest rather than the merits of the dispute, with India exploiting the Cold War to gain the support of the Soviet Union by using or threatening the use of the USSR veto.

Having occupied the bulk of the state, India set about consolidating its control over it. Sheikh Mohammad Abdullah was installed as prime minister. At the same time, India also began attempts to wriggle out of its solemn pledges and commitments to the people of Kashmir, Pakistan, and the United Nations. It alleged non-compliance by Pakistan with one part of the Security Council resolutions or another regarding arrangements for a plebiscite, but rejected proposals by UN mediators for impartial arbitration on differences of interpretation. A suggestion by the US State Department, urging flexibility on legal points, drew a rigid and rude response from Nehru. He 'would not give an inch. He would hold his ground if Kashmir, India, and the whole world would go to pieces.'[13] A joint appeal by President Truman and Prime Minister Attlee on 31 August 1949 for arbitration on differences of interpretation of the UNCIP plan elicited a similarly truculent response.

Proposals[14] made by UNCIP for a reduction of forces on both sides of the ceasefire line prior to the plebiscite were rejected by India.[15] The Security Council decided in March 1950 to replace UNCIP with a Representative, to assist the two countries towards demilitarization. The first Representative, Judge Owen Dixon of Australia, discussed arrangements for the plebiscite, but India refused to concede temporary authority to the UN Administrator. Instead,

Nehru tried to divert the focus by calling for condemnation of Pakistani 'aggression'. Dixon pointed out that the Security Council had made no such declaration and such a question had 'nothing to do with the . . . fairness and freedom of a . . . plebiscite.'[16] Dixon came to the conclusion that India's agreement 'would never be obtained to demilitarization' in any such form as would permit the plebiscite to be conducted in conditions sufficiently guarded against intimidation and other forms of influence and abuse. He then decided to propose either four 'regional plebiscites' or partition conceding 'some areas' to Pakistan, 'some' to India, and limiting plebiscite only to 'the Valley of Kashmir and perhaps some adjacent country.' Nehru indicated interest, calculating that Abdullah could manipulate the plebiscite. Liaquat Ali Khan pointed out that the proposals departed from the Security Council resolutions which envisaged that the 'destiny of the state of Jammu and Kashmir as a whole should be decided by a single plebiscite taken over the entire state.'

The Dispute Festers

The Security Council then appointed Frank P. Graham as its Representative. He took up the question as to the number and character of forces to be retained by India and Pakistan consistent with the holding of a free plebiscite. In his report of 23 December 1952, Graham proposed that Pakistan should reduce the forces on its side to between 3,000 and 6,000, and India to between 12,000 and 18,000. Pakistan accepted, but India rejected the proposal. Graham continued his efforts and made five more reports during his tenure until 1958, but with no result.

Meanwhile, observing that Abdullah's National Conference recommended determination of the future affiliation of the state by the Constituent Assembly, the Security Council adopted a resolution on 30 March 1951 affirming that 'any action that assembly might attempt to determine the future shape and affiliation of the entire State or any part thereof would not constitute a disposition of the State in accordance with the above principle.' The Council also reiterated the principle that 'the final disposition of the State of Jammu and Kashmir will be made in accordance with the will of the people expressed in the democratic method of a free and impartial plebiscite conducted under the auspices of the United Nations.' (All seventy-five members of the 'Constituent Assembly' were 'elected' by the vote of fewer than 5 per cent of the electorate in 1951 without opposition. All belonged to Abdullah's own party.)

In June 1953, Prime Minister Mohammad Ali Bogra opened a dialogue with Nehru in the hope of settling differences bilaterally. After a meeting in New Delhi in August, the two leaders agreed that the Kashmir question 'should be settled in accordance with the wishes of the people of that State' and that 'the most feasible method of ascertaining the wishes of the people was by fair and impartial plebiscite.' The dialogue was soon called off by Nehru, taking the position that the contemplated military pact between Pakistan and USA 'will affect the major questions . . . more especially, the Kashmir issue.' He did not care to explain what the connection was between such a pact and the right of the Kashmiri people to determine the future of their state. Instead, he continued to put forward irrelevant arguments, making convenient use of absurd press reports such as the one that conjured up expansion of the Pakistan army to 'a million men'.[17]

Realizing that his friend Nehru had duped him by solemn promises of plebiscite, in 1953 Sheikh Abdullah sought to retrace his steps, declaring that he had supported only conditional accession to India 'despite our (i.e. Kashmiris') having so many affinities with Pakistan.' In a meeting with Adlai Stevenson, presidential candidate of the United States, in Srinagar, he expressed views in favour of independence for the state. He had also done so earlier in meetings with foreign visitors.[18] Sheikh Abdullah was dismissed in August 1953 because he 'was on the point of demanding that the Indian Army leave the soil of Kashmir.'[19] He remained imprisoned for a decade. The people of the state cursed him for selling out their interests and allowing himself to be used as an instrument in the Indian design.

When the United States began considering a defence pact with Pakistan in 1953, India came up with another specious argument to renege on its commitments on Kashmir. It declared that such arrangements would constitute 'a qualitative change of circumstances' relating to the Kashmir question. Of course, Pakistan's alliance with other countries could neither absolve India of its obligations under UN resolutions nor prejudice the recognized right of self-determination of the people of Kashmir.[20]

India's argument that Pakistan's defence pact with the United States represented 'change of circumstances' releasing India from its obligation under the UN resolutions was totally inadmissible in law and logic. Bad faith was also writ large on India's plea that a decision by Kashmiris in favour of Pakistan would prejudice India's secular character and political unity. This was entirely an afterthought. The law does not permit a state to disown an international obligation. According to Article 25 of the United Nations Charter, 'The Members of the United Nations agree to accept and carry out the decisions of the Security Council in accordance with the present Charter.'

When Pakistan learned that the so-called 'Constituent Assembly' in Srinagar was to ratify the Maharaja's accession, it brought the matter to the attention of the UN Security Council, and on 24 January 1957, the council reminded 'the Governments and Authorities concerned of the principle . . . that the final disposition of the State of Jammu and Kashmir will be made in accordance with the will of the people expressed through the democratic method of a free and impartial plebiscite conducted under the auspices of the United Nations' and reaffirmed that any action taken by the assembly 'would not constitute a disposition of the State in accordance with the above principle.'[21]

As India attempted to wriggle out of its obligations under the UN resolutions, it exploited the Soviet unhappiness with Pakistan's decision to conclude a defence agreement with the United States in order to gain Soviet support for India's position on the Kashmir question. At first the USSR abstained, but it later threw its powerful weight behind India and its statements endorsed the Indian position on Kashmir. The Security Council was henceforth prevented from dealing with the Kashmir question impartially or acting with determination to secure implementation of its own resolutions.

One obstacle after another was thus raised by India to prevent a settlement of the Kashmir question. The dispute itself was—and remains—quite simple. So, too, is its solution. All that it required is the implementation of the pledge in the UN resolutions, accepted by India as well as Pakistan, and to let the people of the state decide the question of the state's accession in a free plebiscite. If it has become complicated, it is because India had made it so.

India's later claim that the Maharaja of Kashmir had the right to decide the question of accession is not congruent with its stance in respect of Junagadh and Hyderabad, the conditional acceptance of the Maharaja's accession, the pledges of Jawaharlal Nehru to the people of Kashmir, or India's commitment in the Security Council resolutions that the question of accession would be decided by the people of the state in a free and impartial plebiscite.

Similarly, India's subsequent argument that implementation of the UN resolutions was subject to the condition of withdrawal of Pakistani troops ignores the record of negotiations. Pakistan was prepared to reduce its forces to the bare minimum, but India refused the UN mediator's suggestion to reduce its forces sufficiently to permit the Kashmiri people to exercise their right of self-determination without fear of duress.

Regrettably for relations between India and Pakistan, and for the peace and freedom of the people of Kashmir, Nehru's pledges of plebiscite to decide the accession of Jammu and Kashmir were a premeditated ruse to mislead the people of the state, Pakistan, and the United Nations. Declassified documents confirm that he never intended to implement the obligations India undertook. In a note dated 25 August 1952 to Sheikh Mohammad Abdullah, Nehru said, 'After some experience of the UN I came to the conclusion that nothing substantive could be expected from it.' On 20 August 1953, Nehru agreed to reiterate the pledge of 'a fair and impartial' plebiscite in a joint communiqué with Prime Minister Mohammad Ali Bogra, but explained in a letter to Karan Singh, the titular head of the state, that 'some kind of an agreement between us and Pakistan' was necessary to preclude reference of the Kashmir dispute back to the United Nations, which might send down another representative to Kashmir, and added: 'The accord was not intended to be implemented.' V. P. Menon, Secretary of the Indian Ministry of States, confessed in a 1964 letter: 'As for plebiscite, we were absolutely, absolutely dishonest.'[22]

NOTES

1. Burke and Ziring, op. cit., 16.
2. Chaudhri Mohammad Ali, op. cit., 226, quoting Alan Campbell-Johnson, *Mission with Mountbatten*, 51–6. On another occasion, Mountbatten repeated the same advice in the following words: 'Normally geographical situation and

communal interests and so forth will be the factors to be considered.' Burke and Ziring, op. cit., 16.

3. S. M. Burke, op. cit., 17.
4. British Foreign Secretary Ernest Bevin expressed regret that 'a warlike spirit has developed' in India. Quoted by G. W. Choudhury, op. cit., 79.
5. Quoted from *Transfer of Power*, Vol. XI, No. 229, in Alastair Lamb, *Kashmir: A Disputed Legacy*, 109. Nehru's assertion that the Maharaja wished to join India either evidenced a preconceived conspiracy, or, if the Maharaja wanted to remain independent, was a deliberate lie.
6. Josef Korbel, *Danger in Kashmir*, 60.
7. Ibid., 63.
8. Pakistan signed the agreement on 15 August; India did not respond.
9. Premnath Bazaz, *The History of the Struggle for Freedom in Kashmir*, 325, quoted in G. W. Choudhury, op. cit., 73.
10. Josef Korbel, op. cit., 71.
11. Quoted in Chaudhri Muhammad Ali, op. cit., 288 from K. Sarwar Hasan, *The Kashmir Question: Documents on the Foreign Relations of Pakistan*, 104.
12. Liaquat Ali Khan quoted in Burke and Ziring, op. cit., 27, from K. Sarwar Hasan, op. cit., 100.
13. Quoted in McMahon, op. cit., 24.
14. For summaries of the various proposals and discussion of their merits, see Lamb, 170–9.
15. US Secretary of State Dean Acheson sent a message to Nehru recommending acceptance of McNaughton's 'realistic approach to the demilitarization issue' and observing that if India did not 'it will be the third consecutive time India will have refused impartial proposals.' Nehru 'exploded' and called the message 'unfriendly'. Quoted in McMahon, op. cit., 60.
16. Quoted in Burke and Ziring, op. cit., 35.
17. Nehru's letter to Bogra dated 9 December 1953, quoted from *Negotiations between the Prime Ministers of Pakistan and India regarding the Kashmir dispute (June 1953–September 1954)* published by Government of Pakistan, Ministry of Kashmir Affairs, Karachi, 1954, quoted in Lamb, 228.
18. In 1950, according to US Ambassador Loy Henderson, 'in discussing the future of Kashmir, Abdullah was vigorous in restating his opinion that it should be independent.' US Department of State, Foreign Relations of the United States, 1950. Vol. V. The Near East, South Asia and Africa, Washington, DC, 1978, 1433–5, quoted in Lamb, 189–90.
19. M. J. Akbar, *Nehru—The Making of India*, Penguin Group, London, 1988, 452.
20. Retired Justice M. V. Tarkunde of India, a respected advocate of respect for human rights, said that 'The offer of plebiscite was not in the nature of a concession made by India to Pakistan, but was a recognition of the right of self-determination of the people of Jammu & Kashmir.' Quoted from 'The Radical Humanist', March 1990, in Bahauddin Farooqi, *Kashmir Holocaust*, 26–7.
21. The UN Security Council first dealt with the matter on 30 March 1950, after observing that a constituent assembly was sought to be created in Srinagar. It reminded the governments and authorities concerned of its earlier resolutions

incorporating the principle of disposition of the state on the basis of plebiscite and affirmed that 'any action that assembly might attempt to take to determine the future shape and affiliation of the entire State or any part thereof would not constitute a disposition of the State in accordance with the above principle.'

22. A. G. Noorani, *The Kashmir Dispute, 1947–2012*, Vol. I, Tulika Books, New Delhi, 27, 41, 42, 176–80.

Chapter 4

The Search for Security

On almost every issue that arose in relations with India, Pakistan found itself faced with New Delhi's refusal to resolve the differences on the basis of principles of law and justice. Whether it was the transfer of Pakistan's share of the assets inherited from British India, accession of princely states, or continued flow of river waters, India sought to impose its own will, in disregard of the principles of the partition agreement between the two countries. Exploiting power disparity, India dismissed reason and equity in negotiations, spurned resort to impartial peaceful means of resolving differences, and did not hesitate to use force or threat of force to impose its own preferences. India's military intervention in Jammu and Kashmir, and its refusal to hold a plebiscite as agreed in Security Council resolutions, injected a sense of urgency to the fledgling Pakistani state's search for ways and means to bolster its capacity to resist dictation.

Pakistan's response to the objective problem posed by the tyranny of power imbalance, and the agony and humiliation of dictation, was in classical style. As other states have done throughout history when faced with a more powerful neighbour intent on exploiting disparity to achieve its inimical aims, Pakistan embarked upon cultivation of sympathy and support wherever it could be found. It sought friends and allies, and assistance to strengthen the 'sinews of statehood'[1] and to preserve its sovereignty and security. The contours of Pakistan's foreign policy were thus shaped by the desperate need for arms to ensure the security of the new state and for funds to finance its economic development.

For economic and defence assistance Pakistan first approached Britain, the only Western country Pakistani leaders knew at first hand. Britain was, however, too exhausted and debilitated following the Second World War to render help. Also, the Labour government was antipathetic to Pakistani leaders, whom it simplistically blamed for wrecking the British hope of maintaining the unity of their Indian empire—'the Jewel in the Crown'. Clement Attlee, prime minister at the time, 'never liked Jinnah' and too many British Labour Party members thought in terms of 'a progressive Congress and a reactionary Muslim League.'

USSR[2]

As Pakistan looked for economic and military cooperation, the Soviet Union was not an option. Having borne the brunt of Nazi Germany's powerful war machine in Europe, with 25–30 million people killed and its economy devastated, it was hardly in a position to provide assistance. Politically, too, the Soviet system was unattractive to Pakistani leaders who were committed to democracy. Moreover, the communist ideology was considered antithetical to Islam. Also, the Soviet leadership looked with little favour upon Pakistan (or India).[3] Moscow perceived the partition as having 'facilitated British domination in both dominions.'[4]

Relations between the two countries got off to an inauspicious start, as the USSR did not even send a customary message of felicitation on Pakistan's independence. Alone among major countries to manifest such discourtesy, the Soviet Union also did not take the initiative to establish an embassy in Pakistan.

On the Pakistani side, too, inherited and inherent factors prejudiced Pakistan against the Soviet Union. The Pakistani administrative elite, nurtured in the British strategic view, suspected that the Soviet state cherished the czarist aim of carving out a land access to the warm waters of the Arabian Sea and therefore posed a danger to Pakistan's security. They also considered communism a secretive and revolutionary movement subversive of law and order. However, Pakistan was by no means hostile to the USSR and in the early years had no interest in the emergent power blocs.

The Soviet record of rapid economic progress evoked admiration and its foreign policy of opposition to colonialism and imperialism made a ready appeal. Progressive artists and *littérateurs* lauded communist ideals of egalitarianism and full employment, sang paeans to socialist ownership of means of production, and denounced capitalism for colonial domination and exploitation of labour for the benefit of the rich. Few spoke or were even aware of Soviet repression at home and its annexation of territories of neighbouring states and imposition of communism over East European countries.

US Invitation to Liaquat Ali Khan: An episode that aroused much attention at the time, and later, involved the invitation to the Pakistani prime minister to visit the Soviet Union, which was accepted but not honoured. The known facts are that President Harry S. Truman's invitation to Nehru to visit the United States was announced in May 1949. At a reception held during Liaquat Ali Khan's visit to Tehran, Ambassador Ghazanfar Ali told the Soviet chargé d'affaires of the prime minister's desire to visit the USSR. Moscow responded within five days. Josef Stalin's invitation to Liaquat Ali Khan was delivered at the Pakistan embassy in Tehran on 4 June. Liaquat Ali accepted it immediately. Each side then suggested visit dates for August, which the other found inconvenient. It was then decided to defer the visit for two months, during which the two sides agreed to establish resident embassies. Follow-up action met further delays. Pakistan designated an ambassador, but Moscow took its time to give *agrément* while failing to nominate its own ambassador. According to an informed Pakistani account, neither side acted with any sense of urgency.[5]

The question as to why the visit to USSR did not take place has remained intriguing. It has been surmised that pique at Truman's invitation to Nehru provoked Liaquat Ali's initiative to solicit an invitation from Moscow. Conversely, it has been suggested that Moscow's immediate response was prompted by a desire to cultivate Pakistan to balance Washington's courting of Nehru. While no evidence is available to corroborate either conjecture, it is known that the US invitation to Nehru, but not to Liaquat Ali, was a disappointment to the Pakistanis, and that announcement of Liaquat Ali's acceptance of Stalin's invitation served to awaken Washington to its omission. Overnight, reported Ambassador Ispahani from Washington, Pakistan began to receive serious notice and consideration.[6] The 'desirability of offsetting the impact of Liaquat's anticipated travel to the Soviet Union, along with balancing Nehru's state visit to the United States, were the main arguments for the invitation to the Pakistani leader.'[7] Washington wanted to reassure Pakistan that there was no change in its policy of 'objectivity, impartiality, and friendly interests in both India and Pakistan.'

There is little evidence to suggest that the US invitation to Liaquat Ali caused Moscow to lose interest in his visit to the Soviet Union. Perhaps the cooling of Moscow's interest was due to Pakistan's harsh anti-communist rhetoric and official discouragement of contacts with the Soviet Union. Pakistan refused passports to poets and writers who wanted to visit the Soviet Union.

Approaches to the US[8]

The United States was the only promising source of assistance. Emerging from the Second World War with its economy intact, it was the wealthiest nation in the world, accounting for over 40 per cent of global production. Also, its democratic system was congenial. It was, however, preoccupied with Soviet expansion in Eastern Europe and the need to stabilize Western Europe through economic and military assistance. US interest in South Asia was rather cursory. However, Pakistan's location next to the Middle East, with its petroleum resources, provided a strategic link of benefit to Pakistan's search for cooperation.

The US was not then alive to the threat in the Middle East, nor was it favourably disposed toward the Pakistan movement. The demand for a state in the name of Islam was difficult for secular America to comprehend.[9] Motivated by wartime priorities and anti-colonial predilections, President Franklin D. Roosevelt believed a free India could make a useful contribution towards the war effort. When Prime Minister Winston Churchill refused to concede the Congress demand for self-government, Roosevelt sent him a strongly worded protest.[10] Apparently unaware of the cooperation the League extended to the Allies by encouraging Muslims to join the armed forces in the war against fascism, Washington considered the Congress as the leading party, and supported a united India. In December 1946, Acting Secretary of State Dean Acheson endorsed the Cabinet Mission Plan.[11] The League tried, within its limited means, to educate opinion in the United States. In 1946, it sent two prominent leaders, M. A. H. Ispahani and Begum Jahanara Shah Nawaz, to Washington. They met Dean Acheson but received little more than a polite audience.

The Pakistani leadership carried no grudge against the United States, however. In May 1947, Mr Jinnah received the US chargé d'affaires in New Delhi and explained to him that Pakistan's foreign policy would be oriented towards the Muslim countries of the Middle East, and they 'would stand together against possible Russian aggression and would look to the U.S. for assistance.'[12]

After Pakistan emerged, the United States showed a friendly predisposition towards the new state. President Truman sent a warm message on Pakistan's independence on 14 August 1947, saying, 'I wish to assure you that the new Dominion embarks on its course with the firm friendship and goodwill of the United States of America.'[13] A high US State Department official, Assistant Secretary Phillips Talbot, came to Karachi in August. A month later, Truman gave a 'sympathetic' response to Ambassador Ispahani's statement about Pakistan's need 'to balance our economy, to industrialize our country, to improve health and education and raise the standard of living.'[14]

Constrained by its desperate needs, Pakistan hurriedly sounded out the US chargé d'affaires for financial assistance. In October 1947, the government sent Mir Laik Ali to Washington to seek a loan of two billion dollars for economic development and defence purchases over five years in order to 'attain a reasonably independent position and . . . to make a fair contribution to the stability of the world order.'[15] To impress Washington, he emphasized compatibility of Pakistan-US interests on the one hand and Pakistan's strategic location on the other, referring to 'the proximity and vulnerability of western Pakistan to Russia.'[16] The US showed little interest, however. Apparently taken by complete surprise at the amount of the aid request, the US politely turned it down, saying it did not have funds of that magnitude. The first rather fumbling request drew a blank, but Pakistan did not give up hope.

Pakistan did not take the US 'no' for an answer and continued to emphasize the commonality of interests. In December 1947, Firoz Khan Noon, a prominent leader and future prime minister, drew an American official's attention to Pakistan's significance as 'the eastern bastion against communism as Turkey is the western bastion.'[17] This point was stressed at the government level as the hostile relations between the USA and the USSR froze into the Cold War. In a meeting with Secretary of State George Marshall in Paris in October 1948, Liaquat Ali Khan said it was 'unthinkable that Pakistan could fall prey to communism' and urged the US to provide economic help to Pakistan and the Muslim nations of the Middle East.[18]

Liaquat Ali Khan visited the USA in May 1950. President Truman received him on arrival in Washington. During his three-week visit, he seized every opportunity to emphasize the commonality of values and interests between Pakistan and the United States. Among these, he mentioned democracy, fundamental human rights, right of private ownership, equal citizenship of all whether Muslim or non-Muslim, equality of opportunity, equality before law, and the moral responsibility of those fortunate in wealth and knowledge towards the unfortunate. He described Pakistan and the United States as 'comrades' in the quest for peace and in translating dreams of democracy into reality. He underlined Pakistan's strategic location 'in relation to communications to and from the oil-bearing areas of the Middle East.' In his speech to Congress, he declared 'no threat or persuasion, no material peril or ideological allurement' could deflect Pakistan from its chosen path of democracy. Though he avoided pointed criticism of Soviet policy, he made frequent references to the communist threat.[19]

Liaquat Ali's statements of desire to enlarge cooperation with the United States impressed the Americans, but the official response to his suggestions for aid was unenthusiastic. Considering South Asia a region of 'secondary importance', the State Department brief for the Pakistani leader's visit simply noted that Pakistan's economic or military requests for assistance had so far 'seemed impracticable'.[20] That appraisal was to come under reconsideration following the Korean War, but it took two years and a change of administration in Washington to formulate a new policy.

The Korean War

North Korean forces moved across the 38th parallel on 25 June 1950. Pakistan promptly issued a statement denouncing the attack as 'a clear case of aggression'.[21] Liaquat Ali, who was still in the United States, endorsed the US decision to invoke the UN Charter provisions for collective security. Pakistan voted for the General Assembly resolution authorizing the UN operation for the defence of South Korea. But when the United Nations called upon members to contribute to the UN action, Pakistan decided against sending a military contingent and limited its contribution to supply of 5,000 tons of wheat for South Korea. Pakistan was willing to send an army brigade only if its own security was assured in the event of Indian aggression. The United States balked at the suggestion for such a commitment.

Pakistan's position, combining principle with manifest constraints of security, was generally well understood at home and abroad. Its low-key policy was seen by the Western countries to contrast favourably with that of India, which sought to exploit the crisis for advancing its own foreign policy objectives. Its support for the UN operation was limited to sending an ambulance unit, but India sought to play a hyperactive mediatory role and presented proposals for settlement of the crisis which were warmly endorsed by Moscow but resented in Washington.

Pakistan's decision against sending forces to Korea proved a blessing. Otherwise, Pakistani troops could have been involved in fighting against the Chinese forces which entered Korea after the UN decided, under American influence, to extend the war into North Korea.

Pakistan's hopes for assistance from the United States continued to be frustrated for the next two years. Meanwhile, political instability increased following the assassination of Liaquat Ali Khan and deterioration of economic conditions, as prices of cotton and jute plummeted after the end of the Korean War. Former foreign secretary M. Ikramullah was sent to Washington at the head of a military mission in October 1951 to press for aid. The US response was again discouraging. It agreed only to sell arms for $10 million and provide technical and economic development assistance under the Point Four Programme. Another such mission headed by Mir Laik Ali was sent by Prime Minister Nazimuddin in July 1952 to ask for an immediate credit of $200 million. The US response was both hesitant and meagre. It agreed only to provide $15 million for wheat purchase. But the US policy toward Pakistan was under steady, if invisible, review in the light of the changing situation in Asia, and especially the Middle East.

Japan

Pakistan supported the conclusion of a Peace Treaty with Japan and attended the San Francisco conference convened in 1951 to sign the treaty. On the question of China's representation, Pakistan supported its participation. When the majority voted against, Foreign Minister Zafrullah Khan voiced regret over the absence of China, whose people had suffered the most at the hands of Japan's erstwhile oppressor regime.

Pakistan's policy on issues in East Asia was appreciated by China, Japan, and South Korea and laid the foundation for friendly relations with these important states. It also served to embellish Pakistan's image in the United States as a moderate and cooperative country. The *New York Times* was so impressed as to praise Pakistan editorially as America's 'one sure friend in South Asia'.[22]

China

Although cultural contacts between the people of Pakistan and China have ancient roots,[23] the two lands remained generally cut off by the Himalayas for most of history. Mindful of China's importance, Pakistan was among the first countries to extend diplomatic recognition to the new government soon after[24] the People's Republic was proclaimed on 1 October 1949, and a year later opened a diplomatic mission in Beijing. Differences of ideology did not obstruct the development of friendly relations between the two neighbours as both conducted bilateral relations strictly in conformity with the principles of non-interference in internal affairs. With bitter experience of foreign domination, China evinced understanding and sympathy for the struggle of other countries of Asia and Africa to maintain their independence and develop their economies. Particularly engaging was China's treatment of small and medium countries on the basis of sovereign equality eschewing big power chauvinism and condescension.

NOTES

1. Lawrence Ziring, Ralph Braibanti, and W. Howard Wriggins, eds., *Pakistan: The Long View,* 304.
2. For comprehensive factual and analytical treatment of the subject, see Hafeez Malik, *Soviet-Pakistan Relations and Post-Soviet Dynamics, 1947–92.*

3. A Soviet spokesman dubbed Gandhi and Nehru as 'lackeys of imperialists' and Stalin considered the leaders of the governments in South Asia as 'stooges'. For Soviet attitude toward India and Pakistan during 1947–53 period, see Maqbool A. Bhatty, *Great Powers and South Asia*, 100–5.
4. *Great Soviet Encyclopaedia*, published in 1953, quoted in Maqbool A. Bhatty, 103.
5. Sajjad Hyder, *The Foreign Policy of Pakistan: Reflections of an Ambassador*, 14.
6. Quoted in McMahon, 70.
7. Dennis Kux, *Disenchanted Allies*, 32.
8. The account of the evolution of Pakistan-US relations has benefited greatly from Robert J. McMahon, *The Cold War on the Periphery*, *America-Pakistan Relations—Documents*, ed. K. Arif, and research by Dennis Kux for his forthcoming book on the subject.
9. Robert J. McMahon, op. cit., 65. According to McMahon, American experts feared that 'the establishment of an independent Muslim state might balkanize the subcontinent.'
10. Dennis Kux, *Estranged Democracies*, 6.
11. Bhutto, *The Myth of Independence*, 38, quoted from *Indian Annual Register*, vol. 2, 88.
12. Dennis Kux, *Disenchanted Allies*, 13, quoting from US documents.
13. *Documents*, ed. K. Arif, 3.
14. Z. H. Zaidi, *M.A. Jinnah Ispahani Correspondence*, 538.
15. Memorandum given by Mir Laik Ali Khan, *America-Pakistan Relations—Documents*, ed. K. Arif, 5.
16. *Documents*, ed. K. Arif, 5.
17. Quoted from US released records in McMahon.
18. Dennis Kux, *Disenchanted Allies*, 28.
19. Liaquat Ali Khan, Pakistan, *The Heart of Asia: Speeches in the United States and Canada, May and June 1950* (Harvard University Press, 1950).
20. Dennis Kux, *Disenchanted Allies*, 34.
21. *Documents*, ed. K. Arif, 33, 35.
22. *New York Times*, 14 September 1951.
23. The Kushan kingdom with Peshawar as capital included Chinese Turkistan. Fa Hian came to Gandhara in CE 401 and Hiuen Tsang (alias Yuan Chuang) came for pilgrimage to Taxila in CE 630.
24. Recognition was announced on 4 January 1950.

Chapter 5

Alliances

Rising security concerns due to India's exploitation of its military and economic dominance and recurrent threats were the determining factors that impelled Pakistan to search for foreign defence cooperation. Britain was unsympathetic because of the priority it attached to relations with the larger India. For the same reason, the United States was reluctant to respond to Pakistan's efforts for provision of military assistance. For several years after the Second World War, the United States expected Britain to ensure the defence of the West's interests in the region East of Suez and followed its advice.

Defence analysts in the United States had begun to recognize the value of Pakistan's geographic location as early as March 1949, when the US Joint Chiefs of Staff noted the strategic importance of the Karachi-Lahore area 'as a base for air operations' against the Soviet Union and 'as a staging area for forces engaged in the defence or recapture of Middle East oil areas.'[1] Others highlighted Pakistan's position as the world's largest Muslim state with the best army in the Middle East and its proximity to the Soviet Union and the oil fields of the Persian Gulf, and even warned that it would be prejudicial to US interests to develop an India policy without taking into account Pakistan's legitimate interests.

Pakistani leaders lost no opportunity to project the country's strategic importance. Speaking to a visiting assistant secretary of state in October 1949, Finance Minister Ghulam Mohammad stressed the 'importance to the United States . . . of the establishment of a bloc of (Islamic) nations . . . as a check to any ambitions of USSR.'[2] Ambassador George McGhee, impressed by the directness of Pakistani leaders and their willingness to support any US-backed efforts to prevent communist encroachments in South Asia, recommended limited American military aid to Pakistan.[3]

Interest in defence cooperation with Pakistan mounted after the Korean War. Analysts in Washington concluded that the North Korean attack, which took place less than a year after the triumph of the Chinese liberation struggle, evidenced an expansionist Soviet design. They were particularly concerned about the security of the Middle East, especially the vital Persian Gulf region with the world's richest petroleum reserves. The rise of the nationalist Mohammed Mossadegh in Iran and nationalization of the Anglo-American Oil Company heightened concerns over upheavals in the Middle East and lent urgency to the need for insulating the region against Soviet political penetration and 'stemming any military advance towards the Persian Gulf and in the Near East generally.'

A meeting of US ambassadors to South Asian countries held in Colombo in February 1951 'favoured the idea of Pakistani participation in the defence of the Middle East.'[4] In April 1951, American and British officials agreed that Pakistan's contribution would probably be the decisive factor in ensuring defence of the area.[5]

Pakistan came to be viewed as a valuable asset. But though sympathetic, Washington remained indecisive 'lest arming Pakistan ensnare the United States in India-Pakistan disputes.'[6] Pakistan's arms procurement missions led by former foreign secretary Ikramullah in late 1951, and by Mir Laik Ali in July 1952, proved infructuous.

Washington's reluctance to make the leap was reinforced by British officials with whom Americans held regular consultations. Considered experts on South Asia, they long opposed American arms supply to Pakistan because, they argued, that would politically and economically antagonize the more important India, foreclose prospects for a Kashmir settlement, and spoil prospects of improved relations between Pakistan and India.[7] In effect, they uncritically endorsed Indian arguments, ignoring the fact that the Kashmir dispute arose because Pakistan was militarily weak and denial of arms to it could hardly improve prospects of a fair settlement. The British were, in effect, conceding India a veto over arms supply to Pakistan, an objective India has pursued ever since. Mountbatten was not alone in seeking to promote Indian domination.

In May 1952, Paul Nitze, the director of the State Department's policy planning staff, wrote a paper deploring Western fragility in the Middle East and recommending direct US involvement in the defence of the region because British capabilities were 'wholly inadequate'. He envisaged assistance to Pakistan to increase its capability to contribute to the defence of the Middle East.[8] By the end of 1952, the Truman administration endorsed the idea of a Middle East Defence Organization (MEDO) that was conceived by London to shore up its sagging position. The problem, however, was that Gamal Abdel Nasser and Nehru opposed the suggestion. British influence in the region had suffered manifest decline.

The post-Korean War perceptions in Washington finally began to crystallize into a search for a new policy. Even before the presidential elections, the US realized it had to take the lead. But the task of launching a major initiative fell to President Dwight D. Eisenhower, who took office in January 1953, and his Secretary of State, John Foster Dulles.

Northern Tier: As the British idea of MEDO proved a non-starter, the US began to search for an alternative. To that end, Secretary Dulles undertook a tour of the Middle East and South Asia in May. Nowhere did he receive a warmer welcome or was more impressed than in Pakistan. Governor General Ghulam Mohammed, Prime Minister Mohammed Ali Bogra, who had replaced Khawaja Nazimuddin a month earlier, and Foreign Minister Zafrullah Khan 'all stressed their allegiance to the anti-communist cause and emphasized Pakistan's desire to join the free world's defence team.'[9] Army Commander-in-Chief General Ayub Khan, convinced that the threat to Pakistan's security could be contained only with the support of a powerful ally, argued that the United States needed to fill the vacuum created by the British withdrawal.[10] His strategic assessment of the threat of a Soviet drive to the warm waters of the Arabian Sea, and Pakistan's potential for opposing it, made a most favourable impact. In a cable to Washington, Dulles said the feeling of friendship in Pakistan 'exceeded to a marked degree that encountered in any country previously visited on this trip.' He was struck by the 'spirit and appearance' of the Pakistani armed forces and their leaders, and had a 'feeling that Pakistan is one country that has [the] moral courage to do its part in resisting communism.'[11] Testifying before the House Foreign Affairs Committee on his return to Washington, he praised the courage and determination of Pakistanis.

Even before Dulles came to Pakistan, the US demonstrated its goodwill, reflecting appreciation of Pakistan's potential importance and friendly disposition. A Pakistani request for the supply of a million tons of wheat to avert a food crisis was processed with exceptional speed. Assistant Secretary of State Byroade recommended prompt action. A US delegation was sent on a study mission to Pakistan in April. Eisenhower approved speedy action. Dulles personally testified before a congressional committee. Within two weeks, Congress gave bipartisan approval, and Eisenhower signed the bill in July. The wheat, valued at $74 million, was delivered free at Karachi.

Sensing the new administration's positive disposition toward Pakistan, India mounted a barrage of criticism, arguing that supply of arms to Pakistan would disturb the 'natural balance' in South Asia. Ignoring international law and practice, India's blind opposition to military aid or sales to Pakistan was obviously motivated by the perverse desire to exploit the existing power disparity to impose its malign agenda on Pakistan.

An even stronger antagonist was US Ambassador to India Chester Bowles, who believed with missionary zeal that India was a democratic counter-model to communist China in the ideological crusade for the mind of the emergent nations. He warned of 'catastrophe' if the US supplied arms to Pakistan, which, he said, would provide the Soviet Union with a golden opportunity to enhance its position in South Asia. The American embassy in India warned that aid to Pakistan would change the course of US relations with India for a long time to come. State Department officials dealing with India agreed: 'India is the power in South Asia. We should seek to make it our ally rather than cause it to be hostile to us. Pakistan is distressingly weak.' Joining the chorus of opposition, Afghanistan made a démarche conveying apprehension that the aid might be exploited by a 'foreign ideology'.

Weightier was the British step to convey consternation, repeating its set warning that aid to Pakistan would antagonize India, wreck negotiations on Kashmir, mar prospects of improved relations between India and Pakistan, and undermine Pakistan's limited capacity to play a valuable role in Western defence plans. Foreign Secretary Anthony Eden even spoke to Dulles who, however, dismissed the British argument, saying India could not claim a right to prevent other nations from lining up with the West.

Dulles publicly spoke of the idea of a defence arrangement of 'northern tier' countries—Turkey, Pakistan, Iraq, and Iran. In July, the proposal was considered and adopted by the National Security Council. Eisenhower approved the proposal. Washington decided in principle to go ahead with the alliance idea, but Pakistan's request for military aid was still obstructed by fear of the consequences. Ayub Khan went to Washington in September 1953, and Governor General Ghulam Mohammed in November, but both were disappointed because they received only assurances of sympathy. Dulles counselled patience and assured them that Pakistan would get aid regardless of India's attitude.

Neither Eisenhower nor Dulles was dismissive of the India factor, however. They abhorred displeasing India. In the hope of preempting Indian objections, Washington informed New Delhi, in 1953, of its intention to provide assistance to Pakistan. Nehru denounced the intention and promptly exploited it to renounce India's pledge of a plebiscite in Kashmir. He made daily speeches against the US policy. The Indian 'public campaign verged on hysteria' with Nehru declaring that aid to Pakistan would be a step not only towards war, but even world war. A veteran foreign observer saw through the Indian design: 'A cardinal underlying Indian purpose was to keep her smaller neighbour weak and isolated for eventual re-absorption. . . .'[12]

The decision was still pending when Vice President Richard Nixon came to Karachi (and New Delhi) in December 1953. He found Ayub Khan 'seriously concerned about the communist threat.'[13] On his return to Washington, he made a strong recommendation in favour of aid. Still, an inter-agency meeting at the highest operational level in January 1954 recommended only a 'modest' amount of aid to Pakistan. It estimated that the Indian reaction would be restrained since the aid would not 'threaten India's present military preponderance in the subcontinent.'[14] Finally, President Eisenhower 'agreed in principle to (US) proceeding with military aid to Pakistan.'

Before announcing the US decision, Eisenhower asked the State Department to make a conciliatory approach to India and explain that the US was not trying to help Pakistan against India, that the arms for Pakistan were part of a regional security package, and offered a similar pact to India. On 24 February 1954, he wrote a letter to Nehru assuring him that if the aid to Pakistan was misused for aggression, the United States would immediately take 'appropriate action, both within and without the United Nations, to thwart such aggression.' He also offered his 'most sympathetic consideration' of a request for military aid by India.

Disconsolate, Nehru gave a point-by-point rebuttal, adding a new argument that the arms supply to Pakistan could trigger Hindu-Muslim tensions in India. Composed in meetings with the US ambassador, Nehru seethed in briefing Indian officials: the US, he said, wanted to check India's power in the region and outflank neutralism.

In the end, India's bluster 'backed the US administration into a corner.'[15] The US Congress was annoyed by the self-serving arguments of Nehru and Krishna Menon. If it did not go ahead with the idea, it concluded, not only would that abort its new proposal, it would be tantamount to giving Nehru a veto over US policy in Asia. Nixon, a vocal proponent of arms for Pakistan, warned it would be a fatal mistake to back down.

The Four Alliances

1. Mutual Defence Assistance Agreement, 1954: Pakistan and the United States signed the first defence agreement on 19 May 1954. The US undertook to provide defence equipment to Pakistan 'exclusively to maintain its internal security, its legitimate self-defence, or to permit it to participate in defence of the area.' The assistance was to be made available under US legislation—the Mutual Defence Assistance Act of 1949 and Mutual Security Act of 1951 relating to the defence of the free world. On its part, Pakistan undertook to cooperate with the United States in measures to restrict trade with nations 'which threaten the maintenance of world peace.' Prime Minister Mohammad Ali Bogra lauded the Pakistan-US agreement. The two countries, he said, 'have a great deal in common' They shared convictions regarding freedom and democracy and spiritual strength to fight the totalitarian concept.[16]

2. South East Asia Treaty Organization (SEATO), 1954): The idea of a South East Asia Treaty Organization came up in 1954 after the French defeat at Dien Bien Phu. It was conceived by the United States in order to create deterrence to communism in general and Vietnam in particular. Dulles did not envisage the inclusion of South Asian countries, but Anthony Eden thought that inclusion of only Thailand and Philippines from the region would make the pact a Western undertaking, and besides, association with India, Pakistan, and Ceylon would provide local military backing. He sent a message to these countries on 18 May inviting them to join talks on the defence of the region. Prime Minister Bogra replied in June that Pakistan should be involved. Acting Foreign Secretary Agha Hilaly told an official of the British High Commission in Karachi that Pakistan would wish to participate in discussions on the defence of South East Asia, East Pakistan being a part of the region. Ambassador Amjad Ali, talking to an official of the department of State in Washington, observed that Pakistan would require equipment to contribute to the defence of the region. Foreign Minister Zafrullah Khan told the American undersecretary of state even earlier, in July, that Pakistan would definitely join if asked.[17]

Pakistan was invited to attend the Manila Conference in September 1954 to discuss the plan for the defence of South East Asia. In his response, Prime Minister Bogra was, however, careful to inform Eden that participation in the conference did not 'imply acceptance of any scheme that might emerge from the discussions in the meeting.' The chief reason for Pakistan's sudden reservations about SEATO was disappointment with the small amount of assistance the United States allocated for Pakistan. Ambassador Amjad Ali told the State Department that Ayub Khan was 'dejected and broken-hearted,' even regretting that Pakistan had joined in a defence agreement with the United States. Dulles thought that Pakistani expectations of US aid were 'self-stimulated'. He asked the US ambassador in Karachi to clarify to the Pakistan government that the US capabilities were limited, and that while it would provide equipment to enable Pakistan to play an effective role in the Middle East, Pakistan itself would have to bear the cost of maintaining its forces. Similarly, the US was not in a position to provide massive economic aid. Dulles believed that it was in Pakistan's interest to join SEATO, but he said it should not do so to oblige the United States. He also considered it imperative to clarify to Pakistan that the treaty aimed at defence against communist aggression and excluded involvement in Pakistan-India disputes.

The message could only add to Pakistan's reservations about SEATO. The government was not satisfied with the first draft of the treaty, which would cover only East Pakistan. Unlike NATO, it provided only for consultations, not joint action, in the event of aggression against one of its members. Nor did the treaty envisage the provision of defence and economic assistance. Keen not to offend China, it did not want the treaty to refer to communism or even appear to permit its possible extension to Formosa.

During discussions in Manila, the conference agreed to a redraft so as to cover the entire territories of the Asian parties. In Article IV, each party recognized that aggression against any of the parties would endanger its own security. However, the United States remained adamant in appending to the treaty the reservation that its obligations would apply only in the event of communist aggression. The treaty did not cover Pakistan against Indian aggression so far as the United States, its most powerful member, was concerned.

In the circumstances, the brief required the Pakistani delegation to first consult the government before accepting the document. However, upon urging by Dulles, Foreign Minister Zafrullah Khan decided to sign the treaty nevertheless. The Pakistan cabinet was surprised and displeased, and some of its members were critical of the foreign minister. Zafrullah Khan offered to resign. On reflection, the cabinet quietly acquiesced in his judgement.

Much has been made in Pakistan of Zafrullah's decision to exceed his brief, but not enough attention has been given to the consequences of a refusal to sign the treaty. Having insisted on an invitation to participate in the conference, it would have been counter-productive to withhold signature. It would have offended other participating states, antagonized opinion in the United States, and thus jeopardized the aid Pakistan so desperately sought. The obvious consequences were clearly unacceptable to the government, which hemmed and hawed for four months but, in the end, ratified the treaty in January 1955, after receiving an assurance from Dulles that in the event of non-communist aggression against Pakistan, the US 'would be by no means disinterested or inactive.'

SEATO members did not consider the 1965 War or the 1971 Indian military intervention in Pakistan to come under the purview of the treaty. After East Pakistan was severed, Pakistan withdrew from the organization in November 1972.

3. Baghdad Pact, 1955: Turkey and Iraq laid the foundation of the Baghdad Pact, signing a Pact of Mutual Cooperation for 'security and defence' in February 1955 in the Iraqi capital. It was not an auspicious start. In the first place, Turkey was unpopular in the Arab world for having recognized Israel. Secondly, Egypt, which was considered by Britain as the key to a defence arrangement in the Middle East, denounced the Baghdad Pact.

On receiving an invitation from Turkey and Iraq to join, Pakistan was not enthusiastic. Disappointed with the amount of US aid, Pakistan was no longer keen to undertake further military commitments in the Middle East. Ayub Khan, then defence minister as well as commander-in-chief of the army, whose opinion was decisive in security matters, was sceptical about the worth of the pact unless the United States also joined. Prime Minister Bogra did not make a commitment when the ambassadors of Iraq and Turkey met him. This position was, however, difficult to sustain. The bilateral agreements Pakistan had signed with Turkey and the United States were conceived as steps leading to a defence arrangement for the 'northern tier'. Pressures mounted from the USA as well as Britain, which wanted a regional arrangement, not so much for the defence of the countries of the region as to shore up its prestige after the setbacks it suffered in Iran and to protect its interests in oil and the Suez Canal.

In June, Ayub Khan was invited to Turkey. Prime Minister Nuri Said of Iraq was also there. He and the Turkish premier, Adnan Menderes, succeeded in convincing Ayub of the advantages of joining the pact, explaining that the United States could be counted upon to support the regional members, and that, in any case, the pact involved no additional commitments. Ayub agreed to recommend adherence by Pakistan. Within days, the Pakistan cabinet approved accession to the Baghdad Pact. Formal action was delayed, first because Pakistan wanted to reserve its position in order to limit defence commitments in case of a war involving Turkey as a member of NATO, and then on account of major changes in the Pakistani leadership in August.

The new prime minister, Chaudhri Muhammad Ali, entertained reservations about joining the pact but was over-ruled by President Iskander Mirza.

On 23 September 1955, Pakistan signed the Pact of Mutual Cooperation in Baghdad; the other regional members included Iran, Iraq, and Turkey. Britain also joined it, but the United States did not become a full member. The US Congress was concerned about the implications of the treaty in the event of a war involving Israel. Instead, the US decided to become an observer and agreed to association with its defence and political committees. Since that did not satisfy Pakistan, the US later signed another defence agreement with Pakistan.

The royal regime in Iraq was not popular to begin with. President Nasser's denunciation of the Baghdad Pact in general—and of the Iraqi government in particular—for breaking rank with the Arab world made it more vulnerable to criticism. In 1958, the Iraqi regime was overthrown in a bloody coup and the country pulled out of the pact named after its capital. Consequently, it was renamed the Central Treaty Organization (CENTO) in 1959.

Pakistan did not see eye to eye with London or Washington on issues in the Middle East. It was historically supportive of the Palestinian cause, friendly with Iran—no less under Prime Minister Mohammed Mossadegh than under the Shahanshah—and sympathetic toward Egyptian aspirations despite incipient reservations about the Neguib-Nasser government's emphasis on Arab nationalism, seemingly downgrading solidarity with non-Arab Muslim countries. Pakistan enjoyed especially close relations with Saudi Arabia, Jordan, and Iraq. There could be no question of Pakistan joining the West against the interests of Muslim nations in the Middle East. At the same time, it hoped for understanding of Pakistan's own security constraints.

Badaber Base, Peshawar: Meanwhile, during his visit to the United States in July 1957, Prime Minister Suhrawardy informed President Eisenhower of Pakistan's agreement to the establishment of a secret intelligence base at Badaber near Peshawar and for permission for US aircraft to use the Peshawar airbase. Ayub Khan was said to have made the decision in the light of his assessment of Pakistan's security imperatives and its economic and military aid needs. Also, Pakistan was interested in the early delivery of B-57 bombers.

Describing the base as a 'Communication Centre', the US did not disclose its exact purpose. Given extra-territorial rights, it operated the base with some 1,200 military and technical personnel, all from the United States. No Pakistani was ever admitted to the base and its purpose was indicated in general terms to a very few high Pakistani officials as being for electronic eavesdropping on the Soviet Union.

Meanwhile, the Peshawar airbase was used by high-level U-2 'spy in the sky' surveillance aircraft for illegal flights over the Soviet Union for photographic intelligence. The base enabled the US to complete a ring of similar bases around the Soviet Union. It was not only the most concrete and strategic benefit the US derived from the alliance, but one that exponentially increased Pakistan's importance in the eyes of the strategic community. The Pentagon, which had played virtually no part in the formation of the CENTO alliance, became its main protagonist. Pakistan did not learn until years later that the facility was also used for the same purpose against China.

For a decade, the base remained an anchor of US military and economic aid to Pakistan. It was also an important factor in restraining Washington from selling modern weapons systems to India.

4. Bilateral Defence Cooperation Agreement, 1959: In the 1959 agreement, the United States made concrete commitments of support to Pakistan's defence. Its Article 1 stated that the United States 'regards as vital to its national interests and to world peace the preservation of the independence and territorial integrity of Pakistan.' It further stated that 'in case of aggression against Pakistan . . . the United States of America . . . will take such appropriate action, including the use of armed forces, as may be mutually agreed upon and as is envisaged in the Joint Resolution to Promote Peace and Stability in the Middle East, in order to assist Pakistan at its request.' In Article II, the United States pledged 'to assist the Government of Pakistan in the preservation of its national independence and integrity and in the effective promotion of economic development.'

The agreement was supplemented by a Formal Note presented by Ambassador James Langley to Foreign Minister Manzur Qadir on

15 April 1959 which stated that 'the United States would promptly and effectively come to the assistance of Pakistan if it were subjected to armed aggression. A threat to the territorial integrity or political independence of the members (of CENTO) would be viewed by the United States with the utmost gravity.'

Islamabad regarded the alliances with the United States as 'the sheet anchor of Pakistan's foreign policy'. Washington, too, was appreciative of Pakistan as a 'wholehearted ally' which undertook 'real responsibilities and risks' by providing facilities 'highly important to (US) national security.'

Such strong mutual support was diluted after Pakistan developed friendly and cooperative relations with China, which the US regarded as an adversary, and the US decided to provide military aid to India, Pakistan's adversary, following its border confrontation with China.

The commitments made in the 1959 agreement did not guide US policy in the Pakistan-India wars of 1965 and 1971. It then took the view that its obligation under the 1959 agreement was subject to the clause 'as may be agreed upon' and limited to a case of 'armed aggression from any country controlled by international communism as provided in the Joint Resolution. The formal note of 15 April 1959 was an executive agreement of a US President lacking the binding character of a treaty that required ratification by the Senate.' Pakistan, however, felt the United States had let it down by failing to honour its obligation when Pakistan invoked this agreement in 1971.

Records are not available to indicate that the Pakistani side comprehended the significance and implications of the reference to the Joint Resolution. The US commitment in this agreement to assist Pakistan in the event of aggression seemed more specific and responsive than any contained in SEATO or CENTO. But when Pakistan tried to invoke the agreement in 1965, the US pointed out that the Joint Resolution on the Middle East limited the US obligation to come to Pakistan's assistance in the event of aggression by a communist state.

In subsequent years, the USSR abused its veto power in the Security Council to prevent adoption of every resolution on Kashmir. The Soviet Union was further outraged by Pakistan's decision to allow a US spy aircraft to use the Peshawar air base for high-altitude surveillance over Soviet territory. After it shot down a U-2 plane on 7 May 1960 and arrested its pilot, Gary Powers, it warned those countries that made their territory available for anti-Soviet intentions, 'Don't play with fire, gentlemen.'[18]

President John F. Kennedy adopted a policy of befriending India in 1961, but he remained sensitive to Pakistan's concerns. The joint communiqué issued after President Ayub Khan's visit to the United States in July 1961 reaffirmed: 'The Government of the United States regards as vital to its national interest and to world peace the preservation of the independence and integrity of Pakistan.' Kennedy also 'affirmed the desire of the United States to see a satisfactory solution of the Kashmir issue.' In conversations with the Pakistani president, he added that settlement of Kashmir was 'a vital US interest' as the Indians kept diverting the economic aid that the US was pouring into India to build armaments. He gave the assurance that he would try to bring Nehru round to a peaceful settlement of Kashmir, and if he failed, Pakistan could bring the matter to the UN Security Council, where the US would support Pakistan. The US kept this promise when the Kashmir issue came before the UN Security Council in May 1962. It joined six other members in support of a resolution that reminded India and Pakistan of earlier Security Council resolutions. The resolution was, however, vetoed by the USSR.

NOTES

1. *Documents*, ed. K. Arif, 15.
2. Ibid., 25.
3. McMahon, 60–75.
4. Dennis Kux, *Disenchanted Allies*, 45.
5. McMahon, 132.
6. Dennis Kux, op. cit., 47.
7. For quotations from the now public US records of British leaders including Prime Minister Winston Churchill and Foreign Secretary Anthony Eden, opposing arms supply to Pakistan, see Robert J. McMahon, *The Cold War on the Periphery*, 134, 144, 149, 167, 170, 171 ff.
8. Quoted in McMahon, 145.
9. Kux, 55.
10. M. Asghar Khan, *The First Round*, 84.
11. Ibid.
12. Ian Stephens, *Pakistan*, Ernest Benn, London, 1967, 220–1.

13. Richard Nixon, *The Memoirs of Richard Nixon*, 163.
14. F. S. Aijazuddin, ed., *The White House and Pakistan: Secret Declassified Documents, 1969–1974*, 4.
15. Dennis Kux, *Estranged Democracies*, 109.
16. *Documents*, ed. K. Arif, 107.
17. Dennis Kux, op. cit., 144.
18. Arthur M. Schlesinger, Jr., *A Thousand Days*, 482.

Chapter 6

The Alliances—Costs and Benefits

No sooner had Pakistan joined the alliances than second thoughts arose on the wisdom of the policy. Particularly corrosive was the harsh criticism of the Baghdad Pact by influential Arab countries. Pakistan's initial policy in the Suez Crisis caused an outrage even at home. Also, Pakistan was suddenly isolated in the kindred community of African-Asian nations who were suspicious of the West and looked upon the Soviet Union as a supporter of the struggle for emancipation from colonial domination and exploitation. Even more concrete were the costs of the furious Soviet reaction. Assured of the Soviet veto in the Security Council, India exploited Pakistan's decision to join the alliance to renounce its obligation for a plebiscite in Kashmir.

The Costs of the Alliances

Arab Criticism: Egypt was quick to take umbrage. Concerned about the implications of the alliances for Arab unity, and Egypt's aspirations to leadership of the Arab world, it denounced the alliance proposal. Radio Cairo said a Turko-Pakistan alliance would be 'a catastrophe for Islam . . . the first stab in our back. The next one will probably occur when Iraq joins the plot.'[1] The Saudi radio echoed the Arab Voice from Cairo when Pakistan joined the Baghdad Pact, calling the decision 'a stab in the heart of the Arab and Muslim states.'[2] Coming from a country that is the cradle of Islam, this allegation ashamed Pakistanis. The Saudi Kingdom invited Nehru to visit. On arrival, he was greeted with banners saying, '*Marhaba, rasool al salam*.' Even its literal meaning, 'Welcome messenger of peace', indicated unconcern for the sentiments of Pakistan, towards which Nehru's message was seldom of peace. Moreover, the slogan was deeply hurtful to sentiments of Pakistanis because they reserve the word '*rasool*' only for the Prophet.

M. Ayub Khan (President of Pakistan, 1960–9). Courtesy of the National Archives of Pakistan.

The Suez Crisis, 1956: President Gamal Abdel Nasser's sudden decision to nationalize the Suez Canal Company in July 1956 was provoked by the American decision to withdraw support for the building of the Aswan High Dam. Revenues from the canal were expected to provide an alternative source of funds. The decision outraged Britain and France, who owned the company. It also worried the United States and other Western countries. Though mistaken in retrospect, they imagined that Egypt's exclusive control over the maritime highway would jeopardize their vital trade interests. Pakistan, too, was similarly misled, on the ground that more than half of Pakistan's trade passed through the Suez Canal. Perhaps that was no more than a rationalization; Ceylon, India, and Indonesia, too, depended on the Suez Canal for trade, but they recognized the political roots of the issue.

Relations between Pakistan and Egypt had suffered on account of the clash between their policies on alliances with the West. Nasser evinced even less comprehension of Pakistan's security dilemmas than the Pakistan government did of Nasser's aim of uniting the Arab world for the defence of its dignity against Israel and its Western supporters. Pakistan disliked Nasser's emphasis on Arab nationalism and relegation of the Islamic bond. The two came into collision over the Baghdad Pact. Iraq's decision to join it was denounced by Egypt as a treacherous blow to Arab solidarity. Its emotional propaganda branded non-Arab Iran, Pakistan, and Turkey as agents of imperialism. Particularly offensive to Pakistan was Nasser's partiality to the Indian stand on Kashmir, failing to take cognisance of the right of self-determination of the Muslim people of the state.

Yet Pakistan was torn by a fundamental contradiction: its national commitment to solidarity with the causes of Muslim nations demanded support for Egypt. Loyalty to allies called for concession to their concern. No other issue in Pakistan's short history posed a sharper and more excruciating dilemma. The government decided on an expedient compromise. Lacking roots in the people, it failed to win credibility for the policy it thought best served the national interest. The people of Pakistan, who were wholly and uncritically supportive of Egypt, denounced it. The government had to correct its course, but only after Pakistan's name had suffered much damage.

Prime Minister Chaudhri Muhammad Ali decided on an objective and balanced approach, upholding Egypt's sovereign right to nationalize the canal, opposing the Anglo-French threat of use of force to resolve the dispute and also recognizing the interests of Pakistan and many other nations 'vitally concerned with the maintenance of the freedom of navigation.'[3] The policy did not meet with popular approval. The masses, the media, and revered veterans of the Pakistan movement of the stature of Fatima Jinnah and Sardar Abdur Rab Nishtar wanted unqualified support for Egypt. Worse, Pakistan's approach lost balance and its diplomacy credit as it came under pressure.

On the way to London to attend the conference of major users in mid-August, Foreign Minister Hamidul Haq Chowdhury personally assured Nasser of Pakistan's support for Egypt's right to ownership and control of the canal. At the conference, however, he succumbed to pressure and decided, apparently without clearance from the prime minister, to join eighteen (out of twenty-two) countries in supporting the suggestion for an international board to supervise the canal. Apparently, he did not think such international supervision detracted from Egypt's sovereignty.

The Pakistan delegation's vote not only provoked a charge of betrayal by Nasser, which was orchestrated by media throughout the Arab world, but also raised a political storm in Pakistan. Pained by the obloquy Pakistan incurred in the Muslim world, political parties including the ruling Muslim League censured the government's policy. Leaders from East and West Pakistan denounced the alliances. The masses came out to protest. Foreign Minister Chowdhury's attempt to explain the vote failed to carry conviction. The press subjected him to harsh censure.

For unconnected internal political reasons, Prime Minister Muhammad Ali resigned in September, and Huseyn Shaheed Suhrawardy became prime minister. He steered the government out of the storm. Chastened by the blunder at the first London conference, Pakistan made amends at the second, held in September. Foreign Minister Firoz Khan Noon was the only delegate to speak out against the proposal to set up a users' association. Instead, he advocated negotiations with Egypt. This did not please the sponsors; Dulles was especially unhappy. But Egypt was delighted by 'the return of the prodigal.' Nasser promptly sent an invitation to Noon to visit Cairo.

Although Suhrawardy retrieved Pakistan's self-respect, the Suez episode confirmed the view of those who regarded alliances as a liability, as Pakistan was seen to have obliged ally Britain and supported its imperialist aim at the cost of a Muslim country with a just cause, and thus allowed itself to be stood in a corner of shame and isolation. He would have been more kindly remembered had he not given gratuitous offence by venting his views, however logical they must have appeared to him, when, asked by a journalist in December 1956 why Muslim countries did not band together instead of getting tied to the West, he said, 'My answer is that zero plus zero plus zero is after all equal to zero!'[4]

Soviet Fury: Pakistani leaders were not enamoured of communism, and some military analysts thought also of the historical Soviet drive towards the warm waters of the Arabian Sea. But the severity of the Soviet reaction went beyond their calculation. Discarding its neutral stance in Pakistan-India disputes, Moscow threw its powerful weight behind India. Promising 'all help' to make India industrially strong,[5] the USSR announced aid for a big steel plant. On a visit to India in December 1955, Nikolai Bulganin and Nikita Khrushchev spited Pakistan by declaring they were 'grieved that imperialist forces succeeded in dividing India into two parts.' The '*Hindi-Roosi bhai bhai*' relationship was reflected also in their reference to Kashmir as 'one of the states of India'. The Soviet leaders also visited Afghanistan and demonstrated their hostility toward Pakistan by announcing support for Pushtoonistan.[6] They also extended a credit of $100 million to Afghanistan, to which they later added $85 million for the Kushk-Kandahar road and the Shindad military airfield.

US Alliance Strengthened

Although the costs of the alliances were high, Pakistan did not—could not afford to—abandon the policy. Guarantees against the ever-present security threat constrained reappraisal. In fact, Pakistan went on to strengthen the alliance with the United States by signing another defence agreement in April 1959.

In the new Cooperation Agreement, the United States went further than before in declaring, in Article I, that it 'regards as vital to its national interests and to world peace the preservation of the independence and territorial integrity of Pakistan.' It further stated that 'in case of aggression against Pakistan . . . the United States of America . . . will take such appropriate action, including the use of armed forces, as may be mutually agreed upon and as is envisaged in the Joint Resolution to Promote Peace and Stability in the Middle East, in order to assist Pakistan at its request.' In Article II, the United States pledged 'to assist the Government of Pakistan in the preservation of its national independence and integrity and in the effective promotion of economic development.'[7]

Records are not available to indicate that the Pakistani side comprehended the significance and implications of the reference to the Joint Resolution. The US commitment in this agreement to assist Pakistan in the event of aggression seemed more specific and responsive than any contained in SEATO or CENTO. But when Pakistan tried to invoke the agreement in 1965, the US pointed out that the Joint Resolution on the Middle East limited the US obligation to come to Pakistan's assistance in the event of aggression by a communist state.

The Benefits of the Alliances

Pakistan's purpose in joining the alliances was primarily to contain the Indian threat, in which the US had little interest. Deterred by the predictable repercussions on its relations with the larger and more influential India, the US did not at first 'dare'[8] to give military assistance to Pakistan. The need to strengthen security in the Middle East with its strategic oil resources impelled the US and Britain to harness Pakistan. With its location close to the Persian Gulf, its military manpower and its friendly predisposition, it was a 'real bulwark,' as Dulles said. But even then, the US remained excessively sensitive to Indian preferences. Eisenhower sent a letter of explanation to Nehru assuring him that the arms given by the US to Pakistan would not be allowed to be used for aggression, and offering to supply arms to India as well.

Benefits were initially meagre. The military aid announced by the United States for 1954, amounting to only $29.5 million, greatly disappointed even the protagonists of the alliance. Stunned, a 'broken hearted' Ayub Khan said, 'It would be better for Pakistan not to be involved in defence arrangements with the United States.' Prime

Minster Bogra told Dulles he would be 'derided'. It was argued that the aid did not compensate Pakistan for the additional risks it assumed by openly allying itself with the United States.

Washington did not expect Pakistani leaders to protest so vociferously. Having first pressed the United States for an alliance, they now seemed to imply it was being forced on them, and that as a result Pakistan was a target of Soviet hostility and therefore entitled to adequate aid to make it secure. If Pakistanis cited the analogy of a man leading a girl up the primrose path and then abandoning her, the Americans compared the Pakistani attitude to that of the girl chasing a man down the aisle and then complaining of gunpoint marriage. Chaudhri Muhammad Ali gave the apt example of 'a man asking for a gun to shoot a mad dog and being given a needle and thread to repair a hole in the trouser!'[9]

Pakistan's concerns were not dismissed in Washington, however. The US increased economic assistance to $106 million for 1954 and boosted military aid for 1955 to $50 million. More significantly, the US soon gave a commitment to equip four infantry divisions, one armoured division and another armoured brigade, provide modern aircraft for six squadrons for the air force, and supply twelve vessels for the navy over the coming years.

Despite Indian protests, US economic and military aid for Pakistan rapidly increased. Annual allocations were doubled after 1959. Altogether, over the 1954–62 period, US economic assistance amounted to $3.5 billion.[10] In addition, the US provided $1.3 billion for defence support and purchase of equipment.[11] From an antiquated, poorly equipped force in 1954, Pakistan's armed forces became a powerful defence machine, with heavy armour and artillery, the latest aircraft and ships, confident of its self-defence capability. Speaking in the National Assembly in February 1957, Suhrawardy expressed satisfaction over the 'dividends' of the country's foreign policy. In the United States, Pakistan had 'a friend and an ally'.[12]

The grievance over the amount of aid was substantially rectified, but Pakistan still considered the aid level incommensurate with the liabilities the alliance was perceived to entail. Its second thoughts continued to grow because of criticism by friends and penalties by adversaries.

Pakistani grievance was no longer so much about the quantity of American aid as about the quality of its political support. The United

States' desire to maintain friendly relations also with India was understandable, but not so a policy that downgraded an ally to a level of parity with a nominally neutral state with a pro-Soviet tilt. With both the USA and the USSR competing for its favours, India was rewarded for hunting with the hounds and running with the hare.

The seeds of disaffection were inherent in the ambiguous bargain. The alliance lacked the bond of a common adversary. Pakistan was focused on the threat from India. The US premise was that Pakistan would play a major part in the defence of the Middle East. Neither side gave enough thought to the glaring contradiction. Having first sought the alliance, Pakistan soon felt it was doing the United States a favour, exaggerating its costs and undervaluing the benefits. Still the mismatch was accepted. Current imperatives prevailed over seemingly remote risks. In 1959, Pakistan entered into another agreement with the United States.

At the popular level, Pakistani dissatisfaction was articulated in the cultural context that expects a friend to be constant and loyal, supportive and self-sacrificing. Having thrown in its lot with the West, it also threw caution to the winds by proudly joining the fight against 'the totalitarian concept'.[13] The 'great disappointment' was particularly due to the American failure to throw its weight behind a just settlement of the Kashmir dispute.[14]

The imperative of national security is primordial. Lacking adequate means to ensure defence against the ever-looming Indian threat, it was perfectly rational for Pakistan to look for alliances to compensate for the glaring power disparity. Opposition to the policy of alliances increased over the years because it cut across other aims and aspirations of the people. Foremost among these was the deep-seated desire of the people for solidarity with other Muslim peoples. They felt they were a part of the *umma,* the global Muslim community. If the state allowed security policy to clash with the national aspiration for support of the cause of a Muslim nation, the people of Pakistan felt torn, and the more open the contradiction, the greater the popular opposition. Nowhere did the opposing priorities clash more glaringly than in the Suez crisis, and nowhere else did they mesh so perfectly as in the Afghanistan crisis a quarter of a century later.

The contradiction could have been reconciled as it was in the final stage of the Suez crisis. A government in tune with public opinion might have done it sooner, but those in power at the time contributed instead to widening the gulf by flouting popular sentiments and antagonising the Egyptian leader.

Popular views in Pakistan about the United States and the Soviet Union were not as clear-cut as those of the government. Political opinion was ranged against the United States and Britain from the beginning because of their support for the creation of a Zionist state in Palestine at the expense of its predominantly Muslim population. The resentment built up as Israel pursued a policy of genocide, depriving the Palestinian people of their national homeland, killing tens of thousands and driving hundreds of thousands into forced exile. The capitalist system was considered abominable, its exploitative nature manifest in the striking gulf between the rich and the poor. By contrast, despite the official heritage of suspicion of Russian expansionism and subversive communism, the popular view admired the Soviet Union for achieving rapid development and redistribution of wealth on an equitable basis. Opinion was swayed by progressive writers and poets with their idealist depiction of socialism, totally oblivious to the reality of Stalinist repression with millions liquidated or terrorized by a brutal and ruthless state machinery invested with arbitrary powers of arrest, torture to extract confessions, and summary justice condemning dissidents to death or slave labour in Siberian exile. The Soviet suppression of religion, prohibition of public prayers, and the demolition of all but a few hundred of the 27,000 mosques and 80,000 churches that existed during the czarist period remained unknown because the carefully selected Pakistani visitors were rarely interested in seeing, much less publicizing, the seamy side of their socialist paradise.

The US policy was to change dramatically after the Sino-Indian border clash in 1962. But even before that, opinion in the United States began to change in favour of India.

Swings of Opinion in the US and Pakistan

Pakistan was not alone in having second thoughts about the policy of alliances. Opinion in the United States, too, began to swing within a few years, illustrated by the radical change in evaluation of neutralism. At first, allies were admired and rewarded, neutral states criticized and penalized in allocation of economic assistance.

In 1954, influential Republican Senator William Knowland opposed the policy of 'rewarding neutralism', and in 1956, Dulles denounced neutralism as 'an immoral and shortsighted conception'.[15] By 1957, neutralism acquired a mantle of respectability; indeed, a position of privilege. Eisenhower endorsed India's neutrality and in internal discussions became critical of his own administration's 'tendency to rush out and seek allies'. He called the alliance with Pakistan 'a terrible error'.[16] As the USSR began assistance to non-aligned India, opinion in the Democratic party and academia in the USA began to advocate increased economic assistance to India. Professors Walt Rostow and Max Milliken of MIT called for aid to India and other countries faced with 'the revolution of rising expectations' in order to enable them to achieve 'take off' under democracy.[17] Adlai Stevenson, Averell Harriman and former ambassadors to India Chester Bowles and Senator Cooper became massive aid-to-India advocates. Calling India 'the hinge of fate of Asia', Senator John F. Kennedy advocated maximum support to India's development in February 1959, warning, 'If China succeeds and India fails . . . the balance of power will shift against us.' He even defended Indian neutrality recalling that during its formative period in the nineteenth century America, too, followed non-involvement.[18]

Opinion in Pakistan was deeply agitated by the change in US policy. While Pakistan was 'taken for granted' by its allies and penalized by the Soviet Union, neutral India was courted by both the US and the USSR. The West was becoming lukewarm in its support for Pakistan on the Kashmir question. The Pakistan government was placed on the defensive. It seemed to have made a bad bargain politically, if not also materially. While Pakistan suffered loss of esteem due to its alliance with the West, neutralism enhanced India's prestige, with the Soviet Union and the United States competing for India's goodwill and giving it aid and assistance. Under pressure of criticism in the National Assembly, Prime Minister Firoz Khan Noon exploded in frustration on 8 March 1958: 'Our people, if they find their freedom threatened by Bharat, will break all pacts and shake hands with people whom we have made enemies because of others.'[19]

General Ayub Khan, during his visit to the United States as army commander-in-chief in April 1958, also emphasized to US officials and military chiefs that 'a definite ground swell' was developing in Pakistan against alliances, because Indian attitudes towards Pakistan had hardened as US aid enabled it to divert its own resources to the purchase of military equipment. Hearing this from one of the architects of the alliance, the US administration was impressed. Secretary of State John Foster Dulles explained that strategic compulsions necessitated aid to India, but, he assured Ayub, the American relationship with India was on an intellectual level whereas that with Pakistan was 'more from the heart'.[20]

Assessing that the military threat of communist expansion had abated, and that the threat now centred on the contest for economic development, the United States decided to focus on economic assistance, overlooking the distinction between allied and non-aligned countries. Even before embarking on a collision course with China on the border issue, India was flaunting itself as a counter-model to China. The world was supposed to be watching 'who would win—India under democracy or China under communism.'[21] Senator John F. Kennedy foresaw apocalypse: 'If India collapses, so may all of Asia.' In 1958, he joined with Republican Senator John Sherman Cooper to sponsor a resolution for enhanced aid to India. Deterioration in India's relations with China due to disagreement over the boundary, and India's support for the secessionist Dalai Lama in 1959, provided a further fillip to burgeoning US support for India. It was proclaimed a 'key country'[22] in the West's struggle against communism. The Eisenhower administration, which had started by cutting aid to India, now swung to the other extreme, increasing the amount from $93 million in 1956 to $365 million in 1957[23] and a record $822 million in 1960. In addition, the US decided, in 1960, to provide $1.2 billion under PL 480 (US Public Law 480 relating to the Global Food Aid Programme) for the export of 12 million tons of wheat to India over the next four years. President Eisenhower also interceded with other Western leaders and the president of the World Bank to enhance economic support for India.

Reacting to the new trends, Pakistan also sought to normalize relations with the USSR. In December 1960, Pakistan signed an agreement with the Soviet Union for exploration of petroleum resources that marked the beginning of an improvement in bilateral relations.

The wooing of India became even more pronounced after John F. Kennedy became president. Although he was not unaware of 'Nehru's talent for international self-righteousness'[24] he regarded India as 'the key area' in Asia. In his inaugural address, he paid high tribute to 'the soaring idealism of Nehru' and placed ardent Indophiles in key positions.[25] The administration provided $1 billion for aid to India in its first budget. Soon, the United States also decided to provide a 400-megawatt nuclear power plant to India.

Pakistan welcomed the opportunity provided by Vice President Johnson's visit in May 1961 to get its message across to the new US administration. He was impressed by the case made by President Ayub Khan for the resolution of the Kashmir dispute and provision of American military equipment.

Ayub Khan's Visit to the US: Kennedy decided to ask President Ayub Khan to advance his visit from November to July 1961 'to exchange views on matters of immediate concern.' In his welcoming speech, he expressed concern over the 'misunderstandings' that had arisen. He was evidently aware of Pakistan's perception of declining US support. During talks, Ayub Khan gave an account of India's stonewalling on Kashmir. Kennedy recognized the urgency of settling the Kashmir dispute and said that it was 'a vital interest of the United States.' He promised to speak to Nehru, and if unsuccessful, to support Pakistan at the United Nations.

When Ayub Khan expressed apprehension over the possible US supply of weapons to India, Kennedy replied that the US did not intend to do so, but 'if a Sino-Indian conflict ever erupted, and India asked the United States for military aid, he would first consult with Ayub before making a commitment.'[26] He also gave an unequivocal assurance that Pakistan had the right to use American equipment freely in defence of its borders.

Ayub Khan told Kennedy he was going to publicly advocate the restoration of the rights of the People's Republic of China in the United Nations. Kennedy commented, 'Let them have it!' Ayub Khan did so during the NBC's 'Meet the Press' and ABC's 'Editors' Choice' TV programmes.

In a 50-minute extempore speech, Ayub Khan told a joint session of the US Congress, 'You have great obligations (and) you cannot hide from them.' While it was 'easy to get tired' of the foreign aid programme, he suggested, 'you had better not get tired at this point.' He assured the congressmen, 'The only people (in South Asia) who will stand by you are the people of Pakistan provided you are also prepared to stand by them.' He received a standing ovation. The previous evening, he had been taken by decorated launches down the Potomac to President Washington's historic house, Mount Vernon, for a glittering banquet, personally planned by Mrs Kennedy. He 'charmed everybody' in Washington.[27] Vice President Lyndon Johnson hosted a reception in the Pakistani president's honour for 600 prominent guests at his Texas ranch.

In the joint communiqué issued on 13 July, 'President Kennedy affirmed the desire of the United States to see a satisfactory solution of the Kashmir issue and expressed the hope that progress towards a settlement would be possible at an early date.' The two leaders also reaffirmed 'the solemn purpose of the bilateral agreement (of March, 1959)' and 'the value of existing security agreements as an instrument against aggression.'

Kennedy's Efforts to Promote a Kashmir Settlement: Four months later, Nehru visited Washington. Kennedy entertained high hopes of the Indian leader, but after talks he felt disappointed. When Kashmir was discussed, Nehru was rigid and dogmatic, ruling out any solution other than perpetuation of the division of the state. Talking to Nehru, Kennedy said after the talks, was 'like trying to grab something in your hand, only to have it turn out to be just fog.'[28] Nehru would answer questions with indifference or lapse into silence. It was partly because at seventy-one his energies were depleted but partly, too, because of his self-centred focus.[29] Like President Truman and Secretary of State Dean Acheson before him,[30] Kennedy found Nehru's sense of superiority 'rather offensive'. Their meeting was a 'disaster'. Nehru's visit was 'the worst' state visit Kennedy had ever had.[31]

Washington was further disillusioned when, in December 1961, India invaded defenceless Goa. 'The contrast between Nehru's incessant sanctimony on the subject of non-aggression and his brisk exercise in *Machtpolitik* was too comic to not cause comment. It was a little like catching the preacher in the hen-house.'[32] Kennedy professed 'shock'. Adlai Stevenson, the US representative to the UN, soared to heights of eloquence in concluding that 'if the United Nations was not to die as ignoble a death as the League of Nations, we cannot condone the use of force in this instance and thus pave the way for forceful solutions of other disputes.' However, neither disappointment with Nehru nor admiration for Ayub Khan had much influence on American policy of support for India in the context of their relations with China.

The United States made an attempt to promote settlement of Kashmir. On 3 January, acting Secretary of State George Ball said the US was 'very serious about it' and would take 'a very strong position'. The next morning, Kennedy told the same thing to the Pakistani ambassador, saying he was conscious of the importance of settling this dispute, as resources of both India and Pakistan were being wasted on 'diversionary arms build-ups'. That afternoon, Kennedy announced that he proposed to appoint World Bank president Eugene Black to lend his good offices to India and Pakistan to settle the Kashmir dispute. Pakistan accepted the offer, but Nehru rejected it.

Kashmir Issue Back at the Security Council: In the meantime, Pakistan decided to move the Security Council to take up consideration of the Kashmir dispute. Contrary to Kennedy's commitment to Ayub Khan, the US administration was hesitant to extend support. On 11 April, Dean Rusk told Ambassador Aziz Ahmed and Zafrullah Khan, then representative to the UN, 'If we are to be helpful in settling this matter in both capitals, then for us to reaffirm our position in the Security Council will affect our ability to be of use. This is our dilemma.' Zafrullah Khan asked Rusk to determine what was holding up progress and who could do what, so that the block could be removed. Assistant Secretary of State Talbot asked if Pakistan would go back to the resolutions of the Security Council. When Zafrullah Khan replied that there was no other way, Talbot commented that India was of the view it was not feasible to implement the resolutions as so much time had elapsed. Zafrullah asked him, 'Is the right of self-determination subject to a time limit?'

The Security Council took up discussion of Kashmir on 28 April 1962. India repudiated its commitment to a plebiscite and Krishna Menon said, 'There has been no commitment at any time by the Government of India that they would take a plebiscite in Kashmir' (sic). Recalling Nehru's statement of 5 March 1948 reiterating India's 'unilateral declaration that we would abide by the will of the people of Kashmir as declared in a plebiscite or referendum,' *The Washington Post* called Menon's statement 'a brilliant piece of double think'.[33]

The Security Council continued to debate the question over two months. Under pressure from India, members from non-aligned countries were reluctant to move a resolution. Finally, in June, the Republic of Ireland agreed, after Kennedy's personal intercession with its president, to sponsor a resolution that reminded India and Pakistan of past resolutions of the Security Council calling for a plebiscite in Kashmir. Seven of the Council's nine members supported the resolution, but it was vetoed by the Soviet Union.

NOTES

1. Quoted from *Dawn* of 22 February 1954 in Burke and Ziring, op. cit., 202.
2. Quoted from *Dawn* of 26 September 1955 in Burke and Ziring, op. cit., 204.
3. Statement issued on 14 August 1956, quoted in Burke and Ziring, op. cit., 185.
4. *Documents*, ed. K. Arif, 125.
5. Burke and Ziring, op. cit., 209.
6. Taking note of the Soviet statements, the SEATO council declared at its meeting in Karachi on 8 March 1956 that 'sovereignty of Pakistan extends up to the Durand Line' and the treaty area included territory up to that line. *Documents*, ed. K. Arif, 116–17.
7. Text of the agreement in *Documents*, ed. K. Arif, 156–9.
8. John Foster Dulles's briefing to Senate Foreign Relations Committee on 3 July 1953, extract in *Documents*, ed. K. Arif, 78.
9. Farooq Bajwa, *Pakistan and the West*, 87.
10. The table below illustrates the level of US economic assistance to Pakistan, including both grants and soft loans. The data for 1953–70 is from *Effectiveness of Aid to Pakistan*, March 1990, Economic Affairs Division, Government of Pakistan, and from 1971 from *Economic Survey*, 1995–96, Finance Division, Islamabad. It illustrates how the aid level rose and fell during the period. (Also see footnote 295).
(Figures are in US $ million)

1953	1954	1955	1956	1957	1958	1959	1960	1961	1962	1963	1964	1965	1966	1967
45	89	114	93	365	305	367	758	668	755	151	140	95	182	223

1968	1969	1970	1971	1972	1973	1974	1975	1976	1977	1978	1979	1980	1981
162	123	28	15	129	110	100	107	108	133	78	79	82	57

11. *Documents*, ed. K. Arif, 285–6, statement by James Noyes, Deputy Assistant Secretary for Defence, on 20 March 1973. Part of the aid was used to build Multan and Kharian cantonments and Sargodha air base.
12. *Documents*, ed. K. Arif, 127.
13. Prime Minister Bogra's broadcast to the nation, 1 October 1954. Extract in *Documents*, ed. K. Arif, 102.

14. Firoz Khan Noon's memoirs, extracts in *Documents*, ed. K. Arif, 163.
15. Quoted from the *New York Times* of 10 June 1956 in Dennis Kux, op. cit., 128.
16. Report of National Security Council meeting of 3 January 1957 quoted in Dennis Kux, op. cit., 154.
17. Dennis Kux, op. cit., 144.
18. Arthur M. Schlesinger, Jr., *A Thousand Days*, 482.
19. Quoted from *Dawn* of 9 March 1958 in Altaf Gauhar, *Ayub Khan*, 113–14.
20. Altaf Gauhar, op. cit., 119.
21. India's ambassador Chagla, quoted in McMahon, op. cit., 260.
22. Walter Lippman quoted in Robert J. McMahon, op. cit., 261.
23. In contrast US aid to Pakistan increased marginally from $162.5 million in 1956 to $170 million in 1957.
24. Schlesinger, op. cit., 483.
25. Chester Bowles, who as ambassador to India advocated the ditching of Pakistan, was given the No. 2 slot in the State Department as undersecretary. Phillips Talbot, an India specialist, became Assistant Secretary of State for the Near East and South Asia, and a Harvard professor known for his sympathy for India, John Kenneth Galbraith, was appointed ambassador to New Delhi.
26. Quoted from US documents, McMahon, op. cit., 280.
27. Ayub 'charmed everybody' during his visit to the USA, 'ingratiated' himself with Mrs Kennedy, and 'shone' at a gala dinner. Quoted in McMahon, op. cit., 280. Vice President Johnson described Ayub as a 'seasoned' leader and a 'dependable' ally. US records, quoted in McMahon, op. cit., 278–9.
28. Schlesinger, op. cit., 485.
29. He 'displayed interest and vivacity only with Jacqueline.' When reminded of this, Kennedy remarked, 'A lot of our visiting statesmen have that same trouble.' Schlesinger, 485.
30. According to US document 690D/760.02, Central File, quoted in Farooq Naseem Bajwa, *Pakistan and the West*, 15, President Truman told Avra Warren, US ambassador to Pakistan, that he had a 'disagreeable' time with Nehru, Nehru's attitudes on disputes with Pakistan were 'silly' and he did not observe 'any inclination on the part of Nehru to be reasonable on the Kashmir dispute.' Truman's Secretary of State Dean Acheson described Nehru as 'one of the most difficult men with whom I have ever had to deal.' McMahon, op. cit., 56.
31. Quoted from *Robert Kennedy in His Own Words*, and Arthur Schlesinger, *A Thousand Days*, in McMahon, op. cit., 281.
32. Schlesinger, 487.
33. Dated 26 May 1962.

Chapter 7

China and Other Countries

China

Pakistan recognized the People's Republic of China soon after the revolution in 1948. Relations were amicable and remained on an even keel despite Pakistan's criticism of communism and its increasing cooperation with the United States, as well as tension in Sino-US relations. Even after Pakistan joined SEATO, China criticized the alliance but not Pakistan. Unlike the Soviet Union, it understood that Pakistan's motivation was the need for security against the Indian threat, and not any hostility towards China or any other nation.

More impressive for Pakistan was China's scrupulous avoidance of any partisan pronouncement on Pakistan-India disputes. It did not seek to strengthen relations with India at Pakistan's expense. Even during a visit to India at the height of the '*Hindi-Chini bhai bhai*' phase in June 1954, Premier Zhou Enlai did not criticize Pakistan.

Pakistan was less careful in its anti-communist rhetoric. At a conference in Colombo in May 1954,[1] Prime Minister Mohammad Ali Bogra spoke of international communism as 'the biggest potential danger to democracy in the region.' At India's insistence, the conference communiqué was more balanced. It called for resistance to interference by 'external communist, [as well as] anti-communist or other agencies.'

Premier Zhou Enlai told the departing Pakistani ambassador that he was hurt by Pakistan's statement, because he regarded Pakistan as a friend. Still, he said, he 'fully understood' Pakistan's circumstances.[2] He expressed the hope that Pakistan would follow principles of peaceful coexistence.[3]

Pakistan did not fail to notice Chinese forbearance and henceforth followed a more balanced policy. At the Afro-Asian summit conference in Bandung in April 1955, Bogra asked for a meeting with the Chinese premier; Zhou Enlai insisted on coming over himself. The meeting was remarkably friendly. Zhou readily accepted Bogra's explanation that Pakistan's membership of SEATO was not directed against China.

In the summit conference, the Pakistani prime minister stated that China 'is by no means an imperialist nation and has not brought any other country under her heel.' He especially praised Zhou, who 'has shown a great deal of conciliation.' Zhou, playing the role of the statesman that he was, helped to reconcile the differences among participants as to whether the communiqué should refer to colonialism only by the Western powers or by both Soviet and Western powers, suggesting that it refer to 'colonialism in all its manifestations.'[4]

The Bandung Conference provided an opportunity for Bogra and Zhou to also discuss bilateral relations. Zhou publicly acknowledged Bogra's statement that Pakistan was not against China, had no fear that China would commit aggression, and, further, that if the United States should take aggressive action under SEATO, Pakistan would not be involved, adding that 'through these explanations we achieved a mutual understanding.'[5]

Prime Minister Zhou's visit to Pakistan in December 1956 led to further development of bilateral understanding. The joint communiqué recorded the shared view of the prime ministers that 'the divergence of views on many problems should not prevent the strengthening of friendship between their two countries. . . . They are happy to place on record that there is no real conflict of interests between the two countries.'[6]

Despite better mutual understanding, US pressure on Pakistan at times led to anomalous stances. On the one hand, Pakistan recognized the People's Republic of China and supported its government's claim to China's seat in the UN. On the other, it did not oppose a resolution sponsored by the United States for the postponement of the consideration of the question of China's representation, and instead abstained in 1952 and 1957, and supported the US manoeuvre for several years up to 1960. Similarly, in October 1959, Pakistan voted for a UN General Assembly resolution calling for 'respect for the fundamental human rights of the Tibetan people and for their distinctive cultural and religious life.'[7]

At other times, offence was gratuitous. In April 1959, Ayub Khan made the extraordinary proposal of joint defence with India. Even after Nehru ridiculed the offer by rhetorically asking, 'Joint defence against whom?', Ayub Khan persisted, forecasting that South Asia would become militarily vulnerable in five years to major invasions from the north.[8] To leave no doubt that he meant both China and the Soviet Union, he issued yet another statement.[9] Perhaps he 'genuinely believed'[10] that Pakistan and India needed to cooperate to forestall the danger. Perhaps he hoped to convince Nehru to realize the desirability of resolving the Kashmir issue in the interest of defending the region. Or perhaps he was trying to humour Washington.[11] Whatever his reasons, Ayub Khan's statements were incongruent with emergent strategic realities and Pakistan's interests.[12]

It is a tribute to the wisdom and foresight of Chinese leaders that Beijing continued to show extraordinary forbearance, overlooking Pakistan's aberrations. Fortunately, these lapsed into limbo. After 1959, friendship and cooperation between the two countries followed a steady and unswerving path and became a crucial factor for peace in South Asia. No other country has been as comprehending of Pakistan's constraints as China.

By 1960, the Sino-Soviet split began to surface. The United States was already hostile to China, with its naval and air power operating close to China's seaboard. Resolutely resisting both superpowers, China was now concerned also about India, which was giving encouragement to separatist elements in Tibet and evincing an imperious attitude on the boundary issue. Beijing understood even better than before the difficulties Pakistan confronted at the hands of India, backed by the Soviet Union. Sharing adversity, the two countries drew closer.[13] By no means so presumptuous as to enter the contest of giants, Pakistan demonstrated the courage to resist the political and economic pressures of its American ally in grasping China's hand of friendship across the Karakorum Range and breaching the ring the USA, the USSR, and India sought to build around China.

Boundary Agreement, 1962

Pakistan approached China in November 1959 with the proposal for demarcation of the border between the two countries. It was desirable to do this in order to pre-empt any problems. Pakistan was encouraged by China's eminently reasonable posture, manifest in its boundary agreement with Myanmar in January 1960 to their complete mutual satisfaction. Its boundary agreements with Nepal and Thailand were also amicably negotiated. In March 1961, Pakistan sent a formal note to China proposing negotiations on the boundary. Beijing was still hesitant because the matter involved Kashmir territory and it did not want to have another argument with India. This problem took time to resolve, but a formula was found whereby the boundary to be demarcated would be between Xinjiang and the contiguous areas, 'the defence of which was under the control of Pakistan', thus by-passing the question of sovereignty over the territory. On 4 May 1962, the two countries announced agreement to begin negotiations.

Started on 12 October 1962, the talks were conducted in a friendly spirit of mutual accommodation, and within two months Pakistan and China reached an agreement (nine days before the Sino-Indian clash).[14] The boundary followed the Karakorum watershed, crossing over K-2, the world's second highest peak. It involved no transfer of territory from the control of either country to the other. Pakistan remembers with gratitude an extraordinary gesture by Premier Zhou Enlai: after the alignment was agreed, the Pakistan government belatedly realized that some grazing lands along the Murtagh River in the Shimshal Pass on the other side of the watershed were historically used by inhabitants of Hunza. It then appealed for an exception to the watershed principle to save hardship to the poor people. Zhou generously agreed to the amendment of the boundary so that an area of 750 square miles remained on the Pakistan side.

The Indian allegation that Pakistan ceded a part of Kashmir territory to China was unfounded. Since a recognized boundary historically did not exist, there could be no question of any such give-away. Pakistan did not transfer any territory that was under its control.

The boundary agreement was motivated by a desire to preclude any controversy between the two neighbours. It was, however, misunderstood by Washington as a tactic of pressure in the context of Kashmir, and considered yet more evidence of 'Pakistan's drift toward Communist China.'[15]

Not too many years later, the USA saw that it was mistaken in its biased assumption of a monolithic communist bloc, its distorted view of China as an expansionist state, and its analysis of the Sino-Indian border clash as a defining moment in the history of democracy's crusade against communism. In the early 1960s, however, Washington was intent on isolating China, and pulling India into its orbit was a dominant passion of the time. Pakistan was seen to be an obstruction, and the United States had no hesitation in pulling levers of pressure in its attempt to bring Pakistan into line.

Sino-Pakistan Entente

A unique characteristic of China's policy toward Pakistan was to observe implicit respect for Pakistan's sovereignty. The Chinese leaders did not even proffer unsolicited advice. During exchanges of views with their Pakistani counterparts, they would describe their own experiences and let Pakistanis draw the conclusion if they so wished. When Pakistan embarked on improvement of relations with the Soviet Union in 1960, the Chinese leaders did not try to hold Pakistan back although Beijing-Moscow relations had begun to sour, and even expressed understanding of Pakistan's reasons.

Relations between Pakistan and China continued to deepen in the wake of the boundary agreement and especially after Pakistan defied Anglo-American pressures to join their policy of support for India against China during the Sino-Indian border war. Pakistan also demonstrated a firm independent stance when, despite sanctions imposed by the United States, it established air links with China, breaching the American strategy aimed at containment and isolation of China. Contacts between the leaders of the two countries became frequent. On their way to countries of the Middle East, Africa, and Europe, Chinese leaders transited through Pakistan, which provided opportunities for achieving closer sympathetic understanding of each other's concerns. In multilateral fora, Pakistan defended Chinese interests.[16]

During his visit to China in March 1965, Ayub Khan was accorded an effusive welcome. Chairman Mao Zedong expressed warm appreciation for Pakistan's support. In the joint communiqué, Pakistan joined China in denouncing the 'two Chinas' policy of the United States. Also, 'the two parties noted with concern that the Kashmir dispute remains unresolved and considered its continued existence a threat to peace and security in the region. They reaffirmed that this dispute should be resolved in accordance with the wishes of the people of Kashmir as pledged to them by India and Pakistan.'

Oman: Gwadar Retrocession

In the nineteenth century, the Gwadar territory on the Balochistan coast had been given to the Sultan of Oman by the Khan of Kalat on the occasion of his daughter's wedding. It was an obvious anachronism in the post-colonial era. Pakistan sought its return and reunion by amicable negotiation through the UK government. An agreement was reached in 1958 by which the fraternal sultanate ceded the territory to Pakistan. Apart from a modest payment, Pakistan agreed to allow continued recruitment of personnel for the sultanate forces from Gwadar. The peaceful transaction ensured the maintenance of friendly relations between Pakistan and Oman as well as continued enjoyment of benefits of employment in Oman by the people of Balochistan.

Indus Waters Treaty, 1960

As Egypt is said to be the gift of the Nile, Pakistan is the gift of the Indus. Of the thirty-seven million acres of land irrigated by canals from the Indus River and its tributaries, in 1947 over thirty million acres were in Pakistan—an area equal to the irrigated lands in Egypt and Sudan. The Indus and its major tributaries rise in or beyond the Himalayas and flow through Indian-held Kashmir or India. Partition gave India a stranglehold over the rivers flowing south into Pakistan. In 1948, India decided unilaterally to cut off supplies to the canals flowing from headworks under its control, ignoring Pakistan's rights under international law. It also embarked on the construction of the Bhakra Dam on the Sutlej, in order to divert the entire water supply of the river.

In 1950, Pakistan proposed arbitration, but India refused. As David Lilienthal, former chairman of the Tennessee Valley Authority, wrote in an article: 'No armies with bombs and shellfire could devastate a land so thoroughly as Pakistan could be devastated by the simple expedient of India's permanently shutting off the source of waters that keep the fields and people of Pakistan green.'[17] In 1952, World Bank President Eugene Black offered his good offices for a solution of the dispute that would provide India additional supplies of water without damage to Pakistan, which the two countries accepted. Negotiations over the highly technical issues took eight years to resolve. The Indus Waters Treaty was signed on 19 September 1960. It allocated the waters of the three eastern rivers (Ravi, Beas, and Sutlej) for use by India, and the waters of the western rivers (Indus, Jhelum, and Chenab) for use in Pakistan, except for (a) domestic and non-consumptive uses of the river waters in the areas under Indian control, and (b) for agriculture, subject to specified limits.

The compromise conceded to India what it wanted, but the World Bank raised the requisite funds for the construction of two large dams at Mangla on the Jhelum and Tarbela on the Indus and 400 miles of link canals from the western rivers in Pakistan to replace the loss due to diversion of waters of the eastern rivers by India. (Three of the seven link canals carry ten times as much water as the Thames, and twice as much as the Potomac.) Of the estimated expenditure of $1.3 billion on replacement works, the treaty required India to pay $170 million, while the United States contributed over $500 million and the rest was donated largely by Australia, Britain, Canada, Germany, and New Zealand.

The Indus Waters Treaty was also farsighted in anticipating problems that might arise in interpretation and implementation of the complex agreement. World Bank experts in law, economics, construction, and engineering foresaw as many contingencies as were likely to arise, so that the treaty provides a self-executing mechanism for their peaceful resolution in a professional manner. In the first place, the Permanent Indus Commission, comprising high-level technical representatives of the two sides, has the responsibility to resolve differences of interpretation and ensure smooth implementation. In case the Commission is unable to agree on a 'question' of interpretation, the matter can be taken up at the level of government; and if governments also cannot agree, the 'difference' can be referred to a 'neutral expert' to be appointed by the parties or, if they fail to agree, by the World Bank. The decision of the neutral expert is binding. If the difference does not fall in the mandate of the neutral expert or the neutral expert rules that it should be treated as a 'dispute', it has to be submitted to a court of arbitration whose award is final.[18]

India-China Border War, 1962[19]

Rooted in contested historical claims to territories along almost the entire length of the Sino-Indian border from eastern and northern India to the disputed state of Jammu and Kashmir, the boundary dispute surfaced in 1958 when the Indian government came to know of the Tibet-Xinjiang road along Ladakh, which the Chinese had started to build in 1951. India protested that the road was built 'through indisputably Indian territory', basing this assertion on the McMahon Line drawn in 1914 pursuant to discussions between Henry McMahon and a representative of Tibet whose claim to sovereignty was contested by the Chinese government. China did not accept the validity of the boundary map 'drawn by a British traveller,' arguing: 'Historically, no treaty or agreement on the Sino-Indian boundary has ever been concluded between the Chinese central government and the Indian government.'[20] It suggested the observance of the line of actual control pending negotiations to delimit the boundary, taking into account both the historical background and the existing realities. India, however, insisted on the acceptance of the McMahon Line. Emboldened by Soviet military supplies and the Kennedy administration's stepped-up economic assistance, while China was under increasing Soviet pressure in addition to continuing US hostility, India adopted a 'forward policy', hoping to negotiate from a position of strength. Its forces undertook aggressive patrolling and built military posts in the disputed area. The easy conquest of Portuguese-ruled Goa in December 1961 made Indian leaders even more reckless. In February 1962, an Indian minister publicly threatened to 'drive out the Chinese forces.' In September, India sent a brigade to Thagla Ridge in the northeast.

On 11 October 1962, Nehru gave a call for battle, declaring 'Our instructions are to free our territory. I cannot fix the date; that is entirely for the army.' China repeatedly warned India to desist from military adventurism. Fighting broke out on 20 October. New Delhi rejected Beijing's offer of ceasefire and ordered the Army to occupy the territory India claimed. General Maxwell Taylor, of the US Joint Chiefs of Staff, commented, 'India might have started the war.'[21] To New Delhi's consternation, the Indian Army was routed. A secret official inquiry by the Indian army, leaked in 2014, held the Nehru government's aggressive deployments responsible for the war. The BJP demanded that the government release the report. Reuters quoted a senior RSS leader saying, 'Our leaders lied to the nation. Result: war lost, territory lost, also loss of face.'

Nehru appealed to the Western countries as well as the Soviet Union for support and assistance against China. Moscow, despite its growing differences with China, was reluctant to side with India in the border dispute. Britain and the United States responded readily, perceiving in the border clash a golden opportunity to pull India into the West's orbit. On 29 October, Kennedy wrote to Nehru offering 'support as well as sympathy.' The US ambassador in New Delhi, John Kenneth Galbraith, had already embarked on efforts, more pathetic than comic, to coax a request for military aid from Nehru himself, playing on his vanity by telling him that 'he is loved in the US as no one else in India' and assuring him that the request would not imply a military alliance. Once Nehru agreed, Galbraith gleefully reported that Indians were 'pleading for military association.'[22] Forgetting his non-aligned professions, Nehru 'reversed policy 180 degrees to seek military assistance from the United States.'[23]

Promptly, the US and UK started sending planeloads of weapons every day, the former on terms to be negotiated later and the latter gratis. Israel, too, responded to Nehru's request by sending a shipload of heavy mortar.[24]

Emboldened by the West's support and assistance, India decided, on 14 November, to mount a division-strength attack in the northeast, leading to large-scale hostilities in which the Indian force was routed.

Although the fighting was still limited to the border, a frightened Nehru flew into panic. In a radio address, he bade goodbye to Assam. Ignoring the nature of the Himalayan terrain and the approaching winter, when snow would block the passes, New Delhi projected a general war, imagining that the Chinese forces would descend into the Gangetic plane. 'In this mood of crisis, the Prime Minister sent off two startling letters to President Kennedy.'[25] The texts of the two letters have not yet been declassified, apparently to spare embarrassment to the memory of 'the father of nonalignment',[26] but officials then working in the Kennedy administration have variously described one of the two as 'a hysterical letter, a silly letter asking us to bomb China,' and a desperate appeal for help 'forgetting the virtues of non-alignment.'[27] Nehru asked the United States to send a dozen squadrons of fighter aircraft to protect India's major cities and two squadrons of B-47 bombers with American pilots to attack Chinese positions.[28]

Kennedy decided to dispatch an aircraft carrier, the USS *Enterprise*,[29] to the Bay of Bengal. To India's, and America's, utter surprise, however, on 21 October China announced a unilateral ceasefire and withdrawal of its forces back to pre-war positions, twenty kilometres behind their claimed boundary, returning to India 'practically all the territory their army gained in the east.'[30]

Pakistan-US Relations Corroded

From its own experience of Indian policy, Pakistan saw that Nehru's tactics regarding the boundary problem with China were of a piece with his postures on Kashmir. He refused to acknowledge the existence of a dispute, claiming the disputed territory was an integral part of India. He spurned Premier Zhou's offers of negotiations and rejected his proposals for mutual withdrawals. He simply wanted China to acquiesce in his interpretation of where the boundary lay.

Pakistan viewed the border conflict as a limited and local affair, precipitated by Indian provocation. The United States and the United Kingdom implicitly accepted, indeed encouraged, Nehru's exaggeration of the Chinese threat and the projection of a border conflict as an invasion and war-threatening occupation of India. Ignoring secret testimony by the chairman of the US Joint Chiefs of Staff, President

Kennedy wrote to Nehru saying, 'Our sympathy in the situation is wholeheartedly with you.' When Nehru approached the US for military aid, Washington seized the opportunity with alacrity and agreed to provide arms to India.

Contrary to the pledge of prior consultation Kennedy gave to Ayub Khan a year earlier, he merely informed the Pakistan president of the US decision by letter on 28 October, saying the arms provided to India would be 'for use against China only.'[31] Kennedy went on to suggest Ayub 'signal to the Indians' that Pakistan would not embarrass them. Such a gesture, he said, would do more to bring about a sensible resolution of Pakistan-India differences than anything else.[32]

In his letter of 5 November, Ayub Khan's reply was statesmanlike. While pointing out that Pakistan could not alter its defensive deployments, as 80 per cent of India's armed forces remained poised against Pakistan—the bulk of them on Pakistan's borders—he agreed not to take advantage of the situation.[33] The answer, he suggested, lay in the settlement of Kashmir.[34]

Meanwhile, in an aide memoir of 5 November 1962, the United States embassy in Karachi reaffirmed America's 'previous assurances that it will come to Pakistan's assistance in the event of aggression from India against Pakistan.'[35] The communication was obviously drafted rather cleverly to create an illusion of assurance without going any further in defining what coming to Pakistan's assistance meant.

As the US and the UK rushed arms to India, opinion in Pakistan was outraged. People felt betrayed, realizing that the arms would enhance India's offensive capability to the detriment ultimately of Pakistan. Speaking 'in anguish and not in anger,' Foreign Minister Bogra said, in the Pakistan National Assembly, that the US failure to consult Pakistan before deciding to rush arms to India was 'an act of gross unfriendliness.' As for the border clash with China, India 'was making a mountain of a molehill.' Keeping the bulk of its forces poised on Pakistan's border, 'India has adopted a strange method of resisting the Chinese.' If friends of Pakistan and India wanted to see good relations between the two countries and settlement of disputes between them, 'Time for reliance on words and assurances has gone.'[36]

Kennedy said he was bewildered as to why Pakistanis were so bitter toward a nation that had done so much to help them.[37] At the same time, he said he understood Pakistani concerns and agreed to launch joint efforts with Harold Wilson to promote a Kashmir settlement.

Negotiations on Kashmir, 1962–1963

Ambassador Averell Harriman and British Commonwealth Secretary Duncan Sandys were charged by their governments to undertake efforts for a Kashmir settlement. They persuaded Nehru to agree, on 29 November, to a joint statement with Ayub Khan for 'a renewed effort to resolve the outstanding differences . . . on Kashmir and other related matters.'[38] But Nehru then made complete nonsense of the statement by declaring that 'an upset of the present arrangement would be very harmful to the people of Kashmir as well as to the future relations of India and Pakistan.'[39] As a result, the proposed negotiations were almost aborted, but Duncan Sandys rushed to New Delhi and obtained a clarification from Nehru that he did not intend to limit the scope of the scheduled negotiations.

Six rounds of meetings were held between December 1962 and May 1963 with Zulfikar Ali Bhutto, Minister for Industries, leading the Pakistan side, while Swaran Singh, Minister for Railways, was leader of the Indian side.

At the first meeting, held in Rawalpindi, India wasted much time on protesting against the Sino-Pakistan boundary agreement, the conclusion of which had been announced the previous day. After the two sides settled down to business, Pakistan proposed that discussion should focus on building on the existing agreement contained in the Security Council resolutions and reports of the UN mediators McNaughton and Dixon (who suggested regional plebiscites in place of a state-wide plebiscite). India merely explained why a plebiscite could not be held.

At the second round, in New Delhi in January, the Indian side took the position that they did not consider old proposals of any value. Swaran Singh refused to consider any solution that involved ascertaining the wishes of the people, putting forward a new excuse that if Kashmiri Muslims voted in Pakistan's favour, the Hindus of India would consider their vote as proof of disloyalty to India, and their safety and security would be in danger. India would be bathed in blood. On the basis of this argument, amounting to the use of Indian Muslims as hostages to blackmail Pakistan and the Kashmiri people, he proposed a 'political settlement', implying partition of the state. Pakistan was willing to probe the idea, provided a division was based on the composition of the population and was acceptable to the people of the state, apart from safeguarding economic and strategic interests, defence requirements, and control of rivers.

The 'political settlement' idea was further discussed at the third round in February and the fourth round in March. The Indian side suggested division of the state along a boundary broadly corresponding to the ceasefire line, with minor adjustments and modifications. It maintained an adamant position on the Kashmir Valley. The Pakistan side indicated a willingness to consider division along the Pir Panjal watershed in northern Jammu, giving Pakistan the districts of Riasi, Mirpur, and Poonch. As India contended the Srinagar-Leh road was essential for defence of Ladakh against China, Pakistan offered to postpone implementation. It further proposed ascertainment of the wishes of the people six months after withdrawal of Indian forces, placing the valley under international control in the interim.

A similar suggestion was made earlier by Ayub Khan through Duncan Sandys. It envisaged placing the valley under international control for five to ten years as an interim arrangement. Nehru was reported to have turned the idea down.[40] Ayub Khan told an American envoy that any compromise would be unpalatable to many people on both sides. He envisaged a settlement that safeguarded 'honour, security, and economic interests.'[41] The idea was, however, soon lost. As the danger of a further flare-up on the border with China receded, Nehru had no incentive in giving even an impression of interest in a settlement with Pakistan.

No progress was achieved at the fifth and sixth rounds in April and May. Instead of narrowing differences, the positions of the two countries became divergent. Before the breakdown of talks, the two sides reverted to their original positions.

President Kennedy was keen to promote a Kashmir settlement and tried to persuade Nehru to join in the effort. However, the priority he attached to this objective suffered as accelerating evolution in the strategic environment opened up opportunities of greater importance to the United States. India emerged as an important factor in the global power and ideological contest, and the value of the regional alliances in Asia was progressively diminishing.

The Changing Strategic Environment

The Sino-Indian border conflict in 1962 coincided with the Cuban Missile Crisis and emergent differences between USSR and China. Kennedy called it 'a climactic period' and 'a new era in history'. The United States saw in the Sino-Indian border clash an opportunity to court and wean India away from neutrality and the Soviet orbit, into the West's embrace. The time also seemed opportune to intensify pursuit of the other objective of building non-communist India as a rival to communist China and an example to other newly independent countries.

At first, the US sought to assure Pakistan that aid to India would not be at the expense of Pakistan's security or the aim of promoting a Kashmir settlement. Kennedy said on 2 November that the US help to India 'in no way diminishes or qualifies our commitment to Pakistan.' Harriman said 'Kashmir is the most important single question.' On 12 December, Ambassador McConaughy told journalists in Pakistan, 'Washington viewed the Kashmir problem as a matter of extreme urgency.' On 20 December, Dean Rusk told Ambassador Aziz Ahmed in Washington the United States had 'a great interest' in a Kashmir settlement'. Despite these reassuring declarations, it was evident that the primary US objective now was to strengthen India against China.

On 20 December, President John Kennedy and Prime Minister Harold Wilson announced the decision to provide $120 million for military aid to India, and help to enable India to raise six additional divisions. Seeking to mollify Pakistan, in a letter dated 22 December, Kennedy assured Ayub Khan the US would 'take any one-sided intransigence on Kashmir into account as a factor in determining the extent and pace of our assistance.' However, other US officials were singing a different tune. Contradicting the president, US ambassador to India Galbraith said, on 28 December, 'The American assistance is in no way contingent on an India-Pakistan agreement on the Kashmir problem.'

Galbraith played a major part in the failure of the Kashmir talks by advising Washington it should not allow the Kashmir issue to cause the US to miss the opportunity to win over India. In view of Nehru's role in the grab of Kashmir, firm and friendly counsel by Galbraith at this moment of crisis might have induced Nehru to consider a salutary reappraisal of his obduracy. But the opportunity was undermined by Galbraith, who opted instead for transitory personal success in winning Nehru over for the US.

By March 1963, little doubt was left about the change in US policy. A committee headed by General Lucius Clay recommended that 'in the interest of our own and free world security, economic and military assistance to India, as well as Pakistan, must continue under present circumstances.' Galbraith's successor, Chester Bowles, declared in May that the United States was 'very anxious to help India' build up military strength against China, adding, 'The only thing to be determined was the amount of military aid that the Indians can absorb.' The joint communiqué issued after talks between President Kennedy and President Radhakrishnan in June stated, 'Both the Presidents recognized the vital importance of safeguarding the freedom, independence and territorial integrity of India for peace and stability not only in Asia but in the world.' On 20 July, Kennedy and Macmillan decided to provide a United States-Commonwealth umbrella to India, to familiarize the Indian air force with supersonic fighter-bombers and planned for further military aid to strengthen India against China.

The United States seemed to believe India could successfully compete with China for leadership of Asia. Its strategic thinkers failed to see that few countries in Asia would accept India's leadership so long as it sought to pursue a hegemonic goal. The Indian proclivity to exploit power disparity in order to impose its own preferences on neighbours was responsible for vitiating its relations with them. Had India played fair on a basis of universally recognized principles of inter-state relations, Pakistan could have been a natural friend. American thinkers deliberately exaggerated the Chinese threat. They completely ignored the unilateral ceasefire and withdrawal of forces by China within days of the border clash, falsifying their premise of Chinese expansionism. The United States was to pay a high price for that assumption in Vietnam. Similarly incorrect was the US belief that US withdrawal from Vietnam would have a domino effect.

As the US policy was changing, so also, it should be added, was that of Pakistan. Whilst its relations with China were amicable from the start, Pakistan took timely steps to remove possible irritants and enhance cooperation with this important neighbour, resisting and defying US pressures and sanctions. As early as 1959, Pakistan proposed demarcation of the Sino-Pakistan boundary, and an agreement was concluded in 1962. The two countries also agreed to commence air services, and for years PIA enjoyed a virtual monopoly on the new corridor to China. Pakistan extended an effusive welcome to Premier Zhou Enlai in February 1964. Enormous crowds lined his route and many stood on rooftops. His talks with President Ayub Khan were marked by convergent views. In the joint communiqué, the Chinese Premier 'expressed the view that the Kashmir dispute would be resolved in accordance with the wishes of the people of Kashmir as pledged to them by India and Pakistan.' The two leaders agreed that an early settlement of the border dispute between China and India 'was necessary in the interest of world peace and the well-being of the peoples of Asia.'

Also, Pakistan took initiatives for normalization of relations with the Soviet Union. On 1 October 1963, Pakistan allowed transit rights to the Soviet airline via Karachi. Appreciating the gesture, Moscow proposed bilateral talks for improving relations. These began two months later and laid the foundation for President Ayub's visit to USSR in 1965.

The Alliance under Strain

The increasing US lurch towards India disturbed Pakistan. The military aid was not very large, but its significance was exaggerated by describing it as 'massive'. If Pakistan-US relations did not deteriorate more than they did, it was partly because Pakistan valued the assistance the US provided and partly because the US attached importance to the intelligence facilities in Peshawar.[42]

President Kennedy was philosophical when he received the new Pakistan ambassador, G. Ahmed, on 11 August 1963, saying, 'We are conditioned by our history. I can well understand your reaction to our extending military aid to India, but allowance must be made for the special circumstances which occasioned our assistance.' George Ball, who was to visit Pakistan as Kennedy's emissary, spoke with less understanding. He told the Pakistani ambassador that the Pakistan-China relationship was 'very dangerous'. A year after ceasefire on the Sino-India border, he still assumed China was intent on attacking India. He wanted Pakistan and India to join in 'common defence' against China. With that thought in mind, he asked Ayub Khan, on 4 September, what exactly Pakistan had in mind in its relations with China. Ayub Khan said it was normalization and Pakistan wanted to reduce its political and military commitments, especially in view of the US aid to India.

The US attitude towards Pakistan further stiffened after Lyndon Johnson succeeded John Kennedy. He took a tough line with Pakistan with regard to its developing relations with China. When he met Foreign Minister Zulfikar Ali Bhutto, who went to Washington to attend Kennedy's funeral, Johnson sternly warned that Premier Zhou Enlai's upcoming visit to Pakistan would jeopardize US economic and military aid to Pakistan.[43] The warning was repeated through General Maxwell Taylor, Chairman of the Joint Chiefs of Staff, who visited Pakistan in December 1963. Johnson wanted Ayub Khan to know that 'Pakistan's flirtation with China was rapidly approaching the limits of American tolerance.'[44]

The US increased aid to India for 1963–4 to $100 million. Its confrontation with China was growing as war in Vietnam reinforced trends in US policy in South Asia. Washington became keener to build up India militarily against China, while Pakistan's entente with China contradicted the US plan for building a coalition of Asian countries against China. De Gaulle's decision to recognize the People's Republic on 27 January 1964 increased Washington's sense of isolation on its China policy. The proposal for a second summit of African and Asian countries placed the US on edge as it apprehended criticism of its Vietnam policy. It considered Pakistan's support for the second Bandung Conference anti-American. Washington, once opposed to neutrality, now supported a summit of non-aligned countries where China would be absent.

Taylor also informed Ayub Khan that US aid to India would be modest—about $60 million a year. 'This was a worthwhile price,' he said, 'for detaching India from the communist bloc.'[45] The United

States actually decided on a $500 million, five-year programme of military aid for India. Ayub Khan was concerned about the enhanced threat to Pakistan from India, which was engaged in a military expansion programme. In a letter to Johnson on 7 July 1964, he protested against the decision that, he said, 'would oblige Pakistan to reappraise CENTO and SEATO'. Johnson's response was even more curt, warning that the US, too, would be obliged to re-examine its relations with Pakistan if it continued to develop its relations with China. The warnings had little effect. Pakistan continued to strengthen cooperation with China. The United States proceeded to 're-examine its relations with Pakistan.'

Ayub Khan's Visits to China and the USSR

Ayub Khan visited China in March 1965. The welcome accorded to him was described as 'magnificent, enthusiastic, elaborate, and colourful.' He held cordial meetings with Chairman Mao and Premier Zhou and spoke of 'lasting friendship and fruitful cooperation' with China. The joint communiqué stressed adherence to the Ten Principles of Peaceful Coexistence, and condemned colonialism and racial discrimination. It reaffirmed that the Kashmir dispute should be resolved in accordance with the wishes of the people of Kashmir as pledged to them by India and Pakistan. At Pakistan's request, no mention was made of Vietnam. The gesture did not impress Washington, however.

A month later, Ayub Khan visited the USSR—the first visit by a Pakistani head of state. He held talks with Leonid Brezhnev and Alexei Kosygin. Foreign Minister Gromyko also participated in the talks. The Pakistan delegation included both Foreign Minister Z. A. Bhutto and Foreign Secretary Aziz Ahmed. The Soviet leaders evinced great interest in Pakistan-India relations. They showed understanding for Pakistan's view on Kashmir. They could not explain why they were supplying arms to India if these were not intended for use against Pakistan. In a separate meeting, Kosygin agreed to consider Pakistan's request for military equipment. Although the joint communiqué did not mention Kashmir by name, it declared 'resolute support for the peoples who are fighting for the right to determine their future in accordance with their own will' and further stated 'that in order to promote universal harmony, international agreements should be implemented.' At Pakistan's behest, the communiqué was moderately worded, and refrained from referring to Vietnam.

Second Afro-Asian Summit

The idea of convening a second Afro-Asian summit had been under discussion among several countries of the region since 1960. It was strongly supported by China, Indonesia, and Pakistan. Even the USSR expressed interest in attending the conference, claiming it was also an Asian country. The conference was to be held in Algiers from 29 June 1965. As the date approached, apprehensions mounted in Washington that the conference, in which North Vietnam would participate, would criticize US policy. In mid-April, a preparatory meeting of eighteen countries was held in Jakarta. Most of the speakers condemned the US bombing of North Vietnam. Foreign Minister Bhutto's statement was moderate, but there could be no doubt of Pakistan's sympathy. Pakistan had earlier declined to send even a token military contingent to join the US armed forces in South Vietnam. The Algiers summit was aborted because of the overthrow of Ahmed Ben Bella and a bomb blast at the conference venue in Club des Pins.

US Reaction

Neither the scrupulous moderation of communiqués issued following President Ayub Khan's visits to China and the USSR, nor even his extraordinary statement in Beijing, suggesting recognition of US 'legitimate interests' in Asia, made any impression on Washington. Instead, the administration was angered by the success of the Pakistan president's visits. It showed no interest in taking advantage of his contacts to open the door to negotiations for a Vietnam settlement. President Johnson was in a truculent mood. On 17 April 1965, he declared the US objective was 'an independent South Vietnam', forgetting, as Walter Lippman said, 'This was not our original position.'[46]

Reputed as a go-getter and wheeler-dealer inclined to use strong-arm methods, and under tremendous stress because of a failing war in Vietnam, President Johnson decided to punish Pakistan. First he cut off a loan for upgradation of Dhaka airport. On 16 April, he announced unilateral postponement of Ayub Khan's visit to the United States, due to begin nine days later. In early July, the United States advised the World Bank to defer the meeting of the Pakistan Consortium to pledge aid to Pakistan. First, it wanted Pakistan to discuss the political issues. The Pakistan government did not bend in the face of the US pressure. Instead, it began to consider refusal to renew the lease for the US base at Badaber.

Regional Cooperation for Development (RCD) and Indonesian–Pakistan Economic and Cultural Cooperation (IPECC)

Allies in CENTO, Iran, Pakistan, and Turkey began to feel the need to supplement and enlarge their one-dimensional military contacts. At a meeting in Istanbul on 22 July 1964, the heads of the three states agreed to promote cooperation in economic and cultural fields, and to that end formed an organization—Regional Cooperation for Development (RCD). A number of industrial projects were later established by two or all three agreeing to share in investment and production. Although the joint projects were relatively small, RCD symbolized the aspiration of the people of the three countries for closer cooperation.

A similar sentiment grew between Pakistan and Indonesia. They both looked upon African-Asian solidarity as a better alternative to the formation of the non-aligned group, which excluded not only Iran, Pakistan, Philippines, Thailand, etc., but also China, the world's largest and most important developing country. India's motivation in keeping China out was transparent. As Sukarno well remembered, Zhou Enlai had out-shone Nehru as a statesman and leader of great acumen and sagacity at the Bandung Afro-Asian summit in 1955. By keeping China out, India wanted to retain the limelight on itself. Pakistan as well as Indonesia realized, moreover, that India nourished hegemonic ambitions. They cooperated closely in preparations for the second Afro-Asian summit. Such multiple commonalities of interest led the two countries to decide on the formation of Indonesia-Pakistan Economic and Cultural Cooperation (IPECC) in August 1965. IPECC, like RCD, has continued to provide a forum for the promotion of cooperation despite changes in the two countries.

NOTES

1. Convened to support decolonization of Indo-China, the summit conference was attended by India, Indonesia, Myanmar, Pakistan, and Sri Lanka. Burke, op. cit., 174.
2. *Hindu,* Madras, of 27 November 1954 quoted in Burke, op. cit., 214.
3. *People's China*, 16 October 1954 quoted in Burke, op. cit., 214.
4. Quoted from George Mc T. Kahin, *The African Asian Conference*, in Burke, op. cit., 178.
5. Ibid.
6. Burke, op. cit., 215.
7. Quoted from UN records in Burke, op. cit., 198.
8. *Times of India*, 24 October 1959.
9. On 9 November 1959, *Reuters* reported Ayub to have said Chinese activities in Tibet and road building in Afghanistan posed a serious threat from the north.
10. Gauhar, 197.
11. In an article in *Foreign Affairs* of July 1960, Ayub Khan said: 'I can see quite clearly the inexorable push of the north . . . in the direction of the warm waters of the Indian Ocean. This push is bound to increase if India and Pakistan go on squabbling with each other.'
12. Prime Minister Z. A. Bhutto said in an article in *Foreign Affairs* in October 1976 that Ayub Khan's joint defence offer was 'humiliating . . . (and) dangerous . . . (as) he was serving a notice to China of Pakistan's hostility.' Extracts in *Documents*, ed. Arif, 325.
13. Mohammad Yunus, op. cit., 131–2.
14. For all these dates see Altaf Gauhar, op. cit., 234.
15. US Embassy, Karachi, press release of September 1963, quoted in Gauhar, op. cit., 245.
16. At the Commonwealth summit in 1964, Pakistan opposed a move to declare opposition to 'the Chinese threat'. Bhatty, op. cit., 165.
17. The article 'Another Korea in the Making' published in *Colliers*, August 1951, quoted in G. W. Choudhury, op. cit., 157.
18. World Bank statement clarified the procedure following Pakistan's reference of the Baglihar issue, *Dawn*, Islamabad, 20 January 2005.
19. Neville Maxwell, *India's China War*; and Stevan A. Hoffmann, *India and the China Crisis*, are two well-known works on Sino-Indian relations.
20. Quoted in Maqbool A. Bhatty, *Great Powers and South Asia*, 105, from Maxwell.

21. Revealed a year later in *The New York Times* of 29 April 1963; quoted by Aziz Ahmed, manuscript, chapter IX.
22. Quoted from John Kenneth Galbraith, *Ambassador's Journal*, in Gauhar, op. cit., 207.
23. Dennis Kux, op. cit., 204.
24. Quoted from Maxwell, op. cit., 410, in Gauhar, op. cit., 504.
25. Dennis Kux, op. cit., 207.
26. Sudhir Ghosh, *Gandhi's Emissary*, 326–38, quoted in Altaf Gauhar, op. cit., 500.
27. Altaf Gauhar, op. cit., 497–517.
28. Kux, op. cit., 207, based on Hoffman, op. cit., 206–8.
29. Ironically, the same ship was considered by India as a symbol of US hostility when it was sent by Nixon in December 1971.
30. Kux, op. cit., 208.
31. Kennedy's letter of 28 October 1962 to Ayub, quoted in Kux, op. cit., 205.
32. Ayub Khan, *Friends not Masters*.
33. Some of the president's colleagues, including Z. A. Bhutto, thought that his decision was a mistake. Ambassador Aziz Ahmed was of the view that it would have been out of character for Pakistan to stab India in the back; also, that would have left an intensely bitter trail, besides antagonising the big powers.
34. The assurance from Pakistan sought by the Western powers was given, though not in so many words.' Quoted from Pakistan's *White Paper On the Kashmir Dispute*, Yusuf Buch suggested in his paper 'Kashmir and the Big Powers' presented at the International Seminar on Fifty Years of Kashmir Dispute, at Muzaffarabad on 24 August 1997.
35. US National Security Archives, NEA/PAB: R K McKEE:gn, dated 23 May 1977, quoted by Altaf Gohar in *Ayub Khan*, 196, Footnote 1.
36. Mohammad Ali Bogra, statement of 22 November 1962, *Documents*, ed. K. Arif, 213–15.
37. US Memo of Kennedy-Shoaib meeting, 9 October 1963, quoted in McMahon, op. cit., 303.
38. A statement to that effect by Ayub and Nehru was announced on 29 November 1962, ref. Gauhar, op. cit., 217.
39. Gauhar, op. cit., 219.
40. *New York Times* of 11 February 1963 quoted in G. W. Choudhury, op. cit., 73.
41. Gauhar, op. cit., 230.
42. Kux, op. cit., 213.
43. Bhutto was 'deeply upset and disturbed' at the discourtesy shown to him, Talbott gleefully noted. A White House aide thought 'Bhutto was asking for it.' McMahon, op. cit., 307.
44. McMahon, op. cit., 314.
45. Quoted by Gauhar, op. cit., 249.
46. *Washington Post*, 17 April 1965, quoted in Aziz Ahmed, manuscript, 276.

CHAPTER 8

The Pakistan-India War, 1965

The Pakistan-India 'Kashmir' war in 1965 was the culmination of the rise and fall of expectations of a peaceful settlement of the Kashmir dispute, popular agitation and state repression in the Indian-held state, jingoism triggered by border clashes in the Rann of Kutch, a limited operation born of frustration and desperation conceived by the Pakistan government to draw international attention, and unintended escalation. In the perspective of history, leaders on both sides seemed to have lost control over actions decided under pressure, provoking like reactions and allowing the build-up of momentum that pushed them into a war neither side had planned.

The fundamental cause of tensions lay in the failure to settle the festering Kashmir dispute. The ceasefire in the state was defined in the 1949 Security Council resolution as the first step toward the holding of a plebiscite under UN auspices to determine the question of the accession of the state. Accepted by Pakistan as well as India, the resolution constituted an international agreement requiring implementation by the parties. But India concocted one pretext after another to evade its obligation. Agreement on the quantum of troops India could retain in the state proved impossible. Even before Pakistan signed a defence assistance agreement with the United States, Prime Minister Nehru began using the assistance Pakistan might receive as representing a change in the situation, though how that could affect the rights of the people of the state defied logic. Then India invented the argument that if the Muslims of Kashmir opted to accede to Pakistan, that would trigger a Hindu backlash and massacre of Indian Muslims. Another pretext for refusal to implement the resolution was that continued hold over Kashmir was a necessity for maintaining the integrity of India; otherwise, its unity would be destroyed.[1] In the process, the pledge to the people of the state and to the United Nations was relegated, as India sought to freeze the status quo and perpetuate its occupation of two-thirds of the state. This was unjustified in law and unacceptable to Pakistan.

Rise and fall of hopes: Expectations rose in 1962, as a result of American and British intercession with India during the Sino-Indian border clash, that purposeful negotiations between Pakistan and India might lead to an acceptable settlement. It was assumed that in order to avert a two-front danger, India would see the need for resolving the Kashmir dispute. Nehru's initial panicky reaction to the border clash fostered hope that India might do so. But optimism was soon betrayed. New Delhi soon realized that Nehru's fear that the border clash was a prelude to a Chinese invasion of India was exaggerated. When the talks commenced, instead of focusing on outlines of a Kashmir settlement, India diverted attention to Pakistan's boundary agreement with China. Evidently, it sought to diffuse issues, relegating the negotiations to an exercise in public relations. The urgency gone, the US and Britain, too, lost interest in pushing India towards a Kashmir settlement. Their aim now was only to suck India into the West's orbit. To that end, they announced a programme for massive supply of sophisticated weapons for India. Instead of inducing flexibility into India's stance on Kashmir, Washington and London emboldened India to revert to rigidity. The Bhutto-Swaran Singh talks were thus doomed. Opinion in Pakistan now blamed Ayub Khan for falling into a trap and missing the opportunity for action to achieve a breakthrough towards a settlement of Kashmir in conformity with their aspirations.

Pakistani disappointment over the failed talks was soon followed by anger when, in October 1963, India initiated legal manoeuvres to erode the disputed status of Kashmir. The puppet prime minister of the state, Bakhshi Ghulam Mohammad, who was installed by New Delhi and sustained in power through rigged elections, announced changes in the constitution of the state designed to bring Kashmir on a par with the states of India. The designation of *sadr-i-riyasat* (president of state) would be abolished, and the title replaced with 'Governor'. Also, the head of government of Jammu and Kashmir would no longer be called a prime minister but a chief minister. Nehru announced in November that a 'gradual erosion' of the special status of Kashmir was in progress. Pakistan protested, denouncing the proposed changes as 'clearly illegal' and a 'flagrant violation of India's commitments.'

Deeply disturbed by New Delhi's moves, evidencing once again the Indian design to annex the state against their will, the Kashmiri people launched an agitation which assumed massive proportions following the theft of *moo-e-muqaddis* (holy hair of the Prophet) from the Hazratbal shrine. Attributing the crime to Indian connivance, the Kashmiri people poured out in a spontaneous eruption. Demonstrations of unprecedented proportions were held in cities and towns across the occupied valley. Even after the Indian authorities announced the recovery of the relic, the agitation did not cease. Instead, it took a political direction with the Kashmiri people demanding an opportunity to exercise their right of self-determination. In the months following December 1963, Kashmir was in the grip of a crisis, with the administration in collapse and India resorting once again to repression against the unarmed Kashmiri people. Pakistan appealed to the UN Security Council, which held lengthy debates in February and May 1964 but was prevented by the threat of a Soviet veto not only from taking any effective action but even from reaffirming its previous resolutions on the Kashmir question. This failure on the part of the apex organ of the United Nations was yet another blow to prospects of peace between Pakistan and India. A proverbial 'unkindest cut' was the remark, by the US ambassador to the UN, Adlai Stevenson, in a conversation with Foreign Minister Bhutto, that the US felt Pakistan kept bringing Kashmir to the Security Council merely for 'internal propaganda'. Clearly, the United States was becoming unsympathetic.

Hopes rose again in April 1964, when Nehru decided to release Sheikh Mohammad Abdullah, the dismissed and imprisoned former prime minister of Indian-occupied Jammu and Kashmir. Called the 'Lion of Kashmir' for leading popular protests against the oppressive rule of the maharaja in the 1930s, he was once again considered a leader of stature capable of bringing peace to the troubled state. His popularity had declined in 1947 when he allowed himself to be duped to endorse Indian military intervention and paraded internationally as proof of Kashmiri preference for India, but it had somewhat recovered after he reminded India of its plebiscite pledge and suffered a decade of incarceration for upholding the right of the Kashmiri people to self-determination.

Whether Nehru wanted only to use Abdullah again merely to pacify the Kashmiri people and divert international opinion, or whether, by now old and sick and possibly penitent for the excesses he had ordered against his friend and ally, Nehru had come round to realize that there was no escaping a settlement acceptable to the Kashmir people remains unclear. Abdullah, however, believed that Nehru wished for a resolution that might satisfy the Kashmiri people.

The assessment that India was inclined to settle the Kashmir question was encouraged by the public stance taken by Jayaprakash Narayan, a leader respected in India for his advocacy of morality in politics. In a courageous article,[2] he exploded some of the myths India had fostered. The highly suspect elections held by India in Kashmir, Narayan argued, did not represent a vote for integration with India. He ridiculed the argument that self-determination by the people of Kashmir would trigger countrywide communal rioting and prove a prelude to the disintegration of India. He argued that it was not only silly but implied that India was held together by force. In essence, Narayan advocated that India should rethink its position in the light of not only its own interests but also those of Pakistan. The two countries, he said, could prosper only if they cooperated.

In this hopeful atmosphere, Sheikh Abdullah came to Pakistan in May 1964. He led Ayub Khan to believe that Nehru and India were sincere in wanting a settlement. After extended discussions of an exploratory nature, he suggested that Ayub should visit New Delhi for a meeting with Nehru. Ayub agreed. The next day, 27 May, Nehru died, and with him perished yet another hope.

The new Indian prime minister, Lal Bahadur Shastri, publicly pledged to continue Nehru's policy, but he did not follow up Abdullah's suggestion for Ayub Khan's visit to India. A brief meeting between Shastri and Ayub Khan at Karachi Airport on 12 October 1964 went off without promise of progress. Not only that, in December 1964 the Indian government resumed moves aimed at the merger of Kashmir with India through the application of the Indian constitution enabling it to impose presidential rule and extend Indian laws to Kashmir. Here again was another proof of Indian deception, speaking of negotiations but acting unilaterally in pursuit of its illegitimate design.

Clash in the Rann of Kutch

The boundary in the Rann of Kutch, a low-lying marsh wedged between the province of Sindh and the Indian state of Gujarat that floods during the monsoon season, had been the subject of dispute between the princely state of Kutch and the Bombay presidency since before 1947. Although the boundary was not demarcated, an area of about 3,500 square miles north of the 24th parallel was contested. After Independence, India claimed the entire territory and in 1956 sent its forces to seize the Chhad Bet high ground. Pakistan protested, but India did not begin negotiations until 1960. Meanwhile, the two countries agreed to maintain a ceasefire. In violation of the agreement, the Indian forces advanced to the north in January 1965 and tried to establish new posts and obstruct Pakistani patrols in the disputed area. Pakistan sent in troops to stop India from solving the dispute unilaterally by force. As both sides strengthened their forces in the Rann, fighting flared up in April. The Pakistani forces surrounded the Indian contingent and could have captured it, but President Ayub ordered restraint. The danger of further escalation was averted partly due to the approaching monsoon. More importantly, the British government persuaded the two sides to agree to a ceasefire on 1 May.

Indirect but intense negotiations were then held through British High Commissioners Sir Morrice James in Islamabad and John Freeman in New Delhi. Foreign Secretary Aziz Ahmed ensured that the agreement, signed on 30 June 1965, provided for a time-bound, self-executing mechanism for settlement of the dispute peacefully. The agreement gave two months for the two sides to try to resolve the issue through bilateral negotiation. If that failed, they would submit the dispute to arbitration by a tribunal, to be constituted within four months, with the UN Secretary General designating its chairman. Both sides further agreed that the tribunal's award 'shall not be questioned on any grounds whatsoever,' that it would be implemented as soon as possible, and that until then the tribunal would remain in being.

Relying on evidence as to where the traditional boundary was, the tribunal awarded 350 square miles to Pakistan, a mere 10 per cent of the territory under dispute.[3] Interestingly, Pakistan was satisfied that the dispute was honourably resolved. India got 90 per cent of the disputed territory but was still indignant. Always wanting to settle disputes on its own terms, it vowed never again to accept third-party mediation or impartial adjudication.

The demonstrated inefficacy of negotiations where one party seeks to impose its own preferred solution on the other has been illustrated over and over again in Pakistan-India disputes, even in comparatively minor disputes including that involving the residual issue of Sir Creek at the western terminus of the boundary in the Rann. Officials of the two countries have held innumerable meetings over three decades but failed to agree on the boundary in the creek, entailing endless suffering for poor fishermen from both sides. Hundreds of them are arrested in recurrent cases of trespass and spend long periods in prison, losing their boats.

In normal circumstances, the agreement to settle the Kutch dispute peacefully might have contributed to improvement of Pakistan-India relations. But circumstances between Pakistan and India are seldom normal. India fumed over what it perceived to be a reverse in the Rann of Kutch. In a statement on 29 April, Prime Minister Shastri threatened that India would fight Pakistan at a time and place of its own choosing. Only Jayaprakash Narayan, who later came to be revered in India as Sarvodaya leader, had the vision and the wisdom to commend the Kutch agreement 'as an object lesson in peace-keeping' which should be applied to all disputes 'including that of Kashmir.'[4] Most Indian politicians and commentators considered the arbitration agreement humiliating and denounced it in Lok Sabha in 'extremely bellicose' speeches.[5] In effect, the Kutch clash, by making India want to settle a score and Pakistan over-confident, proved to be one further stumble toward war, which came within five months as the Kashmir cauldron came once again to the boil.

At the same time as domestic opinion was being fired up by clashes and jingoistic statements, international restraints were weakened. US diplomacy allowed itself to be placed on the defensive during the Kutch crisis. While both sides used American arms, India was vehement in protest against the use of American weapons by Pakistan though it felt free to use Soviet as well as American weapons against Pakistan. Washington announced an embargo on the further supply of arms or spare parts. Apparently even-handed, the decision was weighted against Pakistan because almost all of its equipment was of US origin, while the restriction had little impact on India, whose arsenal was mainly of Soviet origin. President Johnson also ordered discontinuation of any additional US aid or loans. Here again the decision worked to Pakistan's detriment; the World Bank Consortium for India had already met and the US had pledged aid, while the meeting of the Consortium for Pakistan, which was scheduled for later, had to be postponed, contributing to the build-up of a mood of desperation in Pakistan. Americans, Ayub exploded, were 'power drunk'. Pakistan, he said on another occasion, was seeking 'new friends, not new masters.'[6]

Tension built up further when India took additional steps to integrate occupied Kashmir. Abdullah and his colleague, Mirza Afzal Beg, leader of the Plebiscite Front, were arrested in May 1965 on their return from abroad, having had meetings with leaders of Muslim countries during Haj and with Premier Zhou Enlai in Cairo. The Indian moves triggered another popular upsurge in Kashmir with Mirwaiz Mohammad Farooq, leader of the Awami Action Committee, joining the Gandhi-style non-violent disobedience movement. India unleashed its forces to crush the struggle in the state.

Operation Gibraltar

Recurrent popular uprisings in occupied Kashmir and their brutal repression by India and the rise and fall of hopes for a settlement through peaceful means fostered mounting frustration in Pakistan. Official thought in the latter part of 1964 turned to what else might be done to thaw the situation and jolt the world community into recognizing the urgency of fulfilling the pledge given by India, Pakistan, and the United Nations to let the Kashmiri people themselves determine their future. Some in positions of influence believed it was morally incumbent on Pakistan to do something to press for a Kashmir settlement, before India's burgeoning military expansion aggravated power disparity as a result of growing supplies by the US and the concessional sale of the latest MIG aircraft, armour, and artillery by the USSR.

President Ayub Khan, too, was exasperated by India's refusal to agree to a peaceful settlement of the Kashmir question. He was moved by the heroic struggle of the people of Algeria and Vietnam, and his and the army's confidence grew after the encounter in the Rann of Kutch, though he was still averse to war. However, he appointed a group of high-ranking officials to suggest appropriate means. Chaired by Foreign Secretary Aziz Ahmed, it was called the Kashmir Publicity Committee. It reported directly to President Ayub Khan. Although controversy surrounds its precise recommendations, Ayub Khan agreed to the preparation of a plan by the GHQ.

The operation named Gibraltar, prepared by Major General Akhtar Hussain Malik, was approved. Calling for incursions by Kashmiri volunteers into India-held Kashmir, it was based on three assumptions: people in Kashmir would rise to support the guerrillas, a large-scale Indian offensive against Azad Kashmir was unlikely, and the possibility of attack across the international border could be ruled out. All of these turned out to be wrong.[7]

Escalation to War

The volunteers entered Kashmir in August. Poorly equipped for survival in the cold and desolate conditions in the high mountains on the way, they were not joined by the Kashmiri people, who had not been informed or prepared for an uprising. Nevertheless, the guerrillas inflicted heavy damage on the Indian forces. To cope with the situation, the Indian authorities decided to mount a major offensive across the ceasefire line and occupied a large territory in the Kargil area in the north and the Haji Pir Pass between Uri and Poonch, posing a threat to Muzaffarabad, the capital of Azad Kashmir. Now the Pakistani side had no alternative but to respond. It decided to launch an attack in the Chamb area from Pakistan territory. As the force commanded by Major General Akhtar Malik advanced toward Akhnur, a nodal point on the transport and supply link between Jammu and the Kashmir Valley, India decided to up the ante by launching an offensive across the international border. Actions and reactions thus led step by step to a war neither side had planned.

The Indian forces crossed the international boundary before dawn on 6 September. Their offensive aimed at the capture of Lahore, Pakistan's second largest city, twenty miles from the Indian border. The Pakistan army was caught unprepared, but legendary acts of heroism and sacrifice halted the Indian thrust.

The small but highly professional Pakistan air force went on the offensive and attacked a number of Indian bases on the evening of 6 September, inflicting severe losses. The Indian air force launched a counter-attack on 8 September but was checkmated. Particularly bold was the initiative taken by the out-numbered contingent in East Pakistan. It not only rose in defence but took the battle into enemy airspace, bombing targets in India in retaliation of the Indian bombing of Dhaka and Chittagong. Over a few days, the PAF shot down seventy-five Indian aircraft for the loss of nineteen of its own, clearing the Pakistani airspace. The Indian air force then receded to a passive role. Even Pakistan's tiny navy made an audacious foray into Indian territorial waters to attack Dwarka, a naval base 200 miles from Karachi. It captured almost a hundred coastal ships. The Indian navy did not join the battle.

On 9 September, the Pakistan army launched a major offensive in the Khem Karan area towards Amritsar. The armoured division made good progress but then became bogged down as the Indian forces flooded the countryside by breaching an irrigation canal. The Indian army then counter-attacked in the Sialkot area. The biggest tank battle of the war was fought in the Chawinda area, containing the Indian advance aimed at cutting off Wazirabad, a communications nodal point.

Considering the disparity of size and resources between the two countries and their force levels, the Pakistani armed forces can be legitimately proud of their performance in the war. Pakistan made marginally larger territorial gains,[8] but the war ended in a stalemate. Neither side achieved any decisive breakthrough.

The UN Security Council adopted its first resolution on 4 September, calling for a ceasefire and withdrawal of all armed personnel to the positions held by them before 5 August, the date on which, according to UN's information, armed men began to cross the ceasefire line. Neither this nor the resolution of 6 September was acceptable to Pakistan. In reply to Secretary General U. Thant's letter asking for implementation of the ceasefire, Ayub Khan said that a 'purposeful' resolution must provide for a self-executing arrangement for settlement of the Kashmir dispute. India, on its part, was willing to order a ceasefire but not to withdraw from areas in Kashmir.

China took the lead in relieving Indian pressure on Pakistan. On 27 August, Beijing issued a strong protest against Indian 'acts of aggression and provocation' along China's border. Rejecting India's denial, China demanded, on 8 September, an end to India's 'frenzied provocation activities'. On 16 September, China delivered an ultimatum. Unless India dismantled its military structures on the Chinese side of the border, stopped incursions into China and returned livestock and kidnapped civilians 'within three days', it would have to bear 'full responsibility for all consequences'. On 19 September, China extended the ultimatum by three days.[9]

The threat of expansion of the war served to inject a sense of urgency into the deliberations of the Security Council. It passed a resolution on 20 September which went beyond earlier resolutions. Besides demanding a ceasefire and withdrawals, it promised to consider 'what steps could be taken to assist towards a settlement of the political problems underlying the present conflict.' This resolution was accepted by Pakistan and India on 22 September. Not all of Ayub Khan's advisers agreed, but the armed forces, running short of ordnance and spares, favoured immediate acceptance.

In accepting the resolution, Pakistan attached weight to the promise given by the premier organ of the United Nations that it would go beyond a mere return to the *status quo ante* and contribute to the building of permanent peace by promoting a settlement of the 'underlying'—that is, the Kashmir—dispute. The hope thus generated was, however, to prove illusory. In making this pledge, the Council was not moved by Pakistani negotiating strength or the inherent logic of the proposition. The great powers were concerned about the danger of expansion of the war, with China issuing one warning after another to India in the context of the Sino-Indian border problems as well as statements of support for Pakistan.

Stances of Foreign Powers[10]

China's Support: In the 1965 crisis, China extended full support to Pakistan, both directly and implicitly. Foreign Minister Chen Yi and the Chinese foreign ministry used vivid language to manifest their friendship. In transit through Karachi on 4 September, Marshal Chen expressed support for 'the just action taken by Pakistan to repel Indian armed provocations.' On 7 September, China condemned India's 'criminal aggression' against Pakistan and charged India with trying to 'bully its neighbours, defy public opinion and do whatever it likes.'[11] It further declared, on 12 September, that its non-involvement in the Kashmir dispute 'absolutely does not mean that China can approve of depriving the Kashmiri people of their right of self-determination or that she can approve of Indian aggression against Pakistan.'

China responded generously to Pakistan's request for assistance. Apart from providing munitions and spare parts, China was prepared to fly in the material by fighter aircraft. Ayub Khan, apprehending adverse reaction from the United States, asked for their supply by sea.

Allies: The available record does not indicate that Pakistani leaders gave any advance consideration to the applicability of the alliances in the event of war with India. One obvious explanation for the omission could be that they did not anticipate Indian aggression, projecting the conflict to remain confined to the state. Evidently not sanguine about assistance by the allies, they made a belated and half-hearted attempt to invoke the alliances, realizing that not all the allies agreed that India was the aggressor. The SEATO council did not meet even for consultations, and CENTO could not be activated. The UK backtracked after India raised a storm over Prime Minister Wilson's criticism of Indian aggression.

USA: The US response to the outbreak of war between Pakistan and India was one of frustration. Finding its policy in South Asia in shambles, with Pakistan and India using US-supplied arms to fight each other rather than against its enemies, the US adopted a neutral, hands-off stance, leaving it to the Security Council to promote an end to the war. On 8 September, the US decided to stop the supply of arms to Pakistan and India. When the Pakistan foreign minister protested that the US decision to cut off defence supplies amounted to punitive action against an ally, the US ambassador said he considered Pakistan to have provoked the war.

The US view that it was not bound to come to Pakistan's assistance provoked a predictable Pakistani reaction of betrayal. The 1959 bilateral defence agreement had stated, 'The US regards as vital to its national interest and to world peace the preservation of the independence and integrity of Pakistan.' The Ayub-Kennedy communiqué of 13 July 1961 reaffirmed commitment to 'the preservation of the independence and integrity of Pakistan', and the US embassy aide memoir of 5 November 1962 assured assistance to Pakistan 'in the event of aggression from India'. Washington did not interpret the Indian attack as aggression.

'The seeming even-handedness was deceptive,' as Henry Kissinger later noted, because 'the practical consequence was to injure Pakistan, since India received most of its arms either from Communist nations or from its own armouries.'[12]

Washington's hopes of balanced relations with both Pakistan and India proved fallacious, and finding itself reviled in both countries by governments as well as the public, the US sought to wipe the whole slate clean. President Johnson did not respond to Ayub Khan's public appeal, on 13 September, to play a role to establish peace in the region; what stirred Washington, a few days later, was China's ultimatum to India. The US and Britain then began to play an active role in the Security Council in order to secure a ceasefire, promising that they would promote an urgent settlement of the Kashmir question.[13]

Washington did not interpret the Indian attack as 'aggression' and did not agree that it was bound to come to Pakistan's assistance. It merely stated that it was 'acting urgently, as we said we would, to meet this common danger by full support for immediate UN action to end the hostilities.' However, Pakistan had higher expectations of its ally than were founded in the legalistic wordings of the agreements. Foreign Minister of Pakistan Zulfikar Ali Bhutto argued strongly that the spirit of the existing agreements required the United States to help Pakistan in the face of Indian aggression. Omitting the conditions and qualifications specified in the agreements, Islamabad laid emphasis on the main clauses. In the Formal Note of 1959, the US had promised to 'promptly and effectively come to the assistance of Pakistan if it were subjected to armed aggression.' It was committed, in the Ayub-Kennedy joint communiqué of 13 July 1961, to the 'preservation of the independence and integrity of Pakistan,' and in the US embassy aide memoir of 5 November 1962, it had assured assistance to Pakistan 'in the event of aggression from India'. Now, once again, the US had let Pakistan down just as it had done by providing massive military aid to India and failing to use its leverage for promoting a Kashmiri settlement in 1962. Foundations were laid for popular sentiment of US 'betrayal'.

Other Friends: President Sukarno of Indonesia extended memorable assistance, readily agreeing to provide some MIG aircraft. It sent two submarines and four missile boats. By the time they reached Karachi, Pakistan had agreed to a ceasefire. Iran and Turkey provided planeloads of arms and ammunition, though the two CENTO allies could not send equipment imported from the United States, because of American restrictions on transfer to another country. The United States embargoed the supply of defence equipment, including spare parts, which constrained Pakistan because most of its war weapons were of US origin.

No country blamed Pakistan for its attempt to thaw the festering Kashmir dispute, whilst a large number of countries criticized India for aggression across the international border and several provided memorable assistance to Pakistan. President Nasser, though he often favoured non-aligned India, echoed sympathy for Pakistan and endorsed the Arab summit's communiqué, which called upon India and Pakistan to resolve the Kashmir dispute 'in accordance with the principles and resolutions of the United Nations.' Prime Minister Kosygin 'took exception to India's crossing the international border,' reflecting a change in its erstwhile blanket support to India. Prime Minister Harold Wilson was 'deeply concerned' when the Indian forces 'attacked Pakistan territory across the international frontier.' Only Yugoslavia sided with India, and the Malaysian representative in the Security Council, a person of Indian origin, made remarks so offensive as to provoke Pakistan to cut off diplomatic relations.

Ceasefire: Pakistan was at first averse to a ceasefire without a UN commitment to promoting a settlement of the Kashmir question, but it soon came under pressure from its allies, the USA and the UK. Also, its capacity to wage a long war was limited. President Ayub Khan decided to accept the resolution adopted by the Security Council on 20 September. 'Convinced that an early cessation of hostilities is essential as a first step towards a peaceful settlement of the outstanding differences between the two countries on Kashmir and other matters,' the Council 'decided' to consider 'what steps should be taken to assist towards a settlement of the political problem underlying the present conflict' as soon as the ceasefire took effect.[14] Not for the first time did the Security Council fail to pursue its decision, however.

The Tashkent Declaration

With both the United States and the UK not wanting to take an initiative, the field was left open for Soviet diplomacy to promote a post-war settlement. Prime Minister Kosygin offered his good offices to work for a settlement between Pakistan and India. Pakistan was initially reluctant, entertaining misgivings on account of the Soviet Union's pro-India policy ever since Pakistan joined the Western alliances, but it decided to accept the Soviet proposal not only because there was no alternative on offer but also because, in recent years, Moscow had been less partisan. Ayub Khan's visit to Moscow the previous April had ended on a positive note, with the Soviet leaders pleased to be told that Pakistan intended to terminate the lease for Badaber. Also, Moscow now had a stake in ensuring disengagement between Pakistan and India, and thus preventing dangerous polarization between China and the Soviet Union, one backing Pakistan and the other India.

Before going to Tashkent, Ayub Khan visited London and Washington in December. Johnson told him that the alliance between the United States and Pakistan was over.[15] The United States might provide economic aid to Pakistan in future, but that would hinge on Pakistan's willingness to curtail its ties with China. It became evident that Washington had decided to lower its profile in South Asia.

The Pakistan delegation to the Tashkent Conference, 4–10 January 1966, was internally divided on how far to go in pressing for settlement of the Kashmir dispute. The Security Council resolution envisaged some effort to this end. It was not illogical to hope that the Soviet Union would work for progress in that direction. Some believed Pakistan could get India to agree to the creation of a mechanism for settlement. Others were of the view that neither did the stalemated war permit Pakistan to adopt a strong negotiating posture, nor could the Soviet Union be expected to pressure India to agree to settle the Kashmir dispute. Ayub Khan himself was clear about the priority need for disengagement.

The Tashkent Declaration provided for the withdrawal of forces to positions held on 5 August 1965, repatriation of prisoners of war, and return of high commissioners to their posts. The declaration provided for further meetings between the two sides 'on matters of direct concern to both countries.' It made no direct reference to the crucial Kashmir question. Pakistan's effort to include a provision for compulsory settlement of the dispute was opposed by India. Prime Minister Shastri, though he recognized the desirability of a settlement, told Ayub Khan that as a 'pygmy succeeding a giant' his position did not permit him to change India's stance. The Soviets, too, considered the Kashmir question too 'complicated' and the Pakistani demand impractical. Kosygin had to work hard to evolve the ambiguous formulation that the two sides 'will continue meetings both at the highest and at other levels on matters of direct concern to both countries.' Ayub Khan's agreement to this formulation, though eminently rational under the circumstances, was to spark a bitter controversy in Pakistan.

Official propaganda during the war had built up an impression of Pakistani forces having gained great advantage, if not victory, over India. Not for the first time did state propaganda delude its own people. It was difficult enough to understand why Pakistan accepted the ceasefire when Pakistan was doing so well. Even more baffling was the failure to secure any advance toward a settlement of the Kashmir dispute. The Tashkent Declaration came as an anti-climax to the high hopes that propaganda had built up. It exposed Ayub Khan to baseless accusations of squandering at the negotiating table what the armed forces had won on the battlefield. Bhutto later exploited this myth to considerable political advantage.

The provision for bilateral meetings in the Tashkent Declaration papered over the gulf between the two sides on the purpose of such meetings. The cover was torn apart at the first meeting held between their foreign ministers at Rawalpindi in 1966. The Pakistani side interpreted the declaration as requiring recognition of the 'special importance of reaching a settlement of the Jammu and Kashmir dispute.' The Indian side did not agree, joining only in the statement that 'all disputes' should be resolved. According to Z. A. Bhutto, this meant India was willing to hold discussions for settlement of the Kashmir dispute. Swaran Singh, however, said India was willing to discuss any dispute including Kashmir, but India's sovereignty over Kashmir was not negotiable. What then was the purpose of negotiation? The stalemate illustrated the futility of further meetings which were, therefore, not held.

The hiatus in India's logic was obvious also to the people of Kashmir. Just as Pakistan's policy of alliances in the 1950s could not detract from Nehru's pledges and the UN resolutions recognizing the right of the people of Kashmir to self-determination, neither the 1965 war nor the Tashkent Declaration could be a valid reason for depriving them of their inalienable right. Their restlessness was demonstrated in recurrent outbreaks of protests and agitation.

Kosygin was disappointed at the lack of progress in Pakistan-India relations. In 1968, he exhorted the two countries to resolve their disputes, as that would 'meet the vital interests of the two countries as well as of universal peace.' Not for the first time, India ignored an earnest and reasonable appeal.

Post-War Controversy: 'Victory finds a hundred fathers but defeat is an orphan.' The aphorism[16] was illustrated once again after the 1965 war. Controversy continues to envelop history in a fog that has only thickened with contradictory claims and disclaimers by former officials. The records of the period have not been released and it is doubtful they even exist.

A cautious military leader, Ayub Khan initially rejected the plan for sending armed volunteers into Indian-held Kashmir, because it involved unacceptable risk.[17] Although he later agreed, he still believed the incursions would not trigger a war. That he did not anticipate war is also corroborated by his decision to allow a change of command of the Pakistan air force. Air Marshal Asghar Khan, who had led the air force for eight years, was allowed to retire on 23 July, two weeks before incursions began across the ceasefire line, even though his successor, Air Marshal Nur Khan, had been away from the force for six years, seconded to Pakistan International Airlines. Neither the air force nor the navy was informed of Operation Gibraltar, and the fact that the army did not prepare for the contingency of war is further evidence of his anti-war intentions.

From Asghar Khan's account, Ayub Khan emerges as 'kind, intelligent, and shrewd', but not logical. Even as late as 4 September, when war was imminent, 'Ayub Khan did not feel that the Indians would react so decisively,' and 'there was nothing to worry about' as he was assured by Foreign Minister Bhutto, 'Pakistan's incursions into Azad [sic] Kashmir would not provoke the Indians to extend the area of hostilities along the Indo-Pakistan border.'[18]

Zulfikar Ali Bhutto advocated an activist policy, believing it was morally incumbent on Pakistan to do something to press for a Kashmir settlement. But he, too, does not emerge as a farsighted strategist and some of his critics go to the extent of thinking he was devious. They accuse him of deliberately misleading Ayub Khan to believe that in the existing global and regional situation the conflict would remain confined to Kashmir.[19] According to Asghar Khan, Ayub Khan said Bhutto had 'assured' him Gibraltar would not lead to a general war. Other critics attribute the blunder to 'foreign affairs experts' who were alleged to have given a similar assessment.

Assuming that such assessment was, in fact, given, not only those who gave it should be faulted; acceptance of the assessment at face value and calling it 'assurance' projects Ayub Khan as well as his apologists as naïve analysts.

The inescapable fact is that the decision to send armed volunteers across the ceasefire line, however limited its scope, was bound to provoke a reaction. If Bhutto and 'foreign affairs experts' failed to foresee the consequences, they were not the only ones to do so. Nor is it clear whether they had access to the details of the plan. Foreign Secretary Aziz Ahmed told the author at the time of the war that he was taken aback by reports in the press on 9 August. Not only did he not know the date for the beginning of the operation, the number of armed men who were reported to have crossed the ceasefire line particularly surprised him. Quantity made a qualitative difference.

Certainly, hubris fostered by the battle victory in Kutch misled some to believe the Indian political leadership was not bold enough to pick up the gauntlet.[20] Whatever preparations were made for the contingency of war were too little, too late. Not until June was approval given for an additional budgetary allocation of 900 million rupees (then equal to 200 million dollars) to augment ammunition and spare parts reserves. Still another month passed before it was decided to raise one additional infantry division. Some blamed the finance minister, Mohammad Shoaib, for 'myopic' opposition to the army's proposal for two divisions, though it is unclear if he was privy to the decision to send armed volunteers. If not, he was not the only one. Commanders-in-chief of the air force and navy were not even informed of the fateful decision.

Few in the army were aware of the danger of war. Not only were mines not laid on the border with India, but those laid during the Kutch crisis were removed. It was later said that influential retired or serving generals with lands in the area complained that the mines were obstructing agricultural operations on their lands, ironically given to them on the assumption they would contribute to the requirements of defence on the dangerous frontier.

Bilateralism

Disappointment at the failure of Western allies during the war hastened the process of reappraisal of Pakistan's policy of alliances, which had been in progress since 1960, when Pakistan embarked upon efforts for the normalization of relations with China and the Soviet Union. The attempt by the United States and Britain to use the alliances to advance their own interests during the Sino-Indian border clash in 1962 had also served to disillusion Pakistan. Proceeding from the realistic premise that Pakistan had neither the capacity nor any reason to get mixed up in the wrangling of the great powers, it now decided on a policy of lowering its profile in the Cold War. Termed 'bilateralism,' the new policy in effect sought to distance Pakistan from the West and open windows to the East. The idea was different from non-alignment mainly to the extent that Pakistan did not intend to repudiate SEATO and CENTO or denounce the 1959 agreement of cooperation with the United States. Pakistan also resisted the anti-West bias of some of the prominent non-aligned countries, thus hoping to cultivate new friends without offending the existing ones. After he became prime minister, Z. A. Bhutto tried to elaborate this idea and make it into a doctrine in international relations but, as often happens, artificial innovations pass away with their authors.

NOTES

1. '*Hamara sheeraza bikhar jaiga*' (i.e. Our unity would be destroyed), said Atal Bihari Vajpayee in a conversation with the author in 1980.
2. Summarized from *Hindustan Times* of 20 April 1964 in Alastair Lamb, *Kashmir—A Disputed Legacy*, 248–50.
3. The award allocated to Pakistan narrow—up to eight miles deep—stretches of land that surface after the flood season along the northern edge of the Rann while India received the rest, mostly marshy area.
4. Quoted from *Hindu Weekly* of 26 July 1965 in Burke, op. cit., 326.
5. Lamb, op. cit., 256.
6. Statement of 14 July 1965 quoted in McMahon, op. cit., 326.
7. M. Asghar Khan, 75–6.
8. Pakistani forces captured 1,617 square miles of Indian territory and 201 square miles in Kashmir while India gained 446 square miles in Pakistan and 740 square miles in Kashmir.
9. China demand the return of four Chinese inhabitants, 800 sheep, and 59 yaks that India had kidnapped.
10. For details and references see Burke, 338–57, and Gauhar, 340–1 and 347–53.
11. Gauhar, op. cit., 347–8.
12. Henry Kissinger, op. cit., 846.
13. The UK high commissioner in Pakistan gave a 'firm promise' to President Ayub, 'We and others are now determined to settle it.' UN under-secretary Ralph Bunch told the Pakistan ambassador: 'How can you possibly believe that after the war we will forget the Kashmir dispute, as we did earlier.' White Paper, op. cit., 59.
14. UN document S/Res/211 in *Documents* Vol. 2, ed. K. Arif, 115–16.
15. McMahon, 345.
16. Count Galeazzo Ciano: 'As always, victory finds a hundred fathers but defeat is an orphan.'
17. This account, and much of the information here about official discussions during the period, is based on *Ayub Khan* by Altaf Gauhar, *The First Round* by

Air Marshal M. Asghar Khan, a manuscript by Aziz Ahmed, and conversations with senior foreign office officials.

18. M. Asghar Khan, op. cit., 6.
19. Gauhar holds the view that Ayub Khan was influenced by Foreign Minister Z. A. Bhutto and Foreign Secretary Aziz Ahmed. All three were dead before *Ayub Khan* was published in 1993. Aziz Ahmed told the author in 1965 that he was taken completely by surprise when he read newspaper reports on 9 August to the effect that a large number of armed volunteers had crossed the CFL. Apparently, he expected the number to be smaller.
20. Surprisingly for so well experienced a soldier, Ayub Khan held the bigoted notion that 'Hindu morale would not stand more than a couple of hard blows at the right time and place.' Gauhar, op. cit., 329.

Chapter 9

The Legacy of War

The 1965 war precipitated adverse changes in Pakistan's relations with CENTO and SEATO allies who had never endorsed Pakistan's contention that the alliances could be invoked against aggression by a non-communist state. Some of them even disagreed that Pakistan was a victim of aggression. Frustrated that their military assistance, provided in the context of their anti-communist strategy, was wasted in a war between two states they had sought to bolster and befriend, the United States and Britain all but discontinued cooperation with both Pakistan and India. Neither was disposed towards involvement in promoting a peace settlement between Pakistan and India, letting the Soviet Union, their Cold War adversary, take up a role that they had earlier reserved for themselves.

China: Pakistan's acceptance of the Security Council's demand for a ceasefire surprised Chinese leaders, but after Ayub Khan explained Pakistan's constraints[1] they, as usual, showed understanding of Pakistan's decision even though their own view was different. An engaging characteristic of Chinese leaders has been their respect for the right of Pakistan, as also other countries, to determine what is in its own interest.

China's support of Pakistan in the 1965 crisis made a deep impression on the Pakistani people. President Liu Shao-chi's visit to Pakistan in March 1966 was a memorable occasion. In Lahore, Karachi, and Dhaka, his welcome by enthusiastic multitudes was on a scale rarely seen since Independence. His description of Sino-Pakistan relations as *mujahidana dosti* (friendship in righteous struggle) aptly translated the sentiments of the Pakistani people and boosted their morale. Here was a friend the nation could trust and rely on. This friendship, forged in the heat of the war, developed in succeeding years.

To help Pakistan's defence capability after the United States embargoed military sales, China agreed, in 1966, to provide equipment for two divisions of the army as well as MIG aircraft for the air force. It also gave $60 million for development assistance in 1965, a further $40 million in 1969, and $200 million for the next five-year plan. Coming from China, itself a low-income developing country, this assistance was generous. Also, China placed emphasis on the transfer of technology to help Pakistan achieve self-reliance. The Heavy Mechanical Complex, the Heavy Rebuild Factory, the Kamra Aeronautical Complex, and several other industrial plants were later established with Chinese assistance. To provide a land link, the two countries decided, in 1969, to build a road across the Karakorum.[2] China played a major part in the construction of the spectacular Karakorum Highway linking Gilgit in the Northern Areas with Kashgar in Xinjiang, over the second highest mountain range in the world and through the 15,800-foot high Khunjerab Pass. Speaking at the UN General Assembly in October 1970, President Yahya Khan described friendly cooperation with China as the 'cornerstone' of Pakistan's policy. In the communiqué issued after his visit to China the following month, the Chinese reiterated support on Kashmir and Pakistan reaffirmed that 'Taiwan was an inalienable part of China'.

USSR: Pakistan's policy of normalization of relations with the Soviet Union gathered momentum after the 1965 War. The Soviet Union provided credit for development projects in Pakistan. Trade expanded. Pakistan sent a military delegation to Moscow in 1966 to probe the purchase of military supplies from the Soviet Union, and although no agreement was concluded, Moscow did not reject the idea. Ayub Khan visited Moscow in 1967, and before Kosygin returned the visit in April 1968, Pakistan informed the United States of its decision not to renew the lease for the Badaber electronic base upon its expiry in July 1968. Moscow appreciated Pakistan's decision. In 1968, Kosygin announced Soviet assistance for building a steel plant. Later that year, the Soviet Union agreed to sell a small quantity of military equipment to Pakistan. Kosygin visited Pakistan again in May 1969 for a meeting with Yahya Khan, the new military ruler. The Soviet Union committed over a billion dollars in soft loans for thirty-one development projects.[3] Predictably, India raised a howl over this 'unexpected' development. Acquiescing to Indian pressure, Moscow discontinued the further supply of military equipment in 1970, illustrating to Pakistan the limits of bilateralism. In the East Pakistan crisis, Soviet priority reverted to one-sided support for India, leading to a breakdown of the developing links between the two countries.

USA: Already under increasing strain since 1962, the Pakistan-US alliance broke down after the outbreak of Pakistan-India hostilities in the Rann of Kutch and war over Kashmir five months later. The US was antagonized by Pakistani allegations of betrayal. Lyndon Johnson told Ayub Khan in December that the alliance between the United States and Pakistan was over. Military aid was discontinued. Any further economic aid was made conditional on Pakistan curtailing its close ties with China. That was unacceptable to Pakistan.

Neither Washington nor Islamabad renounced the 1959 Cooperation Agreement, however. The US still valued the Badaber base, and Pakistan, not wanting to further antagonize the US superpower, decided to wait until 1968, when the base agreement would expire.

The alliance was torn apart because of the divergent pulls of state interests in a changing world situation. In the early 1960s, the US did not decide to downgrade Pakistan, but the opportunity of pulling India into its own orbit was irresistible in the context of global strategic power and ideological confrontation. Similarly, Pakistan was compelled by its own security interests to improve its relations with China and the USSR.

In retrospect, the damage to friendly cooperation between Pakistan and the United States might have been contained had both sides lowered expectations of each other in the light of evolution in the strategic environment. Kennedy was right, in his observation in 1962, that 'allowance must be made for the special circumstances', but his successor made no such allowance. Pakistani spokesmen unnecessarily emotionalized an objective situation, a tendency that culminated in 1965 in accusing the US of 'betrayal', a charge that could not stand scrutiny. The US was committed under the 1959 agreement to come to Pakistan's assistance in the event of aggression, but it did not accept such an interpretation of the Indian attack across the border. Instead, it held Pakistan responsible for provoking the war. The Gibraltar Operation was Pakistan's own decision, and it was illogical to expect US support in consequential escalation. An ally, especially an unequal one, cannot compel another to underwrite objectives not envisaged in the alliance agreement; the US did not endorse, much less support, the Anglo-French-Israeli attack on Egypt in 1956.

The alliance with Pakistan was conceived by the United States in the context of the threat of communist aggression. The Manila Pact did not identify any source of aggression, and even if aggression was recognized to have occurred, it entailed only the obligation to consult together to agree on measures for common defence. Even that obligation was limited by the United States through a reservation in the treaty to the event of communist aggression. CENTO provided generally for cooperation for security and defence without creating any specific obligations in the event of aggression. When the United States joined the military committee, it clarified that its participation 'related solely to the communist menace'.[4] Britain, too, declared that it promised to defend the region against communist aggression only.[5]

Pakistani failure to consult the US in advance of its high-risk policy in Kashmir and the US failure to assist Pakistan after Indian aggression widened the gulf between the two countries that had opened up as a result of their divergent policies towards China and the increasing US assistance to India after its border clash with China in 1962.

Still, Ayub Khan realized the necessity of mending fences with the United States. Also, tempers cooled down in Washington as some people in high places recognized Pakistan's potential for contributing to better understanding between the US and China. In April 1966, Secretary of State Dean Rusk even asked Foreign Minister Bhutto for Pakistan's help to arrange a meeting with the Chinese foreign minister for discussions on Vietnam.[6] The idea was not, however, pursued. Bhutto, increasingly on the defensive for his role in policies leading to alienation of the United States, was asked to resign. On 12 April 1967, the US announced termination of military assistance to Pakistan (and India), exempting only cash sales of spare parts for the previously supplied equipment on a case-by-case basis.

Nixon Sympathetic: US-Pakistan relations improved after President Richard Nixon took office in 1969. An advocate of close relations with Pakistan since the 1950s and appreciative of its role as an ally, the upbeat tone of Pakistan-US relations was manifest in the strong support the US gave in aid to Pakistan at the World Bank's consortium meeting in May 1969. In October 1970, Nixon told Bhutto that despite difficulties due to Congressional opposition—and 'a psychosis in this country about India'—he 'would stick by (US) friends.' As a mark of his friendship, he decided to make a 'one-time' exception to the Congressional embargo on military sales to Pakistan to provide replacement fighters and bombers, 300 armoured personnel carriers, and four maritime patrol aircrafts in addition to $72 million for food.[7] The US relaxed the ban on military supplies, allowing the sale of a limited number of B-57 and F-104 aircraft.

Channel between the US and China: The Nixon administration decided on 'a new beginning' in relations with China.[8] Following China's split with the Soviet Union, Nixon and his National Security Council advisor, Henry Kissinger, appraised China to be confronted with the 'nightmare of hostile encirclement', in which it might welcome 'strategic reassurance' from improved relations with the United States. Tentative probes were initiated in the fifteen-year-old ambassador-level contacts in Warsaw. In January 1970, the US offered to send a representative to Beijing to consider ideas to reduce tension. The Chinese response was affirmative. To signal serious intent, Nixon started to dismantle obstacles to better relations by relaxing restrictions on travel and trade. Kissinger, well known for his preference for secret diplomacy, used personal friends for confidential contacts with the Chinese embassy in Paris, in order to prepare the ground for a positive outcome of the proposed direct dialogue.

In October 1970, Nixon asked Yahya Khan, in a meeting in New York, to inform the Chinese leaders, during his visit to China in November, that Nixon considered rapprochement with China 'essential'. Upon his return, Yahya Khan conveyed the Chinese response in an elaborately confidential manner. Kissinger was fascinated by Ambassador Agha Hilaly's insistence on dictating the message at slow speed, which he had to take in long hand. For four months thereafter, messages were passed on this Kissinger-Hilaly-

Yahya Khan channel to Beijing in utter secrecy. Pakistan was equally helpful in arranging Kissinger's secret trip for talks in Beijing, 9–11 July 1971.

Beijing and Washington were appreciative of Pakistan's role as an intermediary, but when the news of Kissinger's visit to Beijing broke, Moscow was furious and decided to punish Pakistan for meddling in the triangular power politics by hastily signing a treaty with India that in effect freed India of the fear of Chinese intervention against its design to cut Pakistan into two. Moscow also wanted to humiliate China by making it a helpless spectator of Pakistan's defeat and break-up.

Moscow's reaction to the development was both strong and virulent. Pulling out an old draft from the archives, it promptly concluded a Treaty of Peace, Friendship and Cooperation with India, which in article IX committed the two countries to mutual consultation in the event of an attack or threat of attack in order to remove such threat and to take 'appropriate effective measures' to ensure their peace and security. Apparently not so specific as an alliance, its purpose was unmistakably strategic. The Soviet Union in effect provided India with an umbrella against the fear of intervention by China, thus abetting New Delhi's design to cut Pakistan in to two. It served Moscow's twin objectives of humiliating China and punishing Pakistan for meddling in relations among Great Powers.[9]

Organization of Islamic Cooperation

Israeli aggression against Egypt, Jordan, and Syria in 1967 evoked strong condemnation in the world. The Muslim peoples were stirred, as never before, because of the Israeli occupation of Jerusalem, the first *qibla* of Islam. Mammoth demonstrations were held in Pakistan. Ardent solidarity with the victims of aggression was made manifest not only in words but also in concrete action. Pakistani military deputations in these countries volunteered their services and participated in action. Pakistan's ambassador to the United Nations, Agha Shahi, made an effective contribution to the Arab cause. In reasoned speeches, he supported resolutions in the General Assembly calling for respect for international law and for the rights of the people of occupied territories pending Israeli withdrawal.

Shahi piloted the resolution declaring invalid the measures imposed by Israel to change the status of Jerusalem.

On 21 August 1969, arson inflicted extensive damage on Al Aqsa Mosque, which is associated with the Prophet's Ascension. It triggered a tidal wave of anguish and outrage among Muslims throughout the world. Arab and non-Arab Muslim states joined the first Islamic Summit Conference held in Rabat, on 22–4 September 1969. It adopted a moving declaration reflecting the profound distress of Muslim peoples, agreed to coordinate action to secure Israeli withdrawal from all Arab territories occupied in 1967, and affirmed full support to the Palestinian people in their struggle for national liberation. Also, recognizing that a common creed constituted a powerful bond between Muslim peoples, the leaders decided to institutionalize the conference and established the Organization of Islamic Cooperation (OIC), with a permanent secretariat to be located in Jeddah pending the liberation of Jerusalem.

Criteria for membership of the OIC were defined against the background of India's 'pathetic importuning'[10] for an invitation to attend the Islamic summit, justifying its inclusion on the grounds of its large Muslim population. Recognizing the historic and abiding concern of the Muslim community in South Asia for the welfare of their co-religionists throughout the world, Pakistan—itself an heir to that legacy—agreed to accord representation to the Muslims of India at the conference. But when, by sending a non-Muslim envoy, India failed to observe the distinction between Muslims of India and India as a state, Pakistan raised an objection which was upheld by the conference. If the size of a state's Muslim population was the criterion for membership, many other states such as the USSR and China should have been invited to participate; their Muslim minorities were larger than the populations of some of the participating Muslim states.

NOTES

1. Ayub Khan secretly visited Beijing for this purpose on 20 September. Gauhar, op. cit., 351–3.
2. A jeepable road was completed in 1971, an asphalt road in 1978. The Karakorum Highway, crossing the Khunjerab pass, at 15,800 ft. (4800 m) was opened to adventure travelling in 1986.

3. Quoted from *Asian Recorder*, 1957, in Burke, op. cit., 171.
4. Quoted from *Dawn* of 13 February 1959 in Burke, op. cit., 171.
5. Z. A. Bhutto's note for Ayub Khan, extract in *Documents*, ed. Arif, 250.
6. Hafeez Malik, op. cit., 202.
7. F. S. Aijazuddin, *The White House and Pakistan*, 106–10.
8. Henry Kissinger, *The White House Years*, Little Brown, 1979, 685.
9. Kissinger, op. cit., 767.
10. *Statesman Weekly*, 27 September 1969, quoted in Burke, 374.

Chapter 10

The 1971 Disaster

Shared interest in the protection of cultural, economic, and political rights brought the Muslim people of British India to a common platform, with leaders of Bengal playing a seminal role in the formation of the Muslim League and the formulation of the demand for Pakistan. After the state came into existence, the unity of its two wings, separated by a thousand miles, came under strain as a result of several factors, some of which were inherent in demography and differential colonial legacies and resource endowment, while others arose from narrow and shortsighted politics.

Differences with the distant centre's views began to surface in East Pakistan soon after Independence. A group of students protested when the Quaid-i-Azam said, in a speech in Dhaka in 1948, that Urdu alone would be the national language. Expectations of the people for visible self-rule were disappointed. Few of the senior administrative personnel inherited by Pakistan were from East Pakistan, and some of those who were appointed to East Pakistan did not win the confidence of the people.[1] East Pakistan did not have a sense of participation in the government in distant Karachi. In 1950, the East Pakistan Muslim League asked for 'maximum autonomy'. After elections in East Pakistan in 1954, the Muslim League was eclipsed. The United Front, which won 223 out of 237 seats, asked for 'complete autonomy according to the Pakistan Resolution.'[2] This reversion to the ambiguous text of the 1940 resolution depicted the sea change that had taken place in political opinion after Independence. It ignored the fact that in 1946 the most representative body of elected Muslim League legislators[3] had adopted a unanimous resolution declaring that Pakistan would be 'a sovereign independent State,' thus clarifying the ambiguity of the 1940 resolution, which spoke of 'autonomous and sovereign' constituent units in 'independent States' in the Muslim-majority north-western and eastern regions. The central government's manipulation to deny power to the elected majority in East Pakistan added to the accumulating grievances. Delays in constitution-making and holding of national elections exacerbated East Pakistan's sense of exclusion.

East Pakistan's isolation during the 1965 War and its lack of self-defence capability gave a fillip to the existing demand for autonomy. In March 1966, the Awami League leader Sheikh Mujibur Rahman put forward Six Points[4] calling for a new constitution under which the federal government would be responsible 'only for defence and foreign affairs', for which purpose it would be 'provided with requisite revenue resources' by the federating units. Ayub Khan's highly centralized government equated the demand for autonomy with secessionism. A process of polarization set in, with West Pakistani opinion looking at East Pakistanis as dupes of Indian propaganda and Bengali elites ascribing motives of domination and exploitation to West Pakistanis. Ayub Khan said, 'They are not going to remain with us.'[5]

Alert to the brewing trouble and growing alienation in East Pakistan, India encouraged the separatist sentiment. Operatives of its secret service agency, Research and Analysis Wing (RAW), intensified subversion. In 1966, they met with a group of extremists in Agartala to plan sabotage.[6] A raid on an armoury led to the arrest of twenty-eight people including a few low-level civilians and armed forces personnel in January 1969. The case against them was not without substance, but the government also implicated Mujibur Rahman, though he was in custody during the Agartala Conspiracy. Trial by a special tribunal robbed the proceedings of credibility. Opinion in East Pakistan concluded that the case was concocted for political persecution.

Nature too seemed to collude in the tragedy. In November 1970, a cyclone of ferocious intensity left death and devastation in its trail. A quarter of a million people drowned. The federal government was charged with indifference to the plight of the people of East Pakistan. In the election in December, the Awami League, led by Sheikh Mujibur Rahman, swept the polls in East Pakistan by winning 167 out of 169 seats from the province, sufficient for an absolute majority in the 313-member National Assembly. The Pakistan People's Party led by Z. A. Bhutto emerged with the second largest number of seats, all from West Pakistan, and sought a share in power. The first focus was on constitutional issues. Although Sheikh Mujibur Rahman had earlier told Yahya Khan the Six Point demand was negotiable, after the electoral triumph he became a prisoner of his own extremist rhetoric and lost control over hawks in the party who wanted independence. He declined Yahya Khan's invitation to visit Islamabad for talks. When the President went to Dhaka, he found Mujibur Rahman in no mood for a compromise. Yahya Khan then convened the Assembly for 3 March, hoping the political leaders would settle the issues among themselves. Now Bhutto announced that his party would boycott the Assembly unless the constitutional issues and power sharing were first resolved. Yahya Khan then postponed the Assembly meeting and again went to Dhaka in mid-March. Whether his purpose was to hold talks with Mujibur Rahman or to prepare for imposition of martial law remained unclear. The talks broke down on 23 March when the Awami League proposed Pakistan should be made a confederation. Martial law was imposed on 26 March.

'Almost all nations will fight for their unity, even if sentiment in the disaffected area is overwhelmingly for secession,' observed Henry Kissinger, adding, 'So it was during our Civil War, with Nigeria toward Biafra and with Congo toward Katanga.'[7] But Yahya Khan's decision to use force was a gamble with the dice loaded against Pakistan. Not only was use of military force against compatriots unconscionable, it was foolish to hope 42,320[8] West Pakistani troops could suppress 75 million people in East Pakistan, with India determined to obstruct and prevent the effort through instigation, abetment, and military intervention.

India had started planning to exploit the internal situation in Pakistan years earlier. The Agartala operation instigated by RAW has been mentioned above. On 30 January 1971, an Indian Airlines plane named *Ganga*, on a Srinagar-Delhi flight, was hijacked to Lahore by two Kashmiri youths. They were lionised as freedom fighters on arrival at Lahore airport. Let alone popular opinion: even the usually alert Z. A. Bhutto applauded the 'brave freedom fighters'.[9] Their leader set the plane on fire. New Delhi made furious protests, demanding compensation and immediate surrender of the criminals. Struck by this bolt from the blue, Islamabad was paralysed, too proud to concede to peremptory Indian demands and too weak to control the emotional outburst of popular opinion. Before it knew what was happening, India suspended overflight rights of Pakistan's planes. Subsequently, a Pakistani inquiry tribunal discovered the facts: the leader of the 'hijackers' was a recruit of Indian intelligence, trained and coached for the mission; the 'weapons' given to him and his innocent accomplice were toy pistols and wooden grenades; and the *Ganga* was the oldest plane in the airline's fleet. Pakistan had walked into a clever trap.

After Yahya Khan ordered the crackdown in East Pakistan, the Indian government moved into higher gear. India saw in the crisis an 'opportunity of the century' to cut Pakistan into two.[10] RAW operatives smuggled out Tajuddin Ahmad, an Awami League leader, escorted him to a border village to proclaim the independence of Bangladesh, and installed him as head of the provisional Bangladesh government in Mujibnagar, a house in Calcutta rented by RAW.[11] On 31 March, the Indian parliament adopted a resolution assuring the East Pakistani insurgents that 'their struggle and sacrifices will receive the wholehearted support of the people of India'.[12] Indira Gandhi reassured parliament that she would make timely decisions about the developing situation. Within days, the Indian border police started operating inside East Pakistan. India embarked on an emergency training programme for Bengali army officers and provided military equipment for armed resistance.[13] First secretly and later openly, India began building up a rebel force called the Mukti Bahini. An estimated 100,000 men were trained in guerrilla skills.[14]

Public opinion and the media in the US and Western Europe were outraged by the Pakistani military crackdown. The excesses committed by Pakistani forces were reported at great length, and the number of refugees who entered India was wildly exaggerated. Few bothered to take notice of Indian interference or its rejection of proposals for impartial international inspection. To ease India's burden on account of the refugees, the United States provided $350 million in aid, but that did not dissuade Indira Gandhi from her preconceived purpose. 'The opportunity to settle scores with a rival that had isolated itself by its own shortsightedness was simply too tempting'. All efforts by the international community to promote a political solution were resisted as India 'insisted on terms that escalated by the week'.[15] President Nixon read the Indian design clearly, but the State Department was swept off its feet by popular reaction. He acquiesced to the State Department's decision to embargo delivery of arms to Pakistan.

Pakistan learnt from its own sources, as did the United States 'from sources heretofore reliable that Mrs Gandhi had ordered plans for a lightning 'Israeli-type' attack to take over East Pakistan.'[16] Only its implementation had to be deferred in the light of Chief of Staff General Manekshaw's view that the army needed six to seven months to prepare for war.[17] 'The Indian commanders insisted, at a minimum, on waiting until November when weather in the Himalayas would make Chinese intervention more difficult.'[18]

Indian Strategic Moves: Meanwhile, New Delhi also started negotiations with Moscow with the aim of securing Soviet military and diplomatic assistance in order to reduce the chances of Chinese intervention on Pakistan's side. Moscow was not then hostile and had even reciprocated Pakistan's efforts for improvement of bilateral relations. The withering of the Pakistan-US alliance and the termination of the Badaber base agreement with the United States had removed major obstacles to the normalization of Pakistan-USSR relations. Islamabad did not see any reason for Moscow to assist India in its designs against Pakistan. However, deterioration of Sino-Soviet relations and incipient trends in Sino-US relations had introduced radical changes in the global strategic environment. Islamabad did not realize the impact of its role as a channel between Washington and Beijing. The Soviet attitude was suddenly transformed in July.

Indo-USSR Friendship Treaty: The announcement of Henry Kissinger's visit to Beijing on 9–11 July 1971, and the breakthrough of an invitation to Nixon to visit China, stunned the world.[19] Moscow's reaction to the development was both angry and quick. Taking advantage of the spiralling crisis between Pakistan and India on 9 August 1971, it concluded a Treaty of Peace, Friendship and Cooperation with India. Article IX committed the two countries to mutual consultation in the event of an attack or threat of attack, in order to remove such threat and to take 'appropriate effective measures' to ensure their peace and security. Not as specific as an alliance, its purpose was unmistakably strategic. The Soviet Union, in effect, provided India with an umbrella against intervention by China, allowing it to execute its design with impunity. The Soviet object was 'to humiliate China and to punish Pakistan for having served as an intermediary.' The treaty 'was bound to eliminate fears of Chinese intervention.'[20]

With the Soviet shield in place, and the veto to stymie the UN Security Council in its pocket, India issued orders to the armed forces to prepare for operations.[21] Other preparations, too, were 'excellent'.[22] A policy planning committee was established to ensure political and military coordination at home and the build-up of international opinion through propaganda and high-level visits.

In contrast, conditions in Islamabad were confused and chaotic. The army was said to be operating largely on its own.[23] Yahya Khan 'was oblivious to his perils'; Pakistan's military leaders were 'caught up in a process beyond their comprehension'.[24] Yahya Khan did not inform others in the government of his role in providing a secret channel between Washington and Beijing and did not anticipate the strong reaction it was bound to provoke in Moscow. The importance of the Indo-Soviet Treaty was not correctly assessed; some thought the Soviet objective was only to restrain India.

Indira Gandhi rejected Washington's suggestion for UN monitoring of the border in order to curb guerrilla activities from its territory. By October, Yahya Khan informed Washington that he was willing to grant full autonomy to East Pakistan. A month later, he was even agreeable to a unilateral withdrawal of forces. Any such decision would have been better than the fate that befell the country. Unaccountably, Yahya did not act on these ideas.

Before moving in for the 'kill', Indira Gandhi undertook an international tour. She visited Washington on 4–5 November, mainly to influence public opinion. Nixon was not unsympathetic to India. During the two years of his administration, the United States had given $1.5 billion in aid to India.[25] But he detested the condescension Indira Gandhi exuded, like her sermonizing father,[26] and was opposed to her designs against Pakistan. His conversation with Indira Gandhi was 'a classic dialogue of the deaf', and he 'was disturbed by the fact that although Mrs Gandhi professed her devotion to peace, she would not make any concrete offers for de-escalating the tensions'.[27] She 'denied that she was opposed to [Pakistan's] existence, but her analysis did little to sustain her disclaimer'.[28] As Nixon later recorded in his diary, Indira Gandhi 'purposely deceived me in our meeting'[29] having 'made up her mind to attack Pakistan at the time she saw me in Washington and assured me she would not'.[30] In retrospect, Nixon further lamented, 'how hypocritical the present Indian leaders are' and how 'duplicitous' Indira Gandhi.

Pakistan protested on 21 November that India 'without a declaration of war, has launched an all-out offensive.' By 22 November, Henry Kissinger 'had no doubt that we were now witnessing the beginning of an India-Pakistan war and that India had started it.' While 'Pakistani repression in East Bengal had been brutal and shortsighted,' in his view, and Nixon's, 'it was India's determination to use the crisis to establish its prominence on the sub-continent.'[31]

'From 21 to 25 November, several Indian Army divisions, divided into smaller tactical units, launched simultaneous military actions.'[32] Troops, tanks, and aircraft were used to help the Mukti Bahini occupy 'liberated' territory. Nixon sent another letter to Indira Gandhi informing her of Yahya Khan's offer of unilateral withdrawal, and he also wrote to Kosygin to intercede with her. She was implacable. On 29 November, she told the US Ambassador, 'We can't afford to listen to advice which weakens us.'

On 2 December, Yahya Khan invoked the 1959 agreement asking for US assistance. The State Department argued that the agreement did not oblige the US Government to give a positive response. This view, Kissinger said, 'ignored all other communications between our government and Pakistan.'[33] The 'plain import (of the agreements) was that the United States would come to Pakistan's assistance if she was attacked by India.' As Kissinger concluded: 'The image of a great nation conducting itself like a shyster looking for legalistic loopholes was not likely to inspire other allies who had signed treaties with us or relied on our expressions in the belief the words meant approximately what they said.'[34]

In the event, the White House was stalled by the State Department. Not even a statement was issued. Meanwhile, the military situation in East Pakistan grew more desperate by the day. 'Yahya chose what he considered the path of honour' and ordered a retaliatory attack across the border from West Pakistan on 3 December. This decision, like the others Yahya Khan made, proved ineffectual and merely helped India advance its military plan to commence operations on 4 December.[35]

Speaking in parliament on 16 December, Indira Gandhi announced Lt. General A. A. K. Niazi surrender saying, 'The House and the entire nation will rejoice in this historic event.' Delirious with joy, the parliament gave her a thunderous ovation.[36]

UN: Despite Indian propaganda, the United Nations took a principled position. On 4 December, the Security Council voted 11 to 4 in support of a resolution calling for a ceasefire and withdrawal of forces, but it was killed by the USSR veto. On 7 December, the General Assembly, acting under the Uniting for Peace procedure, recommended a ceasefire and withdrawal of forces to their own territories and the creation of conditions for the voluntary return of refugees. As many as 104 member states voted for the resolution; only eleven voted against and eleven abstained. The overwhelming vote of the world community had no effect on India, however, as it persisted on its ruthless course of aggression in violation of the principles of the Charter.

China: China was supportive of Pakistan and recognized that India was guilty of 'gross interference' in Pakistan's internal affairs. Premier Zhou Enlai assured the Pakistani president that 'the Chinese Government and people will, as always, firmly support Pakistan Government and people in their just struggle to safeguard state sovereignty and national independence.' China continued to supply military equipment under existing agreements and extended political support to the Pakistani position in the United Nations.

USA: The United States upheld the principles of international law and while it did not fulfil its alliance commitments to help maintain Pakistan's unity and territorial integrity, it reviewed its posture on learning that Indira Gandhi was determined to continue fighting 'until the Pakistani army and air force were wiped out'.[37] On 9 December, Kissinger called in the Indian ambassador to warn against such a course. On 10 December, Nixon sent a message to Leonid Brezhnev saying if Indian military operations continued, 'We must inevitably look toward a confrontation between the Soviet Union and the United States. The Soviet Union has a treaty with India; we have one with Pakistan.'[38] The crisis now involved high stakes, and the threat of great power confrontation loomed on the horizon as the USSR encouraged New Delhi in its design, promising that it would initiate military moves if China threatened India. Washington decided it could not allow Moscow to intimidate Beijing if it wanted its China policy to retain credibility. On 10 December, Kissinger met China's representative to the UN, Huang Hua, and briefed him on the steps the US had taken to help Pakistan.

On 9 December, Nixon authorized the dispatch of a task force of eight ships, including the aircraft carrier *Enterprise*, from the Pacific to the Bay of Bengal. The 'objective was to scare off an attack on West Pakistan . . . [and] to have forces in place in case the Soviet Union pressured China'.[39] He stressed upon the Soviets, who had 'proceeded to equip India with great amounts of sophisticated armaments', to restrain India. On 12 December, he sent a 'hot line' message to Leonid Brezhnev saying, 'I cannot emphasize too much that time is of the essence to avoid consequences neither of us wants.'[40] To make the point more concretely, the Soviet authorities were also informed of fleet movements. Evasive at first, Moscow finally responded on 13 December to say that they were conducting 'a clarification of all the circumstance in India'. Kuznetsov was sent to New Delhi to work for a ceasefire. On 14 December at 3 a.m., the Soviet ambassador in Washington delivered a message reporting 'firm assurances by New Delhi that India has no intention of seizing West Pakistani territory'.

At this stage, Poland proposed a resolution in the Security Council which called for the immediate transfer of power to the elected representatives in East Pakistan and a ceasefire and troop withdrawals by both sides. Presumably it had Soviet support and could have, even at this eleventh hour, saved Pakistan from further humiliation. But, as often happens in a crisis, the rush of events overtakes human capacity to make timely decisions. To India's relief, the resolution was not pressed to a vote.

Under mounting US and Soviet pressure, Indira Gandhi offered an unconditional ceasefire on 16 December.

Nixon could credibly claim that his diplomatic signals and the dispatch of the US naval fleet persuaded the Soviet Union to join in pressurising India, thus saving West Pakistan from India's evil design.

Nixon not only demonstrated his long-standing goodwill towards Pakistan, but also manifested a profound understanding of the implications of India and the Soviet Union succeeding in destroying Pakistan. That would have encouraged the Soviet Union 'to use similar tactics elsewhere . . . (and) change the balance of power in Asia. . . . A victory of India over Pakistan would be the same as a victory of the Soviet Union over China.'[41] Nixon's decision to improve relations with China was a part of the same global vision.

It is a sad commentary on the American system that it precluded the United States from fulfilling its treaty obligations towards an ally. As Henry Kissinger explained in a meeting with Prime Minister Zhou Enlai on 10 July 1971, President Nixon and he had 'clearly seen the Indian game from the beginning' but 'failing to grasp the strategic dynamics, the American Congress and media, not to mention South Asia "experts" in the State Department, opposed Nixon's policy and thus became accomplices in the Indian crime against peace and international law. Of course, that does not mitigate the blunders and follies of Pakistani leaders over the years, manifest in the neglect of East Pakistan and its exclusion from due share in power. Political autonomy for East Pakistan would have been consistent with the vision of the founders of Pakistan.'

Tragedy Exploited: The 1971 disaster was an unmitigated tragedy; the country was divided, diminished in self-esteem. The apology rendered by Islamabad to the people of Bangladesh can neither wash away the guilt nor diminish the pain of Pakistanis. Sheikh Mujibur Rahman's daughter has rubbed salt on the wounds even time may not heal. Her heartless distortion of the toll can only distract focus from the inhumanity of fratricidal atrocities and massacres. Prime Minister Z. A. Bhutto established an independent commission headed by the reputable Chief Justice Hamoodur Rehman to inquire into the tragedy. Born in British Bengal, he was a reputable judge in East Pakistan before rising to the Supreme Court of Pakistan. The commission estimated the toll was 25,000. No credible inquiry was ever made by the Bangladesh government. It first ordered and then quashed an official survey 'projecting a death toll of 250,000.' Shaikh Mujibur Rahman pulled the figure of 3 million from thin air. Its first Foreign Secretary and Sheikh Mujib's biographer Sayyid A. Karim wrote that the figure was 'a gross exaggeration'. A 2008 article in the *British Medical Journal* concluded that the number of violent deaths was 'about 269,000.'[42]

Bhutto's New Policy: 1971–1973

On assuming office as president of residual Pakistan in a tortured and turbulent situation, Z. A. Bhutto launched efforts to 'pick up the pieces', bring the nation to grips with the new reality, rebuild morale and confidence, re-orient failed policies both at home and abroad, and rehabilitate Pakistan in the world community. To rescue Pakistan from this predicament, he decided first to turn to friends for sympathy and support.

Even before the 1971 disaster, he had realized the need to mend fences with the United States. After his election victory in 1970, Bhutto told acting US Mission Chief Sidney Sober, 'I'm not-anti-American.'[43] Considering it necessary to reassure President Nixon, he visited Washington on 18 December 1971, and told him that Pakistan was 'completely in the debt of the United States during the recent trying days' and that he now wanted good relations.[44] A rather belated realization, considering that in the 1960s he had advocated 'normalization' of the 'abnormal' relations with the United States,[45] and was responsible for the myth of American betrayal in 1965. President Nixon promised that the US would do 'all within its power'[46] to help Pakistan and that 'the cohesion and stability of Pakistan are of critical importance to the structure of peace in South Asia.'[47]

The first country Bhutto visited after becoming president was China, in January 1972. As always, China extended diplomatic support and economic and military assistance. Bhutto also undertook a whirlwind tour of Islamic countries in the Middle East and Africa which upheld the principles of law for the unconditional release of Pakistani prisoners and the withdrawal of Indian forces from occupied territories.

Britain was unsympathetic. It not only recognized Bangladesh precipitately but also persuaded several countries of Western Europe,

Z. A. Bhutto (Prime Minister of Pakistan, 1973–7). Courtesy of National Archives of Pakistan.

Australia, and New Zealand to do so simultaneously. In disgust, Bhutto decided to quit the Commonwealth.

Little was expected of the Soviet Union. When Bhutto visited Moscow in March 1972, in the hope of moderating its hostility, the Soviet leaders suggested recognition of Bangladesh and negotiations with India for a 'realistic' solution of the post-war problems. It indicated no interest, however, in playing a role. Like the United States, it seemed exhausted by its diplomatic efforts to avoid a confrontation between them during the December war.

Pakistan was left to itself to solve the problems of prisoners of war and recovery of territory occupied by India.

NOTES

1. Of 101 top civil and police officers who opted for Pakistan on Partition, only 18 were Bengalis. Though the number of those who belonged to areas of West Pakistan was also small (35), the issue was politicized so that any non-Bengali was dubbed a 'Punjabi'.
2. The resolution adopted by the Muslim League at its meeting in Lahore on 23 March 1940, demanded that contiguous Muslim-majority units in the north-western and eastern zones should be grouped to constitute 'independent states in which the constituent units shall be autonomous and sovereign.' The popular intent was later clarified by the Muslim League representatives elected by the Muslim masses in a resolution that left no doubt that Pakistan was to be 'a sovereign independent State.' For the texts of the resolutions, see Syed Sharifuddin Pirzada, *The Pakistan Resolution*, Pakistan Publications, Karachi. 1968.
3. The 1946 resolution was adopted unanimously by elected Muslim League legislators who had won 446 out of the 495 seats at stake.
4. For texts of the original and revised formula see Siddiq Salik, *Witness to Surrender*, Oxford University Press, Karachi, 1977, 215–17.
5. Altaf Gauhar, op. cit., 411.
6. Asoka Raina, *Inside RAW*, Vikas Publishing Co., Delhi, 1981, 49.
7. Henry Kissinger, op. cit., 852.
8. Siddiq Salik, op. cit., 101. This figure did not include local raisings and para-military formations.
9. Alastair Lamb, op. cit., 288.
10. K. Subramaniam (director of the official Indian Institute of Defence Studies and Analyses) said on 31 March 1971, 'What India must realize is the fact that the break-up of Pakistan is in our interest, an opportunity the like of which will never come again.' He was also reported by The *Hindustan Times*, New Delhi, to speak of 'a chance of the century'. Quoted in Siddiq Salik, op. cit., 97.

11. Asoka Raina, op. cit., 54.
12. *Bangladesh Documents*, Government of India, Vol. 1, 672, quoted in Siddiq Salik, op. cit., 97.
13. Asoka Raina, op. cit., 57.
14. Siddiq Salik, op. cit., 100.
15. Henry Kissinger, op. cit., 857 and 861.
16. Ibid., 856.
17. Richard Sisson and Leo E. Rose, *War and Secession—Pakistan, India and the Creation of Bangladesh*, University of California Press, Berkeley, CA, 1990, 209.
18. Henry Kissinger, op. cit., 857.
19. President Yahya Khan played the key intermediary role between Washington and Beijing in arranging Kissinger's secret departure from Pakistan for China. See page 122 for channel between USA and China.
20. Kissinger, op. cit., 860.
21. Richard Sisson and Leo E. Rose, 209.
22. V. Longer, *The Defence and Foreign Policy of India*, Sterling Publishers, New Delhi, 1988, 205.
23. The visiting US official Maurice Williams was so informed by Pakistani officials in August. Dennis Kux, op. cit., 197.
24. Henry Kissinger, op. cit., 861.
25. F. S. Aijazuddin, *The White House and Pakistan*, 140–1. (Winston Lord to Henry Kissinger.)
26. Nixon was not alone in finding Nehru insufferable. Secretary of State Dean Acheson said he was 'one of the most difficult men with whom I have ever had to deal.' Quoted from Acheson, *Present at the Creation*, 439–40, in Robert McMahon, op. cit., 56. Truman considered Nehru 'disagreeable' and Kennedy, who publicly praised Nehru's 'soaring idealism', found his sense of superiority 'rather offensive'.
27. Richard Nixon, *The Memoirs of Richard Nixon*, Vol. I, Warner Books, New York, 1978, 651.
28. Henry Kissinger, op. cit., 880.
29. Nixon, op. cit., 652.
30. Ibid., 658.
31. Henry Kissinger, 885.
32. Sisson and Rose, op. cit., 213.
33. Henry Kissinger, op. cit., 895–6. In footnote 7 on 1488, he further says, 'Assurances were given by the Kennedy and Johnson administrations, including a letter from President John F. Kennedy to President Mohammad Ayub Khan on 26 January 1962; an aide-memoir presented by the State Department on 17 November 1962; and an oral promise by President Lyndon Johnson to Ayub Khan on 15 December 1965.'
34. Henry Kissinger, 895.
35. General Manekshaw made this statement in an interview with BBC. Dennis Kux, op. cit., 199.
36. Reports in the Indian press.
37. Henry Kissinger, op. cit., 901.

38. White House Memorandum of conversation between President Nixon and Soviet Minister of Agriculture Vladimir Matskevich, quoted in Dennis Kux, op. cit., 201.
39. Henry Kissinger, op. cit., 905.
40. Ibid., 910.
41. Memorandum of conversation with President Pompidou, 13 December 1972, quoted in Dennis Kux, op. cit., 203.
42. David Bergman, 'The Politics of Bangladesh's Genocide'. *International New York Times*, 6 April 2016.
43. F. S. Aijazuddin, *The White House and Pakistan*, 125.
44. Dennis Kux, op. cit., 204, quoting Memorandum of Conversation of Nixon-Bhutto meeting, 18 December 1971, President's Office Files, NPMP, NA.
45. Z. A. Bhutto, op. cit., 158.
46. Memorandum of Nixon-Bhutto meeting, quoted in Dennis Kux, op. cit., 204.
47. Statement of Policy for the 1970s, issued on 3 May 1973, Documents, op. cit., 207.

Chapter 11

The Shimla Agreement: Negotiating under Duress

For over four months after the ceasefire of 17 December, no foreign power offered to mediate a peace settlement, nor did Pakistan or India take the initiative to call for a bilateral meeting. Then India sent Union Minister D. P. Dhar to Islamabad for preliminary talks preparatory to a peace conference. The talks were held in Murree from 26–9 April 1972. Pakistan had a glimpse of the demands India had in mind at the meeting. Dhar proposed that the peace conference should aim at eliminating once and for all the sources of antagonism between the two countries, and focus on the determination of 'elements of durable peace'. He did not mention Kashmir and made eloquent disclaimers of any intention to impose a solution on Pakistan, but the assurance rang hollow: India was not prepared to release the prisoners of war and withdraw from occupied territory without conditions. The message came through loud and clear. India wanted to dictate a settlement of the Kashmir question. Pakistan, on its part, wanted the peace conference to address issues generated by the war.

The Murree meeting did not resolve the question as to whether immediate postwar issues or the establishment of durable peace (i.e. settlement of the Kashmir question) should receive priority at the summit conference. Dhar and Secretary General Aziz Ahmed agreed to place both the items on the agenda for simultaneous consideration. The compromise was to prove illusory.

The Shimla Conference, even more than the Murree meeting, seems in retrospect a veritable drama in which superb diplomats played skilful roles using words and gestures that masked, but did not conceal, the real aims and intentions of each side from the other. President Z. A. Bhutto and Prime Minister Indira Gandhi, the twin-directors of the drama without a script, were also the principal actors. The chief executives, however, dominated the centre of the stage even when they were not on it, and kept strategic control of the direction in their own hands, letting the officials determine negotiating tactics to suit the evolving situation.

Zulfikar Ali Bhutto, a leader of exceptional intellect and percipience, also excelled in rhetoric and eloquence. A proud man, he had the misfortune to come to the helm when Pakistan lay prostrate in defeat. He must have hated having to negotiate from a weak bargaining position, but comprehended the country's predicament and the traumatized nation's need to be spared further humiliation. His legal education and superb knowledge of the English language stood Pakistan in good stead at the Shimla Conference. He proposed the 'no-prejudice' clause in the Shimla Agreement, which Indira Gandhi accepted, protecting Pakistan's position on the Kashmir question from compromise. His party colleague and able lawyer, Rafi Raza, later disclosed that he had suggested the idea.

Indira Gandhi, petite and seemingly frail in body but robust in mind, was deceptive also in her inarticulate speech. The words at her command did not do justice to the clarity and depth of her thought, but no one could miss the thrust of her remarks. She seemed engagingly shy but was entirely self-confident and unwavering in resolve. A rare leader with a capacity to view her role in history from a vantage point in the future, she spoke and acted with a sense of accountability to her country. The 'iron lady' was also intensely nationalistic and probably never felt happier and more self-fulfilled than on the day when India humiliated Pakistan. Yet she was capable of discerning the limits beyond which the adversary could not be pushed or squeezed, as she demonstrated by reducing demands in the final draft in order to prevent the collapse of the peace conference.

Aziz Ahmed, Pakistan's Secretary General for foreign affairs, was a senior and reputable civil servant, with experience at top levels of diplomacy, having served as ambassador to Washington and Foreign Secretary. He was widely respected as much for his ability and integrity as for his patriotism. Stern of mien and single-minded in pursuit of the national interest, he probably did not win the sympathy of his Indian interlocutors, but even they could not begrudge him credit as a dour negotiator and a hard bargainer.

India's D. P. Dhar, on the other hand, was a charmer. Courteous and sophisticated, he won the trust of his counterparts—which is half the battle in negotiation—by a positive and empathetic approach, often presenting the demands in his brief as requests and recommendations. Although capable of holding his own in argument, he seldom sought to score points. When debate became sterile and unpleasant, threatening to derail negotiations, he diverted attention to the common ground between the two sides and brought discussion back onto a constructive course.

P. N. Haksar, Secretary General in the Indian prime minister's office, became the leader of the Indian official delegation at the conference after D. P. Dhar was taken ill. Peerless in knowledge and erudition, he was also blessed with lucidity of expression to match his clarity of thought. He seemed to relish saying: 'Only the Devil knows what is in your mind; I can only go by the words you use.' But his chuckling at his own wisecrack instantly reassured everyone that he meant no offence. No one could doubt his desire for a positive outcome of negotiations, which cannot be said about T. N. Kaul, the Indian Foreign Secretary, whose unctuous speech contrasted vividly with unmistakable hostility towards Pakistan.

Rafi Raza, an able barrister and special assistant to president Bhutto, was a senior member of the Pakistan delegation at both the Murree and Shimla meetings. He seldom intervened in discussions across the table, but used the weight of his position as a confidant of Bhutto to good effect in informal negotiations with senior Indian officials.

Opening Gambit

Despite formal politeness and courtesies characteristic of conversations between diplomats, and despite the mildness of words that at times camouflaged harsh intent, the wide gulf between the Pakistani and Indian positions was manifest in the opening round of negotiations at Shimla on 28 June. It was reflected more vividly in the initial drafts tabled by India on 29 June and by Pakistan on 30 June. Concise and cold in their content, the drafts were bare of the overlay of protestations of goodwill and noble intentions.

Leaving aside the preambular parts, pledging mutual respect for independence, sovereignty and territorial integrity, the Pakistani and Indian drafts diverged fundamentally in concepts about the outcome of the Shimla Conference. India proposed an elaborate treaty that already comprised eleven articles, with more to be added later to incorporate a Kashmir settlement. It was comprehensive in every aspect of interest to India but, rather surprisingly for the Pakistani side, did not include a word about either withdrawals from occupied territories or release of prisoners, which were, unsurprisingly, the main focus of the unpretentious but pragmatic draft presented by Pakistan.

The two drafts presented an interesting contrast in their selection of principles for the conduct and regulation of relations between the two countries. Whilst the Indian selection betrayed intent to construct a rather peculiar and particularistic framework of principles, with not even a mention of the United Nations Charter, Pakistan emphasized the universally recognized principles of relations between sovereign states. Of course, the most substantive difference between the two drafts centred on Jammu and Kashmir. While India proposed discussion on the Kashmir question and inclusion of the envisaged agreement in the suggested treaty, Pakistan omitted any reference to it because, in its view, the purpose of the Shimla Conference was limited to resolving the problems resulting from the December war.

In the negotiations that followed, both sides tried to give the impression of accommodation, each toning down its own formulations and incorporating portions of the other's draft, but there was little progress on core issues. By 1 July, a sense of gloom set in, as reflected in the second Indian draft. Premised on the failure to bridge differences on substantive issues, it envisaged an interim agreement, leaving the substantive issues for settlement at a subsequent summit. Pakistan declined to join such a charade that would create an illusion of success. Faced with the collapse of the Shimla Conference, India changed tack again. On 2 July, it presented Pakistan with a final draft. That, too, was unacceptable, to Pakistan. A detailed account of the discussions on various issues is necessary for clarification of the obstacles.

Principles of Relations

The omission of any reference to the United Nations Charter from the selection of principles included in the Indian draft was rather peculiar. More than surprising the Pakistani side, it served to bare a design in India's mind to circumscribe and restrict the applicability of some of the Charter principles to relations with Pakistan. Pakistan's approach was, of course, directly the opposite. Its draft emphasized the UN Charter and universally recognized principles of relations between sovereign states, including in particular the fulfilment in good faith of the obligations assumed by them in accordance with the Charter—a pointed reminder that India had failed to implement the obligations arising from the Security Council resolutions on Kashmir.

When the Pakistani side pointed to the flaw in the Indian draft, Haksar explained the omission by arguing that the two countries did not need to invoke 'foreign ideas'. A high-flyer in logic, and a loquacious man, even he found himself flapping in thin air in arguing that the two 'civilized nations should rely on their own wits.' Perhaps unconvinced themselves, the Indian luminaries were unconvincing in their attempt to justify the exclusion of a mention of the UN Charter, which incorporates accepted principles of international law representing the accumulated experience and distilled wisdom of the community of states. Realizing the hiatus in their logic, the Indian side gave up their stand, and reference to the Charter was not only incorporated but given pride of place as substantive point (i) in paragraph 1 of the agreement.

India agreed to make formal deference to the Charter, but resisted Pakistan's suggestion, based on Article 33 of the Charter, that any dispute between the two countries 'will be settled by peaceful means such as negotiation, conciliation, enquiry, mediation, or, should these methods prove unavailing, by arbitration or judicial settlement.' The Indian side suggested that the two countries agree to 'undertake to settle all issues between them bilaterally and exclusively by peaceful means.' Pakistan argued long and hard in favour of retaining the Charter formulation and would have insisted on it were the circumstances normal. But considering the dire situation, it tried to reduce the damage. It suggested amendment of the Indian text so that differences would be settled 'by peaceful means through negotiation or any other peaceful means.' India, however, had the last word and added the qualification 'mutually agreed upon between them.' This version became subparagraph 1(ii) in the agreement.

Arguments on principles of relations and means of settlement of differences, even presented in the abstract, barely concealed their real object. India sought to use its strong bargaining position to compromise and curtail Pakistan's sovereignty and to secure its acquiescence in India's preferences. Pakistan, on the other hand, struggled because of, and in spite of, the constraints of the situation, to safeguard its rights under law as an independent member of the world community. This contest of wills was more vividly illustrated in the discussions on the release of prisoners of war and, especially, on Jammu and Kashmir.

Release of Prisoners: India made the release and repatriation of Pakistani military and civilians prisoners contingent on the concurrence of Bangladesh. India was honour-bound, said Indian interlocutors, to consult and associate with the Bangladesh government over the decision regarding their release. Dhar said he did not 'plead' for recognition of Bangladesh, but in his 'personal opinion' recognition was the key to resolving not only the question of prisoners of war but also 'a number of other matters'. He did not need to elaborate what these other matters were. It was plain from published reports in the Delhi and Dhaka newspapers that Bangladesh would use the prisoners as a lever to pressure Pakistan into agreeing to its demands. Dhaka claimed a share of Pakistan's assets (gold and foreign exchange reserves, aircraft of the national airline, etc.) without reference to its debt and other liabilities. Also, it wanted Pakistan to accept the transfer of all those Urdu-speaking residents of former East Pakistan who had declined to accept its citizenship.

Both Dhar and Haksar told the Pakistan side that India wanted Bangladesh to relent and that it had, in fact, used 'whatever little influence' it had with the government of Bangladesh in favour of forbearance but, they added, Sheikh Mujibur Rahman was an 'emotional' man. They might have believed in what they said, but the Pakistani side could see that India itself was not averse to using the prisoners as a bargaining counter. Dhar's statement that India did not want to use the Pakistani prisoners for any objective of its own was implicitly contradicted by the Indian minister for external affairs three days later. When Aziz Ahmed asked him whether the release of prisoners was linked to settlement of the Kashmir question, Sardar Swaran Singh replied: 'Yes and no'. He wanted these and other issues to be settled as a package.

India seemed to believe that the Pakistani prisoners were a valuable bargaining chip in negotiations because some of them were related to high officials of the armed forces. It calculated that their families would pressure Bhutto's fledgling government to secure their release, obliging it to pay the price India demanded. Bangladesh, too, proceeded on the same assumption, either on its own or upon Indian instigation. India's pledge, that the prisoners would not be released without the concurrence of Bangladesh, further encouraged Dhaka to adopt a hard stance. Nor could New Delhi have failed to see that Dhaka's attempt to use the release of prisoners would add to the bitterness already existing between Dhaka and Islamabad, and vitiate the prospects for early normalization of relations between them. Some in the Pakistan delegation believed that New Delhi's policy was actually based on such a calculation.

The Indian side did not, of course, know that, anticipating the exploitation of prisoners to extract concessions, Pakistani policy planners had decided in advance not to fall into the trap of bargaining over their release. They realized that a willingness to do so would expose Pakistan to blackmail, as no price could then be too high for the ransom of the unfortunate soldiers and civilians. Accordingly, the Pakistan side took the position that the release of prisoners of war was an obligation that the custodian state had to discharge in accordance with the principles of international humanitarian law. Consistent with the strategy, it did not respond to initiatives from the Indian side to link the prisoners to any other issue between Pakistan and India, or Pakistan and Bangladesh.

Withdrawal from Occupied Territory

Security Council Resolution 307 of 21 December 1971 demanded the withdrawal of all armed forces 'to their respective territories and to positions which fully respect the ceasefire line in Jammu and Kashmir supervised by the United Nations Military Observers Group in India and Pakistan.' The first Pakistani draft at the Shimla Conference called for compliance with this resolution. India, however, did not even refer to this matter either in its first draft of 29 June or in the second draft of 1 July. Even its final draft referred to and provided for withdrawal of forces to the international border, but not to the 1949 ceasefire line in Jammu and Kashmir. The Indian formulation about observance of respect for the 17 December 1971 ceasefire line was designed to compromise Pakistan's position on Jammu and Kashmir.

Jammu and Kashmir

Aware of the constraints on negotiations, the Pakistani side would have liked to eschew any discussion on the Kashmir question at Shimla. It soon became obvious, however, that India would not let Pakistan off the hook. It was determined to try to utilize the leverage it then enjoyed in the negotiations in order to secure Pakistan's acquiescence in a settlement of India's preference—legalization of the status quo in Kashmir. This suggestion emerged not only from the statements of Indian interlocutors in the negotiations but also from their drafts.

During the verbal fencing in the negotiations, the Indian side initially avoided direct reference to the Kashmir question. Even the first Indian draft mentioned the subject only in a note at the bottom of the last page. Perhaps Dhar and Haksar were too courteous to raise the issue directly, much less in an abrasive manner. But Foreign Secretary T. N. Kaul could not restrain himself.

As the negotiating session on 30 June was drawing to a close, Kaul, with a smirk on his face, intervened in the discussion and remarked in unctuous Urdu, '*Baqi sub kuch to theek hai laiken aap yeh to farmaeey Kashmir kay mutallaq moaheday main kia kaha jana chaheeye*?' (Everything else is all right, but please tell us what should be said about Kashmir in the agreement?). Aziz Ahmed, leader of Pakistan's official delegation and a minister of state, and reputed for being status conscious and haughty (his pride acquired in colonial Britain's elitist civil service), ignored not only the question but also Kaul, a mere secretary, and continued to talk to Haksar, his counterpart. Kaul, too proud to be thus snubbed and dismissed, persisted with his question, pointedly addressing 'Aziz Ahmed sahib.' On Kaul's second or third attempt, Aziz Ahmed turned a withering glance toward him and replied in cold and calculated cadence, 'If you must, you can say that the Kashmir question will be resolved in accordance with the Security Council resolutions.' Kaul, his face flushed in anger, shut his notebook, its clap echoing in the hushed room, and stood up from his seat to leave as if Aziz Ahmed's reply made further negotiations futile. Surprisingly for a diplomat of his long experience, he forgot that, not being the leader of the Indian delegation, he could not terminate the conference. Haksar had to virtually pull Kaul down by his coat-tails to continue the meeting. Never again during the following two days did Kaul venture another intervention.

There was no escape, however, from the Indian suggestion contained in the note at the bottom of the first Indian draft, which envisaged not only separate discussions on Jammu and Kashmir but an agreement on the question to be included as an integral part of the treaty to be signed at Shimla. Even otherwise, the Indian draft implicitly treated Jammu and Kashmir as part of Indian territory while the Pakistani draft, premised on the disputed status of the state, referred to Jammu and Kashmir only in the context of withdrawal of forces to the 1949 ceasefire line.

Haksar himself took up the subject of Kashmir in the context of India's suggestion for bilateral settlement of differences between the two countries. Recalling Aziz Ahmed's reference to the UN resolutions, he gave his 'preliminary assessment' that if the two countries 'were not capable of making a frontal attack' to settle this question, then India would find it extremely difficult to negotiate with 'anybody else'. The United Nations, he argued, had not led the two countries 'anywhere in the past,' of course omitting to add that this was so because India had turned down each and every proposal by UN mediators to facilitate the implementation of the Security Council resolutions of 1948 and 1949, which envisaged a plebiscite by which the people of Jammu and Kashmir were to decide whether their state should accede to India or Pakistan.

Again omitting to recall that India had not only accepted the UN resolutions of 13 August 1948 and 5 January 1949 for a plebiscite but also pledged to the people of Kashmir that they would be given an opportunity to decide the future of their state, Haksar went on to declaim that India did not accept the concept of self-determination.

The discussion on Kashmir exposed the contradiction in India's stance, manifest from its dual posture. On the one hand, it asserted that the state was constitutionally 'a part and parcel of India', and on the other, it formally proposed discussions with Pakistan for an agreement on the Kashmir question, acknowledging that the status of the state remained disputed. Not only that, Haksar went so far as to declare that there could be no durable peace between India and Pakistan until there was 'some agreement on some principles' on which the question of Kashmir could be settled. Pakistan could readily agree with the linkage between durable peace and settlement of the Kashmir question, but it would not reopen discussion on principles of settlement—the principle had been agreed and affirmed in UN resolutions.

India's effort to secure an agreement on Kashmir was at a dead end, but it was not abandoned. In the context of the discussion on withdrawal of forces from occupied territories, the Indian side took the position that the line to which the forces were to withdraw must have the same sanctity 'all the way from the Arabian Sea to the Himalayan heights.' In essence, India suggested conversion of the new ceasefire line in Jammu and Kashmir into an international boundary; that is, partition of the state. The Indian side even offered 'minor' territorial adjustments. This idea was, however, a non-starter because Pakistan was resolved not to barter the Kashmiri right of self-determination. Finding that a meeting ground between the two sides did not exist on the Kashmir question, India acted more or less as Kaul had done—it virtually terminated negotiations. The second Indian draft, tabled on 1 July, much shorter than the first, was limited in content to principles of relations and progressive normalization measures; 'the question of Jammu and Kashmir, repatriation of prisoners of war and civilian internees, withdrawal of all armed forces to their respective territories and the resumption of diplomatic relations' would be deferred till another meeting. The Pakistani side was not prepared, however, to sign an agreement that settled none of the postwar issues.

On 2 July, the Indian side suddenly decided to delink withdrawals to the international boundary from a settlement of Jammu and Kashmir. Its final draft, given to the Pakistan side in the early afternoon, proposed withdrawal of forces to the international border. As for Jammu and Kashmir, it provided that 'the line of control resulting from the ceasefire of 17 December 1971, shall henceforth be respected by both sides as a Line of Peace.'

Although the offer of withdrawals to the international border was attractive, the final draft was loaded with formulations designed to convert the 'Line of Peace' in Jammu and Kashmir into an international boundary. Faced with a take-it-or-leave-it choice,

Pakistan decided to leave it and so informed the Indian side at about 3 p.m. The conference had reached a dead end.

Dénouement

Addressing a crowded press conference at about six in the evening of 2 July, President Zulfikar Ali Bhutto announced that his delegation would depart the following morning. The expectant audience may have been disappointed, but the officials were not surprised. Not only were they aware that India's final draft of the proposed agreement had been rejected earlier by Pakistan, they also knew that the gulf between the positions of the two countries after five days of intensive negotiations was very wide, with fundamental issues like Kashmir and even sovereignty at stake.

Suddenly, two hours later, near-failure turned into success. Around eight in the evening, a breakthrough was achieved. During the Pakistani president's farewell call on the Indian prime minister, Indira Gandhi agreed to the following deletions and amendments to the Final Draft:

— Paragraph l(vi) was amended with the addition of the words: 'That in accordance with the Charter of the United Nations they will refrain from the threat or use of force against the territorial integrity or political independence of each other.'

— Paragraph 4(ii) was amended to include a no-prejudice clause so as to read: 'In Jammu and Kashmir, the line of control resulting from the ceasefire of December 17, 1971, shall be respected by both sides without prejudice to the recognized position of either side. Neither side shall seek to alter it unilaterally. . . .' Also the words 'as a Line of Peace' were deleted from the Indian draft which had initially suggested that the line of control 'shall henceforth be respected by both sides 'as a Line of Peace.'

— Paragraph 4 was further amended to delete the following subparagraphs: '(iii) Minor adjustments to the Line of Peace in Jammu and Kashmir or the rest of the international border considered necessary by both sides to make the border more rational and viable, may be made by mutual agreement;' and (iv) 'A joint body composed of an equal number of representatives, nominated by each Government, shall be appointed to establish ground rules and to supervise effective observance of the Line of Peace and the rest of the border between the two countries.'

After the Pakistani negotiating team was informed of the agreement, Aziz Ahmed met with P. N. Haksar to clean up the language of the agreed amendments. Ashok S. Chib, Joint Secretary in the Indian Ministry of External Affairs, and Abdul Sattar, Director General, prepared the final documents. Bhutto and Gandhi signed the agreement. The date had already turned, but 2 July remained unchanged in the agreement, which was signed past midnight between 2 and 3 July 1972.

The import of the deletions and amendments that Indira Gandhi conceded cannot be exaggerated by anyone aware of the issues arising from the conflicting aims and objectives of India and Pakistan at the Shimla Conference. Thus:

— India's suggestion for the creation of a bilateral supervisory body, introduced for the first time in the final draft, was an attempt to salvage, at least in part, its aim to secure Pakistan's acquiescence in the status quo in Jammu and Kashmir. It wanted to pave the ground for a call for the withdrawal of the United Nations Military Observers Group in India and Pakistan (UNMOGIP), which had been mandated by the Security Council to discharge specific functions in Jammu and Kashmir, and thus to undermine the validity of the Security Council resolutions. By securing the deletion of the Indian proposal, Pakistan checkmated India's move. If India decided, nevertheless, to refuse cooperation with UNMOGIP, it could not cite the Shimla Agreement to justify its wilful violation of an international obligation.

— Even the addition of the clause 'in accordance with the Charter of the United Nations' in the subparagraph on non-use of force was of considerable, if esoteric, interest against the background of the history of the no-war-declaration proposal. Bhutto did not want to be seen to have given up Pakistan's historical position, which sought to link a no-war pledge to a self-executing mechanism for the resolution of disputes. It also served to strengthen the emphasis on the principles of the UN Charter as the arbiter of relations between Pakistan and India, thus undercutting the Indian aim of roping Pakistan into a non-universal framework of principles that would circumscribe its rights as a sovereign state.

Assessment

Why did Indira Gandhi decide to concede the changes Bhutto sought in India's final draft? Did she think that having cut Pakistan into two and thus neutralized the 'threat' it presented, India should turn to building durable peace in South Asia? Was she under pressure from the Great Powers to conclude a peace treaty? Did she want to appease the world community which was aghast at India's blatant aggression? Was she concerned that the elected leader of Pakistan should not return empty-handed? Or was she beguiled by Bhutto's eloquence and promises?

The Pakistan side could not know what explanations she gave to her cabinet colleagues and officials for reducing India's demands below the rock-bottom level spelt out in the final draft. From the account Bhutto gave to his delegation, it appeared that she was keen to salvage the Shimla Conference from collapse, and decided to accept the changes without which, he told her, the people of Pakistan would reject the agreement. The presence at Shimla of several leaders of Pakistani political parties may have lent weight to this argument.

While only Indira Gandhi could give an authoritative answer, speculation as to why she agreed to dilute the final draft misses the important point that even in the signed text of the Shimla Agreement India extracted a substantial price. Pakistan would not have agreed to some of its provisions were it not for the constraints and pressures under which it was obliged to negotiate in the aftermath of defeat.

Exploiting the 'opportunity of a century', India cut Pakistan into two, first by instigating and aiding separatism in East Pakistan and finally by military intervention. A visceral antagonism towards Pakistan was not yet satisfied, however. Indian diplomacy continued to wage war by other means. Using occupation of territory and prisoners of war as instruments of duress in the post-war negotiations, it set itself three objectives: (1) legitimization of the status quo in

Jammu and Kashmir, (2) construction of a bilateral framework for relations with Pakistan to circumscribe its rights under the UN Charter, and (3) securing Pakistani recognition of Bangladesh. Pakistan's objectives were rather simple: to recover territories and obtain the release of prisoners of war, at the lowest cost to its national interests.

To take point (3) first, no progress whatsoever was made at Shimla on the question of recognition of Bangladesh. Pakistan's refusal to bargain over the release of prisoners weakened what both India and Bangladesh considered a lever of pressure. The miscalculation was to cause considerable embarrassment to India as continued incarceration of these unfortunate soldiers and civilians in violation of international humanitarian law incurred worldwide criticism. Bangladesh was disappointed at the time, but, in the longer run, both it and Pakistan benefited. The delay in Pakistan's extension of recognition until after Bangladesh consented to the release of all the prisoners helped avoid the added bitterness that would have resulted from the attempt to use the prisoners for bargaining, and thus saved the prospect of cooperative relations between the two countries.

Subparagraph 1(ii) of the Shimla Agreement, providing for peaceful settlement of differences, was projected as a triumph of Indian diplomacy. India unilaterally interpreted the provision to mean Pakistan could no longer seek 'third party intervention,' nor raise Pakistan-India issues in the United Nations or any other international forum, nor invoke any peaceful means other than bilateral negotiations without India's concurrence. Pakistan did not then or later accept the Indian interpretation of so-called 'bilateralism'. It maintained that the text of the agreement did not compromise Pakistan's rights under the UN Charter. Firstly, the attempt to interpret one provision in isolation from others is untenable in law. Subparagraph (ii), which makes resort to peaceful means other than negotiations subject to mutual agreement, cannot be read in isolation from the preceding subparagraph (i), which explicitly affirms that the UN Charter 'shall govern the relations between the two countries.' Under the Charter, a state has the right to bring to the notice of the General Assembly or the Security Council any matter which threatens the maintenance of international peace and security. Also relevant is Article 103 of the UN Charter, affirming that obligations under the Charter prevail over conflicting obligations under any other international agreement. In practice, too, Pakistan has not allowed the Indian interpretation to affect its decisions from time to time to bring differences with India to the attention of the organs and agencies of the United Nations. For instance, it filed a petition with the International Court of Justice in 1973 charging India with violation of international humanitarian law in delaying the release of prisoners of war. The Shimla Agreement was no bar to the admission of that petition. Also, Pakistan has continued to exercise its right to raise differences with India in international fora. Pakistan has thus sought to underline the fact that the subparagraph does not prejudice Pakistan's rights under international law. That does not, however, gainsay the fact that, had the negotiating field been level, Pakistan would not have accepted the Indian formulation.

Pakistan's own suggestion for a self-executing mechanism for the resolution of disputes has manifest advantages. It would provide an incentive to the parties to settle the differences through bilateral negotiation, which is the cheapest means of resolving differences. If they fail to settle between themselves, they could agree to invite intercession by a mutually acceptable third party. If that too proves unavailing, the dispute would be referred either by common consent to an arbitration tribunal or by either of the parties to a judicial tribunal. The usefulness of mediation was demonstrated in the successful outcome of the World Bank's efforts in promoting the Indus Waters Treaty, and the efficacy and expeditiousness of arbitration in the matter of the boundary dispute in the Rann of Kutch. In contrast, negotiations between the two countries have a dismal record of failure even in relatively less complicated issues such as the Wullar Barrage and the Sir Creek disputes.

Impartial determination of differences is a necessary component of the strategy for the peaceful settlement and the prevention of use of force. All civilized polities do not merely forbid the use of force but also provide effective means for the peaceful settlement of disputes, so that an aggrieved party can bring the recalcitrant to court for compulsory adjudication of a dispute that they fail to settle between themselves. Regrettably, the community of states has yet to attain that state of civilization. Powerful states prefer instead the present 'state of nature' in which they can exploit power to impose their own will and deny justice to less powerful neighbours.

Firm Stance on Kashmir: On the crucial Kashmir question, Pakistan did not accept the Indian demand for either legitimization of the ceasefire line or an agreement on some new principles for settling the issue. On its part, India refused to withdraw forces to the 1949 'ceasefire line in Jammu and Kashmir supervised by the United Nations Military Observers Group for India and Pakistan' as was required under Security Council Resolution 307(1971).

India's refusal to return to the 1949 ceasefire line was ascribable to transparent political motivation. It sought to convey the message that if Pakistan did not agree to a settlement of Kashmir on its terms, then India felt free to retain the territorial gains it made in war. Otherwise, the gains in Jammu and Kashmir in 1971 were not large. India took more, but mostly uninhabited mountainous land in the Kargil area, while it lost Chamb, which supported an agricultural population of 10,000 people.

Pakistan had no means of compelling India to withdraw to the 1949 ceasefire line. As a result of its refusal to do so, India continues to bear the onus of non-compliance with yet another resolution of the Security Council, thus violating Article 25 of the Charter according to which it is committed 'to accept and carry out the decisions of the Security Council'.

As a consequence of the Indian refusal to withdraw to the ceasefire line, it became necessary for the two sides to keep to the positions they held at the time of ceasefire on 17 December 1971. The term 'Line of Control' was accepted by Pakistan after India agreed to the 'without prejudice' clause. Its design thus nullified, India did not, in the immediate wake of the Shimla Agreement, project the Line of Control as anything more than an interim arrangement. The Indian minister for external affairs stated on 10 October 1972 that the Line of Control was 'obviously a new ceasefire line.' Any other interpretation would compromise India's declared position, claiming the whole of Jammu and Kashmir as an integral part of its territory.

The clause 'Line of Control resulting from the ceasefire of 17 December 1971' could not be deemed to alter the status of Jammu and Kashmir as an outstanding question. The same sentence in the Shimla Agreement that refers to the Line of Control contains also the key 'without prejudice' clause. Obviously, it cannot compromise Pakistan's recognized position that the Kashmir question has to be resolved in accordance with the relevant resolutions of the Security Council.

Also, the Shimla Agreement itself reaffirms, in paragraph 6, that 'a final settlement of Jammu and Kashmir' was one of the outstanding questions, and further, that the establishment of durable peace between the two countries remained contingent on the resolution of this question.

Not much has been said here about the conversations between President Bhutto and Prime Minister Indira Gandhi. This is by no means an attempt to overlook their role or contribution which was, in fact, crucial to the outcome of the Shimla Conference. They were not only the leaders of their delegations but determined the strategy and directed the tactics of the negotiators. Without their eleventh-hour intervention, the Shimla Conference would have been doomed to failure.

What they said to each other in one-to-one meetings is not, however, a part of the record. Neither Bhutto nor Gandhi said much publicly about their conversation. The Government of Pakistan and the Government of India know only what their then leaders chose to tell them. Neither ever said they had secretly agreed to a settlement of the Kashmir question. When Foreign Minister Vajpayee claimed in 1978 that Bhutto and Gandhi had reached a secret understanding on Kashmir at Shimla, the latter publicly rejected the claim as baseless.

Secret Understanding?

Professor P. N. Dhar, one of the secretaries of Indira Gandhi in 1972, claimed in an article in *Mainstream* of 15 April 1995 that the change of nomenclature to Line of Control was 'the core of the Indian solution to the Kashmir problem: the *de facto* line was to be graduated to the level of *de jure* border.' Dhar alleged that 'Bhutto was personally inclined to accept the status quo as a permanent solution of the Kashmir problem', but he said he could not do so, because his 'political enemies at home, and especially the army bosses, would denounce him for surrendering what many in Pakistan considered their vital national interest.' In effect, according to Dhar, Bhutto contradicted in private meetings with Gandhi the views he voiced in public and was prepared, in effect, to betray the Kashmir cause. Invited by the *Mainstream* editor[1] to respond to Dhar's account, the author, a member of Pakistan's delegation at the Shimla Conference, wrote an article that was published in a subsequent issue of the journal.

In the first place, Bhutto made no such remark in any meeting with Gandhi at which members of their delegations were present. As for the one-to-one meeting they held on 2 July, Dhar's account was hearsay. If Indira Gandhi told Dhar that Bhutto had made the statement, it is not uncommon for negotiators to claim self-reconstructed accounts of conversations to embellish their own performance and denigrate that of the adversary. Incredible to those in Pakistan who heard Bhutto express his views on Kashmir in the inner councils of the government before, during, and after the Shimla Conference, Dhar's statement that he gave a secret understanding different from what is contained in the agreement amounts to an allegation of hypocrisy and betrayal against a deceased leader unable to set the record straight, which is, to say the least, in bad taste. Dhar knew that Indira Gandhi had refuted Vajpayee's 1978 claim to the existence of a secret understanding between her and Bhutto at Shimla. The allegation was wholly pointless. No obligation devolves upon a state from an adversary's claim of a secret and oral understanding allegedly given by a functionary, however high his rank. Only agreed minutes of meetings are of any worth as evidence for interpretation of treaties. What binds the parties is the text of the agreement as ratified by them. The Shimla Agreement explicitly regards Jammu and Kashmir as an outstanding question.

Implications of Duress: Aside from the alleged secret understanding, the validity of even an agreement signed under duress is morally, if not legally, doubtful. The Shimla Agreement was negotiated under circumstances characterized by coercion and blackmail. India used occupied territory and prisoners to constrain Pakistan into submitting to its demands. Under domestic law, a contract dictated under duress is not considered binding. International law, too, invalidates a treaty, 'if its conclusion has been procured by the threat or use of force.'[2] Even though states continue to exploit power disparity to impose their will on less powerful states, the validity of agreements under duress has been morally dubious. History records instances of repudiation of treaties after the power equation changed. When Germany denounced the Treaty of Versailles, even those who had dictated it did not insist on its observance. Scholarly opinion went further to blame Britain, France and the United States for the manifestly unfair *diktat* which provoked revanchism and led to the Second World War. Pakistan has not exercised that option.

Professor Dhar claimed that Indira Gandhi proposed to Bhutto that the two countries bury the hatchet and 'agree on the settlement of the Kashmir issue on the lines suggested by India', not by 'an immediate and formal acceptance of the status quo' but in the manner that 'the *de facto* Line of Control was to be graduated to the level of the *de jure* border.' Whilst there is no basis on the record for the claim, India did formally propose the conversion of the ceasefire line into an international boundary in one of its drafts. Those who argue that 'the whole of Jammu and Kashmir is an integral part of India' should remember that at Shimla the Indian government offered to 'give up' a part of the state. The Indian constitution can no longer be a credible excuse for denying the right of self-determination to the people of Jammu and Kashmir.

Finally, whilst opinions may differ as to which side did better in the negotiations, it is apparent that neither did Pakistan escape unscathed in safeguarding its interests nor did India succeed fully in securing its aims. India was persuaded, in fact, to scale down its aims and even the minimum it spelt out in its final draft was further curtailed as a result of negotiations between Bhutto and Gandhi.

Pakistan paid a high price for securing vacation of its territory. Under normal circumstances it would not, and could not, accept the provision regarding bilateral settlement of disputes. The gloom was relieved, however, by the thought that it held no bargaining counters whatsoever. An objective appraisal of the Shimla Agreement cannot fail to marvel at the extent to which Pakistan managed to extricate itself from the clutches of duress. The credit for this achievement goes to the spirit of the Pakistani people who were defiant in adversity and did not want their government to capitulate. Their willingness to bear with the continued incarceration of their soldiers and civilians helped the leadership to set the priorities right. It was important to obtain withdrawals from occupied territories first, not only because this enabled a million displaced people to return to their homes but because delay in withdrawals incurred the risk of prolonging occupation and distress to the refugees.

Unstinted tribute is due also to President Bhutto and officials such as Aziz Ahmed, who not only brought great ability and negotiating skill to their difficult task in an unenviable predicament, but also played their historical roles purposefully and with an inspiring and exemplary sense of commitment.

Normalization with Bangladesh

The brutal separation of East Pakistan was a tragic fact. The government was aware that Bangladesh had to be recognized, but it could not ignore the feelings of a traumatized nation. The government in Dhaka did not make the task easier. Miscalculation led it to believe that Pakistani prisoners of war could be used as a lever of pressure to secure satisfaction of its claim to a share of Pakistan's assets. It further spoke of its intention to try some of the prisoners on charges of war crimes. Indian officials disclaimed, during discussions at the Shimla Conference, that they had encouraged Dhaka to adopt this policy of virtual blackmail. They said Mujibur Rahman was 'emotional'.

Pakistan had few options, but it was obvious that prospects of normalization of relations in South Asia would be severely damaged if India transferred any of the Pakistani prisoners in its custody to Bangladesh for trials. It sought their unconditional release as required under international humanitarian law.

It took nearly two years for New Delhi and Dhaka to realize that the retention of Pakistani prisoners was a lever of diminishing value. Indeed, they became a liability for India, as world opinion became critical of their illegal detention in violation of international humanitarian law. Finally, in September 1973, India, itself having obtained the concurrence of Bangladesh, agreed to release all Pakistani prisoners excepting 195 prisoners Bangladesh said it wanted to try on charges of war crimes. The agreement also provided for the transfer of Bengalis from Pakistan to Bangladesh. On humanitarian grounds, Pakistan accepted the transfer of a substantial number of non-Bengalis. Over 250,000 persons who had served in the government or had family connections were allowed to migrate to Pakistan. Many others, who were said to have 'opted' to leave the land of their settlement for Pakistan, remained stranded. Pakistan, on its part, did not expel Bengalis who wished to remain Pakistani citizens.

Nothing did more to convince Dhaka about the inadvisability of blocking the release of the Pakistani prisoners, or trying any of them, than China's decision to use its veto to bar the admission of Bangladesh into the United Nations. In retrospect, China did a great favour to both Bangladesh and Pakistan. Had Dhaka gone ahead with its intention to try Pakistani soldiers, prospects of normalization of relations with Pakistan would have been obliterated for much longer.

Fortunately for the two countries, the Islamic Summit Conference in Lahore in 1974 provided an opportunity for common friends to persuade Bangladesh to abandon the idea of trying Pakistani captives. Pakistan promptly extended recognition to Bangladesh. Prime Minister Mujibur Rahman attended the Islamic Summit.

The question of apportionment of assets and liabilities continued to obstruct development of normal relations between the two countries. Dhaka claimed a share in the assets of Pakistan. Pakistan denied that, as a part that was sundered by aggression, Bangladesh had a right under international law to any share in the patrimony. On that political ground, Pakistan declined to enter into any discussion on the substance of the issue. Had such a discussion been held, Dhaka would have realized that it was to its advantage to adopt the clean-slate principle, which allowed it to disown responsibility for a share of Pakistan's internal and international debt. An inter-departmental study in Islamabad led to the conclusion that Pakistan's liabilities being greater than its assets, Islamabad could have made out a case for Bangladesh to assume a share of the negative balance.[3]

OIC Summit: The Lahore Summit was a memorable event for the people of Pakistan as for the first time leaders of fraternal states met together to demonstrate mutual solidarity on all issues of common concern. The sagacious King Faisal bin Abdul Aziz captured the mood of Muslim people all over the world with tears of joy in his eyes as he offered Friday prayers along with the highest-level congregation ever assembled at the Badshahi Mosque.

NOTES

1. Subhash Chakravartty was an eminently fair-minded journalist, and doyen of the Delhi corps, whom the author had the privilege to know during his assignments in New Delhi. Substantially the same article was later published, with texts of the agreement and various drafts added, in *Regional Studies*, Islamabad, August 1995.
2. Article 52 of the Vienna Convention on the Law of Treaties, 1969.
3. The author chaired the study.

Chapter 12

Pakistan's Nuclear Programme and Relations with the US

Pakistan's nuclear programme, started in the mid-1950s, aimed at acquiring scientific knowledge and technology for peaceful uses in agriculture and health. It also envisaged the construction of power plants in due course to meet the energy needs of its developing economy. The Pakistan Atomic Energy Commission obtained a small five-megawatt research reactor from the United States in 1962 for the Pakistan Institute of Nuclear Science and Technology (PINSTECH), near Islamabad, under an agreement that provided for inspection and controls by the International Atomic Energy Agency. A few years later, Canada agreed to extend cooperation to Pakistan for the construction of a 120-megawatt nuclear power plant. Completed in 1972, this plant too was placed under the safeguards of the International Atomic Energy Agency.

It became evident in the early 1960s that India was acquiring nuclear technology not only for peaceful purposes but also to develop weapons. While emphasising peaceful uses in public statements, it was establishing the entire nuclear fuel cycle facilities, including production of bomb-grade plutonium, that would give India the weapons option. Facts unmistakably pointed to the conclusion that Indian leaders 'sought to win for their country all the prestige, status and economic benefits associated with being a nuclear power, including the option of building "the bomb" if necessary.'[1] Taking cognisance of the emergent threat to Pakistan's security, and the potential for blackmail in an asymmetrical nuclear situation, Foreign Minister Zulfikar Ali Bhutto said in 1965, 'If India makes an atomic bomb, then we will also do so, even if we have to eat grass . . . an atom bomb can only be answered by an atom bomb.'[2] But his rhetoric was not matched with official action. Few leaders with influence favoured allocation of resources for PAEC to embark on an expanded programme, with a dual-use potential, for which nuclear equipment and technology was then not subject to stringent export controls or intrusive external inspection. In 1966, PAEC proposed purchase of a plutonium separation plant that France was willing to sell, but the ministries of finance and defence opposed the proposal and President Ayub Khan too did not favour the idea.[3] Military leadership apparently believed that a strong conventional defence capability would suffice for deterrence. Meanwhile, Chairman Dr I. H. Usmani built up PAEC's infrastructure by inducting talented youth and sending them to institutions of higher learning in science and technology in Canada, the UK, and the US.

Pakistan vested hope in the Non-Proliferation Treaty (NPT) and actively participated in efforts at the United Nations to promote its early conclusion. It joined multi-pronged efforts for a fair bargain between nuclear-weapon states and non-nuclear states that would provide for the progressive reduction and eventual elimination of nuclear weapons held by nuclear powers, in exchange for the renunciation of the nuclear weapon by other states. At its initiative, a conference of non-nuclear states recommended that nuclear-weapons states should provide 'negative' and 'positive' guarantees pledging (a) non-use of nuclear weapons against non-nuclear states, and (b) assistance to a non-nuclear states threatened with nuclear weapons. Both proposals were conceded in principle, but the pledge on reduction of nuclear weapons in the NPT remained non-binding, and the resolution on security guarantees adopted by the Security Council, of which the five nuclear powers were permanent members, was far from reassuring. Pakistan nevertheless announced its readiness to sign the NPT, provided India did the same. India, however, refused to sign the treaty. Pakistan's reasonableness contrasted with intransigence on the part of India, which championed nuclear disarmament but at the same time persisted in a programme aimed at the acquisition of the weapons option.

The 1971 disaster compelled Pakistan to undertake the proverbial 'painful reappraisal' of its policy of nuclear abstinence. Pakistan's conventional defence capacity had proved inadequate to safeguard its territorial integrity, as East Pakistan was sundered by Indian military intervention to create Bangladesh. India's exploitation of Pakistan's internal political troubles, encouragement and assistance to separatism in East Pakistan, violation of the principle of non-interference in internal affairs, and aggression and military intervention illustrated India's animus, the irremediable imbalance of power, the reluctance of allies to come to Pakistan's rescue, and the powerlessness of the United Nations. Pakistan had to devise its own means to ensure its security and survival.

Soon after taking over the reins of government, President Zulfikar Ali Bhutto convened a meeting of nuclear scientists at Multan in January 1972, and later at Quetta, to review the nuclear programme. Participants included renowned nuclear physicist Professor Abdus Salam. Bhutto's main purpose was to accelerate the nuclear programme to acquire explosion capability. Everyone agreed on the aim, but the task required a range of fuel cycle technologies ranging from mining of uranium to uranium enrichment or plutonium separation and development of design for the explosive device. Professor Abdus Salam agreed to become his adviser. With wide-ranging contacts, he helped in the procurement of technological equipment and admission of scientists into technology institutions abroad. Munir Ahmad Khan, a nuclear engineer working at IAEA, was appointed chairman of PAEC. Bhutto also ensured requisite funds for relevant projects.[4]

The decision to pursue the nuclear option was more easily made than implemented. Pakistan possessed neither fissile material nor explosion technology. Nuclear suppliers were already strengthening controls on nuclear technology transfer. The restrictions were further tightened after India conducted the test explosion in 1974. Canada unilaterally cancelled the cooperation agreement with Pakistan even though, unlike India, it had committed no violation of any agreement with Canada. The United States led other industrialized states in the Nuclear Suppliers Group to tighten restrictions on the export of nuclear technology.

To Pakistan's shock, few countries criticized India for the 18 May explosion. Washington's reaction to the Indian nuclear explosion was particularly muted. Secretary of State Henry Kissinger decided it was futile to fight the *fait accompli*.[5] India-apologists swallowed the pretext that the test codenamed 'Buddha Smiles' was peaceful, although they knew that a nuclear explosion causes irreversible contamination. For that reason, both the USA and the USSR had virtually ruled out explosions for peaceful uses such as digging harbours or canals. The US State Department was not too exercised. As far back as 1961, many of its officials recommended helping India acquire a nuclear explosive to 'beat Communist China to the punch.'[6]

Instead, the United States now focused its non-proliferation agenda on Pakistan. The first target was the reprocessing plant Pakistan was to build with French collaboration under an agreement signed in 1973 providing for application of IAEA safeguards. Moreover, the agreement prohibited Pakistan from replicating the technology for twenty years.

Meanwhile, Pakistan embarked on imaginative diplomacy to counter the pressures of the United States and other industrialized countries. In 1974, it proposed a resolution in the UN General Assembly for the establishment of a nuclear weapon-free zone in South Asia. The UN General Assembly approved the resolution, and support for it continued to increase year after year. India was cornered into virtual isolation, and although that made no dent in its resolve, Pakistan gained the moral high ground internationally and the US pressures on Pakistan were exposed as discriminatory. Also, Pakistan was able to exploit the opportunity to free-ride India's intransigence.

Relations with the United States, 1972–9: In November 1972, Pakistan withdrew from SEATO, but, now keen to maintain good relations with the United States, did not withdraw from CENTO, which was still valued by Washington in the context of its policy on the Middle East. Meanwhile, the Nixon administration continued to manifest understanding of Pakistan's economic and security problems. In March 1973, it authorized a 'one time exception' for delivery of 300 armoured personnel carriers Pakistan had purchased three years earlier.

Prime Minister Bhutto was invited to visit the United States in September 1973. Nixon said, in his banquet speech, 'The independence and integrity of Pakistan is a cornerstone of American foreign policy.' The US also resumed economic assistance, providing $24 million for wheat and $18 million as AID loan, and further agreed to seek congressional approval for $40–50 million as a rehabilitation loan. Also, the Ford administration lifted the embargo on arms sales to

Pakistan and allowed purchase of arms and spare parts worth $160 million. India protested, although it received $1.2 billion in arms aid from the Soviet Union during 1964–73.

The United States did not accept Pakistani professions of peaceful intent concerning its nuclear programme. Bhutto had made no secret of his views. Assessing Bhutto's intention, a State Department official said, 'What he wants is to build a bomb.' In response, Secretary of State Henry Kissinger remarked, 'If you were in his position you would do the same thing,' adding: 'Gentlemen, there is something indecent about our always proving that we are strong by kicking our allies in the teeth. . . . We are going ahead and sending nuclear fuel to India even after they exploded a bomb and then for this little project (reprocessing plant) we are coming down on him like a ton of bricks.'[7] Kissinger's frank and realistic remarks did not, however, change US policy. It tried first to entice Pakistan by offering to sell 120 aircraft if Pakistan agreed to cancel the contract with France for the construction of a reprocessing plant. When Prime Minister Bhutto refused the proposal,[8] the US pressured France to cancel the contract.

As conventional means proved insufficient to defend territorial integrity in 1971, development of nuclear deterrence became an existential imperative. Mr Bhutto's government allocated the requisite resources while dedicated scientists and engineers went to work. An agreement was signed with France for a plutonium separation plant. Also, anticipating international pressures, Mr Bhutto accepted a suggestion by Dr Abdul Qadeer Khan, then working at URENCO, to build a plant for indigenous manufacture of centrifuges to enrich uranium. A. Q. Khan was appointed to head the Engineering Research Laboratories (KRL) in Rawalpindi. He and his talented team of scientists and engineers overcame formidable technological difficulties and obstacles erected by the Nuclear Suppliers Group, which even banned export of non-nuclear components. KRL was built in record time.[9] By 1981, it had achieved the capability to produce weapon-grade material.[10] Meanwhile, PAEC's dedicated teams of theoretical physicists and engineers led by Drs Ishfaq Ahmad and Samar Mubarakmand developed designs for explosive devices[11] and prepared tunnels and monitoring equipment for tests. Several cold tests validated the designs.[12] A timely agreement with China provided for continued supply of nuclear power plants before Beijing acceded to the NPT in 1998. In 2008, Islamabad acquiesced to US pressure and failed to oppose IAEA approval of a US-India agreement by the Nuclear Suppliers Group. The exception to the NSG ban on transfer of nuclear technology to a country not party to NPT manifestly discriminated against Pakistan.

The United States enacted legislation in 1977 and 1978—known as the Symington and Glenn Amendments to the Foreign Assistance Act—which provided for denial of economic aid and imposition of other sanctions and penalties against a country not party to the Non-Proliferation Treaty that imported equipment or technology for production of plutonium and enriched uranium. Nominally aimed at nuclear non-proliferation in South Asia, the law in practice singled out Pakistan; it had a built-in loophole to exempt India and Israel from their purview. Sanctions under the amendment were applied against Pakistan alone. Although India had imported nuclear technology for peaceful purposes and then diverted it to make nuclear explosives in violation of agreements with Canada and the United States, it got away scot-free.

At first, the Ford administration sought to persuade Pakistan to abandon the nuclear programme. Secretary of State Kissinger came to Pakistan in August 1976 and offered to recommend for congressional approval the sale of 110 A-7 aircraft. Bhutto thanked him but said 'No', after all senior officials urged the prime minister to decline.

Relations between Pakistan and the United States slid when Bhutto tried to divert attention from countrywide agitation following the rigged election in 1977 by projecting the United States as his adversary. He misinterpreted an intelligence intercept of a remark by an official of the US mission in Pakistan in April, saying, 'My source tells me the party is over' to mean Bhutto could no longer continue in power. (The officer later explained he was actually correcting an earlier message according to which Bhutto had been detained at a party.)[13] Bhutto, facing domestic protests against rigged elections, used the intercept to allege 'political bloodhounds were after him because of his opposition to US policies on a number of international issues.'[14] In response to Bhutto's accusation, Secretary of State Cyrus

Vance sent a conciliatory letter refuting the charge. Bhutto projected it as an apology.

Until then, the Carter administration had not reviewed the policy of the Ford administration. On 28 April—the same day Bhutto accused the US of conspiring against him—the US navy transferred two destroyers to Pakistan under a long-term lease.

President Carter's policy in South Asia soon became India-centric. Departing from the practice of his predecessors, Carter excluded Pakistan from his tour of Asian countries. Pakistan was concerned that National Security Adviser Zbigniew Brzezinski's concept of 'regional influentials' would encourage and reinforce India's hegemonic ambitions. The slide in Pakistan-US relations accelerated after General Zia ul-Haq took over in July 1977. The offer to sell A-7 aircraft was withdrawn. In April 1979, President Carter decided to apply sanctions against Pakistan: US aid to Pakistan of around $50 million a year was cut off. Noting that the US had taken no action against India even for exploding a nuclear device, Islamabad protested against this 'act of discrimination . . . (applying) different standards to different states.'[15] But it evoked no sympathy at the time. In August 1979, the US was even reported to have considered the option of destroying Pakistan's nuclear capability by an attack on Kahuta.[16] Although the State Department issued a categorical denial, the report illustrated the dangerous deterioration in Pakistan-US relations.

Also, the United States continued pressure on France. In 1978, President Giscard d'Estaing decided to renege on the reprocessing plant contract, inflicting colossal damage to Pakistan's nuclear programme. By then, Pakistan had already paid over a hundred million dollars to the French supplier of equipment. More than a decade later, France agreed to partially compensate Pakistan for the losses.

US Embassy burned, 1979: On 21 November 1979, a mob of students from the Quaid-i-Azam University, infuriated by a false report broadcast by an unidentified radio station alleging US occupation of the holy Kaaba, attacked the American embassy in Islamabad. Local police and a security contingent took four hours to come to the rescue. By then the premises were burnt and an American and two Pakistani staff members had perished in the fire. Pakistan accepted responsibility for failure to fulfil its obligation under international law to protect the diplomatic mission, and immediately agreed to pay compensation. (The students' protest cost the country $23 million.)

Steadfast pursuit of the nuclear programme: Meanwhile, Pakistan continued to make technological progress towards acquisition of the nuclear option. Overcoming obstacles and resisting discriminatory pressures, it succeeded not only in completing the Kahuta plant but also achieving explosion technology. Scientists at the Pakistan Atomic Energy Commission were able to master the design of the nuclear device. By the mid-1980s, Pakistan publicly acknowledged possession of the capability, although it disclaimed having produced nuclear weapons.[17]

Soon other strategic imperatives dictated a different priority to the United States, as a result of the Soviet military intervention in Afghanistan in December 1979. The Reagan administration, which came to office in January 1981, decided to join Pakistan in supporting and assisting the Afghan resistance against Soviet occupation. The nuclear sanctions were relegated, though only for the time being.

Indian plan of attack on Kahuta: After Indira Gandhi returned to power in January 1980, she manifested grave concern about the progress Pakistan had reportedly made towards acquiring nuclear explosion capability.[18] Whether under her direction or on its own, the Indian Air Force conducted a study in 1981 concluding that an attack on the Kahuta enrichment plant was feasible.[19] On 20 December 1982, *The Washington Post* reported that Indian military advisers had nine months earlier prepared a plan for strikes on Kahuta and PINSTECH.[20] New Delhi realized that the attack would result in Pakistani retaliation against nuclear power stations in Rajasthan and Trombay, causing a disaster, as Munir Ahmad Khan, chairman of PAEC, mentioned in a conversation with his Indian counterpart Homi Sethna in 1983.[21] But India did not abandon the idea and considered collaboration with Israel to bomb the Kahuta plant. Learning of it, Pakistan warned it would presume Indian complicity. At the time, the USA was allied with Pakistan as the frontline state in assisting the Afghan mujahideen against Soviet occupation. At Islamabad's request, the US ascertained Israel had no intention of joining in any such attack. In September 1984, reports appeared in the US press of

Indian military planning for an attack on Pakistan's nuclear facilities.[22] Again, before the Brasstacks exercise in early 1987, Rajiv Gandhi considered a pre-emptive attack on Pakistani nuclear facilities, but he was dissuaded by defence analysts.[23]

By 1990, Pakistan was estimated to have accumulated enough enriched uranium for ten or more explosive devices.[24] By then India had built up a stockpile of weapon-grade plutonium for an estimated 100-plus Hiroshima-size bombs.[25]

India's dual-purpose programme:[26] In 1946, Homi Bhaba, an ambitious and brilliant Cambridge-educated physics professor at Bangalore, obtained approval for the establishment of the Atomic Energy Research Committee at Mumbai. Jawaharlal Nehru, prime minister of the interim government, said: 'I hope India will use the atomic force for constructive purposes. But if India is threatened she will inevitably try to defend herself by all means at her disposal.'[27] Two years later, speaking in the Indian parliament, Nehru said, 'I think we must develop [atomic energy] for peaceful purposes. . . . Of course, if we are compelled as a nation to use it for *other purposes*, possibly no pious sentiment of any of us will stop the nation from using it that way'[28] (Emphasis added).

Taking advantage of the permissive environment for international cooperation, India embarked on a programme for acquisition of the entire range of fuel cycle plants. Under the Atoms for Peace plan, the USA provided training facilities for foreign scientists and engineers. Between 1955 and 1974, 1,104 Indians trained at the Argonne Laboratory School of Nuclear Science and Engineering and 'mined' the declassified literature for design and operation of nuclear facilities. India built the first research reactor, ASPARA, in 1955 with the assistance of the UK, which provided the heavy water. CIRUS, a 40-megawatt research reactor suitable for generation of bomb-grade plutonium was built with the assistance of Canada, which accepted the Indian statement that it would use the resultant fissile material for peaceful purposes only. On similar terms, the USA provided heavy water for the plant. In 1961, India began construction of the Phoenix plant for reprocessing plutonium. A US firm, Vitro International, was the contractor for preparing the construction blueprints, while technological assistance was provided by the British Atomic Energy

Commission.[29] In 1963, the US decided to provide two reactors for the Tarapur power plant.

Although Vikram Sarabhai, Bhaba's successor in 1966, was opposed to nuclear weapons on moral and economic grounds, a group of scientists led by Raja Ramanna, R. Chidambaram, and P. K. Iyenger continued work on the project for a nuclear explosion. Meanwhile, the foreign policy establishment protected India's nuclear option in negotiations on NPT under the leadership of Trivedi, who opposed any prohibition on the transfer of nuclear technology for peaceful purposes, calling it 'nuclear apartheid'. Indira Gandhi's government decided not to sign the NPT in 1968. In 1972, she authorized preparations for a nuclear test.

Codenamed 'Buddha Smiles', the explosion on 18 May 1974 was termed a 'peaceful explosion'. Years later, the Indian scientist who played a leadership role acknowledged it was actually a bomb test. Indian politicians and the media considered it a bomb test. 'Monopoly of Big Five Broken', thundered the *Sunday Standard*. 'India Goes Nuclear at Last', crowed *Motherland*. Most parties were ecstatic. Jana Sangh called it 'a red letter day in Indian history'.

International sanctions and tightened export controls slowed down the programme, but India now had proven technology and all the requisite facilities for building a nuclear arsenal. It did not consider it necessary to conduct another test until the Bharatiya Janata Party came to power. Under Prime Minister Atal Bihari Vajpayee's directive, India, on 11 May 1998, tested three nuclear weapons and two more two days later. The US condemned the tests publicly but once again accepted the reality. President Bill Clinton paid an unprecedented six-day visit to India in early 2000. In 2005, President George W. Bush agreed to extend technological cooperation to India for nuclear power plants, proposing an India-specific exception to US non-proliferation laws, as well as to the agreed restrictions of the Nuclear Suppliers Group. An equal criteria-based treatment was denied to Pakistan.

NOTES

1. George Perkovich, *India's Nuclear Bomb*, California University Press, Berkeley, CAL, 1999, 13.
2. 'If India has the bomb, that does not mean we are going to be subjected to nuclear blackmail,' said Zulfikar Ali Bhutto, on 13 August 1966. See Stanley Wolpert, *Zulfi Bhutto of Pakistan*, 112. On another occasion Bhutto said: '[I]f India acquires nuclear status, Pakistan will have to follow suit. . . .'
3. Iqbal Akhund, *Memoires of a Bystander: A Life in Diplomacy*, Oxford University Press, Karachi, 1997, 264.
4. Former PAEC scientists who participated in a meeting in Islamabad on 29 April 2005 to commemorate the sixth death anniversary of Munir Ahmad Khan clarified that the Multan meeting did not discuss the question of making a bomb. Deserved tributes were paid for Munir's seminal role in developing the nuclear programme as PAEC chairman, as well as his extraordinary discretion in public statements, recognizing the danger in flaunting the PAEC's great contribution to the success of the programme.
5. As recounted in Perkovich, op. cit., Kissinger rejected a draft prepared by a state department official (Dennis Kux) that criticized India for undermining non-proliferation efforts. Instead he decided that 'public scolding would not undo the event, but only add to bilateral Indo-US problems and reduce the influence Washington might have on India's future nuclear policy.'
6. Secret State Department memorandum of 13 September 1961, quoted in Perkovich, op. cit., 52.
7. Released record of State Department meeting on 9 July 1976, reported in *Dawn*, Islamabad, 26 December 2007.
8. To his credit, Air Marshal Zulfiqar Ali Khan advised against accepting the conditional offer of sale of aircraft because he believed acquisition of the nuclear option was more important in the longer perspective.
9. A. Q. Khan, Chairman, Khan Research Laboratories, 'The Journey to our Tests', *The News*, Islamabad, Special Issue, 28 May 1999.
10. Shahid-ur-Rahman, *Long Road to Chaghi*.
11. Ibid.
12. Ibid.
13. Dennis Kux, op. cit., 229.
14. Prime Minister Bhutto's statement in parliament on 28 April 1977. *Documents*, ed. K. Arif, 329.
15. Statement by Pakistan Foreign Office, 7 April 1979. *Documents*, ed. K. Arif, 347.
16. *The New York Times* 12 and 15 August report, quoted in Dennis Kux, op. cit., 240.
17. A Pakistani spokesman reiterated on 24 August 1994 that Pakistan had the capacity to produce nuclear weapons but had not actually done so. Former Prime Minister Nawaz Sharif's statement that 'Pakistan possesses the atomic bomb' was described, also by a US State Department official, as having

'something to do with domestic politics.' *Reuters/AP* dispatches of 23 and 24 August 1994.

18. When the author, then ambassador to India, called on her after her election victory, she seemed obsessed about reports of Pakistan's nuclear programme.
19. Perkovich, op. cit., 240, quoting from a research paper by W. P. S. Sidhu.
20. Useful information on the subject is provided in Perkovich, op. cit., 239–41.
21. Perkovich, op. cit., 241.
22. *The Times of India News Service* correspondent from Washington reported on 17 September 1984 that according to *The Washington Post* and *The New York Times*, 'U.S. intelligence agencies recently briefed a senate subcommittee . . . that military advisers had suggested to (Indian Prime Minister) Mrs Indira Gandhi that to prevent Pakistan from making the bomb, India should launch a pre-emptive strike on the Pakistani nuclear facility at Kahuta.' *The Times of India* published the report on 18 September 1984, under a slanted headline: 'U.S. false alarm to Pak of Indian pre-emptive attack.' Also see *The Indian Express*, 19 September 1984, report by H.K. Dua, entitled: 'India concerned over US signal to Pak on Jaguar deployment.'
23. Perkovich, op. cit., 280.
24. Lewis A. Dunn, *Containing Nuclear Proliferation*, Adelphi Paper No. 263 (London: International Institute for Strategic Studies, 1991), 17.
25. Ibid.
26. This section has benefited greatly from George Perkovich, *India's Nuclear Bomb*, University of California Press, Berkeley, 1999.
27. Ibid., 14, quoting from Dorothy Newman, Nehru: *The First Sixty Years*.
28. Jawaharlal Nehru, *Selected Works*, Second Series, Vol. 5, 27.
29. Munir Ahmad Khan, 'Nuclearization of South Asia and its Regional and Global Implications', *Regional Studies*, Islamabad, Autumn 1998.

CHAPTER 13

Relations with India—An Interlude: 1977–1979

Prime Minister Indira Gandhi lost the election in March 1977 as the Indian people handed her a humiliating rebuke for authoritarian rule, imprisonment of most opposition politicians, and draconian curbs on fundamental freedoms during the Emergency in 1975–7. The Janata Party won by a landslide and veteran politician Morarji Desai became prime minister. Coincidently, Prime Minister Zulfikar Ali Bhutto was toppled at about the same time by the Chief of the Army Staff, General Muhammad Zia ul-Haq, in the wake of prolonged and paralysing country-wide agitation.

Little was common between lifelong politician Morarji Desai and professional soldier Zia ul-Haq, but they led an extraordinary relaxation of tensions between India and Pakistan, mainly due to the former's principled policy of non-interference in the internal affairs of other countries and respect for sovereign equality. Islamabad appreciated New Delhi's abstinence from criticism of the Zia ul-Haq government's disregard of human rights. In fact, Mr Desai forbade his cabinet colleagues and government spokespersons from commenting on Pakistan's internal affairs so much so that when the President of India criticized the execution of Mr Z. A. Bhutto, it was said to have precipitated a constitutional crisis in New Delhi. Of course, after the ruthless imprisonment of opposition politicians and draconian press curbs during Indira Gandhi's emergency rule, India was hardly a shining example of democracy.

Détente: The author was fortunate to take up his assignment as ambassador in New Delhi when Mr Desai was prime minister. Shortly after he took charge, a mini-crisis erupted. An embassy staffer was beaten up by Indian police, breaking his nose. When he called at the Ministry of External Affairs (MEA) to register a protest, he was told the man had got involved in a fracas in the bazaar. The lame explanation for several hours of detention was that he had no identity card. The Ambassador avoided recriminations and instead called for observance of principles: members of the diplomatic staff were entitled to immunity from arrest or detention; if any was considered undesirable the embassy could be told to send him back. A couple of days later, he chanced to meet Prime Minister Desai at a Diwali function. The latter, having seen telegrams flying between the Foreign Offices, asked, 'Why are you diplomats spoiling relations?' The Ambassador replied in the same vein as at the MEA. The Prime Minister immediately agreed violence was inadmissible. The next morning, MEA conveyed regrets to the embassy. The storm in the teacup did not spill over.

Mr Desai personally permitted a hospitality assistant in his office, Ms Vimla Sindhi, to visit the ambassador's wife at the residence—their families were friends in Khanewal. Desai's successor, Prime Minister Charan Singh, maintained the friendly stance: he visited the ambassador at a hospital to wish speedy recovery. The solicitous gesture was suggested by Mr Raj Narain, a Union Minister and influential political leader in the Janata Party, famous for his successful petition in Allahabad High Court that unseated Mrs Gandhi for irregularities in the 1973 election.

Cultural Exchanges: Never before had the two countries encouraged cultural and sports exchanges as much as in 1977–9. External Affairs Minister Atal Behari Vajpayee, a notable poet himself, personally invited Faiz Ahmad Faiz, whose poems he read when jailed under Emergency. When Faiz came months later, Vajpayee quipped '*Faiz Sahib itni der sey aye hain aisaa maloom hota hai boht door sey aye hain.*' (Mr Faiz took so long to come it seems he came from far away!) He presided over the function to honour the world-famous poet and listen to his recitation of poems many in the audience remembered by heart. Over the next few years, almost every famous Pakistani artist performed to hearty applause by packed sessions. Great artist Sadequain exhibited his works in major cities. The Hindu University in Varanasi welcomed a visit during which he painted a Qur'anic verse for the assembly hall. Ghazal maestros Mehdi Hassan, Ghulam Ali, Iqbal Bano, and Fareeda Khanum, classicist Salamat Ali Khan, and folksinger Reshma were accorded warm welcomes. For the performance of the qawwali team Sabri Brothers, Indian GHQ asked for forty more invitation cards. Also, the ambassador arranged for renowned sarod maestro Ustad Amjad Ali Khan to visit Lahore for a performance before an enthralled audience of connoisseurs at Al-Hamra. Eminent Urdu writers exchanged visits. National cricket teams drew packed stadia for Test matches—a popular and vicarious means for translating rivalry between the two countries.

A major transformation took place in the projection of Pakistan's image after media editors in New Delhi were persuaded to send reporters to Pakistan for news coverage instead of publishing the content circulated by TASS, which they agreed was hardly a reliable news agency. Pakistani leaders were generous with the time they gave for interviews with reputed Indian journalists. The famous author and columnist Khushwant Singh came to Pakistan several times to meet Pakistani leaders and friends, and contributed his usually friendly pen to portray the Pakistani political and social scene. Another memorable dividend was a prestigious Indian daily's decision to devote the centrefold of the Sunday edition to the text of the interview with the Pakistan president. The reputed interviewer, Mr Inderjit, was faithful in reporting General Zia's replies, straightening out only the syntax. An influential member of the parliament told the ambassador he read the entire text. The Indian Staff College invited the Pakistani ambassador to speak to the class of senior officers—a rare gesture the latter reciprocated by ensuring return by the Pakistani Staff College, which was noted with appreciation.

Although unmarked by any milestones commemorating resolution of bitter disputes, the interlude was memorable for softening hard images, providing an environment for mutual compromise. It is tempting to speculate about the potential inherent in such a transformation. Unhappily, the interlude proved all too brief, leaving hardly a trace in the evolution of relations between the two countries. Yet it can serve to remind leaders and people that good manners and respect for principles of peaceful coexistence can foster an environment of good-neighbourly relations conducive to settlement of differences and disputes. Altogether, it was a welcome interlude.

In recognition of Prime Minister Morarji Desai's contribution setting an example of principled policies among neighbours, Pakistan conferred its highest award—Nishan-i-Pakistan—on the Indian leader in 1991. On his second assignment as ambassador to India, the author had the honour of presenting the award to the respected leader at his apartment in Mumbai. The Indian government did not take official notice, though it did not obstruct the ceremony. Mr Subramanian Swamy, a Union Minister in Prime Minster Chandra Shekhar's cabinet, participated in a personal capacity.

Jinnah House: Foreign Secretary Sardar Shah Nawaz and Ambassador Shankar Bajpai negotiated an understanding in 1978 on reopening consular offices in Karachi and Mumbai. To facilitate implementation, the Indian Ambassador offered to try and secure the lease of Jinnah House in Mumbai for the Pakistani Consul General. President Zia ul-Haq and Prime Minister Desai accorded approval. The implementation had, however, to await vacation of the Jinnah House by the British Deputy High Commissioner. That took two years. Meanwhile, Mrs Indira Gandhi returned as prime minister. The Jinnah House file was pigeonholed. MEA's Special Secretary Kanwar Natwar Singh made personal efforts to expedite approval, but it never came. Khushwant Singh, who called himself 'Pakistan's only friend in India' more than once, raised the question in the parliament of why the Indian government was not implementing the pledge to lease the Jinnah House to Pakistan, but Mrs Gandhi remained unmoved.

Principled Policy: Under the leadership of Morarji Desai, the Janata government's foreign policy adhered to universally recognized principles, refraining from use of threat or use of force against other states and from interference in their internal affairs and indicating respect for sovereign equality and for the right of every state to individual or collective self-defence and peaceful settlement of differences. Some of the outstanding issues between India and its neighbours—Bangladesh, Nepal, Pakistan, and Sri Lanka—were amicably settled. The Janata Party government did not object to Pakistan's uranium enrichment programme, cognizant no doubt that India had tested a nuclear bomb in 1974. Prime Minister Charan Singh's government issued a principled statement criticizing the Soviet intervention in Afghanistan.

In all these respects, Mrs Indira Gandhi, who won the election in early January 1980, reversed the foreign policy pursued by the

Janata Party. Immediately, she tilted towards the USSR and did not join the overwhelming majority of UN members which voted for the resolution calling for withdrawal of foreign forces from Afghanistan. When the author met Mrs Gandhi to felicitate her on election success, the only question she asked was about Pakistan's nuclear programme, ignoring the fact that she had authorized the bomb test in May 1974, calling it 'a peaceful explosion'. The principle of sovereign equality was anathema to her: during the election campaign, she criticized the Janata Party for allowing neighbours to look India in the eye, saying, '*Ab Bhutan aur Nepal bhi hamain ankhen dikhatay hain!*'

CHAPTER 14

Soviet Intervention in Afghanistan–1979

Few other countries are closer to Pakistan in culture and history than Afghanistan. The hope for friendly cooperation was, however, vitiated at the start. On the eve of the establishment of Pakistan, the Afghan government denounced the treaty Amir Abdur Rahman had concluded in 1893 establishing the Durand Line as the boundary with British India. It launched a territorial claim in the guise of support for 'Pushtoonistan', which it wanted to be carved out of Pakistan. Afghanistan was the only country to vote against Pakistan's admission to the United Nations. In the decades that followed, relations between the two neighbours remained strained, though fortunately tensions were kept under control. The Afghan government did not exploit Pakistan's vulnerability during the wars with India. When Sardar Mohammad Daoud assumed power on 17 July 1973, supplanting King Mohammad Zahir Shah, his cousin and brother-in-law, apprehensions of deterioration of bilateral relations rose in Islamabad, as he was a known Pakistan-baiter.

Aiming to use Soviet support to consolidate his power at home and pursue the irredenta against Pakistan, Daoud entered into close relations with the Soviet Union. He was no doubt pleased when Premier Alexei Kosygin exhorted Pakistan to improve relations with 'our friendly neighbour'. However, the embrace soon proved to be a bear hug. By 1976, Daoud appeared to have realized that the Soviets had an agenda of their own. They had penetrated the internal politics of the country, providing support and assistance to the revolutionary People's Democratic Party of Afghanistan (PDPA). To counterbalance the Soviet influence, Daoud embarked on efforts to improve relations with Pakistan, Iran, and other Muslim countries. He and Prime Minister Z. A. Bhutto exchanged visits in 1976. Bilateral relations continued to improve after General Zia ul-Haq assumed power in Pakistan in July 1977. Daoud's talks with Zia proved 'extremely useful'. He asked President Zia 'to give me time to mould public opinion in my country to effect a change . . . to normalize relations with Pakistan.'

Daoud's new policy did not please Moscow or the PDPA. He tried, too late, to control the revolutionaries at home. The contest culminated in a coup on 27 April 1978 that PDPA called the 'Saur Revolution'. Daoud and members of his family were murdered, the constitution was abrogated and a revolution proclaimed by a clique of communist intellectuals. Repeating Daoud's error, they too sought to exploit Soviet support for their own aims, and like him, suffered the same fate, proving the verity, 'Those who foolishly seek power by riding on the back of the tiger end up inside.'

Nur Muhammad Taraki assumed the office of president in the name of the PDPA. The party lacked a popular base. From the beginning, the new regime was faced with opposition in the traditional and conservative Afghan society. Also, the party was riven with rivalry between its predominantly rural and Pushto-speaking Khalq and urban-based Persian-speaking Parcham factions. Infighting led to Taraki's murder in September 1979. He was succeeded by Hafizullah Amin, whose radical reforms evoked even stronger opposition from the Afghan people. Headstrong and defiant of Soviet guidance, he was considered by his rivals in the party, and by the Soviets, to be endangering the stability of the revolution.

On 26 December 1979, the Soviet forces rolled into Afghanistan, eliminated Amin, and installed Babrak Karmal, leader of the Parcham faction, as president in his place. The Soviet pretext of an invitation by the Afghan government for intervention by its forces was obviously false, as its target was none other than the head of that government.

The intervention provoked a deep sense of alarm in Pakistan. Suddenly the buffer disappeared, and the Soviet superpower advanced to Pakistan's borders. The security strategists believed that if allowed to consolidate its hold, the Soviet Union could later leap down the Bolan and Khyber passes to fulfil the historical czarist ambition for access to the warm waters of the Arabian Sea.

Anxiety was enhanced by the realization that Pakistan was deeply divided internally and isolated internationally. The rigging of elections by Prime Minister Bhutto in 1977, the countrywide agitation that brought the economy to the edge of ruin, and Bhutto's overthrow in a military coup and hanging in April 1979 upon conviction on a charge of murder had polarized opinion at home as never before. General Zia ul-Haq's decision to ignore appeals by foreign leaders and the media for clemency had antagonized the whole world.

Pakistan's reaction to the Soviet intervention was visceral, but in deciding policy it sought to exercise prudence.[1] It was 'fully conscious' of the risks of antagonizing and pitting itself against a superpower but also realized that acquiescence in the *fait accompli* would entail even greater dangers. Apart from undermining the sacrosanct principle of inadmissibility of aggression, consolidation of Soviet power in Afghanistan would enhance the danger of Soviet collaboration with India for another military intervention, exposing Pakistan to the nightmare of an Indo-Soviet 'nutcracker'.

Zia's government took two days to decide on its public reaction. The carefully crafted statement did not even name the Soviet Union. Instead, it referred to the 'induction of foreign troops' and described it as a 'serious violation' of the norms of peaceful coexistence and the principles of the UN Charter. Rather defensively, it explained Pakistan's 'gravest concern' in the context of its links of Islam, geography, and non-aligned policy with Afghanistan, and concluded by expressing the hope that 'the foreign troops would be removed from the Afghan soil forthwith.' The element of caution was implicit in avoidance of condemnation.

Non-alignment Policy: Pakistan noted the strong reaction of the United States and West European countries,[2] but, apprehensive of the possibly dangerous implications of involvement in the Cold War, it hitched its diplomacy to the hope of a political resolution of the crisis through the United Nations. It was assumed that Moscow, however cynical, could not dismiss the condemnation of the world, including the Western and especially Islamic and non-aligned nations.

At Pakistan's request, six non-permanent members, all non-aligned, sponsored a resolution in the UN Security Council. It strongly deplored 'the recent armed intervention in Afghanistan' and called for 'immediate, unconditional and total withdrawal of the foreign troops in order to enable its people to determine their own form of government and choose their own economic, political and social systems free from outside intervention, subversion, coercion or constraint of any kind whatever.' At Islamabad's request, the resolution neither named the Soviet Union nor used the stronger word 'condemnation'. It received thirteen votes in the fifteen-member Council but, as expected, was vetoed by the USSR. The resolution was then taken up by the General Assembly under the 'Uniting for Peace' procedure and after a short debate, was adopted on 14 January 1980 by a majority of 104 votes in favour, eighteen against, and eighteen abstentions. Foreign Minister Agha Shahi ably piloted these resolutions.

The USSR suffered a severe blow to its image. Not only the Western bloc but also fifty-six out of ninety-two members of the Non-Aligned Movement (NAM) voted for the resolution while most of the rest abstained. Even India was initially critical. In December, Indian Prime Minister Charan Singh issued a strong statement condemning the intervention. After his government lost the election in January 1980, the prime minister-elect, Indira Gandhi, adopted a pro-Soviet stance. The Indian statement in the General Assembly not only did not criticize the Soviet intervention but even accepted the Soviet explanation that its limited forces would be withdrawn after some time. Indira Gandhi mocked Pakistan's diplomacy of building moral pressure on the Soviet Union, rhetorically asking the Pakistani ambassador: 'Do you expect the UN resolution will force the Soviets to withdraw troops?'[3] Her cynical view was not surprising, as India itself had refused to comply with the UN resolutions on Kashmir. Soon India joined a coterie of Soviet apologists. In the NAM Coordinating Bureau, they sabotaged a resolution on Afghanistan. The outcome did not, however, damage the Afghan cause so much as it did the credibility of the NAM itself.[4]

As part of a campaign to mobilize pressure of world opinion on Moscow, an extraordinary session of the Organization of Islamic Cooperation (OIC) foreign ministers was held in Islamabad on 29 January. Several members spoke in harsh terms. The resolution adopted by the meeting proclaimed a strong indictment of the Soviet intervention. It also suspended Afghanistan's membership of the OIC and affirmed solidarity with the struggle of the Afghan people to safeguard 'their faith, national independence and territorial integrity.'

More critical to the outcome of the crisis than censure abroad was the opposition to the Soviet intervention inside Afghanistan. A traditional people with a sense of pride in their history, having challenged and defeated colonial Britain's invasions a century earlier, the Afghans were engaged in partisan resistance against the PDPA since it grabbed power in 1978. With the arrival of foreign troops to protect and perpetuate a regime with an alien ideology, the resistance was transformed into a people's war.

Pakistan was sympathetic to the Afghan cause, but caution and lack of resources limited the support and assistance it could provide to the mujahideen. The Soviets were threatening in their warnings. Pakistan decided, nevertheless, to provide discreet help. Besides the motivation of solidarity with the Afghan people, self-interest was the clinching rationale of the decision. In fighting for their national survival, the mujahideen would be fighting also for Pakistan's own security and independence.

Although the American CIA also began to provide some assistance to the Afghan resistance, Pakistan's decision to assist the jihad was made autonomously, without foreign instigation. Wary of the consequences, Pakistan was anxious to preclude any impression of acting at the behest of the United States or wanting to push Afghanistan into the Cold War.

The initial thrust of Pakistan's policy was diplomatic in orientation. To that end, it sought to build up greater political pressure on the Soviet Union at the regular session of the UN General Assembly in 1980. A group of like-minded non-aligned countries from Africa, Asia, and Latin America, coordinated by Kuwait, prepared an elaborate draft resolution that suggested the outlines of a political solution. The components included (i) immediate withdrawal of the foreign forces; (ii) preservation of the sovereignty, territorial integrity, independence and non-aligned status of Afghanistan; (iii) respect for the right of its people to determine their own form of government and economic system, free from outside intervention, subversion, coercion or constraint; and (iv) creation of conditions for the voluntary return of Afghan refugees to their homes in safety and honour. The resolution further provided for efforts by the UN Secretary General to promote a political solution that could include guarantees of non-use of force against the security of 'all neighbouring countries'. Similar resolutions with updated text attracted even greater support over succeeding years, rising from 111 votes in 1980 to 123 in 1987. During the same period, negative votes and abstentions combined declined from thirty-six in 1980 to thirty in 1987.[5] Every year, the world community administered a stinging blow to Soviet prestige.

Revival of the US Alliance

Pakistan's decision to oppose the Soviet intervention in Afghanistan was made at a time when its relations with the United States were strained because of the discriminatory sanctions imposed by the Carter administration in 1979.[6] Nor could Pakistan assume that the United States would join in opposing the Soviet intervention; Washington had remained quiescent following the communist coup in April 1978, and President Carter had hardly reacted to the murder of American Ambassador Adolph Dubs.

The Soviet invasion appeared to shake the United States out of indifference, but hardly enough for Pakistan to conclude it could be counted upon to review its policy toward Pakistan. Unknown to Islamabad, US National Security Council Adviser Zbigniew Brzezinski had recommended to President Carter, 'This will require a review of our policy towards Pakistan, more guarantees to it, more aid, and alas, a decision that our security policy toward Pakistan cannot be dictated by our non-proliferation policy.'[7] But Washington did not inform Islamabad of what it contemplated with regard to security guarantees or waiver of nuclear sanctions. Had consultations been held, Islamabad would have sought a guarantee of American assistance in the event of Soviet or a Soviet-backed Indian attack on Pakistan. To that end, it needed the upgradation of the 1959 executive agreement on defence cooperation into a binding treaty. As President Zia ul-Haq later said, the 'credibility and durability'[8] of American assurances was low, founded in the widely held belief that at critical junctures, especially in 1965 and 1971, the United States had betrayed a friend and ally.

Washington acted rather strangely. Without any consultation with Islamabad, the US President announced an offer of $400 million in economic and military assistance for Pakistan over 18 months. Islamabad believed that the defence component would enhance risks of reinvolvement in the Cold War. Moreover, the aid package was 'wrapped up in onerous conditions', and these could affect Pakistan's pursuit of the nuclear programme thus 'denuding (the offer) of relevance to our defensive capacity.'[9] President Zia announced the rejection of the offer, describing it as 'peanuts'. This word ridiculing the amount of the offer gave the wrong impression that what Islamabad wanted was larger aid. Actually, Pakistan was prepared to accept $200 million in economic assistance but not the other half for defence. It was the United States that refused to de-link economic assistance from the defence component. Pakistan's refusal to accept the US aid offer did not affect its steadfast policy of opposition to Soviet intervention. For more than a year, it continued to support the Afghan resistance, also providing it with modest assistance out of its own meagre resources.

Non-acceptance of US aid in 1980 reduced the risk of plunging Pakistan back into the orbit of the Cold War. It also helped in projecting the Afghan cause in its genuine perspective of a liberation struggle. It served, moreover, to save Pakistan's relations with Iran from further strain. The Iranian media perception of Pakistan as a proxy for US interests in the region was painful to Pakistanis, who value Iran as a friend and a fraternal neighbour. The sincerity of Pakistan's solidarity with Iran was illustrated again in April 1980 when it expressed 'shock and dismay' at the US assault on Iran in an attempt to forcibly rescue American embassy staff from captivity, and 'deplored this impermissible act which constitutes a serious violation of Iran's sovereignty.'

Internal Afghan Politics-1980s: Burhanuddin Rabbani, Guldbuddin Hekmatyar, Ahmad Shah Massoud, and Abdur Rasul Sayyaf formed an alliance to establish an independent state. Initially they were conciliatory but by 1984 they had split. Massoud was focused on assembling forces in the Panjshir Valley for the occupation of Kabul. Britain and France gave assistance to Massoud, a Tajik who was ideologically liberal. In two key battles for Kabul, Massoud was assisted by Abdur Rasheed Dostum, an Uzbek warlord. Pakistan's ISPR supported Hekmatyar's Hezb-i-Islami, generously funded and provided with modern arms by CIA and the Saudi government. In the fight against the Soviet Army, the US agreed to channel supply of arms and all assistance to the liberation movement through the Pakistan Army.

US-Taliban Negotiations: President Trump appointed Zalmay Khalilzad to lead the negotiations for a ceasefire and peace with the Taliban. At the end of 2018 and early 2019, he held several meetings with Mullah Abdul Ghani Baradar who was close to Taliban leader

Haibatulah Akhundzada at the invitation of Qatar. The Taliban were said to pledge ban on international terrorists from abusing Afghanistan as a base. The US was said to agree to withdrawal of troops. The Taliban talked only to the US representative and refused to meet with the Kabul regime's representatives.

US Aid: After President Ronald Reagan succeeded Carter in 1981, Washington revived the offer of cooperation with Pakistan. Senior US officials visited Islamabad for talks. By April, the US decided on a new package, with loans and grants amounting to three billion dollars over five years.[10] The amount of $600 million a year for development and defence was a significant improvement over the Carter offer of $400 million for 18 months. The new offer still did not address Pakistan's concerns about defence against the Soviets or Soviet-aided Indian threat. These were taken up during negotiations. The US side explained that Congressional opinion was reluctant to support a formal security guarantee to Pakistan. The administration, however, evinced a reassuring understanding of Pakistan's vulnerabilities as a front-line state. As an earnest of US concern for Pakistan's security, it agreed to consider the sale of forty F-16 aircraft. Also, the five-year programme generated an aura of durability around the US commitment.

On the nuclear issue, the two countries maintained their formal positions, with Pakistan reiterating its intention to continue research and the US proclaiming its non-proliferation concern. But Washington turned the pressure off. Secretary of State Alexander Haig indicated that the nuclear was no longer the priority issue. Acknowledging past discrimination and expressing understanding of Pakistan's rationale,[11] Washington accepted Zia's assurance that Pakistan would not develop nuclear weapons or transfer sensitive technology.[12] Later, it secured Congressional approval for a waiver of the Symington prohibition. Senators and Congressmen who targeted Pakistan for discriminatory sanctions no longer commanded decisive influence.

Pakistan chose not to accept concessional loans for military sales, and instead opted to pay the market rate of interest, so as to safeguard its non-aligned credentials. Islamabad wanted to retain credibility as an independent actor in the hope of persuading the Soviet Union to agree to a political solution of the Afghanistan question outside the Cold War context. In the event, the sacrifice won no appreciation from either Moscow or New Delhi. They denounced Pakistan even though a year earlier India itself had signed a deal with the USSR for the latest MIG aircraft, T-72 tanks and warships, etc. for a give-away price of $1.6 billion on soft terms, though the market value was estimated at $6 billion. In retrospect, Pakistan's more-pious-than-the-Pope posture did not yield commensurate political advantage. Critics unmindful of non-aligned support considered it a costly pose.[13]

Geneva Accords[14]

UN efforts to promote a political solution began in earnest with the appointment of Diego Cordovez, a senior UN official from Ecuador, as the personal representative of the Secretary General in 1981. He found the situation rather bizarre. Before he could convene the first Geneva meeting, Iran declined to participate, arguing that the Soviet withdrawal should be unconditional, and Pakistan was unwilling to meet with the Afghan regime it did not recognize. Cordovez had to persuade Kabul to agree to indirect talks. The Soviet Union refused to join talks, taking the position that its forces entered Afghanistan at Kabul's invitation and would be withdrawn when Kabul no longer wanted their presence, but it sent high-level officials to Geneva to be available for consultation.

Negotiations began in Geneva in June 1982 with exploration of the structure of a settlement that would integrate the components of the UN General Assembly resolution. An energetic, dedicated, and persuasive diplomat of high calibre, Cordovez sidetracked controversy over the past by proposing an agreement on mutual non-interference and non-intervention between Afghanistan and its neighbours as a means of obtaining a Soviet commitment to withdrawal of forces. To satisfy the Soviet demand for American commitment to non-interference, he conceived the idea of guarantees by both super powers. Negotiations were not, however, a serious undertaking at first. Moscow was confident that its mighty forces equipped with the latest weapons would rout the ragtag mujahideen armed with antiquated rifles. It misjudged the situation, as it could not pin down the mujahideen guerrillas, who were supported by the Afghan populace and received sophisticated weapons from the United States for guerrilla warfare.

After the death of the hard-liner Soviet leader Leonid Brezhnev in November 1982, hopes rose for a political settlement. In a meeting with Zia who visited Moscow for Brezhnev's funeral, Yuri Andropov, the new Soviet leader, gave a 'hint of flexibility'. UN Secretary General Perez de Cuellar and Diego Cordovez, who met Andropov in March 1983, received 'new encouragement' for pursuing UN mediation. Andropov counted out to them the reasons why the Soviet Union wanted a solution. Raising his fingers one by one, he mentioned costs in lives and money, regional tensions, setback to détente, and loss of Soviet prestige in the Third World.[15]

Buoyed by the positive signals, Cordovez successfully pressed the two sides in the 1983 April and June rounds of Geneva talks to agree on the components of a comprehensive settlement. These included an agreement on non-interference and non-intervention, guarantees by third states, and arrangements for the voluntary return of refugees. Discussions made good progress. Cordovez was optimistic and envisaged 'gradual withdrawal' of Soviet forces within a reasonable timeframe. But the Soviet-Kabul side dragged their feet, indicating that the hardliners were marking time as Andropov was ailing. After he died, they reverted to the policy of a military solution, which continued under Konstantin Chernenko and Mikhail Gorbachev until the end of the summer in 1987.

The struggle in Afghanistan was unequal, but the mujahideen demonstrated courage and resourcefulness in resistance and did not wilt despite the increasing ferocity of Soviet pressure. Their sacrifices and stamina drew deserved praise and tribute. Assistance to them increased so as to neutralize the Soviet induction of more lethal artillery, helicopter gunships, and bombers for savage and indiscriminate destruction of villages to interdict mujahideen activities. The United States raised covert allocations for supply of arms to the mujahideen from $250 million in 1985 to $470 million in 1986 and $630 million in 1987.[16] The US aid was reportedly matched by Saudi Arabia. China, Iran, and several other countries also provided significant assistance. Pakistan calibrated the flow of assistance to the mujahideen cautiously so as to minimize the risk of spillover of the conflict, but became bolder with time and experience. It realized that a superpower's forces could not be defeated militarily but also that attrition inside Afghanistan combined with blows to its prestige internationally offered the only hope of wearing Moscow down. Negotiations in Geneva and resolutions in OIC, NAM, and the United Nations were a part of that strategy for increasing political pressure.

Diego Cordovez patiently kept the Geneva talks on track, however slow their pace. Altogether, twelve sessions were held over six years. He and the Pakistani side occasionally discussed the question of a compromise between the Kabul regime and the mujahideen, but this subject was not on the agenda. UN resolutions referred to the principle of respect for the right of the Afghan people to determine their own form of government and economic system, but this was not interpreted as requiring replacement of the regime installed by the Soviet forces. Kabul and Moscow at first refused even to recognize the reality of internal resistance. They said 'everything comes from outside.'[17] USSR Foreign Minister Gromyko dismissed the idea of a broad-based government in Kabul as 'unrealistic phantasies'.

Cordovez himself realized the need for a compromise among the Afghans, but as he said, correctly for the time, 'The UN is not in the business of establishing governments.'[18] In 1983, when Andropov indicated a desire for settlement, Cordovez was inclined to favour a role for former king Zahir Shah, who offered to work to unite the Afghans. The idea received enthusiastic support from Afghan exiles. A poll organized by Professor Syed Bahauddin Majrooh, a prominent Afghan scholar who was editing a paper from Peshawar, found that 70 per cent of the Afghan refugees in Pakistan favoured Zahir Shah's return. But this view was rejected by the more powerful mujahideen parties. When Majrooh was later assassinated, opponents of the king were suspected of having organized the crime.

By late 1986, the texts of the agreements having been all but finalized, Cordovez remarked: 'It (is) now true for the first time that the only issue remaining (is) the question of the timeframe (for the withdrawal of Soviet forces from Afghanistan).'[19]

Still evasive on the central issue in 1986, the Soviet side said its forces would be withdrawn four years after the conclusion of the Geneva Accords, while Pakistan asked for withdrawals to be completed in three months. By mid-1987, the Soviets wanted eighteen months for withdrawal while Pakistan went up to seven months. The issue was not to be settled until after the failure of the Soviet military offensive in the summer of 1987. Mikhail Gorbachev then finally decided to abandon the misadventure. By then, the imperatives of democratic and economic reforms at home necessitated an end to confrontation with the West.

In July 1987, Najibullah proposed a coalition offering twelve ministries and the office of vice president to the Mujahideen Alliance. Gorbachev endorsed the idea of national reconciliation to facilitate the process of 'constructing a new Afghanistan.' The Alliance leaders were, however, unanimous in rejecting a coalition with the PDPA. In September 1987, Cordovez put forward a 'Scenario Paper' envisaging a representative assembly comprising the seven Mujahideen Alliance parties, the PDPA, and select Afghan personalities to form a transitional arrangement. Aware of the Alliance's views, Islamabad did not accord the idea much attention. When it was conveyed to them in early 1988, the Alliance leaders ruled out any dialogue with the PDPA. Engineer Gulbuddin Hekmatyar, Professor Burhanuddin Rabbani, and Maulvi Yunus Khalis also ruled out any role for the king. Pakistan did not pursue Cordovez's suggestion. Since resistance against the Soviets still commanded priority, it was considered inadvisable to press the mujahideen lest that divide and weaken the Alliance.

Gorbachev and Shevardnadze succeeded in winning the endorsement of the Politburo of the Communist Party for the policy of terminating military involvement in Afghanistan.[20] The costs of the policy in human and material resources and the obloquy it entailed, even in the Soviet Union's non-aligned backyard, were glaringly disproportionate to any benefits that continued hold over Afghanistan might yield. The new generation of communists no longer shared the pristine ideological fervour of the founders or faith in the inevitability of communism's victory. In fact, the Soviet system was faltering, the economy was in decline, and the people were alienated. The cost of military confrontation and the arms race with the West, occupation of Eastern Europe, tension with China, and finally intervention in Afghanistan had 'ruined'[21] the Soviet Union.

Gorbachev announced, at a press conference in Washington on 10 December 1987, that the Soviet forces would withdraw from Afghanistan within twelve months of the conclusion of Geneva Accords, and further that during that period the forces would not engage in combat. Gorbachev also delinked the question of withdrawal from an internal settlement in Afghanistan. Though he reaffirmed support for 'a coalition on the basis of national reconciliation and the realities of the situation',[22] Moscow was no longer prepared to allow the Alliance's rejectionist attitude to obstruct its decision to extricate the Soviet Union from the Afghan quagmire. Nor was it willing to undertake the removal of the Kabul regime and hand over the government to the Mujahideen Alliance.

Just as prospects for the conclusion of the Geneva Accords brightened, dark clouds suddenly appeared on the horizon in Pakistan. In January 1988, President Zia took the position that the conclusion of the Accords should be postponed until after agreement was reached on the formation of a government in Kabul with the participation of the mujahideen. This took Pakistan's prime minister, Mohammad Khan Junejo, completely by surprise: heretofore Pakistan's refrain was that the only outstanding obstacle to the conclusion of the Geneva Accords was a reasonable timeframe for the withdrawal of Soviet forces. Besides, making the formation of a coalition government a precondition for the conclusion of the Accords seemed a recipe for delaying the withdrawal of the Soviet forces, because the Mujahideen Alliance was known to be averse to the idea of a coalition with the PDPA. Now the Soviets were no longer prepared to wait. When on 9 February, Zia pressed the visiting Soviet First Deputy Foreign Minister Yuli Vorontsov for postponement of the final Geneva round, his comment was withering to the point of insolence. He said, 'For eight years you have been asking us to leave Afghanistan. Now you want us to stay. I smell a rat!'[23]

The logic of Zia's eleventh-hour volte-face was never explained. Pakistan's foreign friends were as mystified as Prime Minister Junejo. His new policy reversed Pakistan's oft-stated position that the only remaining obstacle to the Geneva Accords was an acceptable time frame for the withdrawal of Soviet forces. Zia's changed stance contradicted Pakistan's long-held position. Moreover, it was illogical because Moscow had decided to pull out of Afghanistan. Pakistan could block the Geneva Accords, but it could not prevent the Soviets from withdrawing from Afghanistan either unilaterally or pursuant to an agreement with the Kabul regime. In comparison with these alternatives, withdrawal under the Accords was decidedly more advantageous. The Soviet Union would be internationally bound to withdraw its forces completely within a prescribed timeframe and under UN monitoring. It would be legally bound also to refrain from intervention in Afghanistan.

Pakistan, too, would receive Soviet and US guarantees of respect for principles of non-interference and non-intervention. In contrast, unilateral withdrawal would entail no such commitments.

For Moscow, the residual consideration now was the manner of disengagement so as to avoid danger to their retreating forces and further humiliation for the Soviet Union. It prized the Geneva Accords because contained in them was a commitment to observe principle of non-interference and non-intervention. Pakistan and the United States would be under an obligation to discontinue assistance to the mujahideen. That might save the Soviet friends in Afghanistan from massacre. No less important was their symbolic value. The UN-sponsored agreement would provide a fig leaf to cover the Soviet defeat. As for Pakistan, it could only gain by cooperating in sparing humiliation to the Soviet Union. That would open the possibility for Pakistan to improve relations with this superpower.

Gulbuddin Hekmatyar, an engineer by training but with an impressive grasp of law, contributed to the improvement of the Geneva texts. In a consultation meeting with Pakistani officials, he suggested two significant modifications. He pointed out that Pakistan's signature on an agreement with Afghanistan would constitute recognition of the Kabul regime. Secondly, the agreement would require discontinuation of arms supply to 'rebels' but not to the Kabul regime. He was right on both points.

In friendly conversations at the foreign office in February 1988, Vorontsov was informed that Pakistan would publicly state that the signing of the agreement would not constitute recognition of the Kabul regime. A diplomat of world class, confident in his understanding of his country's policy and decisive in negotiations, he instantly agreed not to make this matter an issue. Nor did he contest the logic of the view that peace in Afghanistan required all sides to discontinue arms supply. On the Soviet side, he convincingly explained, Moscow could not go back on its existing commitments to Kabul. 'Negative symmetry' was not feasible, but when told that in that event 'positive symmetry' would ensue, and the mujahideen, too, could continue to receive supplies, he did not make an issue of the matter. The discussion served to preclude subsequent misunderstanding between Islamabad and Moscow.[24]

The final Geneva round began on 2 March 1988. The talks proceeded in slow motion because the Pakistan delegation did not have authorization to finalize the Accords. On their part, the Soviets conveyed their agreement to reduce the timeframe for withdrawal to nine months. The Kabul representatives still persisted in their objection to the phrase 'existing internationally recognized boundaries'[25] and suggested its substitution by the words 'international borders'. Pakistan considered it an artificial issue. The Geneva talks were not convened to debate the Durand Line. Pakistan had no difficulty in accepting the neutral phrase requiring the two states to refrain from the threat or use of force so as 'not to violate the boundaries of each other'.

The replacement of the Kabul regime was never a part of the Geneva negotiations but, as Diego Cordovez said in a statement issued on 8 April, 'it has been consistently recognized that the objective of a comprehensive settlement . . . can best be ensured by a broad-based Afghan Government' and to that end he agreed to provide his good offices. By that time, Zia realized that the formation of such a government could not be made a precondition for the conclusion of the Accords.

The foreign ministers of Afghanistan, Pakistan, and the Soviet Union, and the Secretary of State of the United States signed the Geneva Accords on 14 April 1988. Pakistan and the United States declared, on the occasion, that their signatures did not imply recognition of the Kabul regime. The US further declared that 'the obligations undertaken by the guarantors are symmetrical' and that it retained the right to provide military assistance to the Afghan parties, and would exercise restraint should the Soviet Union do so too. Pakistan also made the same point, and underlined the right of the Afghan people to self-determination.

The Geneva Accords marked the first time for the Soviet Union to agree to withdraw from a 'fraternal' state. Gorbachev acknowledged that the intervention was a 'mistake'. A Soviet journal blamed 'an inner group of a few Politburo members headed by Leonid Brezhnev (who), discounting the likely opposition of the Muslim world, China, the United States, and the West, decided to take the fateful decision.'[26] Over 13,000 Soviet soldiers were killed and 35,000 wounded.[27] The financial drain was estimated at 100 billion rubles. A classic example of 'imperial overstretch,'[28] the Afghanistan misadventure could well be considered the proverbial last straw that broke the camel's back. To say that, like the United States in Vietnam, the Soviet Union lost the war in Afghanistan due to pressures of domestic and international opinion is by no means to undervalue the courage and heroism of the mujahideen, and the fortitude and sacrifices of the Afghan people.

NOTES

1. For an authoritative account of Pakistan's policy in the Afghanistan crisis, see Former Foreign Minister Agha Shahi, *Pakistan's Security and Foreign Policy*, Progressive Publishers, Lahore, 1988.
2. The US State Department issued a prompt condemnation of the 'blatant' Soviet intervention. President Carter called the intervention a 'grave threat to peace,' proclaimed a boycott of the Moscow Olympics, and suspended arms limitation talks with Moscow. He expressed concern over the Soviet advance to 'within striking distance of the Indian Ocean and even the Persian Gulf . . . an area of vital strategic and economic significance to the survival of Western Europe, the Far East, and ultimately the United States.' West European, too, denounced the Soviet intervention, but with restraint that reflected their desire not to vitiate détente in Europe.
3. The author was the ambassador.
4. Riaz M. Khan, *Untying the Afghan Knot*, Progressive Publishers, Lahore, 1933, 18–20.
5. For detailed table see Riaz M. Khan, op. cit., 40.
6. Also, Washington had remained quiescent following the communist coup by the PDPA in April 1978, and President Carter had hardly reacted to the murder of American Ambassador Adolph Dubs in Kabul in February of that year. Now he was preoccupied with the hostage crisis in Iran.
7. Steve Coll, '*This Ghost War: The Secret History of the CIA, Afghanistan and bin Laden*', quoted in *Dawn*, Islamabad, 19 November 2004.
8. President Zia in NBC-TV 'Face the Nation' interview with Walter Cronkite, 18 May 1980. *Documents*, ed. K. Arif, 394.
9. Statement by Foreign Affairs Adviser Agha Shahi, 5 March 1980. *Documents*, ed. K. Arif, 388–90.
10. The package included $150 million in economic aid for F'82 and $3 billion for economic assistance and military sales credits for the period F'83-F'87. The data below relates to the economic component. *Economic Survey*, 1995–6, Finance Division, Islamabad.

1981	1982	1983	1984	1985	1986	1987	1988	1989	1990
57	88	224	275	302	313	312	346	347	351

(US$ million)

11. In testimony before a Congressional committee on 27 April 1981, Deputy Assistant Secretary of State Jane Coon acknowledged the injustice of past US policy, saying that sanctions were 'applied in the case of one country—Pakistan.' A few weeks later, Assistant Secretary of State James Buckley exuded under-

standing of Pakistan's perception that the threat to its security 'could not be met by conventional and political means.' For texts of statements, see *Documents*, ed. K. Arif.

12. US Department of State, 16 September 1981, *Documents*, ed. K. Arif, 457.
13. The package was carefully negotiated so as to increase the grant component for economic support funds. Still the interest differential on the defence component was initially 8 per cent. As interest rates changed in subsequent years, the differential was reduced. The follow-up agreement remained in force only for three years until 1990 and provided for $700 million a year, and the interest rate on military sales credits was reduced to below the market rate.
14. Riaz M. Khan, *Untying the Afghan Knot*, provides authoritative information on Pakistan's diplomacy and the UN-mediated negotiations leading to the Geneva Accords in April 1988.
15. Riaz M. Khan, op. cit., 107.
16. Selig Harrison, *Inside the Afghan Talks*, 31. Also, Barnett R. Rubin, *The Search for Peace in Afghanistan—From Buffer State to Failed State*, 63–5, and slightly different figures in Riaz M. Khan, 88.
17. Quoted by Diego Cordovez, Rubin, 40.
18. Rubin, 43.
19. Rubin, 77, based on press briefing by Diego Cordovez, 9 December 1986.
20. Shevardnadze told Secretary of State George Shultz on 16 September 1987: 'We will leave Afghanistan . . . I say with all responsibility that a political decision has been made.' Quoted from *Shultz, Turmoil* and *Tragedy*, 1090, in Rubin, 83.
21. Statement by Shevardnadze in a meeting of the Central Committee of CPSU in 1989, after cataloguing over 2,000 billion rubles spent by USSR on maintaining occupation of East European countries, creation of defence structure on the border with China, and in Afghanistan, reported in *Moscow News*, 1989. Author's memory.
22. Riaz M. Khan, 234.
23. This exchange took place on 9 February in the author's presence.
24. The author, then Foreign Secretary, had known Vorontsov for a decade. As ambassadors in New Delhi for four years around 1980 they established amicable relations of mutual trust.
25. This phrase was derived from the 1981 UN Declaration on the Inadmissibility of Intervention and Interference in the Internal Affairs of States.
26. *Literaturnaya Gazeta*, Moscow, 17 February 1988, quoted in Agha Shahi, 93.
27. K. M. Arif, 237, based on statements by General Alexei Lizichev and Prime Minister Nikolai Ryzhkov.
28. Paul Kennedy, *The Rise and Fall of Great Powers*. He ascribes the fall to 'imperial overstretch'.

Chapter 15

Kashmir: The Struggle for *Azadi*

Joseph Korbel, a Czechoslovak member of the UN Commission for India and Pakistan, concluded his book *Danger in Kashmir* with the following perceptive observations:

> The people of Kashmir have made it unmistakably known that they insist on being heard. ... The accession of the State of Jammu and Kashmir to India cannot be considered as valid by canons of international law. ... The issue itself cannot be sidetracked. The history of the case has made it clear that time has only aggravated, not healed the conflict; that neither the Pakistanis nor the Kashmiris will accept the status quo as a solution. ... No high hopes should be entertained that bilateral negotiations will lead to a settlement. ... The United Nations has a principal responsibility to seek a solution.

Korbel's assessment has stood the test of time. Neither has Pakistan accepted the status quo in Kashmir nor have the people of the state given in to Indian oppression and repression. Relations between the two countries have been marred by hostility and conflicts, and decent opinion worldwide and even in India regards India's failure to fulfill its solemn commitment to a UNSC resolution as an indelible blot on its honour.

Resisting Indian duress at the Shimla Conference in 1972, Pakistan neither compromised its own position on the Kashmir question nor allowed any prejudice to the right of self-determination of the people of Kashmir. In speeches in the UN General Assembly, Pakistan continued to draw the attention of the world community to the festering issue. Neither Pakistan nor India took any initiative, however, towards implementation of the commitment in the Shimla Agreement to discuss 'a final settlement of Jammu and Kashmir.'

Meanwhile, groaning under occupation and suppression, the people of Indian-held Kashmir grasped every opportunity to protest against the denial of their fundamental right to self-determination. In 1973, the valley exploded in protest following the discovery of a book in a library in Anantnag with a drawing of the Prophet.[1] As disaffection continued to intensify, the Indian government installed Sheikh Abdullah as chief minister once again to exploit whatever support he still had in order to pacify the people. Hankering for power after a long period in the political wilderness, he submitted to Indian terms. The people of Kashmir denounced him, and the Government of Pakistan condemned him for this new perfidy.[2] For the few years he remained alive, he had to rely on protection by the Indian police.

In February 1984, a group of Kashmiris in England kidnapped an Indian consular official and killed him after the Indian government refused to meet their demand for the release of a popular Kashmiri activist from jail in Delhi. The Kashmiri agitation gathered momentum as Indira Gandhi tried to suppress it by appointing a proven martinet as governor in Srinagar. Jagmohan Malhotra, who had demonstrated his ruthlessness during her authoritarian rule, used his sinister skills by playing Sheikh Abdullah's son-in-law, G. M. Shah, against Farooq Abdullah in 1984. When that did not work, Jagmohan imposed his own direct rule in March 1986. With unrest becoming chronic, Rajiv Gandhi again tried Farooq Abdullah as chief minister but to little avail.

In September 1986, six months prior to the election in Indian-held Kashmir (IHK), several popular political parties formed a United Muslim Front. Believing they could secure their political aspirations through the peaceful electoral process, the Front's young activists galvanized mass support. Over 75 per cent of the electorate turned out to vote. Always unwilling to accept popular opinion in the state, New Delhi panicked. The election held on 31 March 1987 was 'as unfree and unfair as any other'.[3] No one credited the result. The announcement that the United Front had won a token four out of seventy-six seats only added insult to injury. With hope in the peaceful process betrayed, the shocked and thoroughly disillusioned Kashmiri activists decided to resort to 'other means' to secure their fundamental rights.

A popular uprising was thus born. Called Tehrik (movement), it gathered rapid momentum. Peaceful to begin with, the Tehrik organized mass anti-India demonstrations and *hartals* (shutdowns of private business and transport).

As the Indian government responded with a heavy hand, its policy evoked strong condemnation in Pakistan. People demonstrated in cities and towns all over the country. The media condemned Indian atrocities. The Government of Pakistan denounced India for its inhuman policy. Not only was the normalization of Pakistan-India relations halted; much of the progress made since 1972 was reversed.

In IHK, radical Kashmiri youth turned to militancy. An attempt was made to attack Chief Minister Farooq Abdullah in May 1987. Kashmiri youth banded together in armed groups. The largest among them was the Kashmiri Hizbul Mujahideen. Also active were Al Baraq, Al Omar, and others. A Kashmiri politician of the Bharatiya Janata Party was killed in September 1989. In December, the daughter of the Indian Home Minister, Mufti Mohammad Sayeed, was kidnapped but freed unharmed after New Delhi agreed to the demand for the release of five Kashmiris from detention.

Determined to maintain occupation, the Indian government brought Jagmohan Malhotra back as governor in January 1990. During an earlier tenure he had demonstrated a savage streak. 'A rabid communalist,' he now beat 'all previous records of fascist regimes in the world in the matter of unleashing terror and oppression on the innocent people of the state.'[4] Jagmohan proceeded from the premise that 'every Muslim in Kashmir is a militant today. All of them are for secession from India.' Believing that 'The bullet is the only solution,'[5] he 'converted Kashmir into a free-fire zone' imposing 'continuous and indefinite curfews.' Local volunteers who tried to alleviate suffering were 'arrested and mercilessly beaten'. Even free kitchens to distribute food to people confined to their homes were not allowed. Correspondents of the foreign media were prohibited from entering Kashmir. Unseen by the world, the Indian military and para-military forces, already given special powers and immunity from prosecution, now resorted to arbitrary arrests, searches of homes, rape and looting, and punitive destruction of houses.

Jagmohan was removed after months, less for what he did than for his embarrassing rhetoric. His successor, Girish Saxena, added even more ruthless techniques to crush the Kashmiri uprising. Captured militants were subjected to torture until they agreed to assist the armed forces. They were then told to rejoin the militants as embedded informants. The Indian government passed the Armed Forces Special Powers Act (AFSPA), authorizing the use of lethal force and giving immunity from prosecution. Human rights organizations documented the widespread abuses. They published one report after another vividly depicting the inhuman repression by Indian police and armed forces in Kashmir:

> Despite serious criticism, India is continuing its repressive policy against the Kashmiri people to crush their popular movement for right of self-determination. . . .
>
> Widespread human rights violations in the state since January 1990 have been attributed to the Indian army, and the paramilitary Border Security Force (BSF) and Central Reserve Police Force (CRPF). A 145,000 strong force of CRPF was flown into the state at that time. Cordon-and-search operations are frequently conducted in areas of armed opposition activity. . . . Torture is reported to be routinely used during these combing operations as well as in army camps, interrogation centres, police stations and prisons. Indiscriminate beatings are common and rape in particular appears to be routine.
>
> In Jammu and Kashmir, rape is practised as part of a systematic attempt to humiliate and intimidate the local population during counter-insurgency operations.
>
> *Amnesty International*[6]

> Indian forces in Kashmir have engaged in massive human rights violations including extra-judicial executions, rape, torture and deliberate assaults on health care workers. . . . Such killings are carried out as a matter of policy. More than any other phenomenon, these deliberate killings reveal the magnitude of the human rights crisis in Kashmir.
>
> *Asia Watch and Physicians for Human Rights*[7]

> Rape is not uncommon and there is evidence of its employment as an instrument of terror.
>
> *Fédération Internationale des Droigts d'Homme*[8]

> Amnesty International repeatedly expressed grave concern about continuing reports of deaths in custody and of extra-judicial killings.
>
> *Amnesty International*[9]

> Serious human rights abuses, extra-judicial executions and other political killings and excessive use of force by security forces in Jammu and Kashmir and other northern states; torture and rape by police and other agents of Government, deaths of suspects in police custody, arbitrary arrests and in-communication detentions are rampant.

> Researchers for Amnesty International and Human Rights Watch were not permitted to visit Jammu and Kashmir.
>
> *US Department of State*[10]

> The years of armed struggle have taken a heavy toll of lives lost, about which reliable figures are impossible to obtain. According to official (Indian) handouts 19,866 people have died in Jammu and Kashmir since January 1990. . . .
>
> The number of people who have 'disappeared' in Jammu and Kashmir is difficult to estimate because of widespread fear for relatives. . . . According to some observers the number could be as high as 2,000.
>
> *Amnesty International*[11]

> The figures [of those who 'disappeared'] vary between 700 to 2,000. However, the recent statement of Mushtaq Ahmad Lone in the state assembly substantiates the higher figure. . . . He said that the government is aware that 3,257 people are missing.
>
> *Economic and Political Weekly*[12]

The Kashmiri freedom struggle faced a new obstacle after the collapse of the Soviet Union. An imaginary fear of Islam was built up in the West in the early 1990s. Considered an asset so long as it inspired opposition to Soviet expansion in Afghanistan, Islam was now projected as a threat to Western civilization.[13] The word 'fundamentalism' came into sudden vogue to discredit political movements of Muslim peoples, even though their aims were freedom from alien occupation, respect for human rights, and democracy. Exploiting this new environment of prejudice, India labelled Kashmiri activists as extremists, fundamentalists, and terrorists. The United States, which had earlier imposed sanctions on Pakistan because of alleged violation of the Pressler Law, considered placing Pakistan on its list of terrorist states.

To accelerate the favourable change in international opinion, the Indian government adopted a new posture of seeming willingness for political accommodation. It released some of the more prominent Kashmiri political leaders who were under prolonged detention in prisons in India. On returning to Srinagar, they promoted the formation of the All Parties Hurriyat Conference (APHC) in February 1993, bringing together leaders of some thirty political parties and groups.[14] Mirwaiz Umar Farooq, the young grandson of Mirwaiz

Mohammad Yusuf, who founded the Muslim Conference in 1932, was elected as chairman. Recognizing that the question of whether Kashmir should accede to Pakistan or become independent was premature, APHC emphasized the priority objective of ending Indian occupation and rescuing the Kashmir people from repression. APHC has remained united on the common plank of self-determination and the ultimate aim of *Azadi*, a word that can be translated as freedom or independence. While not involved in militancy, most APHC leaders defended armed struggle because India had closed the political option.

The apparent change in Indian policy of opening a political window did not lead to any reduction in the use of force. Actually, repression was intensified through the formation of a militia of captured Kashmiri militants who, unable to withstand torture, turned into Indian agents. Led by Mohammad Yusuf Parray, alias Kuka Parray, they acted as a fifth column against their own kith and kin.

Reacting to Indian atrocities, Kashmiri volunteers from outside IHK, and even former Afghan mujahideen and members of the Pakistan-based Lashkar-e-Taiba, began to enter the occupied state to join Kashmiri militants. India seized on reports to attribute the 'unrest' and 'secessionist attitude' in Kashmir to 'elements' coming into the valley from the Pakistan side to 'fuel the problem'.[15] The government of Pakistan was accused of providing training and arms to Kashmiri militants. Pakistan denied these accusations saying it provided only political, diplomatic, and moral support. The credibility of the denial was undermined, however, by reports that jihadi groups in Pakistan were recruiting volunteers to join the Kashmiri struggle.

A reputable international journal reported in 1999 that 'about 24,000 people have died in the decade-long insurgency, say the (Indian) police. The militants say 60,000.'[16] Through such brutality, Indian police claimed to have achieved 'pacification'. Yet, 'Srinagar still looks like a city dumped inside a maximum security prison with guns poking through piles of sandbags on nearly every corner.'[17]

Appalled by the world's indifference to the plight of the Kashmiri people, thought in official circles in Pakistan seemed to turn once again to what could be done to attract international attention. The Kargil episode was perhaps a consequence of such a consideration. Kargil was described as 'the latest battle in a conflict that has taken tens of thousands of lives over the last decade.' Summary executions of suspected militants and killings of civilians in reprisal attacks took place. No wonder that Kashmiris 'have no love for the Indian security forces, which human rights groups say regularly ransack and burn villages, torture prisoners and assassinate suspects.'[18]

In the event, Kargil too failed to focus international attention on the need to resolve the Kashmir question. Instead, it provided India with another pretext to intensify repression. The toll continued to mount. An independent international study group reported in November 2002:

> The Indian government officially estimates 30,000 deaths in the last twelve years. Kashmiris, including the All Parties Hurriyat Conference, estimate between 80,000 and 100,000 deaths. Most observers estimate there to have been roughly 60,000 deaths.[19]
>
> The deep sense of insecurity (in IHK) can be directly traced to the thousands of disappearances that have occurred over thirteen years with little accountability. Virtually every one in Srinagar knows someone who has been killed, arrested or tortured, and almost no one has been unaffected by the state of physical insecurity.[20]

Following 9/11, India started accusing Pakistan of sponsoring terrorist attacks in IHK. The 13 December 2001 attack on the premises of the Indian parliament was blamed on Pakistan and without any evidence New Delhi proceeded to curtail diplomatic and communications relations with Pakistan. To raise the tension further, it concentrated the bulk of its armed forces on Pakistan's borders and the Line of Control. Pakistan condemned the attack and decided to ban Harkat-ul-Mujahidin and Jaish-e-Mohammad in January 2002.

The Organization of Islamic Cooperation adopted strong resolutions upholding the Kashmiri right of self-determination and condemning Indian repression. OIC's attempts to obtain access to Kashmir for investigation of the grim situation were, however, blocked by India. Pakistan's efforts to secure official cognisance of the plight of the Kashmiri people by the United Nations Human Rights Commission did not succeed. Too many of the member states of the commission took a restrictive view of its competence, were opposed to international prying into their own record, or were disinclined to displease India. Pakistan was obliged to withdraw the draft resolution it had proposed for adoption by the commission in 1994 and 1995.

The United States and some other governments issued statements critical of Indian agencies for arbitrary arrests, torture, and deaths in custody. But some of them also criticized Kashmiri militants for acts of a terrorist nature. Pakistan, too, came under adverse notice for police excesses in Karachi, undercutting its credentials for mobilization of support for Kashmiris.

Formation of a new government in India following the May 1996 elections raised optimism. The manifesto of Janata Dal, the lead party in the coalition government, envisaged discussions with Pakistan to resolve the Kashmir dispute, 'keeping in mind the sentiments of the people of the state.'[21] Also promising was Prime Minister Deve Gowda's statement that he would 'definitely take an initiative to defuse the tension between the two countries.'[22] In a warm letter of felicitations to him, Prime Minister Benazir Bhutto suggested talks 'aimed at the settlement of the issue of Jammu and Kashmir and other outstanding matters between the two countries.' In his response, Gowda made no mention of the core issue. He suggested a 'wide-ranging and comprehensive dialogue' aimed at the realization of 'a firm relationship of trust, setting aside the difficulties that impede amity and cooperation.'[23] These formulations implying relegation of the Kashmir dispute seemed to throw cold water on hopes for a new beginning in Pakistan-India relations. The Indian decision to organize sham elections in the Indian-held part of the state further corroborated the lack of seriousness of its professions for improved relations with Pakistan.

The Hurriyat Conference boycotted the election for the Indian parliament held in May, and the state elections in September 1996. In the past, almost all elections in the occupied state had been rigged, but this was the most farcical exercise in history. Independent media reports eloquently depicted scenes of poor villagers driven at gunpoint to polling stations. Hurriyat leaders were placed under detention and anti-poll protest meetings were prohibited. The National Conference, which has historically provided India with a political front for its annexationist aims, agreed to participate in the state election on the basis of secret understandings reportedly given to Farooq Abdullah by the Deve Gowda government. The popular boycott made it clear that elections under the Indian aegis could not be a substitute for a free and impartial plebiscite under UN auspices.

The toll continued to mount as India persisted in repression. By 2004, the APHC said more than 80,000 Kashmiris had died at the hands of the Indian occupation forces.

5 August 2019: Annexation of the Valley

As has been noted earlier, Kashmiri protest movements had voiced Kashmir's disputes and grievances with the Indian government in Indian-controlled Kashmir from the beginning. These protests became more vigorous after 1989, with Kashmiris in armed conflict with the Indian government based on the demand for self-determination. They became a regular feature whose tempo sometimes slackened but then increased again. In 2008, massive demonstrations occurred after the Indian-administered Jammu and Kashmir state government plan to transfer 100 acres of land to a trust which runs the Hindu Amarnath shrine in the Muslim-majority Kashmir valley. The largest protests saw more than a half million people waving Pakistani flags and crying for freedom at a rally on 18 August. Pro-independence Kashmiri leader Mirwaiz Umar Farooq warned that the peaceful uprising could lead to an upsurge in violence if India›s heavy-handed crackdown on protests was not restrained. The year 2010 had seen a still further increase in the number and intensity of such protests. After an encounter, said to be fake, between local youth and security forces, thousands of youths pelted security forces with rocks, burned government offices, and attacked railway stations and official vehicles in steadily intensifying violence. As observers and scholars confirm, Indian forces have committed many human rights abuses and acts of terror against the Kashmiri civilian population including extrajudicial killing, rape, torture, and enforced disappearances. Amnesty International has accused the Indian government of refusing to prosecute perpetrators of abuses in the region.

On 8 July 2016, the militant leader Burhan Muzaffar Wani was cornered by the Indian security forces and killed. Following his death, protests and demonstrations took root, leading to an "amplified instability" in the Kashmir valley. Curfews were imposed in all 10 districts of Kashmir. Over 100 civilians died and over 17,000 were injured in clashes with the police. More than 600 received pellet injuries and may lose their eyesight. Cellphone and internet services were blocked, and newspapers restricted in many parts of the state.

This lockdown situation prevailed right up to the Pulwama incident on 14 February 2019, the reckless Indian Air Force attack on Balakot on 26 February 2019 and Pakistan's carefully calculated retaliation.

On 5th August 2019, Indian Home Minister, Amit Shah of the BJP told parliament that a decree abolishing Article 370 of the Indian Constitution had been signed by President Ram Nath Kovind and the measure came into force "at once". This Article had been a provision that granted special autonomous status to Jammu and Kashmir. It was drafted in Part XXI of the Constitution, which relates to Temporary, Transitional and Special Provisions. However, it had earlier been understood to have achieved a permanent status. It confirmed that the (Indian Occupied) state of Jammu and Kashmir had a separate status to other states and enjoyed the power to have a separate constitution, a state flag, and autonomy over the internal administration of the state. Article 370, along with Article 35A, defined that the Jammu and Kashmir state's residents live under a separate set of laws, including those related to citizenship, ownership of property, and fundamental rights, as compared to residents of other Indian states. As a result of this provision, Indian citizens from other states could not purchase land or property in Jammu & Kashmir.

The presidential order of August 2019 superseded earlier orders and made all the provisions of the Indian constitution applicable to (Indian occupied) Jammu and Kashmir, based on a resolution passed in both houses of India's parliament with a 2/3 majority.

In addition, the Jammu and Kashmir Reorganisation Act was passed by the parliament, enacting the division of the (Indian occupied) state of Jammu and Kashmir into two "union territories", to be called Union Territory of Jammu and Kashmir and Union Territory of Ladakh. The reorganisation took place on 31 October 2019.

Clause 7 of the original Instrument of Accession that had been signed by Maharaja Hari Singh had declared that the State could not be compelled to accept any future Constitution enacted by of India. The State was within its rights to draft its own Constitution and to decide for itself what additional powers to extend to the Central

Government. Article 370 had ben designed to protect those rights. Article 370 had, among other provisions, limited the central legislative powers over the State to the three subjects of defence, foreign affairs and communications. Article 370 had allowed its own death by permitting plebiscite. Clearly, this would have been one of the reasons for the Indian Government's recent abolition of Article 370 of the Indian Constitution.

These abrupt and fundamentally disruptive measures made possible by Hindu nationalist Prime Minister Narendra Modi's recently achieved huge majorities in the Indian Parliament, are clearly aimed at altering the demographic situation by promoting a large scale influx of both capital and "settlers" from outside the Kashmir region in the manner of the Israeli "settlements" in Palestine.

Subsequently, there was almost continuous curfew in Kashmir from August 2019 to February 2021. Even after that, there continue to be further periodic declarations of curfew for specified periods of time, while in some parts of the region the curfew is almost continuous. Harsh acts, military and police oppression by the Indian authorities are the order of the day, but which, owing to complete blackout of news and a blockage of social media are not being reported and are largely concealed from the world.

In 2020, the Indian government enacted a new 'Domicile Law', allowing certain classes of Indians from other parts of the country to become permanent residents of Kashmir, thus giving 'legal' cover to its designs to alter the demographic balance in the region. Following tensions and some clashes with Chines forces in the Ladakh region, the Indian government used this pretext to issue new laws to expand military bases and create hundreds of thousands of new 'housing units' in the region.

After a prolonged illness, the aging Kashmiri political leader Syed Ali Shah Geelani, who had earlier effectively retired from politics, developed breathing complications and passed away on 1 September 2021 at his home in Srinagar. The Indian government was clearly set on denying him a proper funeral and thereby preventing the risk of any public demonstrations. The police forcibly took away his body and buried it at an unknown place, as his son Nayeem reported. A FIR was registered against his family members for draping his body in a Pakistani flag. Restrictions on travel and Internet were once again imposed in Kashmir shortly after Geelani's death.

Thus, the suffering of the Kashmiri people, especially of the majority Muslim population, continues unabated. Beyond even the denial of their right to self-determination, they have effectively been imprisoned and been subjected to oppression in their own home region.

NOTES

1. *Book of Knowledge—Children's Encyclopaedia*, Lamb, op. cit., 304.
2. Statement by Prime Minister Z. A. Bhutto, quoted in Lamb, 308.
3. Lamb, 331.
4. Justice Burhanuddin Farooqi, *Writ Petition*, 30.
5. Farooqi, 31, quoting *Current*, Bombay, 26 May–1 June 1990.
6. Amnesty International, *India—Torture, Rape and Deaths in Custody,* (New York, 1992), 20–1.
7. Asia Watch and Physicians for Human Rights, Washington, 1993.
8. *Fédération Internationale des Droigts d'Home*, Paris.
9. Amnesty International, Annual Report, 1994, 159.
10. US Department of State, Report on Human Rights Situation in India, 30 January 1998.
11. *'Disappearances' in Jammu and Kashmir*, Amnesty International Report, ASA—February 1999.
12. Gautam Naviakha, 'Internal War and Civil Rights, Disappearances in Jammu and Kashmir', *Economic and Political Weekly*, Mumbai, 12 June 1999.
13. Samuel Huntington, 'Clash of Civilizations,' *Foreign Affairs*, Summer 1993.
14. Prominent leaders included Syed Ali Geelani of Jamaat-i-Islami, Yasin Malik of Jammu & Kashmir Liberation Front, Abdul Gani Lone of the People's Conference, and Mirwaiz Umar Farooq of the Muslim Conference.
15. Statement by Prime Minister Narasimha Rao, *The Hindustan Times*, New Delhi, 8 June 1992. In the detailed account of his life in an Indian prison—*Roodad-i-Qafs*—Syed Ali Gailani, President of All Parties Hurriyat Conference, gives the names of the leaders of the movement for *Azadi* who were detained and murdered by Indian forces.
16. *The Economist*, 22 May 1999, 'Survey India and Pakistan' 10.
17. Ibid.
18. *The New York Times*, 21 June 1999, report by Stephen Kinzer.
19. The International Crisis Group, *Kashmir: The View from Srinagar*, 21 November 2002, 4, footnote 4.
20. Ibid., 11.
21. Quoted in Prime Minister Benazir Bhutto's letter of 3 June 1996 to Prime Minister Deve Gowda, *The News*, Islamabad, 4 June 1996.
22. *Dawn*, Karachi, 1 June 1996, Gowda's statement, report by *Reuters* & *APP.*
23. *The News*, Islamabad, 10 June 1996.

Chapter 16

The Afghanistan Civil War, 1990–1998

The Afghan people suffered grievously in the struggle to recover freedom. A million people perished and some six million people had to take refuge outside their country, largely in Pakistan and Iran. The economic and human infrastructure of Afghanistan was devastated on a scale with few parallels. Already one of the least developed countries, it suffered fearful damage to agriculture, irrigation systems, roads, transport, and educational institutions—indeed, its entire infrastructure. Nor did its travail end with the withdrawal of the Soviet forces. The regime the Soviets installed under Najibullah fought on for nearly three more years. After the proxy administration finally collapsed in April 1992, a protracted war of succession began among the mujahideen political parties, founded apparently in the personal power ambitions of their leaders, but progressively exposing its ethnic basis. For their epic sacrifices, the Afghan people deserved a better fate than the long nightmare of internecine fighting, political disintegration, and economic collapse.

The mujahideen started on a hopeful note of unity after Najibullah's fall. At a meeting in Peshawar on 24 April 1992, the Alliance leaders reached an agreement. An Islamic Council headed by Sibghatullah Mojaddedi was installed for two months, after which Professor Burhanuddin Rabbani was to become president for four months. A transitional government was then to be formed for two years. Mojaddedi abided by the accord, but Rabbani refused to yield power when his term expired. Fighting broke out among the mujahideen parties.

Brokering the Peshawar Accord in concert with Saudi Arabia and Iran, Pakistan worked for unity among the Afghan parties. Gulbuddin Hekmatyar, said to be Pakistan's favourite, did not even figure in the new power structure. Actually, he was respected by Pakistan and other supporters of the Afghan insurgency because 'he fielded the most effective anti-Soviet fighters.'[1]

After Rabbani's refusal to hold elections for his successor led to discord and dissension in the country, Pakistan, Iran, and Saudi Arabia again joined hands to promote another accord among the Afghan leaders. At a meeting in Islamabad on 7 March 1993, the Afghan leaders agreed on the formation of a government for a period of 18 months, with Professor Rabbani continuing as president and Engineer Hekmatyar becoming prime minister. Although the Afghan leaders reconfirmed the Islamabad accord during visits to Saudi Arabia and Iran, it was not implemented. The composition of the cabinet to be 'formed by the Prime Minister in consultation with the President' was not agreed upon. Hekmatyar felt too insecure to even enter Kabul. The accord soon broke down, and Hekmatyar attacked the capital. Though he was repulsed, the attractive city, which had largely escaped destruction during the liberation struggle, was severely damaged as a result of the intra-mujahideen fighting. The United Nations Representative for Afghanistan made spasmodic efforts to promote reconciliation between the Rabbani government and its opponents. Although little progress was achieved toward unity, a certain calm seemed to have descended over the divided country in 1995. The Tajik-dominated Rabbani government ruled over five of the central provinces, Abdur Rashid Dostum's Uzbek militia controlled the northern provinces, and a Pushtoon *shura* or council governed the eastern provinces from Jalalabad while the Taliban controlled the southern provinces.

The Mujahideen Alliance failed to establish an effective central administration. The Northern Alliance received assistance from foreign countries to sustain itself in power, but it did little to establish security, much less begin economic reconstruction of the ruined country. The absence of a national army, financial resources, and administrative reach led to anarchical conditions in the country, with warlords and local commanders trying to impose personal control through intimidation and extortion.

Pakistan's expectations of friendly relations with the government of Islamic Afghanistan received a shock on 6 September 1995, when its embassy in Kabul was sacked by a government-sponsored mob. One employee was killed, the Ambassador and forty officials were badly injured, and the building and all official records were burnt. Still, Pakistan exercised patience and prospects of good relations seemed to brighten in May 1996 when a visiting Afghan government delegation acknowledged liability for the reconstruction of the embassy, even though it pleaded lack of resources to discharge the responsibility.

The Rise of the Taliban

Alumni of religious seminaries, the *taliban* have a history of opposition to intervention by foreign powers. They participated in Afghan armed resistance against the British in the 19th century, the Soviets in the 20th, and the Americans in the 21st. Belief in the supremacy of the Islamic system of government and opposition to penetration of what they regard as un-Islamic culture has been their key motivation. Events since the 1990s have proved that a Pakistani Minister's assumption the Taliban were 'our boys' was a fallacy; that of the Americans that the Taliban were Pakistan's proxy an egregious blunder.

After the liberation struggle, the Taliban retired to their traditional life of prayer, teaching and providing religious guidance. Mullah Mohammad Omar became a prayer leader and a Madrassa teacher in a village near Kandahar. No one has discovered any evidence of his aspiration to political power. The rise of Taliban to power was a consequence of the failure of the mujahideen to forge the unity necessary for peace and stability. Instead, they fought one another in a scramble for power. Meanwhile, each sought to control the territory where he maintained his fighters, but failed to maintain discipline. Local commanders outraged people with corrupt practices, arbitrary tolls, and molestation of innocents. Incensed by a local Mujahideen Commander's rape of two girls, Mullah Omar led a crowd that hanged the perpetrator. Spontaneous uprising in the countryside urged Mullah Omar to rid them of abusive commanders who 'brought suffering on the Afghans and violated Islamic teachings. Mullah Omar set out with forty-five Taliban to punish the culprits. Thus started the Taliban movement in August 1994. Warlords along the way to the north joined the popular movement with their stocks of weapons, and the Taliban whirlwind reached the outskirts of Kabul in April 1996. The Rabbani regime, debilitated by internecine squabbling, fled the capital to Mazar-i-Sharif without a fight. By September, the Taliban controlled the whole of Afghanistan south of the Hindu Kush.

Mullah Omar and his followers were Afghanistan-centric in motivation; hostility to the US was inspired by Osama bin Laden. The Bush administration discounted the inherent strength of the Taliban and blamed Pakistan for their success. In a conversation with the author (then foreign minister) three months before 9/11, National Security Director Condoleezza Rice fulminated against the Taliban and Pakistan. Incredibly, the reputed scholar assumed Pakistan was responsible for the rise of the Taliban, completely losing sight of the fact that Pakistan, under nuclear sanctions that cut off financial aid and arms sales, lacked the means on which influence travels. Fatally underestimating the Afghan national aversion to foreign domination, the US blundered into a futile war on Afghanistan. The Rabbani regime and foreign critics of the Taliban exaggerated the role of Pakistani army veterans they accused of aiding the Taliban. Failing to recognize that the rise of the Taliban was the result of internecine squabbling amongst the mujahideen warlords and popular disgust with their misrule, they also ignored the historical fact that Pakistan had, throughout the struggle against the Soviets, sought to promote unity among the mujahideen leaders, and after the fall of the Najibullah proxy regime, also successfully promoted consensus among them for the formation of a government acceptable to them. On two occasions, in 1992 and 1994, Pakistan collaborated with Saudi Arabia and Iran to successfully persuade the mujahideen to form a unity government. The breakdown of both accords was attributable to the internecine conflict amongst the mujahideen, with different ethnic leaders ranged against one another for domination of the country.

In May 1997, the situation took another dramatic turn as a result of dissension in the Uzbek ranks. Accusing Dostum of pursuing personal power at the expense of the unity of the country, the Uzbek warlord's former foreign minister, General Abul Malik, revolted and invited the Taliban forces to take over Mazar-i-Sharif. It fell to the allies on 24 May. Dostum fled to Turkey. By now Rabbani, the titular president of the country, and Hekmatyar had taken refuge in Iran, and the Taliban controlled some 90 per cent of Afghan territory.

After four days, the Taliban lost control of Mazar-i-Sharif. The Uzbek and the Shiite forces balked at the Taliban attempt to centralize power in their hands. Objecting to the order for surrender of arms, the Uzbek force took the Taliban contingent prisoner on 28 May. A few months later, General Dostum staged a comeback, driving out General Malik, who fled to Iran. The Northern Alliance was revived. Hopes of restoration of peace and unity appeared to recede as the country became divided along geographic and ethnic fault-lines.

The Taliban succeeded in recapturing Mazar-i-Sharif and most of the northern provinces in 1998. They also extended their control to parts of the Hazara areas. Their repeated efforts failed, however, to dislodge Ahmad Shah Massoud from his stronghold of the Panjsher Valley and areas to the north of Kabul, with his artillery launching recurrent salvos on the hapless capital.

Meanwhile, the Taliban established better law and order in the territory under their control than the Afghan people had seen for two decades. Their anti-vice squads received popular support. Security conditions improved. Traffic became orderly and their judicial system provided expeditious, if summary, justice. Men of faith and integrity, the Taliban lived austerely so taxation was light. The vast majority of the people welcomed the Taliban's success in disarming lawless gangs, restoring peace, and providing an administration that was religious, modest, and uncorrupt.

A simple and idealistic group with only religious education, the Taliban lacked sophistication as well as understanding of international law and world politics. They antagonized the inhabitants of the capital, which had been groomed by the Afghan rulers as an island of modernity in a sea of conservative and tribal countryside. The stringent restrictions they imposed upon women evoked denunciation, more abroad than within.

The narrow and extremist interpretation of Islam by the Taliban chief, who was proclaimed head of Muslims (*Amirul-Muslimeen*), offended even Muslim countries, who felt mocked and humiliated by the Taliban parody of their great faith. They castigated the Taliban's archaic interpretation of Islam, especially the corporal punishments. Few Islamic countries endorsed the Taliban version of the *Shariah* law. The Islamic Republic of Iran denounced the Taliban for providing another pretext for prejudice against Islam. Tehran's reservations about the Taliban were founded in a number of factors. Like other neighbours of multi-ethnic and multi-sect Afghanistan, Iran had supported a composite government in Kabul with a due share for Tajiks and Hazaras, just as Pakistan hoped for a due share for the Pushtoons and the Uzbeks. Largely Pushtoon and Sunni, the Taliban were perceived to discriminate against the non-Pushtoons and the Shias. The denial of human rights to women, their confinement and ban on employment outside homes, and the closure of schools for girls earned worldwide obloquy. The entire international community denounced the demolition of the Buddha statues in Bamiyan, an archaeological heritage of world history and civilization. Particularly unacceptable in international law was the Taliban complicity in the abuse of asylum by Osama bin Laden and his followers for their terrorist operations.

Opinion in the West was appalled by the stringent interpretation of the *Shariah* laws by the Taliban, in particular the closure of schools for girls and ban on employment for women outside their homes in Kabul.

Moscow's reaction against the Taliban appeared founded in the apprehension that their religious extremism would be exported to the Central Asian republics, posing a threat to the security and stability of the area the fallen great power now termed as 'near abroad'. Some of these republics also feared that the Taliban entertained 'aggressive designs'.[2]

The UN Security Council adopted a Russia-sponsored resolution on 22 October 1996, condemning Taliban discrimination against women and calling for immediate cessation of hostilities, an end to the supply of arms and ammunition from outside, and resumption of political dialogue among all Afghan parties. The resolution was largely ignored however by the Afghan factions. Efforts by the UN special envoy, Herbert Holl, to promote an intra-Afghan dialogue made little progress.

A Proxy War

Objectively, all neighbours of Afghanistan had a common interest in an end to the civil war, and the formation of a broad-based government in Kabul that would ensure the safety of different ethnic and sectarian segments of the population and create conditions conducive to the return of the refugees. Peace and unity, moreover, would facilitate transit and trade, as well as the construction of oil and gas pipelines, to the benefit of all countries of the region, especially land-locked Afghanistan, which would earn substantial amounts in transit fees. Despite the manifest long-term advantages of peace in Afghanistan, the neighbours seemed stuck in a miasma of rivalries and suspicions.

Foreign military assistance to the warring Afghan parties 'continued unabated throughout 1997,' according to the UN Secretary General. In his report[3] to the Security Council, he cited eyewitness accounts of military deliveries in an unmarked aircraft to the Northern Alliance and in truck caravans to the Taliban. Bitterly denouncing these activities as 'blatant violations of General Assembly and Security Council resolutions,' he mocked these foreign providers who 'enthusiastically proclaim their support to the UN peace-making efforts' but 'continue to fan the conflict by pouring in arms, money, and other supplies to their preferred Afghan factions.' Not surprisingly, their actions 'raised suspicions and worsened relations among the countries in the region.'

Reminiscent of 'proxy wars' of a bygone era, the situation in Afghanistan was tragic for the Afghan people. The 'foreign providers' were said to be engaged in this new 'Great Game' with high stakes in the competition for access to the rich petroleum and gas resources of the Caspian basin. A less Machiavellian explanation could be found in the context of the identical desire of all the neighbours of Afghanistan to save themselves from a further spillover of the Afghan civil war.

Fatal Blunders

Isolated internationally because of their extremist interpretation of Islam, the Taliban invited hostility by their policy of welcoming foreign Muslims and providing them with military training and arms. Many Arab and Central Asian states, as well as Russia, asked Pakistan to detain and extradite their nationals who engaged in subversive activities, abusing residence or transit facilities in Pakistan. Islamabad was not dismissive of the concerns but was reluctant to intervene in the autonomous tribal areas on its border with Afghanistan. Many of the foreign militants had come to Pakistan to join the jihad against the Soviet forces in Afghanistan. Having developed contacts in the areas along the border, and being experts at forging documents and changing addresses, they were difficult to find. Their governments, however, held Pakistan to blame. Algeria and Uzbekistan particularly made strong and repeated protests.

The Taliban failed to see the writing on the wall and grossly misjudged their capacity to resist. The first sign of the gathering storm was Security Council Resolution 1189 of 13 August 1998, condemning terrorist attacks on US embassies in Kenya and Tanzania and calling on all states to take effective steps for the prevention of terrorist attacks and prosecution of culprits. Washington blamed Osama bin Laden for the crime. After the terrorist attack on the *USS Cole*, Security Council Resolution 1267 of 15 October 1999 demanded that the Taliban turn over bin Laden to justice, and imposed sanctions on the Afghan airline. The eight-page Resolution 1333 of 19 December 2000 not only reiterated condemnation of the Taliban and demanded the surrender of bin Laden, but also called upon all states to prevent the supply of arms to the Taliban, curtail contacts with their officials, and freeze their assets or suffer sanctions. The Taliban ignored the demands in repeated resolutions of the Security Council under Chapter VII, and merely went on reiterating their demand for evidence, which was implicitly considered sufficient by the Security Council.

In Retrospect

A more sinister legacy of the Afghan crisis for Pakistan was the spill-over of extremism and weapons from Afghanistan, to which was soon added the influx of narcotics. Modern weapons from Afghanistan proliferated across Pakistan, giving rise to a 'Kalashnikov culture'. Dacoits and sectarian extremists now had more lethal weapons than the police. Hundreds of foreign citizens who came to join the jihad stayed behind in Pakistan, and some of them indulged in acts of terrorism. The bombing of the Egyptian embassy in Islamabad in November 1995 was attributed to them. Also, agents of the Rabbani regime in Kabul perpetrated acts of sabotage in Pakistan. A car-bomb explosion in a Peshawar bazaar killed over forty and wounded a hundred innocent people in December 1995.

The glorification of the mujahideen, however sincere on the part of many in Pakistan, and expedient and cynical on that of the United States with its sole aim of defeating the Soviets, proved equally short-sighted and damaging for both. In Pakistan, it encouraged exploitation of religion for the narrow ends of the regime and skewed and vitiated the balance against the modernist vision of its founding father.[4] It sowed seeds that later sprouted extremism and militancy that were to become a nightmare for both countries.

The Russian people were rightly critical of the Soviet invasion of Afghanistan as 'a great mistake'.[5] Afghans can similarly blame their communist leaders for the disaster that befell their country. Pakistanis alone have few scapegoats. They generally approved of President Zia's policy of support for the Afghans. Few foresaw the consequences of involvement and the grave problems that would emerge in the wake of the conflict. Western supporters of the Afghan struggle, rightly critical of the Afghan warring parties, had themselves to blame for walking away, but had to pay a high price some years later. Pakistan, once praised for 'shouldering great responsibilities for mankind . . . (and its) courageous and compassionate role,'[6] found itself left in the lurch, saddled with the burden of refugees and the consequences of the strife next door.

Was Pakistan's policy misconceived? In retrospect, the answer is easy to give, but, alas, humans are not gifted with prescience and policies have to be devised—and can be fairly judged—in the context of the time and contemporary knowledge. Given the history of Soviet expansionism, Islamabad's sense of alarm in 1979 was not a figment of its imagination. Pakistan was neither in a position to challenge the Soviet superpower nor to ignore the intervention without peril to its security. An alternative to the middle course it pursued seems difficult to conceive even in retrospect. Success and failure can be a measure of policies, but human struggle cannot be appraised in isolation from the nobility of the cause. The Soviet intervention was morally and legally wrong; the Afghan resistance was right. Pakistan's decision in favour of solidarity with the fraternal people of Afghanistan was not only morally right but based on enlightened self-interest.

Could the consequences of the protracted conflict in terms of the Kalashnikov culture and narcotics proliferation be anticipated and obviated? Surely, these could have been minimised if not precluded.

These problems, as well as malfeasance and venality in transactions between the mujahideen and their friends, surfaced during the struggle in Afghanistan. Priorities and vested interests did not permit timely remedies, however.

Were not the Geneva Accords flawed in that they did not provide for the transition to peace and the formation of a government of unity for Afghanistan? The account that has been given above brings out the fact that, from the beginning, the Geneva negotiations had only the limited aim of getting the Soviets to withdraw from Afghanistan. All the parties agreed that the formation of a government was an entirely internal affair of Afghanistan, and the Afghans alone had the right to decide this matter to the exclusion of the Soviet Union, Pakistan, or any other country. The United Nations was understandably reluctant to undertake this task. Until the end of the Cold War, it avoided assumption of a role for the promotion of reconciliation or consensus in any embattled country. Moscow and Kabul were at first dismissive of any suggestion for a role for the mujahideen in the government of Afghanistan except on Kabul's terms. When they later offered accommodation, the mujahideen rejected any truce with the Soviet puppets. Pakistan as well as other friends and supporters backed the mujahideen position. President Zia alone changed his view for reasons that remain obscure, though his unjustified and unlawful dismissal of Prime Minister Junejo in May 1988 provides circumstantial evidence of a personal power motivation. In the event, even he was unable to persuade the mujahideen to meet with Diego Cordovez in pursuit of his mission of promoting a government of unity in Afghanistan.

It was probably too much to expect the mujahideen leaders to reach accommodation with the surrogate regime after the Soviets withdrew, though a government of unity could have saved the country from fragmentation. More tragic was the rivalry for personal power among the mujahideen leaders that prolonged the nightmare for the Afghan people. Also, as a result of the anarchy, the mujahideen themselves were sidelined by new forces in the country. Likewise, the Taliban exclusivism, excess of religious zeal, and permission for a foreign adventurer to abuse hospitality sealed their fate.

Pakistan's interest, as indeed that of other neighbours, lay above all in an end to the civil war and restoration of Afghanistan's unity, which were highly desirable objectives also for the Afghan people themselves. Only peace in Afghanistan could relieve Pakistan and

Iran of the burden of Afghan refugees. Over two million of them still remain in Pakistan, suffering themselves and burdening Pakistan's economy. Peace was a prerequisite, moreover, for the opening of transit facilities without which cooperation with the Central Asian Republics remained blocked.

Could Islamabad influence the Taliban to follow circumspect policies? Not only Tehran but also Washington believed it could. What is obvious in retrospect is the futility of a king-maker role in Afghanistan on the part of any outsider. Like imperial Britain in the nineteenth century, the Soviet superpower failed in its attempt to impose a surrogate government on the Afghans. Pakistan lacked the power and resources to persuade the Taliban to rectify their fatal policies. In contrast, the United States and the West, with their vastly greater resources, would have had a better chance to influence the Afghans. By blaming Islamabad, Washington covered up its own error in walking away from Afghanistan after achieving its Cold War aim and imposing sanctions on Pakistan to further undermine its capacity to play a significant role in Afghanistan. Not until after 9/11 did the United States rectify its blunder—though at much greater cost.

US-Taliban Negotiations: President Trump appointed Zalmay Khalilzad to lead negotiations for ceasefire and peace with the Taliban. At the end of 2018 and early 2019, he held several meetings with Mullah Abdul Ghani Baradar who was close to Taliban leader Haibatulah Akhundzada at the invitation of Qatar. The Taliban were said to pledge ban on international terrorists from abusing Afghanistan as a base. The US was said to agree to withdrawal of troops. The Taliban talked only to the US representative and refused to meet with the Kabul regime's representatives.

NOTES

1. Steve Coll, 'This Ghost War: The Secret History of the CIA, Afghanistan and bin Laden', quoted in *Dawn*, Islamabad, 19 November 2004.
2. Uzbekistan President Islam Karimov, speaking at the OIC Summit in Ashkabat on 14 May 1997, reported in *The News*, Islamabad, 15 May 1997.
3. UN Secretary General's end-of-the-year Report for 1997 to the Security Council, quoted in a despatch by Anwar Iqbal in *The News*, Islamabad, 1 and 8.
4. Lawrence Ziring, *Pakistan: At the Crossroads of History*, Oneworld, 2003.

5. K. M. Arif, op. cit., 327, quoting Eduard Shevardnadze's statement in *Izvestia* of 19 February 1989.
6. President Ronald Reagan, speech welcoming President Zia to Washington, 7 December 1982, *Documents*, 481.

CHAPTER 17

Pakistan-India Disputes and Crises

'All Members shall settle their international disputes by peaceful means in such a manner that international peace and security, and justice, are not endangered.'

UN Charter, Article 2.3

'... the Government of India and the Government of Pakistan have agreed as follows: (vi) That in accordance with the Charter of the United Nations, they will refrain from the threat or use of force against the territorial integrity or political independence of each other.

Shimla Agreement

Despite the pledge in the Shimla Agreement to settle differences by peaceful means, little progress was made towards that objective after 1972. The settlement of Jammu and Kashmir was not even discussed. Other existing disputes continued to fester, and some new ones arose. These disputes and issues are summarized below.

Sir Creek Unresolved: New Delhi reportedly proposed that the demarcation exercise should begin from the seaward side. Multiple surveys and rounds of talks narrowed the differences between the two countries.

Siachen Stalemate: Despite several meetings on Siachen, the two sides were stuck like glaciers, with India insisting on authentication of the 112-kilometre long Actual Ground Positions Line while Pakistan sought disengagement without prejudice to the respective stands of the two countries. Its position was based on the Shimla Agreement which provided: 'In Jammu and Kashmir, the line of control resulting from the ceasefire of December 17 shall be respected by both sides without prejudice to the recognized position of either side. Neither side shall seek to alter it unilaterally irrespective of mutual differences

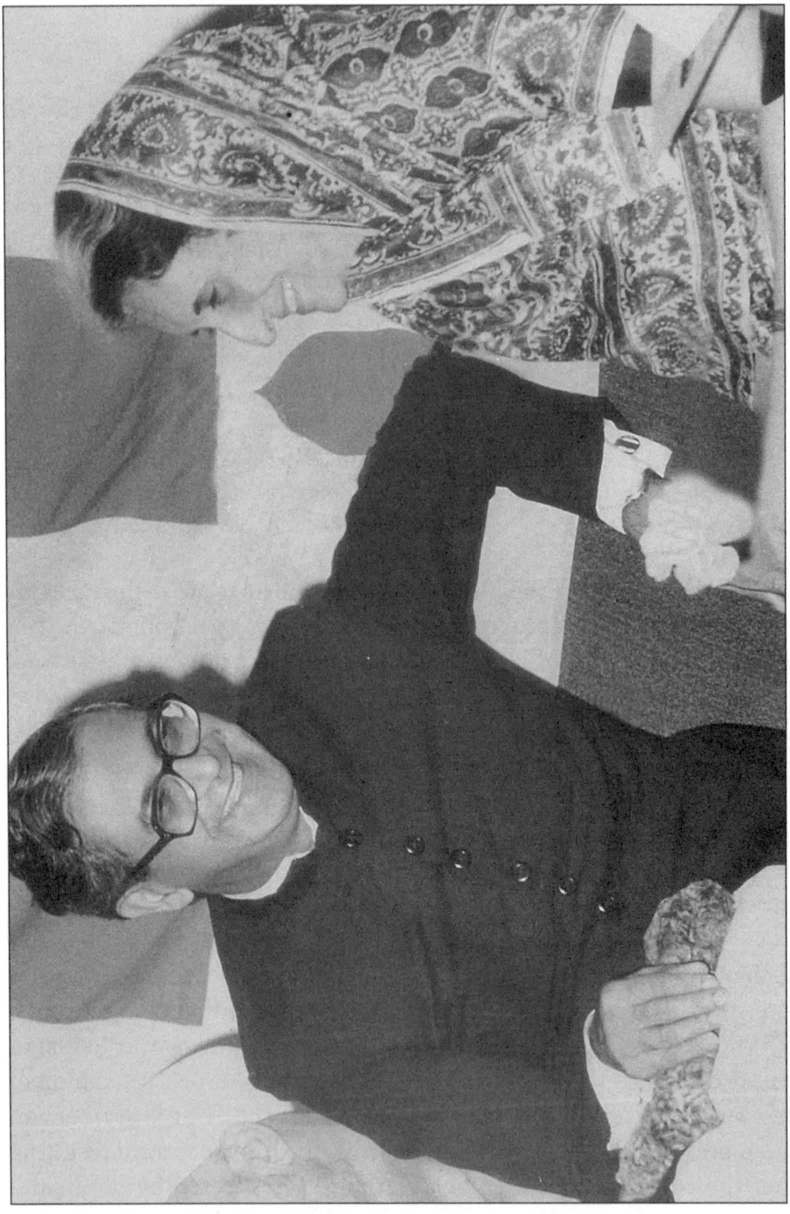

With Prime Minister Indira Gandhi, New Delhi, 1981. Courtesy of Abdul Sattar.

and legal implications. Both sides further undertake to refrain from the threat of use of force in violation of this line.'

Indus Basin Issues: The Indus Waters Treaty allows India to build dams for power generation without obstructing normal flows. Indian plans to build thirty dams have provoked Pakistan's concern because that would enable India to interrupt flows at crucial times for irrigation. Pakistan has had to refer a number of Indian projects for settlement under the aegis of the World Bank. The Baglihar Dam dispute was settled under this provision. Pakistan objected to the Wuller Barrage on the Jhelum; its construction has remained suspended. On the Neelum (Kishanganga) project, the International Court of Arbitration allowed India to divert a part of the flow in the tributary for power generation, provided a part to be determined by the court continued to flow downstream. The planned Nimoo-Bazgo Dam on the Indus tributary, Suru River in Kargil, Chattak, Uri, and other projects would require settlement. Such new problems can be resolved in accordance with the provisions of the Indus Basin agreement.[1]

Sir Creek

The demarcation of the line in Sir Creek, at the western terminus of the Pakistan-India boundary in the Rann of Kutch, has remained unresolved since 1969, when the main dispute was settled by an arbitration tribunal. For most of its length, the boundary was demarcated by the tribunal, which did not consider it necessary to take up the question with regard to the 100-kilometre stretch of Sir Creek because here the boundary between the state of Kutch and the province of Sindh was already delimited by a resolution of the British Indian government in 1914, with the annexed map showing Sir Creek on the Sindh side. Neither side contested that fact before the tribunal. Later, with an eye on the maritime resources, India claimed first that Sir Creek was on the Indian side and then that the boundary should run in the middle of the creek because it was a navigable channel. The changed Indian stance aimed to substantially reduce the area of Pakistan's economic zone.

Pakistan sought negotiations to resolve the difference, but India said it first wanted to complete an air survey of the area. The surveyors general of the two countries met in May 1989 but could not reach agreement, as India no longer accepted the 1914 resolution map, considered authentic during the proceedings of the tribunal. The stalemate has persisted, to the detriment of poor fishermen on both sides, hundreds of who are arrested by the coastguard forces of the two sides, and charged with trespass. In 1999, India shot down an unarmed Pakistani aircraft in the area, killing all its crew and passengers.

Siachen: A Dispute within a Dispute

Descending from the lofty Karakorum Range, at elevations of 6,000 metres or more, the Siachen Glacier traverses part of Baltistan in the Northern Areas of Pakistan. The area was so difficult to access and so inhospitable that no fighting took place here during the hostilities in Kashmir. The ceasefire line, signed on 27 July 1949 under the auspices of the UN Commission for India and Pakistan, is terminated at a point shown on the Map as NJ 9842, some sixty miles (100 kilometres) south of the Karakorum watershed. Thereafter, the last sentence read: 'Chalunka (on the Shyok River), Khor, thence north to the glaciers.' In that direction the notional line extended to the Karakorum Pass.

Following the Sino-Pakistan agreement of 1962 on the provisional boundary between the Xinjiang region of China and the Northern Areas of the disputed state of Jammu and Kashmir under Pakistan's control, the two countries demarcated the boundary from the tri-junction with Afghanistan in the west to the Karakorum Pass in the east. India protested against the agreement, claiming that Kashmir was part of its territory and that the portion west of the Karakorum Pass was 'under Pakistan's unlawful occupation'.[2] The fact of Pakistan's control was implicitly conceded.

No fighting took place in the area in the wars between Pakistan and India. After 1965, the two countries agreed to revert to *status quo ante*. The terminus of the Line of Control resulting from the ceasefire of 17 December 1971 remained the same as that of the 1949 ceasefire line.

In April 1984, India sent a brigade-strength force to occupy a part of the glaciated area. Pakistan protested against this violation of the explicit provision in the Shimla Agreement which prohibited any attempt to 'unilaterally alter the situation'. To forestall further Indian advance, Pakistan also dispatched an army contingent to the area. The forces of the two countries have fought intermittent duels in the highest battlefield in the world. The two sides have lost thousands of soldiers due to frostbite, blizzards, and crevasses.

Of all disputes between the two countries, Siachen is considered as 'arguably the most amenable to a solution that is satisfactory for both sides.' The two countries actually arrived at an agreement in June 1989 to work for a comprehensive settlement based on redeployment of forces to reduce the chances of conflict, avoidance of use of force, and the determination of future positions on the ground so as to conform with the Shimla Agreement.[3] Prime Ministers Benazir Bhutto and Rajiv Gandhi approved the agreement in July 1989. But the Indian army reportedly opposed the pullback. In 1992 talks, the India side raised a new issue demanding 'authentication' of the current positions occupied by the armed forces, a line of control in the 'zone of conflict', and the right to establish a 'civil post' in the area. Although these demands had no basis in the 1989 agreement, the Pakistan side indicated willingness to show the current positions on a map to be annexed to the agreement provided the text affirmed that the map would not constitute the basis of a legal claim to the territory.

Like other disputes, the Siachen issue has festered while thousands of troops have died due to avalanches, frostbite, and altitude sickness.

Salal, Wullar, Baglihar, and Kishanganga Projects

The Indus Waters Treaty of 1960 allows the construction of run-of-the-river power plants but forbids the construction of dams on the western rivers in excess of prescribed limits. Whenever India plans projects that interfere with the flow of the rivers, it is obliged by the treaty to provide relevant data to Pakistan. If the magnitude of the dam is considered by Pakistan to violate the treaty provisions, it is entitled to raise the issue in the permanent Indus Commission. If the commission fails to reach agreement, either side can refer the question for consideration at the level of governments. If even they fail to reach agreement, either side can refer the dispute to the World Bank for the appointment of a neutral expert whose verdict is binding on both parties. Four such issues have arisen since 1960.

The first question arose in the 1970s when India decided to build a dam on the Chenab River at Salal. After the Indus Commission failed to settle the issue, it was taken up at the level of governments of the two countries. India then agreed to reduce the height of the dam so as to relieve Pakistan's concerns regarding interference in the flow of the river.

Another question arose in the early 1980s, when the Indian government embarked on the construction of a barrage on the Jhelum River at the mouth of the Wullar Lake, envisaging the creation of storage. Finding it thirty-three times in excess of the prescribed limit, Pakistan raised the issue in the commission in 1985 where no progress was made. In 1987, Pakistan asked India to discontinue construction pending resolution of the question. After some delay, India suspended work. India then argued that the barrage could be of mutual benefit. Without entering into a controversy over this argument, Pakistan declined to take part in any discussion that would tinker with the provisions of the treaty, its sanctity being too vital for Pakistan. It asked India to first acknowledge that the project was inconsistent with the treaty. India was unwilling to do so, but offered, in 1989, to change the design and operating procedures to eliminate any harmful effects on Pakistan. The two sides then exchanged drafts of a possible compromise. No agreement was reached, however, despite numerous meetings at the level of the commission as well as government. After India suspended implementation of the project because of the uprising in Kashmir, the problem lost urgency.

Meanwhile, still another dispute arose when India decided to build a hydroelectric power project on the Chenab River with a dam at Baglihar upstream from the Salal Dam. The reservoir was far in excess of the prescribed limit, and would enable India to manipulate the flow of the river in a way that would lead to either complete stoppage for up to twenty-eight days during the critical wheat growing period of December to February or opening the flood gates to inundate the land in Pakistan. India did not at first provide the requisite data about the project in advance and then delayed a visit by the Pakistani experts to the site, as required under the treaty. Negotiations at the level of

Indus Commissioners from 2001 to 2004 proved infructuous, as India maintained that the design of the dam did not violate the treaty. The matter was taken up at the level of government secretaries in January 2005, but the stalemate remained unbroken. Pakistan then decided to refer the matter to the World Bank,[4] invoking the treaty provision for appointment of a neutral expert. His verdict of 12 February 2007 upheld three of the four Pakistani objections. As a result, the height of the dam was reduced by 1.5 meters and size of pondage by 14 per cent. India, too, was happy that its position on the spillway gates and power generation capacity of 450 megawatts was vindicated.

After learning that India planned to build a power project on the Kishanganga tributary of the Jhelum River, Pakistan objected on the ground that diversion of the stream would violate the Indus Waters Treaty. The Indus Commission commenced discussion of the issue in 2005.

Consular Missions

Following the resumption of diplomatic relations in 1976, India proposed the reopening also of the consular offices of the two countries, offering to lease Jinnah House in Mumbai for the Pakistani consulate. Since that house, owned by Mr Jinnah until it was taken over by the Indian government as evacuee property, was on lease to the British deputy high commission, and its vacation would entail some delay, India sought permission to open its consulate in advance. Pakistan agreed to this, accepting the Indian promise. The promise was reiterated by the Indian minister for external affairs in parliament on two occasions, affirming: 'The property is at present leased out to the British High Commission and on expiry of the lease in December 1981 it is proposed to lease out this property to the Pakistan Embassy for use by their consulate.'[5] After the house was vacated by the British, Prime Minister Indira Gandhi decided to refuse its lease to Pakistan. Not for the first time was Pakistan to rue its acceptance of an Indian undertaking on trust.

Meanwhile, in August 1980, the Pakistani embassy in New Delhi sought the permission of the Indian government for the purchase of a plot of land for the construction of the consular office in Mumbai. New Delhi refused the request on the ground that the location was 'not suitable'. India was not prepared to help Pakistan acquire an alternative site.

In August 1992, the Pakistan government sent consular staff to open an office in Mumbai. They had to stay in a hotel. Even there, Indian intelligence personnel hounded the Pakistani staff. Pakistan was obliged to close down the office in March 1994. The Indian consulate in Karachi, meanwhile, continued to function even though it was known to the Pakistani authorities that the bulk of its personnel did not belong to the commerce and external affairs ministries of India. After they discovered evidence of subversive activities by the Indian personnel, and their involvement in terrorist activities, the Pakistan government was obliged to order the closure of the Indian consulate in December 1994.

Diplomats of the two countries agreed in 1992 on a bilateral 'code of conduct' for the treatment of the personnel of the missions. This was a superfluous exercise in view of the fact that their privileges and immunities are spelled out in international conventions on diplomatic and consular relations. The problem was not the lack of norms but of the political will to observe international law. Pakistani and Indian governments have repeatedly accused each other of using their diplomatic staff for activities incompatible with their legitimate functions. Apart from vigilance, which is the right of the host government, the authorities have been accused of violating immunities and even resorting to violence against the staff. Whatever the merits of these allegations, it was obvious that instead of contributing to the furtherance of normal relations between the two countries, the consular missions added to bitterness.

Hoping for a new chapter, the two countries agreed, in April 2005, to reopen the consular missions. President Musharraf was reported to have said that India had agreed to lease Jinnah House to Pakistan.

The Brasstacks Crisis, 1986–1987

Another crisis erupted when India decided to hold the largest combined military exercise in South Asian history, codenamed Brasstacks, in the winter of 1986–7.[6] Planned by a 'hawkish and flamboyant'[7] Indian army chief, General Krishnaswamy Sundarji, the exercise was comparable in scale to the biggest exercises by NATO or the Warsaw Pact. It envisaged the concentration of a quarter of a million troops, nine army divisions, five independent armoured brigades, and 1,300 tanks in western Rajasthan, at places hardly fifty kilometres from the Pakistan border, giving the assembled forces the capability to launch a piercing strike into Pakistan to cut off northern Pakistan from the southern part.

Contrary to an existing understanding, the Indian army chief did not inform his Pakistani counterpart of the location, schedule, and scale of the exercise.[8] Specific requests to this effect by the Pakistani GHQ on the 'hot line' and by diplomats in New Delhi were rebuffed. Concerned about the situation, Prime Minister Mohammad Khan Junejo took up the matter with Rajiv Gandhi in their meeting during the SAARC summit in Bangalore in November 1986. He was given to understand that the exercise would be scaled down; this was, however, not done.

As a precaution, the Pakistan army decided to extend its own winter exercises and later, in December 1986, as the crisis escalated, moved some of the formations to forward areas north of the Sutlej River opposite the Indian town of Fazilka and west of the Ravi in Sialkot district. Oblivious to the apprehensions triggered by their own, more massive, force placements in proximity to vulnerable Pakistani border areas, the Indian defence officials termed the Pakistani action provocative. They perceived the Pakistani force dispositions as a pincer posture menacing the security of the troubled Indian state of Punjab, where the Sikh people had been up in arms since the Indian army's assault on the Golden Temple, their most sacred shrine, in 1984.

The crisis peaked in January 1987. The Indian government demanded a pullback of Pakistani forces 'within 24 hours'. Pakistan pointed out that India should first remove the cause of the Pakistan reaction. Both countries placed their forces on alert. Prime Minister Rajiv Gandhi publicly expressed 'tremendous concern'.[9]

The defence committee of the Pakistan cabinet, headed by the prime minister, and comprising chiefs of military services, ministers, and high officials of defence and foreign ministries, which met frequently during the crisis, held an emergency meeting on 20 January. Although the crisis was not of Pakistan's creation, it was decided not to stand on ceremony and instead to take the initiative to try defusing the dangerous situation. Prime Minister Junejo telephoned Rajiv Gandhi and suggested immediate talks, at the level of foreign secretaries, to discuss mutual withdrawal of forces to peacetime locations. The Pakistani delegation arrived in New Delhi on 31 January, and an agreement was signed on 4 February, providing for deactivation of forward air bases and sector-by-sector disengagement and return of forces to their peacetime locations, to commence in the Ravi-Chenab sector in the north. The storm, which had been brewing over several months, passed over within days.

Subsequent studies and research[10] have shown that the Brasstacks crisis brought Pakistan and India closer to the brink of war than any other crisis since 1971. Its basic and direct cause was, of course, the 'mammoth war games'[11] planned by an ambitious Indian army chief. Three wars, chronic tensions rooted in unresolved disputes, inadequate or unreliable intelligence, and deep-rooted mutual suspicions fuelled worst-case assumptions. Besides, some Indian planners hoped for the crisis to spiral into actual confrontation and conflict, giving them an opportunity to exploit the disparity of forces. Scholarly research concluded: 'Brasstacks exercise may have had much larger goals than merely to test the preparedness of the Indian army. These goals appear to have been open-ended.'[12]

To preclude recurrence of unintentional crises, the two sides concluded an agreement in 1991 which specified force thresholds and distances from the border that would require prior notification in the event of exercises or troop movements. Another crisis-prevention agreement concluded in 1991 required advance communication about aircraft flying in proximity to the other side's airspace.

Readmission to the Commonwealth

Britain's partisan role in the 1971 crisis was disappointing for Pakistan. If media criticism of the excesses committed by Pakistani authorities was understandable on humanitarian grounds, the British failure to censure Indian military intervention was reflective of an expedient and unprincipled policy. London did not even allow a decent interval to lapse before it decided to extend recognition to Bangladesh, persuading several countries of Western Europe, Australia, and New Zealand to do so simultaneously. In anger, Z. A. Bhutto decided to pull out of the Commonwealth. A quick analysis revealed that the pullout would not entail any great loss except inconvenience to Pakistani settlers in Britain. National pride would be served by giving a counter-punch to Britain, which looked at the Commonwealth as a source of comfort in its time of decline from a ranking world power status.

If the precipitate decision to quit the Commonwealth was largely Bhutto's, the decision by President Zia to rejoin was no less personal. It was made at the suggestion of visiting British leaders, subject to the condition that re-entry was arranged in an honourable way. For several years, Prime Minister Indira Gandhi frustrated the proposal. She vetoed Pakistan's return at the Melbourne summit in 1980, despite pleadings by the Australian prime minister. Her decision was also quite personal, and surprised even the Indian Foreign Secretary who had earlier told the Pakistani ambassador that India would not stand in the way.[13] Rajiv Gandhi followed his mother's line, justifying the opposition to Pakistan's return to the Commonwealth on the ground that Pakistan was ruled by a dictator. Actually, democratic rule was not a precondition for membership at that time. In any case, India did not abandon its opposition even after elections in 1985, the installation of a civilian government and an end to martial law. Not until after the 1988 election in Pakistan did New Delhi relent. If Pakistan's manner of leaving the Commonwealth in a huff was childish, that of suing for re-entry also did not reflect maturity of decision-making in foreign policy.

War Averted, 1990

Still another crisis erupted in the spring of 1990. As the situation in Kashmir continued to deteriorate, senior military officials in India were reported to have recommended air strikes on targets in Pakistan. Whether their objective was to deter Pakistan or intimidate the Kashmiris, the reports triggered anxiety among analysts that Indian adventurism could precipitate war between the two countries which could escalate to the nuclear level. In May 1990, the President of the United States sent Robert Gates, assistant for the National Security Council, to Islamabad and New Delhi. Although sensational reports[14] depicting an actual nuclear threat were discounted, the United States obviously possessed enough information to consider it necessary to launch an exercise in preventive diplomacy.

Disarmament Issues

Chemical Weapons Convention, 1993: Historically supportive of resolutions in the UN General Assembly for general disarmament, and the limitation, progressive reduction, and eventual elimination of weapons of mass destruction, Pakistan welcomed the Chemical Weapons Convention (CWC) when it was concluded in 1993. As a country that never had a chemical weapons programme, it was satisfied with the CWC's prohibition on production or acquisition of such weapons and the obligation to destroy existing stocks within ten years. Pakistan did not, however, ratify the CWC until four years later, in October 1997, because of its concern over a provision in the convention regarding verification and inspection. This was unprecedented in its broad scope, giving rise to the apprehension that it might be exploited for intrusion into the country's sensitive nuclear facilities. To neutralize the risk, Pakistan stated in the instrument of ratification that it would not allow abuse of the verification provision to degrade Pakistan's defence capability unrelated to the CWC.[15]

India, too, ratified the CWC. Beside satisfying the principle that Pakistan would not undertake asymmetrical obligations in respect of disarmament and non-proliferation treaties, India's ratification of CWC relieved Pakistan's concerns about the use of such weapons against its security, especially because verification provisions make this convention reliable. The importance of this factor was emphatically illustrated by India's obligatory disclosure pursuant to CWC that it had actually produced chemical weapons, in violation of a bilateral agreement with Pakistan, signed in April 1992, prohibiting chemical weapons. The revelation that India did not actually observe that commitment could not but further undermine the credibility of India's pledges in a bilateral framework.

The Comprehensive Test Ban Treaty (CTBT): was conceived in the context of non-proliferation. Its objective was to restrict qualitative improvement of weapons technology by the existing, as well as aspiring, nuclear weapons states. The prospects of the treaty looked promising, as all such states appeared to favour the CTBT. India was one of the sponsors.

Pakistan supported the treaty from the day it was proposed. This stance was consistent with its long-standing policy of joining the vast majority of nations that supported limitation, reduction, and elimination of weapons of mass destruction. Given Pakistan's preoccupation with security in South Asia, its one and only condition was that such measures should be non-discriminatory. That was, of course, a code word with a region-specific purpose.

Pakistan's stance on the CTBT followed the standard line. It favoured the conclusion of the treaty but declared it would not ratify 'unilaterally'. Pakistan sought to ensure, during negotiations in the UN conference on disarmament, to plug any loopholes India might later exploit to change its mind. To that end, Pakistan successfully sponsored a provision which made CTBT's entry into force contingent on ratification by each and every one of the forty-four nuclear-capable states. Moreover, if any such state later renounced the treaty, that would also entitle other states to review their position.

The prospects of the treaty were suddenly clouded, however, when India opposed the adoption of the treaty by the UN General Assembly, explaining its reversal of stance from sponsorship to opposition on the ground of the refusal of nuclear weapons states to give a timetable for total nuclear disarmament. It became evident that the real purpose behind the idealistic facade was to retain the option to conduct nuclear tests. Prime Minister Deve Gowda's government declared it would not sign the CTBT. Foreign Minister I. K. Gujral candidly said on 15 July that India 'will not allow its nuclear options to be restricted in any manner and would take all necessary measures to cope with any threat that might be posed to its security.'

India's refusal to endorse the treaty sealed its fate. Even the slight hope that India might be persuaded by the United States to change its stance vanished when the United States Senate decided against ratification in 1997.

A suggestion was floated in early 2000 that Pakistan should consider signing the CTBT. Keeping in view the distinction between signing and ratification, and the provision in the CTBT text regarding its entry into force, some[16] in the government felt that Pakistan had little to lose and much to gain by signing the treaty. It would cost nothing since the treaty would not enter into force anyway because of

Indian and US refusal to become parties. Many other states, including the United States, had signed the treaty. In doing so, they did not incur any obligation. By signing it, Pakistan, it was argued, could reap considerable benefits. It would deflect and sidetrack international pressures, occupy high moral ground, earn praise for itself, and isolate and expose India. In brief, Pakistan could free-ride known Indian recalcitrance; keep the cake and eat it too. The only problem was that the arguments were too technical and arcane for lay opinion to grasp.

Some of the political parties opposed to the military government sensed an opportunity to exploit the situation by denouncing any unilateral signing. A religious party warned of mass agitation if the government wavered in its resolve. The government, which had never formally approved the suggestion to sign the CTBT anyway, did not pursue the idea.

Although the idea had to be abandoned, its public discussion yielded some benefits. Public opinion in Pakistan became better informed. Foreign governments, especially those of Japan and some EU countries, noted that a section of enlightened opinion in Pakistan favoured a reasoned and rational approach to nuclear issues. The debate also helped soften the impression of a trigger-happy people, generated by popular celebrations in Pakistan (and earlier in India) after the nuclear tests.

FMCT: The Fissile Material Cut-off Convention proposal aims at freezing the production of plutonium and highly-enriched uranium (HEU). Its underlying purpose is to restrict quantitative expansion of nuclear arsenals while that of the CTBT was to restrict qualitative improvement of nuclear weapons.

After the CTBT, negotiated with enormous effort over years, failed to obtain requisite ratifications, the UN Conference on Disarmament appeared disinclined to start negotiations on the FMCT. Later, the CoD sought to revive the proposal and placed it on the agenda of the work programme. That, however, required unanimous vote of its sixty-six members. Pakistan's objection on grounds of principle blocked the proposed inclusion.

The draft text of FMCT focuses narrowly on prohibiting future production of plutonium and highly enriched uranium (HEU). In effect, it would allow states to use their existing stockpiles for further production of nuclear weapons, thus defeating the underlying aim of limitation of nuclear arsenals. Pakistan is concerned that the loophole would enable some states, including India, to expand their nuclear arsenals, and thus aggravate the existing imbalance and undermine strategic stability. To preclude destabilization, it is imperative that the treaty should also provide for reduction of existing stockpiles of fissile materials.

Pakistan has been historically a supporter of proposals for both qualitative and quantitative limitation of nuclear weapons. It was prepared to sign the CTBT if India did. It is also not conceptually opposed to FMCT provided its provisions are consistent with the logic of restricting further expansion of nuclear arsenals.

NOTES

1. M. Rashid Khan, *Crucial Water Issues between Pakistan and India*, quotes award of International Court of Arbitration, *Journal of South Asian Studies*, Islamabad, vol 28, Jan-June 2013.
2. R. K. Jain, ed., *China-South Asian Relations*, Vol. 1, 197.
3. The joint statement issued in June 1989 read:

   > There was an agreement by both sides to work toward a comprehensive settlement based on re-deployment of force to reduce the chances of conflict, avoidance of the use of force and the determination of future positions on the ground so as to conform with the Shimla Agreement and assure durable peace in the Siachen area. The army authorities of both sides will determine these positions.

4. The World Bank was approached on 19 January 2005. For settlement procedure, see section on Indus Waters Treaty, 1960, in Chapter 7.
5. Statements by P. V. Narasimha Rao in parliament on 2 September 1980, and again on 25 March 1982.
6. Kanti P. Bajpai, P. R. Chari, Pervaiz Iqbal Cheema, Stephen P. Cohen, and Sumit Ganguly, *Brasstacks and Beyond*, a joint study.
7. Ibid., 15.
8. The understanding was reached in letters exchanged between Gen. K. M. Arif and Gen. Sundarji's predecessor. Explaining the omission in an informal conversation at Lake Coma sponsored by Steve Cohen in 1995, Sundarji disarmingly told Arif that he was not informed of the 'bloody' exchange of letters!
9. Press conference, 20 January 1987.

10. Apart from the methodically researched *Beyond Brasstacks*, David J. Karl of the Pacific Council on Foreign Policy, University of Southern California, Los Angeles, has written a paper on 'The Impression of Deterrence: Nuclear Weapons and the 1987 Brasstacks Crisis.'
11. Karl, op. cit.
12. Bajpai et al., op. cit., p. viii.
13. The author was the ambassador.
14. Seymour Hersh, 'On the Nuclear Edge' in *The New Yorker*, 29 March 1993.
15. Statement by foreign minister of Pakistan, *Dawn*, Karachi, 26 February 1998.
16. Then foreign minister, the author was the main proponent of the suggestion.

Chapter 18

Nuclear Weapons and Missiles Systems[1]

Nuclear Tests

Pakistan's nuclear weapons development programme made steady progress in the 1980s while remaining within the limits pledged to the United States, but research was speeded up in the face of India's aggressive postures, recurrent plans for airstrikes on Kahuta, the Brasstacks exercise for attack on lines of communication to slice Pakistan in two, and strategic vulnerability due to US disengagement after the withdrawal of Soviet forces from Afghanistan, leaving Pakistan on its own. Washington revived nuclear sanctions after its purpose of humiliating the Soviet Union was served, cutting off economic and military assistance and even withholding the transfer of F-16s and other equipment for which Pakistan had already paid. President Bill Clinton asked Islamabad to roll back the nuclear programme while lifting vigilance on the Indian nuclear weapons programme despite its rejection of CTBT betraying its intentions.

On 11 May and again on 13 May 1998, India conducted multiple nuclear test explosions. Indian leaders threatened Pakistan. Home Minister Lal Krishna Advani boasted of a shift in the balance of power in the region. Another Minister, Krishan Lal Sharma, asserted India was 'now in a position to take control of Azad Kashmir'.

Islamabad was disappointed by India's abandonment of restraint but not surprised—portents of Indian intentions were manifest in its volte-face on CTBT and Bharatiya Janata Party's pre-election statements.

Immediately, the Pakistan government was impaled on the horns of an agonizing dilemma: to test or not to test. It possessed nuclear weapons, had validated their design by cold tests, and prepared sites for test explosions, but a test would entail further sanctions which the country could ill afford, as its international solvency was already precarious due to improvident policies and poor fiscal management in the 1990s, resulting in the build-up of a massive debt mountain of $38 billion with an unaffordable debt-servicing liability of over five billion dollars a year, against annual foreign exchange earnings of hardly ten billion dollars. Eight years of sanctions had further weakened Pakistan's weak economy, and the country was internationally isolated because of its recognition and cooperation with the Taliban regime.

The United States, said US Secretary of State Madeleine Albright, was appalled because 'Indian diplomats had lulled us into thinking that they were not going to take any precipitous action in the nuclear area'. Words apart, US policy now focused on preventing Pakistan from following suit. President Clinton dispatched Deputy Secretary of State Strobe Talbott on a dissuasion mission to Islamabad with a lot of sticks and few carrots. Talbott made out a case for 'restraint and maturity', arguing that 'Pakistanis suddenly had a chance to occupy the high ground in the eyes of a nervous world. They could, literally, cash in by showing restraint. Virtually every dollar of aid that donor countries like the United States and Japan would withhold from India could be offered to Pakistan as a reward for resisting the temptation to test.' Conspicuously missing was credible assurance on the key issue of security.

Talbott's arguments had little appeal because the United States was constant only in its policy of penalizing Pakistan for its nuclear pursuit while acquiescing in India's *fait accompli*. Foreign Minister Gohar Ayub 'fidgeted' as Talbott made opening remarks and 'then unleashed a broadside'. The United States was 'a fair weather friend'.

The cabinet was divided in the meeting on 14 May: only three ministers favoured immediate tests, arguing there would be no other opportunity, three opposed saying Pakistan should wait for more information, while six others straddled the issue. The scientists said there was no substitute for demonstration by hot test.

Prime Minister Nawaz Sharif was clear about the gravity of the moment. Prospects of glory or political ruin stared him in the face. On 18 May, he gave a green signal to PAEC Chairman Ishfaq Ahmad Khan: '*Dhamaka kar dain.*'

More than 150 scientists, engineers, and technicians were flown to the airport close to Chagai. Pakistan Atomic Energy Commission (PAEC) Chairman was there to supervise. Dr Samar Mubarakmand was responsible for preparing for tests. Dr A. Q. Khan and Dr Javed Mirza of Khan Research Laboratories (KRL) came to assist. At 3:16 p.m. on 28 May, young physicist Mohammad Arshad, who had made the largest contribution to the trigger design, was given the honour of pressing the button. Waiting long for the opportunity, the fully-prepared PAEC tested five devices of different designs, sizes, and yields on 28 May and a sixth miniaturized device of advanced design at Kharan on 30 May. Nawaz Sharif declared Pakistan had 'settled the score'. The nation was jubilant. Seismic centres around the world confirmed the emergence of the seventh nuclear power.

Aftermath of Tests: A joint communiqué issued by the permanent members of the UN Security Council (P-5) on 4 June noted that the tests were carried out 'by India and then by Pakistan'. The factual statement differentiating Pakistan from India was due to the just position taken by China: the Indian test and its brandishing of threats left Pakistan obliged to demonstrate that it too possessed nuclear weapons. The Security Council Resolution 1172 of 6 June 1998 condemned both countries and demanded that they refrain from further tests, weaponization and development of ballistic missiles, sign the CTBT, and participate in negotiations on the fissile material production cut-off treaty (FMCT). The Security Council also urged them to resume dialogue in order to remove tensions and encouraged them to 'find mutually acceptable solutions that address the root causes of those tensions, including Kashmir.'

On 12 June, the foreign ministers of the G-8 group of industrialized states (Canada, France, Germany, Italy, Japan, Russia, UK, and USA) issued a communiqué stating they would work for postponement of loans by the International Financial Institutions to the two countries. The penalty was harsher for Pakistan because it faced a grave foreign payments crisis. The government had already frozen foreign currency accounts of Pakistani citizens ($7 billion) offering rupees at the official rate of exchange. The account holders who were assured by law against confiscation suffered losses of 30–40 per cent.

Saudi Arabia demonstrated its traditional solidarity and agreed to provide 100,000 barrels of oil daily on a deferred payments basis. Valued at over $500 million a year, the assistance over five years was later converted into a grant.

The penalties imposed by Western countries were relaxed a year later. The IFCs resumed lending. IMF provided a $1.2 billion credit to Pakistan for structural adjustment. The Paris Club agreed to reschedule some of Pakistan's loans.

India adopted a defiant stance. Prime Minister Vajpayee sent letters to the heads of government of 177 states, justifying the test in the context of India's two nuclear neighbours. Inverting facts, he accused Pakistan of having committed aggression against India thrice. The propagandistic intent of the letters was obvious in Vajpayee's letter to President Clinton which underlined the 'threat' from China. When China protested, India lamely back-tracked, assuring Beijing that it did not regard China as a threat even though Defence Minister George Fernandes publicly called China 'threat no. 1'.

As in 1974, the United States again acquiesced in India's *fait accompli*. Bill Clinton embarked on a six-day visit to India, the longest by a US president, and offered to develop a strategic partnership. Washington abandoned efforts to restrain India from accumulating an increasing stockpile of fissile material. When the time came for further supply of enriched uranium fuel for the Tarapur power reactor the US had supplied to India in the 1960s, Washington asked for no additional safeguards to prevent reprocessing of the accumulated used fuel, from which India could extract plutonium for possible use for weapons purposes. In doing so, it even evaded its own Nuclear Non-proliferation Act of 1978, which prohibited the United States from the export of nuclear materials to a country that did not accept the full-scope inspection and control safeguards of the IAEA. It violated the law, at least in spirit, by arranging for France to provide the fuel. In contrast, Clinton visited Pakistan for five hours. Only under threat of legal action did Washington decide to refund the money Pakistan had paid for F-16s.

Moratorium: Immediately after the Chagai tests, Pakistan announced a moratorium on further tests. It was willing to consider compliance with the Security Council's call for refraining from weaponization and deployment of missiles if India did the same.

The prime ministers of Pakistan and India, in speeches in the UN General Assembly in September 1998, expressed willingness to sign the CTBT by September 1999, when a review conference was to be held. Their statements of intent were, however, hedged by conditions—Pakistan's in the context of removal of sanctions by the United States, and India's with regard to progress in negotiations on nuclear disarmament. In the event, the plan was derailed. After the Vajpayee government fell, New Delhi decided to postpone a decision on signing the CTBT till after the election in October.

On 12 February 1999, Pakistan and India declared in a joint statement that they would continue to abide by their respective unilateral moratoria on further test explosions 'unless either side, in exercise of its national sovereignty, decides that extraordinary events have jeopardized its supreme interests'.

Impact on Security: Pakistan's demonstration of weapons capability had the desired effect on New Delhi. Prime Minister Atal Behari Vajpayee said on 28 May 1998 that the tests had created a 'new' situation. Commentators recognized the need for caution and restraint in the conduct of Pakistan-India relations. In a joint declaration issued on 12 February 1999, the prime ministers of the countries declared, 'The nuclear dimension of the security environment of the two countries adds to their responsibility for avoidance of conflict'. The two sides also agreed to 'undertake national measures to reduce the risks of accidental or unauthorized use of nuclear weapons' and to provide advance notification in respect of ballistic missile flight tests. The prime ministers also pledged to intensify efforts for the solution of outstanding issues, including that of Kashmir.

'The Root Cause': Security Council Resolution 1172, urging India and Pakistan to remove tensions by finding 'solutions that address the root causes of those tensions, including Kashmir', evoked an apparently positive response. The prime ministers of India and Pakistan, in their declaration of 12 February 1999, recognized that 'the resolution of all outstanding issues, including Jammu and Kashmir, is essential' for peace and security and went on to pledge that their respective governments 'shall intensify their efforts to resolve all outstanding issues, including the issue of Jammu and Kashmir.' The words were not followed, however, with any purposeful action. The optimism generated by the Lahore Declaration soon evaporated with the outbreak of the Kargil crisis in May 1999.

Command and Control: Recognizing the need for a high-level decision-making organ to decide issues relating to nuclear policy, Pakistan has established the National Command Authority with the Prime Minister as Chairman. The NCA's Employment Control Committee (with the Foreign Minister as deputy chairman, and Ministers for Defence and Interior and top military officers as members) is vested with authority to define nuclear strategy. The Development Control Committee (with Joint Chiefs of Staff as deputy chairmen, and top military officials as members) is responsible for weapons development and oversight. The Strategic Plans Division (SPD) acts as the NCA's secretariat; it is also responsible for research and development and upgradation and application of custodial controls to ensure against any leakage of technology, and for physical security of the assets against threat of attack or sabotage.

Nuclear Posture: From the inception of the programme, Pakistan viewed nuclear weapons as a means of deterrence and prevention of war, not of fighting one. Islamabad declared commitment to the 'minimum credible deterrence' principle.

The concept was tested in the crisis following a terrorist attack on the Indian parliament on 13 December 2001. Charging Pakistan as responsible for the attack, the Indian government ordered military mobilization on 15 December and deployment of the army with three strike corps and 500,000 troops on Pakistan's borders. The air force moved to forward bases. PIA over-flights were banned. Pakistan, too, undertook counter-deployments. The two countries came to the brink of war. Fortunately for both, the world community was deeply concerned and interceded for restraint, especially the United States, with which a hundred thousand Pakistani troops were cooperating to prevent al-Qaeda and Taliban forces from taking shelter in the border areas. US diplomacy succeeded in defusing the crisis, though the Indian forces did not return to peacetime locations. Six months later, the crisis erupted again following a terrorist attack on an Indian army camp in Kashmir. The Indian army chief declared that the 'time for action has come'. Prime Minister Vajpayee proclaimed, 'India is ready for decisive war.' The Minister for Water Resources threatened to 'scrap the Indus Waters Treaty.' The Navy moved five ships of the Eastern Fleet to the Arabian Sea. War seemed imminent. The US Defence Secretary rushed to the region and once again defused the crisis.

A striking aspect of the crisis was the impact of nuclearization. Pakistan conducted three missile tests to warn of the dangers without actually readying the nuclear force. Actually, Pakistani leadership downplayed the role of nuclear weapons. President Musharraf told a journalist, 'Nuclear weapons are the last resort. I am optimistic and confident that we can defend ourselves with conventional means even though the Indians are buying up the most modern weapons in a frenzy.'[2]

Pakistan has since developed a comprehensive doctrine for defence. Its main components include: (1) Conventional and nuclear forces are integrated to combine the deterrence; (2) Nuclear weapons are a means for war prevention, not war-fighting, to be invoked only as a last resort; and (3) Pakistan would maintain a minimum credible deterrence, not engage in a nuclear arms race.

After India formulated the aggressive 'Cold Start Doctrine' for a surprise attack, Pakistan launched in 2011 a programme to develop tactical nuclear weapons and the short-range Nasr missile for a strategy of 'full spectrum defence'. Washington ignored the provocation by India but expressed concern about the risk posed by deployment of nuclear weapons. Pakistan took appropriate measures to strengthen field security.

Ballistic Missiles: Responding to new strategic challenges, Pakistan started developing ballistic missiles in 1987 and by now possesses multiple short-, medium-, and intermediate-range, solid-, and liquid-fuel, and fixed location and mobile precision-guided missile systems capable of carrying conventional and non-conventional payloads. Khan Research Laboratories, Space Research Commission, NESCOM, and a number of other engineering organizations have contributed to the development of sophisticated design, engineering, and electronic technologies.[3]

Battlefield range missiles include *Nasr* and *Hatf*-I series. Short-range (300–1000 km) missiles include *Ghaznavi*, *Abdali*-I, *Ghauri*-I, and *Shaheen*-I. Medium-range (1500–2750 km) *Ghauri*-II, *Shaheen*-II, and *Shaheen*-III missiles have ranges varying from 500 to 1,050 km. Medium-range *Shaheen*-III can fly 2,500 km while liquid-fuel *Ghauri*-II has a range of 2,000 km. Air-to-surface missiles include *Ra'ad* (*Hatf*-VIII) and B*arq*. In 2005, Pakistan also tested *Babur* cruise missile.

Missile technologies under development in South Asia include anti-ballistic missiles. Precision-guided bombs can zero in on arsenals deep in tunnels. Another threat to deterrent stability is development of cyber 'worms' that can be injected into control systems to disable plants and missiles.

Safety and Security: The government has also taken measures to ensure security of nuclear installations, weapons, and materials. Cooperating with international efforts and benefiting from US experience and cooperation since 2003, the Strategic Plans Division has strengthened vigilance and safeguards for robust security. Pakistan actively participated in President Barack Obama's project of the Nuclear Security Summit since 2010 to secure nuclear weapons and materials against theft by terrorists. On the eve of the fourth summit, high US officials facing a barrage of questions by journalists spoke of Pakistan's 'solid nuclear security cooperation' with the United States, its own Nuclear Security Centre of Excellence, and its 'mature capability' for safeguarding nuclear installations. President Obama's call at the conclusion of the Summit on 1 April 2016 urging both India and Pakistan against developing doctrines (Cold Start by India and deployment of tactical nuclear weapons) was notable for welcoming impartiality.

All countries with nuclear weapons and materials have an obligation to their own to ensure foolproof safety and security remembering the nuclear disaster at the Chernobyl Nuclear Plant in 1986 and the catastrophic meltdown of three of the six power reactors at Fukushima following the earthquake and tsunami in 2011.[4]

The Unauthorized Transfer of Technology: Pakistan was exposed to widespread and enduring embarrassment after inspections by

International Atomic Energy Agency of a pilot centrifuge plant in Iran in 2003 found evidence that implicated Pakistan. Traces of isotopes IAEA collected from Natanz matched the samples provided by Pakistan. The centrifuges transferred to Iran had been earlier used at the pilot plant in Sihala. The government was shocked by the IAEA's finding that A. Q. Khan, popular founder of the uranium enrichment programme, was engaged in illicit transfer of nuclear technology. He and twelve other senior staffers were dismissed. Since then, personnel reliability checks are conducted regularly, and those with 'negative tendencies' are removed.[5]

By far the most lucrative deal of the Khan network involved supply of equipment and technology to Libya. The bulk of the transfer took place after Dr A. Q. Khan was removed as head of from KRL. It involved over twenty complete L-1 centrifuges, a machine shop, uranium hexafluoride, and nuclear bomb designs. Some of the equipment was produced in Malaysia and transferred via Dubai to Libya. Later Colonel Gaddafi decided to give up the project and handed over the equipment and design information to CIA, much of it in unopened crates.

President Musharraf persuaded Dr A. Q. Khan to read a televised statement in February 2004 taking personal responsibility for the transfer of nuclear technology in exchange for a pardon, but the world community did not forgive Pakistan. Sadly, the hero who gave Pakistan the vital enrichment capability was led astray by greed and tarnished Pakistan's image indelibly.

Rudely shaken by the scandal, Pakistan has since devised and introduced stringent personnel reliability verification and material protection, and security programmes that have sealed all strategic plants and organizations against theft of nuclear technology.

Issues and Non-Issues

Non-Proliferation Debate: The academic debate for and against nuclear weapons has necessarily taken place in terms of principles, but few of the participants envisage, advocate, or apprehend the spread of nuclear weapons to many additional states.

Major nuclear powers and some political scientists[6] oppose proliferation basically on the ground that the spread of nuclear weapons would multiply the dangers of their use in war through miscalculation. Medium and small powers, in their view, lack the resources, the mutual learning experience, and the technical safeguards that help the superpowers manage crises. Particularly, states in the Third World are considered to be politically unstable and institutionally immature, if not also deficient in prudence and rationality. For these or other reasons, they could lose control over these weapons, imperilling their own people as well as the world community.

Other political scientists, on both historical and doctrinal grounds, do not share the above view. Some even argue in support of the efficacy of nuclear weapons as a deterrent to war[7] because nuclear weapons 'make the cost of war seem frighteningly high and thus discourage states from starting any wars that might lead to the use of such weapons.'[8] Founded in logic, the deterrence argument is also upheld by empirical evidence. Nuclear weapons have helped preserve peace and prevent military adventures in the past, and there is no reason to expect that the future will be different. Even a powerful state is unlikely to resort to aggression if it concludes that the potential gains are not worth the losses it has to risk. Such a conclusion is not obvious in a conventional environment: leaders may contemplate an adventure in a situation in which even if the adventure fails, the consequences may not be suicidal. Margins are eliminated, however, in a nuclear environment.

It is not necessary to conjure up doomsday scenarios of annihilation in a nuclear Armageddon between superpowers to realize that any use of nuclear weapons would entail an 'unmitigated disaster'.[9] The 15–20 kiloton atomic bombs US dropped on Hiroshima and Nagasaki in August 1945 devastated the two cities and killed 130,000 to 240,000 people; half died in a day and the others over following weeks and months. With improved technology, a single 20 kiloton bomb exploded over a densely populated city could cause 130,000 instantaneous deaths. In addition, over 200,000 people would suffer blast injuries and radiation burns, and many times more would be condemned to a life worse than death due to ingestion of high doses of radiation and the consequent increases in cancer, abortion, and genetic defects. The explosion would also cause destruction of property in a 15-square-mile (38 sq. km) area, and incalculable and irreversible damage to ecology and environment that would make the affected area uninhabitable.[10] Discussing the devastation a nuclear war would cause to the two countries, American, Pakistani, and Indian scientists warn that 'nothing would ever be the same again.'[11]

The awesome potential for destruction invests nuclear weapons with an unequalled power of deterrence. The possibility that nuclear weapons might be used in desperation by an attacked state should foreclose the thought of resort to war in pursuit of a policy of conquest and expansion. This has been the main rationale for the acquisition of nuclear capabilities by states that lack the conventional power to deter aggression.

The contingencies warranting a summons to the weapon of the last resort should be clearly and carefully defined. Deep penetration of a state's territory by adversary forces and large-scale attacks threatening to overwhelm and destroy its defensive capability are types of situations likely to trigger consideration of the use of nuclear weapons. What choice a victim of aggression should make between capitulation and annihilation is a cruel question to which only the people of a state can give an answer.

The 'weapon of defensive last resort' doctrine explained the nuclear policy of most nuclear states, although Britain and France, which could rely on the US umbrella, might have been motivated by Great Power pride and prestige. The Israeli 'never again' rationale was based on the memory of Nazi genocide.

Arguments against proliferation are advanced mostly by states that do not practice the precept they preach. Nevertheless, the arguments are too serious to be dismissed. Miscalculation, for instance, brought the United States and the Soviet Union perilously close to disaster in the Cuban Missile Crisis in 1962.

Nuclear weapons are not a panacea in every conflict. Even with nuclear weapons, a less powerful state 'will face a number of difficult constraints in attempting to construct a survivable deterrent force', especially if it is condemned to live with short warning time, threat of nuclear decapitation, and lack of resources to develop the requisite infrastructure for a survivable nuclear force.

Medium nuclear powers have not considered it necessary to build thousands of warheads. Britain and France are said to maintain 200 and 500 nuclear warheads respectively, and China 450. Theoretically, even a smaller number should suffice to deter, provided the weapons can be delivered on targets of high value. It is inconceivable that a responsible government or leader would risk the nuclear devastation of a single metropolis for the satisfaction of vanquishing an adversary.

A deterrence force must, however, be sufficient. The key to the credibility and efficacy of the deterrent is not numbers but the survivability of the nuclear force. If the adversary develops the capacity for pre-emption and interception, the arsenal has then to be correspondingly augmented, dispersed, and protected in indestructible silos in order to survive a surprise attack. Also, it becomes necessary to develop and deploy mobile missiles.

The Myth of an 'Islamic Bomb': All nuclear weapon states developed the capability in the context of their specific geo-political environment; none was motivated by civilization, religion, or ideology. Pakistan, the first Muslim state to acquire nuclear technology, was motivated solely by the 'never again' resolve after the 1971 disaster. Until then, it had ruled out development of nuclear weapons and even refused a French company's offer of a plutonium separation plant in 1967. President Ayub Khan believed Pakistan could deter Indian aggression by conventional forces.

Years before he became president in December 1971, Zulfikar Ali Bhutto had once rhetorically argued that if Christian, Communist, Jewish, Buddhist, and Hindu civilizations had the right to develop the nuclear bomb, why should Pakistan abstain from producing an 'Islamic bomb?'

When Pakistan actually embarked on the pursuit, Indian propagandists pounced on Bhutto's pronouncement to stroke atavistic prejudices in India and the West. The instigation became all the more sinister after the slogan of 'clash of civilizations' gained currency as a political idea and Osama Bin Laden unleashed terrorism against the United States.

Minimum Credible Deterrence: According to this doctrine, the size of the nuclear arsenal should be the minimum necessary to ensure the credibility of the deterrence. The minimum cannot be defined in static terms. The quantity and quality of the weapons and delivery system have to be readjusted to the adversary's military build-up and capability for pre-emption and interception. The guiding principle is to maintain, preserve, and upgrade the size in order to ensure that a number sufficient for credible deterrence would reach targets.

Nuclear deterrence is not dependent on parity or ratio between arsenals. The Soviet Union possessed deterrent capability during the Cuban Missile Crisis even though its nuclear arsenal was a fraction of the size of the United States. China, which was once threatened by two superpowers, did not seek to match either, bomb for bomb, missile for missile. Its capability remained fractional, but that has been enough for deterrence.

General Krishnaswamy Sundarji, who became a persuasive strategic analyst, once made the memorable remark: 'More is unnecessary if less is enough.' That is an eminently sane view, even though it came under question by hawkish commentators in India who advocate the build-up of a full-fledged strategic arsenal of thermo-nuclear weapons and ballistic missiles of inter-continental range. Over-zealous super-patriots misled the United States and the Soviet Union into a race that rational analysts now consider insane.

Nuclear Arms Limitation: The logic of complete nuclear disarmament does not appeal to nuclear-capable states any more than it did in the nuclear-weapons states. Commenting on the proposal for elimination of nuclear weapons, Zbigniew Brzezinski is said to have remarked: 'It is a plan to make the world safe for conventional warfare. I am therefore not enthusiastic about it.'[12] Even after the Cold War, nuclear powers do not consider a nuclear-free world an acceptable idea. The underlying problem persists: how to make the world unsafe for war, conventional or otherwise? Conventional weapons have not historically proved effective in a deterrence role, which now commands an even higher priority, as nations can no longer afford to fight protracted wars. Great powers have developed high-precision conventional weapons to provide 'strategic' deterrence against conventional weapons. But this option is not in sight of medium powers that lack requisite resources and access to the new technologies.

The concept of arms race implying competitive build-up of arsenals is not applicable to nuclear weapons as credible deterrence is dependent on survivability of strike weapons, not on quantity or quality. China was credited with possession of deterrence even when its nuclear arsenal was a fraction of that of the United States. Consensus also obtains on the imperative of custodial security of nuclear weapons.In March 2015, a study organized by the US Council on Foreign Policy focused on the risk of breakdown of strategic stability between countries with unresolved territorial disputes and cross-border terrorism. Experts warned of intensified risks because non-state actors threatened to penetrate the security of arsenals and mobile systems to gain access to weapons and fissile materials. On 29 August 2015, the White House commented that Pakistan took its responsibilities seriously for securing its nuclear stockpile.

No-First-Use: The Soviet Union first proposed this idea during the Cold War. NATO rejected it because its defence doctrine was predicated on the use of nuclear weapons to deter Moscow from exploiting conventional force superiority in Europe.

A state with peaceful intentions should renounce first-use of not only nuclear but also conventional weapons. India trumpeted the no-first-use of nuclear weapons but reserved the right to use conventional force. It is obviously illogical to seek to keep the cake and eat it too. China's commitment to peace is manifest from its policy of renunciation of first use of nuclear weapons as well as a policy of peace toward neighbours.

India's official doctrine in 2003 proclaimed adherence to No First Use except in response to a chemical or biological strike. In 2010, India's National Security Adviser Shivshankar Menon further elaborated that no-first-use did not apply to nuclear weapon states.

Over-dependence on Strategic Deterrence: Whilst strategic weapons provide unmatched deterrence, they do not eliminate the need for adequate conventional defence capability to cope with situations short of general war. If conventional capacity is eroded, even a local and low-intensity conflict might be misperceived as commencement of general hostilities. Inherent in such a situation is the terrible danger of making the weapon-of-last-resort a weapon-of-first-resort. A responsible nuclear state has an obligation to its own people, as well as the world, to ensure maximum possible delay before invoking the strategic option.

Clandestine Acquisition of Technology: India's polemical approach to nuclear issues was manifest in its attribution of Pakistan's achievement of nuclear capability to the transfer of technology from outside. Pakistan has always been grateful to China for technology cooperation, but India underestimated the capacity and dedication of Pakistani scientists and engineers who successfully assimilated knowledge available in the public domain to develop indigenous designs of nuclear weapons and ballistic missiles. Paying tribute to thousands of Pakistani scientists who dedicated their careers to weapons programme, Dr Samar Mubarakmand said, 'You have done it. Pakistan has done it.'

NOTES

1. Much of the factual information in this chapter has greatly benefited from Brigadier (Retd.) Feroz Hassan Khan's *Eating Grass: The Making of the Pakistani Bomb.*
2. Cited in Feroz Hassan Khan, op. cit., 352, quoting Roger Boyes, *London Times*, 8 April 2002.
3. Khan, Feroz Hassan, op. cit., 247–8. The cruise missiles were developed by reverse engineering the design of US *Tomahawk* missiles that fell unexploded on Pakistan territory in 1998 when US attacked the Osama bin Laden terrorist camps in Afghanistan.
4. Sanger, op. cit., 67.
5. For detailed information on the Khan network's activities see Brigadier (retd.) Feroz Hassan Khan, *Eating Grass: The Making of the Pakistani Bomb*, Stanford University Press, Stanford, 2012, chapter 19, quoting references to published sources of information and briefings provided by SPD.
6. Lewis A. Dunn, *Containing Nuclear Proliferation*; Steven E. Miller, 'The Case Against a Ukrainian Deterrent,' *Foreign Affairs*, No. 72, (Summer 1973); Scott D. Sagan, 'The Perils of Proliferation,' *International Security* 18 (Spring 1994) and others listed by Sagan, 67, footnote 5.
7. Kenneth N. Waltz, *The Spread of Nuclear Weapons: More may be Better*, Adelphi Papers, no. 171 (London, 1981); John J. Mearsheimer, 'The Case for a Ukrainian Nuclear Deterrent,' *Foreign Affairs* No. 72 (Summer 1973); Barry R. Posen, 'The Security Dilemma and Ethnic Conflict,' *International Survival* 35, (Spring 93) and others listed by Scott D. Sagan, himself an opponent, in Sagan, op. cit., 66 and footnote 4 on 67.

8. Kenneth N. Waltz, op. cit., 3.
9. Robert McNamara, *Blundering into Disaster.*
10. S. Rashid Naim, '*Adhi Raat ke Baad*' in Stephen P. Cohen, *Nuclear Proliferation in South Asia*, (Westview Press, Boulder, CO, 1991.
11. Hoodbhoy, Pervez, *Confronting the Bomb: Pakistani and Indian Scientists Speak Out*, Oxford University Press, 2012.
12. Steven E. Miller, op. cit., 73.

Chapter 19

Increasing Isolation, 1990–2001

If, in the 1980s, Pakistan rose from isolation to a position of international respect and admiration for its courageous role in support of the Afghans' struggle against Soviet intervention, the turn of the decade reversed the trend. The process started with a return of the international limelight on Pakistan's nuclear programme and the imposition of sanctions by the United States. The world community, which initially blamed India for repression and gross violation of human rights in Kashmir, became increasingly critical also of Pakistan's interference in the state. Islamabad's declarations that its role was limited to political, diplomatic, and moral support for the liberation struggle were openly questioned. Washington took the lead by considering inclusion of Pakistan in the list of states accused of sponsoring terrorism. As the only state that recognized the Taliban regime, Pakistan was saddled with the responsibility for their policies. Poor governance, reckless international borrowing, and rampant corruption added to Pakistan's increasing loss of prestige. Stringent international sanctions imposed after the 1998 nuclear tests aggravated the economic plight. The Kargil episode projected Pakistan as an 'irresponsible' state. Intervention by the army and the overthrow of an elected government in October 1999 attracted 'democratic sanctions' that tightened the financial squeeze. To cope with the challenge, General Pervez Musharraf's government began the process of rescuing the state from international isolation. It began with earnest internal reforms and stringent austerity that averted further borrowing even before the government's decision to cooperate with the United States in the war on terrorism after 9/11 rehabilitated the state in the international mainstream.

US Sanctions Again

No sooner did the Soviet forces complete their withdrawal from Afghanistan in 1989 than the nuclear issue began once again to dominate Pakistan-US relations. Washington asked Islamabad to discontinue the weapons research programme. When it declined, the Pressler Amendment was activated. Adopted by the Senate in 1985, it required the US president to provide an annual certificate that Pakistan did not possess a nuclear weapon, failing which economic and military assistance to Pakistan was prohibited. So long as the Soviet forces were in Afghanistan, President Ronald Reagan had issued the certificate without much fuss. President George H. W. Bush did the same in 1989, but then the US became intrusive and demanding about the research they knew Pakistan had been carrying on for many years, and the president declined to issue the certificate in 1990. The US immediately cut off $700 million in assistance it was pledged to provide to Pakistan annually during 1988–94. It also declined to permit the transfer of F-16 aircraft and other military equipment for which the US had earlier cleared commercial contracts with manufacturers and Pakistan had paid a billion dollars in cash. An embargo was even ordered on the return of Pakistan-owned equipment sent to the United States for repairs with costs paid in advance. Predictably, the US decision revived bitter memories of Pakistan's past grievances of US refusal to honour commitments. It was manifestly wrong for the United States to renege on the six-year agreement for economic and military assistance. The injustice of refusing to deliver the F-16s for which Pakistan had paid was not rectified until 1995, when President Clinton finally acknowledged it was unfair to keep both the equipment and the cash and ordered reimbursement of the payments Pakistan had made as well as the return of Pakistan's own equipment, which lay ageing in the United States.

Fortunately, international financial institutions and bilateral donors—especially Japan, which was providing $500 million a year—did not follow the US example. Still, the economy suffered a severe jolt and the predicament continued to aggravate as the government failed to adjust budgetary policies and was progressively caught in a debt trap.

Support for the Taliban

Pakistan recognized the Taliban government in May 1997 after it gained control of the capital. Recognition was considered necessary for conduct of normal business, visas for thousands of travellers, and transit trade for landlocked Afghanistan. Islamabad also valued the Taliban's friendly disposition, cooperation, and political support. However, the statement of a Pakistani federal minister calling the Taliban 'our boys' was a figment.[1] The Taliban, like most Afghans, were nationalists and decided their policies to serve their own priorities. Stubborn in pursuit of their agenda, the purblind Taliban paid little heed to Pakistan's suggestions. In dealing with Pakistan, they relied on old madrasa networks and Pakistani religious parties for support, and even tried to export their obscurantist views to promote extremism and sectarian violence in Pakistan. They even refused to extradite proclaimed offenders wanted by Pakistan's judicial authorities for prosecution. Besides, Pakistan, constrained due to nuclear and democratic sanctions, lacked the means on which influence travels.

The Taliban's record of governance was controversial. Eradication of opium cultivation and prohibition on carrying of arms were exemplary achievements. Crime declined, but their stern authoritarian rule, extremist interpretations of sharia law, harsh corporal punishments, confinement of women, and closing of schools for girls converted Afghanistan into a puritanical state. Mullah Omar's decision to demolish ancient Buddha statues in Bamiyan in 2001 provoked universal outrage and condemnation.[2] Particularly suicidal was his decision to allow sanctuary to Osama bin Laden and his followers, who abused it for planning and perpetrating terrorist attacks on the United States.

Mullah Omar persisted in the view that the world was wrong in calling Osama bin Laden a terrorist mastermind. Refusing to heed the writing on the wall even after 9/11, he did not expel al-Qaeda. His recklessness not only doomed the Taliban regime but also exposed Pakistan to dire consequences.

Declining Prestige

Another issue that undermined international goodwill for Pakistan was corruption at high levels. Transparency International, a monitoring organization in Germany, declared Pakistan the second most corrupt country in the world.[3] Poor governance, fiscal extravagance, mounting budgetary deficits, and an escalating debt burden pushed Pakistan to the brink of insolvency. By 1999, the accumulated burden of foreign debt amounted to $38 billion and the annual cost of servicing it to over $5 billion. With exports stagnant at $8 billion, the payments gap widened, and recurrent scams and defaulted loans of nationalized banks raised the spectre of a deep economic crisis and financial crash.

More Sanctions

Not only was Pakistan the target of sanctions after it followed India to carry out tests in May 1998, but its economy was more vulnerable to the aid cut off by countries that had continued to provide loans after the US terminated assistance in 1990, including Japan, which was extending yen credits of $500 million a year. The government resorted to a freeze of $11 billion in foreign currency deposits which the state had attracted by the solemn pledge of transferability. The deposits could now be cashed only in devalued rupees, involving a loss of thirty per cent to account holders expecting payment in foreign currency. The default antagonized hundreds of thousands of people who had trusted the government. Remittances from Pakistanis abroad nose-dived.

Pakistan-India Dialogue, 1997–1999

Dialogue between Pakistan and India, suspended in 1994 because it proved sterile, was reopened in February 1997 at the level of foreign secretaries. The Indian emphasis was, as usual, on normalization of trade and travel, though it was willing to discuss all issues. Pakistan underlined the centrality of the Kashmir issue. The gap between the two positions was not bridged when Prime Ministers Nawaz Sharif and I. K. Gujral held a meeting at Male in May 1997. Gujral reportedly pleaded that his minority government was too weak to make a bold policy shift. Sharif countered by saying that no government in Pakistan, however strong its majority in parliament, could ignore popular opinion in the country.

For the first time since the Kashmir dispute arose, a *hartal* was called by the All Parties Hurriyat Conference in Kashmir when the prime ministers met. A Kashmiri spokesman explained that while the Kashmiri people welcomed these talks, the dispute involved three parties, and any attempt to strike a deal between two without the association of the third would fail to yield a credible settlement.[4] He also appealed that the world community should promote an initiative towards settlement of the Kashmir dispute in order to end the bloodshed and suffering of the Kashmiri people, eliminating regional tensions and the risk of a nuclear war between India and Pakistan.

In June 1997, the foreign secretaries of the two countries met in Islamabad and agreed to recommence dialogue on all outstanding issues of concern to the two sides, and to set up working groups for the purpose. The prime ministers met three months later on the sidelines of a UN summit in New York and exchanged mutual expressions of determination to renew and reinvigorate efforts for durable peace.

Lahore Summit: The prime minister of India, Atal Bihari Vajpayee, visited Pakistan from 20–1 February 1999, travelling to Lahore on the inaugural run of the Delhi-Lahore bus service. He and Prime Minister Nawaz Sharif concluded the most prolific, if not successful, summit with three documents.[5] In a declaration, the two leaders agreed to undertake 'immediate steps' for reducing the risk of accidental or unauthorized use of nuclear weapons and discuss concepts and doctrines, and in a memorandum of understanding pledged to 'continue to abide by their respective unilateral moratoria on conducting further nuclear explosions unless either side, in exercise of its national sovereignty, decides that extraordinary events have jeopardized its supreme interest.' The two sides further undertook to provide each other with advance notification with respect to ballistic missile flight tests.

The Lahore documents were comprehensive and covered the whole gamut of issues of bilateral interest ranging from commitment to 'intensify their efforts to resolve all issues, including the issue of Jammu and Kashmir' to 'condemnation of terrorism in all its forms and manifestations' and 'undertaking national measures to reduce the risks of accidental or unauthorized use of nuclear weapons.'

The summit was a grand, if ephemeral, success. Neither the beginning nor the end of the summit proved auspicious, however. It was greeted with vociferous protests in Lahore against India's brutal repression in Kashmir. On returning to New Delhi, the Indian leaders downplayed the importance of the commitment to resolve the outstanding issues. In Pakistan, influential sections of opinion criticized the emphasis on bilateral negotiations and the failure to mention even the United Nations' principles for governing bilateral relations (as in the Shimla Agreement). The 'Lahore process' glorified by the two sides was considered a convenient alibi to world opinion, and especially influential powers, to abdicate responsibility to promote a just settlement of the Kashmir question.

Particularly insensitive was the reference to the 'sanctity' of the Line of Control. It invested this temporary line with a characteristic that applies to international boundaries and departed from Pakistan's view which maintained that the Line of Control 'resulting from the ceasefire of 17 December 1971' was, like the 1949 ceasefire line, a temporary arrangement to be respected by both sides pending a final settlement of Jammu and Kashmir.

The Kargil Crisis, 1999

A grave crisis erupted following intrusion of armed personnel from Pakistan into the Kargil heights in Kashmir in May 1999. Islamabad denied the facts and attributed the fighting to Kashmiri freedom fighters, recalling that after promising at the Lahore Summit to intensify efforts to resolve all issues including Jammu and Kashmir, Indian leaders in statements on their return to Delhi portrayed insincerity and absence of serious intent. It recalled also that the UN Security Council's call in its resolution of June 1998 for the resumption of dialogue to remove the root causes of tensions, including Kashmir, was not followed up, and that Indian Home Minister Lal Krishna Advani had embarked on a 'proactive' policy, intensified repression in Indian-held Kashmir, resorted to recurrent violations of the Line of Control forcing closure of the Neelum Valley road in Azad Kashmir, and subjected the villages to fierce artillery bombardment. Few foreign countries credited Pakistan's disclaimer, however. Statements issued by the G-8, the United States, Britain, and Germany implicitly blamed Pakistan for the 'intruders' in Kargil.

As armed men penetrated the Kargil-Dras sector and seized high ground threatening the Srinagar-Leh road, an artery in the summer months for stockpiling supplies for Indian garrisons in Ladakh and Siachen, India denounced the operation as a violation of the Shimla Agreement and retaliated with a massive air and army operation to dislodge the guerrillas. Describing them as Islamic militants, Taliban, and regular army personnel, India accused Pakistan of aggression.

Indian bombardment targeted not only the Kargil Heights on the Indian side of the Line of Control but also the alleged supply bases on the Pakistan side. Also, duels raged elsewhere along the Line of Control. In an attempt to defuse the situation, the Pakistani foreign minister was sent to New Delhi on 12 June for diplomatic efforts for de-escalation and dialogue. He was accorded a frigid and hostile reception. India took a rigid, no-negotiation stance, insisting on Pakistani withdrawal of personnel from Kargil before discussion on any other issue. Briefing the press after the meeting, the Indian foreign minister used the word 'demand' three times in one minute.

Meanwhile, concern mounted internationally that the fighting in Kargil might escalate and lead to a general war between Pakistan and India, now declared nuclear states. The Group of Eight (industrialized countries) considered 'infiltration of armed intruders' as 'irresponsible'.[6] The European Union called for 'the immediate withdrawal of infiltrators.' Washington asked Pakistan to withdraw 'its forces' and 'restore *status quo ante*'. Only the OIC backed the Pakistani position by asking for de-escalation and dialogue. China did not criticize Pakistan and called on both India and Pakistan to 'respect the Line of Control'.

Prime Minister Nawaz Sharif sued for the US president's intercession to defuse the crisis. Clinton received Sharif for an emergency meeting on Sunday, 4 July, US Independence Day. He discussed the situation with Prime Minister Vajpayee over the phone and persuaded Sharif to agree to a joint statement which provided for immediate cessation of hostilities, concrete steps to be taken for the restoration of the Line of Control in accordance with the Shimla Agreement, and resumption of a Pakistan-India dialogue as begun in Lahore in February 1999 for resolving all issues dividing India and Pakistan, including Kashmir. President Clinton promised to take a personal interest in encouraging an expeditious resumption and intensification of the bilateral efforts 'once the sanctity of the Line of Control has been fully restored.' Military officers of Pakistan and India later agreed on steps for disengagement. The Pakistani personnel withdrew from Kargil by 16 July.

Reading into the Washington joint statement a US pledge of effort to promote settlement of the Kashmir question was not only a spin aimed at misleading public opinion but a self-deception. From authoritative clarifications given by US administration officials, it became clear that all that the president had promised, after careful prior clearance with New Delhi, was 'personal interest' in promoting the 'Lahore process'.

A US official compared Sharif's dash to Washington to Yahya Khan's request for US help in the face of a rapidly deteriorating situation in the 1971 war.[7] Henry Kissinger had then remarked that the US was asked to be in at the crash-landing when it was not in on the take-off! If Pakistan was mercifully spared that biting sarcasm this time, it was partly because all that it asked was the proverbial fig leaf to cover retreat from an impulsive adventure undertaken without forethought.

Most commentators blamed the Pakistan government for losing sight of strategy in a tactical bid to awaken international attention to the festering Kashmir dispute. Given the power disparity, a military solution was obviously out of question. A war that could escalate to the nuclear level was considered inconceivable. One eminent journalist castigated the government saying, '. . . the original political blunder of approving a strategically flawed and unsustainable plan of guerrilla action was compounded first by diplomatic and domestic mishandling and then by a sudden and inadequately explained policy volte-face.'[8] A provident policy had to steer clear of extremes of bravado and soul-destroying capitulation.

Prime Minister Nawaz Sharif and Chief of Army Staff General Pervez Musharraf were held 'responsible for approving this misconceived operation.' While some described the operation as 'tactically brilliant', others considered it 'a complete fiasco'. A spokesman of the All Parties Hurriyat Conference of Jammu and Kashmir described the Pakistan government's policy as 'unpredictable'.[9] Another APHC leader said, 'First we were excluded, then betrayed.'[10]

Inconsistent and contradictory statements undermined Pakistan's credibility. Its spokesmen disclaimed knowledge of the mujahideen operation in Kargil one day and accepted responsibility for their withdrawal the next day. Shallow thinking was manifest also in pendulum swings from naive bus diplomacy to the Kargil gamble, from glorifying bilateral negotiations in the Lahore declaration to self-deceiving claims of success in inducting American interest in resolving Kashmir. Politics of corruption and crass calculation of immediate political advantage was diagnosed as the main reason for the shallow and myopic policies of the ruling families, along with the absence of long-term thinking and institutional decision-making.

Autopsies of the Kargil crisis by Pakistani commentators underlined agonising dilemmas that Pakistan faced in regard to the Kashmir issue. If it did not act, India could claim to have achieved a final solution; if it did, it incurred the risk of war. Similarly placed were the Kashmiri people: if they did not struggle for freedom, they were considered to have acquiesced in India's illegal annexation; if they did, they were subjected to savage repression, killings, torture, and other excesses no human being should have to suffer in a civilized world.

Misconceived policies and actions not only isolated Pakistan internationally, they also gravely damaged the heroic freedom struggle of the Kashmiri people. Focus shifted from indigenous agitation for self-determination to Indian allegations of its Pakistani sponsorship, from inhuman Indian excesses in Kashmir to restraint in limiting response to its side of the Line of Control, from brutality of Indian forces against the Kashmiri people to bravery on the Kargil Heights.

If the Kargil episode exposed Pakistan to international censure, it also opened a breach between the prime minister and the Army hierarchy. Nawaz Sharif was reported to have blamed the army for keeping him ignorant of the plan for the Kargil operation. A few months later, Sharif dismissed Chief of Army Staff General Pervez Musharraf while Musharraf was on his way back from a visit to Sri Lanka and ordered refusal of landing facilities to the PIA airliner on which Musharraf was a passenger. Musharraf, however, refused to be diverted to another destination, and the Karachi corps commander intervened to save the passengers and crew as the plane ran low on fuel. On return, the chief of staff took over the government in a bloodless coup.

Coping with Isolation

General Pervez Musharraf, chief executive of the new government, focused efforts on improving governance and rectification of Pakistan's fiscal predicament. A decision was taken to stabilize the debt burden, which had grown by $3 billion a year during the 1990s to $38 billion. Since foreign aid was cut off, exports were stagnant at $8 billion, and remittances had declined, so the debt-servicing burden of over $5 billion a year necessitated austerity and belt-tightening. None of the ministers in the sixteen-member cabinet asked for replacement of old cars. Even some development projects had to be postponed. Priority attention was given to accountability and recovery of defaulted loans. By the end of June 2001, efforts had yielded a measure of success; exports increased by 10 per cent, tax revenues increased, and foreign debt remained stable.

Meanwhile, friendly countries maintained solidarity with Pakistan. Saudi Arabia was generous in economic assistance. China and Kuwait provided balance of payments support. Premier Zhu Rongji visited Pakistan in 2001 and announced cooperation in the construction of Gwadar port. Sultan Qaboos of Oman visited Pakistan in April 2001 and extended substantial assistance for economic development apart from taking a 50 per cent share in a joint investment fund. Also, the government's performance persuaded some countries to review sanctions. Prime Minister Yoshiro Mori paid an official visit to Pakistan, announced resumption of suspended aid for development projects, and invited the foreign minister to visit Tokyo. The

With US Secretary of State Colin Powell, Washington D.C., 2001. Courtesy of Abdul Sattar.

United States appreciated Pakistan's assistance for confidential contacts with the Taliban. President Clinton did not omit Islamabad during his tour of South Asia. The US used its influence for containment of Pakistan-India tension and its officials made a valuable contribution to avert the danger of conflict.[11] The International Monetary Fund agreed to provide a loan for balance-of-payments support to Pakistan.

Bound by its rules, the Commonwealth suspended Pakistan's membership but maintained contacts. A Commonwealth ministerial action group delegation was the first to visit Pakistan at the end of October 1999 to meet with the new leadership, if only to encourage them to move towards the restoration of democracy. Privately, some of them recognized the baneful effects of corruption. In a meeting with the C-MAG in September 2000 in New York, the Pakistan delegation urged the UK to join in efforts to reform bank secrecy laws which encouraged corruption, undermined good governance, and siphoned off scarce capital. More than lectures on democracy, reform of these laws in countries like the UK, Switzerland, and Luxembourg would help address the root cause of political instability in developing countries like Pakistan. Despite United Nations and World Bank recognition of the problem of corruption, and the adoption of an international convention on cooperation against corruption in 2004, progress towards rectification of bank secrecy laws remained scant.

The Agra Summit

On New Year's Day 2001, Prime Minister Atal Bihari Vajpayee wrote an article highlighting the need for India to address two outstanding issues: Kashmir and the Babri Mosque in Ayodhya. Regarding Kashmir, he went on to suggest a meeting with the Pakistani president. After a delay of nearly four months, evidently a result of internal debate, he sent an invitation for the two leaders to meet at Agra on 15 and 16 July.

The two leaders held several exclusive meetings. They recognized the need to transform the fifty-year-old confrontation into good neighbourly cooperation. To that end, President Musharraf urged earnest efforts to resolve the Kashmir dispute. Around noon on 16 July, they called in the foreign ministers and informed them of the understanding they had reached to resume dialogue which should be the basis of a declaration to be issued later that day.

Working on the draft[12] already prepared by the foreign secretaries, the two ministers agreed on a declaration text to be recommended to the leaders. President Pervez Musharraf approved it promptly. On the Indian side, the draft was considered in the cabinet committee on political affairs.[13] The meeting lasted over two hours, after which External Affairs Minister Jaswant Singh sought a meeting with his Pakistani counterpart at 6 p.m. to discuss an amendment to the one-line paragraph on Kashmir. After a short and amicable discussion, the foreign ministers agreed to the substance of the amendment desired by the Indian cabinet committee with a slight modification. The apparent hitch thus removed, the Indian conference services officials started making arrangements for the signing ceremony as the Indian minister hoped to obtain formal final approval in 'five minutes'. Once again, the cabinet committee held a long meeting. At about 9 p.m., the Pakistani side was informed that the agreement would not be signed. Held in a blaze of global multimedia coverage, the summit ended on an anticlimactic note, to the surprise of the media people and the disappointment and frustration of the Pakistan delegation.

Before departing Agra for Islamabad, the Pakistani president was told by the Indian prime minister that it had not been possible to reach agreement in the cabinet committee. He did not explain what the disagreement was about, adding only that 'the time was not favourable' and that he would visit Pakistan later to finalize the proposed agreement.

The prospect of another summit helped contain disappointment. Both sides tried to relieve the gloom. President Musharraf declared, 'I came back empty-handed but the summit was not a failure.'[14] Prime Minister Vajpayee also underlined the progress that was made 'towards bridging the two approaches in a draft joint declaration.'[15] In the same vein, Jaswant Singh said, 'I do not characterize [the summit] as a failure. I do term it as yet another step in our march towards finding lasting peace, amity, and cooperation between the two countries', adding, 'We will pick up threads from the visit of the President of Pakistan.'[16] The Pakistani foreign minister gave a similarly positive appraisal: 'The Agra Summit was '*natamam*, not *nakam*' (inconclusive, not a failure).'[17]

The optimism did not last long, however. The Indian side soon started backtracking on the agreed draft. A spokesperson of the Ministry of External Affairs said, 'No agreement was reached. There was no closure of an agreement and no subscription by signature.'[18] A week later, Vajpayee said in the parliament: 'Obviously India's concerns in vital areas—such as cross-border terrorism—will have to find place in any document that future negotiations endeavour to conclude.' Actually, this point was already covered in the draft declaration.

Meanwhile, observers on both sides speculated about what had prevented agreement at the summit. Some identified President Musharraf's breakfast meeting with Indian media luminaries on 16 July as having offended the Indian leaders. The videotape of the question-answer meeting telecast by an Indian commercial channel projected Musharraf's persuasive views on the need to address the Kashmir dispute to a spellbound audience in both countries. The Indian side was said to be angry that he had stolen a march over the Indian prime minister. Actually, there was little new in what he said. He had expressed the same view many times previously. Hours after the telecast, the Indian side had not raised the issue with the Pakistan side, and even agreed to finalize the draft of the declaration.

As for the Pakistani president's reference to Kashmir as the principal obstacle to normalization of Pakistan-India relations, that was no more than a statement of the obvious. Quite apart from the experience of Pakistan and India, normalization has seldom taken place between pairs of countries with serious disputes and differences. Recent examples of the causal link include Portugal and Indonesia over East Timor, Japan and Russia over the Northern Islands, and the US and Cuba over ideological differences.

Another explanation was later given by Prime Minster Vajpayee in a statement in parliament on 24 July, saying, 'Eventually, however, we had to abandon the quest for a joint document because of Pakistan's insistence on the settlement of the Jammu and Kashmir issue as a pre-condition for the normalization of relations.' This was factually incorrect, as the text of the draft declaration confirms. At no point in the negotiations did Pakistan present any 'pre-condition'. Similarly unfounded was the allegation that Pakistan's approach was 'unifocal'.

The draft provided for dialogue on all issues of concern to both sides, including terrorism.

More interesting was the question as to who in the Indian cabinet committee had objected to the draft. Not until months later did a clue appear in the Indian press. A usually well-informed journal attributed responsibility for obstructing agreement to the deputy prime minister, L. K. Advani, dubbing him 'the saboteur of Agra.'[19] When Vajpayee was asked at a press conference to comment on the report, he did not give a direct reply.[20] Four years later, President Musharraf publicly blamed Advani for the failure of the summit. Seven years later, Advani admitted he had torpedoed the summit, now giving a new explanation; namely that in a breakfast meeting with Indian editors, the Pakistani leader had 'blasted India's position on cross-border terrorism and Jammu and Kashmir.'[21] Even this after-thought is hardly convincing. General Musharraf had only made out a case for the resolution of the Kashmir dispute, which most guests appeared to find logical. Perhaps this made Advani unhappy. Otherwise, both Kashmir and terrorism were included among subjects for sustained dialogue at the political level in paragraph 3 of the agreed draft.

Considering that Vajpayee had conceived and canvassed the initiative for dialogue with Pakistan on Kashmir, he was probably disappointed by the outcome, and it can be assumed that he was sincere in his intention to visit Pakistan at a more favourable time to finalize the agreement. In retrospect, it would have been better for the fulfilment of his ambition to improve relations with Pakistan had he asserted leadership to persuade the one or more members of the cabinet committee who vetoed the declaration.

Another opportunity to change the course of Pakistan-India relations was missed as one more agreement fell victim to internal political battles.[22] Three months later, terrorists carried out attacks in New York and Washington that transformed the global situation.

NOTES

1. Cabinet Minister Naseerullah Babar made this factually incorrect remark after the Taliban helped rescue a convoy of Pakistani trucks held up by Afghan warlords.
2. Iran and the Northern Alliance in Afghanistan were similarly critical.

3. Transparency International's report is said to be based on surveys of business houses, etc.
4. Ghulam Nabi Fai, Director, Kashmir Center, Washington, in 'Why the world should care?' in *The News*, Islamabad, 21 May 1997.
5. The documents were the Lahore Declaration, Joint Statement and Memorandum of Understanding.
6. The G-8 summit statement of 20 June 1999, read: 'We are deeply concerned about the continuing military confrontation in Kashmir following the infiltration of armed intruders which violated the Line of Control. We regard any military action to change the status quo as irresponsible. We therefore call for the immediate end of these actions, restoration of the Line of Control and for the parties to work for immediate cessation of fighting, full respect in the future for the Line of Control, and the resumption of the dialogue between them in the spirit of the Lahore Declaration'.
7. Shirin Tahirkheli, *The News*, Islamabad, 13 July 1999.
8. Maleeha Lodhi, *Newsline*, Karachi, July 1999.
9. Comments by Air Marshal (retd.) Noor Khan, Lt. Gen. (retd.) Asad Durrani, Lt. Gen. (retd.) Kamal Mateenuddin and Gulam Nabi Safi, *The News*, 18 July 1999.
10. *The News*, 18 July 1999.
11. Undersecretary of State Thomas Pickering played a key role in contacts with Islamabad while Deputy Secretary of State Strobe Talbott was in contact with New Delhi.
12. The text of the draft is given at Appendix IV.
13. Members of the Committee, chaired by the Prime Minister, were Ministers of Commerce, Defence, External Affairs, Finance, and Home Affairs. Portfolios of Defence and External Affairs were held by one minister.
14. President Pervez Musharraf, Press Conference, 20 July 2001.
15. Prime Minister A. B. Vajpayee, statement in the Indian Parliament, 24 July 2001.
16. External Affairs Minister of India Jaswant Singh, press conference, 17 July 2001.
17. Foreign Minister Abdul Sattar, press conference, 17 July 2001.
18. Report by AFP quoted in *Dawn*, Islamabad, 21 July 2001.
19. *India Today*, November 2001.
20. When a Pakistani journalist asked in an interview with Prime Minister Vajpayee on 1 January 2004 if the agreement was sabotaged by some elements in the Indian cabinet, Vajpayee said 'the draft was written by the two foreign ministers, but it had not had the governmental approval'. *Dawn*, Islamabad, 2 January 2004.
21. L. K. Advani's interview with *Times of India*'s quoted in *Dawn*, Islamabad, 18 March 2008.
22. The two countries agreed, for instance, that the question of the accession of the State of Jammu and Kashmir would be decided through the democratic method of a free and impartial plebiscite, and that the commitment was sanctified in resolutions adopted by the UN Security Council in 1948 and 1949. Later, India gave the resolutions unilateral interpretations and came up with novel explanations to renege on its obligation. The Shimla Agreement and the Lahore Declaration suffered a similar fate.

CHAPTER 20

Post 9/11 Policy

The terrorist attacks on the World Trade Center and the Pentagon on 11 September 2001 triggered a transformation of world politics as profound and far-reaching as the television images of hijacked airliners crashing into the symbols of American military and economic power were surreal. More than three thousand people were killed and material losses amounted to a hundred billion dollars or more. The unprecedented and never-imagined assault on the US mainland was more destructive than the attack on Pearl Harbour in 1941. The American nation was traumatized and seethed with rage and an urge for revenge. President George W. Bush articulated a fierce resolve to hunt down culprits responsible for planning and organizing the terrorist outrage.

The world community reacted with shock. All condemned the attack and expressed condolences and solidarity with the American people. The president of Pakistan issued a strong statement of condemnation and sympathy. He also affirmed Pakistan's readiness to join the United States in the fight against terrorism.

The US media instantly pointed a finger of accusation at Osama bin Laden, naming him as the mastermind behind the terrorist attacks. As these implicated the Taliban government in Afghanistan and speculated about likely US action against it, a sense of crisis and foreboding dominated the air in Islamabad. Because of its geographical location and as the sole supporter of the Taliban regime, Pakistan was bound to face painful choices in the days ahead.

Pakistan's Policy Planning

President Musharraf, who was on tour in Karachi, returned to Islamabad on the evening of 12 September and immediately attended

Pervez Musharraf (President of Pakistan, 2001–8). Courtesy of the National Archives of Pakistan.

a high-level meeting to discuss the grave crisis and its implications for Pakistan. Until then, there had been no contact or communication between the governments of Pakistan and the United States. It was not difficult, however, to surmise that the United States would take military action against the Taliban. Two years earlier, attributing the attacks on US embassies in East Africa to Osama bin Laden and his followers, the US had fired missiles from ships at sea to bomb suspected terrorist camps in Afghanistan, without asking Pakistan for permission to fly over its territory. It was presumable that the US would react with even greater force now. What should be Pakistan's response if the US asked for permission not merely for overflights but also made other, more problematic, demands? The question required anticipation and consideration of Pakistan's options. Whilst it was obvious that Pakistan had to avoid opposition to US policy, and a refusal to cooperate would not only be ineffectual but might also provoke US hostility, it was necessary to evolve a strategy of approach, keeping in the forefront both the national interest and the need for a realistic assessment of the obtaining environment.

It was assumed that major powers would extend cooperation to the United States in punishing the terrorists. None would oppose a likely US decision to mount an attack against the Taliban. No proof would be asked, or considered necessary, of Taliban complicity with bin Laden. Already, a year earlier, the Security Council had condemned and imposed sanctions on the Taliban precisely because they provided bin Laden with sanctuary and a base for terrorist activities. In the new, more grave circumstances, the Security Council would be even more sympathetic to the United States. Some of the major powers might even join in the attack, and the Arab countries and Central Asian neighbours of Afghanistan would probably agree to allow use of landing facilities for US aircraft. India, already canvassing Indo-US cooperation against terrorism, was likely to provide assistance.

The Security Council resolution of December 2000 had imposed sanctions against the Taliban under Chapter VII requiring compulsory compliance. Pakistan had cooperated by closing Taliban-controlled banks and curtailing official contacts. In the graver situation now, a defiant policy course was out of the question. The horizon was dark with dangers. Pakistan might be bracketed with the Taliban, declared a 'terrorist state', and subjected to attacks to neutralize resistance. Pakistan's vital interests would be in jeopardy if India was given a free hand against Pakistan. The Kashmiri freedom struggle might be labelled a terrorist insurgency. Azad Kashmir and Pakistan territory could be attacked under the pretext of eliminating terrorist bases. It was known that in the 1980s, India had pondered an attack on Kahuta. It might again entertain thoughts of targeting Pakistan's nuclear assets.

Objective analysis of the situation pointed to an obvious conclusion: Pakistan had to pursue a strategy that would reduce risks to Pakistan's own security and strategic interests. It had to steer clear of defiance and avoid offence to the United States. The question was not whether Pakistan could exploit its strategic location for economic or political benefits from the United States; the weightier and decisive factor was the predictable cost of non-cooperation. At the same time, long term considerations and cultural and geographical bonds with Afghanistan precluded any actions that might offend the interests or sensibilities of the Afghan people.

The crisis called for a policy that balanced global and regional constraints, immediate imperatives and long-term interests, national priorities and the norms of an international order based on principles of international law. Cautious cooperation in a UN-approved action against the Taliban emerged as the only feasible alternative. Its components would include: (a) Pakistan should join the global consensus; (b) it could not and should not oppose US attacks on targets in Afghanistan; and (c) in the event of US request for Pakistan's cooperation, it should indicate a generally positive disposition and negotiate details later. Such a 'yes-but' approach would allow Pakistan tactical flexibility. It could then also seek modification of US policy and its expectations of Pakistan.

It should be noted that Pakistan's strategy was decided, in broad outline, on the evening of 12 September—still forenoon in Washington—on the basis of objective analysis of contingencies and anticipation of the likely course of events, and before, not after, any specific requests were received from the United States. Until then, US leaders had said little. Public statements by President Bush and administration officials on 12 September were heard in Islamabad either late that night or on 13 September, due to the time difference with Washington.

The clairvoyance of Pakistan's analysis was soon borne out by the events, as world consensus solidified in favour of the United States. The Security Council and the General Assembly adopted unanimous resolutions on 12 September which condemned the terrorist outrage, extended condolences to the United States, and called for bringing the perpetrators, sponsors, and organizers to justice. NATO invoked the treaty provision for joint defence. Canada, UK, Germany, France, and Denmark offered military contingents for a coalition force to attack the Taliban. China, Japan, and Russia expressed solidarity with the coalition. Turkey and the states of Central and South Asia, including India, Bangladesh, and Sri Lanka, indicated willingness to provide logistic facilities, as did several Arab countries.

US Policy

Soon the contours of US policy began to emerge. On 12 September, President George W. Bush spoke of a 'monumental struggle of good versus evil.'[1] Secretary of State Colin Powell announced that the US expected 'the fullest cooperation' of Pakistan. In another statement on 13 September, President Bush said those who harboured terrorists would be treated as terrorists. Asked whether he had made any progress in obtaining cooperation from Pakistan, Bush replied, 'We will give the Pakistani government a chance to cooperate.'[2] The note of warning was unmistakable.

US records that became available three years later confirmed the apprehensions Pakistan had anticipated. In a restricted National Security Council meeting chaired by President Bush on 11 September, Secretary of State Powell said, 'The United States had to make it clear to Pakistan, Afghanistan, and the Arab states that the time to act was now.'[3] Also, the NSC Principals Committee, on 13 September, 'focused on Pakistan and what it could do to turn the Taliban against al-Qaeda (and) concluded that if Pakistan decided not to help the United States, it too would be at risk.'[4]

On 13 September, US Deputy Secretary of State Richard Armitage summoned the ambassador of Pakistan and the Director General of Inter-Services Intelligence, then on a visit to Washington, for a meeting to convey the list of seven steps the United States wanted

Pakistan to take. He was reported to have painted a stark picture: the situation was black or white. Pakistan had a choice to make. Either it was with the US or it was not. There were no half measures. There was no room for manoeuvre. 'The future starts today.' The 'seven steps' were:

- to stop al-Qaeda operations at its border and end all logistical support for bin Laden.
- to give the United States blanket overflight and landing rights for all necessary military and intelligence operations.
- to provide the United States with intelligence information.
- to provide territorial access to US and allied military intelligence and other personnel to conduct operations against al-Qaeda.
- to continue to publicly condemn the terrorist acts.
- to cut off all shipments of fuel to the Taliban and stop recruits from going to Afghanistan.
- if the evidence implicated bin Laden and al-Qaeda, and the Taliban continued to harbour them, to break relations with the Taliban government.[5]

Having decided on its strategy in advance, Islamabad was in a position to give a prompt and generally positive response when the US request was received,[6] with details on some points to be worked out later. The impression that Pakistan had 'totally' acquiesced in US 'demands' was incorrect. Actually, Pakistan's role was to be within acceptable limits. Still, Pakistan made substantial concessions and President Musharraf made that point in his response, suggesting that the people needed to see Pakistan was benefiting from the decision.[7] As the US requests were examined in detail, a couple of points required no action: Pakistan had already condemned terrorist attacks, and it had not provided logistic access to bin Laden. Some misguided *imams* (preachers) in the border areas had encouraged simple youths to go to Afghanistan to fight on the side of the Taliban, but this was never approved or encouraged by the government. Diplomatic relations with the Taliban were to be cut off only if bin Laden was implicated and the Taliban still continued to harbour him. The extent of logistic support to US forces was to be worked out, as was territorial access. Pakistan later allowed the use of three landing strips for logistic purposes and provisions for the coalition forces in Afghanistan were sent via Pakistani ports. However, US war operations were conducted from naval ships or distant bases, not from Pakistani territory. Pakistan did not participate in US military action in Afghanistan.

Consultation with Opinion Leaders

Over a period of about two weeks, the president held lengthy and interactive discussions with a dozen groups of prominent people from various walks of national life, including leaders of political parties, the intelligentsia, media luminaries, *ulema* and *mashaikh*, influential persons from areas adjoining Afghanistan, labour leaders, women, youth, and minorities. He gave them a candid analysis of the costs and benefits of the policy options. Their response was reassuring. They were realistic in their assessment of the gravity of the situation and the need for circumspection. Most—some 90 per cent—agreed with the president's conclusions.

Only the *ulema* (religious scholars) differed. A majority of them opposed cooperation with the US, arguing that right was on the side of the Taliban and religious duty therefore required Pakistan to support them, regardless of costs and consequences. The deductive reasoning was obviously flawed. Moreover, other religious scholars put forward convincing refutation by citing instances from early Islamic history, showing that a leader had the duty to take into account the countervailing circumstances in specific situations before deciding a policy in the best interest of the community. Particularly weighty and relevant were the sagacious decisions of the Prophet (PBUH) to enter into a treaty with the Jews of Madinah after the *Hijrah*, and the Hudaibiya peace agreement with the non-Muslim rulers of Makkah despite the objection of some eminent *Sahaba* (companions).

After the US-led coalition attacked Afghanistan on 6 October, Pakistani religious parties called for demonstrations. Assessing the situation intelligently, the public doubted the wisdom of protest, and participation was limited to a narrow section of opinion. As in other Muslim countries, so also in Pakistan most people realized that the Taliban had provoked the attack and rejected the argument that the war on terrorism was a war against the Muslim world. Islam disapproves and abhors the killing of even a single innocent person. Extremism and violence were not acceptable to the vast majority. That assessment was soon validated by the declining numbers of people who participated in street demonstrations.

The US and the West applauded the Pakistan government for enlightened leadership, and manifested their solidarity by visits to Pakistan. Never before had so many leaders come to Pakistan as in the months after September, one on the heels of the other and sometimes on the same day.[8] They included heads of government of the UK, Germany, Belgium, and the Netherlands, US secretaries of state and defence, foreign ministers of Japan, UK, France, Germany, Greece, and Norway, and the Troika delegation of the European Union. The president of Turkey, prime minister of Lebanon, and foreign ministers of Saudi Arabia, Egypt, Iran, Turkey, and Oman came on visits. Other dignitaries included the UN Secretary General, UNDP Administrator, UNHCR, and UN High Commissioner for Human Rights, the OIC Secretary General, and a number of special envoys.

Economic Cooperation and Assistance

Although Islamabad did not bargain for a quid pro quo, it was not unmindful of the value and importance of its contribution to the fight against terrorism and hence of Pakistan's entitlement to reciprocity by the US and other Western countries. It made known its expectation of the termination of the so-called non-proliferation and democratic sanctions and the resumption of support and assistance. They evinced understanding of Pakistan's hardships on account of past mismanagement and corruption and the rise of international debt and loss in exports due to the destabilizing effect of the military action in Afghanistan, and their response became progressively more forthcoming.

Appreciating Pakistan's key role as a 'frontline state' in the war on terrorism, the United States, the European Union, and Japan dismantled nuclear and democratic sanctions and resumed assistance to Pakistan. Individually or collectively, they agreed to write off or reschedule the debt. Apart from immediate fiscal relief, improvement of relations with major countries yielded long-term aid and trade benefits, as well as an empathetic political environment conducive to the maintenance of peace in the region.

USA: The Brownback-II Amendment authorized the US President to waive 'democratic sanctions.' The Ackerman Amendment in 2004 waived the nuclear sanctions for five years. The US President issued a waiver to allow resumption of economic assistance and military sales. The US agreed to write off a part of Pakistan's debt and immediately provided $600 million as economic aid and $177 million as military and security assistance for 2002. In 2003, the US agreed to provide $3 billion over five years in economic and military assistance. In addition, the Bush administration extended low-interest credits for the purchase of airliners for PIA, expanded trade access with long-term benefits for Pakistan's exports that rose to nearly three billion dollars in 2004, and agreed to sell C-130 transport planes, a P-3 Orion marine surveillance aircraft, TOW anti-tank missiles, and other equipment for defence valued at $1.2 billion. In March 2005, the United States further decided to sell F-16 aircrafts to Pakistan.

Over the period 2001–07, total transfers from the United States to Pakistan amounted to $7.1 billion, including $2.3 billion in military assistance, budgetary support, development assistance, earthquake relief, and $4.8 billion in reimbursement of expenditures on logistic support to US forces in Afghanistan. In addition, the US wrote off $1.6 billion in debt.[9]

EU: The European Union reflected its appreciation of Pakistan's policy in its decisions regarding economic assistance and market access. It joined the US-led efforts to prevent a Pakistan-India war in 2002. Also, its stance on Kashmir reflected recognition of the root cause of the protracted agitation and violence in the disputed state.

Japan: Not misled by false assumptions, Japan had neither exaggerated Pakistan's capacity to influence the Taliban nor adopted a hard stance toward Pakistan after nuclear tests in May 1998. It even considered resumption of development assistance, if Pakistan signed the CTBT. Prime Minister Yoshiro Mori was the only First World leader, apart from Clinton, to visit Pakistan between October 1999 and September

2001. Japan also made an exception to the suspension of aid by providing a loan for the second phase of the Kohat tunnel.

After 9/11, Japan, like most countries, welcomed the change in Afghanistan and appreciated Pakistan's cooperation against terrorism. It decided to provide $300 million as grant assistance and supported Pakistan's case in the IMF and the Paris Club. Prime Minister Junichiro Koizumi invited President Musharraf to visit in March 2002 and accorded him a warm reception. Japan's support in the Paris Club for rescheduling bilateral debt brought substantial relief, as with $5 billion Japan was the biggest creditor of Pakistan. In April 2005, Koizumi announced recommencement of official development assistance that had been suspended after Pakistan conducted nuclear tests in 1998. Until then, Japan's ODA amounted to $500 million a year.

Debt Rescheduling: More substantial was long-term relief in debt servicing as a result of the Paris Club's decision to reschedule $12 billion in bilateral debt at lower interest rates and extended maturities, effectively reducing the burden by thirty per cent.

US Commitment, 2001–9: Pakistan has nourished historical grievances against the United States for going back on its commitments after achieving its immediate objectives. It first welcomed alliances with Pakistan in the 1950s but then allowed them to wither in the 1960s. Pakistan's courageous opposition to the Soviet occupation of Afghanistan was admired by the United States in the 1980s, but as soon as the Soviet forces withdrew, Washington re-imposed nuclear sanctions against Pakistan in 1990, leaving Pakistan in the lurch, without resources to cope with the burden of millions of Afghan refugees, thousands of foreign jihadis recruited by the CIA, and blow back of militancy and Kalashnikov culture from a destroyed Afghanistan.

But no longer was Pakistan alone in hankering after durable commitment. Washington, too, seemed to have recognized the need to contain the volatility that has characterized its past relations with Pakistan. Now, officials in high places in the Bush administration began to entertain doubts about Pakistan's reliability for sustained support to the United States. The Chairman of the key House

Appropriations Committee, which recommends budgetary allocations for financial assistance, questioned the degree of Pakistan's cooperation.[10] Deputy Secretary of State Armitage thought Pakistan had agreed to cooperate because it had little choice, implying it might back out.[11]

This was welcome news to people in Pakistan, who place great emphasis on sincerity, as much in inter-state relations as inter-personal ones: a reflection no doubt of the nation's culture that invests *dosti* (friendship) with characteristics of *ishq* (devotion), and expects a friend to be constant, faithful, selfless, and sacrificing. Only those with knowledge of international relations recognize that such an expectation ignores history. Protection and promotion of the strategic and economic interests of a state is the guiding factor in foreign policy.

Nevertheless, a British statesman's adage, 'We have permanent interests but not permanent friends', is only partly correct, for interests, too, are subject to change with evolution of the environment, and friends are always an asset, especially in adversity. Such a transition of understanding took place in Washington after 9/11. It was realized that the sudden termination of support for Pakistan in 1990, and US neglect of Afghanistan after the Soviet withdrawal, had been a flawed policy. Washington's termination of cooperation with Afghan leaders made them insensitive to its protests about the presence of foreigners hostile to the United States. Pakistan's limited capacity to influence the Taliban was undermined as a result of US sanctions and aid cut off. An objective appraisal of the prevailing situation in the region, marked by tension and instability, and poverty and insecurity that have bred extremism and terrorism, called for a long-term policy and sustained attention on the part of the sole superpower.

After 9/11, US spokespersons repeatedly sought to assure the nations in the region of the durability of their country's new policy, emphasizing especially the continuity of US cooperation with Pakistan. The priorities of the Bush administration during its second term were a 'further broadening of the bilateral relations with Pakistan in economic and security fields,' said Deputy Secretary of State Richard Armitage on his visit to Islamabad after the re-election of President Bush. He noted that Pakistan enjoyed 'broad-based and solid support' in the United States. The 9/11 Commission recommended that the United States should make 'the difficult long-term commitment to the

With Chinese Premier Zhu Rongji, People's Republic of China, Beijing, 2001. Courtesy of Abdul Sattar.

With the Prime Minister of Japan, Yoshiro Mori, Tokyo, 2001. Courtesy of Abdul Sattar.

future of Pakistan sustaining the current scale of aid to Pakistan.'[12] The US Congress passed an act in December 2004 with provisions assuring continued assistance after the expiry of the five-year package in 2009. 'Pakistan has become a vital ally with US in the war on terror,' said Secretary of State Condoleezza Rice. Recalling that 'at one time in our history we did not maintain and continue deep relations with Pakistan after having shared strategic interests during the Cold War,' she assured her Pakistani audience during her visit to Islamabad, 'The US will be a friend for life.'[13]

NOTES

1. President George Bush, 12 September 2001.
2. At a press conference on 13 September 2001, Bush was asked: 'Have you made any progress?' in obtaining needed cooperation from Pakistan and Afghanistan 'which have not necessarily done so in the past'. He replied, 'Won't we? We will give the Pakistani government a chance to cooperate and to participate as we hunt down those people who committed this unbelievable, despicable act on America.'
3. *The 9/11 Commission Report,* W. W. Norton & Co., New York, 330.
4. Ibid., 331.
5. Ibid., 331.
6. Ibid., 332. Whether the US request reached Islamabad on 13 or 14 September is unclear. Armitage made the requests on 13 September, i.e. already 14 September in Islamabad. However, Powell is said to have informed the NSC Principals' Committee on 13 September, 'President Musharraf had agreed to every US request for support in the war on terrorism.' Footnote 38 on page 558 of the *Report* refers to the US embassy, Islamabad, cable of 14 September.
7. Ibid., 331. The US embassy cable reported: 'Musharraf said the GOP was making substantial concessions on allowing use of its territory and that he would pay a domestic price. His standing in Pakistan was bound to suffer. To counterbalance that, he needed to show that Pakistan was benefiting from his decision.'
8. Prime Minister of UK Tony Blair; Prime Minister of the Netherlands Wim Kok; German Chancellor Gerhard Schroeder; and Prime Minister of Belgium Guy Verhofstadt.
9. Ishrat Husain, former Governor of the State Bank, article in *Dawn* of 16 April 2007.
10. Jim Kolby, Chairman of the House Appropriations Committee, referred to 'disturbing' reports that Pakistan had 'balked' at the US request for its forces to go into its border areas and released the extremists arrested after the president's 12 January ban on militant organizations, and although the degree

of cooperation was appraised highly, the subsequent release of the detained extremists was considered inconsistent with the announcement.

11. Armitage told the House Appropriations Committee on 18 April 2002: 'I think they (Pakistanis) have thrown their lot in. I don't think they have a choice.'
12. *The 9/11 Commission Report*, 369.
13. Interview on Pakistan TV, reported in *Dawn*, Islamabad, 18 March 2005.

Chapter 21

On-Off Partnership with the US, 2001–2016

Complying with US demands after 9/11, Pakistan severed relations with the Taliban government, forbade entry of al-Qaeda and Taliban influentials, and arrested a thousand intruders of whom 300 required by the US for prosecution and were transferred to CIA custody. Predictably, the US was hostile not only to the Taliban but also to al-Qaeda, who were suspected as a threat to Pakistan's nuclear arsenal. The Taliban and al-Qaeda hid in the Tora Bora Mountains but were mercilessly bombed. The estimates of the dead varied from 10,000 to three times as much. The infrastructure of al-Qaeda was wiped out. Islamabad also provided transit facilities for military equipment and supplies for US and allied forces and allowed use of air bases Shahbaz in Jacobabad and Shamsie in Balochistan for US operations in Afghanistan. Relations developed into a virtual alliance. A large number of CIA personnel were given visas to operate in Pakistan. While the government stuck to its decision against sending forces to Afghanistan, Pakistan was sucked into support for the US war so that within a few years nearly two hundred thousand troops were deployed along the Afghan border to fight foreign and local terrorists who established hideouts in the mountainous Tribal Areas.

US Pledges

Appreciating Pakistan's cooperation and support, Washington dismantled sanctions, and resumed military and development assistance. Also, Washington used its influence for loans to Pakistan by International Financial Institutions. EU donors, Japan, and Canada resumed assistance and provided debt relief to reduce repayments burden. Aware of chronic doubts in Pakistan about US reliability as a partner, Washington sought to reassure the Pakistani people by pledges of long-term cooperation, illustrated in statements by American leaders and development and military aid programme. In 2004, a 5-year $3 billion aid package was announced. The same year Pakistan was designated as 'a major non-NATO ally' that facilitated access to defence purchases from the United States. Another significant gesture was the generous US contribution for earthquake relief in 2005. In 2006, President Bush pledged to develop a 'strategic partnership' with Pakistan in defence, trade, education, and science and technology. Congressional delegations lauded Pakistan's sacrifices and pledged continuity of support for the strategic partnership. US leaders described Pakistan as a 'pivotal' country and 'a voice of moderation' in the struggle against extremism. President Obama and Vice President Joseph Biden exhibited goodwill towards Pakistan. Secretary of State, Hillary Clinton extolled Pakistan's sacrifices, and acknowledging its concerns about the reliability of US partnership, pledged continuity of mutually beneficial cooperation. Deputy Secretary of State, John Negroponte acknowledged that Pakistani mistrust of the United States had 'some legitimacy' as 'we walked away from them after the Soviets left Afghanistan, and we walked away from them through the 1990s because of the Pressler Amendment.'

In 2009, prominent senators including Kerry, Lugar, and Barman sponsored the Enhanced Partnership with Pakistan Act which more than doubled grant aid from $600 million a year under the 2004 law to $1.5 billion a year for the next five years. In April 2009, at a meeting held in Tokyo, twenty Friends of Democratic Pakistan including the United States, Japan, Britain, Germany, China, Saudi Arabia, and other affluent Arab countries, Turkey, and Iran pledged US$5.7 billion in aid for Pakistan. In 2010, the US made a generous donation for flood relief.

Drones Issue

Unmanned, high-flying airplanes operated by remote control from bases in the United States, drones were used for precision strikes with missiles and bombs on ground targets in the Tribal Areas. In 2004, President Pervez Musharraf gave permission for 'a few strikes.' Prime Minister Yusuf Raza Gilani told the US Ambassador he had no objection 'so long as they get the right people.'[1] Public opinion too remained quiescent until Washington expanded drone strikes and a large number of civilians were killed. The illegal programme provoked a powerful anti-American backlash and worldwide criticism mounted against the violation of international law and 'collateral damage'—a euphemism for murder of innocents. The UN General Assembly adopted a resolution condemning the drone attacks as violation of international law. In 2011, after the US raid in Abbottabad, Islamabad demanded an end to drone strikes.

In November 2013, the issue came to the fore again when a drone strike killed the Tehrik-i-Taliban Pakistan (TTP) Chief, Hakeemullah Mehsud. Surprisingly, it triggered a paroxysm of protests by prominent politicians. The Minister of Interior called for a review of the 'entire gamut of relations with the United States.' Jamaat-e-Islami Chief, Munawar Hasan called Mehsud a martyr and Jamiat Ulama-e-Islam (JUI) leader, Maulana Fazlur Rahman echoed the view saying even a dog killed by Americans was a martyr! Pakistan Tehreek-e-Insaf (PTI) leader Imran Khan decided to blockade the supply route through the Khyber Pakhtunkhwa province ruled by his party. These views did not, however, evoke a popular echo as Mehsud was an arch-terrorist responsible for the death of thousands of Pakistanis. The government, too, did not press the issue. In 2013, during his visit to the US, the Prime Minister only mentioned the subject in the context of the popular reaction in Pakistan. President Obama later imposed 'prudent limits.' The issue all but disappeared from public attention in 2014 and 2015; the US conducted numerous drone strikes killing scores of militants and Islamabad placed routine protest on record.

From 2004 to March 2015, 522 drone strikes were estimated to have killed 3,852 people, 476 of them civilians. Those killed included 22 of the top thirty al-Qaeda cadres, and scores of lower and mid-level militants. Washington claimed that the strikes devastated al-Qaeda morale and diminished recruitment of militants and training of terrorists and suicide bombers. TTP was not on the US priority list except for activists responsible for attacks on US forces in Afghanistan.

Nek Mohammad, Baitullah Mehsud and Hakeemullah Mehsud, notorious for mass murders in Pakistan, all died in drone strikes.

Erosion of Trust

Irrespective of which side was right, the recriminations and the losses suffered by both sides over eight months all but dashed hopes of building a durable strategic partnership. Foreseeing the damaging consequences, *Dawn* had warned the elected representatives against the temptation 'to beat up on the US for its sins of omission and commission.' It recalled that President Obama had 'resisted demands for extreme action against Pakistan' for suspending 'a major supply line' and that 'the world's only superpower' had 'waited patiently for Pakistani policymakers to decide how to reset ties with the US.'

The national daily *Dawn* urged the parliament to put 'interests ahead of emotions.' In a more historical vein *Washington Post* editor, David Ignatius commented that the US and Pakistan 'have the most neurotic, mutually destructive "friendly" relations in the world … . The two countries seem to be sulking all the time … feeling unappreciated and ill-used.' He recalled that a paper General Kayani gave to President Obama on 20 October 2010 described the US as 'intrusive and overbearing … causing and maintaining a controlled chaos in Pakistan (and) that the 'real aim of US strategy is to denuclearize Pakistan.'[7] Both sides would have done well to remember: 'Men remonstrate with friends who are in error, accusations they reserve for the enemies who have wronged them.'[1]

Taliban Insurgency, 2006-2019: It began in 2006, after the Taliban regrouped to mount attacks on US-led International Security Assistance Force (ISAF) and Afghan state and forces siding with the occupation. The Taliban were grateful to Osama bin Laden for al-Qaeda's support and assistance in the liberation struggle and believed the United States was hostile to Islam. The insurgency spread across rural Afghanistan and, by 2018 they had penetrated 60 per cent of the country.

Mullah Omar led a stern authoritarian regime and imposed an extremist interpretation of Sharia law, enforcement of harsh punishments, and confining women to homes, and closing schools for girls, had converted Afghanistan in to a puritanical state. Pakistan did not join the US in the war against the Afghan Taliban nor did it endorse Mullah Omar's domestic or external policies.

Trump's Pakistan and Afghanistan Policy

The US government, especially the military, usually projected an optimistic view of the security situation in Afghanistan. Victory was said to be around the corner. In 2003, the Defence Secretary, Donald Rumsfeld said the war in Afghanistan was ending. In 2008, President George Bush was led to declare that US troops were coming back. President Obama opposed the 'dumb war' in Iraq as well as the war in Afghanistan but he succumbed to pressure of lobbies and instead authorised an increased in force strength—to 100,000 troops. Donald Trump, too, initially favoured withdrawal but his advisers convinced him of an opposite strategy.

On 21 August 2017, President Trump reversed Obama's 'hasty and mistaken' policy of military withdrawal from Afghanistan and declared instead to continue support of Afghan government and military to confront the Taliban. Referring to Pakistan as 'a valued friend *in the past,*' Trump accused Islamabad of providing 'safe havens for terrorist organizations that killed Americans' and warned of 'fast and powerful retribution against the Taliban and other groups that posed a threat to the region and beyond.' The threat to peace, he said, was 'worse because Pakistan and India were nuclear armed states with tense relations that could spiral in to conflict.' He also announced that the US would further develop strategic partnership with India and want it to help Afghanistan in its economic assistance and development.

In December 2017, in his National Security Strategy report, Mr. Trump pledged to strengthen the US role in Afghanistan where state weakness threatened to undermine US interests and warned Pakistan of 'unilateral steps,' against terrorists operating from havens, and urged Islamabad to demonstrate as 'a responsible steward' of its nuclear assets. Even more blistering was President Trump's tweet on 1 January 2018, in which he declared, 'the United States has foolishly given Pakistan more than 33 billion dollars in aid over the last 15 years, and they have given us nothing but lies and deceit, thinking of our leaders as fools. They give safe havens to the terrorists we hunt in Afghanistan, with little help. No more.' Trump's ambassador to the UN, Nikki Haley echoed his undiplomatic language accusing Pakistan of playing a double game.

Pakistan's Prime Minister rejected Trump's allegation of safe havens as an attempt to project Pakistan as a scapegoat for the failed US policy in Afghanistan, cited Pakistan's counterterrorism contribution, and corrected Washington's exaggeration of the 'massive' amounts it gave in aid, pointing out that Pakistan had fought the war against terrorism to decimate al-Qaeda in the region primarily out of its own resources, but that Washington had 'trivialised' Pakistan's sacrifices in the war. Army Chief, General Qamar Javed Bajwa said Pakistan no longer sought US aid.

Mixed Signals: Despite the cut-off of US Coalition Support Funds and security assistance, Pakistan continued to strengthen border security against illegal crossings by Afghan militants, and improved cooperation with the Afghan government so that it extended control over ungoverned territory and prevented TTP from abusing Afghan safe havens for cross-border attacks.

The US Secretary of State, Rex Tillerson visited Islamabad in early October 2017 and undid some of Trump's damage by saying that Pakistan 'is still an important and valued partner for the United States', and describing US-Pakistan ties as 'a respectful relationship' with a long positive history as a key partner for the stability of the region. Defence Secretary, James Mattis came in December 2017, and praised Pakistan Army's contribution in the fight against terrorism. Pentagon quietly opened a channel with the GHQ to broaden dialogue. Assistant Secretary of Defence, Randall G, Schriver testified that Pakistan was not just an important partner but 'absolutely key to our strategy succeeding.'

The Pakistan Foreign Office objected to the singling out of Pakistan on the nuclear issue as 'ironical' because India was the first to conduct explosion tests and introduce nuclear weapons in South Asia. President Trump's remarks about the dangers inherent in nuclear weapons were unbalanced. He ignored facts: because of nuclear capability, Pakistan and India have exercised caution and restraint amidst the tensions that rose in the 1990s. The US technological assistance provided after 9/11 helped Pakistan to seal leaks of nuclear materials and technology. There has not been a single recurrence of criminal activity since. Objective observers noted, too, that costly and prolonged operations by the Pakistan Army rooted out the terrorist infrastructure and there has not been a single instance of penetration of Pakistani nuclear installations by criminal elements. All our nuclear facilities have been secure.

The arguments, old and new, were logical enough but aid was not the make-or-break issue; it was the US demand that Pakistan 'Do more' and Pakistan's response 'No more' which divided the two. Even that was an apparent cause; the underlying reason was the lapse of the common strategic vision for the region. Originally, the post 9/11 US aim was to destroy al-Qaeda; it was not to subvert the traditional power structure in Afghanistan. Pakistan and Saudi Arabia had advised Washington against such interference in 2001. But the US expanded war aims to entrench its favourites in power which provoked insurgencies and rivalries for power.

Meanwhile, American and Pakistani views differed and diverged. In Islamabad's view, political stability in multi-ethnic Afghanistan was dependent on respect for Afghan traditions. Afghanistan descended in to civil war, massive corruption and proliferation of narcotics production and trafficking with the Taliban controlling much of rural Afghanistan. President Donald Trump reversed Obama's strategy, decided to reinforce US troops and mount pressure on Pakistan on the false assumption that the conflict in Afghanistan was fuelled by Pakistan. The accusation was misconceived. The Taliban were never a proxy for Pakistan. Fiercely nationalist like all Afghans, they were patriotic and proud, and historically an integral component of the power structure in their country. In 1992 and 1993, Pakistan, Saudi Arabia, and Iran successfully promoted multi-ethnic consensus among the Afghan rivals for power. A peace and reconciliation process in Afghanistan might have again won support of all the parties.

Exaggerating and distorting the problem of Haqqani Network—two persons were killed by a US drone in three months—and ignoring the tens of thousands of Taliban who, according to a BBC survey in late 2017, could penetrate 66 per cent of Afghan territory at will—and blowing up a 15-year partnership with Pakistan—Donald Trump certainly did not perform a feat of statesmanship. Surprisingly, Rex Tillerson was fired on 13 March 2018 and replaced by the CIA Director, Mike Pompeo.

The Taliban were determined and Trump's new policy did not succeed. The people of Afghanistan had already suffered much—1.5 million lives lost since 1980. In July 2018, the US decided to accept the Taliban condition for direct talks for peace. Secretary of State, Mike Pompeo visited Kabul and a high State Department official also visited Islamabad to probe prospects. The US Special Representative for Afghanistan, Zalmay Khalilzad met with the Taliban and said he expected a peace agreement to be signed by April 2019.

In November 2018, relations between Washington and Islamabad tumbled to a new low as President Trump repeated his earlier tirade alleging Pakistan 'did not do a damn thing for us' in the fight against terrorism,' and that it gave asylum to the 'global terror kingpin', allowing him to live next to the military academy in Abbottabad. He had decided to cut off aid to Pakistan, provoking Prime Minister Imran Khan to advise Trump that instead of making Pakistan a scapegoat to re-assess the reasons for failure despite bringing 140,000 US and NATO troops to Afghanistan, arming 250,000 Afghan soldiers, and spending a trillion dollars. Pakistan, the Prime Minister Imran Khan said that Pakistan had helped the US at a cost of 75,000 dead, US$123 billion in destruction, devastation of tribal areas and dislocation of millions of people.

In Asia, Trump favoured India, Vietnam and other growth markets. Corrupt states like Egypt and Malaysia were ignored and Pakistan was no longer treated as partner. In the Middle East, Trump's policy was brutal in siding with Israel, and openly allied with Saudi Arabia against Iran. The OIC, had, all but disintegrated.

Assessment by Democrats: The Democratic staff of the Senate Foreign Relations Committee issued an unprecedented indictment of a Republican President on the first anniversary of Trump's presidency, accusing him of having 'debased his office, betrayed American values, abandoned our allies and appeased our enemies.' Denouncing Trump's chaotic 'America First' policy for risking in making 'America Alone' and 'America Last,' the document noted that a recent Gallup poll in 134 countries showed that confidence in the US had plummeted to 30 per cent. Accusing Donald Trump of making hasty decisions, a ranking Democrat, Senator Ben Cardin called him the 'most unpredictable Commander-in-Chief in US and free world's history.

In December 2018, in a complete about-turn, President Trump acknowledged in a letter to Prime Minister Imran Khan that Pakistan, too, had suffered in the war on terrorism in Afghanistan and requested Pakistan's cooperation in promoting negotiations with the Taliban for a peaceful settlement. Islamabad said that it was already its policy. Pakistan obliged and played a part in persuading the Taliban to join talks with the United States in December 2018.

Islamabad's Retrospect: The people of Pakistan will have memories of their own: of the pledges of enduring support US made and then being betrayed, of generous aid to the *Mujahideen* in the 1980s and sudden disengagement after Soviet withdrawal in 1989, leaving Afghanistan and Pakistan in the lurch. The people of Pakistan will also draw up their own balance sheet of the costs and benefits of Pakistan's post 9/11 partnership with the US. It incurred much higher military expenditures from its own budget from 2002 to 2017, and suffered US$123 billion in losses in destruction and of the 70,000 people who died in the fight against terrorism. It received lavish compliments for sacrifices and repeated assurances of enduring commitment by George W. Bush, Colin Powell, Condoleezza Rice, Congressional leaders, Barrack Obama, Joseph Biden and Hillary Clinton and then of accusation of lies and deceit by Donald Trump. But the decision was ultimately the US President's: Pakistan was no longer a partner.

NOTE

1. Sanger, *op. cit.* p. 259, quoting a cable of 13 August 2011 from US Ambassador in Islamabad on a conversation with Prime Minister Yusuf Raza Gilani.

Chapter 22

Terrorism

Pakistan supported the world community's efforts to promote international cooperation for the eradication of international terrorism and signed a dozen conventions criminalizing attacks on airliners and ships, taking of hostages, international financing of terrorist organizations. In 1996, it actively participated in discussions for a Comprehensive Convention on International Terrorism. The UN General Assembly was stalemated on whether the convention would be applicable also to violence by self-determination movements. Most of the hundred and forty states that won independence after the Second World War considered armed struggle for freedom legitimate and its suppression as state terrorism.

Rise of Terrorism: Almost from the beginning, religious litigants in Pakistan highlighted doctrinal debates and sectarian controversies. They prevailed on the Parliament to disqualify non-Muslims from holding the offices of President and Prime Minister. The Ahmadis were constitutionally declared non-Mislim. Sectarian organizations raised armed groups— *jaishes, lashkars* and *sipahs* which challenged rivals. An even more fateful milestone in the evolution of terrorism was the consequence of the Afghan jihad and its blowback.

The quantum leap of terrorism in Pakistan took place after 9/11 as religious militants infuriated by Pakistan's support for the US war on Afghanistan rose in rebellion against their own state. Osama binLaden directed his followers to launch 'raids against the Pakistan Army.' Tehreek-e-Taliban Pakistan was formed in 2007 as an umbrella organization to coordinate armed attacks and bombings on militaryand police headquarters, field posts and convoys, crowded bazars, schools, mosques, hotels and hospitals, diplomatic missions, marriage and funeral processions, and railways and buses. By late

2015, the death toll amounted to sixty thousand, including 6,370 military and police personnel and 23,000 civilians. Destruction of public and private assets was estimated at $118 billion.

Al-Qa'eda

Al-Qaeda played a key role in transforming religious militancy into terrorism. Founded in 1988, in Peshawar by Osama bin Laden, a millionaire Saudi Arabian rebel, an Egyptian radical, Aiman Al Zawahiri, and a Palestinian radical, Abdullah Yusuf Azzam. The organization, comprising mostly Arab militants, fuelled hatred against the United States and its European allies for injustices against Muslim peoples, inspired and trained radical groups, and assisted the Afghan Taliban who allowed it a base from which to organize international terrorism.

Afghan Taliban Movement

Tutored at Madrasa Haqqania near Peshawar, the Afghan Taliban from Kandahar region were simple, pious, teachers and prayer leaders, and sought to oppose the infiltration of Western culture. Founded by Mullah Mohammad Omar, the Afghan Taliban Movement was initially aimed at establishing good governance in accordance with their interpretation of Sharia. Unlike the al-Qa'eda, they were Afghanistan-centred in motivation; hostility to the US was advocated by Osama bin Laden. The Bush White House discounted the inherent strength of the Taliban: in a meeting with the Pakistan Foreign Minister two months before 9/11, National Security Director Condoleezza Rice not only fulminated against the Taliban but also inveighed against Pakistan for its support to the Taliban. The US had to pay dearly for the blunder of treating the Taliban as enemies. It realized far too late that the Taliban were insurgents, fiercely tenacious in the defence of their homeland. For over a decade they fought the US superpower and its allies until the latter quit.

Tehreek-e-Taliban Pakistan (TTP)

There were lawless groups operating from the Pakistan's Tribal Areas and Pakistani terrorists banded together in 2007 to form the Tehreek-e-Taliban Pakistan (TTP) as the umbrella organization with Baitullah Mehsud as their Emir. TTP proclaimed jihad against Pakistan. TTP funded its activities from contributions by sympathisers, holdups of banks and businesses and ransom for kidnapped victims. Its sources of heavy arms were mysterious enemies of Pakistan. The terrorists were well-trained and highly motivated. Impressionable adolescents were brainwashed to become suicide bombers, perpetrating mass killings and colossal destruction. The 'madrasa culture' aided the spread of an 'epidemic of violence.'[2] TTP groups operated largely from hideouts in the Tribal Areas where Pakistan did not maintain a large military presence. It took the Pakistan Army several years to build ground facilities for adequate forces. Only after the ravages mounted did public opinion recognize that TTP posed an existential threat.

Islamic State of Iraq and Syria

In 2014, *Al-Dawla al-Islamiya fil Iraq wal Sham* was established in parts of Syria and Iraq. Comprising extremist Sunni militants, the organization announced the establishment of the Islamic Caliphate and named Abu Bakr al-Baghdadi as the caliph. It became notorious for publicized mass execution of Christians, Yezidis, Shia Muslims and Kurds, and destruction of archaeological treasures and revered Sufi shrines. Tens of thousands Muslim extremists from other countries flocked to join the Islamic State of Iraq and Syria (ISIS). An unknown number of Afghan and Pakistani terrorists were attracted by the 'rewards' that ISIS dangled.

Spreading Insurgency: The first major challenge involved the *Lal Masjid* complex in Islamabad after it became a nest of extremism and militancy, stockpiled weapons and trained male and female seminarians to enforce their diktat on the residents. Finally in July 2007, the President decided to summon the army to flush out militants. The action was successful but costly in lives on both sides. Maulana Abdul Aziz's brother was killed and the chief prayer leader was barred from giving sermons at the mosque.

In 2008, the militancy spread to the district of *Swat*. Sufi Mohammad's son-in-law, Mullah Fazalullah led the resistance. The terrorists expelled functionaries of the district administration and closed schools for girls. (Nobel Laureate Malala Yusufzai was a student of one of these schools.) The government then decided to restore its writ. In April 2009, nearly two million inhabitants were evacuated before the army launched an operation. Within two months the terrorists were evicted and the displaced persons returned to their homes.

South Waziristan: In October 2009, a combined military operation, *Rah-e-Nijat*, was launched in the mountainous tribal agency of South Waziristan where TTP terrorists commanded by Baitullah Mehsud, and Uzbek, Chechen and Uighur militants had established hideouts. The Air Force bombed out the shelters and the Army reclaimed the lawless territory. Once again many of the terrorists escaped to neighbouring areas of North Waziristan and Afghanistan.

Karachi: By 2013, Karachi, Pakistan's largest metropolis, business and industrial hub and a centre of modern media, education and entertainment was infested with political mafias, religious and sectarian militants, terrorists and criminal gangs. Targeted killings, kidnappings, robberies, extortion and intimidation, and a dysfunctional politicized administration often shut down the metropolis at will and intimidated the media to cover its propaganda. Finally, in July 2014, the government called in the Army Rangers to the aid of the police. The force arrested tens of thousands of suspects and eliminated 2,800 criminals. In March 2015, 'Nine Zero,' the Muttahida Qaumi Movement's (MQM) head office was raided, a large cache of unlicensed arms was seized, and wanted convicts taken into custody. Militant violence was cut down by nearly half in nine months and law and order situation in the metropolis improved dramatically.

North Waziristan: The Zarb-i-Azb operation to clear out North Waziristan Agency with an area of 3,000 sq. km. was delayed. Some political parties pressed for negotiations with 'good' Taliban. Hardly had the talks begun when the Tehreek-e-Taliban Pakistan (TTP) affiliates carried out terrorist attacks, two in Islamabad and a third on Karachi airport that killed 28 persons and endangered the security of the vital international gateway. In June 2014, the 'talks' option closed and the government decided to launch a 'full scale' air and ground operation. The operation took more than a year; 2,800 militants affiliated with TTP, al-Qa'eda and East Turkestan Islamic Movement were killed, their hideouts were destroyed and arsenals—'enough for 15 years' terror attacks—were captured. By end-August 2015, the terrorists were hunted out from all major towns. Meanwhile, TTP Chief Mullah Fazlullah fled across the border to Afghanistan from where he launched deadly forays across the border.

Terrorism's Ravages: As terrorism gathered momentum from 2006, the TTP attacked public buildings and military camps, and bombed cities and towns, crowded bazaars, schools and mosques, and trained suicide bombers for special operations. Suicide bombers targeted important buildings in the national capital and the Army headquarters in Rawalpindi. The whole country was gripped by insecurity. Most Western banks and airlines closed operations in Pakistan. According to official statistics over 50,000 people were killed by the end of 2014. They included over five thousand Army and security personnel, former Prime Minister Benazir Bhutto, Punjab Governor Salman Taseer, two federal ministers, Punjab Home Minister and high-ranking officials of the Army and civil administration. Losses due to destruction of public and private assets were estimated at 8,264 billion rupees (US$102 billion). In December 2014, the British Prime Minister, David Cameron commiserated with Pakistan for having suffered more than any other country.

Pakistan Army Operations

The Turning Point: The Tehreek-e-Taliban Pakistan (TTP) terrorists sheltering in the mountains in Afghanistan's Kunar province unleashed a deadly attack on an Pakistan Army managed public school in Peshawar on 16 December 2014. Suicide bombers penetrated the premises and mowed down 150 persons, most of them students and staff. The atrocity traumatized the whole nation. Demonstrations and candle-carrying vigils took place across the country.

An all parties meeting decided on a 20-point National Action Plan of counter-terrorism strategy. A ban was enforced on private militias, hate speeches were criminalised and security forces were freed from political interference. The moratorium on execution of convicts was lifted. In January 2015, the parliament expeditiously passed the 21st constitutional amendment to authorise the setting-up of military courts for two years to try terrorism cases. Headed by Maulana Fazlur Rahman, conservative, sectarian madrassas posed the principal obstacle to the success of the new resolve. Hundreds of persons linked to banned outfits continued to teach at madrasas. In September 2015, the Government ordered registration of seminaries and investigation of terrorist funding. But the order proved difficult to enforce due to the prevalent extremism.

By the spring of 2016, the military had recovered almost all the territory lost to terrorists. Terrorists were condemned and loathed by the nation, under hunt for elimination or capture. No one spoke any longer for negotiation with them; their recruiting ground was constricted, propagandists in fear under watch. TTP chiefs had fled to new hideouts in Afghanistan. Terrorism was in irreversible decline, dying but not yet dead. Suicide bombers still could attack soft targets and kill innocent children. Another educational institution—Bacha Khan University—was attacked on 20 January 2016, killing twenty students and a teacher. Another attack on 7 March killed seventeen people in Shabqadar. A TTP affiliate perpetrated still another atrocity in a Lahore park on 27 March, killing seventy-two people, many of them Christians celebrating Easter. On the same day, tens of thousands of Sunni Barelvis assembled in Lahore and Rawalpindi to pray for the executed security-guard-turned-assassin of former governor of Punjab Salman Taseer. Islamabad was paralysed for three days. Shortsighted clerics seemed bent upon carving up Pakistani Muslims into exclusivist sects and sub-sects. Minorities felt fearful, discriminated against, and marginalized.

Counter-Terrorism: Meanwhile, militants worldwide were defaming Islam. The Tehreek-e-Taliban Pakistan (TTP), Al Shabab in Somalia,

Boko Haram in Nigeria, and the Islamic State in Iraq and Syria committed barbarous crimes that outraged humanity, heightened Islamophobia and stigmatized Muslims as targets of hate, suspicion and discrimination. Only men of knowledge realized that religions had been exploited throughout history by extremists in pursuit of criminal aims. The Grand Imam of the prestigious Al Azhar University in Cairo, Egypt attributed terrorism to 'bad interpretations' of the Holy Qur'an' and urged the Muslim community 'to tackle in our schools and universities this tendency to accuse Muslims of being unbelievers.' The Grand Mufti of Saudi Arabia condemned al-Qaeda and ISIS in his Hajj sermon in 2015.

Terrorism Denounced: Terrorism was a paradox: Islam is a religion of peace but too many of its followers were killing innocents. Mainstream Muslims were outraged. All political parties condemned terrorism. Respected scholars began to challenge the extremists. The Grand Imam of Egypt's Al-Azhar University, Sheikh Ahmed al-Tayeb, ascribed origin of terrorism to a 'historical misreading of the Qur'an' and 'intolerant interpretations of Islam' requiring radical reform of religious teaching. Iranian President Hassan Rouhani spoke of the malaise in the Muslim world noting that 'violence, terror and massacres, unfortunately, [took] place in the Islamic world.'

Nexus with Narcotics: Facing military pressure, popular disgust, and diminishing donations, some of the terrorist groups changed track. Religion remained a facade, but they turned to criminal activities for raising funds. Drug money became a principal source of power and influence for leaders of terrorist groups and influential Taliban chiefs in areas under their control.[1]

Jihad:[2] An Arabic word, the root meaning of jihad is to strive spiritually, intellectually, morally, or physically. The Quran ordains 'jihad in the path of Allah.' The Prophet (PBUH) said, 'The highest form of *jihad* is to speak the truth in the face of a tyrannical ruler.' Over time, the word acquired a double meaning, the individual striving to live a moral life and the collective armed struggle against religious repression and unjust war. Muslim and other empire-builders abused religion to inspire their armies.

The right to use force continues to be an exclusive preserve of states for maintenance of peace at home and defence of their right to peaceful coexistence.

Islamophobia

In the wake of 9/11, hard-liners in the United States started hate mongering against Islam and even government agencies began discrimination against Muslim visitors and their own citizens. Evangelical preachers and Zionists joined in whipping up hatred and prejudice. Pastor Terry Jones announced a plan to burn copies of the Quran and did so on 21 March 2011 and again on 28 April 2012. Hostile advertisements in subway stations depicted Jews as 'civilized' and Muslims as 'savages.' US Deputy Attorney General Thomas Perez acknowledged that FBI did not accord equal protection against arson attacks on mosques, burning of holy books, refusing building permits for Islamic centres, bullying of Muslim children in schools, and discrimination in the workplace. A video posted on YouTube in September 2012 by hate-mongers in Los Angeles distorted and vilified Islam. President Obama condemned the 'crude and disgusting' video but pleaded that the law on freedom of speech did not permit ban on blasphemy against any religion.

Pakistan carried little influence to stem the tide of hostility. Too many terrorists in the West were reported to have been incited by extremist seminaries or terrorist groups in Pakistan. Although it was the worst victim of terrorism, the state of Pakistan itself was held to blame for the proliferation of terrorism. India was not alone in pointing an accusing finger at Pakistani state institutions for encouraging terrorist organizations.

The US, ISAF and Afghan government forces meanwhile deployed 100,000 troops; US spent $1,070 billion on the war and $100 billion to build Afghan forces but failed to establish control over the Afghan border region, and placed the entire blame for cross-border violence on Pakistan, the Haqqani Network and Taliban elements. Trump flaunted $33 billion it gave Pakistan in aid over 15 years but not once acknowledged the costs and sacrifices Pakistan incurred in support of the US. The heavy costs from its own meager budget depleted its treasury of resources desperately needed for economic and social development.

Chapter 23

Afghanistan, 2001–2018

Afghanistan Ethnicity and Politics

After 9/11, Pakistan severed relations with the Taliban regime upon its refusal to comply with the UN Security Council resolution. The Taliban abandoned the capital, the rank and file, and melted into the Pakhtun countryside. Mullah Omar and other prominent leaders either went underground or fled to Pakistan. Osama bin Laden escaped to the Tora Bora mountain area and then across the border to Pakistan. The Northern Alliance took control of Kabul, Kunduz, and Mazar-i-Sharif. In December 2001, the United Nations began formation of a new government for Afghanistan. The President of Pakistan prepared a paper in consultation with the Saudi leadership recommending that the government to be formed in Afghanistan should give a fair representation to all ethnic communities: Pakhtuns: 42 per cent, Tajiks: 27 per cent, and Hunzas and Uzbeks: 9 per cent each. It was personally delivered by the Saudi Foreign Minister to the President of the United States, the Prime Minister of the United Kingdom, and the Secretary General of the United Nations. A conference of Afghan elders, held in Bonn under UN auspices in December, approved the provisional arrangements with Hamid Karzai, a Pakhtun, as the interim leader. General Qasim Fahim, a former deputy of Ahmad Shah Massoud of Panjsher, dominated the new dispensation. A majority of important positions were allotted to theTajiks. Uzbeks and Hazaras were also rewarded, but the Pakhtuns received short shrift.

The Pashtuns: Historically a Pashtun nation with a plurality of 13 million (41%) in a country with 35 million population, the Pashtuns share an ethnic link with Pashtuns in Pakistan which is also resilient and durable to fall prey to the exigency of Islamabad's improved relations with the establishment in Kabul. Yet, the Afghan Pashtuns feel alienated and fixing this fractured relationship, although deeply rooted in *Pashtunwali*, would not be easy. Prospects, to say the least, are unclear. The Inter-Services Intelligence Agency (ISI) and the CIA supported Hekmatyar with his base in the valley of Kunduz. The CIA also maintained close relations with Massoud who was assassinated in Tajikistan on 9 September 2001. The Afghan Establishment will continue to look towards US for support and guidance so long as the aid pipeline is open.

The Tajiks: constitute 11 million of the population. The Kabul establishment comprising the bureaucracy, the armed forces and the educated elite has been traditionally dominated by Tajiks, and their share has never been so high as at present. (Uzbeks and Hazaras each number about 9 percent.) The Afghan youth are increasingly aware (63.7 % under 25) that their future lies in Kabul or in other major urban centres. Despite claims regarding national integration, Ministers without any reluctance appoint the entire staff from their ethnic group. None of the appointees, as the current practice goes, survives the dismissal of the Minister. There seem to be a broader and more flexible understanding that Pashtuns are good for business rather than bureaucracy. There is little evidence that the state has adopted it as policy.

As long as they remain in service, Tajik bureaucrats work only for narrow or factional interests. But they do not fade away as non-entities. Instead they join a pool of experienced professionals and move from government to trade, education, think-tanks or civil society. This was happening earlier too. What has changed recently is the scale. Even the National Directorate of Security (NDS) and National Police Force are not immune from this drift.

The Hazaras: A Shia minority, the Hazaras are an enterprising, peaceful people but often victims of sectarian violence. The Afghan government accords them protection as far as possible.

The Uzbeks: Smaller in numbers, their leader Abdul Rashid Dostum built a strong army with arms and funds from Russia. He fought against Russia's enemies; the main target was the Taliban in alliance with the Tajiks.

The Haqqani Group: The Haqqani group is a militant section of Pashto-speaking Afghan Taliban of whom a substantial number migrated to the Tribal Areas of Pakistan in the early 1980s. They played an active part in fighting against the Russian and, later, the American invaders. The main controversy between Pakistan and the United States centred on the alleged protection Pakistan gave the Haqqanis for using Pakistan territory as a base for operations against the Americans and the Afghan state. Their leader, Hibatullah Akhundzada who headed the Quetta Shura, the Haqqani Network, Hezbi Islami, and smaller al-Qaeda groups also joined the insurgency. They often launched terrorist attacks on civilian and security targets. They were finally defeated by the Pakistan Army in 2018.

Afghan Taliban Movement

In 1994-95, Afghanistan dissolved in to total disarray. The Pashtuns from the Kandahar region who had studied at Madrassa Haqqania near Peshawar, a conservative Deobandi institution, organized a Taliban movement of simple pious teachers and prayer leaders. They disbanded the truck mafia, enforced codes of good moral conduct and hanged criminals. In November 1995, they captured Kandahar. A Pakistani Federal Minister described the Afghan Taliban as 'our boys' but this was a delusion as the Taliban, like most Afghans, had their own priorities. In 1996, the Taliban tide swept the country, conquered Kabul and took control of Mazar-i-Sharif, whose mayor, a Massoud ally, defected to them. The Taliban combined Durrani rural culture and Islamic ethos. When Prime Minister Benazir Bhutto sought to open the southern Quetta route to Central Asia, she organized a large commercial convoy which was blocked by the truck mafia. The Interior Minister, Naseerullah Khan Babar persuaded the Taliban to clear the way. In May 1997, Pakistan recognised the Taliban government after Mazar-i-Sharif accepted the Taliban government. Saudi Arabia and UAE followed with their recognition, but the Taliban remained isolated internationally because of their odious human rights record.

The ISI, CIA, and the White House pursued a practical policy. Prince Turki, the Saudi politician, came to Kandahar and asked

Mullah Omar to hand over Osama bin Laden. But this angered Mullah Omar so much that he got up and doused his head with cold water, before rebuking the Saudi royals.

The influential Karzai and Ahmadzai families declared support for the Taliban. Pakistan tried to prevent the Taliban from occupying its territory by crossing the border but this became a long running controversy as the US pressed Pakistan to 'do more' and Pakistan needed time and resources to move forces and enforce its writ in the Tribal Areas. While the US was impatient, Pakistan had its constraints.

Afghanistan War

The Taliban were in no position to defeat the US forces in Afghanistan. Mullah Omar and other prominent Taliban leaders either went underground or fled to Pakistan. The UN convened a conference of two dozen anti-Taliban Afghan influential persons in Bonn in late December 2001, which selected Hamid Karzai, a Pashtun, as the interim leader. A majority of important positions in the new government were allotted to Tajiks, Uzbeks and Hazaras as reward for their support to the US invasion. But they could not win Pashtun acceptance. Even the US and allied forces could not establish the writ so long as they had insufficient troops. In 2003, when the US withdrew a large number of its troops to fight the war in Iraq, the Taliban resurfaced to challenge the US and Afghan forces.

The Taliban Insurgency: It began in 2006, after they regrouped to mount attacks on US-led International Security Assistance Force (ISAF) and Afghans siding with the occupation. The Taliban were grateful to Osama bin Laden for al-Qaeda's support and assistance in the liberation struggle and believed the US was hostile to Islam. By 2018, the insurgency had spread across rural Afghanistan and they were able to penetrate 60 per cent of the country.

Mullah Omar led a stern authoritarian regime and imposed an extremist interpretation of Sharia law, enforcement of harsh punishments, and confining women to homes and closing schools for girls, and converted Afghanistan in to a puritanical state. Pakistan did not join the US in its war against the Afghan Taliban nor did it endorse Mullah Omar's domestic or external policies.

Pakistan-Afghanistan Relations: The relations between Islamabad and Kabul began on an amicable note. President Karzai was friendly and grateful for Pakistan's opposition to Soviet intervention in Afghanistan and for hospitality to millions of refugees. But the situation deteriorated as the Tajiks and their Northern Allies took control of the government.

The Pashtuns including many of the refugees in Pakistan felt alienated and excluded from power. Hekmatyar's Hizb-e-Islami and the Haqqani Network joined a spreading insurgency, some of them using the adjoining Tribal Areas in Pakistan as base for cross-border attacks. President Karzai accused Pakistan of connivance with the dissidents. In actual fact, Islamabad was reluctant to fight any of the old Mujahideen friends.

Mutual Insensitivity: Another factor for the deterioration of relations was Kabul's lack of sensitivity towards Pakistan's security concerns. It allowed India to open consulates in towns close to Pakistan's border, which were used by the Indian intelligence agency, Research and Analysis Wing to incite subversion and sabotage in the FATA and Balochistan Province. Islamabad raised this matter again and again with President Karzai but to little avail. As a result relations between Islamabad and Kabul turned acrimonious. In 2011, Kabul compounded the bitter relationship by its decision to sign a Strategic Partnership Agreement with India. The Karzai regime however, welcomed New Delhi's support and assistance which was much greater than Pakistan could afford. Islamabad did not however, look at this development from Kabul's angle.

The Taliban Government's Record: 1996–2001

During their five year rule, the Taliban eradicated opium cultivation, prohibited carrying of arms and established law and order in the country. But their stern authoritarian rule, extremist interpretation of Sharia law, enforcement of harsh punishments and confinement of women to their homes and closing of schools for girls converted Afghanistan in to a puritanical state. In 2001, Mullah Omar's decision to demolish ancient Buddha statues in Bamiyan provoked universal outrage and condemnation. Particularly suicidal was the decision to allow sanctuary to Osama bin Laden who abused it for planning and perpetrating the 9/11 terrorist attack on the United States. Adamant in pursuit of their agenda, the Taliban paid little heed to Pakistan's suggestions. In dealing with Pakistan, they relied on old madrasa contacts and Pakistani religious parties for support, and tried to export their obscurantist views to promote sectarian extremism in Pakistan. They even refused to extradite proclaimed offenders wanted by Pakistan's judicial authorities for prosecution.

In June 2001, Pakistan's Foreign Minister visited Washington. He exchanged with Secretary of State Colin Powell and the Deputy Defense Secretary the limited information he had about the Taliban. His meeting with Condoleezza Rice was in contrast a disaster — she was rude as she assumed the FM knew more than he actually did and spoke in an offensive manner not realising that the United States with vastly more resources than Pakistan was in a better position to influence Kabul. Actually, she was herself ignorant and did not have a clue about Osama bin Laden's sinister plans and the Taliban's determination to resist US occupation.

Terrorism in Pakistan: The Taliban movement in Pakistan was a product of policies that encouraged and aided religious extremism and militancy. People as well as governments of Saudi Arabia, the Gulf States and the CIA funnelled large sums of money to seminaries that witnessed meteoric expansion. Some of them provided modern weapons. The Taliban were opposed to Pakistan's alliance with the United States and Saudi Arabia and turned their guns on the Pakistani state, army and even civilians. In 2007, a virtual war began between Tehrik-i-Taliban Pakistan (TTP) and the Pakistan Army. The TTP unleashed attacks on Pakistan and Swat was the first battlefield opened by Sufi Mohammad and his son-in-law, Fazlullah. The terrorists were defeated but relocated to the Federally Administered Tribal Areas (FATA) region where they established base facilities, built arsenals and training grounds for attacks across the country. Over 7 years the Pakistan Army deployed 90,000 soldiers and mounted several operations in South Waziristan, Bajaur and Kurram agencies to establish its writ. More than 75,000 people died across the country. Material losses were estimated at $123 billion.

US Fatigue with Wars: In 2009, the new Obama administration came to office in Washington, with a record of 2,323 US fatalities in Afghanistan, and declared a policy of ending the long wars in Iraq and Afghanistan. Vice President Joseph Biden was sceptical of whether the United States could build 'a legitimate Afghan government.' President Obama concluded that the vision of building a modern democratic Afghanistan was too costly to accomplish. In December 2011, he told the Joint Chiefs of Staff, 'The difference we made (in Afghanistan) is unlikely to be lasting … It was a war without winners.' Obama announced an exit strategy that aimed at ending the US combat role, leaving the war to the large Afghan security force assisted by continued US air support. To meet Afghan demands he agreed however, to sign a Security Pact to provide paper assurance to Kabul.

The Karzai Era: 2001-2014: The Hamid Karzai era was remarkable for the transformation of Afghanistan from a war-ravaged, internationally isolated country to a developing democracy supported by the US-led alliance of Western countries. In the eventful thirteen years that Karzai was at the helm, Afghanistan got a constitution endorsed by the traditional *Loya Jirga*, held two presidential and parliamentary elections, received $100 billion in aid for reconstruction of economy and administration, raised a national security force, opened schools for 8 million children, brought women in to politics and administration and broadened the power structure to include all ethnic communities. His many achievements were eclipsed, unfortunately for his place in history, by rampant corruption, narcotics proliferation and, fatally, by Karzai's lack of faith in the system he inducted. All the elections held under his watch were marred by fraud, rigging, and ballot stuffing. In the latter years of his rule Karzai became mercurial and intemperate, and offensive towards the United States. He also ignored the sacrifices Pakistan had made for Afghanistan and accused 'Pakistani power players of trying to control his country's foreign policy.'

Afghan Presidential Election- 2014: In the 2014 elections, Dr. Ashraf Ghani emerged with the largest votes in the one-to-one contest with Dr. Abdullah Abdullah. The announcement was challenged and a threat of division of the country loomed. The United States and NATO allies intervened. President Obama warned that failure to agree to a compromise would 'cost Afghanistan the financial and security support of the United States and the international community.' Secretary of State, John Kerry rushed to Kabul twice and in the final of his thirty telephone calls told the rivals, 'If you do not come to agreement now, today, the possibilities for Afghanistan will become very difficult, if not dangerous ... The United States will not be able to support Afghanistan.'

On 21 September 2014, the two rivals signed a US-brokered agreement providing for Ashraf Ghani to be declared President and Abdullah Abdullah to take a new post as Chief Executive Officer investing in him powers that effectively made him an executive prime minister. The President would head the cabinet of ministers while the CEO would preside over a new council of ministers to implement the executive affairs of the government. Another clause calls for 'parity in the selection of personnel between the President and the CEO at the level of head of key security and economic institutions, and independent directorates.' They took oath of office on 29 September 2014.

The extra-constitutional agreement marked the first time for modern men to rise to power in a country historically dominated by Pashtun dynasts. Both leaders are well-educated and brought wide experience of administration to their high offices. President Ashraf Ghani, a Ph.D. was a World Bank economist. Dr. Abdullah, an ophthalmologist, son of a Pashtun father and Tajik mother, was an associate of Ahmad Shah Massoud, the legendary Lion of Panjshir, and a well-spoken foreign minister in the Mujahideen government of President Rabbani.

Ashraf Ghani's Passing Gesture: President Ashraf Ghani's touching gestures during his priority visit to Islamabad in November 2015 won hearts and minds of the Pakistani people. He laid a wreath at the *Shuhada* (martyrs) Monument demonstrating appreciation for Pakistan's sacrifices in the struggle against terrorism, and made the memorable statements: 'Alone we can strive but together we can thrive' and 'We will not permit the past to destroy the future.' After his meeting with Prime Minister Nawaz Sharif he announced, 'We have overcome obstacles of 13 years in 3 days.' But the dream remained unrealized. The peace process in Afghanistan made little progress. A peace process scheduled for 31 July 2014 was derailed. Mullah Omar had died in 2013.

Afghan Insurgents in Pakistan: The leader and senior commanders of the Taliban insurgents operating inside Afghanistan (comprising the Shura, the top consultative body) maintained an office in Quetta. For years, Kabul and Washington had objected more vociferously to the presence of elements of the Haqqani Network of insurgents on Pakistan territory from where they allegedly mounted cross-border attacks. Pakistan did not approve of their activities, but it was averse to fighting Afghans on its soil, as many of them were friends it had helped in the liberation war. Also, they had sympathizers in the tribal areas. Besides, the Pakistan Army was preoccupied with operations against terrorists. Further, the better armed US and NATO forces and the large Afghan national security forces held responsibility for sealing the border from the Afghan side. Eventually the Pakistan Army's Zarb-e-Azb operation targeted all terrorists. The Haqqani fighters were forced to relocate to the Afghan side of the mountainous border. Incredulous hardliners in the US Congress, however, called for cutting off aid to Pakistan, alleging it 'allowed' the Haqqani Network to carry on cross-border attacks.

Taliban Offensive: The Taliban mounted deadly attacks in July and August 2015. Hundreds of people were killed in Kabul and dozens of soldiers in Kunduz. President Ashraf Ghani blamed Islamabad, declaring: 'We hoped for peace, but war is declared against us from Pakistan territory. ... It is time for Pakistan to prove through action that the enemies of Afghanistan were enemies of Pakistan.' Islamabad condemned the attacks against the elected government as inadmissible. Accusations that the attacks were launched by insurgents sheltering in Pakistan were untenable as the Zarb-e-Azb Army operation had destroyed the infrastructure of all terrorist groups in the Tribal Areas.

The Haqqani Network elements relocated from northern Pakistan and integrated with the Taliban command structure.

Peace and Reconciliation: In 2015, Pakistan used whatever leverage it had with the Taliban to persuade them to enter into dialogue with the representatives of the Afghan government for peace and cooperation. The United States and China co-sponsored and joined a formal meeting as observers. A second meeting was scheduled for 31 July, but the process was derailed by Kabul's disclosure that Mullah Omar had died in Karachi in 2013. The Taliban, having sought to keep that fact secret, had to deal with the fallout. Mullah Akhtar Muhammad Mansour was declared the new Amir, but the Taliban splintered. Mullah Mansour refused to send any representative to attend talks with the Afghan government. Holding him responsible for attacks on US forces in Afghanistan, President Obama authorized a drone attack that killed Mansour on 22 May 2016. The Taliban Shura elected Maulvi Habatullah Akhundzada as the new Amir. He vowed to continue the policy of non-participation in dialogue.

The Friends of Afghanistan supported efforts for peace and reconciliation. A Heart of Asia forum meeting of twenty-two countries in Islamabad on 8 December 2015 emphasized the urgency of an end to civil war in Afghanistan. Afghanistan, China, Pakistan, and the United States tried to revive the peace talks. Islamabad even threatened to expel the Quetta Shura if they did not agree, but the Taliban made participation conditional on withdrawal of all foreign forces, which was exactly the opposite of what Kabul wanted. President Obama announced that he will keep about 8,400 US troops through to the end of his term in January 2017 and that his successor can determine the next move. President Trump has warned against a 'hasty withdrawal' from Afghanistan, saying that 'conditions on the ground, not arbitrary timetables, will guide our strategy from now on.'

Despite Islamabad's intercessions, the Taliban refused to join the peace and reconciliation process as long as foreign forces remained in Afghanistan. The stance evidenced, once again, that they were not anyone's proxy. Now, like Afghan warlords and governors, they raised resources by narcotics trafficking.1 Collapse of the peace and reconciliation process shifted the limelight to the abuse of Pakistan territory by the Taliban and Haqqani Network leaders for cross-border attacks. This problem was not new. The mujahideen had used bases in the Pakistani tribal areas during the war against Soviet occupation.

The Haqqani Network was a legacy. It continued to operate during civil strife in Afghanistan in the 1990s and the Taliban insurgency against foreign forces. Meanwhile, Pakistani terrorists also established hideouts across the border from which they launched attacks on targets in Pakistan. Both countries needed to seal the border against trouble-makers, but both delayed action. Perhaps the problem did not seem urgent. Both knew the main forces of insurgents and terrorists operated from within their countries. The Pakistan military launched a massive operation that drove outlaws out of North Waziristan in 2014–16. The Haqqani Network elements were also forced out. Border fencing was commenced in earnest to inhibit illicit traffic; international law requires states to prevent abuse of their territory for cross-border attacks.

New Taliban Amir: In July 2015, Mullah Omar's long-time deputy Mullah Akhtar Muhammad Mansour was elected as the new Amir. A few Taliban criticised the succession and the peace policy. The chief of the Taliban political office in Doha, Tayeb Agha who was not invited to the Murree meeting, refused to pledge allegiance to the new Amir calling Mullah Mansour a proxy for Pakistan's ISI. Kabul pulled out of peace talks. The Afghan Taliban also announced on 22 September 2015 that the reconciliation process with the Kabul administration would not be resumed as long as 'foreign troops remained in Afghanistan and the government did not revoke its security pacts with other countries.' Mullah Mansour consolidated unity inside Taliban ranks. Siarajuddine Haqqani was appointed a deputy. The decision-making body *Rahbari Shura* comprising 21 members included a Tajik and an Uzbek. Its meetings were held at homes of *Shura* members in Afghanistan.

Terrorist Attacks: In August 2015, as if stung by the charge, the new Taliban leadership launched deadly attacks in Kabul that killed 80 people. President Ashraf Ghani blamed Pakistan. Washington urged Islamabad to do more to stop the Haqqani network from using

Pakistan territory for attacks inside Afghanistan. Islamabad explained that the Army operation *Zarb-i-Azb* had largely destroyed the infrastructure of all terrorist groups in the Tribal Areas. Belatedly, Pakistan realized the globally isolated Afghan Taliban were a liability and asked those in Pakistan to leave the country.

Tehrik-i-Taliban Pakistan (TTP) leader Mulla Fazlullah hiding in Afghan territory carried out a deadly attack on the Pakistan Air Force's Khalid Base at Badaber near Peshawar killing 16 Pakistan Air Force (PAF) personnel. It was evident that the Afghan security force either did not exercise control over the territory or decided not to stop Mulla Fazlullah. He was killed by a US drone in June 2018.

Border Fence: Neither the US nor the Kabul government cooperated with Pakistan in building a fence on the Pakistan-Afghan border. In order to prevent movement of terrorists, smuggling and narcotics trafficking, Pakistan decided in 2018 to build the fence at its own cost. Of the total of 2,600 km. it built 900 km. by January 2019; the remainder—300 km. in Khyber Pakhtunkhwa and 1,400 km. in Balochistan—was expected to be completed in years' time.

US War Costs: Over a period of seventeen years, up until 2018, the US had spent US$1,070 billion on the war in Afghanistan. It placed the entire blame for failure on cross-border violence carried out by the Haqqani Network and the Taliban elements. In 2018, Trump flaunted $33 billion it gave Pakistan in aid over 15 years—$2.2 billion a year—but unlike friends and sympathisers—Britain, China, Germany, Japan, South Korea, and Russia—the US did not once acknowledge the burden and sacrifices that Pakistan had incurred in the war on terror.

The US, International Security Assistance Force (INSAF), a NATO-led security mission in Afghanistan, and the Afghan government meanwhile deployed forces of 100,000 troops; the US spent $1,070 billion on the war and $100 billion to build the Afghan forces but failed to establish control over the Afghan border region, and placed the entire blame for cross-border violence on Pakistan, the Haqqani Network and Taliban elements.

US Economic Aid to Kabul: The US provided $104 billion for the reconstruction of Afghanistan surpassing the inflation-adjusted figure of $103.4 billion US gave to 16 countries of Europe under Marshall Plan after the Second World War. But 'a staggering portion of the money was mismanaged and stolen.' Afghanistan remained dependent on external assistance for over 90 per cent of its GDP of $15.7 billion. The US and other allies were committed to provide $5.1 billion a year for the army and police and $3 billion a year for economic development in addition to the unspent $17 billion in US appropriations.

In 2018, President Donald Trump flaunted $33 billion the US gave Pakistan over 15 years. He did not once mention the staggering human and material losses Pakistan suffered: $123 billion in destruction and 75,000 dead. Not until December 2018 he acknowledged Pakistan had suffered in the war on terrorism.

Afghanistan-China Relations: President Ashraf Ghani's choice of China for his first visit abroad signified recognition of the importance of China in peace, stability, and economic development of Afghanistan and as a source of investment. Already China had signed an agreement to invest 3 billion dollars and shown interest in natural gas and other mineral resources. Mutual cooperation was needed to prevent militants from China's Xinjiang province from abusing Afghan territory as a base for training by the Taliban.

CHAPTER 24

Pakistan–India Relations, 1986–2018

The Brasstacks Crisis–1987

A false crisis erupted when India decided to hold the largest combined military exercise in South Asian history, code-named *Brasstacks,* in the winter of 1986–87. Planned by a 'flamboyant' Indian army chief, Gen. Krishnaswamy Sundarji, the exercise was comparable in scale to the biggest exercises by NATO or the Warsaw Pact. It envisaged the concentration of nine army Divisions, five independent armoured Brigades, and 1,300 tanks in western Rajasthan, at places hardly 50 kilometres from the Pakistan border, giving the assembled forces the capability to launch a piercing strike to cut off northern Pakistan from the south. Contrary to an existing understanding, the Indian army did not inform Pakistan of the location, schedule and scale of the exercise. Specific requests to this effect by the Pakistani GHQ on the 'hot line' and by diplomats in New Delhi were rebuffed.

In November 1986, concerned about the situation, Prime Minister Mohammad Khan Junejo took up the matter with Rajiv Gandhi in a meeting in Bangalore. He was given to understand that the exercise would be scaled down. They also agreed to immediate talks, at the level of Foreign Secretaries. Alexander Gonzalvez and Abdul Sattar agreed on withdrawal of forces to peacetime locations. Foreign Minister Vishwanath Pratap Singh and Prime Minister Rajiv Gandhi personally intervened in negotiations to ensure a positive outcome. Rajiv Gandhi gave one of his official planes for Abdul Sattar to return to Islamabad for a celebratory press conference at midnight. 'A war' was averted!

In December 1986, as a precautionary measure, the Chief of Staff, General K. M. Arif, decided to move an Armoured Division north of the Sutlej River opposite Fazilka and a Brigade west of the Ravi in Sialkot district. Indian defence officials termed the Pakistani pincer posture 'menacing.'

Kargil Crisis–1999

In May 1999, a grave crisis erupted following the intrusion of armed personnel from Pakistan into the Kargil heights in Kashmir. Islamabad denied the facts and attributed them to the fighting to Kashmiri freedom fighters, recalling that after promising, at the Lahore Summit, to intensifying efforts to resolve all issues, including Jammu and Kashmir, the Indian leaders in their statements on their return to Delhi had portrayed insincerity and absence of serious intent. It recalled further, that the UN Security Council's call in its resolution of June 1998 for the resumption of dialogue to remove the root causes of tensions, including Kashmir, was not followed up, and that Indian Home Minister Lal Krishna Advani had embarked on a 'proactive' policy, intensified repression in Indian-held Kashmir, resorted to recurrent violations of the Line of Control forcing the closure of the Neelum Valley road in Azad Kashmir and subjected the villages to fierce artillery bombardment.

Few foreign countries credited Pakistan's disclaimer, however. Statements issued by the Group of Eight (G-8) countries, the US, Britain and Germany implicitly blamed Pakistan for the 'intruders' in Kargil. As Pakistan armed men penetrated the Kargil–Dras sector and seized high ground, threatening the Srinagar—Leh road, an artery in the summer months for stockpiling supplies for Indian garrisons in Ladakh and Siachen—India denounced the operation as a violation of the Shimla Agreement and retaliated with a massive air and army operation to dislodge the guerrillas. Describing them as Islamic militants, Taliban and regular army personnel, India accused Pakistan of aggression. Indian bombardment targeted not only the Kargil Heights on the Indian side of the Line of Control but also the alleged supply bases on the Pakistan side. Also, duels raged elsewhere along the Line of Control. In an attempt to defuse the situation, the Pakistani Foreign Minister was sent to New Delhi on 12 June for diplomatic efforts and for de-escalation and dialogue. He was accorded a frigid and hostile reception. India took a rigid, no-negotiation stance, insisting on Pakistani withdrawal of personnel from Kargil before discussion on any other issue. Briefing the press after the meeting, the Indian Foreign Minister used the word 'demand' three times in one minute.

Meanwhile, concern mounted internationally that the fighting in Kargil might escalate and lead to a general war between Pakistan and India, now declared nuclear states. The Group of Eight (industrialised countries) considered 'infiltration of armed intruders' as 'irresponsible'.

The European Union called for 'the immediate withdrawal of infiltrators.' Washington asked Pakistan to withdraw 'its forces' and 'restore *status quo ante*'. Only the OIC backed the Pakistani position by asking for de-escalation and dialogue. China did not criticise Pakistan and called on both India and Pakistan to 'respect the Line of Control'. Prime Minister Nawaz Sharif sued for the US President's intercession to defuse the crisis. Clinton received Sharif for an emergency meeting on Sunday, 4 July 1999—US Independence Day. He discussed the situation with Prime Minister Vajpayee over the' phone and persuaded Sharif to agree to a joint statement which provided for immediate cessation of hostilities, concrete steps to be taken for the restoration of the Line of Control in accordance with the Shimla Agreement, and resumption of a Pakistan–India dialogue as begun in Lahore in February 1999 for resolving all issues dividing India and Pakistan, including Kashmir. President Clinton promised to take a personal interest in encouraging an expeditious resumption and intensification of the bilateral efforts, 'once the sanctity of the Line of Control has been fully restored.' Military officers of Pakistan and India later agreed on steps for disengagement. The Pakistani personnel withdrew from Kargil by 16 July. Reading into the Washington joint statement a US pledge of effort to promote settlement of the Kashmir question was not only a spin aimed at misleading public opinion but a self-deception. From authoritative clarifications given by US administration officials it became clear that all that the president had promised, after careful prior clearance with New Delhi, was 'personal interest' in promoting the 'Lahore process.'

A US official compared Nawaz Sharif's dash to Washington to Yahya Khan's request for US help in the face of a rapidly deteriorating situation in the 1971 India-Pakistan war. Henry Kissinger had then remarked that the US was asked to be in at the crash-landing when it was not in on the take-off! If Pakistan was mercifully spared that biting sarcasm this time, it was partly because all that it asked was the proverbial fig leaf to cover retreat from an impulsive adventure undertaken without forethought.

Most commentators blamed the Pakistan government for losing sight of strategy in a tactical bid to awaken international attention to the festering Kashmir dispute. Given the power disparity, a military solution was obviously out of question. A war that could escalate to the nuclear level was considered inconceivable. One eminent journalist castigated the government saying, '... the original political blunder of approving a strategically flawed and unsustainable plan of guerrilla action was compounded first by diplomatic and domestic mishandling and then by a sudden and inadequately explained policy *volte face*.' A provident policy had to steer clear of extremes of bravado and soul destroying capitulation.

Prime Minister Nawaz Sharif and Chief of Army Staff General Pervez Musharraf were held 'responsible for approving this misconceived operation.' While some described the operation as 'tactically brilliant' others considered it 'a complete fiasco.' A spokesman of the All Parties Hurriyat Conference of Jammu and Kashmir described the Pakistan government's policy as 'unpredictable.' Another APHC leader said, 'First, we were excluded, then betrayed.' Inconsistent and contradictory statements undermined Pakistan's credibility. Its spokesmen disclaimed knowledge of the Mujahideen operation in Kargil one day and accepted responsibility for their withdrawal the next day. Shallow thinking was manifest also in pendulum swings from naive bus diplomacy to the Kargil gamble, from glorifying bilateral negotiations in the Lahore declaration to self-deceiving claims of success in inducting American interest in resolving Kashmir. Politics of corruption and crass calculation of immediate political advantage was diagnosed as the main reason for the shallow and myopic policies of the ruling families, along with the absence of long-term thinking and institutional decision-making.

Autopsies of the Kargil crisis by Pakistani commentators underlined agonising dilemmas that Pakistan faced in regard to the Kashmir issue. If it did not act, India claimed to have achieved a final solution; if it did, it incurred the risk of war. Similarly placed were the Kashmiri people: if they did not struggle for freedom, they were considered to have acquiesced in India's illegal annexation; if they did, they were subjected to savage repression, killings, torture and other excesses no human being should have to suffer in a civilised world. Misconceived policies and actions not only isolated Pakistan internationally, they also gravely damaged the heroic freedom struggle of the Kashmiri people. Focus shifted from indigenous agitation for self-determination to Indian allegations of its Pakistani sponsorship, from inhuman Indian excesses in Kashmir to restraint in limiting response to its side of the Line of Control, from brutality of Indian forces against the Kashmiri people to bravery on the Kargil Heights.

If the Kargil episode exposed Pakistan to international censure, it also opened a breach between the prime minister and the Army hierarchy. Nawaz Sharif was reported to have blamed the army for keeping him ignorant of the plan for the Kargil operation. A few months later Sharif dismissed Chief of Army Staff General Pervez Musharraf while Musharraf was on his way back from a visit to Sri Lanka, and ordered refusal of landing facilities to the PIA airliner on which Musharraf was a passenger. Musharraf, however, refused to be diverted to another destination and the Karachi corps commander intervened to save the passengers and crew as the plane ran low on fuel. On return, the chief of staff took over the government in a bloodless coup.

Agra Summit–2001

On New Year's Day 2001, Prime Minister Atal Bihari Vajpayee wrote an article highlighting the need for India to address two outstanding issues, namely, Kashmir and the Babri Mosque in Ayodhya. Regarding Kashmir, he went on to suggest a meeting with the Pakistani president. After a delay of nearly four months, evidently a result of internal debate, he sent an invitation for the two leaders to meet at Agra on 15 and 16 July. The two leaders held several exclusive meetings. They recognised the need to transform the fifty-year-old confrontation into good neighbourly cooperation. To that end, President Musharraf urged earnest efforts to resolve the Kashmir dispute. Around noon on 16 July they called in the foreign ministers and informed them of the understanding they had reached to resume dialogue which should be the basis of a declaration to be issued later that day. Working on the draft already prepared by the foreign secretaries, the two ministers agreed on a declaration text to be recommended to the leaders. President Pervez Musharraf approved it promptly. On the Indian side, the draft was considered in the cabinet committee on political affairs. The meeting lasted over two hours, after which External Affairs Minister Jaswant Singh sought a meeting with his Pakistani counterpart at 6 p.m. to discuss an amendment to the one line paragraph on Kashmir. After a short and amicable discussion, the foreign ministers agreed to the substance of the amendment desired by the Indian cabinet committee with a slight modification. The apparent hitch thus removed, the Indian conference services officials started making arrangements for the signing ceremony as the Indian minister hoped to obtain formal final approval in 'five minutes'. Once again the cabinet committee held a long meeting. At about 9 p.m. the Pakistan side was informed that the agreement would not be signed.

The Summit, which was held in a blaze of global multimedia coverage, ended on an anticlimactic note to the surprise of the media people and the disappointment and frustration of the Pakistan's delegation. Before departing from Agra for Islamabad, the Pakistani president was told by the Indian Prime Minister that it had not been possible to reach agreement in the cabinet committee. He did not explain what the disagreement was about, adding only that 'the time was not favourable' and that he would visit Pakistan later to finalise the proposed agreement.

The prospect of another summit helped contain disappointment. Both sides tried to relieve the gloom. President Musharraf declared, 'I came back empty-handed but the Summit was not a failure.' Prime Minister Vajpayee also underlined the progress that was made 'towards bridging the two approaches in a draft joint declaration.' In the same vein, External Affairs Minister Jaswant Singh said, 'I do not characterize [the summit] as a failure. I do term it as yet another step in our march towards finding lasting peace, amity and cooperation between the two countries', adding, 'We will pick up threads from the visit of the President of Pakistan.' The Pakistani Foreign Minister gave a similarly positive appraisal: 'The Agra Summit was '*natamam*, not *nakam*' (inconclusive, not a failure).'

The optimism did not last long, however. The Indian side soon started backtracking on the agreed draft. A spokesperson of the Ministry of External Affairs said, 'No agreement was reached. There was no closure of an agreement and no subscription by signature.' A week later, Vajpayee said in the parliament: 'Obviously India's concerns in vital areas—such as cross-border terrorism—will have to find place in any document that future negotiations endeavour to conclude.' Actually, this point was already covered in the draft declaration.

Meanwhile, observers on both sides speculated about what had prevented agreement at the summit. Some identified President Musharraf's breakfast meeting with Indian media luminaries on 16 July as having offended the Indian leaders. The videotape of the question–answer meeting telecast by an Indian commercial channel projected Musharraf's persuasive views on the need to address the Kashmir dispute to a spellbound audience in both countries. The Indian side was said to be angry that he had stolen a march over the Indian prime minister. Actually, there was little new in what he said. He had expressed the same view many times previously. Hours after the telecast, the Indian side had not raised the issue with the Pakistan side, and even agreed to finalise the draft of the declaration.

As for the Pakistani president's reference to Kashmir as the principal obstacle to normalization of Pakistan–India relations, that was no more than a statement of the obvious. Quite apart from the experience of Pakistan and India, normalization has seldom taken place between pairs of countries with serious disputes and differences. Recent examples of the causal link include the Portugal and Indonesia, over East Timor, Japan and Russia over the Northern Islands, and USA and Cuba over ideological differences.

Another explanation was later given by Prime Minster Vajpayee in a statement in parliament on 24 July, saying, 'Eventually, however, we had to abandon the quest for a joint document because of Pakistan's insistence on the settlement of the Jammu and Kashmir issue as a pre-condition for the normalization of relations.' This was factually incorrect, as the text of the draft declaration confirms. At no point in the negotiations did Pakistan present any 'pre-condition.' Similarly unfounded was the allegation that Pakistan's approach was 'univocal.' The draft provided for dialogue on all issues of concern to both sides, including terrorism.

More interesting was the question as to who in the Indian cabinet committee had objected to the draft. Not until months later did a clue appear in the Indian press. A usually well-informed journal attributed responsibility for obstructing agreement to the Deputy Prime Minister, L.K. Advani, dubbing him 'the saboteur of Agra.' When Vajpayee was asked at a press conference to comment on the report, he did not give a direct reply. Four years later, President Musharraf publicly blamed Advani for the failure of the summit. Seven years later, Advani admitted he had torpedoed the summit now giving a new explanation, namely that in a breakfast meeting with Indian editors, the Pakistani leader had 'blasted India's position on cross-border terrorism and Jammu and Kashmir.' Even this after-thought is hardly convincing. General Musharraf had only made out a case for the resolution of the Kashmir dispute, which most guests appeared to find logical. Perhaps this made Advani unhappy. Otherwise, both Kashmir and terrorism were included among subjects for sustained dialogue at the political level in paragraph 3 of the agreed draft.

Considering that Vajpayee had conceived and canvassed the initiative for dialogue with Pakistan on Kashmir, he was probably disappointed by the outcome and it can be assumed that he was sincere in his intention to visit Pakistan at a more favourable time to finalize the agreement. In retrospect it would have been better for the fulfilment of his ambition to improve relations with Pakistan had he asserted leadership to persuade the one or more members of the cabinet committee who vetoed the declaration.

Another opportunity to change the course of Pakistan–India relations was missed as one more agreement failed, becoming a victim to internal political battles. Three months later, the 9/11 terrorists attacks in New York and Washington transformed the global situation.

Back Channel Diplomacy

The Indian Prime Minister, Atal Bihari Vajpayee said in an interview reported in *Statesman* of 20 May 2004, 'We have an obligation to solve the Kashmir problem. Short of secession, short of redrawing borders, the Indian establishment can live with anything.' General Pervez Musharraf made a moderate suggestion on 25 October 2004 for settlement of the Kashmir dispute by dividing the state in autonomous regions. The people of Pakistan and Kashmir were stunned by his departure from Pakistan's principled position based on UN Security Council resolutions.

The two leaders agreed, however, to establish a 'back channel' to discuss major bilateral disputes. The channel remained active for three years. The exchanges remained secret but progress was said to have been made and understandings reached towards resolution of Kashmir and even settlement of some of the other disputes. The Indian Prime Minister was expected to visit Pakistan to sign agreements on Siachen and Rann of Kutch in 2006. However the visit did not take place due to political instability in both countries. After resignation in 2008, President Musharraf claimed progress had been achieved but nothing concrete was 'finalised and inked.' Two years later former Foreign Minister Khurshid Mehmud Kasuri wrote that a draft on Kashmir 'involved a gradual demilitarization as the situation improved, self-government and a joint mechanism involving Kashmiris from both sides as well as well as the presence of Pakistani and India representatives.'

In 2008, following elections, the PPP government reiterated Pakistan's principled position on Kashmir. Speaking in the UN General Assembly President Asif Ali Zardari reiterated Pakistan's historical position calling for a Kashmir settlement in conformity with the aspirations of the people of the state as pledged to them in Security Council resolutions. Similarly, Prime Minister Nawaz Sharif reiterated the traditional stance after he took office in 2013. The 'understandings' reached in the back channel were reduced to a footnote in history as were the drafts at the Agra Summit in 2001 even though these wee agreed by Foreign Ministers.

Mumbai Terrorist Attack–2008

The sensational terrorist attacks in Mumbai on 26 November 2008, in which more than 160 persons were killed, precipitated grave tension between Pakistan and India. New Delhi attributed the outrage to Lashkar-e-Tayba (LeT). Upon receipt of official report from India, Pakistani authorities detained prominent office bearers of Jamaat-ud-Dawa, the successor of the banned LeT, and asked India for more details to facilitate their prosecution. The information India provided was found inadmissible by the Lahore High Court. In 2015, the chief accused, Zaki-ur-Rehman Lakhvi was granted bail. In the absence of necessary cooperation between the legal authorities of the two countries, prosecution proved frustrating. India protested even though its legal system proved unable to convict the perpetrators of a terrorist attack on the Pakistan-bound Samjhota Express train in 2007 in which 68 persons were killed, 42 of them Muslims. In 2014, the Indian court granted bail to Naba Kumar Sarkar alias Swami Aseemanand, officially described as Hindu extremists.

The controversy over the Mumbai attacks obstructed the dialogue process until 2011, when the Indian Prime Minister invited the Pakistani Prime Minister to witness a Pakistan-India cricket match. A composite dialogue was resumed but made little progress. After elections in 2014, Prime Minister Narendra Modi appeared open to dialogue but made the Mumbai attack settlement an insuperable precondition.

Trade

Between 2008 and 2012, major policy changes took place in relation to Pakistan-India trade. Islamabad reduced the number of items not-importable from India from 1209 to 936 and opened the Wagah route while New Delhi cut its negative list by thirty per cent. In January 2014, negotiations envisaged further relaxation but the understanding could not be finalized. India's exports to Pakistan expanded from US$545 million in 2005 to US$ 2.2 billion in 2014 and Pakistan's exports to India increased from US$250 million to US$406 million in the same period. Indian exports to Pakistan further increased in 2017, averaging Indian Rupees 3.66 billion a month and reaching an all-time high of 24.51 billion Indian Rupees in December 2017.

Pakistan's exports were meanwhile stagnant internationally. Expert analyses further found that India applied its multiple non-tariff regulations ranging from stringent licensing and certification requirements to port clearance delays in a discriminatory manner to imports from Pakistan. Still they were of the opinion that more liberal trade with India with its much bigger market could yield greater benefit as costs and freight would be lower. The Chambers of Commerce and Industry were said to be generally agreeable. Their reservations related to trade in agriculture, pharmaceuticals and automobile spare parts.

From Talks Cut-off to Near War

Modi's first act was to cancel the meeting between foreign secretaries in August 2014 for no reason other than the Pakistan High Commissioner's meeting with Kashmiri Hurriyat leaders for usual consultations preparatory to Pakistan-India talks. In the following months Modi demonstrated his aggressive predisposition again and again: when exchange of fire broke out across the boundary in October he ordered the Indian Border Security Force to act 'fiercely.' He exulted at the heavy casualties the Indian force claimed to have inflicted on inhabitants on the Pakistani side; when Pakistan protested, he said the 'enemy' was 'screaming.' For the first time an Indian Prime Minister publicly called Pakistan an enemy.

In a speech in Dhaka in June 2015 he proudly recalled the active role he, his party and his country had played in aiding the 'liberation of Bangladesh.' There was glaring contempt for international law in his statements of Indian cabinet ministers: Defence Minister Manohar Parrikar publicly advocated use of state terrorism, quipping on 21 May 2015 '*kantey say kanta niklta hai*'—a thorn is used to extract a thorn—and asking 'What is the harm in using terrorists against terrorists!' The statement amounting to legitimization of Indian resort to state terrorism could only further vitiate bilateral relations.

Modi struck a hard position on Kashmir, ordering the Indian Army to unleash 'fierce' attacks across the Line of Control (LoC). Even harsher was the repression he ordered in Occupied Kashmir. His government's stance conformed to the guidelines in BJP's election manifesto, which promised to counter Pakistan's alleged intrusions across the Line of Control and cross border terrorism 'with a firm hand.' The BJP's manifesto devoted larger space to modernization of armed forces and development of the nuclear programme for civilian and military purposes. It further pledged:

'We will leverage all our resources and people to play a greater role on the international high table.'

Indian analysts noted that Modi was building tensions with Pakistan and stroking 'Hindu rage and shame … at what he calls more than a thousand years of slavery under Muslim and British rule.' Such RSS propaganda was 'bound to inflame Hindu-Muslim tensions.' Modi's first meeting with the Prime Minister of Pakistan in 2014 at Modi's oath-taking function was promising. But more indicative of the new Indian policy was External Affairs Minister Sushma Swaraj's remark: 'the talks can be effective and successful only if terrorist activities stop.'

The history of the Kashmir dispute is a tragic tale of violation of the principle of the Partition by Prime Minister Nehru and betrayal of 'friend' Sheikh Muhammad Abdullah and Indian nationalist Kashmiri politicians and a hypocritical pledge by Nehru to a plebiscite under UN auspices to determine the question of the accession of the state to India or Pakistan, of widening power disparity between the two countries, of desire by Prime Minister Atal Bihari Vajpayee for a peace settlement with Pakistan based on maximum autonomy for Occupied Kashmir and lack of a popular mandate for General Pervez Musharraf to negotiate a practical settlement, and a cynical disregard of international law and human rights.

Prime Minister Narendra Modi unleashed a reign of terror in the state. Syed Ali Shah Geelani informed a visiting group of Indians for peace of the reality of the situation in Jammu & Kashmir. At Burhan Wani's funeral, over a hundred thousand people joined the procession. Mirwaiz Omar Farooq told the gathering that the fourth generation of Kashmiris are 'imbued with hate' for India. The Valley was moving towards anarchy. The Hurriyat leadership had agreed to a dialogue but Dr Manmohan Singh and Home Minister P. Chidambaram had 'let us down'. Action on the ground was needed to enlarge the scope for political dialogue. If the 'iron fist and military might' replaced political action, the Kashmir issue would get completely 'Islam-driven', especially as these forces gained in direct proportion to the rise of the Rashtriya Swayamsevak Sangh (RSS), Hindutva and Yogi Adityanath.

Shabbir Shah, a Hurriyat leader, asked 'why are pellets and guns used against us here?' 'India's freedom fighters saw one Jallianwalah

Bagh; we have seen dozens.' Mehbooba Mufti of the Peoples Democratic Party (PDP), was appointed by New Delhi as Chief Minister of Jammu and Kashmir had hardly any influence. She was unceremoniously removed by New Delhi later in 2018.

The Srinagar Chamber of Commerce advocated talks with Pakistan within the framework of the twin assurances that Prime Ministers P.V. Narasimha Rao and Atal Bihari Vajpayee made, stating that the 'sky is limit' for autonomy and that the negotiations should not be confined within the framework of the present Constitution but expanded to '*insaniyat* (humanity), *jamhuriyat* (democracy) and *kashmiriyat*, the traditional Kashmiri ethos)'.

The Deadliest Year–2018: According to human rights groups Indian forces have killed close to 100,000 Kashmiris since 1989. The toll in 2018 was close to 500. Mirwaiz Umar Farooq appealed to humanity against India's repression and killings in Kashmir. Quoting Dr Siddiq Wahid, Vice Chancellor of the Islamic University of Science and Technology in Srinagar, a PhD from Harvard University, the NYT correspondent reported: 'Every Kashmiri is resisting today, in different ways.' The latest are children and grandmothers. When violent protests erupt, the Indian security services blast live ammunition into the crowds killing or blinding people, including school children who are simply bystanders, despite cries from human rights groups.

In December 2018, former Indian Foreign Minister and Bharatiya Janata Party (BJP) leader, Yashwant Sinha said that Government of India was suppressing the freedom struggle of the people of Indian Occupied Kashmir by the use of brute force. According to Kashmir Media Service, Sinha said he had discussions with a senior government official on the situation of the territory. 'I was told there is a doctrine of state—Machiavelli, Chankaya, Metternich, and that doctrine is to use force to quell any rebellion.' 'I told you how the Nepalese hate India. But, the Kashmiris hate us more.' Sinha added that the current Indian government only believed in using force, not consensus, nor democracy, nor *insaniyat* but sheer use of brutal force 'to kill as many as you can'.

Pulwama Attack–2019: On 14 February 2019, a school-dropout Adil Ahmad Dar from Occupied Kashmir rammed an explosives-laden

SUV in to an Indian para-military convoy near Srinagar killing 44 soldiers. Within half an hour New Delhi blamed Pakistan for complicity. Islamabad offered to collaborate in investigations. New Delhi did not provide a report on Pulwama to Islamabad until 28 February; Islamabad said the report contained nothing actionable.

Near War: On 26 February 2019, Indian Air Force (IAF) planes crossed in to Pakistan airspace dropping bombs on Balakot, claiming it had killed 320 militants, then admitting it had not. IAF warplanes attacked again on 28 February. Pakistan Air Force (PAF) Thunderbird fighters shot down two Indian fighter jets. The Indian pilot, Wing Commander Abinandan Varthaman was captured but Pakistan freed him two days later as a 'peace gesture' on 1 March 2019. Islamabad was commended by objective commentators but tensions remained high. Efforts made by the US, China, Saudi Arabia, Russia, Jordan, Turkey and UAE played an important part in de-escalation. Kashmiris in the occupied part blame both India and Pakistan for reducing occupied Kashmir to ruin. At the time there remained great anxiety about Mr. Modi's intentions.

Chapter 25

Pakistan-China: Enduring Entente

A good neighbour is a great blessing
Hesiod (c. 700 BCE)

Founded in the wisdom of ancients and time-honoured good-neighbour solidarity, constantly developing relations between Pakistan and China have entered an even more promising phase following the agreement on the China-Pakistan Economic Corridor signed in 2015. Throughout the travail of religious militancy and terrorism that scared off most foreign economic partners, China stood by Pakistan, and not only maintained cooperation in development but actually greatly enhanced investment in vital fields of energy and communications.

The edifice of 'all-weather strategic cooperative partnership' between the two countries has been built on strong foundations of mutual interests and principled policies. The early record testifies to prescient appreciation by farsighted leaders of the imperatives of peace and security in the region combined with a culture that cherishes 'old friends'. Both adopted supportive stances on issues affecting each other's vital national interests and instinctively refrained from words or actions to please a third country at the expense of the other.

Pakistan established diplomatic relations with the People's Republic of China soon after its establishment on 1 October 1949. It then took the lead for restoration of China's legitimate rights by co-sponsoring a resolution in the UN General Assembly in September 1950 to seat the delegation of the People's Republic in the world organization. Pakistan also displayed foresight in resisting US démarches for sending a military contingent for the war in Korea (1950–53) which expanded into a clash between the US and Chinese forces after the latter crossed the 38th parallel. China, too, was profoundly perceptive. Unlike the Soviet Union, it understood that Pakistan's rationale for joining SEATO was to strengthen its own defence, and not based in any assumption of threat from China. At the Bandung Conference in 1955, Premier Zhou Enlai publicly recognized:

> 'The day before yesterday, after lunch, I paid a visit to the prime minister of Pakistan. He told me that although Pakistan was a party to a military pact, Pakistan was not against China. Pakistan had no fear China would commit aggression against her. As a result, we achieved a mutual understanding although we are still against military treaties.'

Impressed by the equitable boundary treaties China signed with Thailand, Burma, and Nepal, Pakistan took the initiative to propose negotiations on the boundary between China and the Pakistan-controlled Gilgit and Baltistan. The two sides reached quick understanding that the line should follow the watershed. Especially memorable for Pakistan was the gesture Premier Zhou Enlai made by agreeing to an exception leaving a tract of grazing lands north of the watershed in favour of Pakistan, thus sparing hardship to Gilgit farmers.

Equally impressive was the Chinese decision to give exclusive rights to PIA for the routes from Beijing and Shanghai after Pakistan, resisting pressures and economic penalties by the Lyndon Johnson administration, signed a civil aviation agreement with China in 1960. China sympathized with Pakistan's efforts to resist exploitation of power disparity in South Asia. In 1965 and 1971, it denounced Indian aggression and rendered magnanimous economic and defence assistance to Pakistan. China's judicious use of veto in the Security Council in 1972 dissuaded Bangladesh from prosecuting Pakistani military officers.

China's legendary leader Deng Xiaoping reaffirmed 'unswerving support' to Pakistan in 1977 in its struggle to safeguard its national independence and state sovereignty and for the 'exercise of self-determination by the people of Jammu and Kashmir.'[1]

Karakorum Highway: The Karakorum Highway was conceived in 1960s as a strategic project to provide a land link between China's Xinjiang province and northern Pakistan. Reviving the ancient Silk Route, KKH is the highest highway in the world, crossing the Karakorum Mountains via Khunjerab Pass at an elevation of 4,693 metres. Completed in 1979, it is also called Friendship Highway in tribute to the eight hundred Pakistani and two hundred Chinese workers who lost their lives in building the Eighth Wonder of the World. In 2015, the two countries agreed to upgrade and widen and extend the road in order to link Kashgar with Gwadar.

Strategic Cooperation: In the 1970s, a special feature of China's economic collaboration with Pakistan was the emphasis on assistance to establish infrastructure facilities and defence production industries to promote self-reliance. Such facilities included Taxila Mechanical Complex, Heavy Foundry and Forge, and Kamra Aeronautical Complex. After India tested an atom bomb in 1974, China manifested understanding of Pakistan's decision to develop the nuclear option. Alone among nuclear powers, China remained sympathetic to Pakistan. When an earthquake in 1981 destroyed 4,000 centrifuges at the Sihala plant, China assisted Pakistan to tide over the emergency.[2] In the 1980s, China supplied M-11 missiles and technological cooperation that enabled Pakistan to accelerate its indigenous programme and develop the *Hatf* and *Shaheen* series which are the mainstay of its strategic delivery system. In 2005, Pakistan and China embarked on the joint production of JF-17 Thunder fighters and manufacture of naval frigates.

Following the Soviet intervention in Afghanistan in 1979, the Chinese leader Deng Xiaoping (in office from 1978 to 1989) also played a key role in convincing Washington to continue to support Islamabad despite its nuclear programme. He wrote to President Carter applauding his decision to give aid to Pakistan which was playing a key role in the Afghanistan war. He told the US government that Pakistan had its own reasons for the nuclear programme. The world did not complain when India exploded a nuclear device. Pakistan did not start the nuclear race. Now it was playing a key role in the Afghanistan war. There was no other way.[3]

After the 1998 nuclear test explosions, China alone made the just distinction that the tests were carried out 'by India and then by Pakistan.' Furthermore, China alone continued cooperation with Pakistan to build nuclear power plants. Global media sensationalized reports of a bomb design found in the consignment Libya had received from Pakistan. Actually, the six bombs of different sizes that Pakistan tested in 1998 were of advanced designs developed by PAEC's scientists through their research over two decades.

Economic Cooperation: Over the years, China has made seminal contributions to Pakistan's development in key sectors of industry, power generation, agriculture, and communications. Chinese companies submit the lowest bids, arrange credits, and bring engineers and skilled workers who work with dedication to complete projects on time.

Premier Wen Jiabao's visit to Pakistan in April 2005 marked a new stage in the burgeoning relations between 'good friends, good neighbours, and good partners' whose friendship has 'withstood the test of time and international vicissitudes.' China increased credit for a second 340-megawatt nuclear power plant. Gwadar harbour and Ghazi Barotha on the Indus River are among the largest projects built with Chinese cooperation. By 2011, China provided $20 billion in assistance for development projects. Over a hundred Chinese companies were working in Pakistan with ten thousand Chinese engineers and skilled workers. China also agreed to provide assistance for the upgradation of the Karakorum Highway. Bilateral trade rose from $2 billion in 2002 to $10 billion in 2011. To further expand commercial ties and imports from Pakistan, the two countries established a Special Economic Zone for Chinese investment.

Convergence: A notable feature of Pakistan-Chinese cooperation has been reluctance to make demands that might embarrass the other side. As an eminent Pakistan scientist said: 'The Chinese provide subtle help—and only when we ask for it. And we have always been careful not to ask anything that would embarrass them.'[4] Likewise, Chinese friends have been ever considerate of Pakistan's political and financial constraints. Both countries emphasize that China-Pakistan friendship serves the fundamental interests of the two countries, and contributes to peace, stability, and development in the region. Both pursue a policy of peace toward other countries, including their common neighbours Afghanistan and India. Their cooperation is not directed against any third country. In developing relations with other countries, they ensure against detriment to each other's interests and concerns.

Treaty of Friendship, Cooperation, and Good Neighbourly Relations: Signed during Premier Wen Jiabo's visit to Pakistan in April 2005, the treaty pledges the two countries to support each other's efforts to safeguard territorial integrity and promote peace, security, and stability of the two countries and the region. In 2011, the two sides agreed to make the strategic partnership more extensive and productive. The Chinese side has called for respect for Pakistan's sovereignty, independence, and territorial integrity, and recognition and support for its efforts for promoting peace and stability in South Asia. To foster continuity of friendship, Beijing has provided five hundred scholarships for Pakistanis to study at institutions in China and built a cultural centre in Islamabad.

Shanghai Cooperation Organization: China sponsored Pakistan to become an observer in the SCO, established by China, Kazakhstan, Kyrgyzstan, Russia, Tajikistan, and Uzbekistan in 2001 to promote cooperation against terrorism, separatism, extremism, and cross-border drug crimes. Pakistan has actively participated in SCO summit conferences and has been complimented for its anti-terrorism struggle.

During a visit to Pakistan in May 2013, Chinese Premier Li Keqiang said that the all-weather friendship between the two countries 'is more precious than gold.' He declared that 'the integrity, independence, and sovereignty of Pakistan is very dear to China.' The joint communiqué further affirmed: 'China appreciates Pakistan's long-term staunch support on issues concerning China's core interests' and 'will continue to support Pakistan's efforts to uphold its independence, sovereignty and territorial integrity; respect the development path chosen by the Pakistani people according to their national priorities; and support Pakistan in maintaining social stability and economic development.' In June 2016, Pakistan and India were elevated from observer status as members.

Anti-Terrorism Cooperation: The people of Pakistan were outraged when terrorists attacked Chinese workers assisting Pakistan in building development projects. The situation predictably caused great concern to China. The government of Pakistan took immediate steps to provide security to Chinese workers pending military operations that cleared the mountainous region of criminals in 2014–16. No less embarrassing was infiltration by the East Turkestan Movement militants, who took shelter in the mountainous areas along the Afghan border. Friendship with China and the UN Charter principle of respect for the territorial integrity of other states reinforced Pakistan's resolve to prevent abuse of its soil by Xinjiang separatists. Some of them were arrested and handed over to the Chinese authorities. Many were killed in operations by the Pakistan Army.

As Beijing appeared to be reviewing the doctrine of 'self-determination' because of the danger it might generate forces of 'national splitism' and 'ethnic separatism', Pakistan was concerned that the situation might affect China's historical stance on the Kashmir question. Former Foreign Minister Agha Shahi was sent to Beijing. Remembered for his effective advocacy for restoration of China's legitimate rights in the United Nations, he was given a warm welcome. He explained the distinguishing aspects of the Kashmir question: it involved implementation of UN Security Council resolutions of 1948 and 1949, accepted by Pakistan as well as India, that provided for a plebiscite in the state under UN auspices to determine for the question of accession of Jammu and Kashmir to India or Pakistan. Beijing's discerning comprehension of Islamabad's stance precluded misunderstanding between the two countries.

China's Meteoric Rise: Under the visionary leadership of Deng Xiaoping, China decided in the 1970s to accord high priority to industrial and technological development. Reform of domestic and external policies attracted massive foreign investment flows. Big corporations brought modern technology to produce a wide range of producer and consumer goods for export as well as the domestic market. Over a quarter century, the Chinese economy galloped at a double-digit annual growth rate. With a GDP of $10.2 trillion, China has climbed to second place in the world hierarchy by GDP. Adhering to Deng Xiaoping's strategy of focus on economic development and social reform, it has also continued to shun involvement in international 'troubles'.

Meanwhile, China promoted détente with former adversaries and expanded cooperation with developing countries. Combining socialism with market economics and one-party system, it achieved a smooth transition to meritocratic collective leadership alive to public opinion and the imperative need for political reform and containment of corruption. At the global level, China has neither sought nor approved of spheres of influence. Unlike other Great Powers, it does not have any military base outside its territory. It has resolutely maintained that Taiwan is part of China but does not threaten use of force for reunification.

China has built up a modern infrastructure of roads, railways, and communications; workers are educated, entrepreneurs innovative, and leaders forward-looking. The Communist Party still supports state-owned enterprises, but it has not obstructed incentives for the private sector which now accounts for two-thirds of all production and 90 per cent of exports. People are getting richer and 59 per cent are expected to comprise middle class households with annual incomes of $15,000–33,000. Its next five-year plan aims at raising the residual number of poor people out of poverty.

Despite deceleration of economic growth, China's GDP increased by 6.9 per cent in 2015. At a time when American and European economies were struggling to combat recession, the growth rate was still comparable to fast-developing countries. With foreign exchange reserves of over $3 trillion, the Chinese currency remains stable. IMF added renminbi yuan to its basket of reserve currencies—a stamp of recognition of its integration into a global economic system dominated for decades by the US, Europe, and Japan.

President Xi Jinping: Mr Xi Jinping is the first leader born after 1949 to rise from rural grassroots to the helm of the Communist Party and the state. On the way, he distinguished himself in social service, construction, and party-related development work. Since rising to the helm, he has launched multi-dimensional reforms in pursuit of the Chinese dream of national rejuvenation, building 'initial prosperity' in all respects and turning China into 'a modern socialist country that is prosperous, strong, democratic, culturally advanced, and socially harmonious.'

President Xi's vision of international relations, too, departs from traditional power politics. Before assuming the office of president, Mr Xi remarked in answer to a question about the Chinese threat from a journalist in 2012: 'China does not export revolution. It does not export poverty and hunger. What else do you want?' Instead, he envisions a 'new type of great power relations.' The so-called Thucydides Trap—inevitable conflict between a ruling power and a rising power—is no longer applicable.

China is now a developed country that is sharing its wealth to uplift developing countries. It took the initiative to launch the Asian Infrastructure Investment Bank with a contribution of $100 billion to its capital, announced investment of $60 billion in Africa and $46 billion in Pakistan.

China-Pakistan Economic Corridor: A grand project, CPEC aims at building fifty-one energy and infrastructure projects, a land route to link Kashgar in China with Gwadar and the Arabian Sea, and power plants, arterial roads and rail lines to facilitate development in a broad belt of territory along the route. The Chinese banks would provide $46 billion as loans to Chinese corporations which would repay the loans out of profits. The development will benefit the two countries as well as landlocked Afghanistan and the Central Asian republics and countries along the Arabian Sea.

Timelines have been set for the completion of the project. The widening of the Karakorum Highway and implementation of some of the projects has already begun. In addition, Pakistan would expand the existing communications network and promote investment for development of the broad belt of territory in the economic corridor. New industries and businesses are expected to be established by Pakistani and Chinese enterprises. An All-Parties Conference on 28 May 2015 decided to set up a parliamentary committee for continuing oversight so that all constituent political units derive equitable shares in the benefits of the project. To ensure security against terrorism, Pakistan has begun formation of a 12,000-strong armed force.

Cherishing Friendship: Chinese and Pakistani leaders describe the relations between the two countries as an 'all-weather friendship'. Both have friendly relations with many other countries as well but none other is so characterized. Pakistan remains ever grateful for China's understanding, sympathy, and solidarity in critical times. Pakistan supports China's position on Taiwan, Tibet, Xinjiang, and human rights. China speaks of Pakistan's 'tremendous help to

China at crucial moments when China sought to break the external blockade, restore its lawful seat, and achieve the normalization of relations with the United States.'[5]

President Xi Jinping summed up the history of China's relations with 'Iron-Brother' Pakistan in touching words: 'When I was young I often heard moving stories of friendship between China and Pakistan ... Pakistan provided an aerial corridor for China, and supported the restoration of China's legitimate rights in the United Nations.'

NOTES

1. Banquet speech, 18 December 1977, quoted from K. Arif, op. cit., 176 in Spotlight, Institute of Regional Studies, Islamabad, May 2001, 18. Deng Xiaoping was the supreme leader of China from 1978–94 and became famous for quotable sayings (e.g. 'It does not matter whether a cat is black or white, as long as it catches mice.').
2. Feroz Hassan Khan, op. cit., 157.
3. 'Afghan war helped Pakistan keep nuclear option'—report by Anwar Iqbal from Washington, *Dawn*, December 23, 2018.
4. Dr Samar Mubarakmand, reputed scientist, quoted by Feroz Hassan Khan, op. cit., 277.
5. Liu Jian, Ambassador of China to Pakistan, speech on 11 January 2011 at Institute of Strategic Studies, Islamabad.

Chapter 26

International Organizations

The twentieth century has gone down in history with a horrible toll of unprecedented devastation in wars, ideological conflicts, and colonial repression. Over thirty-seven million soldiers and civilians were killed in World War I. The League of Nations, established in 1919 to safeguard international peace and security, was stillborn because the United States, one of the most powerful countries in the world, rejected ratification of the Covenant. The other Great Powers failed to prevent Italian invasion and colonization of Ethiopia, Japanese aggression against China, and German expansion in Europe.

United Nations

After the Second World War, in which over sixty million people were killed, the victorious Allies decided to establish the United Nations with the mandate to save humankind from the scourge of war, but the infant organization was unable to fulfill humanity's expectations as the Soviet Union occupied seven East European countries and sponsored revolutionary movements around the world, triggering the Cold War. Wars broke out in Korea and the Middle East, and Western colonial powers unleashed brutal suppression of liberation struggles in Asia and Africa. The USA and USSR built vast nuclear arsenals. Tensions pushed the Doomsday Clock dangerously close to midnight.

The Charter requires members to refrain from the threat or use of force against the territorial integrity or political independence of any state. A key purpose of the world organization is to bring about settlement of international disputes by peaceful means and in conformity with principles of justice and international law. Other objectives include promotion of international cooperation for solving economic, social, cultural, and humanitarian problems.

Important organs of the United Nations are: (1) the General Assembly, which comprises all member states and has a broad mandate to consider all issues; (2) the Security Council, which has primary responsibility for the maintenance of international peace and security and comprises fifteen members of which five (Britain, China, France, Russia, and the United States) are permanent; (3) the Secretariat, with a mandate to bring any issue for consideration of the GA or the SC; and (4) the International Court of Justice to adjudicate disputes between states that accept its jurisdiction.

Except on procedural matters, decisions of the Security Council require nine affirmative votes; any of the permanent members can veto a decision. All UN members are bound to accept and carry out its decisions. The Security Council is empowered to impose sanctions on parties that fail to comply with its decisions.

Great expectations were in the air in 1945. Humanity looked forward to international cooperation for consolidation of peace and security and promotion of economic development and social progress with better living standards and respect for human rights. The optimism proved ephemeral as the United States of America and the Union of Soviet Socialist Republics pursued clashing aims. The Soviet Union advocated popular revolution, dictatorship of the Communist Party, and socialist ownership of the means of production. In contrast, the United States professed belief in peaceful evolution in world affairs, democracy, and a free market economic system. Their ideological rivalry and contest for influence in world affairs triggered the Cold War; abuse of veto power to prevent adoption of resolutions unacceptable to them or their allies paralysed the Security Council by undermining the effectiveness of the United Nations. The USSR prevented decisions against its occupation of countries in Eastern Europe. The abuse of veto by the United States enabled Israel to defy settlement of the Palestinian question. The Soviet veto obstructed implementation of the Security Council resolutions on Kashmir. Without consensus among permanent members on enforcement action, the organization is powerless.

UN membership grew from fifty-one in 1945 to 104 in 1961, 189 in 2000, and 193 by 2011. Most of the new members became independent as a result of decolonization of the British and French empires.

Prospects of the United Nations brightened after the end of the Cold War in 1991. The Russian Federation, successor to the USSR, began to cooperate in efforts to consolidate international peace and security.

Millennium Summit, 2000: At the turn of the century, the world leaders met in a summit session of the UN General Assembly from 6 to 8 September 2000. The Summit adopted a Millennium Declaration which called for broad and sustained efforts to create a shared future for humanity through international cooperation for development and poverty eradication, protection of the environment, promotion of human rights, and strengthening the United Nations. It also pledged commitment to good governance within each country, transparency in financial, monetary, and trading systems, and more generous development assistance.

60th Anniversary Summit, 2005: Held in September, the UN Summit reaffirmed a strong and unambiguous commitment to the Millennium Development Goals and pledged an additional $50 billion a year to fight poverty, but only five of the twenty-two most affluent countries met the target of 0.7 per cent of GDP for official development assistance, and only six of the rest promised to do so by 2015. Meanwhile, global military expenditure began to gallop in 2002, rising nearly seventy per cent to the colossal total of $1.7 trillion dollars by 2011, with the United States spending more than the next twenty countries combined.

By 2015, UN's global efforts saved millions of lives and improved conditions for millions more around the world. The number of people living in extreme poverty was reduced from 47 per cent of the world population in 1990 to 14 per cent in 2015, thanks largely to the economic strides made by China and India. As many girls as boys now attended primary schools. Malaria took six million fewer lives. Meanwhile, populations continued to grow at an excessive rate in low-income countries.

Reform of the United Nations: The Millennium Declaration called for efforts to make the United Nations a more effective instrument for pursuing global priorities. It reaffirmed the central position of the General Assembly as the chief deliberative policy-making and representative organ, and also called for a comprehensive reform of the Security Council in all its aspects. Secretary General Kofi Annan appointed a sixteen-member high-level panel to recommend clear and effective measures for ensuring effective collective action. The panel's report, released on 1 December 2004, put forward a vision of collective security that would address all major threats to international peace and security. The panel's letter transmitting the report to the Secretary General stated:

> The members of the Panel believe it would be remiss of them if they failed to point out that no amount of systemic change in the way the United Nations handles both old and new threats to peace and security will enable it to discharge effectively its role under the Charter if efforts are not redoubled to resolve a number of long-standing disputes which continue to fester and to feed the new threats we now face. Foremost among these are the issues of Palestine, Kashmir, and the Korean Peninsula.

The panel's report received little attention as the General Assembly got bogged down in disagreement over controversial issues, especially enlargement of the Security Council, funding for implementation of the Millennium Development Goals, and criteria for the pre-emptive use of force in humanitarian emergencies such as genocide.

Enlargement of the Security Council: The proposal for further enlargement of the Security Council was first made in 1993. It was generally endorsed, but the members were divided over the claim of Germany, Japan, India, and Brazil to permanent seats. A group of like-minded states known as the Coffee Club, including Argentina, Italy, Mexico, Pakistan, and the Republic of Korea, joined in opposition, arguing that reform should make the Council democratic, representative and accountable, and reflect the interests of all members, not only the big and powerful states.

A high-level panel appointed by the Secretary General suggested two alternative models for enlargement: Model A provided for the addition of six new permanent seats without veto power, and Model B for the creation of a new category of eight four-year renewable term seats. Model A was supported by Germany, Japan, Brazil, and India while the Coffee Club supported Model B. The argument against permanent seats was founded on Article 24.1 of the Charter in which UN members 'agree that in carrying out its responsibilities the Security Council acts on their behalf.' Accountability could be ensured only through election. The existing permanent members of the Security Council took diverging positions.

Human Rights

Arbitrary rule, bondage, inequality, and male domination persisted through millennia in the old world. Democratic self-rule, individual freedom, and equal rights remained a dream until recent times. Progress finally picked up momentum in the twentieth century. The United Nations Charter reaffirmed faith in fundamental human rights, in the dignity and worth of the human person and in the equal rights of men and women. The General Assembly adopted the Universal Declaration of Human Rights in December 1948. Recalling that disregard and contempt for human rights resulted in barbarous acts which outraged the conscience of mankind, the Declaration proclaimed: 'All human beings are born free and equal in dignity and rights ... without distinction of any kind, such as race, colour, sex, language, religion, political or other opinion, national or social origin, property, birth or other status.' All UN members including Pakistan accepted the Declaration 'as a common standard of achievement for all peoples and all nations.' Since then, the world community has enunciated hundreds of fundamental principles in scores of covenants, conventions, and declarations. Pakistan has signed and ratified most of them.

Pakistan's Record: The constitution of Pakistan requires the state to ensure observance of fundamental rights. The government has made sporadic efforts to raise standards of compliance by additional legislation. However, the abuse of Hudood and blasphemy laws has exposed the country to severe criticism at home and abroad. Religious and sectarian militancy has aggravated the situation. Terrorists have killed fifty thousand people, most of them indiscriminately, but religious and sectarian minorities have often been more conspicuous targets. No less problematic are social practices prevalent among traditional tribes living in a time warp, such as 'honour killings' (*karo kari*), and discrimination against women, which have proved difficult to eradicate despite the laws in force.

Pakistan- Debt, Corruption, and Rescue

Pakistan's Mountain of Debt: With a GDP of $300 billion Pakistan's total debt and liabilities rose to 33.3 trillion rupees by December 2018 (including US$ 99 billion in external debt and liabilities). The country was caught in a debt trap as it had to borrow to pay not only the interest on debt but also the instalments on the borrowed principal amount. Meanwhile, the trade imbalance rose to a record US$40 billion as imports in 1917–18 rocketed to US$66.2 billion while exports of goods and services stagnated at US$29 billion. From December 2017 to December 2018 the Pakistani Rupee depreciated from Rupees100 to 140 to a dollar. The PTI government approached friendly countries and the IMF for rescue from bankruptcy.

Nawaz Sharif Disqualified: In July 2017, the Supreme Court of Pakistan declared Nawaz Sharif disqualified from holding public office because he was not *sadiq* (truthful) and *ameen* (righteous), required under Articles 62 and 63 of the Constitution. In 2018, the National Accountability Court (NAB) convicted Nawaz Sharif of failing to produce the money trail for purchase of Avenfield Apartments in London with funds in excess of his legitimate income and sentenced him to 10 years imprisonment and a fine of 8 million pounds; his daughter Maryam Nawaz was to serve jail for 7 years and 2 years in prison for filing a forged trust deed of a Qatari prince, and her husband Capt. (Rtd.) Safdar was imprisoned for one year for colluding in the crime. All three were jailed in July 2018 but they were granted bail. Nawaz's sons, Hassan and Husain Nawaz remain subject to arrest if and when they tried to enter Pakistan. Sharif's Finance Minister, Ishaq Dar fled Pakistan on the pretence of health treatment in London. He was declared a 'proclaimed offender' as he failed to return for his trial by the National Accountability Bureau.

In December 2018, Nawaz Sharif was convicted by a NAB court for corruption in the Al Azizia Steel Mills case in Saudi Arabia and sentenced to rigorous imprisonment for seven years and a fine of Rs.1.5 billion and US$25 million. Also, perpetual warrants of arrest were issued for Nawaz Sharif's sons.

Leaders in Custody

In October 2018, the National Accountability Bureau (NAB) placed leader of opposition in the National Assembly, Shahbaz Sharif under physical remand for investigation of corruption in the Ashiana Housing Scam. Shehbaz and his son Hamza were detained for misappropriation of public funds for building a 10 kilometre sludge carrier for their Ramzan Sugar Mill at a loss of 213 million rupees to the state and placed on Exit Control List. The court granted bail to Hamza for going to London for medical treatment.

Since January 2019, Khawaja Saad Rafique, a former Railways Minister in the Muslim League (N) government, was held in custody for a month under orders of the Supreme Court of Pakistan for *suo moto* action on charges of corruption involving 60 billion rupees in the purchase of railway equipment. His brother, a Punjab Minister, was also held in custody for corruption involving a housing scam. A Pakistan Tehreek-e-Insaf ruling party minister from Punjab, Abdul Aleem Khan was charged with possession of funds abroad in excess of his income, placed in NAB custody for prosecution in mid-February 2019 and remanded to jail till March 5.

Shahid Khaqan Abbasi, a Pakistani politician belonging to Pakistan Muslim League-Nawaz served as the 21st Prime Minister of Pakistan from August 2017 to May 2018. Abbasi was named prime minister in 2017 after the Supreme Court disqualified Nawaz Sharif, who had served twice as prime minister before and was ousted both times. Abbasi is currently on physical remand in a case pertaining to the LNG case. Khaqan is accused of awarding a 15-year contract for an LNG terminal against the rules while he was petroleum minister in the cabinet of former Prime Minister Nawaz Sharif. The case was closed by NAB in 2016 but was re-opened in 2018.

A Joint Investigating Team probed money laundering by Zardari Group, Bahria Town and Omni Group, involving 172 persons including Asif Ali Zardari, his son Bilawal and sister Faryal Talpur, and Sindh Chief Minister Murad Ali Shah. On the Joint Investigation Team's (JIT) recommendations their names were placed on the Exit Control List (ECL). The Supreme Court ordered a review of the ECL. The Cabinet insisted the names of the PPP leaders should remain on the ECL pending completion of review.

A senior PPP leader, Sindh Assembly Speaker Agha Siraj Durrani was taken in to custody by NAB from 19 February 2019 until 15 March 2019 for interrogation pertaining to alleged embezzlement of public funds, illegal appointments and accumulation of assets beyond his known means of income. He owned 17 properties including a bombproof bungalow.

Friends to the Rescue: On 17 February 2019, an unprecedented US$20 billion investment was pledged by Saudi Arabia's Crown Prince, Mohammad bin Salman, as the first phase for the Supreme Coordination Council to manage, including an $8 billion refinery in Gwadar. It was the first such high-level visit in 15 years by a Saudi leader. In a flattering compliment to Prime Minister Imran Khan the Crown Prince said, 'We were waiting for this kind of leadership to partner with and do lots of things together.'

Earlier, in December 2018, Crown Prince of Abu Dhabi, Sheikh Mohammed bin Zayed Al-Nayhan visited Islamabad to announce loans of $3 billion to bolster State Bank of Pakistan's foreign exchange reserves and $3 billion as deferred payment for oil supply. China invited Imran Khan for talks with President Xi Jinping and Premier Li Kekiang announced a loan of US$2.5 billion in February 2019; It had earlier given $2 billion as loan in July 2018.

International Financial Institutions (IFIs)

The world community has established a number of international agencies to facilitate international cooperation for economic development and monetary stability, expansion of trade, and the provision of multilateral and bilateral assistance to developing countries. Global and regional development banks projected lending $400 billion during 2015–18 to promote sustainable development. IFIs of interest to Pakistan include the following:

International Bank for Reconstruction and Development: Better known as the World Bank, it was established at Bretton Woods in 1944 for the purpose of providing financial assistance for the reconstruction and development of war-shattered economies in Europe. Later, it became the primary vehicle for assistance to developing countries.

International Monetary Fund: Also established at Bretton Woods, IMF is designed to promote international monetary cooperation, help establish a multilateral payments system, lend resources to needy member states to maintain adequate exchange reserves, and facilitate expansion of international trade. Unlike the World Bank, the IMF only provides loans under adequate safeguards. Both expect the recipient states to follow agreed programmes and conditions. Both the IMF and World Bank have weighted voting.

Uninformed opinion in Pakistan often criticizes the World Bank and IMF for 'dictating' political agendas on borrowers. This view misses two essential points: first, they provide funds only upon application, and, second, like any provident lender, they try to ensure that the borrower will utilize the loaned funds in accordance with agreed conditionals that would enable it to repay the loan within the agreed period. Neither writes off defaulted loans.

Asian Development Bank (ADB): was founded in 1966. With its head office in Manila, it has sixty-seven members, forty-seven of them from Asia. Japan and USA each hold 15 per cent of shares. Its capitalization has grown to $165 billion.

Asian Infrastructure Investment Bank (AIIB): was founded on 29 June 2015 with fifty-seven countries as members, including several Western countries (e.g. Germany, the UK, and South Korea), but not the USA and Japan, which did not support it. With its head office in Beijing, AIIB has an authorized capital of $100 billion. China will have 28.9 per cent of the votes. The shares of others will be recalculated after they join. It will be managed by a non-resident board of twelve directors, nine of them from Asia.

Islamic Development Bank: Founded in 1973, ISB is an organ of the Organization of Islamic Cooperation. It has been lending funds to OIC member states. Over the past forty years, it has tripled its authorized capital to $150 billion. Saudi Arabia holds about one quarter of the bank's paid-up capital.

World Trade Organization: Established in 1995, WTO is a global forum for negotiating and administering multilateral trade agreements, resolving disputes among members. It plays an increasingly important role in the promotion of fair and free trade based on binding rules, transparency and predictability, liberalization and reduction in tariffs on industrial products, and the smooth implementation of existing agreements on trade in agricultural products, textiles and clothing, services and intellectual property, and settlements of disputes. After China joined in 2001 and Russia in 2012, WTO has become almost a universal organization.

Expiry of the Multi-Fabric Agreement and reversion of international trade in textiles and garments to normal General Agreement on Tariffs and Trade (GATT) rules from 1 January 2005 was of special importance to Pakistan, as this category accounts for some 60 per cent of its exports. Open international competition was expected to present Pakistan and other major exporters of textile products with an opportunity as well as a challenge.

Two principles that govern all trade-related agreements are 'most-favoured-nation' and 'national' treatment. Both proscribe discrimination, the former in the rate of customs duty and the latter between national and foreign persons. Members of a group may, however, agree to special rates and rules governing intra-group trade. The latest round of trade negotiations, the Doha Round that began in 2001, focused on concerns of developing countries relating to agriculture and textiles, technical barriers, and improvement of dispute settlement mechanisms. Except for a landmark deal on improving customs procedures in 2013, progress in the Doha Round has been slow. The world's top economic powers remained unwilling to lower market-distorting price support and export subsidies on agricultural products, estimated at $400 billion a year. Hopes for progress in Nairobi in December 2015 remained slim.

Meanwhile, many countries reduced barriers through bilateral, regional, and sector-specific agreements. More than fifty countries agreed in 2015 to eliminate tariffs on a wide range of information technology goods. The Trans-Pacific Partnership, scheduled to become operational in 2016, would be the biggest trading group with 40 per cent of the world's GDP. Including USA, Canada, Mexico, Japan, South Korea, and Australia, TPP excluded China and Russia.

South Asian Association for Regional Cooperation: The idea of SAARC was late in conception, slow and faltering in evolution and implementation. Impulses toward cooperation in South Asia have historically been weak, primarily because of political discord between Pakistan and India. Suspicions founded in post-Independence experiences are compounded by asymmetries of size and resources.

Floated by Bangladesh in 1980, the proposal to form a regional forum of cooperation was supported by Nepal and Sri Lanka but greeted with reservation by Pakistan lest the forum be used by India to impose hegemony over the region. However, Islamabad deferred to the preference of friendly countries. New Delhi assumed a calculated posture of reluctance in order to divert attention from the apprehension that India would be the principal beneficiary of the proposal.

SAARC was launched at Dhaka in December 1985. Its charter excluded trade until 1993. The principle of unanimity of decisions and exclusion of bilateral and contentious issues are a protection and a barrier. Even after twenty-five years, the Association lags behind other regional organization in concrete achievement. Progress in trade was slow as the policies of South Asian countries were at odds. India's policy of autarchic development denied access for primary manufactures produced by the other countries of the region while seeking to penetrate their markets for its manufactures. As a result, intra-regional trade remained less than three per cent of their global trade.

In January 2004, SAARC members decided to establish the South Asian Free Trade Area (SAFTA) based on mutual concessions with the Least Developed Countries—Bangladesh, Bhutan, and Maldives—which allowed a longer period for reciprocity. From January 2006, members began reducing tariffs to 20 per cent in two years, and LDCs to 30 per cent, and agreed to further reduce tariffs in five years, allowing LDCs eight years to do so. The agreement provided for each country to maintain a sensitive list of goods for which tariff reductions would be subject to negotiations.

Economic Cooperation Organization: Successor to the Regional Cooperation for Development established by Iran, Pakistan, and Turkey in 1964, ECO was formed in 1985 and expanded to include Afghanistan and six Central Asian republics (Azerbaijan, Kazakhstan, Kyrgyz Republic, Tajikistan, Turkmenistan, and Uzbekistan).

ECO aimed at progressive removal of trade barriers and development of communications and transport links but progress has been slow. The intra-regional trade amounted to $11 billion, or 5.6 per cent of members' global trade, and comprised mainly of petroleum products. The ECO Trade Agreement in 2003 provides for reduction of the highest tariff rates to ten per cent in five years.

Iran completed the Mashhad-Sarakhs-Tajan rail link with the Central Asian railway network via Turkmenistan to Uzbekistan, Kyrgyzstan to Kazakhstan, providing access for the Central Asian republics to international trade via Bandar Abbas on the Persian Gulf. The plan to connect the Iranian and Pakistan railways remains on paper. Iran has not built the Kerman-Zahedan link, nor has Pakistan improved the track from Quetta.

World Crises

Iran's Nuclear Programme: The first big success of international diplomacy in 2015 was the agreement reached by the permanent members of the UN Security Council plus Germany (P5+1) and Iran in September 2015, which in effect defused the crisis over the latter's violation of obligations as a NPT signatory by building nuclear plants outside the safeguards of the International Atomic Energy Agency. Iran agreed to reduce its stockpile of enriched uranium by 97 per cent; cut down the number of centrifuges in operation from 19,000 to 5,060 and mothball the rest; not to enrich uranium over 3.67 per cent for fifteen years; abandon the plutonium plant project; and allow unobstructed access to IAEA inspections and installation of technical means to verify implementation of the agreement. IAEA could seek inspection also of military sites and, in case of Iran's objection, refer the difference to a panel whose decision would be binding. In case of defiance, the sanctions would 'snap back'. Iran also undertook to respect the UNSC embargo on arms procurement for five years and on ballistic missiles for eight years.

The Security Council unanimously endorsed the agreement on 20 July and called for 'full implementation' of the timetable established in it. The world community heaved a breath of relief. Israel alone opposed the accord, but it was stymied by the rare rise of influential intellectuals in support of the accord. Twenty-nine of America's top scientists, including five Nobel laureates, commended the agreement as stringent and innovative. The Republican majority in the Senate opposed ratification but failed to push through a resolution of disapproval. The accord remained binding. Article 25 of the UN Charter requires UN members to carry out decisions of the Security Council.

The IAEA certified on 16 January 2016 that Iran had complied with its obligations. The United States and European countries lifted sanctions and released about $100 billion of Iranian assets. Pakistan welcomed the accord as a breakthrough for peace and cooperation in the region. Termination of UN sanctions unblocked implementation of the Iran-Pakistan gas pipeline project.

Global Warming: The second landmark diplomatic achievement of the year was the agreement reached at the 21st UN conference on Climate Change in Paris in December 2015 on voluntary reductions of carbon emissions. The breakthrough represented a big leap towards restricting global warming within manageable limits: increase in CO_2 emissions will slow down to peak by 2050. Global warming would be held to 'well below 2°C above pre-industrial levels.' But questions persisted regarding whether the approved voluntary reductions would suffice to yield the desired results.

For too long, the world community had remained divided as tension persisted between the rich industrialized and poor developed countries; the former demanded universal emission cuts while the latter argued that those who spewed the bulk of pollutants should assume the brunt of the burden of cutting emissions as well as assist the developing countries to make the transition to clean energy. At the Kyoto conference in 1997, forty developed countries agreed to reduce CO_2 emissions by 5.2 per cent below the 1990 level, but the United States, the largest producer of pollution, refused to accept any obligation and continued to increase emissions. The aggravating toll of climatic disastrous, however, built up momentum for a serious and urgent approach. Presidents Barack Obama and Xi Jinping announced in November 2014 they would reduce emissions by almost 28 per cent by 2030. EU pledged 40 per cent reduction. By then, scientific investigation conclusively established that the global climate was warming and that this was a man-made problem built up by excessive emissions of carbon dioxide and other greenhouse gases due to burning of coal and other fossil fuels since the Industrial Revolution. Over the centuries, the concentration of CO_2 in the atmosphere has increased by 40 per cent and the average global temperature has risen by 0.9°C. The first sixteen years of the 21st century were the hottest on record. Calamitous impacts worldwide included more frequent floods, destructive droughts, disastrous hurricanes, killer heat waves, and monstrous storms that spread havoc. The ice caps on the two poles and glaciers on the Himalayas (the 'third pole') and other mountain ranges are melting. The final report of the UN's Nobel Laureate Intergovernmental Panel on Climate Change forecast greater risks of death and destruction on a wide scale.

The Paris Agreement also committed the rich countries to raise $100 billion annually from 2020 as climate assistance to poor countries. Also, twenty-eight billionaires announced an initiative to fund a renewable energy innovation investment fund. Without innovative technologies to harness solar and wind technologies at competitive cost, global warming will continue.

Pakistan, already water-scarce, is also one of the 'ten most vulnerable countries.' The monsoon cycle has been shifting. Rainfall is concentrated in shorter spells of heavy downpour so that more water is lost in runoffs, reducing seepage to recharge underground reservoirs. Snow season is shifting from January to February, leaving a shorter period for snow to freeze as ice to replenish glaciers. Most of the small glaciers in the Karakorum and Hindu Kush mountains have already melted and larger ones are rapidly shrinking. Reservoir capacity has declined due to siltation so that it now equals a meagre thirty days of requirement as compared to two years in Egypt. Per capita water availability has decreased from five thousand cubic meters in 1950s to a mere eight hundred cubic meters. Pakistan can, and should, build more large and small dams.

Tragedies, Rebellions, and Terrorism in the Muslim World

Palestine: Recent history's most unjust development has been Israel's rise on the ashes of Palestine since 1948, its forcible annexations of Palestinian homeland by the Zionist movement, illegal occupation of the West Bank, Gaza and East Jerusalem, forced displacement of 750,000 Palestinians and confiscations of their lands and demolition of their homes. The United States has vetoed each and every resolution unacceptable to Israel.[1]

Iraq's Wars: Saddam Hussain unleashed a border war on Iran which lasted from 1980–1988 and entailed a million casualties. In 1990, Saddam's army invaded and occupied Kuwait. The UN Security Council authorized intervention and the US led Operation Desert Storm with a coalition of 32 countries which liberated Kuwait in 1991.

The Arab Spring: The Arab Spring was a series of anti-government protests, uprisings, and armed rebellions that spread across much of the Islamic world in the early 2010s. In 2011, it began in Tunisia. Its corrupt President, Zine El Abidin was forced to flee. Fortunately its political leaders succeeded to establish peace.

In **Libya** the rebels rose against the long-time dictator, Muammar al- Gaddafi and traced him to a cave and killed him in 2011; the country has remained divided since.

In **Egypt**, another long-time dictator, Hosni Mubarak was forced to resign, He was succeeded by Ikhwan leader, Mohammed Morsi in 2011–the only elected President of Egypt– but failed to build unity and was ousted by Army chief, Abdel Fattah el-Sisi in 2013, who has ruled the country since.

Only **Algeria** escaped violence. There has been strong opposition to Bouteflika who was expecting to be elected President for the fifth time. He withdrew from the presidential election. The presidential elections are expected to be held in Algeria on 12 December 2019.

Since 2011, **Syria** has been victim of a long and destructive civil war between President Bashar el Asad's Alawite army and Islamic State rebels; 11 million Syrians have been displaced from their homes, 6.5 million internally and 4.5 million across borders – 2.7 million of them moved to Turkey and half a million to other neighbouring countries.

Yemen's President Abdullah Saleh was forced to hand over power to his deputy Abdurrab Mansour Hadi in 2011. The Western part of the country has been largely controlled by Zaidi Houthi rebels. Saudi Arabia charged that Iran was supplying arms to the Houthi rebels. It led a coalition of Sunni Arab states in bombing the Houthi-held area and enforcing a blockade. Thousands of children died of starvation. Michelle Alexander, *The New York Times*, January 21, 2019.

Palestine: The UN Security Council Resolution 181/1948 called for the partition of Palestine into two states and establishment of an international regime for the city of Jerusalem. The Arab countries resisted, but proved militarily weak and politically less influential. The United States and other Western countries supported and assisted the Zionist movement. Israel occupied even more land than the UN plan envisaged. More than 700,000 Palestinians were driven out from their homes in 1948. Tens of thousands have been evicted since 1967. Over 1.5 million live in fifty-two refugee camps in Jordan, Syria, and Lebanon.

Settlement of the Palestine question was stymied from the beginning by Israeli exploitation of power disparity, military superiority, and the US abuse of veto in the Security Council that allowed Israel to defy the world community. The 1967 war ended in disaster. Since then, Israel remains in occupation of the residual Palestinian territory and Syrian Golan Heights in violation of UNSC Resolution 242, which called for (1) 'withdrawal of Israeli armed forces from territory occupied in the recent war,' and (2) 'acknowledgement of the sovereignty, territorial integrity and political independence of every state in the area and their right to live in peace within secure and recognized boundaries …' The 1993 Oslo Accords, negotiated by

ECO countries: Pakistan, Iran, Turkey, Afghanistan, Azerbaijan, Kazakhstan, Kyrgyz Republic, Tajikistan, Turkmenistan, and Uzbekistan

Prime Minister Yitzhak Rabin and Yasser Arafat for co-existence of two states, were betrayed by Israeli extremists. Rabin was assassinated and his successors Ariel Sharon and Benjamin Netanyahu reverted to expansionism by exploitation of military superiority. Israel has subjected the Palestinian people to brutal repression, economic strangulation, and deportations and imprisonment of thousands. In violation of UNSC resolutions, Israel has continued to evict Palestinians from their homes in East Jerusalem and West Bank and built settlements for 500,000 émigré Jews. The Israeli lobby in the United States proved more powerful than President Barack Obama and scuttled his attempt for a freeze on Israeli settlements preliminary to negations for the UN-approved two-state solution.

Gaza Massacre, 2014: Over fifty days of bombardment in July-August 2014, Israel massacred 2,251 Palestinians in Gaza. Israel even targeted schools and camps flying UNWRA flags. More than 30,000 apartments and most of 175 small industrial plants were destroyed. Physical damage exceeded $6 billion.

UN Secretary General Ban Ki-moon condemned the massive toll of death and destruction as 'a moral outrage and criminal act … (that) shocked and shamed the world.' Big demonstrations were held in Belgium, France, and Germany. Outraged protesters shouted Nazi slogans against Jews. The State Department criticized Israel's school bombings as 'disgraceful', but US actions spoke louder: it provided $225 million for arms to Israel and its veto shielded Israel from Security Council sanctions.

After fifty days, the Netanyahu government agreed on 26 August to ceasefire, import of construction materials, and extension of the fishing zone to six miles off the Gaza coast, but its stranglehold has reduced tiny Gaza to a concentration camp teeming with starving people cordoned off by an Israeli navy which even fired and killed some in a mercy caravan aboard a Turkish ship, preventing it from delivering humanitarian aid.

The Arab Spring: Uprisings in the Arab world began with a desperate Tunisian setting himself on fire in December 2010, and spread like wildfire. Longtime dictators were overthrown in Tunisia, Libya, Egypt, and Yemen. Lacking a culture of coalition politics, all the rebellions failed to stabilize democracy except in Tunisia, where human rights activists, lawyers, and labour and business organizations turned the 'Jasmine Revolution' away from civil war to build peace and democracy. They were awarded the Nobel Peace Prize in 2015.

Syria: The Arab Spring fuelled rebellion by the majority population in Syria against the Alawite dictatorship. The rebels supported by the US, France, Turkey, and Saudi Arabia gained control over the eastern part of the country, but the Assad regime hung on to power with the assistance of Russia, Iran, Iraq, and Lebanese Hezbollah. Over the next five years, the civil war morphed into proxy wars between the Iran-led Shi'ite bloc and Saudi-led Sunni states of the Gulf region, and between former Cold War rivals. The US and NATO intervened to assist rebels and bomb arch-terrorists ISIS. Russia intervened with a bomber force and four-thousand troops and tilted the balance in favour of the Assad regime to recapture rebel-held territory. Then President Putin suddenly decided to withdraw the bulk of Russian forces in March 2016, avoiding the risk of getting bogged down. In the civil war since 2011, Syria was all but destroyed: 400,000 people were killed and half of its eighteen million strong population displaced. Five million were forced to seek refuge in Turkey, Lebanon, Jordan, and other countries, and a similar number were displaced internally. The Syrian army, assisted by Iran, Hezbollah, and the Russian air force, controlled a fraction of the country; the larger part was under Islamic State forces or diverse groups of armed rebels supported by foreign powers. Civilians were dying of hunger and disease, but international relief agencies could no longer access the needy.

Yemen Dilemma: Perceiving the Shiite Houthi rebels in Yemen as a proxy of arch-enemy Iran, Saudi Arabia approached the United States, Arab friends, and Pakistan for military assistance to oust the Houthis from power. Washington did not endorse the Saudi assumptions but agreed in order to mollify the key Saudi friend already aggrieved by the US-led nuclear agreement with Iran, agreeing to provide arms and intelligence assistance. Eight Arab countries joined Saudi Arabia in a military assault in March 2015 to dislodge the Houthis and restore the ousted Hadi regime to power. Islamabad, asked for ground, air, and naval forces for intervention in Yemen, was paled on the horns of an agonizing dilemma: refusal and compliance would both jeopardize Pakistan's vital interests. On the one hand, a refusal would disappoint Saudi Arabia, which has been a generous benefactor in need and a dependable friend in deed ever since Pakistan became independent. Over 1.7 million Pakistani workers are gainfully employed in the kingdom. Besides worldly considerations, Pakistan is bound to the kingdom by profound spiritual ties. On the other hand, intervention in a conflict involving different sects was fraught with high risks for a multi-sect Pakistan. The Parliament called for 'neutrality', which offended Arab friends. A UAE minister, Anwar Gargash, threatened that Pakistan would pay a 'heavy price'. Prime Minister Nawaz Sharif tried to retrieve the situation by supporting the UNSC's call for rebels to cease hostilities against the Hadi regime and reassuring Riyadh that Pakistan would send forces for the defence of Saudi Arabia if it was threatened. The provident policy saved Pakistan from a disastrous involvement. Expected to yield swift results, the Yemen operation was continuing a year later. According to UN, bombings inflicted a humanitarian disaster. The ground force sent to Aden was embroiled in a guerrilla war with Yemeni militant groups.

NOTE

1. Michelle Alexander, *The New York Times*, January 21, 2019.

CHAPTER 27

Policy in a Changing World

Sabat ek taghayyur ko hai zamaney mein.
Change alone is permanent.
Allama Iqbal

Foreign Policy Perspective

Foreign policy aims comprise preservation of peace and security, political independence and territorial integrity, promotion of economic and political ties, and cooperation with other members of the world community. Standard means include individual self-defence capability, defence alliances, support of friends, and international goodwill. A look back at the history of Pakistan's foreign policy recalls that the founding fathers emphasized commitment to principles of international law and the Charter of the United Nations as the cornerstone of a strategy for peaceful coexistence. The aims remained constant while policy was adjusted to evolutions in the international environment, especially the changing policies of Great Powers in the South Asian region.

The first turning point in Pakistan's foreign policy, from non-alignment to alliance with the United States, was dictated by the necessity of containing the tyranny of power-disparity. It was unobjectionable in principle as collective defence is a sovereign right affirmed in Article 51 of the UN Charter, and qualified Pakistan for US aid to accelerate economic development and strengthen defence capability.

The dissolution of the alliances was a logical consequence of transformations in the polices of the two allies. Islamabad took steps to consolidate peaceful cooperation with the People's Republic of China, for which Washington penalized Pakistan while disregarding the contradiction with its decision to give military aid to non-aligned India, aggravating the threat to Pakistan. The US refusal to come to Pakistan's assistance against Indian aggression in 1965 led to termination of the alliance.

The third turning point followed the disaster of 1971. Since conventional means proved inadequate to deter Indian military intervention to cut Pakistan in two, Islamabad decided to develop the nuclear option. It involved no breach of law as Pakistan was not a party to the Non-Proliferation Treaty but the United States decided to impose sanctions, cutting off economic assistance and military sales. It also pressured France to renege on its commitment to supply nuclear reprocessing technology to Pakistan. Once again, Pakistan felt aggrieved, and relations with the United States were embittered.

The fourth turning point was a consequence of Soviet intervention in Afghanistan in December 1979. The superpower's advance to its border exposed Pakistan to the nightmare of Indo-Soviet collusion. But past experience inhibited Islamabad from seeking US assistance. Only two years later, when Moscow threatened use of force, did Islamabad agree to negotiate terms of cooperation with Washington in support of the mujahideen struggle for liberation. The alliance proved beneficial, but fizzled out after the last Soviet soldier left Afghanistan and Washington revived sanctions, leaving Pakistan in the lurch having to cope with civil war in a ravaged Afghanistan.

Equally radical was the transformation after 9/11. Pakistan was dragged into partnership in the war on terror, which brought more problems than benefits. The most serious consequence was the rise of religious extremism and ruinous terrorism within Pakistan. The US attack in Abbottabad and bombing of a Pakistan army contingent at Salala drove bilateral relations down to the lowest level, and it took a year of mature diplomacy by both sides to revive cooperation.

Conclusions: The above retrospect on foreign policy permits noteworthy conclusions. First and foremost, the policy decisions were all made autonomously by Pakistani leaders in the light of their own assessment of the nation's interests. The perception that Pakistan was trapped in alliances by the United States is factually wrong: Pakistan took the initiative to ask for US aid within two months of independence in order to strengthen its defence capabilities and economic sinews to consolidate the state, and for seven years Washington refused to oblige. Criticism that non-alignment would have better served Pakistan's interests was uninformed. Pakistan needed aid and the US was the only country after World War II in a position to provide assistance.

Pakistan's decision to develop strategic cooperation with China was also made independently, as was the 1972 decision to develop the nuclear option. Both have stood the test of time. The opposition to Soviet intervention in Afghanistan in 1979 was a strategic compulsion. Had the Soviet leadership exercised foresight and listened to the collective judgment of non-aligned nations, it might have saved the Soviet Union from ruin and spared both Afghanistan and Pakistan unending trouble and travail.

The United States exploited the opportunity to humiliate the Cold War rival but then blundered in 1991 by hurriedly disengaging from the region while Afghanistan was without a viable government. Pakistan was infuriated as the US revived nuclear sanctions it had lifted in 1982. Burdened by millions of refugees and lacking adequate means, Pakistan was unable to cope with chaos and infighting in Afghanistan, the Taliban, and Osama bin Laden. The US 9/11 Commission criticized the precipitate US flight, and fifteen years later, penitent American leaders and Congressmen recognized that Pakistani mistrust of the US 'had some legitimacy' as 'we (Americans) walked away from them after the Soviets left.'

Objectively evaluated, the decisions Pakistani leaders made were eminently logical. Even with hindsight, it is difficult to identify better alternatives. As for the post-9/11 partnership with the United States it was not sought by Pakistan, nor was its rejection a viable alternative.

Pakistan's fury at Washington's decisions in 1965 and 1991 was a product partly of clash of cultures: the United States tended to consider 'friendship' a transactional arrangement while Pakistan invested the word with expectations of loyalty and faithfulness. Still, condemnation of a 'strategic partner' was improvident and unbecoming of a nation pledged to 'friendliness and goodwill towards all.'

A comment is warranted also about relations with India. Too often the tension and hostility between the twin states is incorrectly ascribed to religion and history. Actually, the Partition was decided by consensus between Britain and representative political parties of British India on the basis of exercise of the right of self-determination in territories with a Muslim majority. The Quaid-i-Azam envisioned good-neighbourly relations between the twin states. The relations turned sour because India refused to abide by the agreed principle of Partition and the resolutions of the UN Security Council calling for a plebiscite in the Jammu and Kashmir. Instead, India decided to exploit power disparity to impose its preference. Difference of religion need not be an obstacle to mutually beneficial cooperation between states, as seen in Pakistan's relations with Hindu-majority Nepal as well as with other states irrespective of differences of race, religion, or political systems.

Another memorable point for diplomacy is the reality of power disparity. Great Powers are by definition self-sufficient in defending their security, but middle and small powers need to take greater care to secure peace. Apart from respect for principles of peaceful co-existence, they need to court international goodwill, cultivate friends, and strengthen the United Nations, which was established to maintain international peace and security and promote international cooperation. The United Nations has not always succeeded in resolving international disputes, but negotiations, conciliation, mediation, arbitration, adjudication, and reference to Security Council remain the best means for settlement of disputes.

We can take pride in the right decisions of our leaders and learn lessons from mistakes to avoid repetition. Policies should be reviewed in the light of ever-changing circumstances; aims remain permanent. Our founding fathers envisioned Pakistan as a moderate Muslim state, committed to economic development, political and social progress, and peaceful coexistence in conformity with the universally recognized principles of the United Nations Charter. Better governance and more efficient utilization of national resources are key to financial independence and the world's respect.

Appendices

Appendix I: The Shimla Agreement, 1972

The Government of India and the Government of Pakistan are resolved that the two countries put an end to the conflict and confrontation that have hitherto marred their relations and work for the promotion of a friendly and harmonious relationship and the establishment of durable peace in the sub-continent, so that both countries may henceforth devote their resources and energies to the pressing task of advancing the welfare of their peoples.

In order to achieve this objective, the Government of India and the Government of Pakistan have agreed as follows:

(i) That the principles and purposes of the Charter of the United Nations shall govern the relations between the two countries.

(ii) That the two countries are resolved to settle their differences by peaceful means through bilateral negotiations or by any other peaceful means mutually agreed upon between them. Pending the final settlement of any of the problems between the two countries, neither side shall unilaterally alter the situation and both shall prevent the organization, assistance or encouragement of any act detrimental to the maintenance of peaceful and harmonious relations.

(iii) That the pre-requisite for reconciliation, good neighbourliness and durable peace between them is a commitment by both the countries to peaceful co-existence, respect for each other's territorial integrity and sovereignty and non-interference in each other's internal affairs, on the basis of equality and mutual benefit.

(iv) That the basic issues and causes of conflict which have bedevilled the relations between the two countries for the last 25 years shall be resolved by peaceful means.

(v) That they shall always respect each other's national unity, territorial integrity, political independence and sovereign equality.

(vi) That in accordance with the Charter of the United Nations, they will refrain from the threat or use of force against the territorial integrity or political independence of each other.

Both the Governments will take all steps within their power to prevent hostile propaganda directed against each other. Both countries will encourage the dissemination of such information as would promote the development of friendly relations between them. In order progressively to restore and normalize relations between the two countries step by step, it was agreed that:

(i) Steps shall be taken to resume communications, postal, telegraphic, sea, land, including border posts, and air links including overflights.

(ii) Appropriate steps shall be taken to promote travel facilities for the nationals of the other country.
(iii) Trade and cooperation in economic and other agreed fields will be resumed as far as possible.
(iv) Exchange in the fields of science and culture will be promoted.
(v) In this connection delegations from the two countries will meet from time to time to work out the necessary details.

In order to initiate the process of the establishment of durable peace, both the Governments agree that:

(i) Indian and Pakistani forces shall be withdrawn to their side of the international border.
(ii) In Jammu and Kashmir, the line of control resulting from the ceasefire of December 17, shall be respected by both sides without prejudice to the recognized position of either side. Neither side shall seek to alter it unilaterally, irrespective of mutual differences and legal interpretations. Both sides further undertake to refrain from the threat or use of force in violation of this line.
(iii) The withdrawals shall commence upon entry into force of this agreement and shall be completed within a period of 30 days thereof.

This agreement will be subject to ratification by both countries in accordance with their respective constitutional procedure and will come into force with effect from the date on which the instruments of ratification are exchanged.

Both Governments agree that their respective Heads will meet again at a mutually convenient time in the future and that, in the meanwhile, the representatives of the two sides will meet to discuss further the modalities and arrangements for the establishment of durable peace and normalization of relations, including the questions of repatriation of prisoners of war and civilian internees, a final settlement of Jammu and Kashmir and the resumption of diplomatic relations.

(Signed) Indira Gandhi
Prime Minister, Republic of India

(Signed) Zulfikar Ali Bhutto
President, Islamic Republic of Pakistan.

FINAL INDIAN DRAFT
(2 July 1972)

Agreement on bilateral relations between the Government of India and the Government of Pakistan

1. The Government of India and the Government of Pakistan are resolved that the two countries put an end to the conflict and confrontation that have hitherto marred their relations and work for the promotion of a friendly and harmonious relationship and the establishment of durable peace in the sub-continent, so that

both countries may henceforth devote their resources and energies to the pressing task of advancing the welfare of their peoples.

In order to achieve this objective, the Government of India and the Government Pakistan have agreed as follows:

(i) That the principles and purposes of the charter of the United Nations shall govern the relations between the two countries.

(ii) That the two countries are resolved to settle their differences by peaceful means through bilateral negotiations or by any other peaceful means mutually agreed upon between them. Pending the final settlement of any of the problems between the two countries, neither side shall unilaterally alter the situation and both shall prevent organization, assistance or encouragement of any acts detrimental to the maintenance of peaceful and harmonious relations.

That the pre-requisite for reconciliation, good neighbourliness and durable peace between them is a commitment by both the countries to peaceful co-existence, respect for each other's territorial integrity and sovereignty and non-interference in each other's internal affairs, on the basis of equality and mutual benefit.

That the basic issues and causes of conflict which have bedevilled the relations between the two countries for the last 25 years shall be resolved by peaceful means.

That they shall always respect each other's national unity, territorial integrity, political independence and sovereign equality.

That they will refrain from the threat or use of force against the territorial integrity or political independence of each other:

2. Both Governments will take all steps within their power to prevent hostile propaganda directed against each other. Both countries will encourage the dissemination of such information as would promote the development of friendly relations between them.

3. In order progressively to restore and normalize relations between the two countries step by step, it was agreed that:

(i) Steps shall be taken to resume communications, postal, telegraphic, sea, land, including border pasts, and air links, including over-flights.

(ii) Appropriate steps shall be taken to provide travel facilities to the nationals of the other country.

(iii) Trade and co-operation in academic and other agreed fields will be resumed as far as possible.

(iv) Exchange in the fields of science and culture will be promoted.

In this connection delegations from the two countries will meet from time to time to work out the necessary details.

4. In order to initiate the process of the establishment of durable peace, both the Governments agree that:

Indian and Pakistani forces shall be withdrawn to their side of the international border.

In Jammu and Kashmir, the line of control resulting from the ceasefire of December 17, 1971 shall henceforth be respected by both sides as a Line of Peace. Neither side shall seek to alter it unilaterally, irrespective of mutual differences and legal interpretations. Both sides further undertake to refrain from the threat or the use of force in violation of this Line.

Minor adjustments to the Line of Peace in Jammu and Kashmir or the rest of the international border considered necessary by both sides to make the border more rational and viable may be made by mutual agreement.

A joint body composed of an equal number of representatives, nominated by each Government, shall be appointed to establish ground rules and to supervise the effective observance of the Line of Peace and the rest of the border between the two countries. The withdrawals shall commence upon entry into force of this Agreement in accordance with the ground rules evolved by the above-mentioned joint body and shall be completed within a period of 30 days thereof.

5. This agreement will be subject to ratification by both countries in accordance with their respective constitutional procedures, and will come into force with effect from the date on which the Instruments of Ratification are exchanged.

6. Both Governments agree that their respective Heads will meet again at a mutually convenient time in the future and that, in the meanwhile, the representatives of the two sides will meet to discuss further the modalities and arrangements for the establishment of durable peace and normalization of relations, including the questions of repatriation of prisoners of war and civilian internees, a final settlement of Jammu and Kashmir and the resumption of diplomatic relations.

(Indira Gandhi)
Prime Minister Republic of India

(Zulfikar Ali Bhutto)
President, Islamic Republic of Pakistan

1972 INDIAN DRAFT I
(29 June 1972)

Draft Treaty for Reconciliation, Good Neighbourliness and Durable Peace between the Republic of India and the Islamic Republic of Pakistan

The Government of India and the Government of Pakistan

DETERMINED to put an end to the conflict and confrontation that have hitherto marred the relations between India and Pakistan and work for the promotion of a friendly and harmonious relationship between the two countries and their peoples with a view to the establishment of durable peace in the sub-continent;

CONVINCED of the undesirability of diverting resources from development to defence, and of the need to devote their resources and energies principally to the pressing task of advancing the welfare of their peoples;

UPHOLDING their firm faith in the principles of peaceful cooperation and co-existence between States, non-interference in each other's internal affairs and respect for sovereignty, national independence and territorial integrity of each other;

DECLARING their firm resolve to restore normal and peaceful relations between their countries and to work jointly and unceasingly for maintaining a climate of reconciliation and understanding between their peoples;

HAVE AGREED as follows:

ARTICLE I

The Government of India and the Government of Pakistan attach supreme importance to maintaining a climate for durable peace and preventing the development of any situation capable of causing exacerbation of their relations.

ARTICLE II

The Government of India and the Government of Pakistan affirm their resolve to respect the independence, sovereignty and territorial integrity of each other and refrain from interfering in each other's internal affairs.

ARTICLE III

The Government of India and the Government of Pakistan regard as totally inadmissible recourse to war for the solution of international problems, and hereby renounce the threat or use of force in their mutual relations. In pursuance of this pledge, they undertake to settle all issues between them bilaterally and exclusively by peaceful means.

ARTICLE IV

The Government of India and the Government of Pakistan shall refrain from organizing or encouraging the formation of irregular forces or armed bands, including mercenaries or volunteers howsoever named, for incursion into the territory of the other'

ARTICLE V

In order to concentrate their energies on economic and social development and avoid diversion of resources from development to defence, the Government of India and Government of Pakistan agree to a balanced reduction of their defence forces facing each other and of their stationing and development in areas mutually specified so as to eliminate the possibilities of a sudden outbreak of hostilities.

The Government of India and the Government of Pakistan further agree that joint inspection teams shall be established to ensure effective implementation of agreement entered into pursuant to this Article. The joint inspection teams will submit their report from time to time to the two Governments.

Both sides agree to enter into a Protocol for the implementation of this Article which shall be an integral part of this Treaty.

ARTICLE VI

The Government of India and Government of Pakistan agree that in order to create and maintain a climate of peace, friendship and understanding between the peoples of the two countries, it is essential that all hostile propaganda directed against each other shall cease. They further agree that both countries shall actively encourage the dissemination information to promote the development of friendly relations and cooperation in various fields between the two countries.

ARTICLE VII

The Government of India and Government of Pakistan undertake to identify develop areas of cooperation and common interest between their two people. In order achieve this objective, they shall establish joint commissions or their joint bodies so that areas of cooperation may develop on a firm and long-term basis for mutual benefit. For this purpose, both sides agree to enter into Protocols which shall be integral parts of this Treaty.

ARTICLE VIII

The Government of India and the Government of Pakistan regard commercial, economic and cultural ties as an important and essential element in the strengthening bilateral relations. They agree to promote the growth of such ties.

ARTICLE IX

The Government of India and the Government of Pakistan agree to facilitate visits of nationals of one country to the other through mutually agreed routes for personal, commercial, religious, cultural and other reasons.

ARTICLE X

The Government of India and the Government of Pakistan agree that with a view to the effective implementation of this Treaty, periodic consultations shall be held between the two countries at appropriate levels.

ARTICLE XI

This Treaty shall enter into force upon signature. It shall continue to be in force for a period of ten years in the first instance. It shall continue to be in force thereafter until it is terminated by either party by giving to the other six months' notice in writing.

IN WITNESS WHEREOF, the representatives duly authorized by their respective Governments have signed this Treaty in two original texts, each of which is authentic.

DONE on this the .... day of ....

For the Government of India — For the Government of Pakistan

Note
As agreed earlier, the question of Jammu and Kashmir will be discussed separately. To complete the text of the Treaty, the agreement reached at such discussion shall be incorporated in the form of Articles at an appropriate place in this Treaty, and shall constitute an integral part of this Treaty.

PAKISTANI DRAFT
(30 June 1972)

Agreement on bilateral relations between the Government of India and the Government of Pakistan

The Government of India and the Government of Pakistan are resolved that that the two countries put an end to the conflict and confrontation that have hitherto marred their relations and work for the promotion of a friendly and harmonious relationship with a view to the establishment of durable peace in the sub-continent, so that both countries may henceforth devote their resources and energies principally to the pressing task of advancing the welfare of their people.

In order to achieve this objective, the Government of India and the Government Pakistan have agreed as follows:

The two Governments reaffirm the universal and unconditional validity of the purposes and principles of the Charter of the United Nations as the basis of relations between the two countries, and declare that the breach of these principles cannot be justified in any circumstances whatsoever.

2. The two Governments shall in their bilateral relations adhere to the principles set out in the Declaration on the Strengthening of International Security adopted by the United Nations General Assembly on 16 December 1970, and which was accepted by both India and Pakistan. In accordance with that Declaration, they reaffirm that they will:

(i) respect each other's national unity, territorial integrity, political independence and sovereign equality;
(ii) refrain from the threat or use of force against the territorial integrity or political independence of each other;
(iii) not interfere in any manner whatsoever in each other's internal affairs; and
(iv) fulfil in good faith the obligations assumed by them under the United Nations Charter.

3. Any dispute between India and Pakistan or any situation the continuance of which is likely to endanger peace between them will be settled by peaceful means such as negotiation, inquiry, mediation, conciliation, or, should these methods prove unavailing, by arbitration or judicial settlement.

4. In order to concentrate their energies on economic and social development, the two Governments will, as far as possible, avoid diversion of their resources from development needs to defence purposes, keeping in view the principle of equal security.

5. Hostile propaganda directed against each other shall cease. Both countries will encourage the dissemination of such information as would promote the development friendly relations between them.

6. The two Governments will progressively normalize their relations step by step by:

(i) resuming communications, postal, telegraphic, sea, land and air links, including over flights, in accordance with bilateral agreements entered into by the two Governments in the past and relevant international Conventions and Agreements;
(ii) opening of border posts;
(iii) providing adequate travel facilities to the nationals of the other country;
(iv) resumption of trade and cooperation in economic and other agreed fields as far as possible; and exchanges in the fields of science and culture.

In this connection, teams of experts from the two countries will meet from time to time to work out the necessary details.

7. This Agreement will be subject to ratification by both countries and will come into force with effect from the date on which the Instruments of Ratification are exchanged. The President of Pakistan has declared that this Agreement will require ratification by the National Assembly of Pakistan.

In the meantime, both Governments will take immediate steps to implement Resolution No. 307 (1971) of the United Nations Security Council by:

(i) withdrawing all armed forces to their respective territories and to positions which fully respect the Cease Fire Line in Jammu and Kashmir supervised by the United Nations Military Observers' Group in India and Pakistan, and
(ii) repatriating all prisoners of war and civilian internees in each other's custody in conformity with the Geneva Conventions of 1949.

Also, the two Governments will resume diplomatic relations as from an agreed date.

(Zulfikar Ali Bhutto)	(Indira Gandhi)
President, Islamic Republic of Pakistan	Prime Minister, Republic of India

INDIAN DRAFT II
(1 July 1972)

Agreement on bilateral relations between the Government of India and the Government of Pakistan.

The Government of India and the Government of Pakistan are resolved that the two countries put an end to the conflict and confrontation that have hitherto marred their relations and work for the promotion of a friendly and harmonious relationship and the establishment of durable peace in the sub-continent, so that both countries may henceforth devote their resources and energies to the pressing task of advancing the welfare of their peoples.

In order to achieve this objective, the Government of India and the Government of Pakistan have agreed as follows:

(i) That the principles and purposes of the Charter of the United Nations shall govern the relations between the two countries.

(ii) That the two countries will not use force for the settlement of any differences between them and resolve them exclusively by peaceful means through bilateral negotiations or by any other peaceful means mutually agreed upon between them. Pending the final settlement of any of the problems between the two countries, neither side shall unilaterally alter the situation and shall prevent the organization, assistance or encouragement of all acts detrimental to the maintenance of peaceful and harmonious relations.

(iii) That the pre-requisite for reconciliation, good neighbourliness and durable peace between them is a commitment by both the countries to peaceful co-existence, respect for each other's territorial integrity and sovereignty, non-interference in each other's internal affairs and cooperation on the basis of equality and mutual benefit.

(iv) That the basic issues and causes of conflict which have bedevilled the relations between the two countries for the last 25 years shall be removed bilaterally and by peaceful means.

(v) That they shall always respect each other's national unity, territorial integrity, political independence and sovereign equality.

(vi) That they shall always refrain from the threat or use of force against the territorial integrity or political independence of each other.

Hostile propaganda directed against each other shall cease. Both countries will encourage the dissemination of such information as would promote the development of friendly relations between them.

In order to progressively restore and normalize relations between the two countries, it was agreed that:

(i) Steps shall be taken to resume communications, postal, telegraphic, sea, land and air links, including over-flights.

(ii) Steps shall be taken for the opening of border posts.

(iii) Adequate travel facilities to the nationals of the other country will be provided.

(iv) Trade and cooperation in economic and other agreed fields will be resumed as far as possible.

(v) Exchange in the fields of science and culture will be promoted.

In this connection, teams of experts from the two countries will meet from time to time to work out the necessary details.

This Agreement will be subject to ratification by both countries in accordance with their respective constitutional procedures, and will come into force with effect from the date on which the Instruments of Ratification are exchanged.

Both Governments agree that their respective heads will meet again at a mutually convenient time in the future and that, in the meanwhile, the officials of the two sides will meet to discuss further the modalities and arrangements for the establishment of durable peace and normalization of relations, including the question of Jammu and Kashmir, repatriation of prisoners of war and civilian internees, withdrawal of an armed forces to their respective territories and the resumption of diplomatic relations.

Indira Gandhi	Zulfikar Ali Bhutto
Prime Minister, Republic of India.	President, Islamic Republic of Pakistan

Appendix II: Composite Dialogue, 1997–1998

Joint Statement by Foreign Secretaries, Islamabad, 23 June 1997 (Extracts)

'As decided at their meeting in New Delhi in March 1997 and as directed by their respective Prime Ministers, the Foreign Secretaries of India and Pakistan continued their wide-ranging and comprehensive dialogue on all outstanding issues between the two countries with each side elaborating its respective position. The discussions were held in a cordial and constructive atmosphere. It was also agreed that that both sides would take all possible steps to prevent hostile propaganda and provocative actions against each other.

'With the objective of promoting a friendly and harmonious relationship between Pakistan and India, the Foreign Secretaries have agreed as follows:-

(i) to address all outstanding issues of concern to both sides including inter alia:

Peace and security, including CBMs
Jammu and Kashmir
Siachen
Wullar Barrage Project/Tulbul Navigation Project
Sir Creek
Terrorism and drug-trafficking
Economic and Commercial Cooperation
Promotion of friendly exchanges in various fields.

(ii) to set up a mechanism, including working groups at appropriate levels, to address all these issues in an integrated manner. The issues at (a) and (b) above will be dealt with at the level of Foreign Secretaries who will also coordinate and monitor the progress of work of all working groups.'

Joint Statement by Prime Minister of Pakistan and Prime Minister of India after meeting in New York on 23 September 1998 (Extracts)

'The discussions covered the whole range of bilateral relations. The two Prime Ministers also carried out a detailed review of new developments in the region during the past few months.

'They reaffirmed their common belief that an environment of durable peace and security was in the supreme interest of both India and Pakistan, and of the region as a whole. They expressed their determination to renew and reinvigorate efforts to secure such an environment. They agreed that the peaceful settlement of all outstanding issues, including Jammu and Kashmir, was essential for this purpose.

'The two Prime Ministers noted with satisfaction the agreement reached between the Foreign Secretaries on operationalizing the mechanism to address all items in the agreed agenda of 23rd June 1997 in a purposeful and composite manner. They directed the Foreign Secretaries, accordingly, to resume the dialogue on the agreed dates.'

Appendix III: The Lahore Declaration, 21 February 1999

(Extracts)

The Prime Ministers of Pakistan and India:-

Sharing a vision of peace and stability between their countries, and of progress and prosperity for their peoples;

Have agreed that their respective governments:-

- shall intensify efforts to resolve all issues, including the issue of Jammu and Kashmir.
- shall refrain from intervention and interference in each other's internal affairs.
- shall intensify their composite and integrated dialogue process for an early and positive outcome of the agreed bilateral agenda.
- shall take immediate steps for reducing the risk of accidental or unauthorized use of nuclear weapons and discuss concepts and doctrines with a view to elaborating measures for confidence building in the nuclear and conventional fields, aimed at prevention of conflict.
- reaffirm their commitment to goals and objectives of SAARC and to concert their efforts towards the realization of the SAARC vision for the year 2000 and beyond with a view to promoting the welfare of the peoples of south Asia and to improve their quality of life through accelerated economic growth, social progress and cultural development.
- reaffirm their condemnation and terrorism in all its forms and manifestations and their determination to combat this menace.
- shall promote and protect all human right and fundamental freedoms.

Memorandum of Understanding
Lahore, 21 February 1999
(Extracts)

The Foreign Secretaries of Pakistan and India:-

Reaffirming the continued commitment of their respective governments to the principles and purposes of the UN Charter:

Have on this day, agreed to the following:-

1. The two sides shall engage in bilateral consultations on security concepts, and nuclear doctrines. . . .
2. The two sides undertake to provide each other with advance notification in respect of ballistic missile flight tests, and shall conclude a bilateral agreement in this regard.
3. The two sides are fully committed to undertaking national measures to reducing risks of accidental or unauthorized use of nuclear weapons under their control. The two sides further undertake to notify each other immediately in the event of any accidental, unauthorized and unexplained incident that could create the risk of a fallout with adverse consequences for both sides, or an outbreak of a nuclear war between the two countries, as well as adopt measures aimed at diminishing the possibility of such actions, or such incident being misinterpreted by the other. The two sides shall identify/establish the appropriate communication mechanism for this purpose.
4. The two sides shall continue to abide by their respective unilateral moratorium on conducting further nuclear test explosions unless either side, in exercise of its national sovereignty decides that extraordinary event have jeopardized its supreme interests.
5. The two sides shall conclude an agreement on prevention of incidents at sea in order to ensure safety of navigation by naval vessels, and aircraft belonging to the two sides.

Joint Statement
Lahore: 21 February 1999
(Extracts)

2. Prime Minister Vajpayee 'visited Minar-e-Pakistan, Mausoleum of Allama Iqbal, Gurdawara Dera Sahib and Samadhi of Maharaja Ranjeet Singh. . . .

'3. The two leaders held discussions on the entire range of bilateral relations, regional cooperation within SAARC, and issues of international concern. They decided that

a) The two Foreign Ministers will meet periodically to discuss all issues of mutual concern, including nuclear issues.
b) The two sides shall undertake consultations on WTO related issues with a view to coordinating their respective positions.
c) The two sides shall determine areas of cooperation in Information Technology, in particular for tackling the problems of the 21st century.
d) The two sides will hold consultations with a view to further liberalizing the visa and travel regime.
e) The two sides shall appoint a two-member committee at ministerial level to examine humanitarian issues relating to civilian detainees and missing POWs.

Appendix IV: The Agra Declaration, 2001 Draft Agreement

Having met at their retreat in Agra on 15–16 July 2001 and held wide-ranging discussions on Pakistan-India relations, particularly on Jammu and Kashmir and having affirmed their commitment to addressing each other's expressed concerns, creating an environment conducive to the establishment of peaceful, friendly and cooperative ties, for the welfare of the peoples of the two countries.

Agree to the following:

1. Progress towards settlement of Jammu and Kashmir issue would be conducive towards normalization and will further the establishment of a cooperative relationship in a mutually reinforcing manner.
[Before the amendment the sentence read: Settlement of the Jammu and Kashmir issue would pave the way for normalization of relations between the two countries.]

2. There was progress in the discussions towards an understanding of each other's viewpoints. There was also recognition of the requirement of keeping the door open for future dialogue. There was agreement on continuing the process of dialogue.

3. The two sides will resume a sustained dialogue at the political level on:
   (a) Jammu and Kashmir;
   (b) Peace and Security, including both conventional and nuclear CBMs;
   (c) Terrorism and Drug Trafficking.

4. The following will be addressed at the appropriate level of officials of the two countries:
   (a) Economic and Commercial Cooperation;
   (b) Siachen;
   (c) Wullar Barrage/Tulbul Navigation Project;
   (d) Sir Creek;
   (e) Promotion of friendly exchanges in various fields.

The progress on these issues would be reviewed by the Foreign Minister of Pakistan and the External Affairs Minister of India at their meetings.

5. The President and the Prime Minister further agreed and directed that all these issues be addressed purposefully, constructively and in an integrated manner, with a sense of urgency.

6. There was also agreement on the following dialogue structure:
   (a) Annual Summit level meetings;
   (b) Bi-annual meetings between the Minister of Foreign Affairs of Pakistan and Minister of External Affairs of India;
   (c) Foreign Office consultations at the level of Foreign Secretaries.

7. The two sides will support reactivation of the SAARC process and the holding of the Eleventh Summit on a date convenient to the host country and other Member States of the Association.

8. The President of Pakistan invited the Prime Minister of India to visit Pakistan. The invitation was accepted. Dates would be fixed through diplomatic channels.

9. The President and the Prime Minister also agreed to meet again in New York in September 2001 during the session of the UN General Assembly.

The President of Pakistan thanked the Prime Minister of India for the warm reception and gracious hospitality extended to him and his delegation during their stay, as well as for the excellent arrangements for the visit.

Appendix V: Presidents, Prime Ministers, and Foreign Ministers of Pakistan

Head of State/Government	Foreign Minister
Quaid-i-Azam Mohammad Ali Jinnah Governor General, 1947 to 1948	Mohammad Zafrullah Khan 1947–1954
Liaquat Ali Khan, Prime Minister 1947 to 1951	
Khawaja Nazimuddin Governor General, 1948–1951 Prime Minister, 1951–1953	
Ghulam Mohammad Governor General, 1951–1955	
Iskander Mirza Governor General, 1955–1956 President, 1956–1958	
Mohammed Ali (Bogra) Prime Minister, 1953–1955	
Chaudhri Muhammad Ali Prime Minister, 1955–1956	Hamidul Haq Chowdhury 1955–1956
Huseyn Shaheed Suhrawardy, Prime Minister, 1956–1957	Malik Firoz Khan Noon 1956–1957
Ismail I. Chundrigar Prime Minister, Oct-Dec 1957	
Malik Firoz Khan Noon Prime Minister, 1957–1958	
Muhammad Ayub Khan President, 1958–1969	Manzoor Qadir, 1958–1962 Mohammad Ali Bogra, 1962–1963 Zulfikar Ali Bhutto, 1963–1966 Syed Sharifuddin Pirzada, 1966–1968
Agha Mohammad Yahya Khan 1969–1971	Mian Arshad Hussain 1968–1969
Zulfikar Ali Bhutto President, 1971–1973 Prime Minister, 1973–1977	Aziz Ahmed, 1972–1977

Fazal Ilahi Choudhry President, 1973–1977	
Mohammad Zia ul-Haq President, 1977–1988	Agha Shahi, 1978–1982 Sahabzada Yaqub-Khan, 1982–1987
Mohammad Khan Junejo Prime Minister, 1985–1988	Zain Noorani Minister of State, 1985–1988
Ghulam Ishaq Khan President, 1988–1993	Sahabzada Yaqub-Khan, 1988–1991
Benazir Bhutto Prime Minister, 1988–1990	
Mian Mohammad Nawaz Sharif Prime Minister, 1990–1993	Mohammad Siddique Khan Kanju Minister of State 1991–1993
Benazir Bhutto Prime Minister, 1993–1996	Sardar Assef Ahmed Ali 1993–1996
Farooq Ahmad Khan Leghari President, 1993–1997	
Mian Mohammad Nawaz Sharif Prime Minister, 1996–1999	Gohar Ayub Khan, 1996–1998 Sartaj Aziz, 1998–1999
Muhammad Rafiq Tarar, President, 1998–2001	
Pervez Musharraf Chief Executive, 1999–2001 President, 2001–2008	Abdul Sattar 1999–2002
Muhammad Zafrullah Khan Jamali Prime Minister, 2002–2004	Mian Khurshid Mahmud Kasuri 2002–2008
Shaukat Aziz Prime Minister, 2004–2007	
Asif Ali Zardari President, 2008–2013	Makhdoom Shah Mahmood Qureshi 2008–2011
Syed Yusuf Raza Gilani Prime Minister, 2008–2012	Hina Rabbani Khar 2011–2013
Raja Parvaiz Ashraf Prime Minister, 2012–2013	
Mian Mohammad Nawaz Sharif Prime Minister, 2013–	Sartaj Aziz Advisor for Security Affairs Tariq Fatemi Special Assistant for Foreign Affairs

Dr Arif Alvi
President, 2018–

Imran Khan
Prime Minister, 2018–

Makhdoom Shah Mahmood Qureshi
2018–

Bibliography

Ahmed, Aziz, *Manuscript* (Foreign Policy, 1958–65).

Aijazuddin, F. S., ed., *The White House and Pakistan: Secret Declassified Documents, 1969–1974*, Oxford University Press, Karachi, 2002.

Akbar, M. J., *Nehru—The Making of India*, Penguin Group, London, 1988.

Ali, Chaudhri Muhammad, *The Emergence of Pakistan*, Columbia University Press, New York, 1967.

Ambedkar, B. R., *Thoughts on Pakistan*, Thacker & Co., Bombay, 1947.

Anderson, Perry, *After Nehru*, London Review of Books, 2 August 2012.

Arif, General K. M., *Working With Zia*, Oxford University Press, Karachi, 1995.

Arif, K., ed., *America-Pakistan Relations: Documents*, Vanguard Books, Lahore, 1984.

Azad, Abul Kalam, *India Wins Freedom*, Orient Longman, New Delhi, 1959.

Aziz, Khalid, Apocalypse on the Indus, *Criterion Quarterly*, October-December, 2015.

Bajpai, K., et al., *Brasstacks and Beyond*, Manohar Publishers, New Delhi, 1995.

Bajwa, Farooq Naseem, *Pakistan and the West*, Oxford University Press, Karachi, 1996.

Bazaz, Premnath, *The History of Struggle for Freedom in Kashmir: Cultural and Political, from the Earliest Times to the Present Day*, New Delhi: Kashmir Pub. Co., 1954.

Bhatty, Maqbool A., *Great Powers and South Asia: Post-Cold War Trends*, Institute of Regional Studies, Islamabad, 1996.

Bhutto, Zulfikar Ali, *The Myth of Independence*, Oxford University Press, Karachi, 1969.

Burke, S. M., and Lawrence Ziring, *Pakistan's Foreign Policy*, Oxford University Press, Karachi, Second Edition, 1990.

Campbell-Johnson, Alan, *Mission with Mountbatten*, Atheneum, New York, 1966.

Choudhury, G. W., *Pakistan's Relations with India, 1947–66*, Pall Mall Press, London, 1967.

Connell, John, Auchinleck: A Biography of Field Marshal Sir Claude Auchinleck, London: Cassell, 1959.

Cordovez, Diego, and Harrison, Selig, *Out of Afghanistan: The Inside Story of the Soviet Withdrawal*, Oxford University Press, New York, 1995.

Davenport, et al., *The Plumbat Affair*, London: Andre Deutsch, 1978.

Eichenwald, Kurt, *500 Days, Secrets and Lies in the Terror Wars*, Simon & Schuster, New York, 2013.

Farooqi, Bahauddin, *'Writ Petition' in Kashmir Holocaust—The Case Against India*, ed., Khalid Hasan, Dotcare, Lahore, 1992.

Fukuyama, Francis, *The End of History and The Last Man*, The Free Press (Macmillan Inc.), New York, 1992.

Gall, Carlotta, *The Wrong Enemy*, Houghton, Mifflin Harcourt, New York, 2014.

Gates, Robert M., *Duty: Memoirs of a Secretary of War, 2013*,

Gauhar, Altaf, *Ayub Khan: Pakistan's First Military Ruler*, Sang-e-Meel Publications, Lahore, 1994.

Geelani, Syed Ali, *Roodad-i-Qafs* (My Life in Prison), Institute of Policy Studies, Islamabad, 1993.

Hasan, K. Sarwar, ed., *The Kashmir Question: Documents on the Foreign Relations of Pakistan*, Karachi: Pakistan Institute of International Affairs, 1966.

Hasan, Khwaja Sarwar, *Documents on the Foreign Policy of Pakistan*, Institute of International Affairs, Karachi, 1986.

Hazleton, Lesley, *The First Muslim—The Story of Muhammad*, Atlantic Books, London, 2013.

Hersh, Seymour M., *The Samson Option*, New York, Vintage Books, 1993.

Hyder, Sajjad, *The Foreign Policy of Pakistan: Reflections of an Ambassador*, Progressive Publishers, Lahore, 1987.

Jinnah, Mohammad Ali, *Speeches as Governor General*, 1947–1948, Ferozsons, Karachi.

Jones, Rodney W., *Small Nuclear Forces and U.S. Security Policy*, Lexington, MA: Lexington Books, 1984.

Kadeer, A. A., and Naveed A. Tahir, eds., *Pakistan-Europe Ties*, University of Karachi, 1988.

Kadri, Sadakat, *Heaven on Earth—A Journey through Sharia Law*.

Kadri, Sadakat, *Heaven on Earth*, Farr, Straus and Giroux, New York, 2012.

Kennedy, Paul, *The Rise and Fall of Great Powers*, Random House, New York, 1987.

Khalilzad, Zalmay, *Strategic Appraisal* 1996, RAND, Santa Monica, 1996.

Khan, Air Marshal M. Asghar, *The First Round, Indo-Pakistan War*, Islamic Information Services Ltd., London, 1979.

Khan, Brigadier (Retd.) Feroz Hassan, *Eating Grass: The Making of the Pakistani Bomb*, Stanford University Press, Stanford, CAL, 2012.

Khan, Liaquat Ali, *Pakistan the Heart of Asia: Speeches in the United States and Canada, May and June 1950*, Harvard University Press, 1950.

Khan, Riaz M., *Untying the Afghan Knot*, Progressive Publishers, Lahore, 1993.

Khatab, Sayed, and Gary D. Bouma, *Democracy in Islam*, London and New York: Routledge, 2007.

Khattak, Mohammad Aslam Khan, *A Pathan Odyssey*, Oxford University Press, Karachi, 2004.

Kissinger, Henry, *The White House Years*, Little Brown, 1979.

Klaidman, Daniel, *Kill or Capture*, Houghton Miffen Harcourt, New York, 2013.

Korbel, Josef, *Danger in Kashmir*, Princeton University Press: Princeton, NJ; Oxford University Press: London, 1966.

Kux, Dennis, *India and the United States: Estranged Democracies*, National Defense University Press, Washington, D.C., 1993.

Kux, Dennis, *United States and Pakistan, 1947–2000: Disenchanted Allies*, Woodrow Wilson Center Press, Washington, D.C., 2001.

Lamb, Alastair, *Kashmir: A Disputed Legacy*, Oxford Books, UK, 1991, reprinted by Oxford University Press, Karachi, 1992.

Longer, V., *The Defence and Foreign Policy of India*, Sterling Publishers, New Delhi, 1988.

Malik, Hafeez, *Soviet-Pakistan Relations and Post-Soviet Dynamics*, Macmillan Press, London, 1994.

Mamdani, Mahmood, *Good Muslim, Bad Muslim: America, the Cold War and the Roots of Terror*, Pantheon, 2004.

Marino, Andy, *Narendra Modi—A Political Biography*, Harper Colins Publishers, India'

McMahon, Robert J., *The Cold War on the Periphery: The United States, India and Pakistan*, Columbia University Press, New York, 1994.

McNamara, Robert S., *Blundering Into Disaster*, New York, NY: Pantheon Books, 1986.

McNamara, Robert S., *The Changing Nature of Global Security And Its Impact On South Asia*, Washington, D.C., Washington Council on Non-Proliferation, 1992.

Mendis, Vernon L.B., *SAARC—Origins, Organization and Prospects*, Indian Ocean Centre for Peace Studies, Perth, 1991.

Nehru, Jawaharlal, *Selected Works*, Second Series, distributed by Oxford University Press, New Delhi, 1984.

Nixon, Richard M., *The Memoirs of Richard Nixon*, Warner Books, New York, 1978.

Perkovich, George, *India's Nuclear Bomb*, University of California Press, Berkeley, 1999.

Pirzada, Syed Sharifuddin, *The Pakistan Resolution*, Pakistan Publications, Karachi, 1968.

Qureshi, Saeed Ahmad, *Governance Deficit*, Sang-e-Meel Publications, Lahore.

Rahman, Fazlur, *Islam*, University of Chicago Press.

Raina, Asoka, *Inside RAW*, Vikas Publishing Co., New Delhi, 1981.

Roy, Oliver, *Islam and Resistance in Afghanistan*, Cambridge University Press, Cambridge, 1986.

Rubin, Barnett R., *The Search for Peace in Afghanistan: From Buffer State to Failed State*, Yale University Press, New Haven, 1995.

SAARC Secretariat, *From SARC to SAARC*, Kathmandu, 1995.

Salik, Siddiq, *Witness to Surrender*, Oxford University Press, Karachi, 1977.

Sanger, David E., *Confront and Conceal*, Crown Publishers, New York, 2012.

Sattar, Abdul, 'Reducing Nuclear Dangers in South Asia—A Pakistani Perspective' in *The Non-proliferation Review*, Monterey, Winter 1995.

Savage, Charlie, Power Wars, Little Brown and Company, NY, 2015.

Schlesinger, Arthur M., Jr., *A Thousand Days*, Fawcett Publications, Greenwich, 1965.

Shahi, Agha, *Pakistan's Security and Foreign Policy*, Progressive Publishers, Lahore, 1988.

Shamloo, *Speeches and Statements of Iqbal*, Lahore, 1948.

Singh, Khushwant, *The Lessons of My Life*, Penguin Books.

Sisson, Richard, and Rose, Leo E., *War and Secession—Pakistan, India, and the Creation of Bangladesh*, University of California Press, Berkeley, CA. 1990.

Spector, Leonard S., and Smith, Jacqueline R., *Nuclear Ambitions*, Westview Press, Boulder, CO. 1990.

Stephens, Ian, *Horned Moon*, Chatto and Windus, London, 1954.

Stephens, Ian, *Pakistan*, Ernest Benn, London, 1967.

The 9/11 Commission Report: Final Report of the National Commission on Terrorist Attacks Upon the United States, W. W. Norton & Co., New York, 2004.

Thucydides, *The Peloponnesian War*, ed. Robert B. Strassler, Free Press, New York, 2008.

US Policy Documents, US Government Publications, Washington, D.C.

Yunus, Mohammad, *Reflections on China*, Wajidalis, Lahore, 1986.

Zaidi, A. Moin, and Shaheda Zaidi, eds., *The Encyclopedia of Indian National Congress*, S. Chand & Co., New Delhi, 1976–1981.

Zaidi, Z. H., ed., *Jinnah Papers*, Vol. VI, Quaid-i-Azam Papers Project, Islamabad.

Ziring, Lawrence, Ralph Braibanti, and W. Howard Wriggins, eds., *Pakistan: The Long View*, Duke University Press, Durham, 1977.

Index

D

E

F

G

J